ebusiness

A Canadian Perspective for a Networked World

Fourth Edition

GERALD TRITES
University of Waterloo

J. EFRIM BORITZ
University of Waterloo

PEARSON

Toronto

Vice-President, Editorial Director: Gary Bennett
Editor-in-Chief: Nicole Lukach
Acquisitions Editor: Nick Durie and Kathleen McGill
Marketing Manager: Jenna Wulff
Supervising Developmental Editor: Suzanne Schaan
Developmental Editor: Rema Celio
Project Manager: Marissa Lok and Heidi Allgair, Element-Thomson North America
Manufacturing Manager: Susan Johnson
Production Editor: Heidi Allgair, Element-Thomson North America
Copy Editor: Kitty Wilson
Proofreader: Susan Broadhurst
Compositor: Element LLC
Photo and Permissions Researcher: Terri Rothman M.L.S.
Art Director: Julia Hall
Cover and Interior Designer: Miriam Blier
Cover Image: Jasper James/Getty Images

Credits and acknowledgments for material borrowed from other sources and reproduced, with permission, in this textbook appear on the appropriate page within the text.

If you purchased this book outside the United States or Canada, you should be aware that it has been imported without the approval of the publisher or the author.

10 9 8 7 6 5 4 3 2 1 EB

Library and Archives Canada Cataloguing in Publication
Trites, Gerald
    eBusiness : a Canadian perspective for a networked world / Gerald
Trites and J. Efrim Boritz.—4th ed.

Includes bibliographical references and index.
ISBN 978-0-13-248203-5

    1. Electronic commerce—Management.   I. Boritz, Jefim
Efrim, 1950-   II. Title

HF5548.32.T748 2011   658´.054678   C2011-902270-2

ISBN 978-0-13-248203-5

To my beloved Susan

—GDT

To Naomi … for just being there

—JEB

Brief Contents

Contents

Preface

Although ebusiness is a global phenomenon, Canadian businesses face legal and cultural issues that are unique to this country. *eBusiness: A Canadian Perspective for a Networked World* is the first text to address ebusiness in a Canadian context.

eBusiness: A Canadian Perspective for a Networked World reflects a Canadian perspective on the growth of the exciting field of ebusiness, which has been accepted by a wide variety of business and educational professionals as one of the most significant events to have taken place in business—and across the world—for several hundred years. Educational institutions are developing new courses, programs, and research efforts in an attempt to embrace this area.

The textbook sets out the concepts that guide ebusiness and deals fully with the business strategies and models that have emerged. The companion website and author blog extend these core areas to address new developments and emerging trends on an ongoing basis.

We have also provided a Canadian perspective, which we believe is important for Canadian students despite the fact that ebusiness is a global phenomenon. While ebusiness is global, at least to the extent that various parts of the world have technologies and infrastructures that can support ebusiness, there are distinctly Canadian elements and issues that Canadian students need to learn. In addition, students can relate more closely to cases and examples that are Canadian.

Legal structures and statutes such as the Personal Information Protection and Electronic Documents Act (PIPEDA) are central to the Canadian experience of ebusiness. They are influenced by the activities of the Canadian government in establishing infrastructure, such as the Strategis initiatives of Industry Canada and the digitization of Canada Post. Ebusiness in Canada is also influenced by the activities of Canadian business enterprises, such as the very successful BlackBerry, developed by Research In Motion of Waterloo, Ontario; the ventures of Rogers and others into Web TV; the movement of the banks into virtual banking; and the Canadian capitalists who experienced the rise, fall and subsequent dramatic revival of internet-based business activities in Canada. Books that are not Canadian simply do not discuss these important aspects of Canadian ebusiness.

GENERAL APPROACH

This textbook includes chapters that fully cover the major elements of ebusiness as well as case studies. This format offers instructors greater flexibility in crafting course curricula. The textbook addresses major contemporary trends, such as integrated enterprise systems, cloud computing, social networking and mobile internet-accessible devices, eprocurement, and customer relationship management.

While the emphasis of the textbook is on the macro issues, the companion website presents self-study quizzes, exercises, and problems. Discussion materials on new developments are presented in the authors' blog so that any course can easily encompass them and remain current. Other resources include extra review questions, Glossary Flashcards, and internet exercises.

ORGANIZATION OF THE TEXTBOOK

This textbook is divided into four parts, comprising 14 chapters, an appendix of cases, and a glossary.

Part 1: Ebusiness Models and Strategies

This part places electronic business into an entire business perspective, beginning with an introductory chapter (chapter 1) which discusses some of the basics of ebusiness. It then addresses strategic planning and business models (chapter 2) to ensure that a business mindset is maintained throughout the textbook.

Part 2: Ebusiness Architecture

This part reviews the architecture of ebusiness and explores the impact on business and management of required technologies such as the internet, intranets, and extranets (chapter 3), enterprise-wide and inter-enterprise systems (chapter 4), security and controls (chapter 5), and billing and payment systems (chapter 6).

Part 3: Ebusiness Applications

Starting with supply-chain management (chapter 7), this part examines some of the crucial technologies in ebusiness such as eprocurement, trading exchanges, and auctions (chapter 8), customer relationship management (chapter 9), and business intelligence (chapter 10).

Part 4: Conducting Ebusiness

This part explores the materials needed to integrate the operation of ebusiness within the broader business context, including marketing issues (chapter 11), metrics for performance measurement in ecommerce (chapter 12), privacy, legal, and taxation issues (chapter 13), and small business operations (chapter 14).

NEW TO THIS EDITION

In addition to a thorough review and update of the entire textbook, the following changes have been made to this edition:

- New material has been added on cloud computing, social networking, and mobility. While new material on mobile commerce was added to the previous edition, this aspect keeps changing rapidly and merited additional emphasis in this edition. Various references to these three areas have been included where appropriate in the text. In addition, the following changes have been made:
    - The new material on cloud computing includes additions to chapter 1 (to introduce the concept), chapter 7 (to identify various types of cloud computing approaches and their roles in supply-chain management), chapter 8 (to explain how eprocurement systems have evolved into the use of software as a service in the cloud), and chapter 10 (to show how business intelligence has

gone to the cloud). In addition, an Ebusiness in Global Perspective box on a cloud application has been added.

- The new material on social networking includes the addition of material to chapter 2 on new business models arising from social networking, along with related discussion boxes; a section in chapter 9 on social customer relationship management along with a discussion box covering this topic and new materials on social marketing in chapter 11, with a related discussion box on Groupon; a section on social metrics in chapter 12; and a new discussion box on Facebook privacy in chapter 13.

- Several of the discussion boxes have been changed. The book now contains a box on Wikipedia (chapter 1), three on Facebook (chapters 1, 3 and 13), and a box in chapter 14 that shows how a blog became a business. New material on mobility includes two new discussion boxes in chapter 5, a new discussion box in chapter 6 on a wireless payment system in Africa, and a new section on mobile business intelligence in chapter 10.

- In addition to the changes noted above, the Estrategy, New Business Models, Canadian Snapshots, and Ebusiness in Global Perspective boxes have all been reviewed and updated. Completely new content has been added to half of them.

- The Mountain Equipment Co-op, Monster, Google, TD Canada Trust, BlackBerry, ValueClick, Ntuitive, and Cars4U cases have all been updated and revised. A new case has been added on YouTube.

Features of the Textbook

A special effort has been made to incorporate features that will facilitate learning and enhance an understanding of ebusiness.

- **Ebusiness Mind Maps** at the beginning of each chapter provide students with a visual overview of the organization of the text, and show where each chapter fits into the system of ebusiness as a whole. The mind map illustrates the dynamic relationships among the foundation of ebusiness (models and strategies), the tools of ebusiness (architecture), how these tools are used (application), and the environment in which they are used (conducting ebusiness).

- **Learning Objectives** at the beginning of each chapter summarize the skills and knowledge to be learned in that chapter.

- **Chapter Introductions** provide an overview of the material discussed in each chapter.

- **Key Terms** are boldfaced in the text, defined in the margin of the text, and listed at the end of each chapter. For easy reference, all the key terms and their definitions are collated in a glossary at the end of the textbook.

- **Weblinks** appear in the margin, providing URLs for companies discussed in the text.

- **Estrategy boxes** emphasize the importance of the strategic employment of ebusiness.

- **New Business Models boxes** highlight how technology has had an impact on business models and illustrate how rapid changes in ebusiness require that business models be flexible and adaptable to remain competitive.

- **Canadian Snapshots boxes** highlight Canadian businesses to demonstrate how competition and the Canadian marketplace are changing. These boxes demonstrate how ebusinesses have developed within the Canadian context and some of the difficulties they have faced.

■ **Ebusiness in Global Perspective boxes** address global issues and opportunities in ebusiness. These boxes provide examples of either international companies or companies competing globally, and discuss technological issues related to the management of ebusiness.

■ **Chapter Summaries** recap the issues discussed in the chapter.

■ A **case** at the end of each of the four parts of the text addresses particular issues relevant to those parts.

■ An **Appendix of Cases** includes six decision-based case studies with discussion questions to be used in the classroom or for assignments. These cases provide a mechanism for many of the topics in the text to be applied to current and interesting situations facing ebusiness managers today.

COURSE DESIGN

A major purpose of this textbook is to facilitate a dynamic course design. The topic is so fast-moving that from the time of course design to delivery there are often significant changes. While the course design can focus on the textbook as a core, the use of the website can vary to reflect current needs.

This textbook is intended primarily for undergraduate courses or first courses in ebusiness at the master's level. Essentially, it is for survey courses provided to students who have minimal previous exposure to the subject. There is sufficient material to support a one-semester course.

Potential course designs can include:

1. A chapter-by-chapter, textbook-driven course, with occasional references to the website, lectures, and discussion of problems in class;

2. A topic-driven course, with blended use of the text and the website materials, lectures, and discussion of problems in class;

3. A case-driven seminar course, focusing on particular topics;

4. A web survey that is directed by the organization of the course, but with an emphasis on selected websites.

Accordingly, the textbook can be used to support conventional, lecture- or discussion-based courses as well as seminars using cases and/or web materials.

The authors have found that, for undergraduates, a combined lecture- (maximum half-hour) and discussion-based course (with a variety of other tools) provides the best approach for engaging students. Some classes can focus on problems and others on cases. Of course, combinations of these resources can be used in many classes.

The result is that the resource offers a variety of potential course designs and considerable flexibility in their delivery.

SUPPLEMENTS

The following supplements have been carefully prepared to accompany this new edition.

Student Resources

Companion Website: Visit www.pearsoncanada.ca/trites to find the following resources, updated for this edition by Jennifer Houselander McGrath (Algonquin College) and Nancy Zowkewych (Centennial College):

- Practice tests and self-study quizzes check your knowledge of chapter material and help you focus on what you need to study.

- A frequently updated author blog keeps you current with trends in ebusiness.

- Glossary flashcards help you study key terms.

CourseSmart for Students: CourseSmart goes beyond traditional expectations—providing instant, online access to the textbooks and course materials you need at an average savings of 60%. With instant access from any computer and the ability to search your text, you'll find the content you need quickly, no matter where you are. And with online tools like highlighting and note-taking, you can save time and study efficiently. See all the benefits at www.coursesmart.com/students.

Instructor Resources

Instructor's Manual: This manual, prepared by Ken Dafoe (Conestoga College), includes additional background material for cases, questions to provoke classroom discussions, and exercises as well as a solutions manual.

PowerPoints: PowerPoint presentations, prepared by Andy Igonor (NAIT), consist of customizable slides for lectures.

MyTest: This electronic test bank, prepared by Kelly Halliday (Georgian College), contains multiple-choice, true/false, and short-answer questions that directly assess the content of each chapter. MyTest from Pearson Education Canada is a powerful assessment generation program that helps instructors easily create and print quizzes, tests, exams, as well as homework or practice handouts. Questions and tests can all be authored online, allowing instructors ultimate flexibility and the ability to efficiently manage assessments at anytime, from anywhere. These questions are also available in Microsoft Word format.

Most of these instructor supplements are also available to download from a password-protected section of Pearson Education Canada's online catalogue (www.pearsoncanada .ca). Navigate to your book's catalogue page to view a list of available supplements. See your local sales representative for details and access.

Technology Specialists: Pearson's Technology Specialists work with faculty and campus course designers to ensure that Pearson technology products, assessment tools, and online course materials are tailored to meet your specific needs. This highly qualified team is dedicated to helping schools take full advantage of a wide range of educational resources, by assisting in the integration of a variety of instructional materials and media formats. Your local Pearson Education sales representative can provide you with more details on this service program.

CourseSmart for Instructors: CourseSmart goes beyond traditional expectations—providing instant, online access to the textbooks and course materials you need at a lower cost for students. And even as students save money, you can save time and hassle with a digital eTextbook that allows you to search for the most relevant content at the very moment you need it. Whether it's evaluating textbooks or creating lecture notes to help students with difficult concepts, CourseSmart can make life a little easier. See how when you visit www.coursesmart.com/instructors.

Pearson Custom Library: For enrollments of at least 25 students, you can create your own textbook by choosing the chapters that best suit your own course needs. To begin building your custom text, visit www.pearsoncustomlibrary.com. You may also work with a dedicated Pearson Custom editor to create your ideal text—publishing your own original content or mixing and matching Pearson content. Contact your local Pearson representative to get started.

Acknowledgments

We wish to acknowledge the help of many people during the preparation of this work. In particular, Dr. Boritz wishes to thank his colleagues at the Centre for Information Integrity and Information Systems Assurance at the University of Waterloo for their advice and support, and Ann Bisch and Maya Boritz for their production assistance. We also wish to express a hearty thank you to our developmental editor, Rema Celio, for her cheerful and always helpful prompting and encouragement. We also express our gratitude to the other tremendous Pearson staff who helped us, including Kathleen McGill, sponsoring editor; Heidi Allgair, production editor; and Marissa Lok, Pearson project manager. We would also like to thank our students who have provided us with a great deal of feedback in our courses and assisted in the development of case studies and supporting materials.

Finally, and certainly no less importantly, we wish to thank the people who took the time to review and provide commentary on various chapters:

Darren Charters, University of Waterloo
Lyon Cygman, Mount Royal University
Roger Duckworth, SAIT Polytechnic
Siobhan Fitzmaurice, Sheridan Institute of Technology and Advanced Learning
Elliott Gold, Ridout & Maybee, LLP, Toronto
Margo Karolyi, Mohawk College
Katharine Langille, Red River College
Alexander Pevec, Vancouver Island University
Franklyn I. Prescod, Ted Rogers School of Management, Ryerson University
Karen Woods, Georgian College of Applied Arts and Technology

Gerald Trites, Research Fellow, Centre for Information Integrity and Information Systems Assurance, University of Waterloo

J. Efrim Boritz, Director, Centre for Information Integrity and Information Systems Assurance, University of Waterloo

Chapter 1
Introduction to Ebusiness

Learning Objectives

When you complete this chapter you should be able to:

1 Define *ebusiness*.

2 Identify and explain the foundations of ebusiness.

3 Describe how ebusiness fits into the traditional business environment.

4 Identify and evaluate the major strategies of enterprises that adopt ebusiness.

5 Explain the benefits of ebusiness.

6 Discuss the challenges facing ebusiness and how enterprises are addressing them.

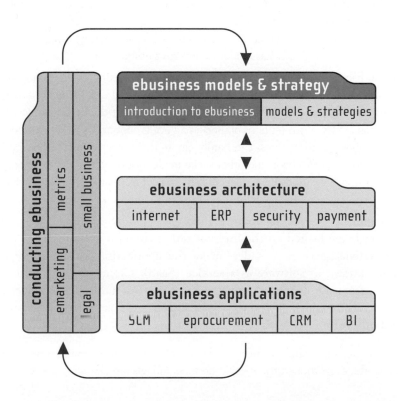

INTRODUCTION

THE REACH OF THE **INTERNET** INTO SO MANY ASPECTS OF OUR LIVES IS REVOLUTION-izing our world. What we have seen so far is only the beginning of a fundamental change that many people have compared to the Industrial Revolution in its scope and potential impact. New types of business have emerged that we wouldn't have thought of only a few years ago. Businesses that have been around for decades have found they need to use the internet and develop new business models to remain competitive or even to survive. Business and society are being changed forever.

During the early years of ebusiness, the media reported phenomenal success stories about the "new economy." With new dot-com companies opening daily, it seemed that upstart companies could launch directly into global markets through the internet and could raise billions on the stock markets with little or nothing in the way of hard assets. They made billionaires of their owners, many of whom had yet to see their thirtieth birth-day. Early success stories included Amazon.com, eBay, E*TRADE Financial, and Research In Motion. More recently, new ventures such as MySpace, Facebook, and YouTube have not only become highly successful businesses but also significant social phenomena. In fact, YouTube became an overnight sensation and was acquired by Google in 2006 for $1.65 billion, after being in existence for only one year.

When the internet was first used in business, in the late twentieth century, it launched a period of unprecedented change, in business and indeed in society in general. Now, in the early twenty-first century, business is using the internet differently than it has in the past. Part of this change comes from mobility, and part from other factors, such as social media and cloud computing:

Mobility. The internet itself is being revolutionized through the spread of mobile units, such as smartphones, iPads, and other internet-capable devices. The large numbers of people using these units has provided unprecedented opportunities to business, as well as new challenges. It has made the internet ubiquitous.

Social media. Facebook, Twitter, LinkedIn and other social media have begun to have a sig-nificant impact on business. Initially, Facebook was a social tool used primarily by people in their teens and twenties. But it has evolved into one of the most significant internet applications today. With millions of users in all age groups and a plethora of information available about them, business can hardly ignore this potential market. So business has been moving into Facebook and other social media not only for marketing purposes but also for customer relationships, collaboration, and public relations. Social media promises to be one of the defining characteristics of the new ebusiness.

Cloud computing. Cloud computing involves applications and other computer resources being hosted on the internet rather than on an enterprise's own com-puter systems. Service providers make the applications available for a fee—a practice known as **software as a service (SaaS)**. Cloud computing frees up the business from the burden of software and infrastructural maintenance. In many cases, it also enables a business to use much more sophisticated systems than would otherwise have been possible.

Many of the traditional business fundamentals continue to make sense in this new electronic world, even though the specific business models are changing and evolving. The search for viable business models, by both old established companies and new internet-based ones, is ongoing, and it will not end anytime soon. This simple fact is at the core of this textbook.

Some of the business models of the dot-com companies did not include any plans about how they would make money on a long-term basis. Napster, the original music-sharing utility, is a case in point. The company offered its service free of charge to users, and it did not have any other plans, such as advertising, to generate money to keep it going. Only after Napster had been in operation for some time and had been challenged in the courts did it begin to charge fees. It is quite possible that, if the courts had not curtailed the company's activities, the original Napster would not have survived for economic reasons.

Napster
www.napster.ca

Now, in the early twenty-first century, the internet has become a central part of the strategy of most businesses; business has embraced the internet as a powerful and essential tool for achieving strategic goals and remaining competitive in the new economy.

Large "old economy" companies have been moving heavily into ebusiness. For example, banks have adopted internet banking, airlines are using online reservation systems, and countless retail outlets now have online sales capabilities. Such business-to-business (B2B) and business-to-consumer (B2C) ventures represent the largest part of ebusiness. Business-to-government (B2G) and government-to-business (G2B) efforts are also showing impressive growth, in the form of government self-service sites. In addition, as discussed more fully in chapter 2, old-economy companies are involved in a wide range of other new areas, including business-to-employee (B2E), government-to-consumer (G2C), and government-to-business (G2B) activities.

Estrategy

Amazon.com: Transforming Estrategy— From Clicks to Bricks

Amazon.com was one of the first companies to sell books on the web. Certainly it was the most widely noticed of the internet startups, and one that caused traditional bookstores, such as Barnes & Noble, to also open websites to sell their product. Amazon started in 1995, with the idea it would be able to take orders over the web and fill them by ordering from suppliers as demand required. Part of the strategy was to be able to supply books without incurring the infrastructure costs that other businesses had to bear, therefore enabling the company to sell at lower prices.

The reality that emerged was that it took Amazon until 2003 to get out of a loss position and actually report a profit for the year. For a time, Amazon's shares rose, despite its losses, but in 2000 the dot-com market corrected itself, and Amazon's shares declined considerably. The shares of the company have since begun to recover.

The reason Amazon had trouble making money was that the company had to spend far more on marketing and infrastructure than it had foreseen. The marketing expenditure had been hard to predict because internet marketing was a new field. Infrastructure costs arose because Amazon found that it was having trouble delivering orders on a timely basis and eventually had to make the decision to develop some of its own warehousing and distribution infrastructure to address this issue. Amazon still relied heavily on order by demand, but it began buffering this approach with some warehouse buying. Of course, that was completely contrary to the original strategy. To deal with the additional costs, the company had to implement a strategy that would generate higher revenues.

Over the past few years, Amazon has undergone a heavy expansion. The company has moved away from

>

being solely a book seller to include numerous other products, including music, DVDs, and clothes. Much of this expansion has occurred though partnerships with other reputable companies, such as Target and gourmet food company Dean & DeLuca. In addition, Amazon expanded into international markets and entered the Canadian market in partnership with Canada Post. Amazon now lets customers list their own items alongside the listed Amazon products in several areas. In response to the realities of the marketplace, Amazon transformed a clearly defined strategy of minimizing infrastructure costs to sell books at a lower price to a strategy that incorporated increased infrastructure costs through warehousing, and it offered new product lines to pay for this expansion.

Adding new products and catering to new markets was a logical way for Amazon to make effective use of its expanded infrastructure. This evolution in strategy allowed Amazon to add to revenues with minimal incremental cost. It is a classic case of transforming internet business strategy.

Amazon.com
www.amazon.com

Questions

1. What challenges arise from Amazon's need to expand into new markets?
2. Comment on the changes in Amazon's business model over the years.

Source: www.amazon.com.

 Ebusiness in Global Perspective

Facebook: A Global Phenomenon

Mark Zuckerberg created Facebook when he was a 19-year-old student at Harvard University. Initially, he called it Facemash, and he used it to post the pictures of students and ask users to rate them as "hot or not." He had hacked into Harvard records to obtain the information. The university administration quickly shut down Facemash, and Zuckerberg faced charges for breach of privacy and stealing data. Eventually, however, the charges were dropped.

Zuckerberg was undaunted, however, and soon launched a new website called The Facebook, (they dropped the "The" later on) based on the concept behind the booklets published by many universities with pictures of students and some basic information about them in order for the students to get to know each other better. At the time, Harvard did not publish a facebook.

The new Facebook site took off quickly, with many thousands of views within a few days. Other universities and schools were invited to join it, and the site quickly grew. On Facebook, users can create profiles with photos, lists of personal interests, contact information, and other personal information. They can communicate with friends and other users through private or public messages and a chat feature, and they can post items of interest and status updates to their Wall. They can also create and join interest groups, some of which are maintained by organizations as a means of advertising.

There have been extensive concerns about privacy, and Facebook has been forced to modify its practices to meet those concerns by such authorities as the Privacy Commissioner of Canada. One of the features it implemented was to enable users to choose their own privacy settings, giving the users the ability to control who can see them and what they can see.

Facebook was incorporated in the summer of 2004. Sean Parker, who had been advising Zuckerberg, became the company's president, and Facebook moved its operations to Palo Alto, California. Facebook launched a high school version in September 2005 and later expanded membership eligibility to employees of several companies, including Apple and Microsoft. On September 26, 2006, Facebook was opened to anyone ages 13 and older with a valid email address.

On October 24, 2007, Microsoft announced that it had purchased a 1.6% share of Facebook for $240 million, thus giving Facebook an implied value of about $15 billion. In October 2008, Facebook announced that its international headquarters would be in Dublin, Ireland. In November 2010, based on an exchange for shares of privately held companies, Facebook's value was imputed at $41 billion, making it the third-largest U.S. web-based company, after Google and Amazon.

During the time it has been in operation, Facebook has grown from a social introduction network for young people

>

to a social networking site for people of all ages. The vast numbers of people regularly using the site have attracted companies to the site for the advertising opportunities. Procter & Gamble recently announced that it would be moving its advertising budget from TV to Facebook. The site has become a major commercial site, with growing importance in the business world. The website is free to users, and it generates revenue from advertising, such as banner ads, although Facebook users click on advertisements less often than do users of other sites. Some speculate that this may be because Facebook users tend to be technologically aware and also tend to be young and rather immune to advertising. But this area has not been extensively studied yet.

A study conducted by compete.com in January 2009 found Facebook to be the most used social networking site in the world. Another study determined the monthly visitors in the United States alone to be around 135 million!

At last count, Zuckerman owned 24% of Facebook, making his personal stake worth about $12 billion.

Facebook
www.facebook.com

Questions

1. What challenges will Facebook face as it moves more completely into the world of business?

2. Are there other user groups that Facebook should be moving to include?

3. What features could Facebook add to enhance its appeal to users?

Sources: www.buzzle.com/articles/history-of-facebook.html; www.webhostingreport.com; www.facebook.com/History; Wikipedia article on Facebook.

Another good example of an old brick-and-mortar company moving to the internet is Sears, which has been a major retailer for many years but now has one of the top-rated ebusiness websites on the internet, grossing over US$18 billion per year. It has made the transition to the world of ebusiness—from "bricks to clicks"—while still retaining its "bricks" presence.

Sears
www.sears.com

Small businesses also continue to enter into ebusiness activities, sometimes to use the internet for marketing and selling products to customers and sometimes to take part in B2B activities, such as buying online. Small organizations face a particular set of issues related to involvement in ebusiness, and this forms the focus of chapter 14.

The global use of the internet has truly created a networked world that is transforming business. Canada is part of this networked world, and Canadian business is going global and using the latest in technology in the process. This book focuses on Canada's unique experience in the world of ebusiness and the new challenges, both domestic and international, that are being met.

WHAT IS EBUSINESS?

IN A VERY BROAD SENSE, ELECTRONIC BUSINESS HAS BEEN DEFINED AS ANY BUSINESS carried out in electronic form. Therefore, if business transactions are carried out by using **electronic data interchange (EDI)**, this is a form of ebusiness. If a bank transaction is carried out by electronic transfers between branches, this is a form of ebusiness. So under this definition, ebusiness has been in existence for a good many years—certainly years before the internet became an economic force.

The growth of the internet has created significant change. It opened up new market channels and wider markets and formed the foundation of ebusiness as we know it. Initially, the use of the internet for selling goods and services was referred to as "ecommerce." More recently, the term "ebusiness" has been used to reflect the fact that the

electronic data interchange (EDI): A structured way of creating electronic "forms" that can be transmitted between trading partners to execute business transactions without the need to generate any paper.

effective delivery of ecommerce requires considerable organizational commitment and change. The term "ebusiness" therefore conveys a much broader meaning, involving the "complex fusion of business processes, enterprise applications, and organizational structure necessary to create a high-performance business model."[1]

This definition of ebusiness connects the idea of business change and structure to the creation of business models that will sustain themselves. Under this definition, ebusiness relies on the whole business—how it is structured, what technology is being used, and how the business is carried out. Therefore, a consideration of ebusiness extends well beyond the use of the internet, although the internet remains central. It extends into a range of management issues, from strategy to execution to supervision, and incorporates the strategic use of information technology to achieve corporate goals.

Accordingly, the definition of ebusiness used in this book is as follows:

> Ebusiness is the strategic use of technology, particularly the internet, to integrate and streamline the business processes, enterprise applications, and organizational structure of a business to create a high-performance business model.

THE FOUNDATIONS OF EBUSINESS
Ebusiness Models

The internet and ebusiness are causing business model changes. Several features of internet-based business have an impact on the business models adopted by businesses, including the following:

- speed
- convenience
- customization
- redefinition of product value
- media flexibility

Speed Certainly, the use of technology has changed the expectations of people regarding the time it takes to satisfy their needs. We can see this impact on society in general. In the early days of technology, there was a widespread thought that it would free up a great deal of time for people—that, thanks to technology, they would be able to reduce their workweeks and take long vacations. It hasn't worked out that way, and today we see people living frantic and rushed lives—in great measure a result of their ability to use technology to respond more quickly to other people and then get on with the next activity on their list. People expect fast turnaround to their requests, especially where technology is involved.

This means that businesses need to construct their business models so that they can deliver their products or services quickly. It also means that if another company implements new technology that results in faster delivery, it may well have a competitive advantage.

Convenience One of the reasons people use the internet is for convenience. When they log onto their bank's website, they can check their current balances without going to the bank branch and standing in line for a teller. They can pay their bills without having to write a cheque, stuff an envelope, and go to a mailbox to mail it. It's all about convenience.

This fact has had a profound impact on the way banks offer their services to the public. Banks have reduced the number of branches, cut their staff, and set up more ATMs in partnership with retail outlets. Generally, it may be said that they have been moving from bricks to clicks. This move has substantially changed their business models—by cutting their infrastructure costs, increasing their technology costs, adding new sources of revenue, and making old sources of revenue obsolete. As they find new ways to add convenience, their mix of old and new changes again, leading to modified business models.

Customization Somewhat related to the idea of convenience is the demand for customized products and services. The use of the internet together with **integrated systems** makes this possible or, to put it another way, is necessary to make it possible. Integrated systems are information systems that are joined together in such a way that they can easily share data with each other. One of the leaders in the provision of customized products was Dell Inc., which was the first major vendor to offer computers for purchase through its website. The distinguishing feature of Dell's site was that customers could select from various options for all components of the computer and build a computer that completely fit their needs. Since then, of course, other vendors have followed suit.

The Dell experience clearly demonstrates the impact of customization on business models. As a result of customization, Dell needed a radically different manufacturing and distribution model to enable it to build and deliver the product after it had been ordered—a very different activity from filling a retail outlet with inventory or selling to retailers so they could fill their stores with inventory prior to the customer buying the product.

integrated systems:
Information systems that are joined together in such a way that they can easily share data with each other.

Dell
www.dell.com

New Business Models

Wikipedia: A Top 10 Not-for-Profit

Prior to the age of the internet, *Encyclopaedia Britannica* was known widely as the world's premier encyclopaedia. It was large (some 20 volumes), and expensive, and aggressive Britannica salespeople sold it door-to-door.

When internet use began to grow, interest in printed encyclopaedias declined, and Britannica tried various electronic formats, such as selling the product on CD, but all these efforts failed. The company then began to develop a website where it could sell its product, but this failed to take off as well. Then, with its very survival at stake, Britannica implemented a radical revision of its business model. The company placed the content of its encyclopaedia on a website completely free of charge, with the idea of using the site to attract advertising revenue. In addition, it included links to other websites, the daily news, banner ads, and an online store. With the crash of the dot-com industry, advertising revenues collapsed. To survive, the company was once again forced to change

its business model. To compensate for lost revenues, Britannica embraced a two-tiered system. Basic searches are still free, but a premium subscription is required for more comprehensive search results.

The consequence of all this was that Britannica's business model changed from one in which it produced and sold expensive books to one where it gave away its prime product on the internet and made its money on advertising and selling its product through an online store to, finally, one in which it makes the product available on a subscription basis.

Britannica and its competitors followed the practice of having their articles written by experts in the field, often renowned experts, and peer reviewed by other experts. This way, they felt that they would safeguard the intellectual integrity of the articles.

This was the world into which Wikipedia was born, and the old-guard companies like Britannica regarded the
>

basic idea as anathema. Even to Jimmy Wales, co-founder of Wikipedia, the idea was revolutionary and somewhat suspect.

While moderating an online discussion group devoted to the philosophy of objectivism in the early 1990s, Wales met Larry Sanger when they engaged in a debate on the subject. They continued the debate offline and became friends. After a few years, when Wales decided to pursue an online encyclopaedia, he invited Sanger to join him. In March 2000, Nupedia was born as a peer-reviewed, open-content encyclopaedia. Nupedia contained expert-written entries on a variety of topics, and the plan was to sell advertising alongside the entries in order to make a profit.

Nupedia grew very slowly, however, because of its cumbersome submission process. Then, in January 2001, Ben Kovitz, a programmer, introduced Sanger to the concept of a wiki. Kovitz suggested that adopting the wiki model would allow editors to contribute simultaneously and incrementally throughout the project, thus breaking Nupedia's bottleneck. However, they couldn't sell the idea to their editors, who feared that quality would degrade. But they continued with the wiki idea separately, and the wiki project, dubbed "Wikipedia," by Sanger, went live on a separate domain five days after its creation.

What happened then was wildly beyond Wales and Sanger's expectations. They expected a lot of rubbish to be submitted but hoped that at least something might come out of it that would be useful for Nupedia. To their surprise, within a few days of launching, the number of articles on Wikipedia had outgrown that of Nupedia, and a small collective of editors had formed. Many of the early contributors to the site were familiar with the model of the free culture movement, and, like Wales, sympathized with the open-source movement. The cadre of early editors helped create a robust, self-regulating community that has proven conducive to the growth of the project.

Sanger was assigned to develop both the Nupedia and Wikipedia projects. In the early years, Wales had supplied the financial backing for the project, but he ran out of money, and Sanger departed. Wales entertained the notion of placing advertisements on Wikipedia but then decided to form a not-for-profit foundation instead. Wales formed the Wikimedia Foundation (WMF), a not-for-profit organization founded in St. Petersburg, Florida, and headquartered in San Francisco, California. All intellectual property rights and domain names pertaining to Wikipedia were moved to the new foundation, whose purpose was to establish general policy for the encyclopaedia and its sister projects. To date, Wales has eschewed the idea of commercial funding or generating revenues through Wikipedia. The project is funded through donations made to the WMF. Wales estimated that Wikipedia was worth US$3 billion.

Wikipedia
www.wikipedia.com

Questions

1. How do the business models of Britannica and Wikipedia compare?

2. What are the business model options for Wikipedia?

3. Do you think Wales has made the right decision in making Wikipedia a not-for-profit organization?

Source: Wikipedia articles on Wikipedia and on Jimmy.

Redefinition of Product Value The ability of the internet to convey a variety of information, services, and other features has led to redefinitions of "product" and "service." For example, when Amazon offers books online, it includes information about the book, reader reviews, sales ranking, related books, and other information. The company has also added to its site other services and products in which it believes its customers are likely to have an interest. In other words, this package including additional information with its prime product (books) means that the package becomes the product. This has the effect of fundamentally altering Amazon's business model, enabling it to charge for some of the additional products. Customers have come to expect packages of this type, and such packages must keep up with consumer expectations and needs at all times.

Media Flexibility The incredible capacity of the internet to grow and change and to convey a variety of content (particularly multimedia, such as voice, video, and music) means that business is continually challenged to offer new features and services to customers before customers demand them. This leads to changing product package content and, consequently, changing business models.

It should be clear from these points and examples that ebusiness models constantly change. They change when businesses enter into ebusiness, and they need constant review to keep pace with the fast-moving times. This need for continual change and improvement emphasizes the need for ebusiness strategy.

Ebusiness Strategy

The changes in and pressure on business models have driven numerous strategic initiatives, some of which are unique to ebusiness and some of which are not. Business models define how a business is going to make money, and strategy defines how it plans to achieve the business objectives within the desired business model. We have already seen, as in the case of Amazon, how business models need to change to survive in the current business environment. This need for change leads to a need for new strategies. In the world of ebusiness, strategy formulation and execution must move fast, and in most cases they must be tied closely to significant business processes in a way that makes them flexible and responsive. This is known as a flexible business design. More often, the desired flexibility cannot be achieved within a single business organization. The organization must look outside to be able to provide products and services or conduct particular business processes. This has led to a substantial incidence of such strategies as outsourcing, partnerships, joint ventures, liaisons, and mergers. Most recently, it has led to outright collaboration with suppliers, customers, and even competitors.

A major result of all these changes has been the creation of ebusiness organizations that transcend traditional business organizations—the creation of virtual corporations. A good example of this is the emergence of integrated companies, where various businesses integrate their supply chains and collaborate to enable them to remain competitive. Essentially, they join forces within an electronic infrastructure to streamline and even reinvent their businesses. This aptly illustrates the fundamental change being wrought by ebusiness.

The Structure of Ebusiness

Ebusiness includes the front-office and back-office information system applications that drive modern business (see figure 1.1). These include the applications that enable information related to the customers to be captured and used to find better and more efficient ways to serve them—the so-called **customer relationship management (CRM)** applications (discussed in chapter 9)—as well as the applications designed to streamline the acquisition of goods and services—**eprocurement** applications (discussed in chapter 8). Ebusiness also includes other information system applications that serve to integrate the systems of a business to streamline its value chain. The streamlining of the internal value chain and the external supply chain is a fundamental strategy of ebusiness that enables businesses to respond quickly to the increasingly stringent demands of ecustomers.

In summary, the definition of ebusiness includes a wide range of business activity—a range that is widening to the point that experts such as Don Tapscott, author of *Paradigm Shift*, *The Digital Economy*, and *The Naked Corporation*, are saying that ultimately all business will be ebusiness.[2] The Canadian Snapshots box illustrates how some companies are using ebusiness. Chapter 2 discusses various ebusiness models and strategies that companies have adopted.

customer relationship management (CRM): The set of strategies, technologies, and processes that enable a business to continuously improve offerings to customers.

eprocurement: The complete business process of acquiring goods and services through electronic means, from requisition through to fulfillment and payment.

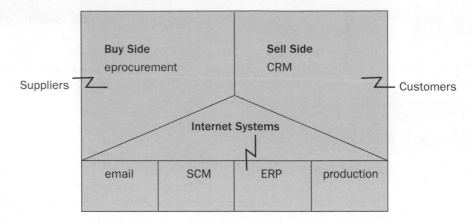

Figure 1.1 Essential structure of ebusiness

Ebusiness encompasses the full range of business activity, from suppliers to customers.

SYSTEMS INTEGRATION

WHILE THE INTERNET IS A CENTRAL ENABLING TECHNOLOGY FOR THE RISE OF EBUSINESS, IT IS not the only one. To make ebusiness work, a great deal of activity must take place behind webpages. Corporate systems need to be organized and integrated in such a way that there is a fast and free flow of information throughout the systems, regardless of the different technologies, functions, and platforms within organizations. This is called **systems integration**. It is necessary to enable companies to respond to the fast-moving pace of business in the information age and to keep customers happy. It is also necessary to enable companies to cope with the growing phenomenon of providing customization of their products for their customers. Increasingly, companies offer to customize their products, and the first time the company finds out the form the customization will take is when it gets the order. The company then needs to obtain the materials and process them in time to meet the high expectations of customers. Systems integration is necessary to enable the company to provide this fast turnaround without resorting to increases in inventory.

Companies use several tools to enable this integration. Where the internet itself is not used, quite often other networks that make use of internet technology are used. Where such networks are internal to the company, they are referred to as **intranets**. Where they extend outside the company, they are called **extranets**.

The use of internet technology in intranets and extranets means that these networks have the same look, feel, and functionality as the web. A user often cannot tell when moving from one to the other or to the internet itself. The difference is therefore said to be *transparent* to the user.

Typically, websites for sizable business organizations are constructed on separate network servers, called web servers. The data on the web servers include the HTML code for the actual webpages, as well as the software being used to construct the storefront on the internet. **HyperText Markup Language (HTML)** is a programming language used to create webpages. The storefront software consists of a shopping basket connected to an online catalogue, which in turn is connected to the main order-entry system of the company, to enable the business to handle orders and other customers requests.

systems integration: The bringing together of various business systems that have different technologies, functions, and platforms so they can conduct business processes in such a way that the user does not see that different systems are being used.

intranet: A computer network within an enterprise that makes use of internet technology.

extranet: A computer network that makes use of internet technology and includes users from outside the organization as well as inside.

HyperText Markup Language (HTML): The programming language used to create webpages.

Research In Motion

Research In Motion Ltd. (RIM) is a high-tech startup company based in Waterloo, Ontario, and listed on the NASDAQ Stock Exchange and the Toronto Stock Exchange. The company, which started in 1984, specializes in producing handheld wireless products, such as the BlackBerry® wireless email unit, various pagers and wireless personal computer adapters, and radio modems. Its major competitors are the Apple iPhone; smartphones fired by Google's operating system, Android; and palmOne, Inc., handheld devices, such as the Zire™, Tungsten™, and Treo™.

RIM has evolved into a leading designer, manufacturer, and marketer of wireless solutions. The company provides platforms and solutions for access to time-sensitive information, including email, phone, internet, and intranet-based applications. RIM technology also enables a broad array of third-party developers and manufacturers to enhance their products and services with wireless connectivity to data.

RIM is now a world leader in small handheld internet-based technology. Its original product—the BlackBerry—has evolved into a personal digital assistant (PDA) with email and internet browsing capabilities and the ability to send and receive voice calls.

In February 2004, Sony Ericsson Mobile Communications and Research In Motion announced plans to enable BlackBerry connectivity on Sony Ericsson mobile phones. The agreement allows Sony Ericsson's Symbian OS-based phones to connect to BlackBerry Enterprise Server and BlackBerry Web Client services for enterprise and individual users. Thousands of companies and government organizations around the world have adopted the BlackBerry services infrastructure. IT departments and consumers are recognizing the productivity benefits that can be gained from wireless access to corporate data and email. The BlackBerry architecture for enterprise customers includes integration capability with corporate information systems and enhanced security.

RIM's "always on" connectivity and push technology, which automatically delivers emails and other data to and from a BlackBerry, has proven to be an efficient and reliable communications platform. Under the agreement with Sony, the BlackBerry services will be able to run on certain Sony Ericsson mobile phones, such as the Sony P900, while maintaining the phone's existing functionality. The P900 phone is a multifaceted device that offers productivity, entertainment, and communications applications as well as full PDA organizer functions and the ability to take colour digital pictures. From RIM's point of view, the agreement provides its end-user customers and carrier partners with additional wireless device choices, while enabling IT departments to leverage their existing BlackBerry infrastructure.

Companies like RIM are leaders in the global wireless market and are establishing Canada as a major presence in this emerging area of ebusiness. But as iPhones, Android devices, and other handhelds vie for top spot among smartphone users, the BlackBerry struggles to retain its top spot among business users. To do so, it is releasing new products that have touch screens that provide a more iPhone-like experience.

Research In Motion
www.rim.com

Questions

1. Why would Sony Ericsson have joined with RIM rather than develop its own products to meet the same needs?

2. What is meant by leveraging "their existing BlackBerry infrastructure"?

3. How would wireless devices add to the value of existing information systems from management and strategic perspectives?

4. How can the BlackBerry compete with the iPhone both among general users and among business users?

Sources: www.rim.net; Research In Motion, "Sony Ericsson and RIM Announce BlackBerry Connectivity Support in P900 Smartphone," news release, www.blackberry.net/news/press/2004/pr-23_02_2004-01.shtml, October 30, 2004.

When SAP is used, for example, the online catalogue is linked to the SAP systems that contain all the product and inventory records and the products that the company wishes to offer for sale at the online store. The data in the main records are located using **Extensible Markup Language (XML)**. XML is a tool that is similar to HTML and is

Extensible Markup Language (XML): A tool that is similar to HTML and is compatible with it but does not rely on single pre-set tags to identify information.

compatible with it but does not rely on single pre-set tags to identify information. Instead, XML provides a mechanism for any document builder to define new XML tags within any XML document.

When an online store is configured, there is the capacity to add graphics to illustrate the products being offered and also the ability to add a shopping cart. Anyone who has shopped online will have seen shopping carts to which products can be added while browsing through the store. Examples can be found on Amazon and on any number of other websites that offer goods for sale online. Eventually, the user will make a purchase by going to a check-out screen that allows payment for the goods using a credit card or any other payment system that the store supports. The online catalogue and the shopping cart software would be on a web server along with the webpages.

Using a web server also facilitates security because it enables firewalls to be strategically located to offer maximum security for both the customer and the company's data. **Firewalls** are separate, highly secure computers, along with related software, policies and procedures, through which access to the network from the internet is exclusively directed. A common configuration is for a firewall to be set up between a web server and the main system. Some companies also set up firewalls outside a web server as well, leaving only the webpages available to the public. The topic of security is explored in chapter 5.

firewall: A separate, highly secure computer, along with related software, policies and procedures, through which access to a network from the internet is exclusively directed.

Tools for Systems Integration

Not all ebusiness is carried out on the internet, but it is undeniable that the rise in the use of the internet, or more specifically the **World Wide Web (WWW),** is the single most important enabler of ebusiness of any type. The World Wide Web is the user-friendly, graphics-capable component of the internet. A good example of this shift to the WWW is EDI, which started on private networks called value-added networks (VANs) but has been moving to the web because of the economies that are possible when using standardized, internet-based systems as opposed to proprietary, private networks. Chapter 3 discusses the workings of the internet and the World Wide Web.

World Wide Web (WWW): The user-friendly, graphics-capable component of the internet.

Businesses achieve the systems integration they need by using intranets to tie together their systems internally and by using extranets to tie their systems to those of their customers and suppliers. They also use tools such as enterprise resource planning (ERP), supply-chain management (SCM), customer relationship management (CRM), and eprocurement to achieve this integration both externally and internally. All these tools are essential to ebusiness and are explored fully in chapters 4 and 7–9. The purpose here is to briefly describe how they fit into a broad perspective on ebusiness.

ERP systems are large software systems that a business uses to automate its activities across their full range. Consisting of the software sold by several major vendors—including SAP, Oracle, and PeopleSoft—an ERP implementation represents a major initiative for any business. Implementation of an ERP system often requires significant changes in business processes to accommodate the software, sometimes to the point of re-inventing the business. On the plus side, ERP systems offer the ability to share a common pool of data across an entire enterprise and to run applications using a very common format. They also enable managers to have immediate access to the latest information about the organization's activities and performance.

The implementation of ERP systems predated the development of ecommerce, and many installations were prompted by the Y2K crisis that was being predicted in the late 1990s (a result of computer systems having to be changed to accommodate the years beginning with the numerals 20- rather than just 19-). The "crisis" turned out to have been overblown, but the event created a strong focus on the software systems used by businesses. The incredible boom in ebusiness and the related need to integrate systems have led to a continuance of interest in ERP systems, and in many companies they are viewed as essential to delivering on ebusiness needs.

CRM systems also are very large information systems, and they present many of the same issues and difficulties as ERP systems. However, CRM systems enable an organization to deliver on its customer needs on a timely basis. They accomplish this by accumulating information about customers and then using that information to offer them a product that is tailored to their needs. The idea of CRM is to be able to acquire new customers, enhance the profitability of all customers, and retain the profitable ones. CRM does not always involve integrating systems with customers, but some of the more advanced systems do. Also, CRM is increasingly being deployed through the use of social media, such as Facebook and LinkedIn. The use of CRM systems, because they involve obtaining and analyzing information about customers, is closely linked to emarketing from a strategic point of view. Emarketing is covered in chapter 11.

LinkedIn
www.linkedin.com

Eprocurement systems are of two main types—buy-side and sell-side systems. **Buy-side** procurement systems essentially involve systems within a business that fully automate purchases by staff and involve electronic contact with outside suppliers, often through the internet or an extranet. **Sell-side** procurement systems, on the other hand, involve systems that are essentially trading communities, or exchanges that link directly to the systems of both suppliers and customers. Many sell-side systems are fully integrated with the systems of their participants. Like CRM systems, eprocurement systems are being developed within social media. These topics are dealt with in chapter 8.

buy-side: The purchasing end of the supply chain, which consists of suppliers and the processes that connect with them.

sell-side: The selling end of the supply chain, which consists of customers and the processes that connect with them.

The use of large integrated information systems such as ERP and CRM led to the availability of large quantities of data within enterprises. The question then arose as to how to make most effective use of those data. Clearly, there was a need to find ways to organize and analyze the data so the best use could be made of them, particularly for strategic purposes. The tool that arose to meet this need was **business intelligence (BI)**, which is the subject of chapter 10. BI is a powerful application, or set of applications, that allows businesses to capture, analyze, interpret, and report on data across an enterprise, thus creating valuable information for the enterprise. Increasingly, all these large systems are moving to the cloud, being provided on a rental basis over the internet.

business intelligence (BI): A powerful application, or set of applications, that allows businesses to capture, analyze, interpret, and report on data across an enterprise, thus creating valuable information for the enterprise.

THE DOMAINS OF EBUSINESS
Business to Consumer (B2C)

As mentioned previously, Ebusiness that involves interaction between businesses and consumers is referred to as business-to-consumer (B2C) ebusiness. In the B2C arena, companies are offering a growing range of goods and services on the internet directly to consumers, often bypassing their traditional distributors. Besides the books that are offered on Amazon, early initiatives in B2C involved the sale of investments, through such sites as E*TRADE Financial and Schwab.com. These sites are particularly interesting, in that the former is an internet upstart and the latter is an old-economy entrant into ebusiness, but both have been successful in their efforts.

A notable example of consumer-oriented ebusiness is banks, which have formed their business strategies around aggressive ebusiness strategies. Banks have been involved in ebusiness for many years; they began to install **automated teller machines (ATMs)** during the 1970s. An ATM is a user-friendly, kiosk-based computer that enables bank customers to carry out their own banking transactions. The process of moving customer service to an automated format, where the customer actually performs the input activity for the bank, proved to be a lucrative strategy. The banks did not have to pay to have this input performed; the customers actually paid them for the "privilege"! The banks installed more ATMs, reduced their staffing, closed branches, and made more money. Then, during the 1990s, the banks moved their ebusiness to the internet by introducing internet banking. After some shaky starts, with concerns about security and sometimes doubtful technology, all banks now offer substantial internet banking services to their customers. People can log on to their bank's website and view their account balances and recent transactions, make transfers of funds, pay bills, manage their investments, and request other services. Internet banking has been very successful and offers even greater cost savings to the banks than do ATMs (see figure 1.2).

B2C has been growing and changing the business environment. Etailing, or electronic retailing, will continue to be an expanding phenomenon as the use of the internet spreads to greater numbers of people.

Business to Business (B2B)

In the business-to-business (B2B) arena, activity has centred on the streamlining of the supply chain by establishing shared systems between suppliers and customers, using the internet or related technology. The **supply chain** is the set of processes that encompasses purchases of raw materials or resources through to final delivery of a product or service

automated teller machines (ATMs): User-friendly, kiosk-based computers that enable bank customers to carry out their own banking transactions.

supply chain: The set of processes that encompasses purchases of raw materials or resources through to final delivery of a product or service to the end consumer.

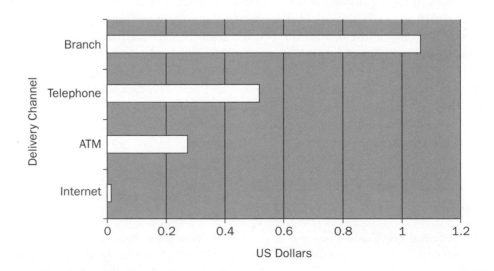

Figure 1.2 Cost of banking transactions (U.S. dollars)

The cost of banking transactions drops dramatically when the internet is used for processing them.

to the end consumer. Activity in the B2B world has focused on the buy-side, which deals with the procurement activity of a business, and the sell-side, which relates to relationships with customers and the consequent marketing and selling activity. In a sense, of course, the two are simply opposite sides of the same coin.

Government to Business (G2B) and Business to Government (B2G)

Many governments of the world make their services available to their constituencies over the internet. Canadian government departments have also been using electronic filing methods. Notable among these is the Canada Revenue Agency (CRA), which has very successfully implemented a system for taxpayers to file income tax returns electronically on the internet, as have the U.S. Internal Revenue Service and U.K. Inland Revenue, among many others. Statistics Canada has been developing a system of electronic filing of reports, and other departments (such as the National Energy Board) have implemented systems for efiling of information. Canadian federal government departments are operating under the general guidance of its Government On-Line (GOL) initiative, which ran from 1999–2005. Similarly, the United States established a comprehensive egovernment strategy in 2002. Governments implement electronic services because of the cost savings that flow from reducing the volume of paper to be handled. In addition, they know from various surveys that businesses and individuals often prefer to be able to deal with the government online. This domain of ebusiness is growing very rapidly and becoming much more important.

THE BENEFITS OF EBUSINESS

WHY HAS THE TREMENDOUS GROWTH IN EBUSINESS OVER THE PAST FEW YEARS taken place? Clearly, there has been a strong interest in the internet, as well as considerable hype, but for it to be adopted by businesses, there must be solid business justification for its use. Put simply, the benefits of using the internet must be greater than the costs; using the internet must result in a satisfactory contribution to profits.

These reasons for the growth in ebusiness generally involve the quest for improved profitability but more specifically include the following:

- increasing sales
- reducing costs
- improving customer service
- responding to competitive pressure
- expanding market reach

Increasing Sales

The internet offers the possibility of increasing sales through various means. It represents a sales channel that can be used to support and augment more traditional channels, such as stores, mail-order catalogues, and field sales personnel. This sales channel also may reach new people, particularly those who use the internet frequently and are comfortable buying online. Finally, the internet offers the possibility of reaching new geographical areas around the globe, many of which were not economically accessible before the advent of the internet.

Reducing Costs

One of the clear advantages of ebusiness is the lower cost of executing transactions, as illustrated so well by the banking business. This lower cost comes from the ability of ebusiness to move the input process from the staff to the customers and outside users, as well as from the reduced necessity to produce, handle, and store paper documents.

An example can be found in airline travel. Under the old reservation system, a customer would call or visit an airline or a travel agent and state his or her requests to an employee, who would then enter those requests into the computer system and generate printed confirmations and tickets. Now all the major airlines have internet reservation systems, which enable the customer to log in and type all their requests into forms provided on the site. Such a system confirms the availability of the flights and the specific requests, such as seating or special meals and then generates tickets that can be mailed from a central point or electronic tickets that are faxed or emailed to the customer. The customer can also obtain boarding passes online, which can then be sent by way of email or text to their BlackBerry or other mobile device. All the input has been carried out by the customer, and no airline employee involvement has been required other than perhaps generating a printed boarding pass and giving it to the customer. Reduced need for customer service personnel leads to considerable cost savings. In the case of the electronic ticket and boarding pass sent by email, the customer is even doing the printing, which points to another of the other reasons internet commerce is cheaper—less infrastructure.

internet service provider (ISP): A company that offers internet access and related services to individuals and businesses for a fee. Connections are offered through telephone lines, cable, satellite, or wireless technology.

Under older, traditional systems, businesses owned hardware and software, and they rented or purchased much of the communications capability. The internet offers a communications platform that is largely cost-free to all users. Certainly, there are internet-related costs, such as fees customers pay to **internet service providers (ISPs)**, and there is still a need for businesses to establish additional internet-related infrastructure, such as new servers and firewalls to ensure security. However, the cost of these additional items, though sometimes considerable, is small in comparison to the cost that would be incurred if the business had to acquire a communications infrastructure comparable to the internet. ISPs are companies that offer internet access and related services to individuals and businesses for a fee. Connections are offered through telephone lines, cable, satellite, or wireless technology.

The use of the internet and its applications for ebusiness involves many different processes carried out in a business. As technology is applied, it is necessary to rationalize and improve these processes to make efficient use of the technological and human resources required. Consequently, ebusiness offers an opportunity to achieve economies in the improvement of business processes, and this is one of the techniques businesses use when entering into ebusiness to reduce costs. It is important to note, however, that the cost reductions derived from business process change come after the change has been executed and is running smoothly; the cost of conversion can be very high, particularly because of issues related to the adaptability of the people involved.

Another cost-reduction measure inherent in ebusiness involves the costs of procurement from suppliers. Automation of these procurement activities should result in cost savings. In addition, more closely tying procurement activities to the processes of the suppliers often leads to improved supplier relations and the resulting opportunity to obtain better prices.

Improving Customer Service

A company's website is an important vehicle for customers and prospective customers to obtain information about the company, its products, and its people. The following are some examples of additional services to customers offered through the web:

- instructions for finding the business, including directions or maps to store locations, bank branches, and so on.

- webpages detailing the specific services offered by the firm and providing contact information for the persons in charge of each area

- reader surveys offered by news sites such as globeandmail.com and CNN.com, where users can quickly vote on an issue and read the real-time results of the vote

- product demonstrations, such as those at websites devoted to automobiles that provide details and working demos of particular models

Responding to Competitive Pressure

Many companies must use the internet for competitive reasons. Part of this reason relates to image: If competitors are doing it, then people will ask why a company in the same market isn't. It also relates to simple economics: If competitors are obtaining financial benefits such as increased sales and reduced costs from using the web, then they will eventually obtain a competitive advantage, and it will be necessary for others in the market to use the web in order to survive.

Expanding Market Reach

The worldwide use of the internet has played a major role in increasing business's interest in using it. One of the major implications is that it allows a business to reach a far wider market than it previously could. The internet offers business the opportunity to reach people all around the world. If companies want to do business in a new country or want to establish direct, cost-effective communications links with existing business partners in other areas of the globe, they can do so through the internet.

Some businesses have used the internet to establish a global market for their products. Of course, there are limitations to this global internet reach. For one thing, there are significant parts of the globe that do not have any internet access or where access is extremely limited. Much of the underdeveloped world falls into this category because it does not have the communications infrastructure necessary to support the internet. As shown in figure 1.3, the number of internet users has been growing consistently since 1995. There seems little doubt that this trend will continue into the foreseeable future around the globe.

The Globe and Mail
www.globeandmail.com
CNN
www.cnn.com

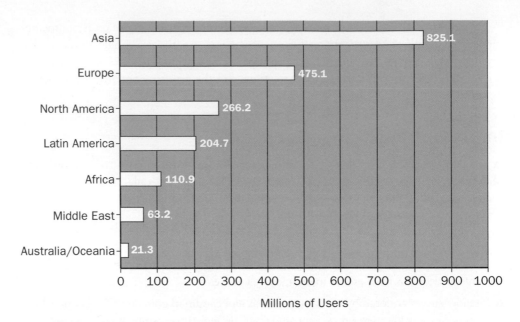

Figure 1.3 World internet usage and population statistics, 2010

THE CHALLENGES OF EBUSINESS
Privacy and Security

As more commercial transactions have taken place over the internet, there have been concerns about the lack of security and privacy. Initially, it was widely acknowledged that there was little or no security available on the internet and that the internet was an environment rife with hackers, viruses, and other threats to data and system integrity. As a result of this lack of security, people were reluctant to allow any of their private information to be transmitted over the internet and were especially reluctant to provide information such as credit card numbers.

This latter point relates to another perceived shortcoming with regard to the internet—the lack of a satisfactory payment system. Since the internet is an electronic medium, hard cash cannot be used to pay for goods or services purchased online. Various other methods have been tried, and for a time, the most common method was the use of credit cards through forms that were filled out offline and faxed to the vendor. Now, the use of credit cards directly online is the most common means of payment on the web.

Security and Payment Systems

Since the early days of the commercial use of the internet, considerable progress has been made in addressing security and payment issues. Security over the internet, at least on commercial sites, has vastly improved in recent years. Many commercial sites have installed firewalls to provide a level of security (see figure 1.4 for the basic structure of a firewall). To augment security, they have also made increased use of **encryption** (the use of a mathematical formula—an algorithm—that is applied to electronic data to render it illegible to anyone without the decoding key) to prevent unauthorized persons from reading data.

encryption: The use of a mathematical formula (an algorithm) that is applied to electronic data to render it illegible to anyone without the decoding key.

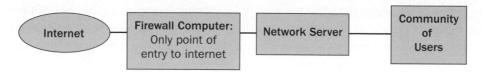

Figure 1.4 Basic firewall architecture

A firewall is placed between the internet and a network to enable outside access to the network to be controlled.

While they have not been overcome, the barriers to the spread of commerce on the internet have at least substantially reduced in recent years. Nevertheless, the most recent surveys indicate that the most prevalent concerns of internet users in conducting business online involve the provision of credit card information and general privacy concerns. The press has reported numerous instances of identity theft, under which the perpetrators find enough information (such as SIN numbers, address and telephone information, employment, etc.) about another person—the victim—that they can reconstruct that person's economic identity and then use that identity to gain credit and actually purchase items and services. The victims eventually find out when their credit rating deteriorates or they begin receiving telephone calls from creditors, demanding payment. The issue of online privacy is being addressed through legislation around the world (see chapter 13 for further discussion).

Many of the privacy concerns of internet users are addressed in Canadian privacy legislation, notably the Personal Information Protection and Electronic Documents Act (PIPEDA). The act was introduced in 2000 and came into effect on January 1, 2004. For the first time, it created an enforceable right to privacy for individuals with respect to the collection, use, and disclosure of personal information by the private sector in the course of commercial activities. As a result of this act, the Office of the Privacy Commissioner of Canada has been established to administer it and act as something of a watchdog on matters concerning privacy of information. In addition, most provinces have established similar legislation, as have the United States, the European Union, and numerous other countries.

Although the new legislation does not deal with all the issues that are important to ecommerce participants, it does address many of them and provides a framework for at least some of the future legislation that will surely follow.

Regarding the topic of payment systems, considerable progress has been made through the banks offering online services, such as the ability to pay bills online. Although internet banking has become routine for many Canadians, true online payment systems are nonexistent or in a pilot phase. For example, many companies, such as telephone companies, notify their customers by email when their bill is ready and offer customers the ability to read the bill on their website. In some instances, the bill can then be paid online or through internet banking or conventional means. However, these systems have not achieved the degree of success that the online banking systems have, and credit cards are still the most common payment method in cyberspace. Although payment systems, such as PayPal, have gained popularity, a universally accepted online transaction system is still not available. **PayPal**, owned by eBay, allows money transfers over the internet in a variety of currencies. Merchants as well as individual users can use the system, and many of them do so.

Other more advanced technologies, not yet used widely for commercial purposes, are beginning to be implemented, principally by credit card companies. An important example is the wireless PayPass card from MasterCard, which will be discussed more fully

PayPal: A payment system, owned by eBay, that allows money transfers over the internet in a variety of currencies.

in chapter 6. Essentially, PayPass is a wireless smart card that offers the capability of buying something in a store simply by waving the card at a receiver near the cash register. A **smart card**, which is not much bigger than a credit card, contains a computer chip that is used to store or process information.

smart card: A card, not much bigger than a credit card, which contains a computer chip that is used to store or process information.

CHAPTER SUMMARY

In a very broad sense, electronic business is normally defined as any business carried out in electronic form. More recently, the term "ebusiness" has been used to refer to the process of carrying out business using the internet as a strategic tool. In this text, ebusiness is defined as the strategic use of technology, particularly the internet, to integrate and streamline the business processes, enterprise applications, and organizational structure of a business to create a high-performance business model.

The rise in the use of the internet is the single most important enabler of ebusiness of any type. Even types of ebusiness that were carried out before the age of the internet are moving to the internet.

The internet and its use in business have been changing due to the proliferation of internet-enabled mobile devices, the introduction of cloud computing, and the spread of social media.

The internet and ebusiness are changing business models. This means that businesses need to construct their business models such that they can deliver quickly to meet expectations. People use the internet for convenience and also to get customized products.

Business models have changed substantially, by cutting infrastructure costs, increasing technology costs, adding new sources of revenue, and making old sources of revenue obsolete. Changing product package content also contributes to changing business models. The changes in and pressures on business models have driven numerous strategic initiatives, some of which are unique to ebusiness and some of which are not. As illustrated so well by the example of Encyclopaedia Britannica (on page 7), business models and strategies have been evolving and no doubt will continue to evolve in the future.

There are numerous domains of ebusiness, principally business to consumer (B2C) and business to business (B2B). In B2C, companies are offering a wider range of goods on the internet. The internet also ushered in the idea of online auctioning and other bidding-related retail systems. Perhaps more importantly, the auctioning idea has extended into business-to-business procurement systems and trading exchanges, where auctioning is perceived as a way for suppliers to become more competitive and responsive to their customers.

Activity in the B2B world has focused on the buy-side, which deals with the procurement activity of a business, and the sell-side, which relates to relationships with customers and the consequent marketing and selling activities. Ebusiness also includes the front- and back-office information system applications that form the engine for modern business. The streamlining of the internal value chain and the external supply chain is a fundamental strategy of ebusiness that enables a business to respond quickly to the increasingly stringent demands of ecustomers.

Businesses achieve the integration they need in their systems by using intranets to tie their systems together internally and by using extranets to tie their systems to those of their customers and suppliers. ERP systems are used in a business to automate its activities across their full range and achieve the required integration.

Buy-side procurement systems essentially consist of systems within a business fully automating purchases by staff and enabling electronic contact with outside suppliers, often through the internet or an extranet. Sell-side procurement systems, on the other hand, involve systems that are essentially trading communities that link directly to the systems of both suppliers and customers.

There are numerous benefits of ebusiness, including increasing sales, reducing costs, improving customer service, minimizing competitive pressure, and expanding market reach. However, there are challenges as well, which largely have revolved around privacy and security and their roles in the making payments on the internet. There has been considerable progress in meeting these challenges through better security techniques and payment systems.

Key Terms

automated teller machines (ATMs) (p. 14)

business intelligence (BI) (p. 13)

buy-side (p. 13)

customer relationship management (CRM) (p. 9)

electronic data interchange (EDI) (p. 5)

encryption (p. 18)

eprocurement (p. 9)

Extensible Markup Language (XML) (p. 11)

extranet (p. 10)

firewall (p. 12)

HyperText Markup Language (HTML) (p. 10)

integrated systems (p. 7)

internet (p. 2)

internet service provider (ISP) (p. 16)

intranet (p. 10)

PayPal (p. 19)

sell-side (p. 13)

smart card (p. 20)

software as a service (SaaS) (p. 2)

supply chain (p. 14)

systems integration (p. 10)

World Wide Web (WWW) (p. 12)

MyEbusinessLab Tools for Online Learning

To help you master the material in this chapter and stay up to date with new developments in ebusiness, visit the MyEBusinessLab at www.pearsoned.ca/myebusinesslab. Resources include the following:

- **Pre- and Post-Test Questions**
- **Additional Chapter Questions**
- **Author Blog**
- **Recommended Readings**
- **Commentaries on Current Trends**
- **Additional Topics in Ebusiness**
- **Internet Exercises**
- **Glossary Flashcards**

Endnotes

1. R. Kalakota and M. Robinson, *E-Business 2.0: Roadmap for Success* (Reading, MA: Addison Wesley, 2000).
2. D. Tapscott and D. Ticoll, *The Naked Corporation* (Toronto: Viking Canada, 2003).

Chapter 2
Internet Business Models and Strategies

Learning Objectives

When you complete this chapter you should be able to:

1 Describe the key elements of an internet business model.

2 Explain the similarities and differences between B2C and B2B models.

3 Explain the similarities and differences between models based on "bricks," "bricks and clicks," "clicks and bricks," and "clicks."

4 Describe key revenue-generating approaches used by internet business models.

5 Define and explain the importance of ebusiness strategy.

6 Describe the relationship between internet business models and business strategy.

7 Identify the key areas addressed by a strategic plan.

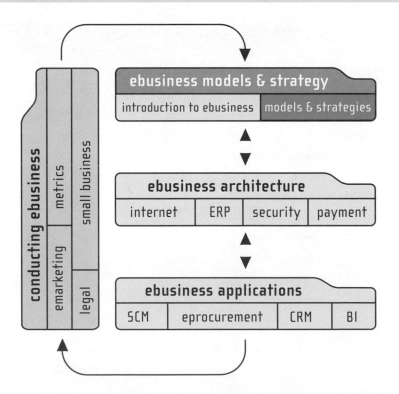

INTRODUCTION

Broadly, a BUSINESS MODEL MAY BE DEFINED AS THE MANNER IN WHICH A BUSINESS organizes itself to achieve its objectives, which normally involve the generation of profits. Although there are various views about what components should make up a business model, we will consider the following eight components:[1]

1. *External forces.* Political, economic, social, and technological factors, pressures, and forces from outside the entity that create opportunities for the entity or threaten its business objectives.

2. *Markets/formats.* The domains in which the entity may choose to operate and the design and location of the facilities.

3. *Customers.* The individuals and organizations that purchase the entity's output.

4. *Core business processes.* The processes used to develop, produce, market, and distribute an entity's products and services.

5. *Core products and services.* The commodities that the entity brings to the market.

6. *Alliances.* The relationships established by an entity to attain business objectives, expand business opportunities, and reduce or transfer business risk.

7. *Resource management processes.* The processes by which resources are acquired, developed, and allocated to the core business activities.

8. *Strategic management process.* The process by which the entity's mission is developed, its business objectives are defined, business risks that threaten attainment of the business objectives are identified, business risk management processes are established, and progress toward meeting business objectives is monitored.

An **internet business model** represents the manner in which a business uses the internet to support, amplify, or develop its overall business model. An ebusiness **strategy** is the sum of all the choices that a business makes within these eight categories and how it fits them together to offer unique value to its customers that differentiates its ebusiness model from those of its competitors. In other words, the term "business model" denotes a general description of how a business structures its activities to earn profits, while the term "strategy" focuses on the specific choices in that set of activities that are aimed at giving the entity a unique position in its industry and, thereby, a competitive advantage. Once all the choices are made, however, there is little distinction between an entity's business model and its business strategy and these terms become interchangeable.

According to Michael E. Porter, "The essence of strategy is choosing to perform activities differently than rivals do.... Competitive strategy is about being different. It means deliberately choosing a different set of activities to deliver a unique mix of value."[2] Porter cautions against a strategy based on price competition. The internet is a very competitive environment that can lead to relentless price reductions, to the point where most entities will find it difficult to earn a profit. This leaves room for only a very small number of players with very cost-effective operations in any particular sector or domain. Instead, Porter recommends competing on quality, features, and service.

Traditional business models have usually revolved around a central product or service. The idea was that a business would acquire or make goods and sell them for amounts

business model: The manner in which a business organizes itself to achieve its objectives, which normally involve the generation of profits.

internet business model: The way in which a business uses the internet to support, amplify, or develop an overall business model.

strategy: The sum of all the choices that a business makes to offer unique value to its customers that differentiates its business model from those of its competitors.

in excess of cost. Often, a business would add services or accessories to augment its profits or customer satisfaction, but the central feature of the traditional business model was the sale of a product or service at an amount in excess of its cost. This model fits the traditional industrial environment very well. Manufacturing organizations, such as Ford Motor Company, exploited this model by adopting a mass-production model that enabled them to reduce unit costs and selling prices and still generate profits. Much traditional business literature has been devoted to the idea of maximizing revenues, minimizing costs, and generating competitive advantage.

During the last few decades of the twentieth century, there was an increase in the number of organizations that sold services rather than goods. These organizations, including various types of professional firms (such as accountants and consultants) and, increasingly, technology-related service firms, have followed a model similar to that of traditional manufacturers. They have focused their efforts on a service or related package of services, hired people with the skills to provide these services, and sold their time and skills to their clients at a price in excess of the costs they had to pay. As the environment has changed, the nature and scope of the services that companies offer has changed, but companies continue to follow the same basic business model of selling something in excess of its cost. This chapter discusses business models and strategies that are being used to exploit the advantages of doing business on the internet.

External Forces

As mentioned earlier, an internet business model involves the use of the internet as a strategic tool for generating profits and achieving other business objectives. The internet is a technological factor that creates the business opportunities described in this chapter. Chapter 3 describes the technologies that are the driving forces for internet-based business models. The New Business Models box illustrates a new, disruptive business model for the music industry that was enabled by the internet. During the dot-com boom (also called the tech bubble) from August 1995 to March 2000, numerous media reports and articles by influential business executives suggested that the internet "changes everything" so that "old economy" business models no longer apply. This view gained widespread acceptance as companies like Amazon.com and E*TRADE Financial raised huge amounts of capital in the stock market without ever having made a profit. Some business writers pointed to the success of these ventures in raising capital and announced that the old rules didn't apply anymore.

When the tech bubble burst, the dramatic declines in the share prices of dot-com stocks acted as a reality check and renewed the realization that a business needs to make money in the long term and therefore needs to have a viable business model. While this does not seem like a radical insight, the exuberance about the possibilities arising from the innovative use of the internet had blinded many investors to this simple reality. Although the tech bust represented a setback for many internet-based businesses and the failure of many dot-com startups, ebusiness continues to represent a rich mine of opportunities, and numerous internet-based business models have developed in recent years.

Technological developments associated with the internet are an external force underlying ebusiness. Other external forces include legal and regulatory forces that determine how ebusiness is conducted in many jurisdictions. For example, some governments' and marketers' intrusions on internet users' privacy have led to the development of privacy protection technologies and processes. Laws and regulations aimed at protecting intellectual property have constrained certain business models and boosted others. Chapter 13 addresses legal and regulatory forces that create opportunities and constraints on how ebusiness is conducted.

Markets/Customers

Writings on ebusiness use broad classifications such as business to consumer (B2C) and business to business (B2B) to discuss categories of markets and customers. For example, Amazon.ca operates in the business-to-consumer (B2C) domain. Other widely used B2C models involve the provision of services such as auctions (eBay), travel reservations (Expedia), and financial services (President's Choice Financial).

While the business press devotes a great deal of attention to B2C models, B2B models actually represent a much higher proportion of ebusiness activity conducted in

Expedia
www.expedia.ca

President's Choice Financial
www.pcfinancial.ca

Ariba
www.ariba.com

the economy and often involve multi-year, large-volume, high-value contracts between business partners. For example, Ariba Inc. arranges reverse auctions where prequalified suppliers bid on contracts offered by a buyer. In contrast to a regular auction, where a seller offers goods to many buyers who compete by bidding up the sale price of the goods being auctioned, a **reverse auction** has one buyer offering a supply contract to many sellers who compete by bidding down the supply price for the contract. Other examples of B2B models involve the sale of office supplies (STAPLES Business Depot), job listings (Workopolis), and cloud computing services (Salesforce.com).

Staples Business Services
www.staples.ca

Workopolis
www.workopolis.com

Salesforce
www.salesforce.com

In addition to B2C and B2B models used for conducting ecommerce activities on the internet, business-to-employee (B2E) internet models support the ebusiness activities of many entities. For example, B2E is used in websites that enable employees to register for benefits, monitor the status of their benefits, and update personal information as necessary, as well as in websites that provide employees with training and procedural guidance.

It is important to recognize that governments can utilize internet business models to enhance the delivery of services to citizens and to secure services from business entities. Various levels of government in Canada use the internet to deliver services to citizens. The objective of the federal Government On-Line (GOL) initiative is to provide easy and seamless access to services that may involve more than one government department or other levels of government, while protecting the confidentiality of information and users' rights to privacy.[3] Some examples of government-to-consumer (G2C) ebusiness activities include online tax filings (Canada Revenue Agency), driver's license renewal kiosks, and information dissemination over the web (provincial and federal governments). Examples of government-to-business (G2B) activities include tax filings (Canada Revenue Agency) and the open bidding system on government contracts (Business Access Canada).

Government On-Line
www.tpsgc-pwgsc.gc.ca/
apropos-about/fi-fs/ged-gol-eng.
html

Canada Revenue Agency
www.cra-arc.gc.ca

Government of Canada
www.canada.gc.ca

Business Access Canada
www.canadabusiness.
mb.ca/home_page/guides/
guides_by_department/
public_works_and_govern-
ment_services_canada/
business_access_canada/

While labels such as B2C and B2B can help focus discussion, considering them in isolation can be misleading because they are definitely not mutually exclusive. Figure 2.1 illustrates a common internet business scenario, where a business can be involved in B2C, B2B, and B2E domains at the same time. A consumer purchases goods or services over the internet from a business (B2C) that also sells its goods or services to another business (B2B). The two companies operate internal intranets for their employees and other insiders (B2E) and connect with each other through an extranet, which is an expanded portion of a company's intranet or a restricted portion of the internet.

An example of a company that uses its website to sell to both consumers and businesses is Rogers' Chocolates, of Victoria, British Columbia. Its website has a section for resellers, who will buy the company's products and resell them in their stores. In other words, in this case Rogers' Chocolates is acting as a wholesaler, but it does so within the same website it uses for retailing to end consumers.

Rogers' Chocolates
www.rogerschocolates.com

Core Business Processes

Most businesses today have some degree of internet presence. The "bricks vs. clicks" label is used to distinguish the degree to which core business processes depend on the internet. Figure 2.2 illustrates the continuum of internet business models, based on the bricks-vs.-clicks dichotomy. The "clicks" label is applied to business models that are solely or predominantly based on the internet (these are also called "pure plays"), whereas the "bricks"

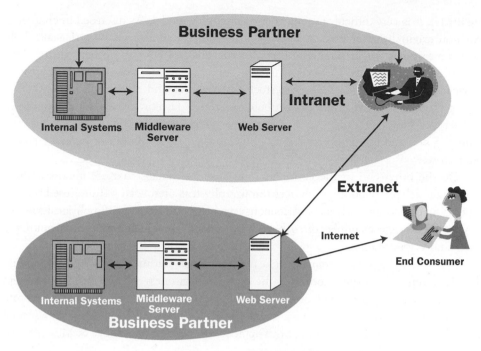

Figure 2.1 Types of ebusiness relationships and interactions

An ebusiness can be involved in a variety of relationships and interactions with customers, suppliers, and other entities.

label is applied to business models that are solely or predominantly based on provision of goods and services through physical outlets such as stores or branch offices.

Pure-play ebusinesses are completely focused on the internet, with physical sites devoted solely to housing the management and operations personnel and ebusiness technology infrastructure. Some examples of pure-play internet business models are Google, Yahoo!, eBay, and Twitter. Pure plays typically deal solely with electronic goods and services rather than physical goods or services. Unless the goods or services being provided

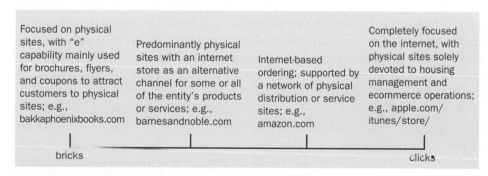

Figure 2.2 Continuum of internet business models

Internet business models range from "bricks" to "clicks," with many variations between these two endpoints, even within the same product or service sector.

are digital, it is very difficult to implement a pure-play model. As discussed in chapter 1, Amazon originally attempted to implement a pure-play model whereby it would hold no inventory but would simply broker sales on behalf of book publishers, distributors, and specialty bookstores. However, Amazon found that to provide satisfactory customer service, it had to have warehouses to stock the high-demand physical products (books, DVDs, electronics) that it had to distribute in a timely fashion or risk losing business to competitors. However, unlike some of its competitors—including Barnes & Noble in the United States and Indigo Books & Music in Canada—Amazon did not build a chain of retail stores.

On the other end of the continuum are business models that are almost entirely focused on delivering goods or services through physical sites, with websites used primarily to display brochures, flyers, and coupons to attract customers to the physical sales or service sites. Some examples of such business models are McDonald's, Shoppers Drug Mart, and Canadian Tire.

Between these two extremes lies a continuum of ebusiness models with varying degrees of reliance on the internet for the conduct of business activities. A step up from the "bricks" model is the use of a web storefront to create an alternative channel for some or all of the entity's products or services, as if the ecommerce website were simply a special type of store or branch. Examples of this approach include Indigo Books & Music, Sears, Future Shop, and Royal Bank of Canada.

Another step up from the web storefront is the use of internet-based sales channels for users to order goods and services, supported by a physical distribution network. Examples of such business models are Netflix, Amazon, 1-800-Flowers, Grocery Gateway, and President's Choice Financial.

Some analysts have observed a growing convergence between pure-play ebusinesses and traditional offline businesses. This has led some to predict the disappearance of the "e" in ebusiness due to the adoption of ebusiness models by all businesses. Others predict that customers will use websites primarily to research their purchases but will continue to make their purchases in physical stores, limiting the growth of some ebusiness models; however, statistics on online shopping behaviour contradict this view and instead show a continuing expansion of ecommerce activity.[4] Even during the sharp pullback in technology spending after the tech bust, ecommerce spending and revenues continued to grow significantly.[5]

Some of the most exciting developments in business today stem from innovations that are made economically feasible and compelling by the networking aspects of the internet: always-open stores, elimination of geographical barriers in the supply and demand chain, pervasive use of auctions to replace fixed prices, continuously gathered customer feedback to rate products and services, seamless delivery of digital goods and services, and many other such innovations.

Some B2B processes appear to be similar to B2C processes; however, often the B2B models are more complex than their B2C counterparts, from both revenue and cost perspectives. Revenues are often generated under some form of long-term agreement that defines the terms of business between the supplier and the customer. The process of negotiating, establishing, and maintaining these arrangements adds complexity and cost to the business model, but once in place, it results in a long-term relationship rather than the unpredictable, one-off nature of much B2C commerce. For example,

STAPLES, Business Depot, and Dell have specific webpages devoted to their major business customers that are similar to those used by retail customers, except that they are customized for each major business customer, listing pre-negotiated items for sale at pre-negotiated prices. To arrange its reverse auctions, Ariba employs specialist industry consultants who help buyers create the supply specifications, pre-qualify suppliers, set up the auctions, and manage the auction processes, supported by proprietary software developed for this purpose.

As mentioned earlier, B2B business dealings often involve long-term arrangements that are documented in legal contracts containing specific performance requirements by the parties to the relationship, often including financial penalties for failing to comply with the terms of the agreement. Many of the contractual arrangements with "downstream partners" (companies closer to the point of sale) implicitly require the B2B entity to manage its "upstream partners" (companies closer to the point of production) to facilitate the fulfillment of obligations to downstream partners. As a result, entities involved in B2B commerce must invest a great deal of attention and effort to managing their B2B relationships and create and maintain trust in those relationships.

Core Products and Services/Revenue Models

There are usually considered to be 11 ebusiness revenue models:[6]

1. *Merchant model*—Sales of non-digital and digital products (per unit or volume price)
2. *Direct sales by manufacturer model*—non-digital and digital products (per unit or volume price)
3. *Manufacturer service model* (indirect revenue)
4. *Subscription model* (includes free trial model)
5. *Utility model* (service fee)
6. *Infomediary model* (service fee)
7. *Licensing model* (licensing fee)
8. *Advertising model* (fee per ad displayed)
9. *Affiliate model* (commission on sales generated)
10. *Community model* (advertising-type fees)
11. *Brokerage model* (transaction fee per transaction and/or percentage of order value)

From this list of models, it is possible to identify the following five subsets: direct sales of products and services (categories 1 and 2), sales of intellectual property/information (categories 4, 5, 6, and 7), intermediation (category 11), advertising (categories 8, 9, and 10), and non-revenue (3 and not-for-profit sites). A noteworthy reference source on these models is a website maintained by Michael Rappa (**http://digitalenterprise .org/models/models.html**). This section provides examples of these revenue models and illustrative products and services.

1. Merchant Model Wholesalers or retailers of goods and services (online retailers are often referred to as "etailers") exemplify the merchant model. If a business sells and

iTunes
www.apple.com/itunes

Kindle
www.amazon.com/kindle

Blackberry App World
http://appworld.blackberry.
com/webstore/

channel conflict: A situation
in which various sales channels
for a single organization
operate in competition with
each other.

Nike
www.nike.com

Cisco Systems
www.cisco.com

AOL
http://aol.ca

Globe and Mail
www.theglobeandmail.com

BusinessWeek
www.businessweek.com

distributes only over the web, it is a pure-play etailer (e.g., Apple iTunes Music Store, Amazon's Kindle eBook store, and BlackBerry App World). If it also has a traditional brick-and-mortar presence, it is referred to as a "bricks and clicks" or "clicks and mortar" operation, or a "surf-and-turf" site. Such sites are often based on online catalogues. A good example of a bricks-and-clicks retail operation is Sears. Its very successful entry into web retailing was made easier by its long history of selling through a catalogue. By 2010, online shopping had grown to about 10 percent of U.S. retail spending, and a large proportion of sales that were not made over the internet were facilitated by the internet. In fact, many brick-and-mortar stores have added in-store kiosks and other web-enabled devices to mimic the type of information that shoppers can get when shopping online at home.

2. Direct Sales by Manufacturer Model Product manufacturers can use the web to sell their products directly to customers. As discussed earlier, there are several variations of this model, depending on to whom the manufacturer sells. If it sells to end consumers, then this effectively opens a new distribution channel, which streamlines the distribution process by bypassing wholesalers and distributors. However, this situation can also create **channel conflict**, a situation in which various sales channels for a single organization operate in competition with each other. Distributors may not approve of this system and may even rebel, as was the case with Levi's when it started selling jeans directly to customers online. Still, by using the web to sell to customers, manufacturers can better track buying habits and preferences—thus creating a considerable advantage. Nike has been able to satisfy its distributors as well as maintain a direct-sales website. One customization special feature Nike offers is the ability for customers to custom-build their own shoes. Perhaps the most widely cited example of the effective use of the manufacturer direct sales model is Dell.

If a manufacturer uses the web to sell to other manufacturers, wholesalers, and distributors, then it takes on the form of a B2B site rather than a B2C operation. Sometimes the two kinds of sites are combined (as with Dell.ca), where the site is available to consumers but there is a login page (i.e., secure area) for large business customers, government entities, wholesalers, or distributors to obtain special pricing or other special services. Either way, the use of the web has the potential for greater efficiency than the traditional means of distribution.

3. Manufacturer Service Model Product manufacturers that use the web to provide customer service for their products employ the manufacturer service model. By using the web for this purpose, a company can help support its sales growth and reduce the cost of maintaining extensive technical support personnel. An often-cited example of the effective use of the web for customer service is Cisco Systems.

4. Subscription Model Some businesses have users subscribe to their site, paying a monthly or annual fee, in order to view some or all of the content or obtain other services. This model has seen uneven success because of the general reluctance of web users to pay for content. For example, AOL provides access to the internet and to its extensive online content for a monthly fee. Netflix provides DVDs to subscribers by mail and, increasingly, over the internet. Newspapers offer some of their content for free and require subscriptions to view the full content. The *Globe and Mail* provides an example of this approach. Some print publications, such as *BusinessWeek*, allow their subscribers to access their online editions at no additional cost. Subscription models often use free trial subscriptions to persuade customers to sign up for a full subscription. Music sites like Napster and Rhapsody use the subscription model to offer music streaming to customers.

5. Utility Model The utility model is a user "pay as you go" site. It offers specific services "on demand" for a fee. Usually it is necessary to open an account to make use of the services and to facilitate the charges. The utility model offers an advantage over subscription sites in that the user has to pay only for the content he or she specifically wants. For example, Skype enables users to place telephone calls from their computers to reduce long-distance charges by telephone companies. Access time is metered and charged to the user's Skype account, which is replenished by a charge to a credit card number. The development of good micropayment systems (discussed in chapter 6) would be a boost to sites implementing the utility model, as they could charge small amounts for small services.

Skype
www.skype.com

6. Infomediary Model Sites that build on the economic value of information about people's purchasing habits are referred to as "infomediaries." These sites offer something free to users and, in exchange, ask them to provide information about themselves and their buying habits. Sometimes a registration process is required for users to enter the site. The data collected this way are then sold to other businesses that must pay a service fee for having their ecommerce activity monitored and analyzed by the infomediary service provider. An example of an infomediary is BizRate.com. BizRate provides an online merchant-rating service that merchants subscribe to. Online shoppers fill out a short survey each time they shop at a BizRate member site. BizRate uses the survey to assign ratings to the online merchants on various dimensions that are then displayed on those sites. BizRate also provides detailed analyses to its clients to help them improve their ratings. Online shoppers benefit from the ratings by being able to select merchants based on their performance as reflected in customers' ratings.

BizRate.com
www.bizrate.com

7. Licensing Model Licensing models are often applied to long-lived intellectual property such as software. Licensing revenues are often based on a formula that takes into account the number of locations and users. The customer pays a one-time licensing fee to be able to use or resell the software. Software that is used to enable ecommerce such as that sold by Ariba, Perfect Commerce, JDA Software and Cornerstone OnDemand are examples. Such software is part of the infrastructure of an ebusiness, along with computer equipment, facilities, networks, and support personnel.

Perfect Commerce
www.perfect.com

JDA Software
www.jda.com

Cornerstone OnDemand
www.cornerstoneondemand.
com

8. Advertising Model From an economic point of view, advertising on the web works similarly to the way it works in traditional media, such as radio and television. Content is provided on the website (either free or at a bargain discount) that is intended to attract people, and advertisements are placed on the site for a fee paid by the advertiser. Quite often, the site makes its profits from the advertising revenue rather than from the content itself. On the web, the advertising model has been prevalent, as users have become accustomed to receiving free content. The advertising messages on the web often take the form of **banner ads**, which are icons containing advertising messages that, when clicked, take the user to the site of the advertiser. Sometimes the fees payable on these banner ads are dependent on the **clickthrough counts** on the banner ad. The click-through count is the number of times that users have clicked on a banner

banner ad: An icon containing an advertising messages that, when clicked, takes the user to the site of the advertiser.

clickthrough count: The number of users who have been shown a banner ad and who have clicked on it to take them to the website to which it refers.

ad to take them to the website to which it refers; software on the website automatically keeps track of these counts. The clickthrough rate is the proportion of users to whom a banner was shown that clicked on the banner ad to take them to the website to which it refers. Since a single user could click on a banner ad several times, clickthrough counts do not necessarily result in an accurate count of individual users who use the ad. Banner ads and other online advertising methods are discussed in more detail in chapter 11. Clickthrough counts and other metrics used by advertisers are discussed in more detail in chapter 12.

The advertising model is viable only when there is a sufficiently large volume of user traffic on a site. Therefore, the strategies followed by advertising sites tend to focus on volume generation by offering diversified content and a wide array of services, such as email, chat, news, and message boards. Generalized portal sites such as Yahoo! and MSN and social networks such as Facebook and Twitter exemplify this approach. In contrast to these sites, Google provides one main service: It is a highly rated search engine that has attracted a large volume of traffic and, with it, significant advertising revenue.

Yahoo! and MSN allow the user to customize the interface to show items of particular personal interest, thereby becoming personalized portals. Numerous other generic sites offer this capability to develop user loyalty while maintaining a high volume of traffic. There is also a value-added element to personalized portals through improved access to information that may be more relevant to the user.

The idea behind a personalized portal is that users will use it as their own entry point onto the internet. Ordinary portals attempt to do this as well, but personalized portals seek to lure the user into using the site regularly because they allow the user to structure the site to cater to his or her particular interests.

Some portals target a defined user base, such as sports enthusiasts, investors, or homebuyers. Such specialized portals seek large volume, but because they can't count on volumes as large as those of general portals, they often charge a premium for their advertising. The premium is supported by the claim that users with a particular interest are on the site, and because their interests are known, product advertising can be targeted to them. As users become more sophisticated in using the web, specialized portals are likely to grow in number. Music sites like Grooveshark and Spotify use the advertising model to offer free music streaming to their customers.

Other sites use the "incentive marketing" approach, which involves paying visitors for viewing some content, filling out forms, or entering contests. Payment takes the form of some kind of point scheme, similar to frequent-flyer programs offered by the airlines. An early entrant to this kind of site was Cybergold, which offered an "earn and spend community" by bringing together advertisers interested in incentive-based marketing. Cybergold was subsequently bought by MyPoints.com Inc. Advertising methods and emarketing are discussed in more detail in chapter 11.

9. Affiliate Model A good example of an affiliate model is a banner ad exchange. A company can join an affiliate program through an affiliate manager site, such as Affiliates World, which offers a point of contact for those interested in exchanging banners. Sometimes, this type of arrangement involves payment of commissions to the sites hosting banner ads when sales are made to customers using them to enter the site. For example, Example Inc. might enter into a banner arrangement with Amazon under which an

Grooveshark
www.grooveshark.com

Spotify
www.spotify.com

MyPoints.com
www.mypoints.com

Affiliates World
www.affiliates-world.com

Amazon banner ad is placed on the Example website. Amazon tracks the entry points of people entering its site and therefore knows which visitors have entered Amazon through the banner ad on Example. Amazon can also track when those people buy goods and how much they spend. It can then pay a commission to Example for the sales.

For Amazon, this is a way of building sales. For Example Inc., it is a way of generating some revenue from Amazon, with no risk and very little cost. Amazon was a pioneer with this type of model and was granted a broad-ranging patent on the process that some observers feel may inhibit the activities of others in the field.

10. Community Model Community sites depend on user loyalty and community identification for their viability. The sites are usually built with volunteer labour and feature a variety of content from the community, usually provided free of charge, although sometimes the site charges to host the content. Challenges for these sites are to provide adequate functionality and stay current. They can present opportunities for businesses to advertise and to provide a convenient access point to their own sites. A successful community site can function as a portal to local businesses, acting almost as a virtual shopping mall. Funding for these sites is sometimes solicited as donations from community members.

Social networking sites segment their users in numerous ways to sell targeted advertising to marketers. Segmentation requires access to a variety of information about users, much of which is personal. This creates a tension between users' privacy concerns and social networks' economic objectives to sell advertising. Privacy issues are discussed in more detail in chapter 13.

A unique example of a community site is Wikipedia. In this community, participants contribute both content and funding to maintain open access to knowledge for all internet users.

11. Brokerage Model Brokers are often referred to as *market-makers* because they bring together buyers and sellers and facilitate transactions between them. Brokers generate revenues through a variety of transaction fees and commission charges for the transactions they enable or facilitate. There are a large number of brokerage sites, and they take on a variety of specific forms, including the following:[7]

- classifieds
- virtual malls
- market exchanges
- buy/sell fulfillment sites
- auction brokers
- reverse auctions
- transaction brokers
- metamediaries
- search agents

As the following discussion illustrates, there are many types of **brokerage sites**, but it is clear that one feature they have in common is that they bring together buyers and sellers to facilitate business transactions on the web. Chapter 8 discusses in more detail how some forms of brokerage sites operate on the internet.

brokerage site: A site that brings together buyers and sellers to facilitate business transactions on the web.

Digital Distribution of Music: An Evolving Business Model

During the late 1990s, Napster turned the music industry on its head by facilitating the transfer of free music between people connected to the web. The industry at first directed its efforts to legal battles with Napster over copyright issues—and won. But soon, new file-sharing services that launched were more difficult to combat. It was clear that the rules of the game had changed, and the industry needed to find new ways to deal with the distribution of music over the internet that would be economically viable for the industry and for artists.

In October 2002, Roxio responded to the industry climate and bought Napster's assets. A year later, it launched a legal version of Napster. In 2010 Napster was acquired by Best Buy. Napster now requires customers to use proprietary software to access its online music selection and pay for the music they download. With over 2.5 million songs to choose from, customers pay US$0.99 per song and US$9.95 for a full album. Napster also offers a subscription service that enables users to listen to an unlimited number of songs streamed over the internet for US$9.95 per month. Many users have opted for streaming music rather than downloading it. This is comparable to a rent vs. buy decision.

While Napster boasts of a brand recognition ratio of 92.5 percent, first-mover advantage goes to Apple's iTunes.com, launched in April 2003. Like Napster, iTunes requires customers to use proprietary software to access its online music store. The number of music offerings on iTunes is over 6 million songs, and the prices for downloading are similar to those at Napster. In addition to downloadable songs, iTunes also offers downloadable audio books, movies, videos, and television shows.

Recently, a new business model for free downloadable music has appeared. Sites such as Grooveshark, Pandora and Spotify stream music over the internet and earn their revenue through advertising for free subscriptions and through fees for premium subscriptions. These sites also encourage music sharing through social networks such as Facebook and Twitter.

Some analysts believe that consumers will be put off by the need to pay for these services, preferring instead to exchange unlimited songs over the internet for free. Peer-to-peer software such as Gnutella and LimeWire enables users to share an unlimited quantity and variety of songs at no cost. Copyright laws dealing with this issue vary. While music labels have attempted to discourage illegal sharing of music through several high-profile lawsuits against downloaders, their ability to continue may be hampered by the courts' failure to grant them the right to obtain information on user identities from internet service providers. As a result, some observers feel the market for this type of service is still vague and uncertain.

Although the volume of paid music downloads has grown over the past few years, so has the volume of illegal downloading. Recent (2010) data from the U.K. indicates that fewer than one-third of music downloads are paid for, supporting claims that paid-for music models will not succeed in the long run.

Napster
www.napster.ca

iTunes
www.apple.com/itunes

Grooveshark
www.grooveshark.com

Questions

1. How do the three business models (download, subscription based streaming and advertising supported streaming) described in this case respond to the realities of purchasing music in the age of the internet?

2. What aspects of these business models are likely to be viable, and what do you think will still need to be done to improve them and keep pace with changes in customer demand for music, videos, and movies?

Sources: W. S. Mossberg and K. Boehret, "A New Prescription for Watching iPod Video," *Wall Street Journal*, December 27, 2006, http://solution.allthingsd.com/20061227/myvu-ipod-videos/; www.napster.com, accessed December 27, 2006; PressPass, www.microsoft.com/presspass/features/2003/oct03/10-15musicservices.asp, accessed December 27, 2006; "Downloading Costs U.K. Music Industry," *The Globe and Mail*, December 17, 2010: B8.

Classifieds Many sites provide advertisements similar to the classified ads in newspapers. The broker charges for the listings, regardless of whether a transaction ultimately takes place. An example of this kind of site is workopolis.com, which lists job advertisements for jobs across Canada. Employment agencies also use this site to find jobs for people and to find people for jobs.

Workopolis
workopolis.com

Virtual Malls As the name indicates, a virtual mall is a site that hosts a number of online merchants. The mall charges fees for setup, listings, and transactions. Yahoo! provides a good example and also illustrates the combination of a mall with a popular portal site, assisting businesses to attract a large volume of visitors to the site. Amazon and eBay also provide facilities for merchants to set up shop through their infrastructures.

Yahoo! Canada shopping
http://yahoo.shoptoit.ca

Market Exchanges Market exchanges are a part of the business model often referred to as *trading exchanges*, and they have been one of the fastest-growing types of B2B business. Figure 2.3 illustrates a typical market exchange. In market exchanges, pricing of transactions can be determined through simple offers, negotiations, or auctions. A good example of a market exchange is ChemConnect Inc., which is now the biggest online exchange for chemical trading. Trading exchanges are more fully discussed in chapter 8.

ChemConnect
www.chemconnect.com

Buy/Sell Fulfillment Sites A buy/sell fulfillment site takes customer orders to buy or sell a product or service. This is a very widely used model, ranging from online financial brokerages, such as TD Waterhouse WebBroker, where customers place buy and sell orders for transacting financial instruments, to online auto brokers such as CarsDirect.com, to online travel agencies such as Expedia.ca. In this kind of site, the broker charges a transaction fee, but it is often a lower fee than can be obtained offline because the cost of executing transactions on the internet is lower, and the savings can be passed on to the customer. For example, Hotels.ca lists discounted hotel rooms, charging a listing fee to the hotels and a transaction fee to the customer at the time of the reservation (and payment).

TD Waterhouse WebBroker
https://webbroker.
tdwaterhouse.ca

CarsDirect.com
www.carsdirect.com

Expedia
www.expedia.ca

Hotels.ca
www.hotels.ca

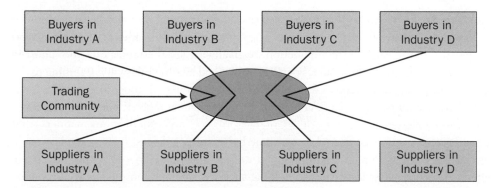

Figure 2.3 Structure of a market exchange

A market exchange provides a vehicle for suppliers to connect with buyers. The exchange provides the tools for buyers to list supply requirements, for sellers to register their supply offers, a price-setting mechanism such as an auction for buyers and sellers to negotiate a price, and a fulfillment process for the resulting transactions.

Groupon
www.groupon.ca

Groupon negotiates special offers from providers of goods and services on behalf of subscribers. It sells vouchers for claiming the items purchased from suppliers and retains a significant portion of the revenues that it collects on behalf of its suppliers, remitting the rest.

Auction Brokers An auction broker is a site, like eBay.com, that conducts auctions for sellers who list their products on the site. The broker charges the seller a fee, which is typically scaled to the value of the transaction. Normally the seller establishes a minimum bid and then accepts the highest offer. Specific offering and bidding rules vary according to the site. Auctions are very effective ways of maximizing revenues, although they require a sufficient number of participants to compete for a given item at a given place and time. The internet enables remote participants to interact online in an **asynchronous** manner—that is, with activities not conducted in real time but involving delays, such as sending email messages for others to pick up and respond to at a later time. This asynchronous nature eliminates many physical barriers to holding auctions, and auction models are becoming widespread on the internet. Chapter 8 discusses in more detail how various types of B2C and B2B auction sites operate on the internet.

asynchronous: A term for activities that are not conducted in real time but that involve delays.

Reverse Auctions Whereas a standard auction involves a seller auctioning goods to a group of buyers, a reverse auction has sellers competing to fill a buyer's order. A notable example of a reverse auction broker site is Priceline.com, with its patented "name your own price" model that was first applied to airplane ticket purchases. Guru.com is a site devoted to matching freelance professionals who wish to sell their services with buyers who have projects that need to be completed. Guru.com uses a reverse auction whereby the freelancers bid on the contracts posted by the buyers; the lowest bid wins.

Transaction Brokers A transaction broker facilitates the completion of a transaction by enabling payment. For example, credit card companies are transaction brokers that receive fees from merchants for facilitating payments for customer purchases. PayPal is an example of a third-party transaction broker that operates on the internet to facilitate settlements for purchases for a small fee per transaction. PayPal provides a plug-in "shopping cart" that sellers can easily add to their websites. A buyer purchases items by depositing funds into the seller's PayPal account. The seller then retrieves the funds from its PayPal account.

Metamediaries Metamediaries are intermediaries that gather and coordinate the products and services offered by other intermediaries that specialize in specific areas. A good example is Edmunds.com, which links numerous automobile sellers, service providers, and automobile buyers; organizing information from numerous disparate sources for a unified view of a group of products and related services, such as specific car models, accessories, financing, and insurance. OneSpout is a metamediary that aggregates all of the Canadian deals offered by various deal sites.

Search Agents A search agent is a site that uses an intelligent software agent, or "bot," to search the internet for the best price for a good or service that a buyer wants. Examples of this type of site are RoboShopper, mySimon, and Shopbot.

As the previous discussion makes clear, there are many approaches to offering goods and services over the internet. While some analysts have challenged the validity of some of the models discussed in this section, all these models are in use today, and the ultimate proof of their validity will be the degree to which they are accepted in the marketplace. As most businesses begin to take advantage of the internet for at least some of their activities, they are implementing these models, sometimes creating new variations of them. As they gain experience and observe the strengths and weaknesses of their ebusiness models, businesses will often combine them with other models, seeking to create a unique value proposition for their customers; for example, news sites may offer both subscription and utility services, as well as infomediary and licensing opportunities.

Alliances

Research on ebusiness models emphasizes the importance of various types of relationships, including the networking benefits of partnerships, alliances, and other collaborative associations that can help companies leverage their resources and competencies to create competitive advantage. However, Michael E. Porter believes that some entities have forfeited their proprietary advantages by engaging in misguided partnerships and outsourcing relationships that rob them of their distinctiveness.[8]

Resource Management

A key component of an ebusiness model is resource management. As noted in the introduction, resource management refers to the processes by which resources are acquired,

Guru.com
www.guru.com

PayPal
www.paypal.com

Edmunds.com
www.edmunds.com

OneSpout
http://onespout.com

RoboShopper
www.roboshopper.com

mySimon
www.mysimon.com

Shopbot.ca
www.shopbot.ca

Priceline.com
www.priceline.com

Guru.com
www.guru.com

Emodel at eLong

eLong is one of China's leading web-based travel companies, providing one-stop travel services including tourist information, map functionality, 24/7 call center reservation support, and online booking through its websites **www.eLong.com** in Chinese and **www.eLong.net** in English.

eLong is partly owned by Expedia and has its headquarters in Beijing. It provides information and travel booking services to a variety of customers, for both leisure and business travel. Through web technology and a call center, eLong provides access to information on 17,000 hotels in 618 cities across China and enables customers to make hotel and air ticket reservations through both online and offline channels. Through its network of international connections, eLong also makes it possible for customers to make travel reservations for cities throughout the world.

Ctrip.com is China's leading travel service enterprise and eLong's main competitor. Like eLong, it was founded in 1999, but unlike eLong, Ctrip is headquartered in

Shanghai and has five times as many employees as eLong. Both companies are listed on the NASDAQ stock exchange in the United States.

The online landscape for travel in China has changed dramatically over the past decade. In the past, eLong and other online travel search engines could reliably aggregate the best airline deals for travellers in one place. But now travellers can often go directly to the airlines' own websites for the best deals and specials on fares around China. The airlines often see online travel sites such as eLong often as rivals.

elong
www.elong.net

Questions

1. Discuss the business model eLong is using. What are its strengths and weaknesses?

2. What forces protect eLong? What forces threaten it?

Source: www.elong.net.

---

developed, and allocated to the core business activities. In an internet-based business model, as in most other business models, a key resource is capital. Capital can be raised from friends, family, venture capitalists, banks, and equity markets, depending on the entity's stage of development. That capital is then used to acquire or develop other resources, such as people and technology, that will implement the business model. In many cases, the entity will outsource some of its activities to firms with specialized competencies in areas such as web hosting or IT infrastructure provisioning. It will need to have processes to identify alternative suppliers, select the most appropriate supplier, and enter into a contract for the required services that protects the entity's interests. When the entity develops its own technology or business process, it will need to have sound project management processes in place to prioritize projects, staff them, and effectively manage project activities. To effectively align the resource management activities with the entity's strategic objectives will require a performance measurement system that utilizes metrics linked to strategic objectives to guide and motivate entity personnel to take actions that are congruent with the entity's strategy. Subsequent sections of this book deal with these issues extensively.

INTERNET BUSINESS MODELS AND BUSINESS STRATEGY

WHILE IT IS CLEAR THAT MANY BUSINESS MODELS ARE BEING USED TO DELIVER value through the use of the internet, these models are not all mutually exclusive. They can be combined in numerous ways to achieve business goals. For example, an etailer may make use of the simple merchant model but also may use its site to advertise its brick-and-mortar business. It may enter into banner exchanges and make money through banner ad commissions, or it may enter into other affiliate programs, virtual malls, and market exchanges.

The specific model or combination of models that a business uses helps to define its internet or ebusiness strategy. The ebusiness strategy will determine the value proposition that differentiates the entity's ebusiness offerings from those of its competitors, a distinctive value chain tailored to its value proposition and to choices of how various elements of the ebusiness will fit with each other and with aspects of the larger enterprise. Will the site be used as a stand-alone initiative? Or will it be used to complement the existing business or even to launch a new type of business? The business models described earlier in this chapter provide a menu for business strategists to consider when addressing these questions.

The previous discussion has identified a number of revenue models for ebusiness. However, as noted at the beginning of this chapter, a business model includes other components in addition to the approach a company will take to generate revenue. It also includes a set of related business operations and outlines the model's cost structure, required investments in tangible and intangible assets, and other factors. To achieve profitability, an internet business model must not only generate revenue but must also do so utilizing effective business processes that are executed and managed by competent, motivated personnel and supported by an appropriate technology infrastructure. This is discussed in parts 2 and 3 of this book.

FITTING THE EBUSINESS STRATEGY INTO THE CORPORATE STRATEGY

FOR MANY BUSINESSES, THE PROCEDURAL ASPECTS OF CORPORATE STRATEGIC PLANNING are a well-established feature of management. Strategic plans are developed periodically, sometimes every year and sometimes every few years, with annual updates. They require employees from across the organization to be involved in determining goals, strategies, and work activities.

As illustrated in figure 2.4, most strategic planning exercises involve a process of developing a broad vision, considering the constraints and assumptions that constrict or guide that vision, and defining strategic objectives for the business that come as close as possible to the vision. The strategic objectives must recognize the constraints, which might be based on resource restrictions, environmental constraints such as legal and regulatory stipulations, and other matters. Each year, the process of strategic planning normally involves reviewing the previous year's plans and updating those plans to reflect new trends and events or even a changed vision. Then the various stakeholders draft, review, and analyze a plan. Finally, the plan is approved, and action begins.

The process illustrated in figure 2.4 should result in a strategic plan that addresses five key areas:[9]

1. Arenas where the entity will be active, including the product categories, market segments, geographical areas, core technologies to be employed, and value-creation stages.

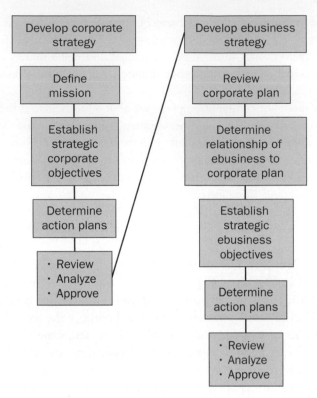

Figure 2.4 The strategic planning process

Strategic planning for ebusiness must fit with the strategic planning for an enterprise as a whole.

2. Vehicles for moving towards goal achievement, such as internal development, joint ventures, licensing or franchising, and acquisitions.

3. Differentiators that represent competitive advantages, such as image, customization, price, styling, and product reliability.

4. The speed and sequence of moves, such as the speed of expansion and the sequence of initiatives.

5. Economic logic for obtaining returns on investment, such as being the lowest-cost producer due to scale advantages or scope and replication advantages or obtaining premium prices for outstanding service or proprietary product features.

Of course, the strategies and objectives in this kind of a plan relate to the success of the business as a whole. The ebusiness strategy must fit into the corporate plan. See the Estrategy box for an example of how an ebusiness strategy can support the overall corporate strategy of a business.

How the ebusiness strategy fits into the corporate plan depends on the extent to which the business is involved in ebusiness. If it is a pure-play situation, where the only business is ebusiness, then the corporate strategic plan will be the same as the ebusiness plan. At the other end of the spectrum, where ebusiness is a small part of an overall business, a separate ebusiness strategic plan may be prepared. If this is the case, there needs to be a process through which the objectives of the ebusiness plan are compared to the corporate objectives for consistency of purpose and aligned with them.

Ebusiness planning must be done in conjunction with, or in a manner consistent with, the entity's IT strategy and its overall corporate strategy. Ebusiness planning involves the following activities:

- Defining how ebusiness can help the entity achieve its overall objectives. This step involves analyzing the entity's overall vision and mission; analyzing the industry, the company, and its competition; and identifying areas where ebusiness can contribute to the entity's success, considering issues such as whether to be a leader or follower, the geographical scope of the ebusiness, the technologies to be utilized, and the value-creation opportunities made possible by those technologies. An approach to industry analysis that is widely used is the Porter Five Forces analysis, which considers these five forces as the basis for a company's strategy: (1) the barriers to entry in the industry, (2) the threats posed by substitute products or services, (3) the bargaining power of suppliers, (4) the bargaining power of buyers, and (5) the rivalry among existing competitors.[10]

- Assessing gaps between the entity's current IT resources and performance capabilities and its desired strategic objectives. This step involves analyses such as SWOT (strengths, weaknesses, opportunities, and threats) to identify technology, competency, and resource limitations, as well as opportunities.

- Formulating strategies to fill gaps. Strategies can be (1) competitive—competing head-to-head on price, cost, quality, and service; or attempting to outflank competitors by attacking them indirectly; (2) defensive—blocking competitors with patents and other barriers; or (3) cooperative—relying on alliances, partnerships, and joint ventures. Developing these strategies creates an ebusiness model to achieve the entity's strategic objectives. This model will specify the value propositions offered to customers, how revenues are generated (i.e., what products and services are provided and how), what resources are required, and what costs are incurred to support core ebusiness activities.

- Performing a risk assessment aimed at identifying weaknesses in the ebusiness model and compensating for them.

- Defining the IT policies, infrastructure, applications, business processes, information architecture, and information flows designed to serve the ebusiness model and compensate for any weaknesses and risks identified in the risk assessment phase.

- Defining a tactical plan that includes the sequence of anticipated acquisition or development and implementation steps, resource requirements (human, technological, operational, and financial), and project management requirements.

- Measuring ebusiness performance, as discussed in chapter 12.

It should be clear that the process of strategic planning for ebusiness presents numerous coordination and communication challenges in an organization. Not only do the various types of planning—corporate, IT, and ebusiness—need to be consistent, but the various stakeholders in the organization need to be involved, and their individual perspectives and objectives must be reconciled. When the business is an established one, the challenges are compounded, in that the business likely has had strategic plans for some years before the advent of ebusiness, and the introduction of the ebusiness must therefore take place in the context of established hierarchies and organizational structures, which may be resistant to change. On the other hand, when the business is a new internet startup, the whole organization depends on the ebusiness, and the importance of finding viable business models and developing successful strategies is not only more critical but must be built from the ground up.

Many—and maybe most—new dot-coms have failed because they are not successful in finding business models and strategies that can work to make them economically viable. The problems that many businesses have experienced in venturing from their traditional spheres of activity to ebusiness can often be traced to the same general failures. Even when a business finds a successful strategy, there is no assurance that it will continue to work very long. The world of ebusiness and technology changes so quickly that strategic plans must be constantly reviewed and reassessed, and the business must remain flexible in its approach to be able to adapt to the changes that will inevitably take place.

CHAPTER SUMMARY

Broadly, a business model may be defined as the manner in which a business organizes itself so as to achieve its objectives, which normally involve the generation of profits. Most often, a business model is defined in terms of how a business plans to generate revenues, the costs it must incur to generate the revenues, the investments that its stakeholders must make to fund the business development and operations until they generate positive net cash flows, and other critical success factors that enable the business to make money on a long-term basis. A major aspect of strategy for ebusiness is how the business plans to use the internet for these purposes.

An internet business model involves using the internet as a tool for implementing a business model. Numerous internet-based business models have developed in recent years, including B2C and B2B variants, pure-play as well as bricks-and-clicks approaches, and numerous traditional as well as innovative revenue-generating and cost-containment activities.

The specific model or combination of models that a business uses helps define its internet or ebusiness strategy. The models provide a menu for business strategists to consider when addressing strategic questions.

For many businesses, the procedural aspects of corporate strategic planning are a well-established feature of management. Corporate plans are developed, and ebusiness plans must fit into the corporate plans. The manner in which the ebusiness strategy fits into the corporate plans depends on the extent to which the business is involved in ebusiness. In a pure-play situation, where the only business is ebusiness, the corporate strategic plan will be the same as the ebusiness plan. Where the ebusiness is a small part of the overall business, there may be a separate ebusiness strategic plan prepared. Because ebusiness includes elements of IT, an IT plan must be prepared or incorporated into the ebusiness plan. All these plans must be consistent and coordinated with each other. The process of strategic planning for ebusiness presents numerous challenges of coordination and communication in an organization.

Key Terms

asynchronous (p. 36)

banner ad (p. 31)

brokerage sites (p. 33)

business model (p. 23)

channel conflict (p. 30)

clickthrough count (p. 31)

internet business model (p. 23)

reverse auction (p. 26)

strategy (p. 23)

MyEbusinessLab   Tools for Online Learning

To help you master the material in this chapter and stay up to date with new developments in ebusiness, visit the MyEBusinessLab at www.pearsoned.ca/myebusinesslab. Resources include the following:

- **Pre- and Post-Test Questions**
- **Additional Chapter Questions**
- **Author Blog**
- **Recommended Readings**
- **Commentaries on Current Trends**
- **Additional Topics in Ebusiness**
- **Internet Exercises**
- **Glossary Flashcards**

Endnotes

1. T. Bell, F. Marrs, I. Solomon, and H. Thomas, *Auditing Organizations through a Strategic-Systems Lens: The KPMG Business Measurement Process* (Montvale, NJ: KPMG Peat Marwick, LLP, 1997).

2. M. E. Porter, "What Is Strategy?" *HBR OnPoint* (November–December 1996): 61–78.

3. "Information Technology: Government On-Line." *Report of the Auditor General of Canada to the House of Commons* (November 2003): 6.

4. C. Ranganathan, et al., "Managing the Transition to Bricks and Clicks," *Communications of the ACM* 46, no. 12 (December 2003): 308–316; P. Prasarnphanich and M. L. Gillenson, "The Hybrid Clicks and Bricks Business Model," *Communications of the ACM* 46, no. 12 (December 2003): 178–185.

5. T. J. Mullaney, H. Green, M. Arndt, R. D. Hof, and L. Himelstein, "The E-Biz Surprise," *BusinessWeek* (May 12, 2003): 60–68.

6. M. Rappa, *Business Models on the Web*, www.digitalenterprise.org/models/models.html, accessed January 1, 2007.

7. D. Tapscott, "Rethinking Strategy in a Networked World (or Why Michael Porter Is Wrong about the Internet)," *Strategy+Business* (Third Quarter, 2001): 1–8.

8. M. E. Porter, "Strategy and the Internet," *Harvard Business Review* (March 2001): 63–78.

9. D. Tapscott and A. D. Williams, "Wikinomics," series for the *Globe and Mail*, www.theglobeandmail.com, December 2006–January 2007.

10. M. E. Porter, *Competitive Strategy: Techniques for Analyzing Industries and Competitors* (New York: Free Press, 1980).

PART 1 CASE STUDY
GOOGLE—SEARCHING THE WORLD

Google is one of those new ventures that has become so successful that it has become part of the modern lexicon. People say they will "google" something to find out about it, which means they will search the web for relevant information. In 2006, *Webster's* dictionary added "google" as an entry in its latest edition.

Google started small, like so many other modern successful new business ventures, and there was even a garage involved. This is not a new phenomenon: Henry Ford built his first car in a small workshop behind his house and launched the Ford Motor Company with his own capital, along with a group of 11 friends. However, Google stands out because of the scale and speed of its growth, as well as the fact that it started as an idea that became a school research project while the two founders—Larry Page and Sergey Brin—were computer science students in 1995. It must be the most successful school project of all time—at least financially!

Page and Brin's idea was to build a search engine that made use of backlinks to judge the popularity of a site. Backlinks are incoming links to a site—that is, the site where visitors are coming from. When they tested their first prototype, their new search engine was called Backrub. By late 1996 and into 1997, Backrub was experiencing a growing reputation around campus as an effective search engine.

As the two young men developed their new technology, they found that they needed space to store large amounts of data. In an approach that became a feature of Google, they acquired several terabytes of disk space at discounted prices, using their personal credit cards, and built storage facilities in Larry's dorm room—Google's first data centre.

They began to look for investors to finance a new company for their new search engine, but at first they had no luck. People couldn't see the benefits of a better search engine. Then they approached Andy Bechtolsheim of Sun Microsystems. He saw the potential and wrote them a cheque for US$100,000 on the spot. Page and Brin were so unprepared for this that they had to incorporate their new company before they could cash the cheque. Several more hits with friends and acquaintances, and they had US$1 million to start their new venture.

Page and Brin hired a third person, Craig Silverstein, and the three set up shop in September 1998, in a friend's rented garage. Google was still in the beta-testing phase, but it was gaining a widespread reputation and handling more than 10,000 search queries per day. That year, they were written up in *USA Today*, and then *PC Magazine* listed Google on its Top 100 Web Sites and Search Engines list for 1998. By early 1999 the company was prospering, and it moved to Palo Alto, California. There were eight employees, and the number of search queries had grown to 500,000 per day. In mid-1999 Google attracted venture capital to the tune of US$22 million.

The company ran out of space again and built new headquarters—the Googleplex—in Mountain View, California. Staff numbers continued to grow. Revenue grew as well, primarily from advertising that Google let companies attach to search results.

Clientele also grew in numbers. In 1999 AOL/Netscape selected Google as its web search engine, raising search levels to 3 million searches per day. That same year, Google went global, signing on a major Italian portal and adding versions of the search engine in

10 different languages so people could search in their own languages. Growth continued at a phenomenal rate, with the company earning several major awards and, in June 2000, it officially became the world's largest search engine. That was the year it began tying its advertising into keywords. For example, when searches were entered for, say, "New York," the return search would include advertising of products that might be of interest to the searcher, such as a blip from Amazon.com listing books about New York. This means of earning revenue has worked well for the company. But it wasn't Google's only source of revenue. The company owned its own unique search technology and signed up companies to use it on their sites. By the end of 2000, after signing a partnership with Yahoo!, Google was handling more than 100 million search queries a day.

Google continued to add features that enhanced its role as a search engine. For example, it added the Google Toolbar, which made it easy for people to use the search engine without going to the Google website. The Google Toolbar also opened the way for the company to make available to users any new products it introduced. Since its introduction, the Google Toolbar has been downloaded by millions of users. It now contains applications such as Google Maps (which allows easy access to detailed maps of most parts of the world), Blogger, Calendar, Gmail, Notebook, and Picasa (a photograph management utility).

Because Google relies largely on advertising for its revenue, most of the applications it offers are free. This gives Google tremendous competitive clout, and it has been a factor in some of the mergers it has engineered over the past few years.

Other ways that Google has found to build on its search expertise have included Google Image Search, which was launched with 250 million images to search, and Google Catalog Search, which made it possible to search more than 1,100 mail order catalogues, greatly facilitating online shopping. Then Google began to search its own search records, with the issuance of Google Zeitgeist, a retrospective on the search patterns, trends, and top search terms of the year. This service was intended to provide a take on the current concerns of humanity—what people are searching for in their lives as well as on the web. Google characterized it as "a real-time window into the collective consciousness."

During 2005, Google ran into controversy when it announced that it was going to scan thousands of books into databases and make them available for searching. Much of the concern related, of course, to the copyright implications of doing this. Moreover, copyright laws vary considerably around the world, as do copyright privileges after the copyright has expired. Therefore, the publishing industry saw Google's book initiative as a major threat. This view was exacerbated when it was learned that Google had decided not to follow the usual process of obtaining permissions from the book companies. Instead, Google made deals with five large libraries, including the New York Public Library, to digitize their entire collections. The libraries would receive digital versions of their holdings in return. Google wouldn't be able to reproduce the books using this approach, but it could produce what are called in the industry "snippets," or small excerpts from the books.

These concerns led a number of large publishing companies, such as McGraw-Hill, Penguin, and Simon & Schuster, to sue Google for copyright infringement. Google defended its position vigorously, arguing that any publisher could keep its books from being digitized simply by sending a list of titles to Google. Then, in August 2007, Google announced that it would temporarily halt the project to respond to concerns.

Another expansion Google introduced in February 2002 was a new search appliance. It was "packaged" in a bright yellow box and was referred to as "Google in a Box." It was designed to search the internal records of companies, such as their intranets, websites, and university networks. Organizations from Boeing to the University of Florida have implemented this tool to search their own data stores.

One of the lines of business Google started was Google Video, which allows users to search the net for videos to watch. In 2006, Google announced the acquisition of YouTube, another relative newcomer to the world of ebusiness—and a successful one at that. The purchase was accomplished with an exchange of Google shares for YouTube shares.

YouTube, although successful, was still trying to find a viable business model, and it knew it had to start making money. Google had proven itself a master of finding innovative ways to use advertising on the web as the core of its very successful business model. Thus the hope was that Google could lend its expertise to the operation and turn the tremendous user loyalty to YouTube into a hugely profitable enterprise. At the time of the merger, the announcement indicated that the two companies would retain their separate identities.

Shortly after the merger, Google and YouTube announced that they had signed distribution deals with record labels and CBS. This meant they had their eyes on the lucrative music video market.

In 2005, Google launched a music search feature that delivers a mix of information on artists and titles, including links to albums, reviews, and where to buy information for a wide range of musicians and performers. In 2006 the Google Video store was launched, featuring titles from numerous partners, as well as the ability to view or download them using a new Google Video Player.

For most people, Google's new products were hard to keep up with. But many users were interested in participating in new products, so Google opened up Google Labs. With Google Labs, new ideas are presented to people to acquaint them with new prototypes, and developers receive feedback that helps them refine their projects for success.

Other recent products include the following:

- Google News, which was launched in September 2002, offers access to 4,500 leading news sources from around the world. Headlines and photos are automatically selected and arranged by a program that updates the page continuously.

- Froogle, a product-search service launched in test mode in December 2002, continues Google's emphasis on innovation and objective results. Searching through millions of relevant websites, Froogle helps users find multiple sources for specific products, delivering images and prices for the items sought.

- Blogger, a leading provider of services for people who have their own weblogs (blogs), found a new home at Google in 2003, when Google acquired Pyra Labs.

- Google AdSense offers websites of all sizes a way to easily generate revenue through placement of highly targeted ads adjacent to Google content.

- Local Search, which was released in 2004, facilitates searches for local facilities, businesses, and so on. It is for users who need, for example, a tire store that is within walking distance or a grocery store close enough to deliver fresh food.

- Google Talk is a free way to actually speak to people anytime, anywhere via Computer Plus, an instant message service.

- Google Desktop offers quick access to files, email, news, photos, weather, RSS feeds, stocks, and other personalized web content.

In April 2004 Google filed with the U.S. Securities and Exchange Commission for an initial public offering (IPO). August saw the IPO of GOOG introduced on NASDAQ through the little-known "Dutch auction" process, which is designed to attract a broader range of investors than the usual IPO often does.

Later that year, Google moved heavily into the mobile world, investing hundreds of millions of dollars in a project allowing searches to be made through cellphones. While mobile advertising is still a relatively small market, advertisers and wireless experts expect this to change, so Google may be onto something. One significant company, for example, has forecast the mobile ad market increasing to an incredible US$2.2 billion by 2010. Google also extended its initiatives with cellphones by moving into China, with the formulation of a partnership with China Mobile, the world's largest mobile telecommunications carrier, to provide its users with Google Mobile Search. The mobile initiative, however, was not restricted to Google Search. Google Calendar was made available for mobile devices, as was Picasa. In addition, Picasa had the ability to link photos and albums to Google Maps, also available on certain phones and PDAs. Finally, Google SMS was offered, to enable people who are away from their computers to get instant, accurate answers to queries (like local business listings, dictionary definitions, or product prices) quickly and easily through text messaging.

Google Maps has a dynamic online approach. Users in North America can find location information, navigate through maps, and get directions quickly and easily. Google Maps also features easy navigation and detailed route directions, and it can locate businesses related to a particular query.

Next Google acquired Keyhole Corp., a digital and satellite image mapping company, and created Google Earth. This technology enables users to virtually fly through space, zooming in to specific locations they choose and seeing the real world in sharp focus, right down to individual buildings, streets, and businesses. Later, Google announced that it had entered into an agreement with Second Life to integrate Google Earth with that virtual world. Second Life has its own geography, but it would be an important addition, and one that would be of considerable interest, to have a geography that corresponded with real earth, although this would lead to issues as well. For example, would a business that owns property on Yonge Street in Toronto have a right to set up business in the corresponding place in Second Life?

Google Earth has proven to be very popular, and Google improved it with add-ins such as Google SketchUp 6, which is a 3D software modelling tool that enables buildings and topography to be presented in 3D in Google Earth. In a related move, Google improved Google Maps, with the addition of the ability to see up-to-date traffic info for 30 major U.S. cities. At about the same time, Google announced licensing and support for businesses wanting to embed Google Maps in their websites or internal applications.

While introducing a plethora of interesting and innovative new products, Google has continued to pay attention to its revenue base, which still depends heavily on advertising. It added AdWords to expand its access to local businesses. Then it started with click-to-play video ads, followed by a partnership with MTV. Most recently, to help advertisers understand their click streams and how visitors access their websites, it integrated AdWords with Google Analytics.

Google Checkout was introduced to provide consumers with a convenient and efficient way to shop online and help merchants achieve a better, more efficient business by tying together Google Search and Google AdWords. In the first six months, Google signed up thousands of merchants and millions of buyers, and later in the year it announced a waiver of all transaction processing fees for merchants for the year, as a way to continue building on that momentum.

Looking to diversify, Google announced an advertising partnership with eBay, a distribution agreement with Adobe, a strategic alliance with Intuit, an agreement with Dell to install search software on Dell computers, and plans to bring web content to a major ISP in the United Kingdom. Google also recently announced the significant acquisition of DoubleClick, which is intended to bolster Google's advertising business.

In 2008, Google released an open source browser called Chrome to compete with Microsoft's Internet Explorer and, more importantly, the first version of its Android operating system (OS) for mobile devices. This was followed in 2010 by the release of its own Android-based mobile phone called Nexus One. The Android OS has become very popular and is viewed as a competitive alternative to Apple's iPhone.

Despite the numerous products and services launched by Google in the intense growth period since its IPO, virtually all of its revenues still came from one source: advertising. In December 2010 Facebook surpassed Google in the number of users, although Google still had much higher revenues. Some were predicting a decline in Google's search engine marketing model in favour of social searching and social marketing.

Questions for Discussion

1. Comment on the interplay between Google's business strategy and its business model.

2. How has Google's company acquisition program supported its business model and business strategy?

3. Which Google products have moved beyond the company's original strategic focus on searching information? What do these products indicate about the strategic direction of Google?

4. Does Facebook represent a threat to Google? Why?

Sources

S. Brin and L. Page, *The Anatomy of a Large-Scale Hypertextual Web Search Engine*. (Stanford, CA: Stanford University, 1998).

J. Martin, "Get Right with Google," *Fortune Small Business* 16, no. 7 (September 2006): 70.

http://en.wikipedia.org/wiki/Google

www.google.com

Chapter 3
Evolution and Applications of the Internet

Learning Objectives

When you complete this chapter you should be able to:

1   Describe the internet, its history, and its overall significance.

2   Describe how the internet is appropriate for ebusiness.

3   Identify the components of the internet.

4   Identify the relationship between the internet, extranets, and intranets.

5   Describe situations in which the internet, extranets, and intranets are used for ebusiness.

6   Explain what a virtual private network is and how it can facilitate ebusiness transactions.

7   Describe how the use of the internet is evolving to support social networking and information sharing through blogs, wikis, and mashups.

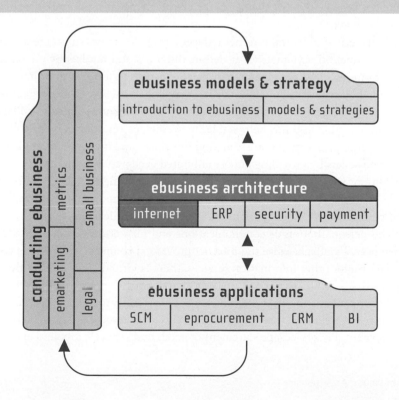

INTRODUCTION

Everyone knows what the internet is—or do they? It is the world's largest communications network, connecting millions of computers from more than 100 countries. In fact, the internet is a network of loosely connected networks whose size and number of users are growing rapidly. The internet works over virtually any type of connection, ranging from dedicated fibre-optic cables to coaxial cables to telephone lines to satellite connections to wireless frequencies. The internet links people and organizations large and small in every part of the world. This global linking, or networking, aspect of the internet is its main strength. In fact, the more people and organizations get connected to the network, the more valuable it becomes, because more people can interact with each other. Some of the main features of internet technology that make it attractive to business are that it is used globally; it is easy to implement on almost any technology platform; it is reliable; and it is fast.

More technically, the internet connects uniquely numbered computing devices that relay information from point to point using the **Internet Protocol (IP)**, or IP with other protocols layered on top of IP. IP is a set of rules for sending and receiving messages at the internet address level. IP was created to provide a mechanism for routing a data packet to its destination. The most common protocol used in addition to IP is the **Transmission Control Protocol (TCP)**. TCP uses a set of rules to exchange messages with other internet points at the data packet level. TCP ensures reliable, flow-controlled data packet delivery. IP provides the addressing system that enables computers to be logically connected so they can send messages to each other, while TCP provides the mechanism for subdividing the information being sent into small packets (that is, data packets) and sending and correctly re-assembling those packets of information at their destination. From these basic but robust components has sprung the globe-spanning network of networks that has become the key enabler of the ebusiness models and strategies that are the subject of this book.

Due to its universality, the internet reduces barriers to competition created by space, time, and information asymmetries. It defeats distances and borders by enabling people with similar interests who are separated by great distances to interact in online communities, enabling buyers and sellers from far-flung regions of the world to interact online in electronic marketplaces, and enabling co-workers to share knowledge and collaborate in ways that would otherwise not be possible. It overcomes time zones by enabling buyers and sellers to interact asynchronously around the clock, and it creates level playing fields for buyers and sellers by providing almost unlimited access to information.

In addition, while the internet has the capacity to bring together vast networks of users, a key feature that distinguishes it from other mass media, such as radio, television, and newspapers, is that it permits interactive communications between sender and receiver and personalization of communications and marketing to suit individual tastes and preferences. Finally, because the internet provides a common and reliable communications platform for other information services, there is virtually no limit on the software applications that can be layered on it to enhance the basic communications capabilities of TCP/IP. For example, business technology applications can be added to support management, investor relations, treasury and finance, human resource management, research and development, IT services, procurement of goods and services, inbound and outbound

Internet Protocol (IP): A protocol that uses a set of rules to send and receive messages at the internet address level.

Transmission Control Protocol (TCP): A protocol that uses a set of rules to exchange messages with other internet points at the data packet level.

logistics, operations management, marketing and sales, and after-sales support. All of these applications will be discussed in subsequent chapters of this book.[1]

As impressive as this network is, the popular conception is that the internet just grew, with no particular planning or control. The fact is, however, that the internet is not just a random network that grew up by accident. There is a very definite structure to it that is not widely known, and there are specific organizations that manage it. To have an understanding of ebusiness, it is useful to know what the internet is, how it is structured, and who the major players are in its operation and governance.

In this chapter we will review the history of the internet and learn about its components and how they enable ebusiness models and strategies.

HISTORY OF THE INTERNET

In 1968, the U.S. Defense Advanced Research Projects Agency (DARPA) formed a network intended for sharing research and development work among corporate, academic, and government researchers. As this was during the Cold War, one of the specifications was that the network should be designed to withstand a nuclear attack. On this new network, called ARPANET, each computer had a unique address, and any computer could communicate with any other computer by specifying its unique address. An **IP address** was formed by concatenating four 8-bit segments of data, where each segment could represent a number ranging from 0 to 255 (e.g., 207.236.71.45). Since the internet was conceived as a network of networks, one part of this address was used to identify the network address and another part was used to identify the specific computer (often called the "host") on that network.

When the internet was created, it was thought that this numbering scheme, called IPv4, that permits 2^{32} unique addresses, would suffice indefinitely. However, as the use of the internet exploded, it became clear that there would soon not be enough addresses for all the devices that people were connecting to the internet. As a result, a new IP addressing system called IPv6 is currently being implemented, albeit slowly. This system will enable 2^{128} unique addresses and should suffice for the next several centuries.

Since IP addresses are just a series of numbers, it became clear that people could not remember the IP addresses of all the devices that they needed to communicate with, so a **domain name system** was created to help people easily identify computers using mnemonic names rather than numbers. Numerous top-level and second-level domains were created, and **domain name services (DNS)** were created to facilitate lookups of IP addresses that correspond to names. For example, top-level domains include .com, .net, .org, .edu, .gov, .num, .arpa, and country codes such as .ca. Second-level domains relate to the name of a particular organization. For example, facebook is a second-level domain name, which, when combined with the top-level domain .com becomes facebook.com, which most people would recognize as Facebook's domain name.

At about the same time, DARPA began the development of **packet switching**, a method of transmitting data by breaking it up into small segments, or packets, and sending the packets individually in a stream. The packets are not necessarily sent together but rather are disassembled, transmitted separately, and then reassembled when they arrive at their destination. After successfully trying out packet switching on media such as radio, the possibility arose of using these packet-switching methods as a

IP address: An address used in a scheme that provides an address for every physical device on the internet to enable any device to communicate with any other device.

domain name system: A method of translating names into IP addresses.

domain name service (DNS): An internet site that provides a table for translating domain names into IP addresses.

protocol for transmitting data between computer systems. Previously, this would have been very difficult, as different computers used different technologies. The introduction of a standard protocol made it possible to transmit data between many different types of computers, as long as they had the protocol installed on their computers. A **protocol** is a special set of rules that the sending and receiving points in a telecommunication connection use when they communicate. Protocols exist at several levels, including hardware and software levels. Both end points must recognize and observe a protocol to be able to understand the contents of transmissions. Protocols are often described in an industry or international standard.

The new protocol could also be used by entire networks, and if two or more networks had the protocol installed, then those networks could be linked together and could share data. Since each computer, also referred to as a node on the network, had its own unique address, every computer could still be accessed on this network. Thus, the ARPANET became a system of linked networks.

TCP/IP: A set of protocols based on Transmission Control Protocol (TCP) and Internet Protocol (IP).

A set of protocols was developed based on TCP and IP. Together, these protocols are referred to as **TCP/IP**.

As the research program grew, it became necessary to form a committee to guide the work. As a result, the Internet Configuration Control Board (ICCB) was formed, which was renamed the Internet Architecture Board (IAB) in 1983. In that same year, TCP/IP protocol was declared by the U.S. Defense Communications Agency to be the standard protocol for the ARPANET.

As knowledge of and the role of the internet expanded, it gained growing support from several U.S. government organizations. A coordinating committee was formed that became known as the Federal Networking Council (FNC). It liaises with the Office of Science and Technology Policy, which is headed up by the President's Science Advisor, and is responsible for setting science and technology policy affecting the internet.

The Canadian Internet

internet backbone: An organized and managed communications system, often based on fibre-optic cables, that forms the central connection for a section of the internet.

In Canada, the internet began in earnest in 1990, when CA*net was created, with support from the National Research Council. The purpose of CA*net was to provide internet connectivity between universities and research organizations in Canada through a unified high-speed network. CA*net linked over 20 regional networks across Canada, most of them provincially oriented, such as ONET in Ontario, BCNET in British Columbia, and ARNET in Alberta. For several years, CA*net was the only internet backbone in Canada. An **internet backbone** is an organized and managed communications system, often based on fibre-optic cables, that forms the central connection for a section of the internet. In partnership with Bell Advanced Communications CA*net operated until March 31, 1997, when it was superseded by CA*net II.

asynchronous transfer mode (ATM): A switching technology that organizes digital data into 53-byte cell units and transmits them using digital signalling technology. A cell is processed asynchronously relative to other related cells; in other words, not necessarily in a pre-specified sequence.

In 1995, Canada entered the world of asynchronous transfer mode (ATM) networks, which transmit data faster than previous networks, with the introduction of the National Test Network (NTN) in partnership with Bell Advanced Communications, AT&T Canada, and Teleglobe Canada. **Asynchronous transfer mode (ATM)** is a switching technology that organizes digital data into 53-byte cell units and transmits them using digital signalling technology. A cell is processed asynchronously relative to other related cells; in other words, not necessarily in a pre-specified sequence. NTN was one of the first national ATM networks in the world, although access was initially limited to specific researchers and labs located at universities and other research facilities across the country. In 1997, NTN was upgraded to form the basis of CA*net II by linking it with international organizations using IP. The core capacity of CA*net II was 155 megabits per second (Mbps). Data transmission speed is measured in **megabits per second (Mbps)**, which means a million bits per second and states the number of data bits that are transmitted per second on a particular medium. Gigabits means a billion bits. Terabits means a trillion bits. Bell Advanced Communications and AT&T Canada jointly provided the underlying ATM networks, while Teleglobe provided a connection to Europe.

CA*net II connected to individual universities, government labs, and research institutes through Regional Advanced Networks (RANs), which operated in every province. Approved organizations could access CA*net II directly through any of the 15 gigabit points-of-presence operated by RANs and the three participating carriers. A **point of presence (POP)** is an access point to the internet that has a unique IP address. An internet service provider (ISP), which is a company that sells access to the internet, has at least one point-of-presence on the internet. In 1998, the federal government began working with CANARIE Inc. (a Canadian not-for-profit corporation supported by its members, partners, and the federal government) to build a national R & D internet network, CA*net 3, based on fibre-optic technology. **Fibre optics** transmit information as light impulses along a glass or plastic wire or fibre. Fibre-optic media carry more data than conventional copper media and are less subject to electromagnetic interference. Most telephone company long-distance lines are now fibre optic.

megabits per second (Mbps): A measure of speed for data transmission. Megabits means a million bits per second and states the number of data bits that are transmitted per second on a particular medium.

point of presence (POP): An access point to the internet that has a unique IP address.

fibre optics: The transmission of information as light impulses along a glass or plastic wire or fibre.

International Governance

The IAB remains the coordinating committee for internet design, engineering, and management (see Figure 3.1). It was formed by the Internet Society (ISOC), a not-for-profit organization established in 1992 to provide leadership in internet-related standards, education, and policy.

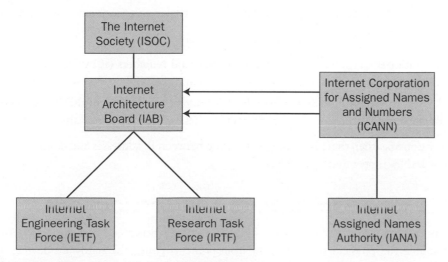

Figure 3.1 Internet Governing Organizations

Today, the IAB is an independent committee of researchers and professionals with an interest in the technical strength and growth of the internet. The IAB meets quarterly to review the condition of the internet, approve any proposed changes or additions to TCP/IP, set technical development priorities, and discuss policy matters that may need the attention of the internet sponsors.

The IAB has two extremely important continuing task forces:

the Internet Engineering Task Force (IETF), and

the Internet Research Task Force (IRTF).

The Internet Engineering Task Force The IAB established the IETF to help coordinate the operation, management, and evolution of the internet. There was a recognition that the internet had grown to geographically dispersed networks and, perhaps more importantly, had moved from experimental to commercial deployment. Of course, since that time, the commercial applications on the internet have grown exponentially, and the importance of the IETF to ebusiness has also expanded tremendously.

The IETF has responsibility for specifying the short- and mid-term internet protocols and architecture and recommending standards for IAB approval, providing a forum for the exchange of information within the internet community, identifying relevant operational and technical problem areas, and convening working groups to explore solutions.

The IETF is a large, open community of network designers, operators, vendors, and researchers concerned with the internet and its protocols. The work of the IETF is performed by a large number of working groups. The working groups tend to have a narrow focus, such as particular security issues or encryption standards, and are normally disbanded when their project is completed.

The Internet Research Task Force The IRTF was formed to promote research in networking and the development of new technology. Since the distinction between research and engineering is not always clear, there can be an overlap between the activities of the IETF and the IRTF. The IRTF is generally more concerned with understanding than with products or standard protocols. The IRTF is a community of network researchers, generally with an internet focus, and is organized into a number of research groups that focus on subjects such as the development of privacy-enhanced email software.

ICANN and IANA Two organizations work closely with the IAB:

the Internet Corporation for Assigned Names and Numbers (ICANN), which coordinates the domain name system, and

IANA, the Internet Assigned Numbers Authority, was formed in the 1970s to coordinate various protocols for the internet, including the very important IP addresses.

As mentioned earlier, there is a close relationship between IP addresses and domain names, so now IANA is operated by ICANN.

INTERNET TECHNOLOGIES AND APPLICATIONS

THE INTERNET VALUE NETWORK CONSISTS OF THE BACKBONE AND RELATED NETWORKS that enable the physical traffic to flow from point to point, the hardware devices and related infrastructures that enable the network to function, the software that is used to implement the various protocols and applications that run on the network and its devices, the information content that is stored on network devices and transferred upon request, and the service providers who manage all aspects of these activities. From a business perspective, these components provide a myriad of business opportunities for network technology providers, software developers, content creators, content aggregators, service providers, and social network creators.

Electronic Mail

The most important internet application continues to be electronic mail, or email. Several email protocols are used today. The oldest and simplest internet mail protocol is SMTP, which stands for Simple Mail Transfer Protocol. The most widely used protocol today is POP3, which stands for Post Office Protocol version 3. Other widely used protocols are IMAP, which is a superset of POP3, and MIME, which stands for Multipurpose Internet Mail Extensions, an extension of SMTP designed to support binary attachments and rich file types. At one time, email seemed to be a straightforward utility service with little additional business opportunity attached to it. However, the creators of Hotmail, Yahoo! Mail, Gmail, and the BlackBerry have demonstrated convincingly that email is a killer application that can be the basis for adding valuable services. For example, it can be used for viral marketing, search-engine marketing, generating web storage revenues, and generating sales of email-enabled telephones.

Canadian Snapshots

The Berkman Study on the Canadian Internet

A study published by the Berkman Center for Internet & Society at Harvard University in February 2010 created some controversy in Canada. The study stated, "Canada still presents itself as an internet leader even though it now offers substandard web access compared to other countries."

Canadian internet providers denounced the study as wrong and based on faulty data.

The study went on the say that Canadian internet systems are slow and expensive. The strategy of government regulators was also the focus of some criticism in the study, stating that there has been a much greater emphasis on connecting remote areas in the country rather than on developing the latest and fastest technologies. The study seemed to ignore the fact that Canada is a very large geographic area, and that connectivity over such great distances has always been a tremendous challenge.

The critics who wrote the study stated that the result of these strategies is that Canada is poorly positioned for the future – that the lack of emphasis on the development of new technologies, such as 3G (and now 4G) runs the risk of leaving the country in a technological backwater.

A Telus spokesman pointed out that the study used high-speed radio service WiMAX rates, which are expensive but are used only in rural areas. He went on to say that Telus "doesn't advertise its 100 megabit per second services because they're available only to high-rise apartments and condos."

This meant, the study concluded, "Canadians are paying $189 per month for their internet service, while the real truth is $35 to $45 a month."

Rogers, Bell, and Shaw are all planning to move into fibre-optic-based communications services but their prime targets are city-centric locations like condos, apartments, and hotels. Along with Telus and Videotron, these companies control approximately 81 percent of the Canadian market for broadband services.

Competition has been a major issue in the Canadian broadband industry. There are few players, and research shows that the highest prices for the lowest speeds are

>

offered by firms that own both a telephone system and a cable system. "In speed, Canada is a weak to midpack performer." Carriers such as Bell that provide infrastructure for other services can impose bandwidth caps, the study said.

On the other hand, the Canadian Radio-television Telecommunications Commission (CRTC) has said that Canada has the highest internet penetration of G7 countries. However, this does not necessarily mean that Canadian customers are getting the best deal by relying on existing cable and telephone companies to provide competition.

There have been critics of the Berkman study, pointing out that it is out of date and even that there was political motivation to support its obstensibly prime objective of encouraging the U.S. FCC to develop a new connectivity policy.

The Berkman study was conducted on behalf of the largest U.S. internet service providers, who wanted to be placed under the jurisdiction of the FCC to stop other companies from investing in their broadband networks.

In response to critics of the Berkman study, the authors mounted a rebuttal, pointing out that very few homes in Canada can tap into the ultra-high speeds offered by fibre-optic. Canada is behind some other countries in the provision of this infrastructure. Since the study was released, Canadians have invested heavily in fibre-optic, and have been implementing it for in-home service. Roll-outs continue in 2011.

The study also used its own independent analysis, as well as OECD data and other sources where those seemed better. This meant that the data were substantially better than the critics indicated.

The study acknowledges that cable and DSL services have been available in some parts of Canada since 1996, when SaskTel became one of the world's first telecommunications carriers to offer it. By the end of 2008, broadband was available to almost all city households in Canada.

At the time of the study, however, fibre-optics availability for Canadian home internet use constituted just .01 per cent of the country's broadband subscribers, substantially lower than countries like Korea (39%), Japan (44%) and Sweden (20%).

Some of these comparisons are difficult and potentially misleading. For example, most Japanese people live in high-density apartments where the provision of high-speed internet is much easier than in Canada, where more people live in single-family homes.

BERKMAN CENTER FOR INTERNET & SOCIETY AT HARVARD UNIVERSITY
http://cyber.law.harvard.edu/pubrelease/broadband/

Questions

1. What does the Berkman study mean to efforts in Canada to improve its internet service?
2. Are there unique circumstances in Canada that might have contributed to some of the conclusions in the Berkman study?

Source: *The Toronto Star*, February 24, 2010, www.thestar.com/news/sciencetech/science/article/770697--we-overpay-for-slow-old-internet-study.

The World Wide Web (WWW)

After email, the next most important internet application is the World Wide Web. Initially, the web was viewed as a way of enabling users to easily access documents stored on remote computers. However, new conceptions of the web, labelled Web 2.0, focus on its social networking aspects. Some see the next evolution of the web, labelled Web 3.0, leading to a universal, network-accessible knowledge base.

The internet, as we have seen, is a collection of interlinked networks. In a real sense, the internet can be viewed as a very large client-server network, and is often discussed in those terms. A client-server network can be analysed in terms of clients connecting to servers, as illustrated in figure 3.2. The figure shows a series of three **clients**, which are the computers with which users gain access to and operate applications on the network. The

client: A computer that is used by a network user to gain access to and operate applications on the network.

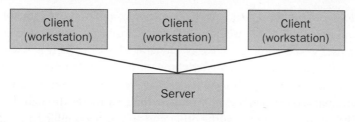

Figure 3.2 Client-server network

A client-server network can be analysed in terms of clients and servers.

server is a large central computer that forms the nucleus of a network and contains the network operating system, as well as case-specific network-based applications. The server is a passive computer that awaits processing requests from clients.

Figure 3.3 expands the diagram in figure 3.2 to specify some of the major characteristics of the World Wide Web as a client-server network. Users use their computers (called clients) to communicate with a special set of servers on the internet, known as web servers, with the help of web browser software running on the client computers. A **web server** is a server attached to a network that is dedicated to specific applications that must be run on the World Wide Web, used by web users, or interfaced very closely with the web. Servers are owned by the company where the user works or by an ISP with which the user has signed a contract, such as Rogers, Sympatico, or Interlink. The ISP then connects to the regional network, or directly to an internet backbone such as CA*net, and through that to a web server at the website targeted for communication. The website is identified by a **uniform resource locator (URL)**, which is the address of a resource on the World Wide Web. The URL contains the name of the required protocol followed by a colon (normally http:), an identification that a web server is the target (such as // www), and a domain name that identifies a specific web server followed by a slash (e.g., gm.com/), and perhaps a specific file name (such as index.html)—all of which makes **http://www.gm.com/index.html**. Increasingly, the letters "www" are no longer required, as web servers are assumed unless otherwise specified. Index pages are often assumed as

server: A large central computer that forms the nucleus of a network and contains the network operating system, as well as case-specific network-based applications.

web server: A server attached to a network; it is dedicated to specific applications that must be run on the World Wide Web, used by web users, or interfaced very closely with the web.

uniform resource locator (URL): The address of a resource on the World Wide Web.

General Motors
www.gm.com

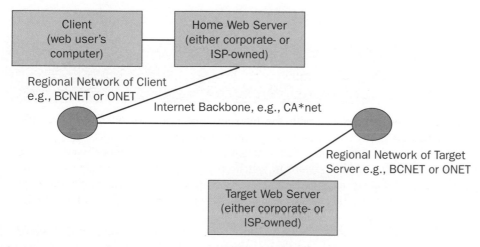

Figure 3.3 Overview of the World Wide Web network

This figure specifies some of the major characteristics of the World Wide Web as a client-server network.

well. If a user logs into the World Wide Web, for example, and wants to shop for a General Motors car from home, he or she would connect and log onto the web server of a local ISP. Then the user would enter the URL of General Motors (which is **www.gm.com**). A signal would go from the user's computer's browser to the ISP's router and then would be forwarded through the best path to GM's primary web server. Since TCP/IP is being used, the various packets in the message will take different routes through the networks, but will all arrive at the same server at the other end and be reassembled according to the instructions embedded in the packets.

However, what a person sees after logging onto the internet is typically only a part of the internet—the World Wide Web. When the internet was first implemented, it had several specialized applications, including Gopher, Veronica, and FTP. These were simply sets of functionalities for certain specific purposes. For example, Gopher and Veronica were used to find and retrieve certain kinds of information, and FTP was used for transporting large files or data sets. None of these functions were user-friendly, which created serious limitations on the usefulness of the internet for non-technical people. User interfaces were character-based rather than graphical or icon-based, and required the knowledge of various commands that users had to enter in command lines to make the system work.

In 1993, however, a new tool emerged in the form of a user-friendly, graphics-capable interface that enabled users to connect to and navigate websites on the internet. It was known as Mosaic. This new interface software, which became known as a **web browser**, led directly to the emergence and popularity of the World Wide Web on the internet. Mosaic evolved to become Netscape Navigator, one of the most significant pieces of software that helped make possible the internet as we know it. Navigator (or Netscape Communicator, which includes Navigator) was once the most popular web browser, with over 90 percent market share. It is now estimated that Microsoft's Internet Explorer enjoys 90 percent of the browser market. The World Wide Web still provides a bridge to the older technologies that remain on the internet, such as FTP, to facilitate file transfers and other functions through the use of icons rather than requiring the old commands.

web browser: Software with a user-friendly, graphics-capable interface that enables users to connect to and navigate websites on the internet.

New Business Models
Television in the New World

Hulu, purveyor of online television, has been reconsidering its business model. So far, it has offered up content for free and obtained its revenue from advertising. This time-honoured business model is a popular one on the Web.

The world keeps changing, however, and there are signs that this business model will need to change. The concept of online TV and movies and other videos has been catching on lately. Many people like to watch TV and videos on their computers, and more are now watching them on their BlackBerry devices and other smartphones. With the high resolution possible on premium mobile devices, TV and movies become very watchable.

The problem for the advertising model when people want to watch on their handhelds is, of course, airtime and data cost. Nobody wants to spend money to watch commercials. So Hulu is considering going to a subscription model.

But would a subscription model work well? It would definitely need to be carefully thought out. Hulu has several options. It could run a subscription model along with

>

an advertising model and let customers decide which they want to use. Those who can afford a subscription will be able to watch TV and movies without enduring ads, while students and others with limited funds will be able to choose the advertising option. Hulu could also offer those who pay for the subscription route some premium content to make their investment worthwhile.

With the growing convergence of television and computing devices like home PCs and mobile devices such as smartphones and iPads, the competition for online television is heating up fast.

YouTube, for example, is the web's biggest carrier of videos. If it decided to go more heavily into television content, it would be a major competitor for Hulu.

Traditionally, much content has been offered on the internet for free. However, attitudes about this approach are changing to an attitude of saying if the information is worthwhile then people should pay for it.

Hulu
www.hulu.com

Questions

1. What are the risks and benefits to Hulu of going to a subscription model?

2. What will Hulu's competitive environment be like in a few years?

Sources: Kimberly Hill, "Will Hulu Do the Subscription Dance?" *E-Commerce Times*, April 22, 2010, www.ecommercetimes.com/story/Will-Hulu-Do-the-Subscription-Dance-69838.html?wlc=1272550402; *BusinessWeek*, April 23, 2007, 20; and M. Ingram, "Is Facebook the Next Google, Is It More Like Lindsay Lohan?" *Globe and Mail*, May 24, 2007, B3.

HyperText Markup Language (HTML)

HyperText Markup Language (HTML) is a specialized coding language that is used to encode content so it can be displayed in a web browser. It tells the web browser how to display the words and images in the file on a webpage. Figure 3.4 shows the HTML source code for the main webpage of the website for the University of Waterloo Centre for Information Systems Assurance. **Source code** is the format in which a program is written that can be read by humans and that is then converted into a different format that the computer can recognize. In the source code in figure 3.4 can be seen the metatags that are used to identify the contents of the page. **Metatags** are coding statements in HTML that identify the content of a website. In this case, the metatags are near the top of the figure, and can be identified by the word "meta" that begins the code inside the angle brackets. Metatags are used by search engines to identify webpages. Accordingly, the words included within metatags on a website are very important, since they help web users find the site when they enter a search request on a search engine. Other lines in the source code reproduced in figure 3.4 show the content that appears on the actual page that web users will see.

HyperText Markup Language (HTML): A specialized coding language that is used to encode content so it can be displayed in a web browser.

HyperText Transfer Protocol (HTTP)

HyperText Transfer Protocol (HTTP) is a set of rules used in exchanging files (e.g., text, graphics, sound, video) for display on the World Wide Web. It is by far the most common protocol used for reading webpages on the web. As will be discussed in chapter 5, several security protocols have been developed for use with HTTP to ensure the security of files and messages that need to be exchanged during ecommerce.

HyperText Transfer Protocol (HTTP): A set of rules used in exchanging files (such as text, graphics, sound, and video) for display on the World Wide Web.

Extensible Markup Language (XML)

Extensible Markup Language (XML) is similar to HTML in that they both contain symbols to describe the contents of a page or file. While HTML describes the content

Extensible Markup Language (XML): A markup language similar to HTML in that they both contain symbols to describe the contents of a page or file; but while HTML describes the content only in terms of how it is to be displayed and interacted with, XML describes the content in terms of what data is being included.

```
<?xml version="1.0" encoding="iso-8859-1"?>
<!DOCTYPE html PUBLIC "-//W3C//DTD XHTML 1.0 Transitional//EN"
"http://www.w3.org/TR/xhtml1/DTD/xhtml1-transitional.dtd">
<html ><!— InstanceBegin template="/Templates/uwcisa.dwt"
codeOutsideHTMLIsLocked="false" >
<head>
<!— InstanceBeginEditable name="doctitle" >
<title>UWCISA</title>
<!— InstanceEndEditable >
<meta http-equiv="Content-Type" content="text/html; charset=iso-
8859-1" />
<meta http-equiv="content-type" content="text/html;charset=iso-
8859-1">
<meta name="description" content="The key objectives of the
Centre are to stimulate relevant research, support the develop-
ment/delivery of educational materials, communicate about impor-
tant ISA issues and Centre activities and promote interaction
among ISA educators and practitioners.">
<meta name="KeyWords" content="UWCISA, CISA, Centre for
Information Systems Assurance, Information Systems Assurance,
Information Systems Audit and Control, Accounting, Accountancy,
University, Waterloo, education, auditing, finance, taxation, CA,
accountant, accountants, ">
<PARA />
<!— InstanceBeginEditable name="head" >
<!— InstanceEndEditable >
<PARA />
<style type="text/css">
td img {display: block;}h2 {
font-family: Arial, Helvetica, sans-serif;
color: #006699;
}
p {
font-family: Arial, Helvetica, sans-serif;
}
h3 {
font-family: Arial, Helvetica, sans-serif;
color: #006699;
}
</style>
```

Figure 3.4 A website's source code

This is a sample of the source code for the main webpage of the University of Waterloo Centre for Information Systems Assurance.

Source: Reprinted with permission from University of Waterloo Centre for Information Systems Assurance.

only in terms of how it is to be displayed and interacted with, XML describes the content in terms of what data is being included (e.g., "phonenum" for phone number). This markup language provides more flexibility in execution of the file; for example, in XML, a phone number can be stored, displayed, or dialled. The data described can be in a separate server; thus, XML can be used to gather information from across the internet.

Common Gateway Interface (CGI)

Common Gateway Interface (CGI) is a method used by a web server to pass a user's request that has come over the internet to an application. It also receives data from the application that can be sent back to the user. This is necessary because web servers can only handle HTTP requests for HTML files, and they require other servers to process other requests. It is a standard internet-based method and therefore can be recognized by web servers around the world.

All these technologies are needed to be able to use the World Wide Web for business purposes. The web is a vehicle for communication, and tools such as CGI, and other programming aids beyond the scope of this book, such as ASP, JSP, PHP, and ColdFusion, are becoming important tools to allow interaction between users and web servers. Although the web worked for some years without XML, XML is becoming an essential part of the web because of its power, flexibility, and its multiple-language support.

Another technology that is not a part of the core set of technologies, but that has become important to the display of webpages, is Java. **Java** is a programming language that was originally invented by Sun Microsystems for the purpose of enhancing webpages. It is the programming language that is used, for example, to create many of the little animated icons one sees moving about on webpages. Since its inception, its use has grown markedly beyond webpages to include many business and ebusiness applications. Various other technologies are used on the web for similar purposes, such as Flash and Shockwave, but while important for modern webpages, they are not considered core technologies.

Common Gateway Interface (CGI): A method used by a web server to pass a user's request that has come over the internet to an application. It also receives data from the application that can be sent back to the user.

Java: A programming language that was originally invented for the purpose of enhancing webpages and is used to create animations and moveable, interactive icons.

Website Design

Apart from the protocols and technologies required to enable users to browse the World Wide Web, the key components of the web are the websites that contain the content that users seek to access. This content can range from documents such as catalogues of products available for sale to photos, music files, video files, information databases, and various applications such as calculators, search tools, and other resources. Links that connect to content within a website, applications, users, and other websites are a major element of a website.

All websites are not created equal, however. Some are more attractive than others due to the content they provide or due to design features that set them apart from others. Key quality indicators of a website include reputation/recognition, access speed, content, simple page layout, navigability, ecommerce capabilities, shopper friendliness, service orientation, customization/personalization features, connectivity to other users and relevant sites, community, global perspective, effective fulfillment capabilities, and trust indicators. Each of these is briefly described below:

1. *Reputation/recognition.* An effective, memorable, or branded URL; word of mouth or buzz; and off-internet advertising as well as internet-based ads and links can help build the reputation/recognition and user base that all websites crave.

2. *Access speed.* Fast load of first page, limited use of graphics in downloaded files, and use of effective compression techniques can help to reduce download times and prevent loss of users due to download delay.

3. *Content.* A catalogue of goods and services offered, paying attention to emotional as well as informational content, is a key design feature.

4. *Simple page layout.* A clear, well-organized, product/service focus is superior to uncontrolled clutter.

5. *Navigability.* Ease of access to key pages, memory aids, short search trees, effective search tools, and a short time to checkout are essential, unless a site is intended for entertainment or extended information search.

6. *Ecommerce capabilities.* A registration form can help to screen users and gather personal information to help customize/personalize the shopping experience; other key features are a shopping cart with memory capabilities, credit card validation and approval, security features to protect privacy and confidentiality of information, order tracking, and delivery options.

7. *Shopper friendliness.* Personalized greetings, attention to shopping enjoyment, and personal interaction through chat and other features help to create a shopper-friendly environment.

8. *Service orientation.* Product quality, product variety, information accuracy and currency, and comparison shopping features are valued by shoppers; it is a good idea to limit impulse buying to reduce regret and minimize returns and complaints; also, shoppers like to know the total product cost (including tax, shipping, duties, etc.) before finalizing a purchase; otherwise, they may abandon the shopping cart.

9. *Customization/personalization features.* Log-in registration, cookies, personal email, and personalized page configuration help personalize the shopping experience and put shoppers at ease.

10. *Connectivity to other users and relevant sites.* Chat, instant messaging, email, and other links are becoming essential connectivity aspects, especially in social networking sites.

11. *Community.* Product reviews, ratings by other shoppers, statistics on top products, and member areas reduce user uncertainty and encourage completion of orders.

12. *Global perspective.* Multi-language and multi-currency support, and cross-border delivery are consistent with the value proposition of the internet.

13. *Effective fulfillment capabilities.* Product availability; reliable and timely delivery; no shipping shock due to unspecified duty, shipping, or other costs; and efficient reverse logistics are essential.

14. *Trust indicators.* Features to protect against credit card abuse; disclosure of business practices; privacy policies and controls; assurances about privacy, security, and processing integrity though trust marks and other disclosures; and dispute resolution mechanisms help to create and maintain trust in a site.

INTRANETS AND EXTRANETS
Intranets

An intranet is a network that is internal to an organization and uses internet technology. Since these technologies include the use of browsers, the network appears to users to be the same as the internet. Since it uses the same protocols as the internet, such as

TCP/IP, it can interact seamlessly with the internet. Intranets have all of the advantages of the internet, including ease of use, compatibility with other systems, and simplicity.

Intranets play an important role in the ebusiness strategies of many organizations. Initially, they were used to convey to employees information that once was printed—documents such as procedure manuals, personnel manuals, policy statements, and major announcements. Essentially, they were used to save printing costs and to speed up the dissemination of information.

In the next step of their evolution, intranets began to be used by employees to input information into corporate applications. For example, they have been used to input time reports on assignments in process and make changes to personnel information such as addresses and telephone numbers. Essentially, applications like these on intranets transfer the input process to employees, empower employees to maintain their own records, and support those who are travelling by giving them remote access to their organization's intranet. This last use is an example of how intranets support and facilitate ebusiness, as they enable employees to work from outside their offices, or in clients' offices, and input timely information for management and others with whom they must collaborate.

Extranets

Extranets are networks that are available to users inside and outside of a company and use internet technology. If a company is successful in opening an application up to customers, then the intranet that was available only to employees will become an extranet, because it will also be available to customers.

Extranets have all the advantages of intranets but extend those advantages to outside parties—most often, suppliers and customers. Accordingly, a prime purpose of the use of intranets and extranets is to automate and streamline the supply chain. For suppliers, extranets are used to enable companies to place purchase orders online and for the suppliers to fill those orders. On an extranet, companies can place their catalogues online, and their customers can place orders online. All of the documentation can be in electronic form, and if the applications are sophisticated enough, all of the transactions can be executed online.

An extranet can also be an excellent way to deal with inquiries about availability, delivery times, and other customer concerns, and to provide promotional information to customers. For suppliers, extranets have been extended to implementing joint applications such as vendor-managed inventory (VMI) applications, in which the suppliers manage the company's inventory levels by monitoring quantities on hand and automatically replenishing the stock when needed. Extranets are critical to contemporary ebusiness. They reduce costs, improve the timing of business transactions, and foster key business relationships. These are the reasons why extranets have proven to be powerful and popular business tools adopted by a growing range of companies. The Ebusiness in Global Perspective box describes how Gmail at Sanmina-SCL uses an extranet to build parts sales and illustrates how ebusiness can help the overall business to succeed.

Gmail at Sanmina-SCI Corporation

Since 2008, numerous companies have adopted internet-based applications. This approach, usually referred to as "cloud computing," or "computing in the cloud," avoids the need to install and maintain the apps.

Manesh Patel, CIO of contract manufacturing firm Sanmina-SCI Corporation, drew some sideways glances and even criticism when he decided to switch his 16,000 users from the Outlook/Exchange email system to Gmail, Google's "email in the cloud" system.

Patel was cautious at first, partly because he had to sell the idea to firm management. He spent a year investigating, testing, and evaluating the process that would be needed to adopt Gmail. Eventually, he determined that the savings were too big to ignore. Also, he did not view email as a critical application but one that is essential, but not one that would give the company a competitive advantage if done better than others. This left some additional scope for innovation. On the other hand, Patel knew that a broken email system can be a significant competitive disadvantage. So there was definitely a potentially large downside.

One of the big concerns of companies moving to the cloud is security, and Patel's team looked at this aspect carefully. However, they managed to set up Gmail within the company's corporate single sign-on infrastructure, taking the security to a reasonable level. They recognized that Google had more resources than they did.

Overall, the transition went well. Patel did have one regret: not requiring users to attend training classes prior to implementation. He and his team had felt that everyone either knew how to use Gmail and Google Calendar or would pick them up quickly. Also, of course, they were busy. However, they quickly realized after cutover that people didn't know quite enough, and there were a lot of calls to IT support for assistance.

There were a few other hitches. Some user interface features, such as drag and drop, won't work until browsers integrate the emerging HTML 5 specifications. Gmail's threaded approach to organizing the inbox bothered some employees, who were used to Outlook's folder-based approach to organizing messages. Also, calendar updates on BlackBerry devices could go only one way: Changes could be downloaded to the BlackBerry, but changes made on a BlackBerry couldn't be uploaded to the main servers. Patel and his team managed to fix these issues, however, over the following summer.

After studying Gmail, the company concluded that it would do most of what Outlook/Exchange did for them and still achieve cost savings. It was estimated that the cost of Gmail would be less than half of what they had been paying to run Outlook/Exchange. They would save around $10 per user per month and since they had 16,000 users, their total savings would total in the vicinity of $1.9 million a year.

Patel felt that the long-term benefits of Gmail were important. They included flexibility and the ability to integrate email and calendaring functions into a more socially networked, collaborative environment. They also felt that the other Google applications could be adopted to foster the atmosphere of collaboration. So the plan also included the idea of making effective use of other Google applications.

Sanmina-SCI Corporation
www.sanmina-sci.com

Questions

1. What are the pros and cons of using Gmail for corporate email?
2. Is it likely that more companies will adopt cloud-based email services?

Source: Robert L Mitchell, "Why a Billion Dollar Corporation Entrusted its E-mail to Google," *Computerworld*. April 28. 2010.

VIRTUAL PRIVATE NETWORKS

Many extranets and intranets run on the internet in order to save the cost of acquiring broadband network capability, dedicated telephone lines, and the other paraphernalia that is necessary to set up a conventional network. The major feature of an intranet or an extranet that distinguishes it from a normal website in this circumstance is the existence of a login requiring a user ID and a password to obtain access. Clearly, having a network on the internet exposes it to the well-known security shortcomings of the internet. A good hacker can find the intranet or extranet by surfing the internet and only has to crack the ID and password to gain access—a comparatively easier job than if the network is set within the bounds of the corporate networks.

One answer to these concerns that has been adopted by many companies is the **virtual private network (VPN)**, which is a secure and encrypted connection between two points across the internet. VPNs transfer information by encrypting the data in IP packets and sending the packets over the internet by a process called tunnelling. **Tunnelling** is a process in which data packets are transmitted over the internet by including an additional header that establishes its route through the internet. This adds some assurance and security to the transmission process because it is known where the data are and where they are going at all times. The route to be followed by the data is called a tunnel. Most VPNs are built and run by ISPs and have been used to replace remote access and international proprietary networks.

By using the internet, VPNs reduce networking costs and staffing requirements. In this respect, VPNs are somewhat akin to outsourcing, but with better cost reductions. Using VPNs for international networks is quicker than waiting until links can be established by carriers.

When a user sends data through a VPN, the data go from the user's PC to a firewall, which encrypts the data and sends them over an access line to the company's ISP. The data are then carried through tunnels across the internet to the recipient's ISP. From that point, the data travel over an access line, through another firewall, where they are decrypted and sent to the recipient's PC.

virtual private network (VPN): A secure and encrypted connection between two points across the internet.

tunnelling: A process in which data packets are transmitted over the internet by including an additional header that establishes its route through the internet.

How VPNs Facilitate Ebusiness Transactions

VPNs are driven by a need for wide-ranging networks that have the advantages of the internet in terms of cost and availability, but without the disadvantages of the internet in terms of security. By providing a secure environment, VPNs address the internet's limitations and, as a consequence, add considerable flexibility to a company's network options. In other words, they make the internet a more viable business system.

VPNs are used as a framework in which to develop extranets as well as intranets. Extranets range outside a company and, therefore, tend to serve the need for wide area networks. Intranets, on the other hand, are internal to a company. However, in large companies, the network must cover a large geographical area, and may well be global in scope.

EVOLVING INTERNET TECHNOLOGIES AND APPLICATIONS

AN INTERNET TECHNOLOGY THAT HAS BEEN GROWING RAPIDLY IN RECENT YEARS is Voice over Internet Protocol, or VoIP. In addition, a series of developments that have collectively been termed Web 2.0 have fostered new interactions and collaboration over the web. Blogs, wikis, mashups, and social networking services are examples of these developments. The goal of Web 3.0 is to create a semantic web.

Voice over Internet Protocol (VoIP)

Voice over Internet Protocol (VoIP): A set of protocols for carrying voice signals/telephone calls over the internet.

blog: A website maintained by individuals or a group to provide an ongoing stream of information about personal experiences, opinions, or some specific topic of interest.

Skype
www.skype.com
Amazon
www.amazon.com
Xanga
www.xanga.com
Technorati
www.technorati.com
MyBlogLog
www.mybloglog.com
wiki: A group-editable webpage.

Wikipedia
www.wikipedia.com
Socialtext
www.socialtext.com

Voice over Internet Protocol (VoIP) is a set of protocols for carrying voice signals/telephone calls over the internet. VoIP can dramatically reduce the cost of telephone calls as well as enhance the telephone experience through the addition of numerous services such as three-way calling, call forwarding, caller ID, and auto redial. VoIP phones can integrate with other internet services, such as routing incoming calls anywhere the recipient connects to the internet, address book management, message or data file exchange, audio conferencing, and video calling. Many companies are now offering to replace conventional phone services with VoIP at much lower cost. One well-known VoIP service is Skype.

Blogs

Web logs, or **blogs**, are websites maintained by individuals or groups to provide an ongoing stream of information about personal experiences, opinions, or some specific topic of interest. Blogs can contain text, graphics, pictures, videos, and links to other blogs and websites. Sites such as Xanga enable users to easily set up blogs. Sites such as Technorati enable searching of blogs. Sites such as MyBlogLog link communities of bloggers. Some businesses have created blogs to communicate with customers, investors, and other interested parties. Some businesses sponsor blogs maintained by individuals in return for promotion of their products or services.

Wikis

Wikis are group-editable webpages. These pages can enhance collaboration on projects involving knowledge management. The best known example of a wiki is the group-edited online reference source Wikipedia. One company uses a wiki service provided by Socialtext to create meeting agendas and host training videos for new hires. Wikis can reduce the need for extensive emails among a group by providing a website where materials can be posted and edited by a group of interested participants. Some entities have found that their employees prefer to use wikis instead of their corporate intranets.

Mashups

mashup: A website or application that combines content from simple existing web services to create a new service.

social network: A loosely linked community of individuals with some common interest.

Flickr
www.flickr.com
YouTube
www.youtube.com
del.icio.us
http://del.icio.us

Mashups are websites or applications that combine content from simple existing web services to create a new service. For example, HousingMaps is a mashup that combines information on rentals from Craigslist with Google map services to show pushpins on maps of various regions that users can click on to get detailed information. BookBurro takes book information from Amazon.com and accesses other stores to show price comparisons.[2]

Social Networking Services

Social networks on the internet are loosely linked communities of individuals with some common interest. Typically, a set of founders initially sends out messages inviting people to join the network. New members then invite others, creating a social network.

Social networking services such as Flickr, YouTube, del.icio.us, LinkedIn, MySpace, and Facebook enable people to share photos, videos, and bookmarks; update address books; create and view profiles of network members; and create new links. Social networking site Twitter asks its members "What are you doing?" and they can answer by instant messenger, mobile phone, or on the web and have their answers routed to networks of friends or "followers."

Some businesses have started experimenting with social networking services to identify sales leads and hiring prospects. Ning provides tools that enable any individual or organization to create their own social networks. However, the use of such social networking tools can also carry risks. For example, customers could create networks of their own, which could include an "I hate your business" network. Or, ads on the network could advertise competitors' products or services.[3] Salesforce.com provides tools that enable users to upload virtually any type of "document" and then attach it to other documents, such as sales reports. Users can control who can see, download, or modify the documents. Users can also post comments or ratings that other users can see and monitor. Users can also subscribe to RSS feeds that alert them whenever relevant information is added or changed.[4] The Estrategy box provides an example of how Facebook is pursuing a strategy based on its success as a social networking service.

LinkedIn
www.linkedin.com

MySpace
www.myspace.com

Facebook
www.facebook.com

Twitter
http://twitter.com

Ning
www.ning.com

Salesforce.com
www.salesforce.com

HousingMaps
www.housingmaps.com

BookBurro
http://bookburro.org

Estrategy
Strategy at Facebook

Facebook was started by Mark Zuckerberg, a Harvard dropout, and two classmates in 2004. By April 2006, it was the seventh-most-visited site on the internet.

In fall 2006, rumour had it that Viacom, which owns MTV, VHL, and Comedy Central, offered $750 million to buy Facebook, but Zuckerberg turned down the deal. Pundits were astonished and dismissed the valuation, saying Facebook's owner was foolish. They said he would never see that kind of money again.

Facebook is a social networking site, similar to MySpace, which had attracted tremendous attention before being snapped up by News Corporation for about $600 million. Facebook started out as a social networking site for college students. When it opened itself up to non-students in September 2006, it was roundly criticized for abandoning its niche, but traffic doubled shortly afterwards. Although its market share is lower than that of MySpace in the United States, the situation is reversed in Canada. In fact, 15 percent of the worldwide Facebook user base is in Canada.

Also in fall 2006, rumour had it that Yahoo! offered $1.6 billion for Facebook. Once again Zuckerberg declined to sell. And once again pundits claimed that he had missed a big opportunity.

Instead of selling out, however, Facebook has continued to roll out new features. For example, it created a classified advertising network that enables Facebook members to list and share items. Facebook is also looking to create partnerships with companies that want to reach its millions of monthly users. Many companies already have set up Facebook pages and use them for communicating with customers and employees. One aspect of Facebook's user network that partners such as eBay have found appealing is that Facebook users have been younger than the average eBay user. However, this is changing. Recent reports show that older adults, even seniors, are joining Facebook, making it very much a mainstream application. In fact, 11 percent of users are over the age of 35, and the fastest-growing demographic is users over 30.

Facebook's growth in the fall of 2007 was staggering. More than 1 million new users signed up every week—200,000 daily—totalling over 50 million active users. Facebook received 40 billion page views a month. Facebook has also seen huge growth internationally; Facebook users' passion , or addiction , to the site is unparalleled: More than half use it every day, and users spend an average of 19 minutes a day on Facebook. Facebook is the sixth-most-trafficked site in the United States and the

>

top photo sharing site, with 4.1 billion photos uploaded . The most recent estimate of its value was in the $15 billion range, based on Microsoft's investment in 1.6 percent of the company for $240,000.

Facebook
www.facebook.com

Questions

1. What accounts for the remarkable success of Facebook?
2. What strategic risks does Facebook face?

Sources: S. Rosenbush, "Omigod, That Site Is Totally Hot," *BusinessWeek*, April 10, 2006, 13; V. Vara, "EBay Eyes Teenager Social Sites to Spur Growth," *Globe and Mail*, March 1, 2007, p. B17; S. H. Wildstrom, "Harnessing Social Networks," *sinessWeek*, April 23, 2007, 20; www.crunchbase.com/company/facebook; M. Ingram, "Is Facebook the Next Google, or Is It More Like Lindsay Lohan?" *Globe and Mail*, May 24, 2007, B3.

The Semantic Web

semantic web: A version of today's web that will include technology to understand and process human language.

One problem with the internet is that although the technology is universal, sharing information on the internet is limited by culture and language. Webpages are typically coded in HTML, which defines how information looks on a webpage but not what it means. A web browser looking at HTML-tagged information cannot tell the difference between dates, postal code numbers, and telephone numbers. The goal of Web 3.0 is to create a **semantic web**—a version of today's web that will include technology to understand and process human language. Thus, a web browser looking at semantically tagged information would know the meaning associated with every item displayed on a webpage, not just its appearance on the page. The browser would be able to tell the difference between a date, postal code, and telephone number because these items would have attached tags that would represent these concepts. This project is led by Tim Berners-Lee, the creator of the World Wide Web and the protocols that enable it to function on the internet. His vision is to create a web based on frameworks that define the meaning of various concepts and the tagging of all information in accordance with those frameworks, making it possible to exchange and share information across language and other barriers.

CHAPTER SUMMARY

The internet is the world's largest network, connecting millions of computers from more than 100 countries. The size of the network and the number of users are growing rapidly. It began as a military project in 1968, when the U.S. Defense Advanced Research Projects Agency (DARPA) formed a network intended for sharing research and development work among corporate, academic, and government researchers. They formed a new network called ARPANET and a protocol to make it work—Transmission Control Protocol/Internet Protocol (TCP/IP).

In Canada, the internet took shape in 1990, when CA*net was created. It evolved from there to include the major providers, such as Bell, Telus, and others, utilizing the established telephone networks in the country. A network of networks evolved with major points of presence (POP) across the country that individuals and businesses can gain access to through their internet service providers (ISPs).

The Internet Architecture Board (IAB) is the main coordinating committee for internet design, engineering, and management. The IAB established the Internet Engineering

Task Force (IETF) to help coordinate the operation, management, and evolution of the internet. The IETF is a large, open community of network designers, operators, vendors, and researchers concerned with the internet and its protocols. The Internet Research Task Force (IRTF) was formed by the IAB to promote research in networking and the development of new technology.

The World Wide Web (WWW) is a special set of servers on the internet, known as web servers, that is equipped to communicate with web browsers.

The main technologies used on the internet are TCP/IP, HyperText Markup Language (HTML), HyperText Transfer Protocol (HTTP), Extensible Markup Language (XML), and Common Gateway Interface (CGI).

An intranet is a network that is internal to an organization and uses internet technologies. Since these technologies include the use of browsers, the network appears to users to be the same as the internet. Since it uses the same protocols as the internet, it can interact seamlessly with the internet.

Extranets are networks that are available to users outside of a company and use internet technology. On an extranet, companies can place their catalogues online, and their customers can place orders online. Extranets are critical to contemporary ebusiness. They reduce costs, improve the timing of business transactions, and foster key business relationships.

Many extranets and intranets actually run on the internet, in order to save the cost of acquiring broadband network capability, dedicated telephone lines, and the other paraphernalia that are necessary to set up a conventional network. Clearly, having a network on the internet exposes it to the security shortcomings of the internet. A virtual private network (VPN) is one solution that has been adopted by many companies. A VPN is a secure and encrypted connection between two points across the internet. It can transfer information by encrypting the data in IP packets and sending the packets over the internet by a process called tunnelling. Most VPNs are built and run by internet service providers and have been used to replace remote access and international proprietary networks.

Emerging internet technologies and applications include VoIP, blogs, wikis, mashups, social networking services, and the semantic web.

Key Terms

asynchronous transfer mode (ATM) (p. 52)

blog (p. 66)

client (p. 56)

Common Gateway Interface (CGI) (p. 61)

domain name service (DNS) (p. 51)

domain name system (p. 51)

Extensible Markup Language (XML) (p. 59)

fibre optics (p. 53)

HyperText Markup Language (HTML) (p. 59)

HyperText Transfer Protocol (HTTP) (p. 59)

internet backbone (p. 52)

Internet Protocol (IP) (p. 50)

IP address (p. 51)

Java (p. 61)

mashup (p. 66)

megabits per second (Mbps) (p. 53)

metatag (p. 59)

packet switching (p. 51)

point of presence (POP) (p. 53)

protocol (p. 52)

semantic web (p. 68)

server (p. 57)

social network (p. 66)

source code (p. 59)

TCP/IP (p. 52)

Transmission Control Protocol (TCP) (p. 50)

tunnelling (p. 65)

uniform resource locator (URL) (p. 57)

virtual private network (VPN) (p. 65)

Voice over Internet Protocol (VoIP) (p. 66)

web browser (p. 58)

web server (p. 57)

wiki (p. 66)

MyEbusinessLab Tools for Online Learning

To help you master the material in this chapter and stay up to date with new developments in ebusiness, visit the MyEBusinessLab at www.pearsoned.ca/myebusinesslab. Resources include the following:

- **Pre- and Post-Test Questions**
- **Additional Chapter Questions**
- **Author Blog**
- **Recommended Readings**
- **Commentaries on Current Trends**
- **Additional Topics in Ebusiness**
- **Internet Exercises**
- **Glossary Flashcards**

Endnotes

1. M. E. Porter, "Strategy and the Internet,"*Harvard Business Review* (March 2001): 63–78.

2. R. D. Hof, "Mix, Match, and Mutate,"*BusinessWeek*, July 25, 2005, www.businessweek.com/@@76IH*ocQ34AvyQMA/magazine/content/05_30/b3944108_mz063.htm, accessed July 5, 2007.

3. S. H. Wildstrom, "Harnessing Social Networks,"*BusinessWeek* (April 23, 2007): 20.

4. M. Ingram, "Social Networking Gets a Corporate Face,"*Globe and Mail*, April 12, 2007: B8.

Chapter 4

Enterprise-wide and Inter-enterprise Systems

Learning Objectives

When you complete this chapter you should be able to:

1 Describe what is meant by enterprise-wide systems.

2 Describe how enterprise-wide systems fit with ebusiness strategy.

3 Identify the key features of enterprise systems.

4 Describe how inter-enterprise systems are created.

5 Evaluate the structures for setting up enterprise and inter-enterprise systems.

6 Explain how enterprise and inter-enterprise systems are crucial to ebusiness.

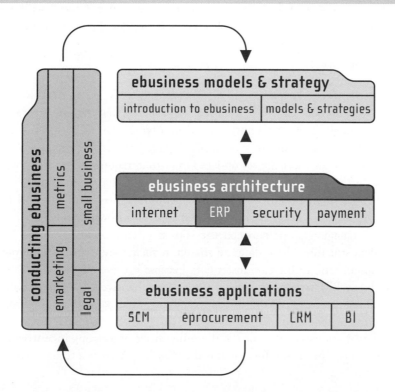

INTRODUCTION

ENTERPRISE-WIDE SYSTEMS ARE ANY INFORMATION SYSTEMS THAT ARE DEPLOYED THROUGHout an enterprise. They are intended to make information available to all personnel in the enterprise who need it, regardless of where the people are located. They are based on the concept that personnel should have confidence that the information they have is as accurate and up-to-date as what others in the enterprise are receiving and, therefore, everyone is "on the same page." They also are intended to gather data using one piece of software to optimize the organization of that data and, therefore, make it easier to access and manage.

Enterprise-wide systems became widely used as business enterprises spread out around the globe and as management decisions were pushed down in organizations so that local managers had more autonomy to make decisions but still needed to be up-to-date on activities in the rest of the organization. Such systems take many forms, including enterprise resource planning (ERP) systems (described below), supply-chain management (SCM) systems (see chapter 7), and customer relationship management (CRM) systems (see chapter 9).

There are different ways of effectively creating enterprise-wide systems other than by purchasing a single large software package. Some companies link together disparate systems by using tools such as middleware and Extensible Markup Language (XML). The linked set of systems can be referred to as an enterprise-wide system. **Middleware** is a general term for any software or programming that links together or communicates between two separate and different programs. Middleware is often used to enable an ERP system to pass data back and forth between it and a legacy system. A **legacy system** is an old, usually outdated application that has not yet been replaced or upgraded. ERP systems are discussed in the following sections. The advent of ebusiness spurred the development of enterprise-wide systems because an enterprise can use an enterprise-wide system to integrate its data and systems so the supply chain can respond quickly to customer needs.

ERP SYSTEMS

ENTERPRISE RESOURCE PLANNING (ERP) SYSTEMS HAVE ALL THE CHARACTERISTICS of enterprise-wide systems. However, what sets them apart is that they are created as enterprise systems, and all the functionality needed in a typical large enterprise is built into the same set of software. They are specifically designed to enable personnel throughout an organization to view the same set of data rather than requiring it to be moved across applications. In this way, ERP systems overcome the traditional functional "silos" that have historically inhibited the free flow of information in enterprises. Figure 4.1 shows a traditional data structure where each functional area has its own data, tied into separate applications. Communications between the silos is often difficult. Figure 4.2 shows a centralized data structure where data are shared, reducing and perhaps eliminating the need for communications just to transfer data because everyone has access to the same data. Accordingly, ERP systems are large, have a comprehensive set of functionalities, and utilize centralized databases to hold the data of an organization so that all personnel are, in fact, reading the same data.

Many organizations saw the turn of the millennium as a strong incentive to implement ERP systems. The reason for this was the Y2K bug. **Y2K** is a term referring to the

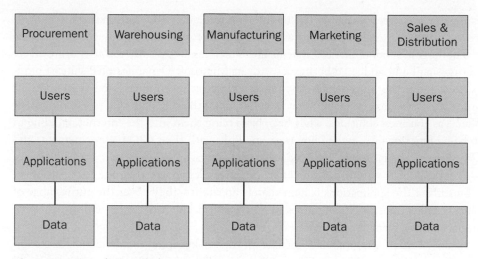

Figure 4.1 Traditional data structure

In this data structure, each functional area has its own data, tied into separate applications.

year 2000 and was a common abbreviation to categorize the computer glitches that were widely predicted to take place when the calendar turned to the year 2000. Organizations around the world were faced with a mixture of incompatible legacy systems that, in many cases, were not able to handle the change in dates from the 1900s to the 2000s. Faced with this looming deadline, many organizations tried to make the best out of the situation and replaced their outdated and often incompatible systems with new ERP systems. Since ERP implementations are massive undertakings that require a business to be analysed, a positive side effect was that organizations were often able to initiate business process reengineering (BPR) through best practices built into the software.

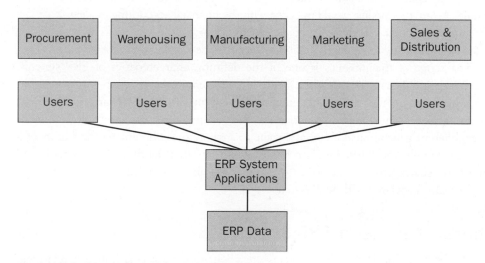

Figure 4.2 Centralized data structure

In this data structure, data are shared.

Business process reengineering (BPR) involves fundamentally rethinking and radically redesigning existing business processes to add value or prepare for new technologies.

The largest vendors of ERP systems are Oracle and SAP. Microsoft is aggressively targeting small and mid-sized businesses with its Microsoft Dynamics ERP suite of products. Because of the importance of systems integration in ebusiness and the important role that ERP systems can play in that integration, all these vendors are positioning their products as ebusiness solutions. They have been tying them into the internet, building in web-based functionality, and adding in strong links with their CRM, eprocurement, and SCM systems. The latter are discussed in later chapters.

A typical ERP system has numerous modules. When we examine such a system, the breadth of the applications is immediately apparent—they cover the entire range of business applications, including areas like financial accounting, sales and distribution, materials management, and human resources.

Financial accounting modules include all the bookkeeping requirements for a company. These modules collect all the transactions of the company and assemble them into financial statements and other reports regarding profitability and financial position. As with other modules, the financial accounting reports can usually be used on a "drill-down" basis, where the overall financial results can be presented in a report, and then theuser can access progressively more detailed reports according to division, geographical area, and even particular stores by clicking on selected numbers in the report. In this way, detailed information about the company can be made available throughout the organization.

Sales and distribution modules capture and record data about individual sales and then pass the necessary information to the shipping area of the company. The data on sales and shipments are then passed along to the financial accounting module for inclusion in the bookkeeping records and the financial reports.

Materials management modules are used to manage all the materials that go into the production of the final product. For example, if automobiles were being built, this module would keep track of the inventories of the individual components, such as engines, seats, fenders, and headlights. Detailed specifications and costs of these components would also be kept in this module. Again, this module would integrate with the financial accounting module.

Human resources modules, of course, include the payroll system as well as all the records the company must maintain about the personnel in the organization.

The scope of the modules is one of the defining characteristics of ERP systems. Another defining characteristic is the fact that the system works across an entire organization, whereas companies that do not employ ERP systems often have a variety of different systems in place, some based on functionality (i.e., financial reporting software), some to cover different geographical areas, and some to support the different business units of a company. Finally, the sheer size of an ERP system is another defining characteristic, and one of the characteristics that leads to many of the implementation and management issues usually associated with ERP systems.

Characteristics of ERP Systems

Client-Server Systems ERP systems are client-server systems built on relational database systems. A **client-server system** is a network configuration that evolved from networks built around central computers (servers) to provide computing power to the users on their own desktop computers (clients). A **relational database system** is a logical database model that relates data in different tables within the database by sharing a common data element (or field) between them. The common data element can serve as a reference point in the tables to other data elements in a data record.

relational database system: A logical database model that relates data in different tables within the database by sharing a common data element (or field) between them. The common data element can serve as a reference point in the tables to other data elements in a data record.

There are various forms of client-server systems, and the differences between them are primarily defined by strategic objectives. There are three basic elements to any information system: data, processing (applications), and output (display). The strategic forms of client-server systems are derived from the idea that these three system elements can be distributed between the client and the server in several ways. The processing element, for example, can be distributed to the clients, giving rise to a form of client-server system called a *distributed processing system*. Systems that simply have servers and clients are referred to as *two-tier client-server systems*. When the applications are distributed to servers dedicated to applications (i.e., when the processing is done), the system is referred to as a *three-tier client-server system*. If the data are distributed to the clients, the resulting system is known as a *distributed data client-server system*. Most ERP systems are configured as three-tier client-server systems, which means they have applications servers available in the organization. A system like this makes the applications more manageable, making it possible to place them closer to the user groups who are responsible for using them. This is illustrated in figure 4.3.

Recently, there has been a strong movement to extend the distributed client-server model to the internet through the use of web-enabled applications. For example, SAP has invested a great deal in a system called mySAP, which extends the capabilities of ERP to the internet. Its leading competitor, Oracle, also developed a new web-enabled version of its software, and then introduced an integrated package called Oracle E-Business Suite. Web-enablement is crucial to the effective use of ERP systems in ebusiness, since it makes the integration of the ERP systems with the internet much more effective and seamless.

The integration of the web and ERP products is having an impact on the basic architecture of ERP systems, to the point that some vendors are touting their products as having moved from a client-server system to a network-computing architecture. Oracle, for example, in announcing version 11*i* of Oracle Applications, made such a statement, arguing that a client-server model is too rigid. The company pointed out that, in a network-computing

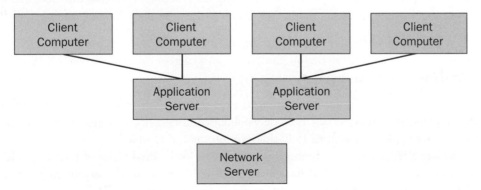

Figure 4.3 Three-tier client-server system

This graphic shows the basic structure of a three-tier client-server system, with the clients in the top row, the application servers in the middle row, and the network server in the bottom row.

model such as the internet, the architecture of the network is fluid, placing the data, processing, and output where it makes sense. In fact, the initial configuration of an ERP system can reflect this flexibility. It does become much more difficult, however, to change the system after the initial configuration. This is sometimes referred to as the "wet cement" theory: The system is quite malleable at first but tends to set firmly after implementation.

Relational Databases The fact that ERP systems are built on relational database systems is an important feature of ERP systems, since they provide the central vehicle for gathering and holding data for the enterprise. All ERP systems use a relational database for this purpose, with some providing more flexibility than others as to how the database can be organized. Relational database systems, through the use of separate files linked together by common fields, enable the storage of vast amounts of information that can be easily accessed by the user through the use of user-friendly interfaces or data-retrieval languages. A very common database used for ERP systems is Oracle, which underlies the Oracle Applications ERP system. Oracle also is one of the most common database systems used for SAP. Others are Microsoft's relational database system, SQL Server, and IBM's DB2.

Packaged Software *Packaged software*, commonly known as COTS (commercial off-the-shelf) software, is written by software development companies, bought off the shelf, installed, and then operated. ERP systems are a form of packaged software, which is very different from that developed in-house. While the program code for packaged software is not normally changed, the program itself does need to be customized as much as possible to the specific company adopting it. Such customization must be carried out by using the functionality contained within the software as provided. Because of the size and complexity of ERP systems, the customization process is in itself a large and complex project and usually leads to changes in business processes.

Business Process Reengineering (BPR) Business process reengineering is one of the characteristics of ERP systems in a broad sense because all ERP systems require so many changes in business processes that BPR is needed to fit the software into the business or, more correctly, to fit the business to the software. By definition, BPR means that the business processes being carried out by the organization must be substantially changed to accommodate the processes that are built into the software. These changes can involve changing the steps carried out during the processes, changing who does them, combining them, or replacing them. BPR is one of the most difficult components of ERP implementation projects.

Implementing ERP

Hershey Foods Corp.
www.hersheys.com

Several notable news stories have emerged over the years about spectacular failures of ERP implementation projects. One widely publicized story concerns Hershey Foods Corp. and a major implementation in 1999 that ran into serious trouble.[1]

In late 1999, Hershey announced that problems in the final phase of its ERP implementation project had resulted in delays in filling its orders to the extent that it was taking them more than twice as long to fill orders as previously. The announcement was made during their busiest season, when back-to-school and Halloween orders were flooding in. Retailers scrambled to find other suppliers, and Hershey lost out significantly, particularly with the lucrative Halloween trade. To make matters worse, there were reports that many of those customers stayed with the other suppliers they had found for the Christmas season as well.

The impact of all this on Hershey's financial statements was substantial. The company's reports showed that, in the third quarter of 1999, sales were down about US$60 million from the same period in 1998, and net income fell by US$20 million. For the fourth quarter, sales were down US$42 million and earnings were down US$11 million from the fourth quarter of 1998.

In a statement released with the third-quarter results, Hershey CEO Kenneth L. Wolfe said, "Our third-quarter sales and earnings declined primarily as a result of problems encountered since the July start-up of new business processes in the areas of customer service, warehousing, and order fulfillment. These problems resulted in lost sales and significantly increased freight and warehousing costs."

Hershey's implementation plan involved replacing about 80 percent of its legacy systems with a system that included SAP R/3 combined with other software from Manugistics and Siebel Systems. The implementation team was formed in early 1997, with a view to going live by the spring of 1999. It was a tight deadline, with little room for error. As with many ERP implementations at the time, they were driven to meet the Y2K deadline. They also had a strong interest in preparing themselves for the emerging twenty-first-century world of ebusiness.

As always with major projects, some things went wrong, and the pressure wrought because of the tight deadlines skyrocketed. The timetable slipped, and the last phase of the implementation, which included the critical functions of warehouse management, transportation management, and the order-to-cash process, was moved to the third quarter. This happened to be the company's heaviest shipping season. The company couldn't keep up, and orders couldn't be filled in time, customers were unhappy, and lower earnings followed.

Hershey, SAP, and the press had lots of reasons and excuses for this outcome. Lack of adequate training was frequently cited. Also, some pointed to a lack of distribution capacity, although it's hard to see how this factor could be attributed to the implementation process. One author put forward the view that Hershey's computer network just couldn't handle the new system, and that Hershey didn't check it out well in advance—a classic systems sizing issue. (**Systems sizing** is the process of ascertaining the volume and processing requirements that will be placed on a new information system, and thereby determining the size of system required, including hardware and software.) Hershey wouldn't have been the first company to run into this oversight. It's not unusual for an enterprise to implement a complicated system only to find its infrastructure can't handle it. This is especially true of an ERP system, which is huge, causes a heavy traffic flow, and requires a high capacity for data transmission and storage. With a big-budget implementation, it makes sense to do everything possible to eliminate risks, and one of the first places to look is to check the platform on which the system is intended to run.

There were no reports from Hershey as to whether it checked its network before starting the implementation project, so it's not known whether this was the problem or not. Some reporters thought it might have been, pointing out that with a full probe of the network, modelling it and profiling the applications that would run on it, Hershey could have checked the impact of the SAP R/3, Manugistics, and Siebel systems on its network. By doing this, it

systems sizing: The process of ascertaining the volume and processing requirements that will be placed on a new information system, and thereby determining the size of system required, including hardware and software.

could have seen the loads those applications were going to put on the network, and would have been able to identify problem areas. Put another way, thorough testing of the system, including stress testing, might have done the job. **Stress testing** is a process consisting of high-volume entry, processing, and output of test data designed to determine whether the system has the capacity to handle the volumes that will be required of it.

Another issue was training. Some informed people felt that this was the main problem—that Hershey underestimated the amount of training required and so the people running the system couldn't cope. Even with a modern high-tech system, the people running it are critical to the process. An enterprise must make sure the people have the skill sets needed to operate and support the new system, and that proper processes are in place for supporting the users (see the Ebusiness in Global Perspective box for an example).

Integrating ERP

ERP systems offer the most direct way of integrating an organization's systems. If, for example, all the modules of SAP are implemented, then all those modules, which likely represent the activities of the different functional areas (silos), will share the same data and therefore be able to "talk to" each other easily. The major challenge that arises is that the enterprise's business processes need to be modified to fit the processes built into the ERP system. The larger the system, the bigger this challenge is likely to be. On the positive side, the interface with users is standard across the modules, minimizing the training required for personnel who change their jobs within the company. (Table 4.1 on page 80 provides an outline of the steps in ERP implementation, as recommended by Oracle.)

Another way to integrate an ERP system is to implement a number of systems in an organization by choosing the best fit for particular functionality—a "best-of-breed" approach. This enhances the possibility of attaining a good fit between the business processes and the software, requiring less business process change. However, more time must be spent during implementation on the interfaces between the systems, and sometimes these interfaces don't work as well as the users would like. The Estrategy box outlines a best-of-breed approach that Dell Inc. used. The essential point is that good integration is essential for ebusiness purposes.

Ebusiness in Global Perspective

HP's Global SAP Rollout

In 2002, HP launched a US$110 million ERP consolidation project and SAP rollout that it called GSO, named after the company's Global Supply Operations unit. The project was originally due to be completed within three years. By 2007, however, it was still not finished, although Peter Ginouves, director of finance at the GSO unit and a leader of the project, hinted that it should be done during that year. He added that "having three years to do something of this magnitude is extremely aggressive. Three years just zips by doing something of this scale." He maintained, however, that he still expected the project cost to remain within the US$110 million budget.

During 2003, HP suffered bad publicity after a poorly executed migration to SAP AG's ERP software in its server

>

division. Its GSO project therefore followed hard on the heels of a major problem in the ERP implementation area.

The difficulties with the GSO project were blamed primarily on a lack of adequate internal processes. The GSO unit provides spare parts and repair services across the company and has annual revenue of US$2 billion. HP officials acknowledged that the aggressive schedule from the beginning didn't allow for adequate mapping of business processes or the implementation of change management capabilities.

Joshua Greenbaum, an analyst at Enterprise Applications Consulting in Berkeley, California, said, "The obvious object lesson is that the complexity of these projects requires even tech-savvy companies like HP to stop, slow down and make sure they are getting all the little details right." He added, "Redemption is possible if you catch the mistakes before you're too far down the road."

The goal of the GSO initiative is to consolidate 250 systems—some of them 20 years old and custom-written for HP, Compaq, Digital, and Tandem systems—around a core ERP backbone based on SAP Enterprise 4.7. The existing systems also include varying instances of SAP, as well as an "alphabet soup of just about everything," Ginouves said.

Because of its difficulties with the previous project, the implementation team needed to establish immediate credibility. The 350-member team therefore scrambled to do a rapid deployment in 2002, installing applications such as SAP's materials management module but linking them to HP's legacy systems. In its haste, the team neglected to focus enough on business process management and failed to craft full end-to-end workflows, according to Ginouves.

By March 2004, it was clear that the project would take five years instead of three, and that it would likely only at best break even instead of achieving the expected 35 percent return on investment. HP developed a revised plan on the basis of achieving high double-digit returns on the remaining investment of US$40 million–US$45 million.

"Any large changes within organizations are challenging without a good change management program," said Dan Duryea, a supply-chain architect at the GSO.

Accordingly, the GSO decided to take a new approach that involved driving collaboration among business users and IT staffers to get a more thorough mapping of its business processes.

To achieve this objective, it adopted the NetProcess tool from IntelliCorp Inc. to map complete business processes, such as procuring a part and delivering it to a customer. The resulting process models can be summarized and shared with executives or segmented into task-level detail for use by HP's programmers.

Prior to adopting NetProcess, the project team had been using PowerPoint, Word, and Visio documentation tools, which didn't enable adequate communication among the employees implementing the system and, in any event, weren't designed specifically for business process documentation.

HP
www.hp.com

Questions

1. Why would business process documentation be so important to the success of the HP project?

2. What other approaches could have been taken to the basic issues that HP was trying to resolve in this project?

Source: M. Songini, "HP Struggles with Second SAP Project," *Computerworld*, March 14, 2005, www.computerworld.com/softwaretopics/erp/story/0,10801,100366,00.html, accessed April 2, 2007.

Estrategy

Best of Breed at Dell

When Dell Inc. decided to implement enterprise-wide systems, it chose the ERP software of Glovia International for inventory control, warehouse management, and materials management as part of its strategy. Dell also chose i2 Technologies' supply-chain management system and Oracle's order management system to implement what is known as a best-of-breed strategy. The concept of a best-of-breed strategy is to choose specific functionality

>

from a variety of software packages instead of relying on one all-encompassing product. Then the packages need to be knit together by using middleware and other linkages.

The company had tried to implement SAP's R/3 ERP system in 1994 for manufacturing applications, but had felt it to be "too monolithic" to be able to keep up with Dell's changing business needs. After trying to implement the system over the following two years, it finally cut back the effort in 1996, using SAP only for human resources. Dell had tried to customize the product to match its business model, but found SAP couldn't keep up with the very rapid changes in this area.

Dell management pointed out that the Glovia software was scalable on Dell hardware, but also flexible enough to integrate with the other software they had chosen to run. In addition, they felt Glovia had the capability to break into smaller pieces for implementation.

This was before SAP modularized its software to offer the same capability.

Dell undertook a global implementation of Glovia in 2000, with approximately 3000 Dell employees in the United States, Ireland, and Malaysia slated to use the software.

Dell Inc.
www.dell.com

Questions

1. Based on what you know of Dell, evaluate the company's best-of-breed strategy against a single-vendor strategy.

2. What are the risks of a best-of-breed strategy?

3. Which strategy—best-of-breed or single-vendor—is likely to remain valid for the long term?

Source: Informationweek.com, May 11, 1998.

Table 4.1 Steps in ERP Implementation

These steps are recommended by Oracle in its methodology for implementation of an ERP system.

Phase 1: Definition
1. Set up and organize the project team.
2. Conduct project team orientation.
3. Plan the implementation project.
4. Identify and document the overall business and system requirements.
5. Define the future business model of the organization.
6. Describe the application and information technology architectures.
7. Develop a training plan for team members.

Phase 2: Operations Analysis
8. Collect the business process information and requirements.
9. Fit the required business processes to the standard built-in ERP processes.
10. Develop the business requirements scenarios and the gap analysis.
11. Refine the applications and technology architectures.
12. Prototype business processes.
13. Begin consideration of the feasibility of the business process design.

Phase 3: Solution Design
14. Develop detailed documentation of business procedures.
15. Consider and set specific application configuration options for customization.

>

16. Design any custom extensions, interfaces, and data conversions.

17. Determine process and organizational changes required to enable implementation.

Phase 4: Build

18. Code and test the customization carried out, including all enhancements, conversions, and interfaces (development team).

19. Create and execute performance, integration, and business system tests.

Phase 5: Transition

20. Conduct data conversion.

21. Conduct final training for the users and support staff.

22. Conduct a production readiness check.

Phase 6: Production

23. Cutover to production.

24. Fine-tune the system to make sure it is actually running as it was intended.

25. Begin the process of regular maintenance.

26. Turn over the system to the continuing management of the organization.

27. Begin ongoing support by the continuing IS personnel.

Source: "Using Oracle Applications" (Boss Corporation, Indianapolis, 2000). Reprinted with permission of NetLedger Inc. All rights reserved.

Oracle recommends these steps in its methodology for implementation of an ERP system.

Middleware

As mentioned earlier in this chapter, the term *middleware* describes any software that is used to link applications together. Middleware differs from software that imports and exports information between applications in that middleware involves the creation of a direct linkage through which data can flow uninterrupted. For example, accounting applications such as Simply Accounting by Sage Software have functions in their menus that specifically allow data and reports to be imported from and exported to spreadsheets for further analysis. Such software is *not* middleware because it requires the import and export functions to be executed. The use of middleware between applications like accounting software and spreadsheets is seamless (i.e., it is not seen by the user). The data moves as though it were still in the same application.

Middleware is used in enterprise systems because it is important that data move freely and easily across the enterprise. While the large systems such as ERP and CRM systems are sophisticated enough to minimize the use of middleware, they do not eliminate that need. The process of using middleware to knit applications together across an enterprise is known as **enterprise application integration (EAI)**. EAI involves planning, implementing, and managing the ability of applications in an enterprise to share information efficiently, often including legacy systems and ERP systems.

Sage
www.sage.com

enterprise application integration (EAI): The process of planning, implementing, and managing the ability of applications in an enterprise to share information efficiently, often including legacy systems and ERP systems.

One example of middleware is Microsoft Message Queue Server (MSMQ). This software is designed to enable application programs to communicate with other application programs through a built-in messaging system that asynchronously sends and receives messages. Database systems, such as Sybase, DB2, and Oracle, are also used as middleware by providing a direct linkage to specific data and a repository of data that is in transit. Data often reside on networks, mid-range, and mainframe systems, and database systems can provide direct, read/write access to integrate that data into an application. Such linkages are used in ebusiness to build data warehouses, automate sales forces, and integrate internet-based applications.

Extensible Markup Language (XML)

In chapter 1, Extensible Markup Language (XML) was defined as a very powerful tool that is similar to and compatible with HTML but does not rely on single pre-set tags to identify information. Instead, XML provides a mechanism for any document builder to define new XML tags within any XML document. This means that in addition to being a markup language, XML is a meta-language that can define new tags. Data can be tagged within a system using XML and then found quickly by an XML-enabled browser.

With XML, the tags always accompany the data and, since the tags identify the data, an application reading the data can tell what the data represent. For example, an XML document might be a report that shows the total sales of a company. The XML tag will be sent to another application and that application will read the tag, recognize the data as sales for a particular period, and process the data accordingly. Of course, in order to do this, the application needs to be "XML enabled," which means it must contain the software code that enables it to read and interpret the tags.

This ability of XML to send tags along with the data has led to the use of XML for the integration of systems across the internet and internally, and between the CRM and ERP systems, the accounting systems, and any other components of the supply chain. The internet application sends an XML request (tag) back to the source data within the applications, which then sends that specific data back to the internet application. The whole process should be very fast and seamless.

XML is not just a single technology, but rather has been referred to as a family of technologies. It is built on specifications that represent agreements within the information systems (IS) community. The core specification is XML 1.0, which defines what "tags" and "attributes" are, but there are several other parts of XML. For example, XLink describes a standard way to add hyperlinks to an XML file, and XPointer and XFragments are syntaxes for pointing to parts of an XML document. The details of XML are quite complex, but such detail is not needed to gain an understanding of the applicability of XML for ebusiness.

COLLABORATIVE AND INTER-ENTERPRISE SYSTEMS

Collaborative systems and inter-enterprise systems are becoming increasingly common as electronic business becomes more sophisticated and companies become more interlinked. **Collaborative systems** are information systems that interact between enterprises to enable them to work together on common business initiatives and ventures. Inter-enterprise systems arise because of the growth in collaborative ebusiness between enterprises and their customers, suppliers, personnel, and competitors.

collaborative systems:
Information systems that interact between enterprises to enable them to work together on common business initiatives and ventures.

Collaboration with Customers

An early form of collaboration with customers arose out of the customization of products and the involvement of customers in the customization process. Levi Strauss & Co. was an early innovator in this area. Through its website, Levi Strauss offered customers the option to create their own jeans by inputting their own measurements and then ordering them over the web. By having the ability to create a pair of jeans that fit their measurements in the way they wanted, customers were essentially collaborating in the design of those jeans. The collaborative system in this case was the internet. There had to be a way for the input measurements to reach the sales order system within the company, and that would also be part of the collaborative system. This, of course, would require integration of these two parts of the system.

Levi Strauss
www.levi.com

Another example is Cisco Systems, one of the world's leading suppliers of technical network equipment, such as routers, hubs, and switches. Cisco has initiated several applications that use the web as a vehicle for collaboration with customers. For example, customers can sign into a website with interactive chat rooms and whiteboard tools that allow customers to interact with Cisco representatives to discuss technical problems. The whiteboard tools are used to exchange drawings to explore possible solutions to issues. This initiative was successful and was later expanded to include the capability for customers to simultaneously interact with company representatives using the telephone and the web. The truly collaborative element comes in when customers click on a "help" button to request an immediate telephone call from a Cisco representative and establish a link between their respective web browsers. As the customer and the representative speak on the telephone, they can navigate the web together using their linked browsers, sharing electronic documents and completing shared forms on the website. This linked browser system is a good example of a collaborative system based on the use of the internet.

Cisco Systems
www.cisco.com

Collaboration with Suppliers

Several automobile manufacturers are involved in collaboration with their suppliers, to the point that some are saying that the car manufacturers could eventually be out of the car manufacturing business, acting instead as coordinators of the activities carried out by their suppliers. Ford Motor Company is a good example of a company that uses collaborative techniques for product design. Before the advent of collaborative systems, Ford would send drawings of a new product to a supplier, who in turn would add in its components and send the drawings back to Ford, who would then pass the drawings along to other suppliers involved in that particular product. Through a process of revision and circulation among suppliers, the ultimate product would evolve. Naturally, this process took a considerable amount of time, even though the drawings were transmitted electronically, because it was a linear process, with each participant revising the drawings in succession.

Ford Motor Company
www.ford.com

To improve on this process, Ford adopted a system it called "digital mockup," which operates on a website and enables all of the suppliers to work on the design at the same time. This meant the process changed from a sequential one to an interactive, fully collaborative activity. As with the other examples, the internet is the prime enabler for this collaborative system. Ford has had success with this type of system, and uses a very similar system for its "World Car" design, under which collaborators from around the world work together on the system to design new cars. Collaborative systems of this type are spreading not only throughout the automobile industry, but also in other industries as well.

More recently, we have seen an upsurge in the movement of automobile manufacturing out of North America to Asian countries, such as China, Korea, and Japan, through the process of outsourcing. While outsourcing arises out of economic origins not necessarily related to ebusiness, nevertheless the existence of technology for collaborative purposes is crucial in implementing and managing outsourced business processes.

Collaboration with Personnel

For several years, Lotus Notes has been used in businesses for purposes of collaborative work on projects. The advantage of Lotus Notes is that it is designed for collaboration by enabling personnel on a project to file their papers in a central location and have them fully accessible by other team members, regardless of their location. It was ideal for consulting assignments for large companies, because consultants in Toronto, Halifax, and Vancouver, for example, could work using Lotus Notes, which would maintain their files on a central server, say in Toronto, and enable all of the consultants to view, review, comment on, and even change that documentation. In this way, the working paper files for the entire consulting job could be assembled in a central location on a coordinated basis and thus eliminate duplication and minimize inconsistencies as the job proceeds, rather than just at the review stage. This system can be used between companies as well as within companies.

Collaboration with Competitors

Trading exchanges—such as Covisint, discussed in chapter 1—provide an excellent example of collaboration with competitors. More than 2000 trading exchanges were formed during the dot-com boom, in virtually all industries. One of the objectives of this approach was to go public with the exchange company, thereby raising capital for the trading exchange on the stock market. Since the initial bubble in the stock market with dot-coms, however, this aspect of trading exchanges has largely ended. In addition, many trading exchanges have gone out of business. Even Covisint had to change its business model and ownership to survive. However, numerous trading exchanges still exist, and provide a good example of collaborative commerce.

Managing Inter-Enterprise Systems

Most of the collaborative systems described in the preceding sections are at least partially based on the internet. Indeed, the internet has been the prime enabler for virtually all such collaboration in recent years. As collaboration increases in intensity and scope, and as it becomes more complex, the systems will also grow and become more difficult to manage. The management of the systems is being approached in different ways—by outsourcing, by placing the systems management in the hands of a separate entity (such as an exchange), by establishing a management agreement with one or more of the participants in the collaboration, and by having each of the participants manage the part of the system that simply falls within its own system. The management approach depends in part on who the owner of the system is and who is designated as the system manager, which are matters that can be covered in any agreement entered into to govern the collaboration.

When a collaborative system is adopted, specific processes need to be changed, as some will be reallocated between the partners or taken on by a separate entity. As a result, job descriptions change and the need for personnel changes, because of the efficiencies achieved, which often involves staff reductions and cutbacks.

Canadian Snapshots

Big Changes at Sobeys

During 2000, Sobeys Inc., one of Canada's largest food retailers, was immersed in an implementation of the SAP ERP system. In December of that year, the company experienced a five-day database crash that left them scrambling to fill the shelves in their stores just before the busy Christmas season.

Shortly before that, on November 25, the company had announced the appointment of a new president and CEO, Bill McEwan, who moved in from the position of president and CEO of the Atlantic Region of the Great Atlantic and Pacific Tea Company, Inc. (A&P). Prior to joining A&P he was vice president, Market Development, Coca-Cola Beverages Ltd.

On January 24, 2001, Sobeys announced it was abandoning SAP's distribution system but planned to retain SAP's payroll and financial systems. "We do have a meeting set up with [SAP]," said Stewart Mahoney, vice president of Treasury and Investor Relations for Empire Company Limited, parent company of Sobeys. Empire holds 65 percent of Sobeys. "We will be having thorough discussions on the phase-out . . . of that (distribution) system." He said that the decision was precipitated by the crash of the database system in November. He also announced that a new information officer would be joining the company shortly.

After these events, the company announced that it would record an after-tax special charge of $49,900,000, or 82 cents per share ($89,100,000, or $1.47 per share pre-tax), due to its decision to abandon the SAP distribution system. The next day, Sobeys stock dropped by 16 percent.

SAP, of course, announced its disappointment, referring to the recent shuffling in the Sobeys management structure as possibly being behind any technological trouble. "When companies change executive management, this sometimes results in changes in a company's information technology strategy," SAP's news release stated. SAP said it had a strong team at the company and that it had worked on the problems with the IBM database, which had been identified as a central issue.

McEwan said the SAP software couldn't deal with Sobeys' large transaction volume and that the company had plans for a new system that would provide "better functionality in half the time." He added: "We have come to the conclusion that what appeared to be growing pains with the implementation of these enterprise-wide systems are in fact systemic problems of a more serious nature. We have determined that there is insufficient core functionality in the SAP software component of our enterprise-wide systems to effectively deal with the extremely high number of transactions in our retail operating environment."

Industry analysts said that retail companies represent some of the most difficult businesses for the implementation of enterprise-wide solutions, given the large numbers of transactions and the wide range of products. It requires careful training of the staff, which some reports stated might have been lacking at Sobeys, although Sobeys disagreed.

After Sobeys announced its decision to discontinue further development and implementation of the SAP enterprise-wide software and systems initiative, SAP had to be phased out of operation in Sobeys Atlantic Division and 30 corporate Sobeys stores in Ontario. The operations of Sobeys Quebec, Sobeys West, Serca Food Service, and the remaining 379 stores in Ontario had not been converted to SAP.

Sobeys
www.sobeys.com

Questions

1. What was the most likely cause of the difficulties with the ERP implementation at Sobeys?

2. What does this situation indicate about the importance of an ERP implementation to a supply-chain business, particularly a business that relies on internet sales (which of course Sobeys does not)?

Source: I. Smith, *History of Nova Scotia*, chap. 76, www.littletechshoppe .com/ns1625/nshist76.html, accessed November 11, 2004.

Lawson Enters the ERP Hosting Market

Lawson is a mid-market applications vendor that has had a long-standing relationship with IBM. In early 2007, Lawson announced plans to enter the hosting market and use more of IBM's middleware.

The idea was to build on Lawson's existing Total Care maintenance and support program by offering a new ERP hosting service. Lawson Total Care Platinum would cover software delivery, hosting, support, and application management services. Lawson said the offering would be available on a monthly subscription basis, with customers having to commit to at least a year's service.

Customers had been asking Lawson to provide hosting for its ERP applications for some time, but it lacked the necessary resources to offer the service on its own. Lawson had previously encouraged users to go with third parties, but customers made it clear they would prefer to deal with a single organization. So Lawson looked for a hosting provider with global reach and service capabilities.

In planning its new service, Lawson considered several hosting providers and then chose IBM because of its obvious global capabilities. In addition, it negotiated attractive pricing. Customers signed a hosting deal with Lawson that committed to 99.7 percent system uptime. Subsequently, Lawson announced that IBM's WebSphere would be the core middleware for all future versions of its applications. After that deal, Lawson realized there were other pieces of IBM software it should have bundled into its stack and went back and negotiated with IBM to add the WebSphere Enterprise Service Bus.

Still later, Lawson announced that IBM would resell Lawson's S3 and M3 applications in North America, targeting small to mid-size businesses. IBM also pledged to help develop the software for users in the financial services, fashion, and food and beverage industries. It was reported that some Lawson operations in Europe began negotiating with IBM about their own reselling arrangements, using the North American agreement as a framework.

IBM had previously resold Lawson software outside North America, notably the M3 applications, but without the benefit of a formal arrangement.

Lawson
www.lawson.com

Questions

1. What are the pros and cons to Lawson's customers of using hosted ERP systems as opposed to their own?

2. Why is it likely the customers have been clamouring for hosted services?

3. What are the implications to Lawson of IBM reselling Lawson software?

Source: C. Martens, "Lawson Enters Hosting Market with Best Buddy IBM," *Computerworld*, March 6, 2007, www.computerworld.com.au/index .php/id;127203155, accessed April 3, 2007.

CHAPTER SUMMARY

Enterprise-wide systems are information systems that are deployed throughout an enterprise to draw together data and make that data available to anyone who needs it. Such systems may be single systems such as enterprise resource planning (ERP) or customer relationship management (CRM) systems, but also can be smaller systems linked together using middleware, Extensible Markup Language (XML), or other tools. Ebusiness spurred the development of enterprise-wide systems, since they are necessary to enable an enterprise to fully integrate its supply chain to respond quickly to customer needs.

ERP systems have all the characteristics of enterprise-wide systems. They have different modules, like financial accounting and sales and distribution, that cover the full range of a business's activities. Implementing ERP systems is a major activity, involving considerable risk. Implementations usually require considerable process change and reengineering. With the large systems in particular, the business processes must be changed to fit the software rather than changing the software to fit the existing processes. ERP systems that are implemented across an organization offer the most direct way of integrating systems.

Middleware is used in enterprise systems because it is important that data move freely and easily across the enterprise. While the large systems like ERP and CRM systems are sophisticated enough to minimize the use of middleware, they do not eliminate that need. The process of using middleware to knit applications together across an enterprise is known as enterprise application integration (EAI).

XML is used for the integration of systems from the internet back into the basic information systems of the company, the CRM and ERP systems, the accounting systems, and any other components of the supply chain. The internet application sends an XML request back to the source data within the applications, which then sends that specific data back to the internet application.

Different types of collaborative systems exist within companies and between companies that work together. The most common collaborative systems are based on the internet. A good example is a trading exchange's system that is linked to the systems of the participants through the internet. In such a case, the collaborative system consists of the exchange system, the internet linkages, and those parts of the participants' systems that are linked to the rest of the system.

Key Terms

business process reengineering (BPR) (p. 74)

client-server system (p. 74)

collaborative systems (p. 82)

enterprise application integration (EAI) (p. 81)

enterprise-wide system (p. 72)

legacy system (p. 72)

middleware (p. 72)

relational database system (p. 75)

stress testing (p. 78)

systems sizing (p. 77)

Y2K (p. 72)

| MyEbusinessLab | Tools for Online Learning |

To help you master the material in this chapter and stay up to date with new developments in ebusiness, visit the MyEBusinessLab at www.pearsoned.ca/myebusinesslab. Resources include the following:

- Pre- and Post-Test Questions
- Additional Chapter Questions
- Author Blog
- Recommended Readings
- Commentaries on Current Trends
- Additional Topics in Ebusiness
- Internet Exercises
- Glossary Flashcards

Endnote

1. The Hershey Foods story is reproduced with permission from G. Trites, *Enterprise Resource Planning— The Engine of e-Business* (Toronto: Canadian Institute of Chartered Accountants, 2000).

Chapter 5
Security and Controls

Learning Objectives

When you complete this chapter you should be able to:

1   Identify the security risks of internet-based business.

2   Describe generally how ebusiness is made secure.

3   Identify the major components of security systems for ebusiness.

4   Identify and evaluate the major security strategies.

5   Explain the major issues in implementing good security.

6   Describe the significant types of security tools available.

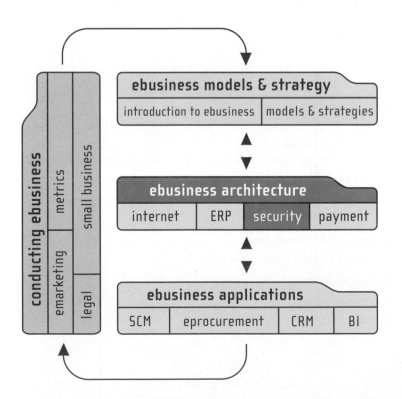

INTRODUCTION

EVERY INFORMATION SYSTEM IS SUBJECT TO THE RISKS OF ERROR, FRAUD, MALICIOUS acts, and disasters. **Risk** is the probability of an event occurring and leading to undesirable consequences, such as lost revenues, excessive costs, misappropriation or destruction of assets, unreliable information, erroneous decisions, unauthorized disclosure of confidential or private information, competitive disadvantage, disruption of business activity, or legal or statutory sanctions. An **error** is an unintentional act or omission that leads to undesirable consequences. Errors include accidents, improper use of system features, lapses in system maintenance, and flaws in system design, development, or implementation. According to the National Computer Security Association, over half of the security risks that companies face are attributable to carelessness, errors, or omissions rather than to malicious acts. **Fraud** is an intentional act that relies on deception to misappropriate assets or obtain other benefits. **Malicious acts** intentionally lead to the destruction of facilities, hardware, software, or data, or unauthorized disclosure of confidential or private information. Malicious acts include hacker attacks, viruses, sabotage, vandalism, and terrorism. **Disasters** are acts of nature such as floods, storms, tornados, earthquakes, fires, power failures, or other events that can lead to destruction of assets and disruption of business activities. Every company faces these risks to some extent and needs to assess the degree of risk that can be tolerated and design appropriate countermeasures if the risks it faces are greater than its tolerable level.

risk: The probability of an event occurring and leading to undesirable consequences.

error: An unintentional act or omission that leads to undesirable consequences.

fraud: An intentional act that relies on deception to misappropriate assets or obtain other benefits.

malicious act: An intentional act that leads to the destruction of facilities, hardware, software, or data or unauthorized disclosure of confidential or private information.

disaster: An act of nature such as a flood, storm, tornado, earthquake, fire, power failure, or other event that can lead to destruction of assets and disruption of business activities.

WHAT ARE THE KEY RISKS FACED BY EBUSINESSES?

EBUSINESS RISKS ARISE FROM THREATS THAT ARE EITHER NOT PREVENTED FROM occurring or are not promptly detected and corrected when they occur. Risks of errors or omissions are created or magnified in ebusiness because it constantly creates new services, business models, processes, technologies, and fulfillment processes, and because it commonly entails outsourcing.

New Services   Internal risks associated with new services include lack of standards, regulations and rules, and support systems. External risks associated with new services are natural hazards, legal issues, and environmental issues.

New Business Models   The internet has facilitated the introduction of new business models that face unique risks not encountered by traditional offline business models. These include revenue leakage, poor image, and inability to foster trust and confidence on the part of business partners.

New Processes   Ebusiness enables businesses to integrate with their customers and suppliers in a manner that was not possible before (e.g., real-time information processing associated with just-in-time manufacturing). Such arrangements are often accompanied by strict product specifications and product deliveries, with penalties for non-compliance written into their contracts. If the company develops a reputation for failing to meet such contractual obligations, then this can also impair its ability to obtain additional business.

New Technology   Ebusinesses use leading-edge technologies that may have issues associated with scalability, security, availability and processing integrity. In addition, such

Estrategy

Combating Online Fraud

When British Columbia Securities Commission (BCSC) staff looked at the Genius Funds website, they became immediately suspicious. The site was offering extravagant returns that were impossible to achieve with real investment strategies. BCSC had been contacted by a bank after two clients attempted to wire money to an account in Australia so they could invest in the funds.

One fund offered 1.9 percent per day, and another one offered 9 percent per week. Since the promulgation of online scams such as phishing, social engineering, and other scams for parting bank customers from their money, banks have become cautious when customers come to them with unusual requests to transfer funds. In this case, the bank became suspicious of the Genius Funds offerings (called high-yield investment programs [HYIPs]) and attempted to dissuade one customer from following through with the wire transfer. However, another customer insisted on sending $25,000 to the account in Australia. That was when the bank contacted the BCSC.

HYIPs can be very appealing to unsuspecting investors. They offer high returns from enacting complex trading strategies on the investor's behalf. Often they are supported by specialized chat rooms where scammers give advice about the schemes with the best payouts. Some schemes do in fact pay for a short period of time, but often these payments are merely Ponzi schemes designed to draw in more and larger investments.

The Genius Fund website was sophisticated. It was translated into seven languages and had promotional YouTube videos and a Facebook site. It claimed to be operating out of Cyprus, with accounts in Australia and elsewhere.

Regulators such as BCSC have limited tools to combat online scams such as this one. They can issue a warning notice to the public, but the public may not see it. They can also issue a cease trade order for the security, but they may not be able to find the identity of the perpetrators or, if the website is in another jurisdiction, they may not have the authority to issue such an order. BCSC took these actions but feared that they would not be sufficient to protect unsuspecting investors.

BCSC decided to use the web to combat this fraud. Patricia Bowles, BCSC's director of communications, used her online blog to start posting articles questioning the claims made on the Genius Funds website. She also used Twitter to post messages, asking people to spread the word. In addition, the Cyprus Securities Commission issued a warning that the fund was not licensed to operate in Cyprus, contradicting the information posted on the Genius Funds website.

Initially, when "Genius Funds" was typed into a search engine, a series of links to articles with glowing reviews would appear. However, after Bowles's campaign caught on, each time "Genius Funds" was typed into a search engine, a series of links to negative articles appeared, warning potential investors about the scam. Thanks to a two-month campaign in February and March 2010, Genius was effectively exposed and shut down.

British Columbia Securities Commission (BCSC)
www.bcsc.bc.ca

Questions

1. Whose is responsible for stopping online fraud, such as websites with false information or phishing?
2. Was there anything else that the BCSC could have or should have done in this case?
3. Are there any risks associated with BCSC's approach?

Sources: Janet McFarland, "B.C. Regulator Uses Web to Fight Online Fraud," *Globe and Mail*, June 12, 2010, B1–B2; www.bcsc.bc.ca/release.aspx?id=9678; www.bcsc.bc.ca/release.aspx?id=9852.

systems may not be able to integrate with existing systems. Also, the extensive use of the internet in ebusiness poses particular issues related to security, confidentiality, and privacy.

New Fulfillment Processes   The online fulfillment process has brought expectations of "instant" deliveries resulting in real-time procurement requirements. Such expectations give businesses less room for error within their supply chains.

Outsourcing IT Activities   It is common for ebusiness entities to outsource various aspects of their IT activities to outside service providers, ranging from website hosting to fulfillment to the entire IT infrastructure. In many cases, outsourcing of parts of ebusiness systems splits the responsibilities for controls, with the attendant risks of non-performance and insufficient monitoring by the outsourcing service provider. If not properly defined and monitored, such outsourcing arrangements can lead to a loss of control over the entity's ebusiness activities.

In addition to the business risks caused by ebusiness innovations, entities face the risks of abuses attributable to malicious attacks perpetrated by employees and parties external to the entity, such as fraudsters, hackers, and vandals.[1] The following are the most common abuses involving malicious acts that have been reported by various surveys (in order of frequency of occurrence):

- infection by malicious pieces of code (e.g., virus, Trojan, worm)
- installation or use of unauthorized software (e.g., adware, spyware, personal apps)
- use of official computers for illegal or illicit activities (e.g., pornography, email harassment)
- installation of unauthorized hardware
- use of official computers for personal profit (e.g., gambling, spam, managing personal ecommerce websites, online investing)
- physical theft, sabotage, or intentional destruction of equipment, especially laptop theft
- denial of service attacks (i.e., deliberate attacks to disable an entity's communications systems, preventing it from providing services)
- website or web server attacks
- abuse of passwords that are not secure
- electronic theft, sabotage, or intentional destruction or disclosure of proprietary data or information
- financial fraud

As mentioned previously, more than half of the damage suffered by entities experiencing security breaches is attributable to carelessness, errors, or omissions. Thus, an entity's security program must address its users' security awareness, procedural guidance and training, compliance incentives, and compliance monitoring. However, although it is important not to overlook the threats posed by acts of nature and human errors and omissions, it is equally important not to underestimate the risks that intentional malicious acts pose to ebusinesses. It is also noteworthy that annual Computer Security Institute/Federal Bureau of Investigation surveys indicate that a major source of such threats are individuals inside the corporation or organization, such as disgruntled employees, followed by external hackers.[2] In 2010, hackers used a Trojan program called Zeus to collect customers' personal login information for several thousand U.K. bank accounts and steal millions of dollars over a period of several months before being caught. Foreign corporations and foreign governments are consistently reported threat sources, albeit at a much lower frequency. In 2010, Google accused the Chinese government of sponsoring hacker attacks against its systems to gain access to the identities of dissidents.

Studies of the impact of hacker attacks and system outages on stock prices of ebusiness entities indicate that security breaches involving access to confidential data and website outages are associated with significant stock price declines.[3-5] These findings indicate that stakeholders are sensitive to ebusiness risks and reinforce the importance of measures to address threats that might result in risks. A **threat** is a condition or force that increases the risk of error, fraud, malicious acts, or disaster. It is important to recognize that there is always a risk that one or more events could happen and lead to undesirable consequences. Not all risks can be prevented. For example, nobody can prevent an earthquake from happening; the only thing that can be done is to take steps to ensure that the consequential losses will be minimized. For example, **viruses**—computer programs that are inserted into computer systems on an unauthorized basis, unknown to the system owner or user, and with an intent to take some action on that computer that can be mischievous or malicious—will continue to be developed, and even with virus protection software installed it is likely that at some time a virus will succeed in penetrating the protective barrier provided by the anti-virus software. By having backups of its software and data, a company can minimize the consequences of a virus attack.

threat: A condition or force that increases the risk of error, fraud, malicious acts, or disaster.

virus: A computer program that is inserted into computer systems on an unauthorized basis, unknown to the system owner or user, and with the intent to take some action on that computer that can be mischievous or malicious.

CONTROLS

THE ENTRY OF A COMPANY INTO EBUSINESS RAISES SOME UNIQUE CHALLENGES, and business has adopted various security strategies to deal with them (see the New Business Models box). These challenges centre heavily around the use of the internet as a vehicle of communication with customers and business partners, as well as an integral part of the IT platform.

Preventive, detective, and corrective measures to reduce the risk of error, fraud, malicious acts, or disaster to an acceptable level are known as **controls**. There are two broad categories of controls—general and applications controls. Within each of these broad categories there are several types of controls. Following is an overview of controls generally, then an examination of those controls that are particularly important to ebusiness.

All controls are guided by strategy, policy, and implementation procedures. Indeed, strategy and policy are essential parts of a security system, as they involve institutionalizing the degree of risk that is acceptable and the knowledge and culture among personnel that is necessary to implement security procedures and make them effective.

control: A preventive, detective, or corrective measure that is designed to reduce the risk of error, fraud, malicious acts, or disaster to an acceptable level.

General Controls

General controls are controls that are not unique to a particular application or applications. There are several categories of general controls:

general control: A control that is not unique to a particular application or applications.

- security management
- physical and logical access controls
- system acquisition or development controls
- system maintenance and change controls
- operations controls
- business continuity controls

Security Management The policies and procedures that management adopts and implements to guide the security program of an enterprise fall under the security management category. These policies are approved by top management, often as a result of a strategic security plan, and are then monitored by a security committee. Security personnel, such as security officers to manage the access controls, are appointed, and policy manuals are distributed to appropriate personnel to ensure that everyone is aware of the policies and procedures.

Physical and Logical Access Controls There are two kinds of access to a computer system—physical access and logical access. **Physical access controls** are measures that an enterprise takes to safeguard the physical safety of a resource by restricting access to it. These controls include many security features like fences, surveillance equipment, alarms, and security guards. They also include locks on computer consoles, server rooms, and gates. Any measures designed to protect the physical security of the system fall under this category.

physical access control: A measure to secure the physical safety of a resource by restricting access to it.

Logical access controls are controls that are included in software to permit access by authorized personnel in accordance with the privileges granted to them, and to prevent access by unauthorized personnel. They involve the use of user IDs, passwords, biometrics, and the granting of permissions and rights by the security software. **Biometrics** are access controls that rely on physical characteristics such as signatures, fingerprints, palmprints, voice recognition, and retina scans to authenticate the identity of a user before permitting access. An access control technique used on the web to prevent unauthorized software from masquerading as a person involves presenting a set of distorted squiggly letters and numbers that people can decipher but computers still cannot. This technique is called **CAPTCHA**, which stands for "completely automated public Turing test to tell computers and humans apart." Contexts in which it is important to prevent software from filling in information on a website include registering for a service such as email, participating in opinion polls, adding comments to blogs and user rating sites, and repeatedly entering a password in an attempt to guess it. Figure 5.1 illustrates one type of CAPTCHA. Other types include randomly rotated pictures that people can turn right side up but computers cannot and selected audio phrases for the visually impaired.

logical access control: A control that is included in software to permit access by authorized personnel in accordance with the privileges granted to them and to prevent access by unauthorized personnel.

biometrics: Access controls that rely on physical characteristics such as signatures, fingerprints, palmprints, voice recognition, and retina scans to authenticate the identity of a user before permitting access.

CAPTCHA: Completely automated public Turing test to tell computers and humans apart.

Logical access controls can be established at various software levels. If they are established at the applications level, they are considered applications controls. If they are established at the operating system or the database level, they are considered general controls. To look at it another way, if the access controls affect more than one application, they should likely be considered to be general controls. Figure 5.2 illustrates the basic levels of software at which security can be implemented.

Firewalls One of the most important elements of control over the security threats posed by the internet is the use of firewalls. In reality, they are not walls at all, but rather computers or routers added to a network system with very high security capabilities. Firewall

Figure 5.1 Example of a CAPTCHA

A CAPTCHA is an automated technique for telling computers and humans apart.

Source: www.google.com/recaptcha/captcha, accessed January 2, 2011. Used with permission.

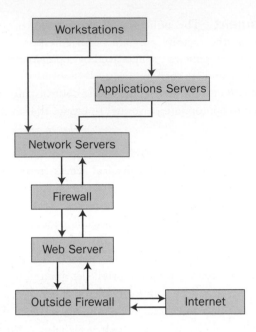

Figure 5.2 Security software structure

Basic layers at which security is established.

computers must be installed at the only point of entry between the internal network and the internet. If they are not the only access point, they cannot be effective, because hackers and other intruders will be able to enter the system through the least secure point.

Firewalls must be a part of the overall security policy of a company and must also be accompanied by specific policies that determine how the firewall is configured, who has access to it, and how the firewall actually works. Normally, a company involved in ebusiness will make use of two firewalls, as shown in figure 5.3. The reason for this is that when a network is connected to the internet, it must have a web server that can be accessed by way of the internet. Of course, this exposure to the internet can add unnecessary exposure to the network if it is not controlled. Control is achieved by having a firewall placed between the web server and the internet, referred to as the "outside firewall" in figure 5.3, and an inside firewall placed between the web server and the internal network itself.

Using these two firewalls provides protection because each firewall can be configured to play a role appropriate to its placement. The outside firewall is set to accept transactions that only call upon the web server, and it restricts the types of transactions to those that the web server is authorized to handle. The inside firewall is set to process only those requests to network data that, again, are authorized. For example, the inside server might be set to accept requests to display information on company products, but to reject requests to gain access to payroll information. There are many ways that firewalls can be configured, but all are done with the same objective—to enforce the security and data access policies of the enterprise.

Intrusion Detection Systems An entity should be equipped with monitoring devices and processes for real-time monitoring of security threats to alert appropriate personnel

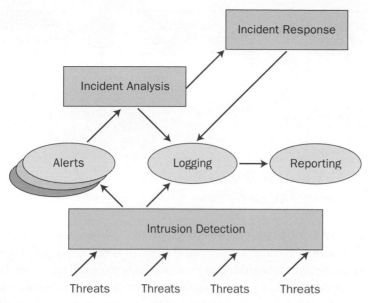

Figure 5.3 Platform structure for ebusiness security system

The relationship of a network system to its firewalls.

of the occurrence of unusual activity, allowing them to act in a rapid manner. Unusual activity should be detected and transmitted to the appropriate person (e.g., a security administrator).

An **intrusion detection system (IDS)**, as shown in figure 5.4, monitors devices and processes for security threats and can alert security personnel of the occurrence of unusual activity as it occurs. An IDS generates alerts based on a "threat score" determined from an analysis of user activity. A passive IDS performs various network-related surveillance activities, including monitoring, logging, and flagging anomalous behaviour. An active IDS can log users off the network or close off access through the firewall.

The difference between a firewall and an IDS is that an IDS has an extensive database of attack signatures or patterns, which allows it to detect intrusions dynamically. In contrast, firewalls either permit or block connections based on a comparatively small number of criteria and do not track related activity patterns.

A potential problem with some IDSs is that they generate a large volume of false-positives, like the "cry wolf" problem, thereby making it difficult to identify the real attacks. An active IDS that is poorly tuned can undermine productivity and service delivery by preventing customer access. Thus, IDSs must be continuously monitored and updated. Configuring the IDS alert threshold involves a delicate balance between ensuring that all threats are detected and false positives are minimized.

intrusion detection system (IDS): A system that monitors devices and processes for security threats and can alert security personnel of the occurrence of unusual activity as it occurs.

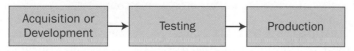

Figure 5.4 Intrusion detection, incident analysis, and incident response

An intrusion detection system analyses, logs, and reports threats to security personnel who respond to them as required.

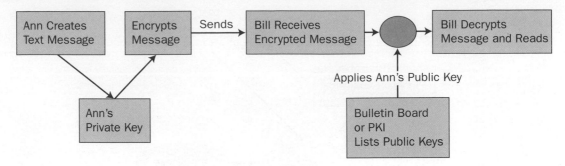

Figure 5.5 Directories for system development

System development activities progress through three directories.

System Acquisition or Development Controls   When new applications systems are acquired from system vendors or developed in-house, it is very important that the systems that emerge from the process be those that management approved. This means that through the acquisition or development process there must be good control to ensure that errors or omissions are not introduced during the programming, testing, or implementation phases.

Control during the acquisition or development process is normally accomplished by setting up different directories (or sometimes even separate systems) on which to carry out the installation, programming, testing, and implementation phases. Figure 5.5 illustrates this process. Programs are written in the development area. They are then tested in the testing area by the programmer and others. The prime control over these different areas is that access is restricted to those who need it. The development area is accessible only by the programmers, and testing is accessible only by those doing the testing. Once they are felt to be ready, and the users and management have signed off on them, the new programs are "promoted" to the production area. This is the area where the programs actually run and use the data of the enterprise to execute procedures and create reports. The process of following this established approach and obtaining appropriate approvals is crucial to ensuring that the programs that are actually placed into production in the enterprise are the proper ones.

System Maintenance and Change Controls   After programs are developed and implemented, they are continuously subjected to changes to introduce corrections or enhancements. This process, usually referred to as system maintenance, must undergo controls similar to development controls, since the same risks and threats exist.

Operations Controls   Control over the operations of a computer system include the operation of servers, scheduling of jobs, and maintenance of system infrastructure. Operations controls are often in the hands of technical support people in the organization. Often, these people have particular parts of the operations assigned to them. Operations controls include such activities as review of system logs, monitoring system activity, and review of exception reports on system activity.

Business Continuity Controls   Ebusiness systems must always be available to organizations and accessible to authorized users. This is especially critical for ecommerce systems as downtime can be costly and even disastrous. Therefore, steps must be taken to keep systems running continuously. If an outage is encountered, the company must be able to restore the system to operation and recover data and programs affected by the outage in a timely manner. This means the enterprise must have a business continuity plan that maps out the steps to be followed in the event of a system failure or disaster. A **business continuity plan** ensures that a business can continue to operate after a disaster or other event occurs that could otherwise disable the computer systems for a lengthy period of time. The steps must be detailed and the plan must be carefully tested. Normally, testing is done in as much detail as possible, and all the steps must be documented in detail. Of course, the testing should be repeated periodically and documentation kept up to date.

Part of the business continuity plan is a disaster recovery plan. A **disaster recovery plan** is a detailed plan of action that enables an information system to be recovered after a disaster has made it inoperable. An effective disaster recovery plan normally addresses at least the following points:

- the nature of potential disasters that might pose a risk (power failures, floods, fires, storms, terrorist attacks, etc.)
- the roles and responsibilities of information systems personnel and users in an emergency
- detailed scripts for all personnel involved in the operation
- a contact list, including home phone numbers, of information systems personnel and external service providers
- critical processing priorities (to guide the order in which systems will be restored)
- procedures to be followed for testing, reviewing, and updating the plan
- the backup hardware to be used and its location and access requirements
- the location and availability of backups of systems software, applications, data files, databases, and documentation
- the offsite storage locations and access requirements of all backups, including a copy of the plan itself
- power requirements and contingency plans if power is down
- communications requirements and contingency plans if communications are down
- detailed procedures for rebuilding the system on the backup computers, including estimated time for completion

Applications Controls

All applications that a business uses consist of four basic areas: input, processing, output, and storage. Thus, applications controls must be established for each of these areas. In addition, another category that has assumed increased importance is communications controls.

Input Controls Input controls include those that validate the input, such as check digits and input masks. **Check digit controls** perform a calculation on a set of digits, such as an employee ID number, and then add the result of that calculation to the number. This enables the integrity of the set of digits to be checked whenever required. **Input masks** establish formats for input areas in a screen that allow certain numbers of characters and/or digits to be entered.

Processing Controls Processing controls include those discussed previously, under "System Acquisition or Development Controls" and "System Maintenance and Change Controls," which help to ensure that only properly tested and approved processes are used in applications. Other processing controls include log monitoring to ensure that

business continuity plan: A plan which ensures that a business can continue to operate after a disaster or other event occurs that could otherwise disable the computer systems for a lengthy period of time.

disaster recovery plan: A detailed plan of action that enables an information system to be recovered after a disaster has made it inoperable.

check digit control: A control that performs a calculation on a set of digits, such as an employee ID number, and then adds the result of that calculation to the number.

input mask: A means to establish formats for input areas in a screen that allow certain numbers of characters and/or digits to be entered.

all processing steps were completed, process status checking to ensure that all program steps were executed without error or interruption, and reconciliations of input and output control totals to ensure that the programs processed completely and accurately all the information submitted for processing. **Control totals** are totals based on counts of records, monetary values, or hashes that are used to reconcile inputs and outputs and thereby control completeness and accuracy of processing. A **hash** is a total based on a field that is not expected to change (e.g., total of all employee number fields in a file) and is therefore useful for ensuring that no unauthorized additions, changes, or deletions have occurred in a file of records containing that field. **Time stamping**—the process of adding a tag containing the time that a record is created, modified, or moved—is used to control the timeliness of data processing and the currency of information.

Output Controls

Output controls include controls over the distribution of reports, including access to online reports. If reports are in paper form, then output controls determine the printer that is used, where it is located, and who has access to it. Such controls also include procedures to have the output picked up by authorized personnel for distribution. If the reports are online, access controls are established to determine who can view the reports.

Storage Controls

Storage controls include controls over physical and logical access to databases, tables and other files that are used for processing and for producing reports. Such controls include procedures to classify and label the stored information according to who is entitled to access it, when and how and to check access requests against the access privileges granted to the users requesting access.

Communications Control

Communications controls are particularly important in ecommerce to ensure that commitments made over the internet are not repudiated due to the inability to establish the authenticity of the sender and/or receiver or the integrity of the message in transit. A major communications control is encryption (see figure 5.6), which is discussed further in the sections that follow. Encryption is one of the most important control tools used in ebusiness to protect the confidentiality of information. **Message digests** are control totals (similar to check digits) that are used to control the completeness, accuracy, and validity of data transmissions. A message digest calculates a unique number from the content of a message that can then be added to the message and checked by recalculating the number to ensure that the message has not been tampered with. **Digital signatures**, encrypted message digests that can be decrypted only with a key that authenticates the sender's identity, combine encryption and message digests to ensure the authenticity of transmitted messages.

Encryption

Encryption techniques are fundamental to control over the communications process, a process that is central to ebusiness. Encryption is the conversion of data into a form called a cipher, which is very difficult to read without possession of a code called a "key." The encryption is achieved by applying an algorithm, or formula, to the data bits that comprise the data, converting it into the cipher. The key is a set of data that can be applied to the cipher to decipher it, that is, convert it back to the original data. Application of the key is referred to as the decryption process.

Encryption is used in various aspects of ebusiness, including email, transmissions to execute banking transactions on the internet, and other sensitive transmissions.

---

control total: A total based on a count of records, monetary values, or hashes that is used to reconcile inputs and outputs and thereby control completeness and accuracy of processing.

hash: A total based on a field that is not expected to change (e.g., total of all employee number fields in a file) and that is useful for ensuring that no unauthorized additions, changes, or deletions have occurred in a file of records containing that field.

time stamping: The process of adding a tag containing the time that a record is created, modified, or moved.

message digest: A unique number calculated from the content of a message that can then be added to the message and checked by recalculating the number to ensure that the message has not been tampered with.

digital signature: An encrypted message digest that can only be decrypted by a key that authenticates the sender's identity.

UN vs. BlackBerry

How the tables have turned for BlackBerry maker Research in Motion Ltd. (RIM)! For years, the BlackBerry was the gold standard in security of smartphone communications. The BlackBerry had the cachet of being used by the president of the United States, as well as an army of legislators, due to the security of its communications. Now, RIM is facing demands for access to its encrypted data.

Many governments have accepted the use of encryption technology to protect privacy and confidentiality of emails. But officials in some jurisdictions have balked and are demanding that RIM allow them access to its customers' emails. The following are some examples:

In China, where government agents routinely monitor citizens' email messages, RIM's plans to offer BlackBerry service were delayed by two years while the company attempted to persuade the Chinese government that the BlackBerry would not pose a security threat.

Saudi Arabian authorities have threatened to ban the BlackBerry service, on grounds that the BlackBerry Messenger service was being used by Saudi youth to meet members of the opposite sex.

The United Arab Emirates, where RIM reportedly has 500,000 users, has threatened to ban the BlackBerry Messenger service as well, on grounds that data were being exported offshore and managed by a foreign commercial operation.

India threatened to shut down BlackBerry service, citing suspicions that terrorists used BlackBerry services to plan a 2008 attack in Mumbai that killed 166 people.

Indonesia is involved in a dispute with RIM that is similar to those mentioned above.

Most recently, Hamadoun Toure, Secretary General of the International Telecommunication Union, reportedly stated that RIM should give law enforcement agencies around the world access to its customer data to help them combat terrorism. Civil libertarians assert that these are merely attempts by authoritarian governments to intimidate RIM into granting them the ability to spy on citizens.

RIM asserts that it cannot access data sent via its devices and that it complies with all legal requests for data, such as phone logs, even if it cannot provide the text of emails.

Research in Motion Ltd.
www.rim.com

Questions

1. Should governments have access to encrypted BlackBerry data?

2. How should we balance rights to free speech and privacy on the internet with the pursuit of criminals and terrorists?

3. Would your views on this issue differ if the UN or another non-governmental entity were given access to encrypted BlackBerry data?

Sources: Raphael G. Satter, "UN Says Blackberry Data Should Be Shared," *Globe and Mail*, September 3, 2010, B7.

The major web browsers—including Microsoft Explorer, Mozilla Firefox, and Google Chrome—include strong encryption capability.

There are various strengths available in encryption, measured by the length of the key. For standard browsers, 128-bit encryption is commonly used. For internet banking, the banks in Canada require 128-bit encryption technology in order for their customers to obtain access to internet banking.

Encryption works like this: A person initiating a transaction generates and uses a key and then provides that key to the recipient to enable the transmission to be decrypted. This can be done on a symmetric basis or an asymmetric basis. When it is done on a symmetric basis, the sender of the message simply provides the recipient with the same key used for encryption.

The asymmetric approach, illustrated in figure 5.6, is carried out by using a system of private and public keys, which are created together in pairs. A **private key** is a code

private key: A set of data used to encrypt and decrypt data transmissions that is known to one person only.

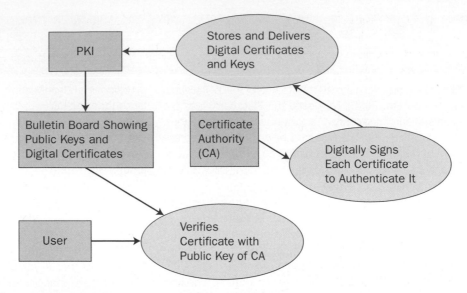

Figure 5.6 The asymmetric encryption process

Sample method of encryption.

used to encrypt and decrypt data transmissions that is known only to the person who generated it. A **public key** is a code used to encrypt and decrypt data transmissions that is made known to outsiders, and can be obtained by the recipient of the message. In a typical transmission, Ann might send a message to Bill that she wants to keep secret. She encrypts it with her private key and when Bill receives it, he decrypts it using her public key. Only her public key will decrypt a message encrypted using her private key.

Because the public key works on the message, Bill knows that Ann sent the message, which establishes the property of authentication of the user. **Authentication** confirms that a particular person or server is, in fact, the person or server that is identified in a transaction. In addition, since the public key worked in the decryption, Ann cannot deny she sent the message, establishing the property of **non-repudiation**.

On the other hand, if Ann wants to make sure that only Bill can open the message, she will encrypt it with Bill's public key. Only his private key can open the message and, of course, only he has that key. In practice, a combination of symmetric and asymmetric encryption is adopted, usually by using the **Secure Sockets Layer (SSL) protocol**. The SSL protocol is a security protocol associated with TCP/IP that establishes a secure communications channel between web clients and servers. The **Secure HyperText Transfer Protocol (S-HTTP)** provides security for transmission of messages over the World Wide Web. Note that S-HTTP is different from HTTPS, which is related to SSL. Secure protocols such as SSL and S-HTTP are commonly used by banks and other ecommerce sites to encrypt transmissions between a user and a web server. Without a secure protocol, much ecommerce activity would not be feasible.

Under the SSL protocol, a system of server authentication is used by making use of server-related digital certificates administered by certificate authorities (CAs) and digital signatures. **Digital certificates** are electronic documents that contain the identity of a person or server and the related public key. **Certificate authorities (CAs)** are organizations that issue digital certificates and sign them with digital signatures to establish the authenticity of the certificates. Using SSL involves a series of interactions between computers called negotiations when a browser contacts a web server. First, the browser obtains the server certificate and examines the digital signature on it. The digital signature would have been placed on the certificate by the certificate authority using the CA's own private key. The browser checks that this is a CA that it trusts and then decrypts the signature with the CA's public key, thereby establishing the authenticity of the CA. The browser gets the public key by accessing the CA's online database. The browser and the server then agree on a master key for the session, and that master key is used to encrypt and decrypt all transmissions for that session. The master key is generated by the browser and then sent to the server, encrypted with the server's public key. Because the master key can be opened only by the server for which it is intended, the identity of the master key is secure. From that point on, the encryption process for that session is carried out on a symmetric basis.

S-HTTP is an extension of HTTP that enables individual messages to be encrypted. In contrast, SSL encrypts all the transmissions for a session. The S-HTTP protocol was designed for transaction confidentiality, authenticity/integrity, and non-repudiation of origin (i.e., it can authenticate the user, whereas SSL can only authenticate the server), and thus it is particularly desirable for ecommerce and online banking transactions that may arise spontaneously while a user is browsing a website. According to its developers, the protocol emphasizes maximum flexibility in choice of key management mechanisms, security policies, and cryptographic algorithms by supporting option negotiation between parties for each transaction. Thus, S-HTTP does not require the user to have a public key or a public key certificate. Option negotiation is used to enable clients and servers to agree on how a message should be encrypted, with numerous options being available.

Public Key Infrastructure (PKI) The importance of digital signatures for business, and the essential role that public and private keys play in them, means that there is a need for a great many keys. Since the public keys must be accessible by anyone, they need to be stored in a database that is accessible to the public. In addition, there is a need for a reliable system for managing the keys—one that is secure and backed by a reputable organization. This is where a public key infrastructure (PKI) is used.

Public key infrastructure (PKI) is a system that stores and delivers keys and certificates as needed and also provides privacy, security, integrity, authentication, and non-repudiation support for various technological and ebusiness applications and transactions (see figure 5.7). A PKI system manages the generation and distribution of public/private key pairs and publishes the public keys accompanied by certificates that confirm the

public key infrastructure (PKI): A system that stores and delivers keys and certificates as needed and also provides privacy, security, integrity, authentication, and non-repudiation support for various ebusiness applications and transactions.

DATA STATUS	
Data at Rest	**Data in Transit**
Data in mainframes, internal networks, applications, etc.	Data moving through communications media, on laptops, etc.

Figure 5.7 Flow chart for PKI systems
This chart shows the parties and procedures involved in the use of a PKI system.

identity of the key owner. All of this is included in open bulletin boards accessible by the public—or at least by all the people who need to know the information. (The latter qualification recognizes that certain PKI systems are set up by companies that choose to make the databases available only to their corporate personnel and their business partners rather than to the general public.)

A PKI system structures its data—the keys and CAs—in a logical fashion for orderly management and accessibility. A user's public key and identification are placed together in a certificate. The user's certificate authority then digitally signs each certificate to provide the necessary authentication, which can be verified by using the CA's public key to verify the CA's signature on the certificate. With this system, any user can get any other user's public key from a bulletin board to verify its authenticity.

In summary, PKI integrates digital certificates, public-key cryptography, and CAs into a total, enterprise-wide network security architecture. A typical PKI system for an enterprise encompasses the issuance of digital certificates to individual users and servers, end-user software, integration with corporate certificate directories, tools for managing certificates, and related services and support.

VPNs and Security In chapter 3 we looked at virtual private networks (VPNs), noting that they include (1) the use of firewalls, (2) tunnelling through the internet, and (3) the use of encryption.

Firewalls are, of course, a prime tool for adding security to a network. They are usually deployed as part of a VPN system if they are not already in place. The concept of tunnelling means that messages are directed through predetermined paths on the internet. This has security implications, since the path through which the messages are directed can be made secure to minimize the opportunities for unauthorized persons to intercept those messages through sniffing techniques. **Sniffing** is the use of electronic devices attached to transmission lines that can detect and capture data transmissions on those lines. Newer models of sniffing devices can work on wireless transmissions as well.

As previously discussed, encryption is one of the key techniques for protecting information residing on, or transmitted through, the internet. VPNs are set up by installing VPN software, which always includes the ability to encrypt messages being sent and to decrypt them when received. This means that even if messages are intercepted through sniffing, they cannot be understood by an unauthorized person.

sniffing: The use of electronic devices attached to transmission lines that can detect and capture data transmissions on those lines. Newer models of sniffing devices can work on wireless transmissions as well.

Drive-by Hacking

The abundance of wireless networks has led to a proliferation of drive-by hackers, who position themselves within range of a wireless network, which may or may not be secure, and log into that network. Then they can use the network to access the internet and download files. There have been cases where drive-by hackers have downloaded illegal pornography, thus transferring the potential blame for this activity from themselves to the owners of the network. With the growing popularity of wireless networks for home use, this activity has moved to the suburbs and residential neighbourhoods.

Wireless networks offer some attractive advantages, such as the ability to connect a single computer to a high-speed internet connection and then connect to it a wireless base station configured for use with laptops in the house, enabling the laptop users

Ebusiness in Global Perspective

Mobile Viruses

Nokia Corporation has the distinction of being the first company whose mobile phones became infected by viruses, which had previously affected only computers. Starting in 2004, several mobile phone viruses appeared in Asia and spread around the world. Particularly targeted was the Symbian operating system favoured by Nokia. Most of the viruses were embedded in downloadable games.

Fortunately, the consequences for users were mild. One of the viruses, named Cabir, drained the phone's battery. Commonwarrior and Mabir sent messages, including copies of themselves to other phones via the Multimedia Messaging Service (MMS). While this did not harm a phone, it ran up costs for the phone's owner. Locknut and Hobbes. A froze up phones.

Cabir and Commonwarrior were able to spread through Bluetooth, jumping to nearby phones that were available to them. This led to rumours of phone viruses transferring to a car's computer system via the Bluetooth link that enables hands-free use of mobile phones by connecting the driver's mobile phone with the car speaker and in-dash entertainment system.

One expert dismissed concerns raised by this rumour, on the grounds that it was unlikely that a virus could harm the electronic components that it could reach via Bluetooth. He also noted that mobile phones run operating systems that are difficult targets—hence less tempting targets—for virus writers than are the billions of networked computers around the world.

Another expert expressed fears that smartphones that synchronize data such as calendars, contacts, and files with desktop computers using Bluetooth could become infected and transfer viruses and other malware to corporate networks.

Nokia
www.nokia.com

Questions

1. Are mobile phone viruses such as the ones that attacked Nokia phones a concern? Why?

2. How can individuals protect themselves from phone viruses and other mobile malware?

3. How can companies protect themselves from phone viruses and other mobile malware?

Sources: Grant Buckler, "Cellphone Acting Sick? Might Be a Virus," *Globe and Mail*, May 19, 2005, B11.

---

to compute and access the internet from anywhere in the house—in the study, the kitchen, in front of the fireplace—anywhere. Increasingly, people use their networks to do their internet banking, manage their personal financial software, and generally carry out activities that involve the recording of a lot more personal information than ever before.

Wireless network systems, such as the popular Wi-Fi (which uses the 807.22(b) protocol) include security features as part of their standard package. The most common is **WEP (Wired Equivalency Privacy)**, a security protocol designed to provide a wireless local area network with security and privacy comparable to that of a wired local area network. However, the "default" condition of the networks when they are delivered is that encryption is *not* enabled. There is no security unless it is specifically configured during the installation process. When it is enabled, hackers need to obtain and enter the encryption key, which can be as much as 30 alphanumeric characters long, depending on the type of system and the strength of the encryption. High encryption of 128 bits is available for wireless networks.

Because home users often do not enable the available WEP security, they can be vulnerable targets for hackers. Drive-by hacking is a popular pastime for certain illegal hackers and criminals and, as surveys carried out by the experts show, one that stands a good chance of success. There have been numerous instances where the lack

WEP (Wired Equivalency Privacy): A security protocol designed to provide a wireless local area network with security and privacy comparable to that of a wired local area network.

of security in place in wireless networks has been tested by experts. Typically, a wireless expert with a handheld computer drives or walks around a district where there are likely to be wireless networks installed and tries to gain access to those the computer detects.

Purchasing computer systems with a default of no security has been common in the industry for years. The situation is rather like purchasing a car and having it delivered with the doors open and the keys in the ignition. Removing the keys from a new car and locking the doors to prevent theft is typical practice. Similarly, for wireless networks, encryption needs to be enabled to prevent theft of the information on the computers. When installing a new wireless network, the setup routine will normally ask whether to enable encryption. The answer should be yes.

WEP, when enabled, provides a basic level of security, but it has limitations. For more effective protection, other security measures that should be taken, such as turning off the base station when it is not in use, monitoring the use of the network, and restricting the access to the base station to specific computer ID numbers.

SECURITY POLICIES

It is clear that an essential element of good security is a set of security policies that establishes the acceptable transactions that can be carried out through internet connections. These policies should be centrally defined and must be consistent with, or part of, the overall corporate security policies. Security policies are a starting point for the security framework within an organization. They link management's objectives and the operational procedures implemented to achieve them. They are also formal statements of organizational and managerial intent: Standards define minimum performance requirements, and guidelines provide behavioural direction. The core policies should describe the function of the security program, outline oversight, establish roles and responsibilities, identify laws and regulations requiring compliance, and outline a framework for asset classification, asset management, change management, and exception management. The policies, standards, and guidelines should be approved and periodically updated in response to changes in the environment, technology, and business requirements identified through systematic monitoring of these factors.

Prior to developing security policies, the company should conduct a risk assessment to determine where the risks are. This will enable the policies to address the risks that actually exist. The policies should be comprehensive, and approach security from a full end-to-end perspective rather than just as a series of components (e.g., firewalls, passwords). Security policies should be integrated into the overall policies governing the entity's ecommerce activity.

Business objectives should be the foundation for security aims and initiatives. The following are some common security goals:

- complying with service-level agreements, defined external and internal commitments, and any other contracts
- complying with laws and regulations

Outsourcing Security at First American Bank

In recent years, outsourcing has been a strategy in almost every area of business activity, including IT. Many security people feel, however, that security should not be outsourced, especially at the large and conservative companies. But in the past few years, the option of outsourcing IT security—through an enterprise known as a managed security service provider (MSSP)—has grown in popularity and respectability. Companies have been handing over key parts of their security structures to MSSPs, including firewalls, anti-virus software, virtual private networks, and intrusion detection.

Some of them, like First American Bank, are relatively small companies that have big security concerns. At that bank, a vice president got a call at 2 a.m. from a technical analyst at the Unisys security command centre. The analyst detected suspicious activity but hadn't been able to isolate and identify the source of the trouble. He said that if the problem wasn't solved soon, the network would have to be shut down as a security precaution. The VP gave the go-ahead to shut down the network.

A short while later, the security analyst determined that a malicious attack hadn't occurred after all; instead, the problem was network interference, caused by local telephone lines. The network was brought up again, and the VP went back to sleep. The analyst, or others like him, continued to monitor the bank's network on a 24/7 basis. The VP's attitude was "Better safe than sorry."

Security is extremely important to a bank, as a lack of security could raise questions about the bank's trustworthiness and lead to a loss of customers. First American had entered into internet banking and didn't fully understand all the security risks posed by the internet. For these reasons, and also because it did not have sufficient staff resources to mount a sophisticated security system internally, the bank decided to go with the e-@ction security solution offered by Unisys.

When it was asked to provide the service, Unisys did a three-day security assessment, which included an inventory of the bank's IT systems, discussions of the bank's growth plans, and a thorough evaluation of the bank's existing security systems. When the assessment was complete, the bank compared the cost of the Unisys service with the cost of developing an in-house, round-the-clock network-monitoring operation such as that of the e-@ction security solution, and Unisys got the contract.

MSSPs, like most other services, don't promise 100 percent reliability, so companies using such services might also buy hacker insurance. But companies are buying into MSSPs more frequently, for reasons similar to those of First American, and because they can't keep up with all the latest security threats or respond to them appropriately on their own.

Unisys
www.unisys.com

Questions

1. If First American Bank had not gone with the Unisys service, what issues would it have had to address?

2. What are the risks to First American Bank of adopting an MSSP?

3. Discuss the matters First American Bank would have had to consider in making the decision to adopt the Unisys service.

Source: G. V. Hulme, "Security's Best Friend," InformationWeek, July 16, 2001, www.informationweek.com/story/showArticle .jhtml?articleID=6505999, accessed July 16, 2001.

- protecting data confidentiality
- making certain that unauthorized persons or systems cannot inadvertently or intentionally alter data without being detected
- ensuring that the information accessed is genuine
- making the data accessible and usable
- logging transactions and data exchanges
- verifying the identity of a person engaged in a business transaction

Determining the right level of security is a difficult balance; too little security opens the company to attacks, while too much security slows system performance and can impact employee morale and customer satisfaction. All those who will be affected by a security policy should be invited to collaborate in its development. Such a process can increase employee buy-in to the policy. Care should be taken to ensure that the security policy is suitable for the entity's business partners.

When security policies are developed, they should be documented and approved by the board of directors for distribution to staff. The major components of a security policy are outlined below.

Security Administration

A security policy needs to cover the duties of the persons responsible for security administration, including the person in charge of security and the administrators of the various networks, operating systems, databases, and applications. It also needs to establish to whom the person in charge of security will report. Increasingly, that person is reporting to higher levels of executives, and often has responsibilities for privacy as well as security.

For controls to be enforced and meaningful to employees, upper management must play an active role. Senior management should establish that security has high visibility in the arenas of corporate governance and business processes. The latter may require management to realign lines of communications, authority, and responsibilities. The entity must ensure that there are resources available to implement the security program defined by policy. If the security function is in-house, it must have a budget sufficient to employ knowledgeable IT staff with tools and authority to ensure a secure IT infrastructure. If there are no resources available in-house then outsourcing should be considered. The vendor selected should be reputable and trustworthy.

Whether in-house or outsourced security is used, it will require a budget sufficient for the type of security program required. The amount to be expended must be aligned with the severity of risks faced and the organization's capacity to respond. In this regard, the security budget needs to be linked to the overall corporate mission of generating value for the owners and employees of the organization.

Effective budgeting for security is complicated by the fact that the amount of spending is not a guarantee of the level of security achieved. Also, effective spending on security can lead to invisible outcomes, in the sense that any security incidents prevented are, inevitably, invisible. This, in turn, can lead to the perception that the spending is pointless and can be cut back. Security is largely a fixed cost that does not depend on the volume of data. Some security measures are inexpensive and merely require attention to detail. A by-product of security measures is a potential increase in the overall efficiency and effectiveness of the business.

Standard Operating Procedures

Security standards adopted by an organization's security group should be based on an accepted information security standard such as ISO 17799. Security standards represent agreed-upon performance requirements against which operating procedures can be assessed. At present, several competing standards cover similar ground but are organized differently and have varying levels of acceptance by different professional groups and jurisdictions. Once an organization adopts a standard, it will need to translate the standard into operating procedures that fit its circumstances so that this standard will become part of the daily duties performed by the organization's personnel (e.g., new passwords, access log review). Because exceptions are bound to arise, the standard should explicitly establish procedures to be used for exceptions to standard operating procedures.

Information Management

Many companies include in their security policy an information management policy that describes the importance of the corporate information and identifies the "owner" or custodian of the information. This policy includes details such as all applications and data used in the organization, a description of the level of security required for each application or data set, and identification of appropriate business managers as custodians of the applications and data.

Privilege Management

As an entity's use of ebusiness expands, its user base can include employees, customers, suppliers, and business partners. To effectively manage such a diversity of users requires centralized control of user privileges by the security management unit. The most basic privilege in a computerized business system is access. However, very quickly an entity will find that it must distinguish what types of access to permit to what types of assets, to whom and under what circumstances—who can do what, to what, and when. Thus, entities must identify who can gain physical access to system facilities and resources and under what circumstances, and who can read and write to various files and which software functions they can use under what circumstances. To implement effective access controls will require the establishment of user registration and authorization, identification and authentication, and the creation of user privileges and permissions based on the **principle of least privilege**—granting the minimum privileges required by individuals to complete the tasks they are responsible for and no more. While this principle may seem obvious, low adherence to this principle is a major contributor to system vulnerabilities. Many software systems are configured for maximum privilege by default. Also, many organizations are not prepared for the administrative and user management issues that arise when the principle of least privilege is enforced as the underlying basis for access control.

principle of least privilege: A principle which suggests granting to each individual the minimum privileges he or she requires to complete the tasks he or she is responsible for and no more.

Physical Security

Procedures to be followed with regard to safeguarding the physical safety of the hardware, software, and communications infrastructure in an organization are normally covered in the security policy. This includes control over servers, the related network/telecommunications equipment, and workstations, as well as access to the premises. With the increasing use of mobile devices such as laptops, smartphones, and other handhelds and their capacity to store vast amounts of information, it is important to consider security measures for such devices in a security policy.

Logical Access Control

An organization's policy with regard to logical access control should focus on the user IDs and password system adopted by the company. It should also include the policy guiding the assignment of access rights to specific user IDs, such as which screens, programs, and data a user can access and what actions they can perform on them (e.g., read, write to, change, execute). The policy is often broken down into access to personal computers, access to networks, and access to any other unique components of the system to which personnel might be granted access, such as intranets, database systems, and the internet. A security policy should also address controls over giving access to temporary personnel (e.g., contract workers, consultants, customers).

End-User Computing Policy

The end-user portion of a security policy sets out the responsibilities of users who use corporate computers and systems. It is important for reminding users of their responsibilities for the security of the system, and for defining those responsibilities. The policy should include items such as reminders that users must comply with corporate security policies and procedures, take care of corporate equipment, and use the company's computer resources and information only for authorized business purposes.

The end-user policy also normally sets out responsibilities for backing up data, protecting against viruses, keeping passwords secret, and taking other precautions for protecting the privacy of corporate data. The end-user policy also normally identifies the software brands that will be supported by the company.

A major issue with regard to end users is that they often have access to powerful programs and tools that can be used to construct ad hoc information systems. Sometimes such ad hoc systems can become, unofficially, a critical part of the overall information system and, therefore, need to be safeguarded. To provide proper control over such "unofficial" systems, the security policy needs to define the controls that apply to ad hoc systems and the levels of system that might require different levels of control.

Software Acquisition, Development, Maintenance, and Change

It is important in most organizations to take precautions to ensure that any applications are developed or modified using techniques that provide for data integrity and appropriate audit trails. A security policy on software development and maintenance should define a procedure for setting up and managing the various directories that are used in the process, such as development, testing, and production. It should include the process for review and approval, who owns the programs, and the required documentation and access rights to various parts of the system that are used in development and maintenance.

Impact of Data Mobility

Due to an increase in ebusiness as well as the use of wireless devices, the internet for data transmission, and wide area networks, data are much more mobile than ever before. In some cases, data are lost during transmission or when they are resident in a foreign databank.

Security policies need to recognize this phenomenon. Accordingly, they should determine where the data in an organization go, when they are transmitted, and where they reside at various points in the business cycle. The first step is to classify data according to their status, as illustrated in figure 5.8.

By having a security policy that classifies data by status, a company can "follow the data," which move through many different platforms and technologies. Data protection should lean heavily on the use of encryption, as this is the main security tool to protect data within and outside an organization, whether data are at rest or in transit.

Personnel Management

Highly qualified IT personnel are necessary to enable an enterprise to operate and manage the system, but there is a risk to having them, in that they have the skills to circumvent established controls. Therefore, a security policy must deal with the area of personnel management, including training and education. This includes matters such as distribution of duties, confidentiality agreements, passwords, and control over equipment.

Security Monitoring

The security policy should provide for a compliance verification and auditing program to ensure that the procedures established to implement the policy are followed. Monitoring of systems activity is crucial in establishing a secure system, as it helps the security personnel identify inappropriate activities both on the part of staff and on the part of unauthorized intruders. Security personnel should consider the use of automated tools for this purpose. The security policy should establish how monitoring will take place, who will carry it out, and the reporting procedures for events that occur, such as usage anomalies and security violations. The security policy should also provide for a regular, ongoing vulnerability assessment and management program.

Security compliance procedures (e.g., auditing, monitoring) need to be balanced with employee productivity and satisfaction. Overly intrusive measures can be viewed as an invasion of an employee's personal space. Compliance procedures should be

DATA STATUS	
Data at Rest	**Data in Transit**
Data in mainframes, internal networks, applications, etc.	Data moving through communications media, on laptops, etc.

Figure 5.8 Location of data by status

It is important to classify data according to their status.

complemented with information sessions that make security an integral part of the corporate culture. A memorandum must be issued to users to advise them that monitoring is being done; it should discuss the type and frequency of monitoring, and the implications of breaching security.

Disaster Recovery, Contingency Planning, and Insurance

The basic existence and general nature of a disaster recovery plan should be outlined in the security policy. This policy should stress the importance of the plan, and also cover who is responsible for it and generally how it is administered. One of the essential elements of disaster recovery and contingency planning is the provision for backup of systems. The security policy should therefore contain detailed guidance as to the backup procedures in force within the company for all systems, including communications. An important element of a contingency plan is insurance. The security policy should define the risks that should be insured.

Periodic Updates of Security Policy

Security policies should be periodically reviewed and updated to take into account technological changes, business changes, and the entity's experience with security incidents, vulnerability, assessments, and compliance enforcement.

CHAPTER SUMMARY

Every information system is subject to risk of error or fraud. Preventive and corrective measures that deal with the threats to a system (and thereby minimize the risk borne by the system) are known as controls. All controls are guided by strategy, policy, and implementation procedures, which involve institutionalizing the degree of risk that is acceptable, and by the knowledge and culture among personnel that is necessary to implement security procedures and make them effective.

There are two kinds of controls: general and applications controls. General controls include security management, physical and logical access controls, system acquisition or development controls, system maintenance and change controls, operations controls, and business continuity controls. Applications controls include input, processing, output, storage, and communications controls. All controls must be approached in a holistic fashion. This means that the ebusiness controls must be completely integrated with and consistent with the controls over the enterprise's information systems generally.

The entry of a company into ebusiness raises some unique challenges, and business has adopted various security strategies to deal with them. One of the most important elements of control over the security threats posed by the internet is the use of firewalls, intrusion detection systems, and encryption. All threats must be covered by good security policies, which establish the acceptable transactions that can be carried out through the internet connections.

Encryption techniques are fundamental to control over the communications process, a process that is central to ebusiness. The major web browsers such as Microsoft

Explorer include encryption capability. Most encryption is carried out by using pairs of private/public keys to encrypt and decrypt messages and other data transmissions.

The Secure Sockets Layer (SSL) protocol makes use of these keys along with the certificates issued by certificate authorities. Under the SSL protocol, a system of server authentication makes use of server certificates administered by certificate authorities and digital signatures. Access to the public key is accomplished by accessing the CA's online database. The master key is generated by the browser and then sent to the server by encrypting it with the server's public key.

Public key infrastructure (PKI) is a system that stores and delivers keys and certificates as needed, and also provides privacy, security, integrity, authentication, and non-repudiation support for various technological and ebusiness applications and transactions. A PKI system manages the generation and distribution of public/private key pairs, and publish the public keys accompanied by certificates that confirm the identity of the key owner.

Comprehensive security policies should be developed that view security from an end-to-end perspective and that are integrated into the overall policies governing the entity's ecommerce activity. Prior to developing security policies, the company should conduct a risk assessment to enable the security policies to address the risks that actually exist. In developing their security policy, companies need to trace the flow of data, and determine how to protect data wherever they are and be able to know if data are in transit or at rest. Security policies should be periodically reviewed and updated to take into account technological changes, business changes, and the entity's experience with security incidents, vulnerability assessments, and compliance enforcement.

Key Terms

authentication (p. 100)

biometrics (p. 93)

business continuity plan (p. 97)

CAPTCHA (p. 93)

certificate authority (CA) (p. 100)

check digit control (p. 97)

control total (p. 98)

control (p. 92)

digital certificate (p. 100)

digital signature (p. 98)

disaster recovery plan (p. 97)

disaster (p. 89)

error (p. 89)

fraud (p. 89)

general control (p. 92)

hash (p. 98)

input mask (p. 97)

intrusion detection system (IDS) (p. 95)

logical access control (p. 93)

malicious act (p. 89)

message digest (p. 98)

non-repudiation (p. 100)

physical access control (p. 93)

principle of least privilege (p. 107)

private key (p. 99)

public key (p. 100)

public key infrastructure (PKI) (p. 101)

risk (p. 89)

Secure Hypertext Transfer Protocol (S-HTTP) (p. 100)

Secure Sockets Layer (SSL) protocol (p. 100)

sniffing (p. 102)

threat (p. 92)

time stamping (p. 98)

virus (p. 92)

WEP (Wired Equivalency Privacy) (p. 103)

MyEbusinessLab — Tools for Online Learning

To help you master the material in this chapter and stay up to date with new developments in ebusiness, visit the MyEBusinessLab at www.pearsoned.ca/myebusinesslab. Resources include the following:

- Pre- and Post-Test Questions
- Additional Chapter Questions
- Author Blog
- Recommended Readings
- Commentaries on Current Trends
- Additional Topics in Ebusiness
- Internet Exercises
- Glossary Flashcards

Endnotes

1. A. Briney, "Security Focused: Survey 2000,"Information Security 5, no. 1 (September 2000): 40.
2. Computer Security Institute, 2003 Computer Crime and Security Survey (San Francisco: Computer Security Institute, May, 2003).
3. K. Campbell, L. A. Gordon, M. P. Loeb, and L. Zhou, "The Economic Cost of Publicly Announced Information Security Breaches: Empirical Evidence from the Stock Market," Journal of Computer Security 11 (2003): 431–448.
4. M. Ettredge and V. J. Richardson, "Assessing the Risk in E-Commerce" (proceedings of the 35th Hawaii International Conference on System Sciences, IEEE Computer Society, 2003).
5. J. H. Anthony, W. Choi, and S. Grabski, "Market Reaction to E-Commerce Impairments evidenced by Website Outages"International Journal of Accounting Information Systems 7(2) (2006): 60–78.

Chapter 6
Billing and Payment Systems

Learning Objectives

When you complete this chapter you should be able to:

1 Describe the characteristics of payment systems that have been used on the internet.

2 Describe how billing and payment techniques relate to corporate strategy.

3 Identify and describe the emerging electronic bill presentment and payment systems.

4 Describe the advantages and disadvantages of these systems.

5 Evaluate the suitability of billing and payment methods for various ebusiness scenarios.

6 Discuss the trends most likely to prevail in the future.

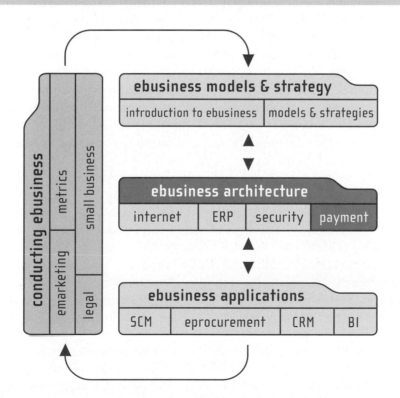

INTRODUCTION

EVER SINCE ENTERPRISES BEGAN TO OFFER GOODS AND SERVICES FOR SALE ON THE web, there has been a need for some kind of system to enable sales to be completed by paying over the web. The ability to complete sales in this way is viewed as being good for business. Moreover, it is much less expensive to carry out payment transactions on the web as compared with other methods. In figure 1.2 (see page 14), for example, it was shown that the cost to a financial institution of conducting a transaction through a bank branch amounts to over US$1, while conducting that same transaction over the internet costs only 1 or 2 cents. This is a remarkable fact that clearly provides an incentive for businesses to move payment transactions to the internet.

In business-to-consumer (B2C) commerce, if customers can pay online, there is a greater chance that they will buy, as opposed to a situation where they must go offline to pay. In business-to-business (B2B) commerce, there is also an economic incentive to have online billing and payment, as there is a tendency for numerous transactions to be carried out with the same regular customers. The savings in serving these customers can be dramatic, and, on the other side of the coin, the savings for the customers in procurement costs can also be significant.

The need to process small payments (micro payments) to pay for music downloads or other low-cost purchases creates an additional incentive to develop convenient and inexpensive payment methods.

Credit cards have been the main payment method used for online purchases. However, the shortcomings of credit cards in the real world have become even more evident in cyberspace; credit card fraud on the internet is widespread, and credit card transactions can be costly to merchants. It has been difficult to develop an alternative system that is secure, convenient, and accepted by enough people to make it economically viable. The need for security is clear: If there is too great a chance their money will be lost in a transaction, either through fraud or error, consumers will not use the system, and if they do, legal issues will arise for the businesses using the system. Such a system must also be convenient. People using the web tend not to want to spend a significant amount of time just to purchase something online. Finally, a system must gain acceptance by the customers, the financial institutions, and the vendors in order to be viable.

Thus, early on in the development of ecommerce, making payments over the internet was seen as both a problematic issue and an opportunity for the development of new digital currencies and payment methods. There were numerous attempts to develop online payment systems, but almost all of them failed to achieve acceptance. Some of the most visible of them have included DigiCash, CyberCash, Beenz, Flooz, Mondex, NetCash, NetCheck, First Virtual, Intell-A-Check, and NetCard. However, out of all the experimentation that has occurred over the years, some innovative methods have, in fact, found traction. The most successful and innovative alternative online payment system developed so far is PayPal. It is growing rapidly, but it has far to go before it can be viewed as having truly universal acceptance.

Apart from the problems associated with payment processing on the internet, it is important to recognize that the internet also offers a means of enhancing existing methods of billing customers and reducing the costs associated with printing and mailing billions of paper invoices, bills, and statements. In the balance of this chapter, we will discuss online payments, initiatives to make credit card use on the internet more secure, the PayPal system, and electronic billing.

CHARACTERISTICS OF TRADITIONAL PAYMENT SYSTEMS

Electronic Data Interchange (EDI)

Electronic data interchange (EDI) is a way to conduct transactions, including payment transactions, in electronic form. It is based on the use of widely accepted standards for formatting data in EDI transmissions. Persons using EDI must be signatories to an EDI agreement and must have their information systems configured to be able to recognize and process the transactions.

EDI has been used for many years as a means of settling payments, especially in the B2B world. Traditionally, EDI systems have made use of value-added networks (VANs) as a platform for operation. **Value-added networks (VANs)** are privately owned networks that are rented to users, along with a package of related services, to operate their EDI systems by providing an environment within which they can work, and by connecting them to their customers and suppliers. Generally, EDI has been costly and, in its "traditional" form, has been used most often by very large companies. Since the internet has become more widely used for conducting business transactions, EDI has moved from VANs to the web. The web is a much more cost-effective platform for EDI transactions than VANs, because access to it is much less expensive and the technology is widely recognized and used, making it easier to communicate with various other organizations. The use of the internet for replacing or augmenting existing VANs for EDI transactions is a logical step in streamlining payment systems for B2B commerce.

Normally, organizations using web-based EDI set up a web browser interface that links with the corporate systems. For payment purposes, the links would be with the cash systems to enable the payments to be processed through the corporate bank accounts. Such linkages would not be direct, because of security issues. The conversion of EDI systems from VANs to the internet involves many security issues because of the difficulties of securing the internet and the involvement of cash. In addition, it involves integration of the systems within the company, with the internet, and with the other parties to the system over the internet.

> **value-added network (VAN):** A privately owned network that is rented to users, along with a package of related services, to operate their EDI systems by providing an environment within which they can work, and by connecting them to their customers and suppliers.

Cash

The issue of introducing electronic payments systems for both B2B and B2C purposes leads to the question, what characteristics are required of payment systems in general for them to be effective? It is instructive to consider the characteristics of that most traditional method of payment—cash.

Cash can be carried easily from store to store and therefore can be characterized as portable. In addition, it is widely acceptable by stores, other companies, and other people, which means customers can be reasonably confident that it will be accepted by stores for payment of goods. In addition, there is normally no need to identify oneself in order to gain acceptance of the cash. Therefore, cash has the characteristics of portability, acceptance, and anonymity. Cash also provides for an instant transfer of value from the buyer to the vendor.

Portability While traditional cash cannot be transported on the web, the transportability feature is relatively easy to achieve in the case of electronic cash, as it only requires that the payment be capable of being transported over electronic media.

Acceptance The means of achieving acceptance have proven to be much more elusive. The acceptability of cash at one time was based on its value relative to gold. There was a commitment by the government that any bank note could be turned over to the government of Canada for gold, equal in value to the denomination of the bank note. During the 1970s, this approach was abandoned, and no such commitment of the government has existed since then. The acceptance of the dollar now rests on the strength of the economy, the stability of the currency, and the extent to which it is used. Since Canada generally has a strong economy and a stable government, acceptability has not been a problem in recent years.

On the internet, acceptance of electronic cash has not been easy to achieve except in the form of prepaid money cards that can be loaded on the internet but are spent at offline retail sites. An interesting development has been digital currencies created by companies such as e-gold (United States), WebMoney (Russia), NetPay (Panama), GoldMoney (United Kingdom), and several others.[1] Many of these companies claim that their currency is based on and backed by gold deposits.

Anonymity The anonymity provided by cash is of particular interest in web-based transactions and may be the most important attribute due to widespread concerns about the privacy of personal information on the web. Any system that is set up to protect the privacy of information will be advantageous for this reason.

Instant Transfer of Value The idea that cash provides an instant transfer of value is an important one. This is not necessarily the case for other methods of payment. If a credit card is used for payment, for example, the vendor must send the signed voucher to the sponsoring or financial institution for payment in cash. The vouchers themselves cannot be used to purchase something. The transfer of value, therefore, takes some time, the actual length of which varies according to the type of card and the method used to process payments. Cash has none of these problems; it can be used immediately by the vendor for purchases.

Digital Cash

Of the various online payment systems that have been invented and tested so far, ECash, developed by DigiCash, is the closest to approximating the attributes of cash. The product did not gain acceptance, and the company itself went bankrupt, but the attempt is interesting and revealing for those interested in the challenges of developing an online cash payment system.

ECash was built on public key cryptography—involving the use of a private key to sign messages and a public key to verify signatures. For example, if Laura wants to send a

M-PESA

Many parts of Africa have never had the communications infrastructure to support even telephone lines, let alone sophisticated modern communications. However, with the advent of wireless capabilities, this has been changing. The best example is the proliferation of cellphones. At present, there are millions of cellphones in Africa many in areas where phone service was previously nonexistent or difficult to obtain. In Kenya alone, statistics show that there are more that 6.5 million mobile phones in the country.

This spread of mobile phones has made it possible for many Africans to bypass the earlier stages of ecommerce and now to tap into electronic communications, data transfer, and the internet. Accordingly, there is an opportunity to develop new applications that are uniquely useful to Africa. Electronic transfer of cash is one of those applications.

One such new application is a service called M-PESA, which is offered by Safaricom Kenya, a leading mobile phone service operator. Safaricom has about 5 million subscribers.

The service enables subscribers to send large amounts of money instantly. The service is also inexpensive, costing on average about $1 to send or receive money. As soon as it launched, M-PESA became serious competition to existing money transfer agencies, including the government-owned Postal Corporation. Within two weeks, M-PESA had about 10,000 subscribers and had transferred over $100,000.

The system works quite simply. The customer deposits money in an account at one of Safaricom's shops and is issued an evalue voucher on his or her M-PESA account. The voucher can then be accessed by phone and cashed at any appointed agent in the country. A mobile phone needs a subscriber identity module (SIM) card to operate the M-PESA account and access the money transfer menu that allows account funds to be managed.

Although the M-PESA service has been extremely successful, many people naturally have been concerned about security. The system utilizes a pin code, which restricts access to individual accounts.

Many rural Kenyans live in abject poverty and have to rely financially on relatives in the cities. Transferring the needed money to them from relatives in the cities has been very difficult in the past. In many cases, they would use postal money orders, which are cumbersome and slow. When they don't have the time to wait for a money order, some have simply placed the money in an envelope and given it to a bus driver to deliver, which presents obvious risks. The M-PESA service avoids these problems. The money can simply be transferred to an agent in the destination area. In cases where the money has been lost in transit, the customers have been able to get it back.

Even bigger than the transfer of money to rural areas is the transfer of money from outside Kenya, from relatives who have relocated and want to send money home to their families. M-PESA is working on a service that provides for such international transfers. Migrants send approximately $93 billion back to Africa each year. Safaricom will need to deal with currency exchange rates and money laundering laws.

Questions

1. What potential is there for further development of M-PESA in the future?

2. What other cash transactions could M-PESA be used for?

Source: Noel Mwakugu, Money transfer service wows Kenya, BBC News, 3 April 2007, http://news.bbc.co.uk/2/hi/africa/6510165.stm.

private message to George, she encrypts it with her private key, and when he receives it, he applies her public key to verify that it was sent by her. With this approach, George is able to authenticate Laura as the sender. Because the message was unencrypted with her public key, it means it could only have been encrypted with her private key, because her public key is the only key that will unencrypt a message encrypted with her private key. Her public and private keys are key pairs. No other keys will act with them. Since it can be demonstrated that her private key was used, and that she is the only person with access

Safaricom Kenya
www.safaricom.co.ke

to that key, she cannot argue she didn't send it, so the ECash system has the feature of non-repudiation. This encryption system can be used for any business documents. Under the ECash approach, Laura would generate a note and sign it with her private key—a digital signature. The bank would verify the signature with its own private key and charge her account. It would send to Laura the signed note and a digitally signed withdrawal receipt for Laura's records.

Laura would then send the signed note to George to pay for some goods. George would receive the note, use the public key of the bank to check the bank's digital signature, and then send the note to the bank, which would credit George's account and return an electronic deposit slip to him. George would then send the merchandise to Laura along with a receipt. With this system, ECash would fulfill most of the characteristics of old-fashioned cash. Although it would not be portable, it would be easily transferable by electronic means. It would also provide an instant transfer of value, as the cash would be deposited in the vendor's account when the transaction takes place. However, ECash did not succeed.

Digital Cheques

Cheques have been used for many decades for settling business transactions and have many of the attributes of cash. They differ from cash largely in that they are not anonymous and carry a greater risk to the vendor accepting them because the bank might not honour them. For this reason, cheques are most useful for dealing with long-term, regular customers. Several attempts have been made to emulate cheques in the digital environment. One of the digital cheque products was called NetCheck.

NetCheck, like DigiCash, made use of cryptography to provide the signatures and endorsements that are used in processing paper-based cheques. Except for the fact that NetChecks were electronic, they operated in exactly the same way as paper-based cheques, could be used with existing chequing accounts, and contained all the same information, although they did provide for the inclusion of additional information. Like DigiCash, however, NetChecks did not gain enough acceptance to enable them to be used widely in daily commercial activity and the product has disappeared.

One significant electronic project is sponsored by the Financial Services Technology Consortium (FSTC), which has done some important work on electronic cheques in a project that led to the development of eCheck (discussed below).

 New Business Models
Transferring Cash with Visa

The search for new and viable case payment mechanisms continues, despite the failure of numerous upstarts over the past few years and the difficulty of finding a method that is reliable and gains acceptance.

Of course credit cards are one of the most time honoured and consistently used payment methods on the internet. Their familiarity and user friendliness has contributed to this, as has their reliability and the fact that the

>

banks effectively guarantee users against loss from fraud in most circumstances.

So it is no surprise that companies like Visa are looking at ways to expand on their base and provide a wider range of options for their customers. A new plan that Visa has been working on contemplates the use of Visa cards to actually transfer cash from a person's Visa card to another card or a bank account.

Cash transfers using e-mail have been in place for some time within the online banking services offered by the banks. In those services, customers log into their personal accounts and then go to cash transfers. They fill in the name and email address of the recipient, the dollar amount and a security question. The system generates an email message to the recipient, who then clicks on the bank they use and the message then takes them to the online banking logon. After they login, they designate the account into which they want the funds to be deposited and the money is then deposited, completing the transfer.

Under the new Visa plan, the process is somewhat similar. The difference is that people can use their Visa card to transfer money to another Visa card, debit card or bank account. The money will be transferred by using the recipient's mobile telephone number or email address. The recipient would receive the message, enter her/his own Visa number, and receive the money as a deposit or a credit on a card.

To launch this new initiative, Visa partnered with two other companies - Fiserv Inc. and CashEdge Inc. Both already provide payment services to banks, which should help in getting the service started. Many previous attempts to launch payment services failed because they were not adopted by the banks. In addition, Visa already has about 1.85 billion cards in circulation worldwide, which gives it a good head start

Questions

1. Is this new service likely to be more successful than previous attempts to develop online payment systems?

2. Who would be interested in buying this service?

Source: *http://www.cio-today.com/news/Visa-Unveils-Plastic-Payment-Service/story.xhtml?story_id=13000EVIA2QY&full_skip=1*

FSTC Projects

The FSTC's eCheck project was an early attempt to establish standards for electronic cheques. The idea was that eChecks do all the following:

- contain the same information as paper cheques
- are based on the same rich legal framework as paper cheques
- can be linked with unlimited information and exchanged directly between parties
- can be used in any and all remote transactions where paper cheques are used today
- enhance the functions and features provided by bank chequing accounts
- expand on the usefulness of paper cheques by providing value-added information

The eCheck project is now completed, but it established several important technological advances:

the first use of digital signatures to sign a markup document

the use of smart cards to perform digital signing

the use of smart cards to reduce the incidence of identity theft

the widespread use of public key infrastructure, built and operated by the banks

eChecks were planned to work in exactly the same way as paper cheques, except for the electronic base. An electronic cheque writer would create an eCheck and electronically send it to the payee. The payee would deposit the eCheck by electronically conveying it to the bank, and then receive credit, and the payee's bank would clear the eCheck to the paying bank. The paying bank would validate the eCheck by checking the digital signature and then charging the cheque writer's bank account for the eCheck. eChecks would include digital signatures, digital certificates, and other encryption-based features.

An electronic cheque under the FSTC approach would be created by a smart card "chequebook" that would include a digital signature for the cheque along with all the information that would be included on a normal cheque. The cheque would then be delivered by means of an electronic transmission and cleared through an electronic clearinghouse.

Somewhat related to the electronic cheque project is another project underway by the FSTC on cheque imaging. This is a process involving the creation of a digitized image of a cheque by the payee's bank at the time of deposit. The bank then sends the digital image, not the original cheque, through the payment clearing system. The purpose of the project is to speed up the payment process and reduce the opportunity for fraud. From a business perspective, cheque imaging has appeal because it substantially reduces the costs of processing cheques. Many banks have now implemented cheque imaging and are phasing out the provision of paper cheques to customers.

One of the big problems with this system is that images have large file sizes. When they are transmitted, therefore, they require a very wide bandwidth, to the point that it would strain the existing bandwidth normally available in some parts of the world. Another issue is that the legal system has not recognized imaged cheques, adding some uncertainty about their use for consummating business transactions.

Credit Cards

Throughout the economy, electronic payments through credit cards, debit cards, and pre-authorized payments now exceed cheque payments and are growing. This growth has benefits, such as cutting down on cheque fraud and providing opportunities to better analyse and track economic activity. However, electronic payments have drawbacks that have reportedly stalled the growth of ecommerce.

When commerce over the web began, the payment mechanism often took place offline. Typically, a website would provide a page that people could download, print, and fax to the company. In addition, many people would review websites for research and comparison purposes and then go to the store to buy the goods. While this is still common, it was much more common when web-based commerce began. Slowly, the idea of providing people with the capability of inputting their credit card information into the website itself and completing a transaction online became more common. The issue that companies had to deal with, however, was that the security provided on the website needed to be significantly increased. Where credit cards are used for payment, numerous systems offer customers the opportunity to register by entering information about themselves, including their credit card information, in a personal profile that is kept in a secure area by the vendor. Then when the customer enters the site to buy products, that customer needs only to log into the personal profile and does not need to enter all the additional information many times over. The vendor has an interest in setting up the personal profile to make it easier for the customer to buy, and the customer has an interest in doing this to save the time required to input information every time. An additional advantage of this system is that the credit card information is only entered and transmitted once per vendor, reducing the risk of detection by unauthorized parties during transmission.

The demand for a credit card payment system with good security is related to the needs of both the company and the customer. From the customer's point of view, good security is necessary to ensure that his or her credit card information is not made available to other people who might make illegal use of it. In addition, for reasons of personal privacy, customers normally do not want any information about themselves to be passed along to others without their knowledge and permission. From the company's point of view, good security is necessary to safeguard their customers' interests—and to avoid the possibility of litigation being brought against the company if a web customer's reasonable expectations about security are not met.

As a consequence, most websites that accept credit cards have adopted measures such as encryption using the **SSL/HTTPS protocols**. Normally, when a user enters a secure part of a website, a warning will appear on the browser screen that indicates that he or she is entering a secure area. In the case of Microsoft's Internet Explorer, a small lock icon in the lower corner of the screen will move into a locked position. When the user moves out of the secure area, a warning to this effect will also appear, although there is an option in the browser to turn off these warnings at the discretion of the user. In addition to encryption, many online businesses have also submitted themselves to independent trust audits as additional assurance for customers.

However, despite the use of encrypted transmission of credit card information, credit card fraud is still a major problem. In fact, although overall credit card fraud has fallen by two-thirds over the past decade, online credit card fraud is triple the rate of bricks-and-mortar fraud, accounting for average losses of 14 cents of every $100 spent. This may not seem like much, but it adds up to hundreds of millions of dollars, since online retail accounts for more than 10 percent of the value of all credit card transactions.[2] Although most sites use encryption to ensure the privacy and integrity of the credit card information during transit across the internet, most credit card fraud is committed by using stolen card numbers. In most cases, only a name, credit card number, and expiry date are necessary to order goods and services online and have them shipped virtually anywhere in the world. Since it is not difficult to obtain someone's credit card number, it should not come as a surprise that fraud is rampant. For example, one scam is to sell goods in an online auction, receive payment from the buyer, and then, using a stolen credit card, purchase the same item from another online retailer who ships the item to the buyer. Online merchants are generally liable for bogus charges, since there is no physical card to check. As a result, some overly cautious retailers reject suspicious-looking, but legitimate, orders, estimated at 6–8 percent of all orders, hurting their profitability. According to the Canadian financial services industry, in 2008 credit card fraud represented $408 million, or about 0.17% of the $241 billion of retail sales. More than 70,000 cards were lost or stolen, and 210,000 were used fraudulently.[3]

To curb this growing problem, several initiatives have been undertaken. On the technology side, the industry put high hopes into new electronic encryption and authentication initiatives such as **Secure Electronic Transaction (SET) protocol**, a method of securing credit card transactions with encryption and authentication technology. Unfortunately, many of these initiatives hoped that consumer's cards would soon be converted to smart cards and, additionally, that smart card readers would become widespread in consumer devices such as

SSL/HTTPS protocols: Protocols for sending encrypted data from a web browser to a server.

Secure Electronic Transaction (SET) protocol: A method of securing credit card transactions using encryption and authentication technology.

personal computers. Unfortunately, smart cards were not as successful as originally hoped, and even today most bank cards are not equipped with smart card capabilities.

Many online merchants, for example, will only ship to the billing address of the credit card holder. In addition, credit card companies have developed new systems to verify the legitimacy of a credit card user without the need for additional hardware (see the Estrategy box on page 127).

In addition to the issue of credit card fraud, there is the issue of transaction costs. Merchant accounts offered by credit card companies cost 3–10 percent for each transaction, depending on the creditworthiness of the merchant and the sales volume. For example, Moneris is one of the largest North American processors of credit card and debit card transactions, handling payments for Visa, MasterCard, and American Express. To use Moneris's system, a company must purchase an SSL certificate. This enables the payment transactions to be encrypted. Customers can enter their credit card information and address on the business website when purchasing goods or services rather than using another site, such as PayPal, to process a payment. Moneris charges a one-time setup fee of $525 plus a monthly fee of $52. In addition, Moneris charges 3 percent for transactions worldwide, regardless of size, plus 25 cents per transaction.[4]

Debit Cards

Canada has one of the highest rates of use of debit cards in the world. There were an estimated 37 million debit cards in Canada in 2009, and debit card use is growing much more rapidly than credit card use. In 2007, the volume of transactions conducted with debit cards rose above that of credit cards.[5] Merchants prefer debit cards because they can avoid credit risk and the costs of late payments, postage, employee theft, and cheque-clearing fees. Other benefits include increased customer loyalty and the ability to track spending.[6]

Innovative uses of debit cards include prepaid cards to pay employees (for example, hourly workers without chequing accounts), replacing traveller's cheques with prepaid cards, and other types of prepaid cards. For example, the reloadable cash cards at Tim Horton's have attracted numerous customers since their inception.

Of course, debit cards are not immune to fraud. Thieves reportedly use hidden cameras to record victims' personal identification numbers (PINs) at automated teller machines (ATMs) and obtain copies of their debit cards. In 2009, about 238,000 cards were reimbursed for being subject to this type of "skimming" fraud. This is up from 49,000 cards in 2004.[7]

Smart Cards

Smart cards are a payment method that has received some support from financial institutions, but they have not yet achieved wide acceptance. Smart cards contain chips with memory, software, and their own operating system. The software includes algorithms and electronic keys for security as well as loyalty programs. One such implementation that has been field tested several times in North America and other parts of the world is MasterCard's Mondex electronic cash system. (Visa has a similar product, called Visa Cash.)

Mondex utilizes a smart card, which is a plastic card that looks like a credit card but contains a microchip that is used like a purse to store information about cash transactions and cash on hand. The card also contains some security features, designed to protect transactions between it and another Mondex card. It also contains security that restricts access to the information on the card. Mondex is easily transportable over digital connections, telephone lines, and the internet, since it is electronic.

The idea is that the card would be "loaded" by the owner at a bank or at a Mondex-compatible ATM and then used at retail and other locations to buy goods, rather like a debit card, except that it is paying out the money stored in its own memory rather than having to log into the buyer's bank account. In this way, Mondex can act as an electronic substitute for cash.

Mondex can be applied in two broad areas, unlike ECash. While ECash can be transported over communications media, it was never designed to be carried by a person like real cash. Mondex, however, can be used in both arenas—the card can be carried around by a person, and the signals can be sent over the internet. This additional flexibility brings it closer to the functionality of real cash.

The acceptability of smart cards depends on their recognition by financial institutions, which in Canada has largely been accomplished, at least in principle. For example, although financial institutions have been slow to implement Mondex, most of the banks still say that it will be launched. There have been field tests in several cities in Canada, including Guelph, Sherbrooke, and Toronto. In addition, Mondex's acceptance for use by people in stores depends on the extent to which the stores themselves have adopted the card readers that are necessary to make the system work. In this respect, the card's progress has been extremely slow to date.

One of the most significant recent developments is the implementation of cards containing chips to replace the traditional magnetic strip credit and debit cards. A PIN will replace a signature. Merchants will not need to store paper receipts. This has been widely implemented in Canada for both debit and credit cards, with the result that many merchants are now equipped with card readers that can read embedded chips. Whether this will lead to increased use of smart cards like Mondex and Visa Cash remains to be seen.

Mondex
www.mondex.com

Across Canada, well over 1 million merchants process payments with Visa or MasterCard. Thus, converting the infrastructure to smart cards will ultimately cost hundreds of millions of dollars, but banks and credit card companies believe that the security and convenience of the cards will make this a worthwhile conversion. If smart cards are combined with personal card readers that can be connected to the internet, this will revolutionize billing and payment systems for ecommerce. This is a global project for Visa, MasterCard, and other payment organizations. Europe is already moving quickly in this direction.[8]

PayPal

Credit cards have become the de facto standard for payments on the internet. However, as mentioned previously, credit card transactions are usually quite expensive and are accepted only by professional online merchants. For small transactions between individual users, PayPal has become a good alternative to sending a cheque through "snail mail." PayPal, which is owned by eBay, is the world's largest online payment service, with more than 200 million member accounts in 190 countries and a payment volume of more than $60 billion in 2008.[9]

PayPal
www.paypal.com

To send money, a user must simply open an account with PayPal. After a deposit is made with PayPal, sending money is easy. A user simply specifies the email address of the recipient, and the transfer is completed. If the recipient is not a PayPal member yet, he or she receives an email with instructions on how to open an account and receive the payment. By storing credit card and bank account information at PayPal, customers can shop from anywhere without giving out financial information. PayPal can also be used to request money and, for a fee, to accept credit card payments. Since PayPal is owned by eBay, it is not surprising that the system is heavily tied in with the eBay auction platform to facilitate payments between eBay members. Because of the success of eBay, PayPal has also been very successful. Much of PayPal's business comes from eBay, with the balance generated by other users seeking the convenience and security that it offers. In fact, thousands of small business owners have turned to PayPal to conduct their back office transactions because of the convenience and security that it offers.

PayPal was founded in November 1999 by Max Levhin and Peter Thiel. The internet was growing at a rapid rate in the early years of the web but lacked a real system for facilitating payments between individual users on the internet. PayPal was founded with the intention of providing a fast and secure way to conduct transactions over the World Wide Web. The venture became an instant success. Within its first year of operation, the company had attracted more than 1 million customers and had secured $100 million in equity financing. The success of PayPal quickly inspired competitors, most notably American banking giant Citibank, to start their own internet payment systems. None of its competitors, however, managed to replicate PayPal's success. In February 2002, the company went public. It didn't take long for eBay to notice the success of PayPal. After all, the payment system was a perfect fit for the auction house. Many of its members already used the service to pay for their eBay purchases. In July 2002, eBay purchased PayPal for US$1.3 billion. The transaction made sense for eBay: PayPal could be tightly integrated with the eBay auction site, and transaction fees could provide an additional source of revenue for the company. Since acquiring PayPal, eBay has linked the PayPal payment services into the auction process. Every auction and every Buy It Now listing now offers the ability to pay for the purchase by using the PayPal service. This integration has been a win-win situation for both companies. eBay members have an additional payment choice, and PayPal has gained a large number of customers. The majority of PayPal's revenues now stem from payments processed as a result of an eBay auction. Of course, this also means additional fee revenues for eBay/PayPal.

PayPal Services What makes PayPal so appealing to many internet users around the world is the fact that all it takes to receive money is an email address. The service lets its users send money securely, cost-effectively, and conveniently to virtually any person or business with an email account. To send money, a credit card or a chequing account is required. The process is quite simple. To transfer $50 to pay for an eBay purchase, a buyer creates a PayPal account and specifies the email address of the recipient. The $50 is then charged to the credit card of the sender. After confirming receipt of the money, PayPal automatically contacts the recipient of the payment. If the recipient is already a known PayPal customer, the money is instantly transferred into his or her PayPal account. If not, PayPal asks the recipient to supply his or her bank information for an electronic transfer of funds. Alternatively, PayPal can also send a cheque to the recipient of the money. In addition to sending payments, PayPal customers can also send a "money request," which is somewhat like a traditional invoice. After receiving the request, the recipient can use the PayPal service to send a payment.

PayPal offers three levels of service. Its basic level, the Personal Account, lets users send and receive money for free. Charges do, however, apply for all credit card transactions. The second account type is called the Premier Account. The Premier Account offers additional services such as lower fees and no limit for receiving credit card payments, special online tools, and an ATM debit card for direct access to funds received via PayPal. The company also offers a Business Account, which provides better reporting capabilities as well as access to multiple logins.

PayPal originally offered payments only in U.S. dollars. More recently, however, it has also introduced payments in other major currencies. Other features that have been added to the service include the ability to download transaction histories and to use mobile devices such as BlackBerrys and mobile phones to access PayPal accounts. PayPal's main source of revenue is transaction fees. Fees are charged for all credit card transactions on a sliding scale according to the volume of transactions. For example, in Canada, businesses with monthly sales of less than $3000 pay 2.9 percent plus 55 cents for each transaction, while for sales between $3000 and $12,500 the fee is 2.5 percent plus 55 cents per transaction. There are no setup fees. In addition, the service also charges a fee for all funds received with a Premier or Business account. Fees also apply to withdrawals from international banks as well as for currency conversions. Comparisons between fees charged by PayPal and credit card companies indicate that PayPal's fees are significantly lower. For example, downloading a 99-cent song from iTunes would cost 16 cents or more through a credit card processor and only 9 cents through PayPal.

Security at PayPal As discussed earlier, a sound ebusiness architecture is vital to the success and the survival of any ebusiness. PayPal is a case in point. As with its corporate parent eBay, security and a reliable infrastructure are vital to PayPal's continuing and uninterrupted operation. Since the company processes financial transactions and handles very sensitive information, issues like security, fraud protection, and data security are paramount to the success of the company. After all, the success of the service depends on the trust and confidence of its users. Compromised user data could prove disastrous, as the PayPal service stores very sensitive financial information about its customers. To protect itself, PayPal relies heavily on encryption technologies. All sensitive data that are exchanged between PayPal's servers and the web browsers of users are encrypted using 128-bit SSL encryption. PayPal's servers are protected both electronically and physically. The systems are housed in secure facilities. They are located behind firewalls to protect them against hacker attacks. Of course, even the most sophisticated security and protection schemes don't help against fraudulent users. A classic example of fraud at PayPal is the use of stolen credit cards. Some criminals try to use the PayPal service to send money to themselves with a stolen credit card. This type of fraud can never be completely eliminated, but it can be reduced through the use of technology.

PayPal claims that merchants suffer less fraud when using its service than with credit card services. PayPal and eBay combined employ more than 1000 people to fight fraud. PayPal says it has developed risk models to detect fraud, as well as a patent-pending method of verifying buyer bank accounts. PayPal has also developed a fraud detection system called Igor. The system is a sophisticated data mining solution that continually scans

PayPal's various databases and cross-references them to detect potential cases of fraud. If, for example, many accounts have been created within a short period of time under a single address, the system "flags" the accounts and alerts a member of PayPal's anti-fraud team. As a result, PayPal estimates its merchants' losses are 0.17 percent of revenues, compared with average losses of 1.8 percent for online merchants that take credit card payments.

Nevertheless, PayPal cannot afford to rest on its laurels. It must stay ahead of the fraudsters who make it the most attacked payment service on the internet. Cyberthieves target its account holders through "phishing"—that is, using emails to fool account holders into revealing critical account information that enables crooks to empty victims' accounts. PayPal's stringent anti-fraud measures designed to address such issues—when a buyer has a dispute with a merchant, PayPal can freeze the merchant's account while it investigates—have caused some dissatisfaction among its account holders. Thus, PayPal must also work on improving its customer service to overcome complaints about frozen assets, rude customer service, and billing errors.

Customer Relationships—PayPal Style PayPal's databases contain a wealth of information about its millions of customers. They include very sensitive information, such as name, address, phone number, email address, and other contact information. Most importantly, PayPal stores bank account and/or credit card data for its customers. This information is a burden on the company, because it needs to be protected at all costs. But it is also a very valuable asset. As discussed earlier, data can be used (or "data mined") to detect potential cases of fraud. PayPal's data are aggregated in its customer relationship management (CRM) system. In addition to regular customer data, the CRM system can be used to store and analyze additional information, such as click-stream data and log-file data. The potential use of this collection of data is enormous. For example, the data can be used to analyze whether a customer is eligible for a PayPal debit card. The marketing potential of this information is also substantial. If, for example, the system identifies a very attractive customer with a large transaction volume, PayPal could offer the customer a Premier Account at a preferential rate. Its affiliation with eBay also provides both PayPal and eBay with additional opportunities. PayPal's and eBay's databases could be cross-referenced and analyzed, for example, to gain additional knowledge about customers.

PayPal seeks to be the standard for online payments. In fact, PayPal has surpassed American Express in the number of accounts; however, it has far to go to match the two biggest credit card companies—Visa and MasterCard (see the Estrategy box). For comparison, Visa and MasterCard have 1.2 billion and 680 million cardholders, respectively. Visa's payment volume is more than $3 trillion. However, PayPal is growing much more rapidly than the credit card companies.

Online "Instant" Credit

Major purchases of electronic goods such as computers and home theatre systems may exceed a purchaser's credit card limit. Thus, some online merchants (for example, Dell) offer lease options to qualified purchasers. An online credit system enables customers to go through an online credit screening process that results in them being able to purchase high-priced goods on an instalment basis, enabling them to convert a large one-time charge into a series of smaller monthly payments. For example, a merchant may subscribe to a

Fair Isaac
www.fico.com

Layered Security for Credit Cards

Credit card fraud has become a major issue around the world. As a result, many consumers are afraid to give out their credit card numbers over the internet. The most common fear is that a credit card number will fall into the wrong hands during transit across the internet. Also, there have been many instances of hackers and others obtaining credit card numbers from stolen databases, laptops, and mobile devices and then using them for illegal purposes. To address these issues, online merchants have invested heavily in state-of-the-art encryption technologies. Most consumers feel safe when they see the reassuring 128-bit encryption lock on the bottom of their computer screen. Encryption is a necessary element of security, but it is not sufficient to deal with cases of fraud.

Major credit card companies, including Visa and MasterCard, have implemented layered security to help fight the credit card fraud battle. Visa, for example, has issued a process called Verified by Visa, which adds an additional pin that is needed to make purchases. When a consumer makes a purchase on the internet, the merchant is identified as a Verified by Visa user, and an additional request for the pin comes up to verify the consumer. MasterCard has a similar product, called SecureCode.

Both Visa and MasterCard have also added a code to the back of their cards called the Card Verification Value 2 (CVV2), which is a three-digit security number. The CVV2 proves to the merchant that the consumer is in possession of a real card, which helps to prevent the type of fraud where the criminal only has the card number.

The credit card companies have also been implementing new cards that contain chips containing additional verification information that is transmitted to the credit card company, but this is not helpful for online sales. For Verified by Visa, a cardholder simply has to visit the Visa website and pick a password, which is then associated with the user's account. To make an online purchase, a customer proceeds to the online checkout as usual and submits his or her credit card number. The customer is then prompted to enter a Visa password to approve the transaction. As an added layer of protection for the customer, this online password is directly transmitted to Visa, not to the online merchant, for verification.

Although many initiatives to make online transactions more secure have failed to garner widespread support, verification has been well accepted. Many companies, such as Westjet, Air Canada, and Wal-Mart, have joined the program.

Visa
www.visa.com

Questions

1. How effective do you think Verified by Visa and CVV2 are in preventing fraud? What more can be done?

2. View the webcast at www.visa.ca/en/merchant/VbVwebcast2009/index.html. Do you think the idea of layered security is heading in the right direction, as a response to credit card fraud? Why?

Sources: www.visa.ca/en/merchant/products/vbv/index.jsp
www.mastercard.com/us/personal/en/
http://www.mastercard.com/ca/personal/en/cardholderservices/index.html

service such as that provided by Fair Isaac Corporation, which has created a credit score formula called FICO. Fair Isaac uses 22 data items in 5 categories gathered from 3 major credit bureaus to calculate a score from 300 to 850. The 5 categories are payment history (35 percent), length of credit history (15 percent), new credit (10 percent), types of credit used (10 percent), and debt (30 percent). The score is then used to grant credit and to set the rate of interest on the lease. The monthly lease payments are then charged to the customer's credit card or bank account.

Mobile Payments

Since the mid-1990s, consumers have been promised that cash and plastic cards are going to be a thing of the past.[10] At various times, it has been said that almost every version of mobile technology could be used for payments, including smartphones and wireless smart cards. One company even foresaw that microchips embedded in our clothes would make payments, as we know them, obsolete. Most of the promised payment technologies, however, have never made it past their field test phase, and socks and pants still refuse to pay our bills. It is interesting to note that some of the promised technologies actually have succeeded; for example, smartphones like the BlackBerry and iPhone are widespread. And progress is being made in their use as payment devices. For mobile payment (m-payment) technology to succeed fully, widely accepted standards are required and need to be backed up by reputable organizations, similar to the way that credit cards have developed.

The following section gives a brief overview of two different wireless payment technologies. There are many more technologies out there, and new ones are constantly being developed. Although none of the existing wireless payment technologies have reached a "critical mass" yet, some of them have been quite successful when implemented for a specific purpose or within a particular region.

Wireless Smart Cards The most widespread m-payment systems are wireless smart cards based on **radio frequency identification** (RFID) technology. RFID technology uses radio waves to transfer data between a reader device and an item such as a smart card.

radio frequency identification (RFID): Technology that uses radio waves to transfer data between a reader device and an item such as a smart card.

The technology is simple and inexpensive to deploy. It works by adding a sophisticated wireless chip to a smart card, which can be read by a corresponding reader device. There are several reasons why RFID technology may be the most attractive and promising alternative for m-payments. First, the transmitter chips are cheap and can be mass-produced. Second, the technology does not require a power source such as a battery. Third, the system can be made to be secure, although this is an ongoing issue. Data that are sent between the chip and the reader can be, and usually are, encrypted, and the content of the chip can be read only if the reader device is in close proximity. The fourth, and probably most important, point is that the technology has proven itself in the field and is already in use. In Canada, the best-known payment processing applications of RFID are the Esso Imperial Oil Speedpass system and Shell's similar easyPAY system.

Speedpass
www.speedpass.com

Customers who register for the Speedpass system are issued a plastic key fob with a built-in RFID transmitter. To buy gasoline, a customer only has to wave the key fob in front of the pump to authorize the transaction. The charge is then automatically added to the customer's credit card. A significant security problem with this system is that if the fob is lost, the finder can easily use it at a pump, because there is no password or access code attached to the fob. When the owner discovers the loss, he or she would call the company to cancel the number associated with the fob and replace it with a new number.

PayPass
www.paypass.com

MasterCard is currently testing its own RFID system, called PayPass, in the Orlando, Florida, area. Customers are given a regular MasterCard credit card, which also contains a RFID chip. At participating locations, a customer need only wave his or her card in front of the card reader to approve the transaction. The PayPass program is very promising, because it is backed by MasterCard. Since the cards have a normal magnetic strip, the cards are also "backwards compatible" with the existing credit card infrastructure.

A Canadian company founded in 1985, Telpay has kept up with the times, offering a number of services designed to enable businesses and institutions to make payments electronically. Originally founded as a division of Comcheq Payroll Services, Telpay was the first organization to provide Canadians with the ability to pay by phone. Today, Telpay serves 250 financial institutions and thousands of other businesses, making it Canada's largest, independent epayment provider.

Currently Telpay carries $12 billion in epayments annually and makes it possible for its customers to facilitate epayments 24/7 to anyone in Canada.

Telpay offers a number of products. For example, Telpay for Business facilitates business payments to any individual, supplier, organization, or government department in Canada. Payment details are sent with each payment and can be imported into most accounting systems. Telpay for Business reduces payment costs by as much as 50 percent compared to cheques. Telpay also offers consulting on ebilling. Telpay for Business is a major player in the epayment field in Canada.

Telpay Over the Counter and Telpay Online enable financial institutions to offer their customers low-cost electronic payments by providing front-end payment and banking technology. This can be done online, in a branch, or over the phone. Customers can pay any bill and make funds transfers to any account in Canada. Customers can make all their payments electronically to other businesses and to governments.

Telpay BillerConnect and Telpay Now enable bills to be sent and paid electronically, which is cost-effective and efficient for both the biller and payer. Telpay also offers consulting services on electronic billing.

An international payment module is available, which makes it possible for customers to make payments in all major international currencies. The system requires an agreement with a foreign exchange provider and also accounts for exchange differences for the customers.

Telpay systems are designed to meet common operational and control standards. For example, they facilitate double signatures on payments and enable signing officers to review and approve by email that is security protected.

There is also a direct deposit module for payroll that works with common payroll programs, importing and handling the distribution data. Payroll payments can also be split to different destinations, such as credit cards or utility bills. Deposits can be sent to four different bank accounts.

A user reported that Telpay is easier, faster, and cheaper to use than electronic funds transfer (EFT) provided by the banks or payroll companies such as ADP. It provides a full audit trail. Most importantly, bills can be paid from anywhere in the world.

Telpay
www.telpay.ca

Questions

1. What other services could Telpay offer to utilize current technology?

2. How do you think Telpay has changed since its founding in 1985?

Sources: K2 Enterprises Canada, TelPay Enhances Its Online Payment Services, www.telpay.ca; www.salmon.ca/Mm200808%20Telpay.htm.

Mobile Phones Since most people today already own a mobile phone, these devices are obvious candidates for m-payments, especially smartphones, which have powerful abilities to run applications. Mobile phones with embedded chips based on **near-field communication** (NFC) use magnetic field induction to transfer data between the mobile phone and a reader device, similar to the process described for wireless smart cards. NFC technology uses magnetic field induction to transfer data between a reader device and another device such as a mobile phone. As NFC devices are extremely inexpensive, they can be embedded in all mobile phones.

There are two main advantages to using mobile phones for m-payments. First, mobile operators usually have the necessary billing information for customers and a billing

near-field communication (NFC): Technology that uses magnetic field induction to transfer data between a mobile phone and a reader device.

infrastructure in place. Second, most people carry their mobile phones with them almost all the time. The big advantage is that consumers don't need any additional devices. On the merchant side, systems can be employed under which very limited additional hardware is required, and in some cases existing transaction technology can be used.

One problem with mobile phones is that there are still no standards when it comes to processing payments. European operators who tried mobile phones as payment devices failed to agree on interoperability standards when conducting their field tests. As a result of this, mobile phones are still not really a viable payment alternative for general usage.

Nevertheless, some interesting applications have been developed. One example is a new system to pay parking fees in Austria. The system, developed by Siemens, allows drivers to send a text message with their license plate number and the requested parking time to traffic authorities. The fee is automatically charged to the driver's mobile phone bill. An advantage of this system is that frequent trips to the parking meter to pay for additional time are no longer necessary. Ten minutes before the parking time expires, a reminder text message is sent. The driver can then add more parking time simply by sending another text message to the system. The fee is added to the mobile phone invoice of the driver.

Another interesting application is a soft drink vending machine that accepts wireless payments. The concept is simple and not tied to any specific mobile system. A customer simply dials a 900 toll number printed on the machine. As soon as the number is called, the machine will dispense the drink, and the charge will be added to the phone bill. This type of application could also be used for online payments, as the user only has to use his or her mobile phone and does not need to disconnect from the internet. In addition, there would be no danger of accidentally installing an unwanted dialer. The use of 900 numbers in a payment system is controversial and could leave the door open for fraud. Nevertheless, it may be a viable m-payment alternative in the short run until more standardized systems have been established.

In Japan, many cellphones come with embedded chips that let subscribers transfer funds, pay some bills, buy train tickets and movie tickets, and make purchases at vending machines and convenience stores.[11] Edy is a major contactless payment method that is accepted by more than 40,000 stores in Japan. The system is jointly operated by NTT-DoCoMo, the country's largest mobile phone operator, and Sony. Phones with embedded NFC devices can eliminate the need for plastic debit or credit cards, and many Japanese smart card services are migrating to mobile phones. It is interesting to speculate whether phone companies may begin to compete with banks for transaction processing and funds transfer business.[12]

Electronic Bill Presentment and Payment Systems

So far, we have discussed payment systems. With the growth of ecommerce, there has been a great deal of interest among businesspeople in developing efficient and effective systems for billing and payment over the web—in other words, systems that incorporate online billing as well as payment. The average person receives about 10 bills per month, and about 45 percent of Canadians with internet access pay at least some of their bills online, mostly through bank websites, more than at ATMs or bank branches. U.S. businesses send out about 30 billion bills per year at an average cost of 90 cents each for printing, processing, and postage. Electronic bill presentment promises to be about 40 percent cheaper, representing a significant savings. In addition, electronic bill presentment and related payment processes promise more predictable cash flows to companies, representing another significant potential benefit. However, there is little perceived benefit to consumers from receiving numerous ebills and then visiting company websites to view the bills. Unless people can receive most of their bills at one site, electronic bill presentment will languish. While a number of companies have attempted to exploit the opportunity implied by such savings, banks have been protecting this territory.[13]

Canada Post

The billing and payment system referred to as epost was developed by Canada Post Corporation and the Bank of Montreal. The epost system is an electronic mailbox that people can use for several mail functions, including the ability to receive and pay bills through the epost website. Individuals must register with the site and select the bills they wish to receive online from those available through epost. Then the bills will be received electronically and can be paid online by using a credit card or electronic funds transfer through a bank's payment system.

Canada Post's epost
www.epost.ca

As far as possible, epost emulates traditional mail in an electronic environment. It makes use of high security and provides an electronic post office box free of charge. All pieces of mail are stamped with an electronic postmark to guarantee they have not been opened or tampered with. The security environment includes firewalls and 128-bit SSL encryption technology. Canada Post has been attempting to become the trusted provider in this area; however, to date it has met with little success, and banks have been protecting this territory vigorously by expanding their own services in this area.

Banks

On their websites, banks have provided systems for billing and payment that are among the most popular of this type of service. For several years, banks have offered their customers the capability to log into their online banking pages at their websites. Online banking has offered customers the ability to use a user name and password to log in and view their bank account balances and transactions. They also have the capability to transfer funds from one account to another and pay bills. Ultimately, it will likely be possible for people to deposit and withdraw funds from their home computer, but this will depend on the introduction and integration of smart card technology with smart card readers that plug into the user's computer or phone adapter.

A relatively new addition to the online offerings of banks is email payment. In Canada, five major banks have adopted the Interac Email Money Transfer service developed by Acxsys Corporation. After logging in and navigating to the appropriate webpage, a customer enters the name and email address of the intended recipient. Then the system requires that the customer enter a question to which only the recipient would know the answer. After the sender clicks the send button, the recipient receives an email instructing him or her to go to a website to answer the question and transfer the money immediately to his or her bank account. If the recipient doesn't have online banking privileges, or if his or her bank isn't part of the Interac service, the funds are deposited to the recipient's account after a period of a few business days. The system works very quickly and efficiently. Email payment systems show considerable promise because of their convenience and ease of use.

Acxsys Corporation
www.acxsys.ca

In recent years, banks have expanded their online services to include electronic billing. While online bill payment has been possible for quite a while, it has been used in relation to bills mailed through the snail-mail system. For example, a customer receives a bill—say, from American Express—and then goes to the online banking function on his or her bank's website to pay it online. To make this payment, the customer would need to select American Express from the list of participating organizations as the organization that would receive payment, and then make the payment. Once the selection is made, it would remain in the customer's profile and would not have to be selected from the main list again.

With the addition of electronic billing to their online banking functions, participating organizations can elect to have their bills sent to customers electronically rather than by regular mail. This means that bills can be transmitted faster and more cheaply, and paid online just as the mailed bills would have been paid. This approach is gaining support from many organizations and has a great deal of potential for the future.

CHAPTER SUMMARY

Payment systems have traditionally included cash, cheques, credit cards, and debit cards. Attempts have been made to emulate all of these in digital form for use on the internet. Early attempts to develop digital cash and electronic cheques have failed to gain acceptance by financial institutions and users.

Credit cards continue to be a prime method of payment, but concerns about their cost and security remain. However, the Financial Services Technology Consortium (FSTC) has been seeking ways to improve on the use of electronic payment systems. Public/private key encryption techniques are a prime way to provide security. The Secure Electronic Transaction (SET) protocol uses public/private key technology, encryption, and digital certificates to enable the cardholders to check that online parties are valid merchants qualified to accept their particular credit card, and also allows merchants to validate that the prospective customer has a valid card. Where credit cards are used for payment, numerous systems offer customers an opportunity to register by entering information about themselves, including their credit card information, in a personal profile that is kept in a secure area by the vendor.

Smart card systems have been promoted for decades as alternatives to both credit and debit cards. A smart card is used like a wallet to store information about cash transactions and cash on hand. It also contains security features that restrict access to the information on the card. One such system, Mondex, has received support from financial institutions, but has developed very slowly. One of the most significant recent trends was the implementation of smart cards to replace magnetic-strip credit and debit cards in Canada. With these cards, a PIN replaced a signature, and the merchant does not need to store paper receipts.

PayPal is the most successful online payment system and offers an alternative to the use of credit cards for online purchases. PayPal offers lower fees than credit cards and has a lower rate of fraud. Owned by eBay, it has been growing rapidly and is becoming known around the world. New money transfer systems, such as the email payment systems offered by banks, may catch the interest of people and become competitors to PayPal in the future.

Some newer payment systems also show considerable promise. These include the use of mobile phones and PDAs to execute payment transactions, and wireless smart cards with embedded RFID chips. Online "instant" credit is also an interesting development for encouraging online purchases of large ticket items.

With the growth of ecommerce, there has been a great deal of interest among businesspeople in developing efficient and effective methods of billing and payment systems over the web. As a result, the billing and payment systems in place have evolved considerably, and continue to do so. The principal billing and payment systems in current use include those established by Canada Post, banks, and vendors. Canada Post's epost system is an electronic mailbox that people can use for several mail functions, including receiving and paying bills. Banks have also provided systems for billing and payment that are among the most popular of this type of service. For several years, banks have allowed customers to log into their online banking pages on their websites. In some cases, vendors themselves have also offered online billing and payment systems on their sites. Most of these systems are similar to those of epost and the banks; they offer the ability to transmit and receive bills electronically, view them on the company website, and then pay them online using a variety of payment methods.

Key Terms

near-field communication (NFC) (p. 129)

radio frequency identification (RFID) (p. 128)

Secure Electronic Transaction (SET) protocol (p. 121)

SSL/HTTPS protocols (p. 121)

value-added network (VAN) (p. 115)

MyEbusinessLab Tools for Online Learning

To help you master the material in this chapter and stay up to date with new developments in ebusiness, visit the MyEBusinessLab at www.pearsoned.ca/myebusinesslab. Resources include the following:

- Pre- and Post-Test Questions
- Additional Chapter Questions
- Author Blog
- Recommended Readings
- Commentaries on Current Trends
- Additional Topics in Ebusiness
- Internet Exercises
- Glossary Flashcards

Endnotes

1. B. Grow, "Gold Rush," *BusinessWeek,* January 9, 2006, 69–76.

2. R. Bernier and A. Carter, "Swiping Back at Credit Card Fraud," *BusinessWeek,* July 11, 2005, 72.

3. http://www.rcmp-grc.gc.ca/count-contre/cccf-ccp-eng.htm.

4. M. Ryval, "PayPal Clicks with Entrepreneurs," *Globe and Mail,* April 11, 2006, p. B6.

5. http://canada.creditcards.com/credit-card-news/canada-credit-card-debit-card-stats-international.php

6. E. Pooley, "Debit Card Banks on Small Purchases," *Globe and Mail,* August 12, 2004, p. B7.

7. www.rcmp-grc.gc.ca/scams-fraudes/dc-cd-fraud-fraude-eng.htm.

8. S. Avery, "Smart Cards to Make Credit, Debit Dealings Easier and Safer," *Globe and Mail,* October 11, 2005, p. B9.

9. M. Ryval, "PayPal Clicks with Entrepreneurs," *Globe and Mail,* April 11, 2006, p. B6.

10. M. Der Hovanesian, "The Virtually Cashless Society," *BusinessWeek,* November 17, 2003: 125–126.

11. I. Rowley, "$5,000? Sure, Put It on My Cellphone," *BusinessWeek,* June 6, 2005.

12. "The End of the Cash Era," *Economist,* February 17, 2007, 71–73.

13. J. Alsever, "Here's the Hook: Gifts for Online Bill Payers," *New York Times,* November 28, 2004, p. 7.

PART 2 CASE STUDY
eBAY—THE WORLD'S AUCTION PLACE

When Sir Tim Berners-Lee invented the World Wide Web at the CERN research lab in Switzerland, he could not possibly have imagined the impact of his invention on our daily lives. During the "gold rush" times of the dot-com revolution, a few visionaries saw potential in the new technology and founded companies in their university dorm rooms, b asements, or garages. Giants like Yahoo! and Amazon.com started this way. Although some of the early pioneers broke new ground by effectively using the internet as a new sales channel, many of the new ventures had business models that were not well thought out, or not considered at all. When Jeff Bezos founded Amazon, he didn't really develop a fundamentally new business model. Instead, he took the traditional catalogue mail-order business model and adapted it to the internet. In the early years of the web, most ecommerce sites consisted of a website where products were simply listed, similar to traditional mail-order catalogues. Progressive ecommerce ventures allowed for online ordering, but in many cases one still needed to call the company to order the goods. This period in internet time became known as the brochureware phase. Many online retailers today still follow this rather traditional approach.

eBay, the online auction company, was different. Instead of selling goods and services itself, it acted as an intermediary between buyers and sellers. The company, which today is the largest online trading exchange in the world, has created a completely new business model of a type that is only possible on the internet. Almost everyone in the world has heard of eBay. According to the company's mission statement, eBay aims "to provide a global trading platform where practically anyone can trade practically anything." Although the company originally started as an online flea market, it is now used not only by individual buyers and sellers around the world but also by many companies and even governments as a way to efficiently buy and sell goods and, to some extent, services.

To be fair, eBay founder Pierre Omidyar probably did not intend to develop a revolutionary new ecommerce model when he launched eBay as a hobby in his living room in September 1995. Rumour had it that Omidyar launched eBay as a trading exchange for his girlfriend who collected Pez dispensers, but this story has since been revealed as a publicity tactic. Word about eBay spread quickly around the internet, and people soon began to use it as a trading platform for a wide range of goods and services. The venture quickly outgrew Omidyar's living room as it gained popularity with internet users around the world.

Omidyar has since given up his position at the helm of eBay. He is now a full-time philanthropist but continues to serve as the chairman of the board of directors at eBay. The company realized that the time had come to transition from a "startup leadership" to a more "managed leadership." In March 1998, Meg Whitman was hired as new president and CEO. Although she did not have a background in technology, she did have substantial management experience through positions at Bain and Company (a consultancy), Disney, and Florists Transworld Delivery Inc. Under her leadership, the company continued to grow rapidly and, in 1999, eBay went public. The company is now listed on the NASDAQ stock market. Whitman went on to other things in 2008.

eBAY: A SOPHISTICATED GLOBAL FLEA MARKET

On an average day, millions of items are listed on eBay. People from around the globe use the eBay platform every day to buy and sell items in countless different categories. Virtually everything is traded on eBay, including books, antiques, collectibles, electronics, home furnishings, sporting goods and memorabilia, and movies and DVDs, to name just a few of the categories. Almost every item imaginable can be found on eBay. Expensive items such as cars and real estate are also traded. Even airplanes and other unusual items have been sold (and, of course, bought) on eBay. The company, which calls itself a community, has tens of millions of registered members from around the world. In addition to its main website, eBay.com, the company also operates localized sites in more than 20 countries, including Canada, Australia, Germany, Japan, the United Kingdom, and India. eBay is also present in the Latin American and Chinese markets through its investments in MercadoLibre and EachNet.

Traditionally, auctions were the best way of selling something while obtaining the best selling price possible. Although this process is efficient, it is also cumbersome. Auctions were usually conducted by auction companies, who sold items for their owners on commission. Items had to be physically transported to the auction houses and potential buyers had to physically gather at the auction house. This made auctions a very complicated form of trading, and they were typically only used for trading certain kinds of goods. eBay's business model, which combines the traditional auction method with the global internet, has brought auctions into everyone's home and office.

eBay has become so successful because it combines the traditional price-finding technique of auctions with the all-familiar yard sale. In a sense, eBay has created a sophisticated global flea market. Users register with the eBay website and list an item they would like to sell. If, for example, Tony in Toronto wants to sell the ugly old painting from his basement, he can simply list it on eBay. He creates an account, lists his painting, and specifies a starting bid price. His painting is immediately listed on the eBay website. Over the next few days, interested buyers can submit their bids for the painting, just as they would in a traditional auction. At the end of the auction period, Heather from Halifax has won the auction for the beautiful antique painting, which would look great in her living room. She sends Tony a cheque, and he ships the painting. After the transaction is completed, Heather can rate Tony as a seller on the eBay website. Her review becomes part of Tony's eBay profile and can be seen by other potential future buyers. This feature is very useful in creating trust in the eBay community. A positive rating can have a substantial impact on the sales prospects of a seller, and it can give the buyer confidence that he or she can trust the seller. A bad rating, on the other hand, can severely hurt a seller's chances of selling an item at a decent price. The rating system is an important aspect of eBay, since buyers and sellers don't know each other and are often several thousand kilometres apart. Since eBay would not work without trust, it is important that buyers have a way of finding out about other buyers' previous experiences with a seller.

eBay also offers a variety of additional transaction options. In addition to its auctions, the company offers a Buy It Now option, where goods can be purchased immediately at a fixed price. In addition, eBay operates a special section called eBay Motors, which is dedicated to buying and selling vehicles.

eBAY'S REVENUE MODEL

eBay never takes ownership or possession of any of the items sold on its trading platform. Instead, the company earns its money with a two-tiered fee structure. First, it charges an "insertion fee" for each listing. A second transaction fee, or "final value fee," is charged after an auction has ended. These fees are always paid by the seller. As the sale price increases, the fee gradually decreases.

EXCHANGING PAYMENTS AT eBAY

Initially, one weak spot of eBay was the exchange of money between the buyer and the seller after an auction has ended. In a traditional ecommerce setting, customers typically pay for their purchases with a credit card, which (in most cases) also provides reasonable protection against fraud. In the early years of the internet, the web lacked a satisfactory method for allowing people to exchange payments with each other while offering reasonable assurances of trust and security. The only two options were, in many cases, cheques and money orders—which had to be done offline and were obviously not the best solution for either the buyer or the seller. This payment dilemma proved to be especially difficult for eBay, since it depended heavily on its members' ability to exchange payments. To address this problem, eBay acquired PayPal, an online payment system that lets users exchange payments directly over the internet.

REASONS FOR eBAY'S SUCCESS

The success of eBay is truly astonishing. No one would have expected that an online trading site for Pez dispensers would, within such a short time span, become a global auctioning powerhouse. There are several reasons eBay has achieved such success, but mainly, it was a good idea at a good time. Before the arrival of the web, no one could have imagined the possibility of linking individuals around the country and around the world together to enable them to trade directly with each other.

Peer-to-peer is a buzz word in the technology industry. The term, first coined by music-sharing service Napster, refers to a network without any central control. Although eBay does have a "central point" in its network, it can be argued that eBay turned commerce into a peer-to-peer network: Every participant can trade with everyone else, and everyone can be a buyer as well as a seller. This truly is a new concept compared to the "old" mail-order type business models.

Another important reason for eBay's success is the small risk it takes compared with other trading companies. Since the company only acts as an intermediary, it does not have to worry about storing inventory or shipping orders to a customer. During more difficult economic times, eBay will most likely earn less commissions and fees, but it is never faced with having to write off parts of its inventory. This essentially minimizes the risk for the company and makes eBay's business model very scalable.

A third reason for eBay's success is its combination of auctions with the internet. Collectibles have long ago stopped being the primary market for eBay. Instead, many businesses and even governments have found in eBay an efficient platform and a viable alternative to their old ways of doing business. Even some large companies now offer their products or surplus production on eBay. In addition, eBay has proved very useful in determining the right price for a product. It has become practice in many companies to use eBay as a price-finding tool. By simply offering a new product on eBay, a seller can quickly determine how much buyers are willing to pay for an item. Using eBay to find out this information has often proven to be more accurate than many marketing estimates—without the need for lengthy and expensive market analysis studies.

THE COMPETITION

Its unique combination of success factors has made eBay one of the prime dot-com companies, one that has largely been unmatched. Although there are and have been other auction websites on the internet, none have posed a serious challenge for eBay's predominance. Some of eBay's larger dot-com rivals, however, have moved into the auction business. Search engine giant Yahoo!, for example, offers auctions. In addition, Yahoo! has made it possible for smaller businesses to offer their goods as part of the Yahoo! shopping portal. This service aggregates smaller sellers under the Yahoo! umbrella.

Another more serious competitor is online retailer Amazon. The company, which started as an online bookstore, has also become an ecommerce powerhouse. Amazon now offers, either directly or through partners, a full assortment of goods. In addition to its traditional "etailing" business, Amazon has also begun to offer used goods through several different sales channels. Amazon.com Auctions offers eBay-style auctions. Amazon Shops let individuals and small businesses set up a presence in Amazon's online mall, similar to Yahoo!'s shopping mall. A third offering by Amazon is called Amazon Marketplace. Amazon Marketplace lets Amazon customers and other businesses list their new and used products alongside those of Amazon. If, for example, a customer wants to buy a Nokia mobile phone on the Amazon website, he or she would be offered a new phone by Amazon, as well as (potentially) cheaper offers on Amazon Marketplace. Before Amazon Marketplace, a customer might have compared the Amazon offer to an offer from eBay. By allowing competition with itself on its own site, Amazon has made a strategic move to keep customers away from eBay.

POTENTIAL THREATS

As powerful and stable as eBay is at the moment, there is also a substantial potential for threats. All of the factors that have contributed to eBay's success, which were described earlier, could also lead to problems for the company. The very scalable infrastructure is easy to replicate. Theoretically, one computer in an entrepreneur's living room, connected to the internet, is enough to create a competitor. Other larger companies may also be interested in a piece of the pie. The offerings of Yahoo! and Amazon are good examples of this trend. By becoming too large, eBay could also be trying to be too many things to too many people. More specialized sites may be better able to cater to certain market segments.

eBay's success has been remarkable, but it can't take anything for granted, as the internet continues to pervade business and there are new entries into the world of ebusiness every day.

eBAY ARCHITECTURE

In the early days of the web, a hosted website with some basic information about a company and an email address were enough to establish an internet presence. This has since changed, and global ebusinesses like eBay now require a well-structured (ebusiness) architecture and stable infrastructure. Ebusiness architecture refers to the IT infrastructure of a company, but covers a wider spectrum of issues, including everything a company needs to conduct its business and to remain in business. For a pure-play ebusiness such as eBay, its architecture starts with its IT infrastructure. This includes all of the technology needed for the company to conduct its day-to-day operations, such as servers, data storage systems, and networking technologies. For a company such as eBay, IT infrastructure is clearly a major enabler to remain competitive. After all, a bricks-and-mortar auction house can still hold auctions without electricity. eBay, of course, would be shut down completely without power.

Although the specific technology infrastructure of eBay is well beyond the scope of this case, it does deserve some attention, as it is a good example of the growing pains of a company. When Omidyar first developed eBay in his living room in 1995, the system was quickly written in the C++ programming language. eBay calls this original system eBay Version 1. As the company grew, eBay's systems grew along with the company. Although the system was continually expanded and eventually became eBay Version 2, it was nevertheless still based on the original Version 1 written on Omidyar's personal computer. As eBay continued to grow, it became increasingly difficult to maintain a system that was originally intended for only a few users and adapt it for millions of users. eBay also became more and more concerned about outages, which began to occur at increasingly frequent intervals as the site grew. One outage lasted almost three days. Not only did lengthy outages erode customer and investor confidence in eBay as a company, they also translated directly into lost revenues. In 2000, eBay decided that it needed to change its entire technology infrastructure to be able to continue growing and to remain competitive. For Version 3 of the eBay system, the company established the following architectural principles and objectives:

- performance, scalability, and availability
- business continuance
- functionality, with the specific need to absorb business changes
- security, including authorization/authentication protocols and data integrity
- open-standard components for vendor product interdependence

This list shows that eBay tried to move from an undefined and unstructured system that evolved during the early years of the company to a more structured and defined ebusiness architecture. In 2001, eBay decided to use a very scalable infrastructure solution which is based on the J2EE Java platform.

SUPPLY-CHAIN MANAGEMENT AT eBAY

Although eBay is widely known for the auctioning of goods between individuals, it has become much more than that. Since its beginning, eBay has extended into the business supply chain of established businesses of all sizes, facilitating both the purchase and sale of goods. In fact, this ebusiness startup may have initiated a new approach to the automation and integration of business supply chains.

One example of a business using eBay as a sales channel is Reliable Tools Inc., a machine-tool shop that listed some items on eBay in 1998 because of an industry downturn. The products included heavy machinery, such as a 2300-pound milling machine. The items, even the huge machinery, sold quickly, and since then Reliable has become a regular eBay customer. By 2003, it was up to $1 million in monthly eBay sales, which constituted 75 percent of its total business. Prompted by this success and others, eBay established an industrial products marketplace that in 2004 grossed sales of US$1.2 billion, and continues to be highly profitable.

eBay also has established a market for selling automobiles online, called eBay Motors. To start this line of business, eBay bought an existing auction company that specialized in cars for collectors, Kruse International, for US$150 million in stock. Then it arranged a deal under which it would include listings from the online classifieds site AutoTrader.com. It also arranged insurance and warranty plans, and shipping and inspection services.

In a related move, Toyota Motor Sales U.S.A. Inc. was the first automaker to sign a contract for exclusive automaker sponsorship on eBay. As part of the agreement, Toyota launched a site from which it showcases its entire new vehicle line-up, links to item listings on eBay, and special promotional offers.

As a result of these initiatives, sales of cars and car parts through eBay topped the US$5 billion mark, putting eBay ahead of the number-one U.S. auto dealer, AutoNation, in number of used cars sold. About half of the sellers are bricks-and-mortar dealers.

eBay also started another line of business: It began offering third-party equipment financing by Direct Capital Corporation through a new service on its site. This new service provides business buyers with financing options for industrial equipment and information technology. The equipment financing applies to a broad range of categories, including computers, networking, telecom, construction, agriculture, metalworking, restaurant, commercial printing, and medical equipment. "Buyers can preserve working capital, leverage significant tax advantages, and bundle in shipping costs," said Jim Broom, CEO of Direct Capital. "Sellers benefit from the reimbursement of eBay final value fees, attracting more buyers, and have the added assurance of selling to pre-approved bidders."

Use of the equipment-financing program is streamlined for both sellers and buyers. Sellers simply enrol in the program and include a link to the financing service within their eBay item listings. Buyers complete an online application and, once approved, are able to purchase items on eBay up to a specified financing amount. Once a transaction is completed on eBay, Direct Capital will remit to the seller, via PayPal, the purchase price of the item, the eBay final value fee, and any associated PayPal fees. The equipment financing program can be accessed via eBay Business. More recently, eBay has also been in negotiations with a major partner to provide small-business lines of credit.

A very significant feature of all the new big business entrants into eBay is that they are not all using the auctioning method, which of course was eBay's signature from the beginning. Giant companies such as Sears and Walt Disney are selling brand-new items there as well. More than a quarter of the offerings are listed at fixed prices familiar to mass-market consumers. In this way, eBay is entering the mainstream of mass retailing, probably the largest market segment in the economy.

Equipment Financing for eBay

http://financing-center.ebay.com/ebaybusiness/

As a result of all this new activity, eBay has morphed into something quite different than what it was when it started. It has changed from an auctioning site, used largely by individuals selling off used and odd-lot items, into a large-scale collaborative ebusiness. In 2007, people bought and sold over US$59 billion in merchandise on eBay. Meg Whitman referred to this phenomenon "the eBay economy."

A collaborative business requires a collaborative approach to management. It's important to make all the participants feel like they are in charge of their own business activities, and not to annoy them to the point that they want to leave. The big-business participants are really customers of eBay as well.

The whole eBay environment is very transparent. Through the web, eBay's participants have access, 24/7, to every trend, every sale, and every new regulation in the eBay world. The spread of information means that everyone has more power, but this can make life miserable for managers who fail to adapt. The key for management is to embrace the transparency and use it to turn customers and vendors into collaborators and colleagues.

One of eBay's more unique institutions is called the "voice of the customer" under which, every couple of months, eBay brings in a dozen or more sellers and buyers to ask them questions about how they work and what else eBay needs to do. Also, at least twice a week, it holds hour-long teleconferences to poll users on almost every new feature or policy, no matter how small.

This means the company must take a laissez-faire approach to management, based on co-operation and finesse rather than coercion and force. eBay's executives must follow this approach as well, polling the populace through online town hall meetings and providing them with the services they identify or appear to need. It's a very dynamic approach, a different approach to management.

eBay Toyota Showroom
http://motors.shop.ebay.ca/
Toyota-/6016/i.html

The collaboration also extends to collaboration among the customers themselves. By rating each other on transactions, for example, both buyers and sellers build up reputations they must then strive to maintain. This sets standards of behaviour that reinforce eBay's business model—and its appeal. Other companies can learn from this approach. Some have, such as Microsoft. Its world of software keeps growing as a result of the thousands of companies and programmers who add their own applications. As Harvard Business School Professor David B. Yoffie has observed, "You get the incredible leverage of other people doing all your work for you."

While eBay has grown tremendously in the world of big business, it still has a strong interest in maintaining its customer base among the individual users who like to use it to buy and sell items online on an auctioning basis. This is arguably what made eBay what it is in the first place. Therefore the activities that eBay gets into to accommodate the big customers must not alienate its huge traditional customer base. It's a high-wire balancing act.

In addition, eBay wants to continue to expand its traditional business, which means it needs to continue to try to attract new customers, many of whom find the process of registering, listing items on the site, packing them up, and mailing them to be cumbersome and confusing. Moreover, there is the problem of fraud, which has been well-publicized and possibly acts as a deterrent for some.

The more eBay moves into the big business arena, the more difficult it will be to balance the needs of its two major groups of constituents. Can its laissez-faire collaborative approach survive? Also, eBay must continuously look at how it can make its website as easy to use as possible to attract more small business and individual users. It may well require simplifying payments, reducing the hassles of shipping goods, and cracking down on the rising number of crooks who are prowling the site. But this would require management to push through the necessary reforms, which may require a more forceful management approach.

The future of eBay depends on maintaining a partnership between the company and those who sell on its website.

Questions for Discussion

1. What lessons does the eBay experience offer for the management of other ebusinesses?

2. What are the implications of moving to fixed-price retailing for eBay? Is fixed-price retailing compatible with eBay's traditional auctioning approach?

3. How does eBay management structure the strategic initiatives of eBay to balance the interests of small business and individual users with those of big business users?

4. What should the main elements of eBay's business strategy be for the next year?

Sources

C. Davis, "Expand Your Business with eBay," National Business Association, www.nationalbusiness.org/nbaweb/Newsletter2005/2082.htm, accessed October 15, 2007; G. S. Black, "Is eBay for Everyone? An Assessment of Consumer Demographics," SAM Advanced Management Journal, January 1, 2005, www.accessmylibrary.com/coms2/summary_0286-19154096_ITM, accessed October 15, 2007.

Chapter 7
Supply-Chain Management

Learning Objectives

When you complete this chapter you should be able to:

1   Describe the process and components of supply-chain management (SCM).

2   Identify and describe the forces affecting SCM.

3   Explain how ebusinesses can use technology in SCM.

4   Contrast the traditional supply chain with the internet-enabled supply chain.

5   Outline how business process reengineering can be carried out and why it is necessary as part of implementing SCM.

6   Describe partnership strategies and implementation concerns for SCM.

7   Describe order fulfillment/delivery/reverse logistics issues related to SCM.

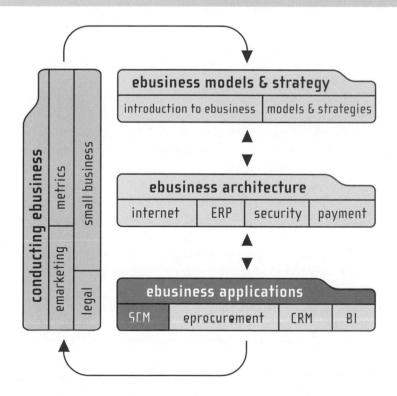

INTRODUCTION

In *the world is flat*, Thomas L. Friedman (New York: Farrar, Straus & Giroux, 2005) describes the "ten forces that flattened the world," many of which relate to the information technology–enabled supply chain.[1] The proliferation of a standardized, internet-based platform, made more accessible through the introduction of the web browser (via HTTP), led to interconnectivity and permits the dynamic updating (via DHTML) of information accessible on demand to users from sources around the globe. Internet-based technologies provide more effective ways for corporations to communicate with stakeholders. The convergence of desktop computers, modems, global communication networks, standard protocols (e.g., TCP/IP, SMTP, X.400, X.25, HTML), and standard applications (e.g., Excel, Word) established a basic interoperable platform for information storage, manipulation, and communication. The proliferation of tools (e.g., wireless technology, file sharing, laptops, tablets, smartphones) that make data digital, mobile, personal, and virtual, is predicted to further enhance all the other forms of collaboration. Workflow software, which enables software and hardware interoperability, allows for diverse processes to be integrated and optimized with little regard to their physical location.

All of these tools have made the corporate supply chain highly automated, often managed by computer-based logistics and optimized by third-party logistics service providers. Information flows resulting from this development are significant both in terms of amount and importance to the success of the business. As a result, supply-chain management (SCM) has become an increasingly important component of corporate strategy over the past several years. Driven by the need for companies to reduce costs and prices while improving customer service and product quality, SCM is also recognized as an essential aspect of ebusiness implementation. Customers making web-based orders tend to expect very fast service, which means that the supply chain must be particularly efficient.

The supply chain is the set of processes that encompasses everything from purchases of raw materials or resources through to final delivery of a product or service to the end consumer. Therefore, the supply chain includes sourcing, transportation, manufacturing, distributing, wholesaling, retailing, and final delivery of goods. The chain is not necessarily a linear or simple process: some authors have suggested that "supply web" is a more appropriate term to describe the complex interrelationships involved in the supply chain.

SCM involves the oversight of materials, information, and finances as they move in a process from supplier to manufacturer to wholesaler to retailer to consumer. It involves coordinating and integrating these flows both within and among companies.

Dell Inc. is an excellent example of a company that has been able to maximize the efficiency of its supply chain to allow for reduction of costs, reduced inventories, increased speed of delivery, and customized (made-to-order) products for its customers over the web or by direct telephone order. (See the New Business Models box for a discussion of Dell's make-to-order approach.) Throughout this chapter, both the strategic and technological aspects of SCM will be discussed.

supply-chain management (SCM): The process of coordinating and optimizing the flow of all products or services, information, and finances among all players of the supply chain.

Supply-chain management (SCM) is the process of coordinating and optimizing the flow of all products or services, information, and finances among all players of the supply chain, from raw material provider to the end consumer. SCM includes functions such as forecasting the demand for various types of materials, ordering from suppliers in economic order quantities, inbound logistics, warehousing, manufacturing, outbound logistics, sales, and delivery to the end consumer. Therefore, we can say that the supply chain includes upstream, internal, and downstream components, all of which need to be effectively managed.

Innovations in Supply-Chain Management at Dell

Dell Inc. is widely recognized as a leader in the sale of customized computers through the web. Users can log in (www.dell.com), design the computer they want, and order it online. Dell's job is to source the components, assemble, and ship the computer in the very short timeline that online customers have come to expect. A key to Dell's ability to achieve this performance is its use of SCM. Dell is one of the world's leading companies in SCM. Its make-to-order approach to ebusiness was recognized early as an industry-changing concept that involved numerous changes to the supply chain. The initial goal at Dell was to reduce inventories, increase efficiency, reduce obsolescence, and facilitate the delivery of custom products to customers. To achieve this goal, Dell began to "substitute information for inventory." By 1998 Dell had reduced its inventory levels to approximately seven days but was not satisfied. Compared with many traditional industries and other competitors, seven days was a risky inventory level that could result in stockouts and poor customer service.

Supply-Side Streamlining

Dell decided that it was necessary to increase the level of information sharing with key suppliers to better facilitate planning. Customized webpages for top suppliers were created that allowed access to Dell's forecasts, sales data, customer information, defect rates, and other product-related information. In addition, Dell began to require its suppliers to share the same types of detailed information, to allow for improved planning at their point in the supply chain. Through effective communication, high-technology solutions, and sound planning, Dell has reduced inventories for many items to a level measured in only hours rather than days—creating a true just-in-time inventory system.

After establishing strong links with suppliers, Dell also extended its communications through the supplier portal **valuechain.dell.com**, allowing for more complete exchange of information between suppliers and the company. In late 2000, Dell extended the portal with a web-based supply-chain initiative (coined DSI2) aimed at improving forecasting further up the supply chain. The goal was to share information with second- and third-tier suppliers and increase the effectiveness of the complete supply chain (see figure 7.1).

Customer Focus

Dell has also worked to implement SCM on the customer portion of its supply chain. To improve sales and customer

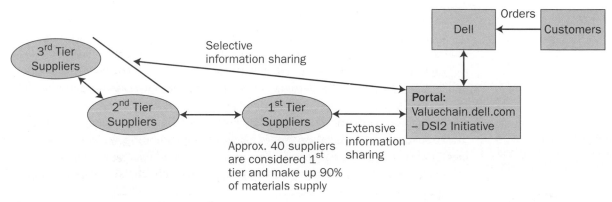

Figure 7.1 Dell's supply-chain configuration

Dell's supply chain involves information sharing by its members.

>

service, Dell created "Premier Pages" for many of its business customers (80 percent of its business), which aimed to reduce the complexity of ordering. The Premier Pages were established in conjunction with customers such as Ford Motor Company, and held information on pre-approved product configurations and established pricing—effectively taking several steps out of the traditional purchase order process. Ford estimates that this initiative alone saved US$2 million in procurement costs and is very satisfied with its relationship with Dell.

Service Enhancement

After achieving great success in the core of its supply chain, Dell decided to apply similar management concepts to its customer service and support divisions. Again focusing on the customer, Dell set goals to provide high-quality service, on time, and at reasonable prices, as a means of bolstering commitment to the brand. To improve its service area, Dell decided to partner with UPS SonicAir for parts inventory management and distribution to ensure its important same-day and next-day services. Through effective partnership and supply-chain strategies, Dell has achieved a 95 percent service level for parts availability and on-time delivery. Considering that Dell handles approximately 60,000 calls per day, this is an impressive accomplishment.

Calls are screened first at the high-tech call centre, where staff connect through the internet to the customer's machine to identify any problems. Each product is embedded with diagnostic equipment so that Dell is able to analyze many functions remotely, as well as access product information and configuration to ensure parts availability. Unless the call is handled remotely, the service request is logged and Dell's service processes take effect.

Dell uses electronic data interchange (EDI) and web technologies to relay service requests immediately to both SonicAir and a technician to facilitate planning on a tight schedule. At that point SonicAir's logistics system ensures that required parts are moved to the appropriate location and confirms the schedule with Dell. Technicians are scheduled to work at either a repair depot or the customer's location, and arrival of the parts and technician is coordinated.

Despite the sophistication of Dell's supply chain, the company was scoring poor marks on customer service and losing sales because of it. The blogosphere was full of uncomplimentary stories about Dell. Thus, in 2005 Dell launched a Direct2Dell blog to hear about customer service issues, followed by IdeaStorm.com to get input from customers. Apparently, Dell's cost-cutting supply chain, extensive use of outsourcing and offshoring, and reliance on call centre metrics that motivated efficiency of call handling over effectiveness of service were undermining Dell's other supply-chain successes.

Dell
www.dell.com

Questions

1. Dell enjoyed success in its strategy for several years. What went wrong? What should it do now?

2. What other industries do you think would benefit from Dell's supply-chain model?

Sources: Jeff Jarvis, "Dell Learns to Listen," *BusinessWeek*, October 29, 2007, 118–119; A. Saccomano, "Dell Computer Builds Service," *Traffic World 259*, no. 4 (1999), 26–27; "Dell Aims Web-Based SCM Program at Forecasts," Electronic Buyers' News (August, 2000); T. Stein and J. Sweat, "Killer Supply Chains," InformationWeek (November 1998).

A number of terms are used interchangeably with or are closely related to SCM, such as "value-chain management," "integrated logistics," "integrated purchasing strategies," and "supply-chain synchronization." Keep in mind that many business terms are adapted to suit specific industry and company preferences. "Logistics" is the term you may commonly hear used and is now considered by some to be nearly interchangeable with "SCM." Traditionally, **logistics** is the process of planning, implementing, and controlling the efficient and effective flow and storage of goods, services, and related information from point of origin to point of consumption. In essence, the supply chain integrates a number of very important topics in ebusiness. For instance, business-to-business (B2B) ecommerce is an essential component of managing the buy side or the sell side of the supply chain. Business-to-consumer (B2C) ecommerce is an essential component of managing the sell side of the supply chain for organizations that deal directly with the end consumer. B2B

logistics: The process of planning, implementing, and controlling the efficient and effective flow and storage of goods, services, and related information from point of origin to point of consumption.

has been affected substantially by SCM, as well as eprocurement and trading exchanges, which are discussed in more detail in chapter 8. Both B2B and B2C have been shifting to the customer focus of business through customer relationship management (CRM), which is the topic of chapter 9. In this chapter, SCM is discussed from an inter-organizational perspective to facilitate an understanding of its importance to success in ebusiness.

THE TRADITIONAL SUPPLY CHAIN

IN THE TRADITIONAL SUPPLY-CHAIN MODEL (SEE FIGURE 7.2), SUPPLIERS PRODUCED goods in the most efficient manner for their business (typically large batches), and sent large orders to customers (either retailers or wholesalers). This system was referred to as the **push system**, where vendors produce product and the end consumer chooses whether or not to purchase what has been made. The suppliers produce goods based upon their efficiencies and push them to customers, rather than relying on demand to determine production. The system was most effective in the early days of manufacturing, as a means of driving unit costs down and bringing prices within the reach of most people. The best example of this is the mass production assembly-line techniques used by Henry Ford. The system worked best for highly standardized products in markets where there was very high demand. The movement of large orders was considered to be a cost-effective method of production, but it required inventory to be held at various stages of the supply chain. The manufacturer would hold raw materials as well as finished goods, while downstream members of the supply chain would each hold inventories of their own. Creating large batches of product was considered efficient for each individual company, but supply chains became burdened with excess inventories. As buyers became more discriminating, and markets more narrowly defined, the traditional push system grew less cost-effective because of increased production costs, storage costs, cycle times, obsolescence, and consumer wait times.

Early attempts to improve the efficiency of the supply chain involved the use of EDI to transmit business documents between supply-chain firms. Interestingly, the railroad companies were behind this innovation, followed by retail store chains such as Sears and Kmart and auto giant General Motors. Despite the efficiencies of sending electronic documents through EDI, many firms were unable to drastically improve performance due to difficulties in setting standards for the EDI format across many supply-chain members. In addition, the information being transferred was often based on data that came from legacy systems that lacked timeliness and, thus, accuracy.

push system: A supply-chain model in which suppliers produce goods based upon their efficiencies and push them to customers, rather than relying on demand to determine production.

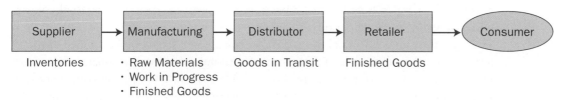

Figure 7.2 The traditional supply chain

The traditional supply chain was focused on efficiency of production gained through batch manufacturing that often resulted in excess inventories throughout the supply chain.

Common attempts at SCM have focused on reducing inventories and achieving greater levels of efficiency within the value chain. However, simply reducing inventory levels along the chain may not be enough in the modern business environment. Thus, Walmart promoted radio frequency identification (RFID) tags as a SCM efficiency measure aimed at improving the speed and accuracy of information flows in the supply chain and to reduce stockouts.

FORCES AFFECTING SCM

THE RAPID PACE OF CHANGE IN THE BUSINESS WORLD TODAY HAS AFFECTED SCM in a number of ways. The following are some of the major forces of change:

- globalization
- mass customization
- price sensitivity
- customer focus and time to market
- just-in-time inventory and inventory reduction
- enterprise resource planning
- outsourcing

Globalization

While companies continue to expand their global presence, challenges to the efficiency of the supply chain become more complex. For example, establishing a reliable transportation and delivery system in a foreign country is complicated by domestic policies, tariffs, and customs regulations. When customers are waiting for delivery, the supply chain needs to perform well. Slow delivery from a foreign supplier can result in lost sales, disgruntled customers, and negative publicity. (The impact of globalization on ebusinesses is also discussed in chapter 13, in connection with privacy, taxation, and other legal aspects of doing business over the internet.)

Mass Customization

The advent of ebusiness has shifted some of the power from companies to consumers, resulting in consumers asking for products or services that are tailored to their specific needs. The internet and computer technology have played a major role in enabling businesses to meet the needs of consumers more easily by simplifying the process of customization, data capture, and information sharing with partners in the supply chain. For example, Dell allows customers to customize their computer system by selecting various components ranging from internal random-access memory (RAM) to external colours, while providing a very rapid turnaround time. To support this service successfully, Dell must be able to quickly establish production plans, purchase required components, and arrange shipping of its products. This form of customization is very popular with customers and, for a time, gave Dell a tremendous competitive advantage. However, eventually Dell's competitors such as HP developed ways of competing against Dell; for example, by creating more attractive looking computers that were pre-configured with the most popular features and therefore required no customization, and were competitively priced due to economies of mass production as contrasted with mass customization.

Price Sensitivity

The internet provides individuals with the ability to easily compare prices and gather product information. As a result, customers are becoming increasingly sensitive to price. When combined with customer preference for customized products discussed earlier, this shift requires businesses to have a very strong grasp of their competition and their supply-chain partners. Internet companies like Priceline.com have also changed the nature of pricing—consumers can now name their price and allow a company to accept or reject their offer. Auctioning sites have had a big impact on pricing as well, since auctioning has made its way into B2B through trading exchanges and sites like eBay.

Customer Focus and Time to Market

The ability to create and deliver new products has become critically important in many industries. Not only is it necessary to be able to innovate and develop high-quality products, it is crucial to be able to do so quickly and continuously. Competitors Intel and AMD are examples of high-tech chip manufacturers that focus on time to market to maintain their coveted market share of the computer industry. A combination of research and development, partnerships, and SCM allows these companies to continually create high-quality products at "internet speed."

Just-in-Time Inventory and Inventory Reduction

Inventory control has been a key objective of participants in the supply chain for many years. However, limited or ineffective data sharing and communication have traditionally been major obstacles to reducing inventories. The increasing use of the internet has improved the ability of firms to share information with other supply-chain members, even to the point of sharing common inventory management systems. Having common information is most effective because all members of the supply chain can then work in concert to reduce inventories while meeting customer demands and maintaining order fill rates. Walmart is known for its extensive information systems and its sharing of information with its suppliers to enable them to manage store inventory so that it is at an optimal level. From Walmart's perspective, an optimal level of inventory is one that minimizes stock outs while maintaining the lowest possible amount of inventory so as to minimize storage and handling costs for Walmart.

Enterprise Resource Planning

Enterprise resource planning (ERP) applications have become the norm in large organizations and, to a great extent, help an organization to facilitate SCM. With legacy systems, firms could spend days or even weeks trying to integrate data from sales, inventory, and purchasing systems to effectively plan for future production. This lack of data integration has been largely overcome with ERP systems, which use centralized databases, allowing companies to ensure that everyone is using the same data and to make decisions in real time. Through the use of centralized data, and the linking of the applications that utilize that data, ERP is an effective tool for integrating the supply chain and thus expediting SCM.

Outsourcing

Outsourcing is an arrangement whereby companies shift facilities and activities (including IT infrastructures, platforms and applications) to outsourcers and then integrate them into their global supply chains. Offshoring shifts facilities to offshore outsourcers. Outsourcing and offshoring are increasing and require supply-chain managers to make important supplier selection decisions. For example, in December 2010, the U.S. space agency NASA outsourced its end-user computing services to HP in a $2.5 billion contract covering up to 10 years. HP will provide, manage, secure, and maintain these essential IT services to support NASA's core business, scientific, research, and computational activities.

While many outsourcing decisions are made for cost-reduction purposes, particularly the extensive offshore outsourcing to places like India and Korea, strategically, the decision is also often made to focus on core competencies. The supplier effectively becomes a partner who can dramatically affect the ability of the business to meet its objectives. Coupled with customization and time-to-market forces, outsourcing requires that the supply relationships be strong and well managed. The outsourcing partner must be willing and able to react quickly to required product changes and demand fluctuations. Many of the concepts discussed earlier in this book, such as the use of extranets and cloud computing, can be helpful in establishing effective outsourcing strategies by allowing the supplier to access crucial information on a timely basis.

When an entity outsources significant parts of its operations, it can realize significant benefits. However, it can also encounter risks, such as loss of control over the outsourced operations, inability to monitor performance by the outsourcing service provider, conflicts of interest with the outsourcing service provider, and loss of in-house expertise in the outsourced functional areas. Additional potential issues can arise from cultural differences, unclear ownership and accountability, and inconsistent standards.

Outsourcing contracts should be entered into only after a thorough analysis of the benefits and risks. It is important to include provision for the entity to oversee the outsourced operations to the extent necessary, because it remains responsible for the operations it outsourced and will be held accountable for them by its customers.

THE INTERNET-ENABLED SUPPLY CHAIN

THE INTERNET ECONOMY HAS RESULTED IN DRASTIC CHANGES TO THE ENTIRE supply chain. The push system of old is being replaced by a **pull system** of production. In a pull system, the production of suppliers is determined by the needs of customers who request or order goods, necessitating production. Instead of manufacturers pushing products on to the market, the internet-enabled supply chain (see figure 7.3), is driven by the customers who initiate orders (often for specific or customized products) that result in information flows being passed upstream to suppliers such as manufacturers, distributors, or wholesalers. In some organizations, no product is made until the customer order is known (e.g., Dell), while in others the customer order results in updates to supplier orders so that appropriate inventory levels can be maintained. The major change from the traditional supply chain is that the predominant information flow is upstream as opposed to downstream.

The internet supply chain has also resulted in substantial changes to more than just information flows. Early in the electronic age, some analysts felt that major changes to supply chains would result in disintermediation, and that many businesses would fail if

pull system: A supply chain in which the production of suppliers is determined by the needs of customers who request or order goods, necessitating production.

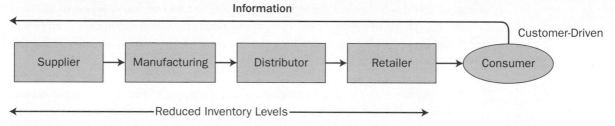

Figure 7.3 Internet-enabled supply-chain information flows

In the internet-enabled supply chain, the customer drives the process, and information flows primarily upstream.

they did not counteract this phenomenon. **Disintermediation** is a change in the supply chain where the provider and consumer interact directly with each other, thereby eliminating the need for an intermediary. The two major categories of disintermediation are (1) when the supplier of a good or service circumvents another member of the supply chain, such as a distributor, and provides the good or service directly to the end consumer and (2) when a new intermediary enters the market using a new business model (often lower cost) to drive out existing intermediaries.[2]

The air travel industry is an example of an industry that has seen some level of disintermediation take place in the area of bookings (see figure 7.4). In the past, nearly all airline

disintermediation: A change in the supply chain where the manufacturer or service provider and consumer interact directly with each other, thereby eliminating the need for an intermediary.

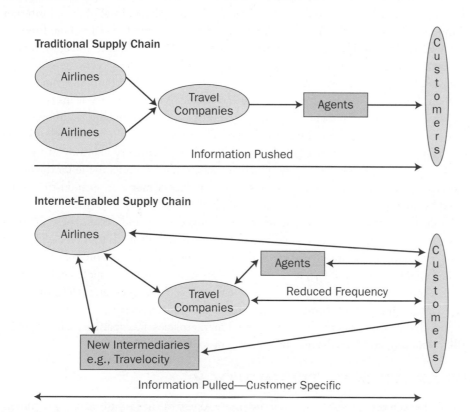

Figure 7.4 Travel industry information flows

The travel industry supply chain has been drastically changed by ecommerce and the internet.

and other travel were booked through travel agents, who had exclusive access to information and provided it to the customer. The airlines, hotel chains, car rental chains, and other travel suppliers provided information to the travel companies which, in turn, rolled out that information to their agents. The agents would then provide information to interested customers. Reliance on manual processes reduced timeliness and accuracy of information.

With the advent of internet communication, the process of booking a trip has been completely transformed. Customers now have access to a great deal of information from a variety of sources on the internet, including information directly from the airlines and other travel suppliers. Thus the travel industry has undergone disintermediation in both major formats. Customers can book flights now in a variety of ways: online directly with the airline, online with new services like Travelocity.com, or through a travel agent. Essentially, the booking area of the travel industry has shifted from a push system to a pull system, whereby the customer can extract information from a variety of sources and make an informed decision.

Some travel agents feel that their services will remain in demand because they are better able than websites to offer travel packages and provide customized solutions and recommendations to travellers. While this may be true to a degree, travel arrangements are one of the most widely used services on the internet. Customers can comparison shop quickly and easily in the comfort of their homes at their own pace, forcing the industries involved to ensure they offer high-quality, reliable service.

Other industries are experiencing disintermediation. For example, banking has undergone a transition, with tellers having largely been replaced by ATMs and internet banking. Apple iTunes, Netflix, and Amazon have disintermediated brick-and-mortar music, video rental, and book stores. However, not all attempts at disintermediation have been successful. Levi's attempted to offer custom jeans directly to consumers through its website, but was faced with difficulties when retailers and distributors became angry and when demand fell short of expectations (customers preferred to try jeans on before purchase). WebVan and Grocery Gateway attempted to disintermediate traditional grocery stores by organizing direct from warehouse deliveries based on a web-based ordering system. This business model has failed miserably, although Grocery Gateway was pulled out of bankruptcy by Longo's Grocery, which appears to have found a niche for the delivery service. As business continues to change, we can expect many other industries to be affected by changes in the internet-enabled supply chain.

While disintermediation has significantly changed some industries, these changes simply force these industries to compete in different ways. This leads to a process known as reintermediation. **Reintermediation** is the process by which companies use the internet to reassemble buyers, sellers, and other partners in a traditional supply chain in new ways. Examples include New York–based Newview Technologies and Houston-based ChemConnect Inc., which bring together producers, traders, distributors, and buyers of steel and chemicals, respectively, in web-based marketplaces. Companies such as Apple, Netflix, Amazon, and Expedia are the pioneers of reintermediation.

reintermediation: The process of using the internet to reassemble buyers, sellers, and other partners in a traditional supply chain in new ways.

INTEGRATION OF TECHNOLOGY

As discussed previously, changes in many aspects of the business environment, including technological changes, have greatly affected how an entity manages its supply chain. While SCM has been strongly affected by the growth of the internet, other technologies such as extranets, enterprise resource planning applications, business intelligence software, application service providers, and other technologies also contribute to the evolution of SCM.

Use of Extranets

Sharing information between supply-chain members has been made significantly more manageable through the use of extranet technologies. For supply-chain members to reduce costs and increase efficiency, information needs to be shared in a reliable, cost-effective manner. Extranet technologies have reduced the usage of EDI as an information-sharing technology due to the simplified and more economical process of using internet technologies. Even so, the cost of providing information on an extranet is much more manageable if an organization's supply chain is fully integrated through the use of technology like ERP.

Extranets allow companies to share information in a much more timely manner than was previously possible through EDI. The use of EDI required inter-organizational standards to be developed, since a request for a shipment would be sent to a supplier and require a reply. Extranets basically automated previously existing processes. Extranet/internet technology allows for the demand forecast to be adjusted constantly, giving the supplier advance notice and allowing for production planning changes to take place sooner. This increase in timeliness of information shortens the production-to-delivery time frame and reduces supply-chain costs. Effective information sharing is a critical element in enabling companies like Dell and Walmart to become highly effective supply-chain managers.

Walmart is famous for sharing its information with suppliers. Its Retail Link system processes tens of thousands of supplier queries per week, providing updates about invoice status, product sales per store, effects of markdowns, and returns on inventory and other detailed information. Retail Link helped Walmart shift responsibility for inventory management from in-store managers to suppliers. By sharing information gathered from store cash registers with suppliers such as Procter & Gamble, Walmart encouraged quicker replenishments and leaner inventories, giving both suppliers and the retailer higher margins.

Thomson Consumer Electronics Inc. made extensive use of an extranet to facilitate communications and information sharing in its supply chain. Analysis of Thomson's customers was carried out through a survey, which revealed that its supply-chain effectiveness was considered weak in on-time delivery and stockouts. As a result, Thomson implemented an integration project by using an extranet and i2's SCM system (see figure 7.5). Customers such as Best Buy, Circuit City, and Kmart agreed to provide detailed information on sales and forecasts to Thomson. Thomson used i2 software [now JDA Software] to analyze the information internally and update its plans and forecasts that were shared with its suppliers. In effect, the extranet facilitated communications and allowed supply-chain members to improve planning. Thomson's supply-chain strategy improved its supplier relationships, increased sales, and reduced rushed shipments due to last-minute decision making.

ERP in SCM

ERP systems have truly become the backbone of ebusiness. To improve decision making in the digital economy, it is essential to have access to up-to-date information. ERP systems allow for effective monitoring of the entire organization and provide essential information

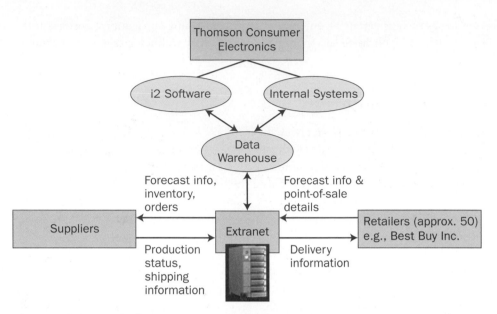

Figure 7.5 SCM at Thomson Consumer Electronics

Thomson Consumer Electronics uses an extranet along with sophisticated applications to control its supply chain.

SOA at Austin Energy

In 2004, Austin Energy in Austin, Texas, launched a service-oriented applications (SOA) project with the objective of streamlining and speeding up its response to emergency power problems. SOA essentially involves the automation of business processes used in providing specific services, and the ordering of those services so they can be provided in a useful sequence. Technology used generally involves Web services and XML—to provide metadata about the processes—along with certain conventional protocols, such as SOAP.

In order to implement SOA, Austin Energy employed consultants from IBM and used some of IBM's application packages. The programs were written in Java, which meant their programmers had to be retrained. Eventually the plan was to implement as many as 75 new applications. They determined that the cost would be no more than maintaining the legacy systems, which the SOA would replace.

Austin Energy's first operative SOA application, called AECall, was completed on May 3, 2006. The very next day, a storm tore through the area, putting some 52,000 customers out of service. It was a major stress test of the new system.

The AECall system was intended to process calls through Austin Energy's call centers. In a three-day period during the storm, the application processed more than 20,000 calls per day; this would have been impossible with the previous application, which was limited to fewer than 4000 calls per day.

As with most other SOA systems, the data used in the applications—in this case, data about customers—is resident in numerous databases, and web services are used to query those databases and draw out the needed data to initiate a power restoration process.

The new application passed the test with flying colours. Austin Energy credited the success of the application and

>

to the functions of SCM. The major difficulty in legacy systems was coordinating and synchronizing data sets to ensure that inventory levels, purchasing requirements, and production plans were all based on accurate and consistent information to meet upcoming orders. In today's business world, a manager is constantly aware of customer demand information and can quickly revise purchasing, staffing, financial, and production information when using an ERP system.

Business Intelligence Software

In an era of information overload, it is essential for companies to have strong data analysis tools to identify critical operating information. At Walmart, data warehousing and data mining assist in better understanding which items sell and which do not; which tend to sell with other specific items; and what types of people shop at particular Walmart stores. That means better decisions in merchandising, inventory, and pricing.

A number of software tools and techniques have emerged to turn raw data into business information, such as data-mining techniques, decision support systems (DSS), and, most recently, business intelligence software. As discussed in the previous section, ERP systems allow organizations to capture data, and many of these systems include analysis tools such as SAP's Business Warehouse (BW) and Executive Information System (EIS) modules. The SAP EIS functions enable high-level reporting of data, and are intended to simplify the analysis of data for information appropriate to decision makers. Most organizations, however, have traditionally determined that custom reports are necessary for their specific organization, which is where the BW module is targeted. This data warehouse allows for customized queries and reporting to be carried out, based on the SAP data.

Business intelligence and specialized software from SAS, Oracle, IBM Cognos, and many other suppliers can improve the usability, impact, and understanding of critical data. Chapter 10 delves more deeply into the features, capabilities, and uses of business intelligence software.

Cloud Computing

Cloud computing is a new term for delivering and consuming IT resources, such as servers, data storage, network bandwidth, and even applications over the internet. The term "cloud computing" stems from the cloud symbol used to represent the internet. There are three well-known cloud service types:

Software-as-a-service **(SaaS)** SaaS uses cloud computing to deliver a specific application (e.g., salesforce.com) over the Internet. The most popular applications being moved to the cloud include email, archiving, CRM, and storage.

Platform-as-a-**service (PaaS)** PaaS is a cloud-based development environment (e.g., Google App Engine, Microsoft Azure) where customers can build their own applications that run on the provider's infrastructure and are delivered to users via the Internet.

Infrastructure-as-a-**service (IaaS)** IaaS, as its name implies, provides customers with a complete Internet-accessible infrastructure including processing, storage, network bandwidth, and other resources upon which they can run multiple operating systems and applications. Providers in the IaaS category include Hosting.com, GoGrid, and FlexiScale.

Cloud computing is gaining popularity due to features such as on-demand access to IT resources, self-service features, rapid elasticity, measured service (i.e., pay-as-you-use), resource pooling, and broad network access. Cost savings and agility are the two biggest reasons that companies are adopting cloud computing. The pay-as-you-use cost model and reductions in required capital expenditures enabled by cloud computing are some of the top reasons that companies are adopting cloud. Also, cloud computing provides dynamic scaling to quickly provision and de-provision IT resources, which adds tremendous business value to new programs and initiatives that companies need to launch in a timely manner. Some industries are moving to the cloud faster than others, with the top three adopters being technology, financial services and legal/professional services.

Cloud computing also highlights issues related to information security, availability, privacy, confidentiality, and integrity. Access controls take on special significance when access to information is available through a cloud. Availability and accessibility of data through the cloud is also critical, since lack of access will prevent any activities that depend on such access. Privacy is governed by the laws of the entity's home jurisdiction. There may be restrictions on movement of data to other, less privacy-conscious jurisdictions. Protecting the confidentiality of business information may be required as one of the terms of doing business with certain business partners, and providing such protection can be more complicated in a cloud computing environment. Finally, information integrity depends on controls over completeness, accuracy, timeliness and validity that are more complex to enforce in a cloud computing environment. Users of cloud computing services should not take information security, availability, privacy, confidentiality, and integrity for granted. They would be well served by service auditor reports on controls at the service organization.

The growth of cloud computing is affecting SCM in a number of ways. It is allowing companies to access software through the internet without hosting and maintaining the systems in-house. To date, logistics and supply-chain software have experienced difficulty in providing technology through the cloud computing model because customization is often required for each business. However, as standards develop and ERP providers increasingly move toward cloud computing models, the provision of SCM technology through the internet will become much more commonplace.

Strategic SCM

To operate effectively, an organization must employ its technology strategically. The adoption of leading-edge technology will yield little benefit unless it is used to facilitate corporate goals, and the same is true of SCM software and applications. The technology to be chosen for SCM must be carefully planned and coordinated so that benefits may be achieved through integration and information.

Boeing recognized that its supply chain was in crucial need of revision in 1997, when delays forced the closure of its production facilities. Since that time, Boeing has planned extensively to build its new technological infrastructure, which consists of its ERP backbone (provided by SSA Global Technologies [now Infor]), forecasting software (provided by i2 Technologies [now JDA Software]), factory floor software, and internet communication tools.[3] Each of the applications was implemented with a common goal in mind—to turn Boeing's assembly line and supply chain into a highly efficient operation. Starting with a backbone ERP system, Boeing added applications that would allow it to more specifically target areas crucial to its success. Given that the lead time to order a plane was approximately three years in the late 1990s, it was essential to be able to forecast several years in advance to achieve supply-chain effectiveness. As such, Boeing adopted i2 Technologies's forecasting software to allow for advanced planning, and also changed many manual processes to EDI and internet transactions. For example, customers were enabled to order parts through the Boeing PART webpage. In addition to adopting technological solutions, Boeing carried out product changes to streamline internal processes. The core components of the aircraft were redesigned to allow for a more assembly line–like production process, with customization taking place at the end of the process wherever possible.

Boeing provides a good example of a company that made strategic use of technology: It established a strategic vision for its supply chain, adopted technological applications in support of that vision, and made process changes internally and externally in support of its strategy. Strategy, not technology, must drive the business. However, since new technologies can dramatically affect companies' competitive position, business strategy must be aligned with the evolution of business-relevant information technology.

Infor
www.infor.com

JDA Software
www.jda.com

Boeing
www.boeing.com

BUSINESS PROCESS REENGINEERING

BUSINESS PROCESS REENGINEERING (BPR) WAS POPULARIZED WITH HAMMER AND Champy's *Reengineering the Corporation* and reflects the requirements of corporations to initiate change to fundamental business processes as a result of the changing business world. Hammer and Champy define a business process as "a collection of activities that takes one or more kinds of input and creates an output that is of value to the customer."[4] Business process change can occur at three major levels—streamlining, reengineering, or organizational change.[5] Streamlining involves relatively minor changes or "tweaking" of existing business processes to facilitate changes occurring in the business. Reengineering is defined as "fundamental rethinking and radical redesign"[6] of existing processes and is therefore a large undertaking. Organizational change has been described as the creation of a process organization by modification of organizational structure. In a process organization, new management-level positions are created that focus on maximization of process efficiency. As discussed in chapter 4, ERP systems such as SAP require that specific processes be adopted to facilitate the technology's "best practices" model. The adopting corporation's current processes often determine the extent of change required, because streamlining may be adequate in cases where processes are similar.

As discussed in the previous section, the evolution of internet technologies affecting IT infrastructure and software is requiring that companies change business processes to integrate them with the technology changes and thereby to maintain their competitiveness. In terms of SCM, business processes include procurement processes, internal operations, sales processes, and numerous other fundamental processes in the business. The adoption of ERP, forecasting tools, SCM, and eprocurement are all changes that will require an organization to re-evaluate and often revise its business processes.

Ford Motor Company was involved in an often-cited BPR initiative in the early 1990s. At that time, Ford's North American accounting department employed 500 people in its accounts payable area, and management thought that by rationalization and automation, this could be reduced to 400. However, it then noticed that Mazda (partly owned by Ford in Japan) had an accounting workforce of only 5 people doing essentially the same task! By reengineering the process, much of the paperwork and cross-checking associated with the department's tasks were either eliminated or automated. As a result, Ford achieved a 75 percent reduction in headcount, not 20 percent.

Ford used to have its purchasing department prepare a three-part purchase order—one part each for purchasing, the vendor, and accounts payable. When goods were received, the receiving department prepared a multi-copy receiving report and sent one copy to accounts payable and kept the other. The vendor prepared a multi-copy invoice and sent a copy to accounts payable. More than 500 people worked in accounts payable matching 14 different data items on the 3 documents and trying to reconcile all the mismatches. Payments were delayed, vendors were unhappy, and the process was time-consuming and frustrating for all the parties.

In Ford's reengineered system, purchasing agents enter their purchase orders into a database application and forward an electronic copy to the vendor. Vendors ship the goods but send no invoice. When goods arrive, the receiving clerk enters three items of data into the system: part number, unit of measure, and supplier code. The computer matches the receiving information with the outstanding purchase order data. If they do not match, the goods are returned. If they match, the goods are accepted and the computer sends an electronic funds transfer payment to the vendor. The reengineered system has saved Ford a significant amount of money and time, and has been a widely quoted example of BPR.[7]

Many organizations have achieved tremendous results through reengineering. IBM's senior vice president of technology and manufacturing stated, "As we set out to reengineer our company, we knew that having world-class information technology simply wasn't enough. Since speed and efficiency were fundamental elements of our strategy, we needed entirely new approaches to our operations management."[8] Through technological innovation and reengineering of operations, IBM saved hundreds of millions of dollars (see the Ebusiness in Global Perspective box for more information).

TRUST AND PARTNERSHIPS OF THE SUPPLY CHAIN

WHEN ORGANIZATIONS BEGIN TO MORE CLOSELY INTEGRATE WITH SUPPLY-CHAIN members, it is often necessary to align processes more closely with other organizations. For example, assume that a key supplier of e-Co wishes to be able to quickly monitor demand to adjust its production plans. To facilitate this information sharing, e-Co may decide to use an extranet to share inventory levels, customer orders, and sales forecasts with this supplier. However, e-Co has always been very cautious in releasing information related to sales, and it also guards its forecasts closely. In addition, e-Co's production manager meets with the purchasing department manager once every two weeks to establish appropriate purchase order amounts. For the extranet to provide useful information, e-Co will have to modify business processes such as budgeting and ordering. Therefore, the duties of the production and purchasing managers will also change. This simple example illustrates how information sharing and technology adoption can result in tremendous change within an organization; ebusiness must be willing to embrace change to achieve success.

Sharing information is a difficult task in a business world where traditionally information has been safeguarded. In this section, partnership formation is discussed in further detail from the perspective of managing relationships.

Forming partnerships and strategic alliances in the supply chain are as crucial to supply-chain success as the technology and information systems. Appropriate sharing of critical information will not take place unless both exist. Establishing strong lines of communication is the first step in ensuring that supply partnerships will succeed. Since the technology is only an enabler of the information sharing, decisions need to be made about what information should be shared, when, and who is responsible for it. Clarifying these basic terms early will help to develop trust.

cash-to-cash cycle: The length of time from purchasing materials until a product is manufactured.

Ebusiness in Global Perspective

Refining the Global Supply Chain and Service Call Management at IBM

IBM Corporation is one of the world's largest technology companies, operating in more than 160 countries worldwide. The range of services and products provided by IBM includes manufacturing, software design/sales, personal computers, servers, and after-sales service. Revenues were over US$90 billion in 2004. Operating on such a large scale requires IBM to have an effective supply-chain strategy in place, ensuring that research and development, purchasing, manufacturing, delivery, and sales channels are all properly integrated to deliver products on time, within budget, and of superior quality.

Global Supply-Chain Reengineering

In the mid-1990s, IBM decided that inventory levels were too high and that customer service levels could be improved. Operations analysts began reviewing the supply chain and determined that the length of time from purchasing materials until the product was manufactured (called the **cash-to-cash cycle**) was excessive. The results of a long cash-to-cash cycle include increased inventory levels, customer service delays, excessive write-offs of obsolete inventory, and high dealer discounts.

To improve the global supply chain, IBM needed to develop a strategic approach to improvement. Management

>

determined that in-house expertise within the IBM Research division would be able to assist in the development of a simulation tool that was named the Asset Management Tool (AMT). The AMT is a sophisticated optimization tool that examines inventory levels, forecasts, supplier information, and products to develop optimal supply-chain plans. In addition, AMT must be able to integrate foreign currency transactions, duties, tariffs, and tax concerns to make accurate decisions. Given that IBM deals with such large volumes of product, the AMT needs to carry out many analytical functions. For example, AMT analyzes products manufactured in all countries to identify common parts requirements, and carries out detailed analysis of shipping and purchasing costs, combined with activity-based costing methods, to determine whether all parts should be sourced from common locations or sourced from the nearest company. This analysis can now be carried out across the 3000 hardware and 20,000 software products and analyzed in further detail by supplier. Essentially, AMT demonstrates the need for advanced systems in large organizations that can accommodate uncertainty.

Service Call Management

IBM also recognized that the increasing complexity of its Global Services division was an area where effective planning could improve results. Dealing with approximately 22,000 service calls per day, more than 7000 service representatives need to be scheduled throughout the world. At first glance, one could assume that this task could be simple: Just give each representative three or four service calls per day. However, the diverse products, parts availability, language, location, call/problem complexity, and service representative expertise make the task overwhelming.

Once again, the IBM Research division was called in to help develop a customized solution, after a manager recognized the similarity of the situation's complexity to chess. The IBM Research division had been able to develop algorithms for the chess match between then-world-champion Gary Kasparov and IBM's Deep Blue computer. The programming was designed to handle the multiple iterations of moving chess pieces and was also able to develop an advanced call centre management system for Global Services.

The solution is able to analyze huge volumes of data to reduce customer response time and minimize idle time, travel costs, and delays by focusing on the integration of data. Available service reps are first assigned to service calls as they come in (by qualifications), and then the system begins to optimize the assignments through global and local locations by analyzing costs and other factors. The schedule needs to be recomputed every 10 minutes to ensure that new service calls are allocated in an optimal manner—often juggling the calls already within the system. IBM estimates that the time spent at service calls has been reduced by 10 to 35 percent through better assignment and that idle time has decreased as much as five-fold in some locations.

IBM
www.ibm.com

Questions

1. In a large company like IBM, how can management be sure that the supply-chain initiatives are improving operations?

2. Can other organizations effectively manage service calls like IBM without the use of high-technology systems?

3. What complications does the global operation of IBM add to the SCM process?

Sources: www.ibm.com, accessed April 19, 2004; B. Dietrich et al., "Big Benefits for Big Blue," OR/MS Today (June 2000).

Supply-chain success can often be attributed to the development of a relationship based on trust. Trust involves one party having confidence in, or relying on, another party to fulfill its obligations. The existence of trust in a relationship reduces the perception of risk associated with opportunistic behaviour and allows each party to believe that its needs will be fulfilled in the future by actions taken by the other party.[9] As in personal relationships, trust is formed over time and begins with honest and open communication among parties. Having appropriate managers involved in the partnership development is key to success.

The relationship of trust can be created more quickly if discussions centre on the following:

- realignment
- service-level agreements
- performance measurement
- dispute resolution
- security

Realignment

The creation of a supply-chain partnership does not simply entail setting up an extranet and sharing information. In many cases, realigning work responsibilities, selectively outsourcing, and realigning decision-making will help achieve success. For example, many organizations have realigned the decision making related to purchasing by moving toward vendor-managed inventory. **Vendor-managed inventory (VMI)** is the process by which suppliers take over monitoring inventory levels through the use of technology and are responsible for replenishment of stock. Walmart has adopted the use of VMI for many of its products, thus reducing the reliance on internal decision-making and allowing suppliers such as Procter & Gamble to be responsible for their own products. Research has shown that VMI often leads to reduced inventory levels and substantially lower stockout rates,[10] as suppliers are keen to ensure that consumers are always able to purchase their products.

vendor-managed inventory (VMI): A process by which suppliers take over monitoring inventory levels through the use of technology and are responsible for replenishment of stock.

Selective outsourcing may be necessary or economically feasible in some supply chains for functions that are traditionally problematic. For example, if both partners evaluate the outcomes as positive, transportation of rush orders may be outsourced to courier companies to reduce costs and improve delivery times. Outsourcing may also mean the movement of work from one organization to another in the supply chain to improve overall supply-chain effectiveness and reduce costs. Outsourcing decisions will vary by industry but should always be made on the basis of improving customer value, reducing complexity, and/or controlling costs.

Service-Level Agreements

A service-level agreements (SLAs) are fundamental to service provision from the perspective of both the supplier and the recipient.[11] An SLA essentially documents and defines the parameters of a supplier–customer relationship. The quality of the service level agreement is therefore a critical matter that merits careful attention.

An SLA is wide in scope, covering all key aspects of the service to be delivered and such issues as problem management, compensation (often essential in terms of motivation), warranties and remedies, resolution of disputes, and legal compliance. It essentially frames the relationship, and determines the major responsibilities, both in times of normal operation and during an emergency situation.

Performance Measurement

To ensure high performance, measurements are needed to test the performance of each link in the supply chain. The downstream links need to provide fast response to any market opportunity, while the upstream links need to effectively support any sales made. One criterion that could be used to measure the performance of a vendor is late orders, how late they were, and the financial value of the orders. This measurement is specific and motivates all the parties to do what is good for the chain as a whole.

Performance measurement is a complex task in any setting, and ebusiness changes the dynamics of performance measurement by changing the dynamics of information and rate of change. To allow supply-chain partners to contribute positively to the partnership and later evaluate the relationship, partners should create joint metrics for performance measurement. Establishing the terms by which success will be measured at the onset allows partners to develop plans to meet those goals.

Performance measurement goals should be established for delivery timelines, decision effectiveness, quality procedures, and any other outcomes that are considered important to the relationship. The partnership can also make use of benchmarking studies to establish realistic goals, which can later be reevaluated. For example, Walmart uses Bridgepoint software to assess supplier performance and identifies opportunities to improve cycle times and other performance measures. Suppliers can review these results in scorecards posted online.

Dispute Resolution

Given that we are in an age of lawsuits and expensive legal battles, it is wise, as with other business functions, to take dispute resolution into account in supply-chain planning. Supply-chain partners need to document and plan ahead for areas of concern such as security, copyright, and asset title when changes to the supply-chain process take place. Intellectual property rights covering trade secrets, trademarks and copyright concerns need to be dealt with up front so that partners are willing to share critical information without the risk of losing a "trade secret." In addition, simple changes to the process can result in confusing terms of title that should be clarified with contracts and partnership agreements. As in health, prevention (of disputes) is the best medicine.

Security

Sharing information digitally poses additional concerns about security in the supply-chain partnership. Managing changes to how confidential information is shared and how work responsibilities are defined is often a major task. Thus, security issues arising from remote access and data warehouse sharing over extranets or virtual private networks, should be clearly documented and monitored to ensure that security breaches do not occur. Partners need to establish policies that each is comfortable with, and they may monitor the compliance continually (and seek inclusion in internal and external audits as well).

When processes are outsourced, security issues are extremely important because the company retains responsibility for the security, integrity, confidentiality and privacy of the data being used by the outsourcer. Such data can include confidential information about suppliers and sensitive personal information about customers.

ORDER FULFILLMENT/DELIVERY

ORDER FULFILLMENT HAS EMERGED AS A CRITICAL COMPONENT OF THE SUPPLY chain in the ebusiness era. During Christmas 1999 and in the early 2000s, fulfillment failures and difficulties tarnished the reputations of many etailers, including toy sellers and electronics retailers. The inability of many dot-coms to deliver goods on time for Christmas tarnished the growth of ecommerce and disappointed a number of children waiting for Barbie and Hot Wheels models, or computer systems. Since that time, a number of new fulfillment possibilities have emerged, and organizations—both brick-and-mortar and dot-com—have dedicated substantial management and financial resources to modifying the fulfillment process.

The 1999 ecommerce problems were to a great extent the result of unexpected demand, combined with underdeveloped supply chains and inventory control, and unrealistic delivery promises. In addition, some supply chains lacked full integration on the B2B end, which resulted in increased pressure on etailers to take late shipments and turn them into on-time deliveries, often at excessive costs. Admittedly, at the early stages of ecommerce, demand was unknown; however, many of the early etailers had committed relatively little to planning and were focused on other important areas, such as security and advertising. General business studies have taught us that a business is an integrated enterprise, and emphasis on select functional areas at the expense of others often leads to failure.

Order fulfillment is a set of processes involved in delivering a product to a customer. It consists of many procedures grouped into the main areas of order processing, warehousing, and shipping and transportation planning (see figure 7.6). Order fulfillment is the front-end and back-end processes necessary to convert an order into a sale by completing the company's responsibility of providing a product or service. **Order processing** includes activities that take place during the fulfillment of an order, such as credit checks, inventory availability determination, shipping, billing, replenishment requests and accounting. A great deal of the work in order processing is now automated through ERP and internet-based systems.

order fulfillment: A set of processes involved in delivering a product to the customer. It consists of procedures grouped into the main areas of order processing, warehousing, and shipping and transportation planning.

order processing: A set of activities that take place during the fulfillment of an order. These include credit checks, inventory availability determination, accounting, billing, and replenishment requests.

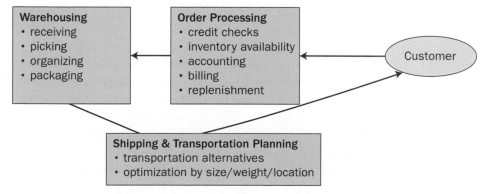

Figure 7.6 The order fulfillment process

Order fulfillment includes many business processes in areas such as order processing, warehousing, and shipping and transportation planning.

Warehousing refers to all tasks involved with handling inventory. This includes processes such as receiving orders of inventory from suppliers (if not previously in stock), as well as picking, organizing, and packaging goods for delivery. Initial attempts by online sellers to have suppliers package orders for shipment direct to the consumer had to be revised, as customers began ordering multiple products and were dissatisfied with receiving multiple deliveries. Consider, for example, Wine.com (originally Virtual Vineyards), an etailer of wines and other gift products. When a customer ordered wines from the California region, Wine.com would relay the orders to individual vineyards for shipment to the consumer. Ordering wine from more than one vineyard would result in an inconvenience to the customer, who might receive delivery at various times. As a result, Wine.com needed to centralize its fulfillment centre into a warehouse to provide quality service to customers An alternative to creating a fulfillment centre is to outsource the handling and consolidation of shipment to shipping companies such as UPS, FedEx, DHL, and Purolator. Many consumers do not know that many of the multi-part shipments they receive, such as computers from Dell, are actually packaged by shipping companies on behalf of the vendor.

Shipping and transportation planning (STP) is the process of transporting finished goods to the consumer quickly and efficiently. STP requires businesses to coordinate all their orders cost-effectively by analyzing sizes, weights, packaging, and transportation alternatives. Like many other ebusiness functions discussed in this book, STP and order fulfillment require the use of sophisticated technologies to implement.

Walmart announced in June 2003 that it planned to require its top 100 suppliers to put radio frequency identification (RFID) tags on shipping crates and pallets by January 2005. This would result in the deployment of nearly 1 billion **RFID tags** with embedded electronic product codes (EPC) for tracking and identifying items at the individual crate and pallet level. RFID tags can gather and track a variety of data related to products, materials, and more, though Walmart initially focused on using the technology to further improve inventory management in the supply chain. The tags can store more detailed information than conventional bar codes, enabling tracking of items at the unit level. Walmart's announcement provided a thrust to the wider acceptance of RFID, which has since experienced higher adoption rates.

Fulfillment is similar to the "moment of truth" in service organizations, whereby delivery of a quality service or product is the only thing that a customer truly sees. The moment of truth is the critical moment in a service transaction when the customer's expectations are met, exceeded, or disappointed. The customer is not aware of or concerned with how complex the supply chain is or the number of processes involved—the customer wants to receive what was ordered, when it was promised, and at the cost quoted. To meet these needs, many companies have chosen to outsource the fulfillment function to remain focused on core competencies. For example, Toys "R" Us decided to outsource its fulfillment function for online orders to Amazon so it could focus on inventory management and procurement, which are complicated processes in the toy industry.[12] Amazon had strong fulfillment capabilities in place and could capitalize on existing infrastructure, allowing Toys "R" Us to control internal functions, manage its upstream supply chain, and concentrate on its new estrategy.

A growing number of outsourcing companies are emerging, including some of the well-known courier companies like FedEx and UPS. UPS signed an agreement with

Samsung Electro-Mechanics Company in fall 2000 to provide outsourced global SCM services. The UPS Logistics Group offers services such as supply-chain analysis, transportation, brokerage, and financing to companies wishing to move SCM outside of the organization.[13] Samsung determined that its focus should remain on quality, production, and management, and UPS offered a competitive price, leading technology, and proven expertise.[14] Partnerships and outsourcing with firms such as UPS and FedEx have allowed many organizations to reduce the demands of SCM. While outsourcing is common, it can be an expensive alternative to in-house management and should be carefully evaluated. The size of an organization, product features, industry, and complexity of the supply chain will all affect the costs of carrying out SCM.

Large organizations with established management structures and supply-chain expertise can develop top-performing fulfillment systems by capitalizing on technological structures already in place. ERP systems hold a great deal of the information required to develop efficient fulfillment, such as inventory information (quantities on hand and on order, delivery information, backorders), customer information (credit limits, shipping addresses), and financial information (sales prices, shipping cost information, etc.). To leverage the information in the ERP system, it is necessary to ensure that fulfillment is based on ERP data and integrated with the SCM system to deliver real-time updates. Order status information needs to be provided back to the ERP system from custom applications (such as shopping cart applications or shipping partner data, so that data need not be entered twice) and allows customer service to provide meaningful feedback to customer service calls. The Canadian Snapshots box explores one company's solution to the technological side of SCM.

Canadian Snapshots

Descartes Systems Group

Descartes Systems Group is a Waterloo, Ontario-based provider of inter-enterprise execution software for SCM. The company's products are geared towards delivery-sensitive organizations with short time-to-plan horizons. For these companies, successful execution is essential to success: Delivery is a component of product value, and failure to perform may be catastrophic to their business. Descartes' product family offers a complete portfolio of software solutions that streamline the entire order-to-delivery process.

Market Differentiation

Descartes differentiates itself through the broad functionality of its solutions, application of leading edge technologies, and its inter-enterprise focus on the supply chain. Descartes designs solutions from an inter-enterprise perspective for global companies with multiple trading partners. By approaching the supply chain from this perspective, Descartes has created a complete order-to-delivery solution that companies can rely on to manage their current and emerging supply-chain requirements.

Descartes offers an integrated solution for the highly fragmented software application market for logistics industries. Descartes provides three value-added networks (VANs) to serve as a central communications infrastructure for companies. Millions of logistics-related messages are exchanged via the Descartes VANs each month to provide companies with real-time vision into their supply chains. These messages are also recorded in the VANs' data repositories. Descartes integrated software solutions provide a means of querying the information about actual logistics activities that take place throughout a company's

>

Warehousing concerns have resulted in major changes within ebusiness as companies strive to reduce delivery times while controlling costs. The classic example is that of Amazon. Amazon's original business model was to operate as an online sales organization with no inventory on hand. Amazon chose to move from a pure-play ebusiness model to a bricks-and-clicks business that holds some inventory in strategically located warehouses throughout the United States. Amazon now stocks high-volume books in high-tech warehouses and has the ability to better meet its objectives of shipping overnight for most customer orders. Wine.com has taken a similar approach by using warehouses as storage points for high-volume items and as receiving points for integrating and packaging orders. Many online retailers have found that it is often necessary to hold some inventory to provide rapid customer service and delivery.

As shipping and transportation companies embrace technological advances in business, it becomes easier to provide high levels of customer service. UPS and FedEx allow customers to track packages on the internet by entering an identification number. The ability of these transportation service providers to deliver information at all stages of the delivery channel is made possible through information systems, mobile wireless devices and internet technology. In an age where delivery speed is often measured in hours or days, this type of information becomes crucial to success. The combination of wireless and internet technologies is creating excellent opportunities for transportation and other companies to gain substantial benefits throughout the fulfillment process—improving customer service, increasing revenue, and controlling costs all at the same time.

REVERSE LOGISTICS

reverse logistics: The internal processes for handling customer returns, either for a refund or for repair or replacement under warranty.

INTERNET RESEARCH HAS DEMONSTRATED THAT RETURNING PRODUCTS IS BOTH A concern for buyers and an important issue for sellers. **Reverse logistics** is the internal process through which customers can return items purchased, either for a refund or for repair or replacement under warranty. Having an effective mechanism for dealing with returns is helpful in making sales but also must be designed to guard against fraud.

Brick-and-mortar businesses that have been in the catalogue sales business have dealt with the problem of returns for many years. However, pure online stores need to establish policies, drop-off locations, and credit procedures to effectively handle returns. For instance, clothing etailers quickly found that customers would purchase a medium size and a large size of the same style and then return the item that did not fit properly. Without proper procedures in place, the return of items can be very costly—incurring shipping costs, banking and transaction costs, and the expense of storing and dealing with excess inventory. Policies that assist with returns include many elements that are common to retailing, such as time limits on returns, responsibility for shipping costs, and reasonable use limitations for warranty-related concerns. Establishing clear policies and communicating them to customers assists greatly in controlling reverse logistics.

Outsourcing has once again become an important strategy in dealing with reverse logistics. For example, Buy.com Inc. determined that having an effective delivery system encouraged customers to purchase products and have confidence in the company. Initially, Buy.com allowed customers to make returns by calling and obtaining an authorization code, and then later a mailing label would be sent to the customer for the product's return. The process was cumbersome and slow, so Buy.com outsourced the function to UPS. Customers now obtain authorization for returns online and can enter their authorization code into the returns section of the website, which enables them to print out their own packaging label from UPS. The package can then be dropped off at a UPS location or picked up by the courier service. Once again, customer service has dominated.

C-COMMERCE: THE FUTURE

THE GARTNER GROUP COINED THE TERM COLLABORATIVE COMMERCE (C-COMMERCE) in a strategic planning note examining the future of ebusiness.[15] C-commerce is the application of technologies to allow trading partners to synchronize and optimize their partnerships, and is performed in collaboration. As SCM and other applications have developed, as described in this chapter, c-commerce has emerged as a fundamental component of SCM by facilitating strong relationships, fuelling efficiency, and driving customer-oriented decisions. For example, Walmart's SCM program, known as Collaborative Planning, Forecasting, and Replenishment (CPFR), aims to sell as much product as possible without either the supplier or Walmart having too much inventory. Some analysts believe that Walmart saves 5 to 10 percent in cost of goods through the use of technology in its streamlined supply chain. The reason Walmart has had so much success is that its SCM practices have benefited not only the retailer but its suppliers as well.

Essentially, c-commerce is the advanced stage of many of the topics discussed in this chapter. It involves employing technology to improve partnerships, gain efficiency in processes, make effective decisions, and satisfy customers. Trading exchanges and customer relationship management are part of the development of c-commerce, as discussed later in this book.

collaborative commerce (c-commerce): The application of technologies that allow trading partners to synchronize and optimize their partnerships and that are performed in collaboration.

CHAPTER SUMMARY

Supply-chain management (SCM) is the process of coordinating and managing the product, information, and financial flows among members of the supply chain. As ebusiness has emerged, SCM has become an important aspect of success by allowing businesses to gain efficiencies and improve customer service in a fast-paced environment. The internet-enabled supply chain has a customer focus from the beginning, whereby the entire chain is driven by the pull of the customer.

Technology is an important component of SCM. Enterprise resource planning systems provide the backbone for information exchange. The internet provides the medium through which much communication and "collaboration" take place. Extranets and other technologies allow partners to securely share information in a convenient, cost-effective, and user-friendly manner.

Strategy plays a key role in SCM by setting the direction for partners to work toward. Like many other aspects of business, technology is a critical tool for SCM, but success is achieved by making strategic decisions and effectively managing the people who employ the technologies. Companies like Dell have employed SCM to achieve their goal of providing customers with customized products, at a competitive price, in a short period of time.

Key Terms

cash-to-cash cycle (p. 159)

collaborative commerce (c-commerce) (p. 167)

disintermediation (p. 151)

logistics (p. 146)

order fulfillment (p. 163)

order processing (p. 163)

pull system (p. 150)

push system (p. 147)

reintermediation (p. 152)

reverse logistics (p. 166)

RFID tag (p. 164)

shipping and transportation planning (STP) (p. 164)

supply-chain management (SCM) (p. 144)

vendor-managed inventory (VMI) (p. 161)

warehousing (p. 164)

MyEbusinessLab Tools for Online Learning

To help you master the material in this chapter and stay up to date with new developments in ebusiness, visit the MyEBusinessLab at www.pearsoned.ca/myebusinesslab. Resources include the following:

- **Pre- and Post-Test Questions**
- **Additional Chapter Questions**
- **Author Blog**
- **Recommended Readings**
- **Commentaries on Current Trends**
- **Additional Topics in Ebusiness**
- **Internet Exercises**
- **Glossary Flashcards**

Endnotes

1. Thomas L. Friedman, *The World Is Flat* (New York: Farrar, Straus & Giroux, 2005): 48–172; especially section on supply chaining: 128–141.

2. P. Evans and T. S. Wurster, Blown to Bits: *How the New Economics of Information Transforms Strategy* (Boston, MA: Harvard Business School Press, 2000), 237.

3. T. Stein and J. Sweat, "Killer Supply Chains," InformationWeek (November 9, 1998).

4. M. Hammer and J. Champy, *Reengineering the Corporation* (New York: HarperCollins Publishers, 1994), 35.

5. G. Trites, *Enterprise Resource Planning—The Engine for E-Business* (Toronto: CICA, 2000).

6. M. Hammer and S. Stanton, *The Reengineering Revolution* (New York: HarperCollins, 1995).

7. J. Peppard and P. Rowland, *The Essence of Business Process Reengineering* (London: Prentice Hall, 1995).

8. B. Dietrich et al., "Big Benefits for Big Blue," OR/MS Today (June 2000).

9. K. R. Moore, "Trust and Relationship Commitment in Logistics Alliances: A Buyer Perspective,"*International Journal of Purchasing and Materials Management* 34 (1988): 24–37.

10. H. Lee, "Creating Value through Supply Chain Integration,"*Supply Chain Management Review* (September/October 2000).

11. "The Service Level Agreement," IT Infrastructure Library, Office of Government Commerce, www.itil-itsm-world.com/itil-sla.htm, accessed April 19, 2004.

12. B. Tedeschi, "Internet Merchants, Seeing Landscape Shift, Adapt to Survive,"*New York Times*, December 18, 2000.

13. UPS Global website, www.ups-scs.com, accessed April 19, 2004.

14. Samsung Digital World website, www.pressroom.ups.com/pressreleases/archives/archive/0,1363,3827,00.html, accessed April 19, 2004.

15. B. Bond et al., *C-Commerce: The New Arena for Business Applications*, Gartner Group research document (August 1999).

Chapter 8

Eprocurement, Trading Exchanges, and Auctions

Learning Objectives

When you complete this chapter you should be able to:

1   Explain the eprocurement process and why eprocurement is important in today's business world.

2   Outline the major benefits of eprocurement and what types of goods are often procured.

3   Describe trading exchanges, the functions they perform, and the issues they face.

4   Describe the different types of auctions, how an auction is carried out online, and the auctioning process.

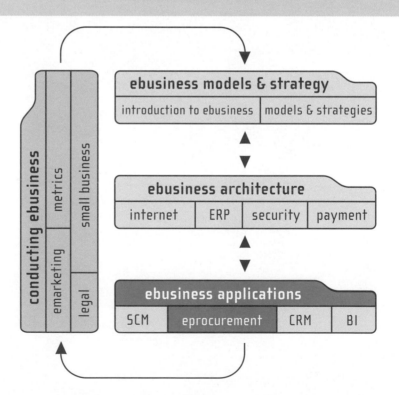

INTRODUCTION

BUSINESSES BECAME INTERESTED IN EPROCUREMENT AS A MEANS OF CUTTING costs and improving efficiency in the early 2000s, particularly for B2B ecommerce. The benefits of B2B transactions, eprocurement, and trading exchanges are now being realized by many companies. A variety of strategies have been adopted in the B2B arena in an attempt to capitalize on the benefits. For example, the Marriott and Hyatt hotel chains moved their procurement staffs outside the organizations into a joint venture called Avendra LLC, specifically formed for eprocurement purposes. Raytheon, a large U.S. defence contractor, has used its own in-house eprocurement efforts to "rationalize" its number of suppliers and cut costs, while also using outsourced procurement services from Ariba Inc.[1] While a variety of strategies are used, one thing is clear: Eprocurement is a critical area of ebusiness that will continue to evolve for the next several years, as companies strive to achieve completely digital, integrated B2B ecommerce. In this chapter we will examine the eprocurement process, trading exchanges, implementation challenges, and directions for future development.

Eprocurement can be defined broadly as the complete business process of acquiring goods through electronic means, from requisition through to fulfillment and payment. The process of eprocurement involves more than just the purchasing of goods, as it deals more broadly with the complete cycle, including selection and payment.

Marriott
www.marriott.com

Hyatt
www.hyatt.com

Avendra
www.avendra.com

Raytheon
www.raytheon.com

THE EPROCUREMENT PROCESS

THE EPROCUREMENT PROCESS IS ILLUSTRATED IN FIGURE 8.1. THE PROCESS VARIES somewhat by organization, but a simplified analysis of the components will allow a better understanding of the concept. Once a firm identifies a need for a good or service, an employee would begin the selection process to find a good or service to fill the need. This process could be carried out through catalogues, either online or through a corporate intranet, through a trading exchange, or by examining websites of potential vendors. Other possibilities such as negotiated prices and auctions will be discussed later. Once the employee has identified the specific good or service to be procured and an appropriate supplier, he or she would create a requisition electronically and forward it to the appropriate signing officer if approval is required. Purchases of specific types of goods or those within certain dollar limits may be automatically approved by the system.

The approval of the requisition will result in the creation of a purchase order that will be transmitted to the supplier firm. The transmission could take place in various formats, including EDI (Electronic Document Exchange) or XML (eXtensible Markup Language), or through a secure internet channel in a customized format. The transmission of the purchase order may occur directly through a trading exchange, through the internet, or through a proprietary VAN (Value Added Network), depending on the technology strategies of the firms involved.

The supplier firm may then carry out all its fulfillment processes and arrange for transportation to the buyer firm, if required. In the case of a purchase of goods, once the buyer receives the goods, the payment process will begin. The receiving information should be entered in the buyer's ERP/accounting system to update inventory, and when the invoice is received, it is matched to the receiving information and purchase order to confirm receipt of the entire order, as well as pricing information. The accounts payable will be

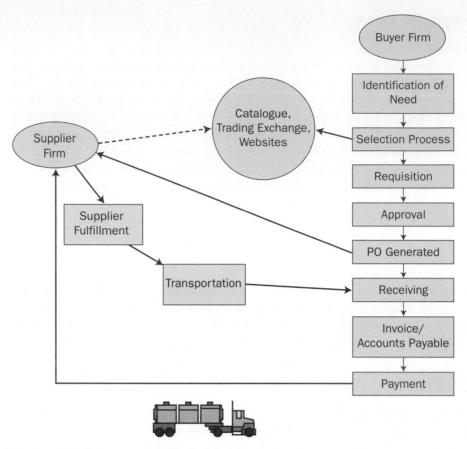

Figure 8.1 The eprocurement process

Eprocurement encompasses the steps of the procurement process that are carried out in an integrated, electronic form.

paid in the normal sequence by the buyer, and again the format of this would depend on the particular circumstances.

Surprisingly, the level of integration in the process achieved by many large companies has been rather limited. For example, Texas Instruments claimed that it wanted to improve its own capabilities and those of its suppliers by integrating systems to increase the number of products acquired through eprocurement. A great deal of information was passed through email and spreadsheets and then later re-keyed into their ERP system, leading to inefficiencies and errors.[2] Many organizations have identified improved integration as a key issue for stimulating B2B transactions through trading exchanges and eprocurement.

Goods and Services Procured

When eprocurement began, it was primarily used for the purchase of office supplies and maintenance, repair, and operating (MRO) items. As businesses began to realize its potential for cost savings, the range of purchases increased to include computer equipment and corporate travel services. Later, eprocurement expanded into production-related goods such as raw materials.

It is important that processes for eprocurement take into consideration the types of goods and services being acquired so that eprocurement can be efficient and effective. As with paper-based transactions, the dollar value and urgency of a purchase can affect how well processes function and how quickly they occur. Despite this, it is important to keep electronic processes under control. Consider the following example from Microsoft, where Bill Gates discovered inefficiency in digital processes:

> I thought every company had this kind of explicit review for expense approval. I learned I was wrong when I demonstrated our intranet to a group of CEOs. Paul O'Neill of Alcoa, which is the world's leading producer of aluminum, came up to me after my talk and asked, "It's great that everything is digital and efficient, but why should you have to review expense reports? You've got better things to do with your time."[3]

This example illustrates exactly what businesses must be careful not to do—simply automate paper processes. In this case there was no need for Bill Gates to authorize the travel expenditures of senior-level vice presidents, even though doing so may have taken only a relatively short amount of time. As with many other aspects of ebusiness, processes often need to be modified or reengineered when they are moved to an electronic environment.

Businesses will need to consider whether or not to allow automatic approval on particular types of goods or services being acquired. For example, it may be reasonable to establish budgeted amounts for basic office supplies that are purchased through specified vendors, rather than deal with individual purchase order review and approval. The expenses may be audited later for control purposes, but the time saved should exceed the cost of any potential employee wrongdoing.

MRO Expenses MRO expenses are an area where automatic approvals may be delegated to specific individuals or otherwise streamlined. For instance, the production manager may have approval to create a purchase order up to a specific dollar limit so that machine breakdowns can be efficiently handled. If downtime within a manufacturing business is expensive, then allowing the production manager to deal with a problem quickly would benefit the business, whereas a detailed process of approvals could delay the repair and affect the bottom line.

Travel Services Travel services and meals and entertainment costs represent a major expense for many of today's service-based businesses. Therefore, the ability to process travel services in an integrated fashion has the potential for major cost savings. Microsoft saw this potential in the late 1990s and established a partnership with American Express so employees could access negotiated rates and discounts through the eprocurement portion of the corporate intranet, which was named "MS Market." Allowing employees to book their own travel at approved rates resulted in more than just improved rates—it also satisfied employees who wished to manage their own schedules and have the flexibility to make changes if necessary.[4]

Computer Equipment The acquisition of computer equipment represents another major category where businesses have begun to use eprocurement. Not only can computers be acquired through exchanges and vendors' websites, but increasingly corporate intranets can be linked to specialized pages of the vendors. For example, Dell has created "Application Management" pages (see figure 8.2) for many of its

Figure 8.2 The medium and large business home page of Dell.ca

Dell Premier Pages allow corporate and other large customers to access tailored webpages and preconfigured systems. The pages provide excellent service and ease of use.

Source: Dell Canada, www.dell.ca <http://www.dell.ca>, © 2011 Dell Inc. All Rights Reserved.

customers, which provide for preconfigured systems, which allows computer systems within budget limits to be purchased with little involvement of supervisors and technical support staff.

Production Items   The cost savings and benefits obtained through eprocurement for non-production items have led many businesses to look to eprocurement for production items (also referred to as direct spending), such as raw materials and product components. There are, however, some significant differences between production and non-production goods, making this transition more difficult. For example, non-production goods can be acquired more easily through poorly integrated systems, since the coordination of the arrival date of the goods and the update of related information in the system is less critical. Production items need to be acquired within specific time frames to keep manufacturing schedules and maintain inventory levels, both for internal planning purposes and for customer notification. Also, production items may need to be customized. Therefore, production items need to be obtained and tracked through an integrated eprocurement system, or information will need to be re-keyed.

The eprocurement of production items has other important concerns, such as product quality, payment terms, delivery arrangements, and supplier capabilities for collaborative product design. Essentially, when a business considers using eprocurement, trading exchanges, or auction models to procure production goods, price is only one part of the buying decision. Item quality, availability, and predictability and timeliness of delivery are also important considerations.

Estrategy

Public Works Decides Against Reverse Auctions

In September 2006, Michael Fortier, minister of Public Works and Government Services Canada, announced the discontinuance of a controversial plan that would have seen federal suppliers compete against each other in reverse auctions to drive down prices. The plan was recommended by A.T. Kearney in a $24 million consultants' report.

This announcement was a major change of direction for the department's procurement overhaul strategy, a strategy that had sparked an unprecedented revolt among suppliers, who feared they would be put out of business. The announcement came less than a week after Public Works dismissed the two private-sector executives recruited to lead the overhaul project.

In the announcement, Fortier said that after listening to suppliers' complaints, he decided to scrap the reverse auctions idea and reopen discussions with industry groups on a new buying strategy for the 34 goods and services commonly purchased by the department. He added that he felt procurement reform can be achieved without the use of reverse auctions.

Officials in Fortier's office later stressed that the minister was not backing down on his target to save $2.5 billion in procurement costs over 5 years out of the $13 billion a year spent on goods and services. "It's still the target," said spokesperson Jean-Luc Benoit. "We have to find a way because it is in the fiscal framework and the minister is committed to achieving those savings."

The government also announced that it is going ahead with competitions for its pre-approved supplier lists or "standing offers," which have been on hold since the controversy began in June. Fortier also asked the Conference Board of Canada to mediate in the talks between his department and three of the biggest and most complicated purchases: temporary help, IT professional services, and office furniture.

Public Works has been under fire since suppliers discovered that the work of procurement specialists A.T. Kearney, Inc. was behind an unexpected decision to make suppliers compete in reverse auctions—live, online auctions in which the lowest price wins. Critics said that the government fell into the same trap as most companies and governments do—the consultants hired to lead the changes offer solutions around the products their firms sell. In this case, A.T. Kearney provides a service that does reverse auctions, known as eBreviate. There is a tendency in these situations for consultants to fit the problem to their solution.

Reverse auctions gained popularity in the 1990s, by promising big savings for buyers and turning the traditional auction on its head by reversing the roles of the buyer and seller. With a reverse auction, sellers fight for the right to supply, and the lowest price wins.

Critics say the practice has never achieved the savings promised, destroys buyer–supplier relations, leads to retaliatory pricing, and violates the government's own contracting principles of fairness, openness, and integrity.

The remaining question is whether, without reverse auctions, the government will be able to reach its goal of $2.5 billion in savings. One senior bureaucrat said the projected savings are "built on quicksand with no validity, and should be discarded."

Alan Williams, a former assistant deputy minister for procurement, said reverse auctions may work for the private sector, which is driven by profit and return on investment for shareholders, but the government juggles many stakeholders and policy objectives and has to weigh the

>

repercussions of its decisions on departments, industry, and taxpayers.

"The public sector has a moral obligation to work on a higher ethical plane. The government's objective isn't to wring out every last cent, but to make sure industry makes a fair profit, departments' needs are met, and Canadians are well-served. It has to balance," Williams added.

Questions

1. Why would reverse auctioning have elicited such a negative response from suppliers?

2. Based on the facts provided, how would you evaluate the process followed by Public Works to plan and set up the eprocurement plan?

3. What strategies might Public Works follow to achieve its goals?

Source: K. May, "Public Works Scraps $24M Procurement Plan," *Ottawa Citizen*, September 08, 2006, A1. http://www.cata.ca/Media_and_Events/ Press_Releases/cata_pr09080601.html Material reprinted with the express permission of: Ottawa Citizen, a division of Postmedia Network Inc.

Supplier Selection and Approval

Supplier selection is critical in managing costs in the procurement process. There may be several vendors for any given product to be purchased, and considering the number of products purchased routinely by a company's purchasing department, unless careful attention is paid to costs, those costs could spiral out of control. For repetitive purchases, contracts should be negotiated with selected suppliers, and terms should be established for delivery, pricing, and quality. In the case of non-repetitive purchases, employee requests to purchase a product may involve a request for quotations (RFQ) being sent to suppliers inviting them to submit a bid for that purchase contract.

When detailed evaluation is required for a new purchase, perhaps because of its size, supplier evaluation may be required. The potential evaluation of suppliers begins after determining that a purchase need exists (or is likely to exist) and the development of materials specifications occurs. For routine or standard product requirements with established or selected suppliers, further supplier evaluation and selection is not likely necessary, and the approval process may be started. However, potential sources for new items, especially those of a complex nature, require thorough investigation to be sure that purchasing evaluates only qualified suppliers.

Final supplier selection occurs once purchasing completes the activities required during the supplier evaluation process. Errors made in supplier selection can be damaging and long-lasting. After bids have been received, and/or the negotiation has taken place, the sourcing team will select a supplier, and then move on to authorize the purchase through the purchase approval process.

After the supplier is selected or a requisition for a standard item is received, purchasing grants an approval to purchase the product or service. This is accomplished through an electronic drafting of a purchase order (PO), sometimes called a purchase agreement. The purchase order details critical information about the purchase: quantity, material specification, quality requirements, price, delivery date, method of delivery, ship-to address, purchase order number, and order due date. Note that firms are increasingly using computerized databases to perform these processes, and are moving toward a "paperless" office.[5]

Several technology solution providers are targeting this area of strategic sourcing of purchases, also known as esourcing. These strategic sourcing solutions are designed to replace the traditional paper-based, labour-intensive processes of identifying and evaluating suppliers, automatically performing those processes to help enterprises identify the optimal supply network.[6]

The cost savings of consolidating purchases with a few suppliers can be substantial. For example, Bristol-Myers Squibb claims to have saved US$20 million per year by consolidating its purchases from both Dell and IBM with eprocurement.[7]

Benefits of Eprocurement

The benefits of eprocurement to businesses are still being discovered, but indications so far are that the practice has a tremendous payoff. Some of these benefits involve cost and efficiency, strategic procurement, and authorized suppliers.

Cost and Efficiency   The benefits of eprocurement are many, including price reductions and process efficiencies. Recent studies have found that companies reported benefits such as faster order times, convenience, time savings, easier price comparisons, and cost savings.[8] While the initial jump to adopt eprocurement was to create more competitive markets and reduce prices, a number of businesses claim that the "primary benefit lies in streamlining internal processes."[9]

Paper-based procurement is laced with inefficiencies such as approvals of all purchase orders, despite the dollar amount or importance. In addition, the length of time to process a purchase order has been reduced by many businesses by nearly 75 percent due to the removal of "the paper chase." Microsoft claimed to have significantly reduced its paper forms related to procurement from 114 to 1.[10] The reduction in cost and increase in efficiency also results in a reduced administrative workload for procurement staff.

Strategic Procurement   With the implementation of eprocurement in a business, the staff from the procurement area will be able to focus efforts on more important tasks, such as strategic sourcing and supplier relations. As discussed in chapter 7, efficient supply chains depend on reliable suppliers, and the ability of staff to spend more time developing relationships is very beneficial. In addition, procurement staff may become involved in managing procurement processes that now occur through electronic means.

Authorized Suppliers   Another area where eprocurement has shown benefits is in consolidating buying from a small number of approved suppliers.[11] By controlling whom employees may order from, a business should be able to demand improved pricing by increasing volume. For example, the impact of consolidation could be tremendous for a large business with tens of thousands of employees, all of whom purchase their own office supplies at the local supplier. Limiting employees to the suppliers in the eprocurement system can reduce maverick buying. **Maverick buying** is the unauthorized purchase of goods by employees through non-routine and poorly controlled means, such as acquiring office supplies with petty cash. In addition to potentially reducing the costs of goods purchased, controls required by eprocurement can reduce the volume of small transactions and payments required, thereby increasing the efficiency of related transaction-processing operations.

maverick buying: The unauthorized purchase of goods by employees through non-routine and poorly controlled means, such as acquiring office supplies with petty cash.

The benefits of eprocurement are broad in scope and will vary by organization. However, one thing is clear—eprocurement is a strategy that all ebusinesses are working on now, or will be working on in the near future.

TRADING EXCHANGES

B2B TRADING EXCHANGES ARE INTERNET-BASED SITES IN WHICH BUSINESSES CAN SELL OR purchase products and services or share information to advertise products and services. Trading exchanges reduce reliance on other forms of communication in the procurement/selling process, as illustrated in figure 8.3. At the outset, more than a thousand trading exchanges were formed, but within a year the limited growth in trading through these exchanges led many of the startups to shut down. Since that initial shake-out, several strong exchanges have survived, are operating successfully today, and offer extended benefits to eprocurement activities on the buy side and sales opportunities on the sell side.

Trading exchanges may also be referred to by a number of different names in practice. Terms such as "hubs," "ehubs," "marketplaces," "consortiums," and combinations of these (sometimes with "B2B" added) are used in trade literature and magazine publications. In this book, we will refer primarily to "trading exchanges," that being the most comprehensive term.

Trading exchanges can be grouped into two major categories in terms of products and services exchanged: vertical and horizontal. **Vertical trading exchanges** are those that have an industry or specific market focus, such as health care or energy products and services. **Horizontal trading exchanges** are those that have a product or service focus, such as computers or office equipment, and that do not target any specific industry. Figure 8.4 illustrates the concept of vertical and horizontal trading exchanges.

Trading exchanges are also categorized as either public or private, depending on the controls in place and any access limitations. A **private exchange** is a trading exchange that limits participation to specific buyers and sellers—normally related to the exchange provider's supply chain. For example, when General Electric first began its Global eXchange Services (GXS), it was limited to a few specific buyers who were soliciting goods and services from sellers who had been given access to enter the exchange. GXS has evolved over time and continues to provide exchange services such as network

vertical trading exchange: A trading exchange that has an industry or specific market focus, such as health care or energy products and services.

horizontal trading exchange: A trading exchange that has a product or service focus, such as computers or office equipment, and that does not target any specific industry.

private exchange: A trading exchange that limits participation to specific buyers and sellers—normally related to the exchange provider's supply chain.

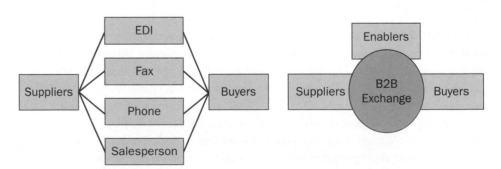

Figure 8.3 Trading exchanges' facilitating role

Trading exchanges can consolidate numerous forms of communication into one medium.

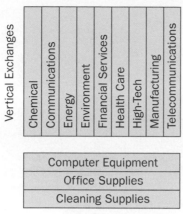

Figure 8.4 Vertical and horizontal trading exchanges

Trading exchanges are often categorized as either vertical or horizontal, based upon the way they operate.

infrastructure, software, hardware, and consulting services to major clients like JCPenney and Procter & Gamble.[12] Private exchanges continue to evolve and vary in the methods by which they allow sellers and buyers to join.

Public exchanges are those in which buyers and sellers register to join, and there are few limitations to joining. Public exchanges have not had tremendous success in the B2B market, however, as enterprises have had difficulty integrating their ERP/EDI systems with the exchanges, especially since the enterprise would have to implement the integration itself.

public exchange: A trading exchange in which buyers and sellers register to join, and there are few limitations to joining.

Trading Exchanges' Evolution to SaaS

Trading exchanges operate with a variety of service levels and allow for varying degrees of integration. The functions of a trading exchange can range from simplistic, in which members share company information and then conduct transactions offline (similar to the brochureware phase of the internet), to catalogue sites, to fully integrated collaborative environments (see figure 8.5 on page 180). In the collaborative environments, contract terms and payment can be carried out completely online and integrated with the buyer and seller back-end systems, and products and services may even be designed online.

During the early 2000s, the provision of software services by third parties became more prevalent. While companies had previously focused primarily on running their own software COTS (commercial off-the-shelf software), they began to "rent" software from outside providers of full application suites. This process became known as "software as a service" (SaaS). Because these applications are accessed over the internet, SaaS based applications became known as "cloud computing." Now, cloud computing is a major and growing segment of the use of software in ebusiness.

Covisint
www.covisint.com

software as a service (SaaS): Software made available over the internet by independent providers to users who pay on a subscription or pay-as you go basis.

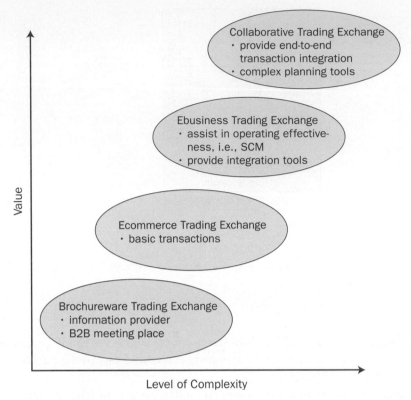

Figure 8.5 Progression stages for trading exchanges and marketplaces

B2B trading exchanges range from basic brochureware sites to complex collaborative environments.

Some of the most successful trading exchanges evolved to become SaaS providers. For illustration purposes, we will discuss SaaS in relation to Covisint, which originally was an automotive trading exchange, but has evolved into a SaaS provider in the cloud.

Covisint was formed in the spring of 2000 by General Motors Corp., DaimlerChrysler AG, and Ford Motor Company. In subsequent years, it expanded into other industries and broadened its services, Covisint is currently owned by Compuware Corporation and now aims to create a business community of buyers, sellers, designers and engineers.

Compuware provides software, experts, and best practices to ensure their applications work well. Compuware solutions provide enterprise-wide applications over the Internet for leading organizations around the world, including 46 of the top 50 Fortune 500 companies. Compuware is therefore a leading SaaS (or cloud) provider.

Under the Compuware umbrella, Covisint has followed a development plan to move far beyond the use of the exchange for procurement to providing services for supply-chain management, collaborative product development, and eprocurement capabilities. The company's goals relate to figure 8.5, which shows the progression stages from an ecommerce trading exchange to a collaborative trading exchange and then a SaaS provider.

Halcrow's Global Procure-to-Pay Project

Halcrow is a consultancy that specialises in the provision of planning, design and management services for infrastructure development worldwide, including those in transport, water, maritime, property and power commissions in over 80 countries. Halcrow is owned and managed by its 7000 employees, tightening their connection with the company.

Specific projects in which Halcrow has been involved include the United Kingdom's High Speed 1 Crossrail and large sections of the highways run by the U.K. Highways Agency. Internationally, the company has worked on Korea's Busan-Geoje Fixed Link, CityCenter Las Vegas, and Abu Dhabi's Yas Island, home of the United Arab Emirates's Grand Prix circuit. For its eprocurement system, Halcrow installed a solution from Proactis, which included purchase-to-pay, supplier relationship management, catalogue management, and e-invoicing technology solutions. Purchase-to-pay refers to the processes that occur from the time of initial requisitioning of a purchase through to the actual payment.

"Once we recognised the need for a spend control solution, we started to look at solutions that would provide us with greater visibility and control over the procure-to-pay cycle; from approving suppliers, authorising staff purchases, and processing invoices for payment," said Julian Ward, group supply-chain manager.

"We identified a number of vendors that specialise in eProcurement solutions and Proactis provided the best fit for our organisation. They have a strong portfolio of solutions that accelerate performance across the entire procure-to-pay cycle and extensive experience of managing UK and international roll-outs," said Ward.

Some important features of the Proactis solution include the ability to direct staff to preferred suppliers and deploy user friendly order templates, contracts and catalogues. The system streamlines the procurement and purchasing processes, reduces the cost of procurement, improves transparency, and contains steps to ensure compliance with company policy. Some of the efficiency is achieved by improving efficiency in accounts payable and automating the processes that manage the receipt, matching and approval of supplier invoices and statements.

After implementing Proactis in Halcrow's 23 U.K. offices, the plan is to extend the solution globally to all offices.

Proactis is widely used around the world. It offers procurement solutions, which help organisations automate the buying cycle where they find, evaluate and engage suppliers, enabling more effective collaboration. Their purchase-to-pay solutions enable organisations to eliminate labour-intensive manual registration of invoices, speed up invoice matching and approvals and gain control of "after-the-event" purchase claims.

Halcrow
www.halcrow.com

Questions

1. What are the advantages to Halcrow of implementing the Proactis system?

2. What are the challenges to Halcrow of implementing the Proactis system?

Source: www.proactis.co.uk/newsevents/news-archive/2010/october/halcrow-completes-first-phase-of-global-proactis-procure-to-pay-project.aspx.

For Buyers Trading exchanges offer buyers the ability to search, select, and acquire goods and services in an efficient manner from numerous suppliers. Suppliers can register with an exchange to list their products in catalogue form on the exchange so that buyers may seek their products.

In addition to hosting catalogues, trading exchanges can facilitate trade by providing extra services that buyers may consider valuable. For example, an exchange could provide reviews of potential suppliers in terms of quality and past customer satisfaction. It could also work closely with buyers to deal with issues such as integration, technology requirements, and training. See table 8.1 for a listing of a number of services that could be offered by trading exchanges.

Eprocurement in the Oil Industry

For some time, the oil industry has recognized the difficulty of duplicating cost savings achieved in other B2B sectors, given that 60 to 80 percent of its spending is on complex products and services with variable pricing based on multiple factors. As a result, the industry and its suppliers have largely focused on improving transaction efficiencies.

In the industry, eprocurement typically accounts for between 20 and 30 percent of spending on MRO assets and services. One industry spokesperson said that the development of ebusiness tools has helped on the transactional side, but hasn't made a huge difference in pricing because suppliers don't like the idea of being commoditized, given the specialist nature of their exploration and production (E & P) products and services and very established relationships. Suppliers resent being steamrollered into dealing with a host of new exchanges and intermediaries, where previously they had established direct relationships.

After industry members started to form their own eprocurement portals, the suppliers baulked at the concept and formed their own consortium—OFS Portal—primarily to handle catalogue content, effectively as a price sheet, with strict controls on the provision of e-invoices and on confidentiality. Chevron threatened to stop procuring from suppliers who didn't use its marketplace. However, the suppliers called Chevron's bluff and its exchange—Petrocosm—collapsed in April 2001. Chevron now uses the Ariba supplier network in North America and has undertaken a few pilot projects in various other countries. Most of its suppliers deal through this network, but a couple of major ones still deal direct.

In May 2005, Trade Ranger, a major emarketplace used in the industry, was forced to change its business model several times and then was acquired by Hubwoo Group—a leading global provider of on-demand eprocurement solutions, which annually handles €5 billion of spending in a variety of sectors, such as chemicals, oil and gas, and rubber.

Shell Corporation has pioneered many ebusiness initiatives and resolutely stayed with Trade Ranger after it was acquired by cc-hubwoo. Dave Conway, vice president, Supply Chain, for Shell E&P, said that the emarketplace is appropriate for about 50 percent of the company's transactions on an annual basis. He won't reveal details of savings, but says: "cc-hubwoo helps us streamline and get efficiency in transactions, removing the administrative burden, speeding up transactions and building transparency."

Surprisingly, optimizing transactional efficiency hasn't reduced the number of procurement managers. "Improved efficiency means procurement managers can be more involved in developing our sourcing strategies from concept design through to placing contracts and managing contracts after award. We've actually increased our procurement organization, and their time has been freed up to focus on more strategic issues, managing relationships around supply performance," said a Shell spokesperson.

Shell also favours reverse auctions. "We're proud to have done over 10,000 sourcing events since 2000, worth over $10 billion," says Conway. "Our strategy is to use the best-in-class reverse auction provider, because we think it is important to have deep integrity and a consistent approach throughout the process, with internal rules that are well communicated to suppliers. We take into account the value offering of the supplier, and award to the best value offering, based on cost of change, demonstrated performance capability, new technology or ability to deliver products and services by a certain time. Just as in a traditional sealed bid, we incorporate these transformation factors into the online reverse auction."

Shell has also recognized that reverse auctions are not appropriate for some complex tenders. "We've learned what is appropriate over the last six years, and have gained a more joined up view with the supply base on this issue."

Hubwoo
www. hubwoo.com

OFS Portal
www.ofs-portal.com

Questions

1. How have the special characteristics of the oil industry affected the eprocurement implementation strategies of companies such as Shell?

2. Would reverse auctions be more acceptable in this industry rather than in government? (See the Estrategy box on page 175.)

Source: B. Davis, "Digital Evolution," *Petroleum Review*, December 2006.

Table 8.1 Potential Trading Exchange Services

Trading exchanges have the potential to provide numerous value-added services to members on both the buy side and sell side of transactions as they increase in complexity.

- Supplier certification, reputation
- Transportation management
- Product life cycle management
- Warehousing and inspection
- Risk mitigation services
- Catalogue display/maintenance
- Financing
- Product configuration
- Derivative instruments
- Community news, employment, etc.
- Returns processing, repair claims
- Payment processing/order management
- Order explosion/routing
- Workflow and business rules

- Contract administration
- Tariffs and duties assessment
- Planning, scheduling, forecasting
- Promotions/campaign management
- Profiling and personalization
- Authentication/security
- Complex pricing
- Private markets, negotiated terms
- Post-sale support, warranty programs
- Receivables management
- Scrap management/reverse logistics
- Inventory availability
- Partner/team selling and promotions
- Back-order management

Covisint offers a number of services to its buyers. Members of the exchange can carry out procurement activities through catalogue methods, or use auction or reverse auction methods. Other services at Covisint include supply-chain optimization, integration of supply chain technologies, and hosting of applications to allow for collaborative design and development of new products in a virtual workspace. It allows buyers to deal more efficiently with suppliers, to reduce costs, and to make gains in effectiveness by using collaborative tools.

For Suppliers Suppliers to trading exchanges are attempting to attract additional business through a medium that allows for efficient sales to take place. By listing products and services on a public trading exchange, a supplier may be aiming to reach new customers across a range of industries. On the other hand, a supplier may join a private trading exchange to more efficiently and effectively deal with customers it has sold to previously.

Covisint offers suppliers access to a huge market, as well as an exchange backed by leading players in the automotive industry. Suppliers can look forward to accessing customers on a more cost-effective basis, and can also look forward to using collaborative functions to become more closely involved in the design process. Covisint also allows suppliers who deal with several customers within an industry the ability to use one major interface to conduct business, thus simplifying the process for employees. These functions should develop strong bonds between trading partners who successfully participate and demonstrate their ability to provide input and meet commitments.

Issues for Trading Exchange Providers

B2B trading exchange providers have a huge challenge ahead of them to deliver on the demands of both buyers and suppliers over the coming years. In addition, those exchanges that have gone through the initial public offering (IPO) process, whereby they raised capital to fund their operations by selling shares to the public, are faced with high expectations from shareholders. The challenges ahead for B2B trading exchange providers include integration, profitability, governance, and legal issues.

Integration: Making It Work Early participants in B2B trading exchanges provided only basic services, such as corporate information on products and contact details. Exchanges, however, have moved quickly beyond that point, and participants now demand the ability to conduct transactions in real time and integrate the data into their own back-end systems. By early 2001 only about 5 percent of companies involved in trading exchanges had achieved full integration of processes with back-end ERP systems.[13] The difficulty is that exchanges may facilitate transactions between companies that use dozens of different back-end systems. For those that are moving into the SaaS environment, however, integration is less of an issue, since the provider uses integrated systems.

Web services have been a viable approach for ebusiness that has changed the way business applications are developed and how they interact. The primary goal of **web services** is to provide a mechanism for applications to communicate with each other from different systems across the internet, based on standards such as XML, SOAP (Simple Object Access Protocol), WSDL (Web Services Definition Language), and UDDI (Universal Description, Discovery, and Integration). In essence, a web service consists of four key components: a message that is exchanged, application software that acts as a service requester or a service provider, shared transport mechanisms that enable the flow of the message, and a service description of these components (i.e., the service itself, the messages that are exchanged by the service, and the service's interface). These descriptions may be machine accessible and processable for use in service discovery systems and in service management systems. Since the service is wrapped up in an interface with a service description, one service is independent of the interaction of other services.

Advances in technology and improvements to existing standards will assist in the process of integration; however, as in most other areas of technology, complexity also continues to rise. XML is used as a tool to assist in integration, even though initially many of the ERP systems were unable to adequately deal with the language. Exchange enablers such as Ariba and Commerce One have established partnerships with leading ERP vendors such as SAP and Oracle to address these very issues. Collaboration in the technology area must continue to be developed in order to facilitate B2B integration.

Profitability B2B trading exchange providers initially struggled with the same issue faced by the failed dot-coms—notably, how to charge for services. It is essential that exchange providers adopt pricing schemes that will allow them to become profitable enough that they can continue to grow and invest in new technologies. Similarly, exchange providers struggle with the issue of whether fees should be based on per-transaction amounts, dollar amounts traded, or a membership sign-up fee.

Covisint, for example, began by charging no fees to encourage participation, but later changed to a fee-per-transaction system to cover the costs of operating the exchange. Other exchanges tie fees more closely to services offered and utilized by the particular customer. Establishing a pricing model for an exchange is not dissimilar to determining pricing in any other business—determine what drives costs, estimate costs, evaluate the market, and establish a profitable pricing system.

web services: A mechanism for applications to communicate with each other from different systems across the internet.

Governance   B2B trading exchange providers encounter additional issues when they attempt to establish policies and procedures to govern their operation. Some of the concerns that may arise include: Who can join the exchange on both buyer and supplier sides? Are data owned by the exchange or individual members? Do members have the ability to demand access to data? Are members restricted in their rights to participate in or own other exchanges?

Responses to the issues noted above vary depending on the format of the exchange. Private exchanges and public exchanges address these concerns in different manners, but each has the same objective—to provide the most value possible to all members of the trading community.

Restricting membership in an exchange may be necessary. As mentioned previously, the exchange may provide a service of supplier accreditation, which effectively limits membership to those suppliers who pass the codes of accreditation established. In other circumstances, however, exchanges will experience pressures from members not to allow competitors to join, in an effort to keep a competitive advantage. Exchanges must clearly document methods by which membership is restricted and enforce policies to achieve consistency and provide a valuable service to members.

Data confidentiality is a key concern to all members. Consider the repercussions if DaimlerChrysler were to find out through Covisint that Supplier X had been giving General Motors a better price and higher service levels. In this age of litigation, this situation would likely lead to several costly lawsuits. Details on data confidentiality and data ownership must be clearly laid out in the exchange's policies to prevent situations such as those described here.

The rights of members are another area of concern for exchange governance. Covisint exchange members, for example, are not restricted from using other exchanges, but the question of their commitment arises when you consider that several of the founding members also operate their own private exchanges. Private exchanges will need to address the issue of member rights if they want to stimulate a community of collaboration where members are not competing directly with the exchange and/or borrowing valuable resources from the exchange itself.

Legal Issues   The growth in the size of B2B trading exchanges and the establishment of Covisint has brought attention to legal issues surrounding B2B trading. The sheer magnitude of Covisint in its early days when it brought together the large automobile manufacturers sparked the U.S. Department of Justice and the U.S. Federal Trade Commission to examine the impact of such exchanges on competition and antitrust laws. Covisint was given approval to go ahead based on its policies, which did not strictly limit competition, despite some concerns by suppliers that they would be heavily pressured to reduce prices. Legal issues that could arise are far-reaching and should be carefully considered in advance by exchanges, both public and private.

AUCTIONS

INTERNET-BASED AUCTIONS HAVE BEEN POPULARIZED BY THE SUCCESS OF EBAY IN developing a model for trading goods between disparate individuals. Indeed, eBay itself is often used by organizations as an eprocurement portal. The development of internet-based auctions, however, has not been limited to consumer-to-consumer transactions, as businesses have begun to embrace the concept for purchasing and procuring all types of goods. Auctions have been built into trading exchanges as one major method of carrying out transactions and have also been employed by government organizations to conduct commerce online.

History of Auctions

The internet has brought attention to auctions recently, but auctions do not have a short history by any means. Some historical researchers claim that auctions actually date back to 500 BC, when marriage and slave auctions were carried out. Other auctions have also been traced to ancient Rome around AD 100, where auctions took place in the atrium auctionarium. Documentation on these auctions is limited, and approximately a thousand years passed before information regarding auctions was again written down. By the mid-1500s auctions again were documented in France, the Netherlands, and China for slaves, estate auctions, and fine art.[14]

Modern auction giants such as Sotheby's and Christie's were formed in the late 1700s in Britain to sell books, art, and other valuable collectibles. Globalization began to take place in the auction industry in the post–World War II era, as Sotheby's and Christie's expanded internationally with their high-quality and prestigious auctions.

Sotheby's
www.sothebys.com
Christie's
www.christies.com

Canadian Snapshots

Eprocurement in Canadian Governments

Canadian governments have put billions of dollars into IT over the years, and one notable success story some of them have achieved is eprocurement, where IT enablement of the purchasing function has brought some very real tangible benefits, at least to jurisdictions that have implemented sophisticated: online tendering and bidding systems.

For example, on the eprocurement site of the British Columbia government, BC Bid, prospective bidders on government projects can find a range of information related to a relevant tender. Some government online procurement sites stop at making available tender forms for download. But BC Bid provides a variety of additional services to its suppliers and potential suppliers. For example, suppliers can register for the site's bid-watching service by creating a profile of the types of government contracts that would be of interest to them, and when one becomes available, the site automatically sends an email. This approach is great for suppliers because it means they will not miss a bidding opportunity. On the other hand, they might be facing greater competition from a larger number of bidders.

Moreover, the BC Bid site does not just make available bid documents for downloading. Companies can also post their bids and proposals online. Thus, the site contains more than just information; it also offers interactivity. The result is easier and cheaper bidding, so the government should get more participants in each bid. While each bidder may lose a greater proportion of their bids, their total number of bidding opportunities should expand. Also, bidders will be able to bid from a distance, again resulting in more bidders.

An effective bidding system requires careful design of an eprocurement site to encourage bids and to ensure that bids and contracts made on it are binding. There should, for example, be a requirement for bidders to register on the site, and they should be required to agree to sensible and fair terms and conditions.

Sometimes, site operators make the terms too one-sided by inserting provisions that are very onerous for users. Such overreaching terms are sometimes found to be unenforceable in the courts.

>

Auctions made their way to the internet in 1995, when Aucnet, a Japanese company, began selling automobiles at auction. eBay followed closely in September 1995, with its storybook beginnings as a technology to assist the fiancée of Pierre Omidyar (eBay's founder) to sell Pez dispensers over the internet. During 1999, eBay purchased Butterfield & Butterfield to transform itself into a bricks-and-clicks organization, and Sotheby's formed a joint venture with Amazon.[15] By 2001 hundreds of auction sites had begun to replicate and expand upon the model of eBay, including internet giants like Yahoo! and Amazon. By 2007, they had become an accepted part of the landscape.

eBreviate
http://ebreviate.com/solutions/technology.html

Types of Auctions

Auctions, both physical and virtual, can take a variety of formats in terms of how the process is conducted and how the winner is determined. The auction format is generally tied to the type of product being sold and the audience where the auction is taking place, in an effort to achieve the maximum revenue for the seller of an asset, or the lowest price for the purchaser of an asset.

A number of different names have been assigned to auctions. The following are the most common types of auctions:[16]

1. *English auction*. In an **English auction** the bidding occurs through an ascending price process when buyers gather in a common location (physical or digital) during specified periods of time. This is the form of auction most would be familiar with, as both estate auctions and online auctions are usually run on this model.

2. *Yankee auction*. A **Yankee auction** is similar to an English auction except that multiple items are sold by price, quantity, and earliest bid time. This type of auction can be used by businesses that are buying products where price is not the only factor to consider and quantity available is a key consideration, such as purchasing supplies where a small quantity would be insufficient and would necessitate buying from multiple suppliers.

3. *Dutch auction*. **Dutch auctions** use a descending price format whereby the auctioneer begins with a high price, and buyers can bid on specific quantities of inventory as the price falls. This type of auction can be used for perishable goods or any other type of commodity in which the process is predicted to have good results. The buyers must purchase the goods they wish to obtain before the price falls to a level such that demand rises enough to deplete the inventory.

English auction: An auction in which the bidding occurs through an ascending price process when buyers gather in a common location (physical or digital) during specified periods of time.

Yankee auction: An auction format similar to an English auction, except that multiple items are sold by price, quantity, and earliest bid time. This form of auction can be used by businesses that are buying products where price is not the only factor to consider and quantity available is a key consideration.

Dutch auction: An auction that uses a descending price format, whereby the auctioneer begins with a high price, and buyers can bid on specific quantities of inventory as the price falls.

4. *Reverse auction.* **Reverse auctions** again use a descending price format but in this case the buyer creates the auction to receive bids from potential suppliers. Suppliers must bid lower than the most recent bid in order to gain the sale in this auction-type format, which has been used quite frequently on the internet through trading exchanges and other formats.

5. *Sealed-bid auction.* A **sealed-bid auction** is often used for products/services where price is only one consideration in the decision. For example, construction contracts often go through a sealed-bid process, as the buyer will consider capabilities, product quality, timelines, and past experience of the contractor before awarding the contract.

6. *Vickrey auction.* The **Vickrey auction** format is an ascending price format in which the highest bidder wins the auction but must pay the price submitted by the second-place bidder. The objective of this auction type is to encourage the price upwards by allowing the buyer to pay the next highest price.

A number of variations on these auction types exist where conditions of anonymity, "opting out," and restrictions are used to control the process. A number of studies have been conducted that indicate that the outcomes Of many of the auction formats are very similar in nature, with a few minor exceptions.[17]

The most common formats of auctions used on the internet to date have been English auctions for consumer-to-consumer (C2C) transactions (such as those on eBay) and reverse auctions for B2B transactions (such as those often used Ariba's FreeMarkets). The English auction format appears to work well in the C2C arena and could also be used in the B2B arena for selected products and services. In addition, governments are being strongly advised to adopt auction models to become more efficient and effective in carrying out their mandates.[18]

The reverse auction model, as noted above, suits itself particularly well to addressing the needs of buyers looking to procure products and services in a cost-effective manner. Ariba's FreeMarkets, for instance, assists numerous customers through the reverse auction process and claims to reduce costs—often by as much as 50 percent.[19]

EDS Canada used a reverse auction to acquire contract technical staffing services after first issuing a **request for proposals (RFP)**. An RFP is the first stage in a procurement process whereby the buyer communicates its needs to potential suppliers, who will then submit tenders based on the requirements. The RFP process was used to short-list qualified suppliers in terms of qualitative aspects such as service capabilities, experience, and guarantees. Initial requests for pricing information were included in the RFP, but it was made clear to suppliers that pricing details would be dealt with later. In association with eBreviate, the procurement solutions arm of A.T. Kearney, Inc., EDS provided the six short-listed candidates with information on the auctioning process. In discussing the time involved to carry out the reverse auction, Patricia Moser, director of Global Purchasing, commented that turnaround time was quite impressive since, "We knew that the bids we were receiving reflected the going market rate for our size and type of organization. Instead of having to go through a research house for this information, we were able to get this information during the auction."[20] EDS Canada was able to successfully carry out the auction, and within two months had hired a labour contractor for a two-year period, using a new purchasing strategy. Previously, this process would have taken up to six months, and would have involved a lot more administrative work.

E-auction Requirements

To successfully carry out online auctions, either to sell or buy products or services, it is necessary to properly plan and administer a process that uses the appropriate technologies. For auctions to be fair to participants, the process requires full disclosure and security procedures, which prevent the "rules of the game" from being broken. In addition, e-auctions must provide the capability to integrate data, notify users of recent information, and process/facilitate payments.

Full Disclosure   To function efficiently, auctions must provide participants with all relevant information related to the prospective purchase or sale. In addition to basic descriptions of product or service types and quantity information, it is necessary to provide details on quality levels, warranty programs, transportation agreements, payment terms, and after-sale support mechanisms. In essence, an auction will only work properly when participants are aware of what they are getting involved in. Similar to the "viewing period" in traditional auctions, where buyers are given time to view the items for sale and determine their own preferences, the disclosure of information in an e-auction will yield better results and create more active participation. Where possible, emerging technologies, such as streaming video and collaborative discussions, should be used to provide visual support to the disclosure of information.

Integration   The use of auctions creates some unique considerations for integration of the auctioning system with the back-end ERP system. For sellers, it is important that the ERP system can be integrated with the auction's front end or the auction provider's system to capture pricing and shipping information, so that the transportation-planning process can be carried out effectively. Buyers can also benefit from integration if details on incoming shipments, cost information for acquired assets, or upcoming expenses can be captured.

Notification Mechanisms   Auction providers, whether external (such as FreeMarkets) or internal, must develop notification mechanisms that are effective at ensuring that all participants in an auction are up to date at all times. Early auction sites used email extensively for communication, but developments in the area have led to the use of push technologies, which allow the auction server to frequently update clients directly through the internet browser. Information relating to the current status of the auction can be critical in gaining new business for sellers or cutting costs for buyers, so it is essential that mechanisms are in place to provide details. EDS Canada's first e-auction made use of timed bidding, whereby if any bid was placed during the last 10 minutes of the auction time block, a 15-minute extension would be added to ensure that other suppliers had an adequate opportunity to resubmit.

Auction Security   Auction security is crucial to ensure that the process is executed appropriately and that hackers are unable to sabotage an auction. In addition, it is necessary to ensure that information that is meant to be confidential is in no way breached, or the use of auctions in the future could be compromised. For example, if a product's design and manufacturing details are released to a potential buyer but the auction mechanism inappropriately releases the information to a competitor in the auction, the reputation of the auction provider and buyer could be damaged. To prevent this type of mishap, the auction process needs to use cryptographic techniques similar to those used by other electronic transactions. In addition, the auction process needs to adequately create audit trails so participants can develop confidence that the technology will conduct the auction according to the rules and award business to the appropriate supplier.

Payment Capabilities   The requirement for payment capabilities differs depending on the nature of the auction, the products or services, and the participants (whether B2B or C2C). However, the ability for auction providers to facilitate payments will become increasingly important. Early in the life of eBay, the potential for the business was limited due to the lack of convenient payment mechanisms. The growth of numerous payment schemes for online commerce (such as PayPal), however, has allowed eBay to successfully grow and for consumers to sell to one another by paying for goods through online mechanisms. Similarly, B2B transactions with unknown suppliers have been limited by payment mechanisms. Technology advances are helping in this area as well (see chapter 6), while other services like escrow payments and funds transfer are also helping to make these transactions possible.

The Auctioning Process

The process of conducting an auction online varies depending on the type of auction and the rules adopted, but the basic process is presented in figure 8.6.

Auction Configuration   The auction initiator (who may be either the buyer or seller) and auction enabler must establish the preliminary requirements for the auction at the beginning of the process. The auction type (English, reverse, etc.) must be decided upon, as well as the details of the products or services involved (quantity, quality, etc.). In addition, the configuration will control the timing details of the auction, minimum bid amounts, minimum bid increments, auction closing rules, and other details.

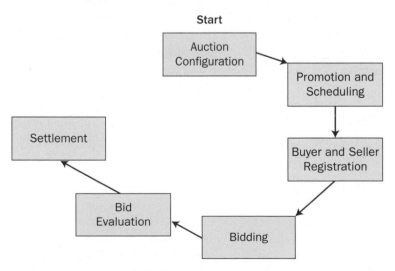

Figure 8.6 The auctioning process

The auctioning process must be carefully executed to be efficient and effective.

Promotion and Scheduling   In coordination with the auction enabler, the initiator will carry out promotion and advertising consistent with the strategy for the auction. This may involve simply notifying a number of potential participants that the initiator is familiar with, or an advertising campaign to a broad or targeted audience. This stage of the process may also involve soliciting participants from other exchange or auction providers to expand the number of participants to improve the outcome of the auction.

Buyer and Seller Registration   In this step of the process, both the buyer(s) and seller(s) must register with the auction provider and deal with such concerns as sharing of cryptographic keys, contact information, and other basic details. At this stage, the process can be either "open" or "by invitation only," depending on the preferences of the initiator of the auction. Participants may be investigated or evaluated at this phase as well to ensure that they meet standards they have claimed (e.g., ISO certification) and to verify credit if necessary.

Bidding   The bidding phase of the auction may last for minutes, days, or weeks depending on the parameters outlined at the configuration stage. While this stage is primarily concerned with carrying out the auction and executing the process, it may also include a training element. For example, new participants may be able to use a demonstration to evaluate the bidding process and train members of their firm. There may also be a number of standby mechanisms, such as the ability to use fax or voice in the event of bidding process problems. Once the bidding has begun, this stage essentially carries out the details of the configuration by controlling minimum bid increments and notifying participants of changes in auction or bid status.

Bid Evaluation   The evaluation of bids may be automatic or may involve human intervention depending on the format of the auction chosen. For example, a reverse auction may automatically notify the "winner" at the end of the bidding time period, whereas a sealed-bid auction would simply notify participants that their information had been received and they would be contacted later. If factors other than price are involved at this stage, the process is complicated; however, alternative methods can be utilized, such as pre-screening participants for qualitative factors (as EDS Canada did).

Settlement   The final stage of the process involves settlement of contractual terms, payment, and transfer of goods. The ordering and method of carrying out this stage may differ based on a number of factors, but the key is to execute payment and enter a valid contract. This stage may be entirely electronic (besides delivery of tangible goods) or may involve an in-person meeting, again depending on the preferences of the parties involved.

The auction process as described here could take only a few hours in total or could occur over a period of months. The importance of the process is that each of the stages needs to be thoroughly planned and executed, taking into account the auction requirements discussed earlier for an auction to be successful.

The Future of Auctions

The use of auctions in the procurement and sale of goods is likely to continue to grow over the next several years. Some pundits go so far as to predict the demise of fixed prices in business, with a move to dynamic pricing.[21] **Dynamic pricing** is the use of market-based, negotiated prices for transactions, which some analysts argue can be easily

dynamic pricing: The use of market-based, negotiated prices for transactions.

```
┌─────────────────┐    │ Automobile Metamarket
│                 │    │
│ Fully integrated,│    │ • Auto manufacturers
│ informational, and│   │ • New car dealers
│ transactional   │    │ • Used car dealers
│ marketplace     │    │ • Newspaper classifieds
│                 │    │ • Auto magazine
└─────────────────┘    │ • Peer and expert opinions
                       │ • Financing companies
                       │ • Insurance companies
                       │ • Mechanics
                       │ • Service shops
                       │ • Spare parts dealers
```

Figure 8.7 An automotive metamarket

The consolidation of auctions and B2B exchanges may lead to the creation of metamarkets such as this automotive market.

accomplished through internet-based auction technologies. While the demise of fixed pricing is unlikely, the increasing use of auction models for conducting business will continue to occur.

To facilitate the improved use of auction models to carry out commerce, the idea of metamarkets and meta-auctions has been discussed. Essentially, a metamarket would result in the linking of all related auctions and markets together to form a large base of participants with common interests. Figure 8.7 provides an example of a metamarket for the automotive industry. The difference between this concept and the concept of industry exchanges is that the metamarket would allow for various exchanges and auctions to integrate all the participants to achieve a critical mass, which would lead to a more efficient market of "frictionless commerce."[22]

Eprocurement, trading exchanges, and auctions will continue to converge and be more easily integrated with back-office technologies over the coming months and years. The creation of metamarkets is an ideal that may only occur in the distant future, but it gives competitors in this area something to strive for.

CHAPTER SUMMARY

Eprocurement has become an important ebusiness initiative in the last few years. Recognizing the potential for reduced administrative costs, increased turnaround time, and improved pricing, businesses have begun to embark upon eprocurement initiatives to automate paper processes. The major success factors for eprocurement are the ability of organizations to integrate digital procurement data into the ERP system and the flexibility of the organization to modify existing business processes.

Trading exchanges form an important part of an overall eprocurement strategy. Exchanges provide a medium through which buyers and suppliers can transact business in an efficient manner. Horizontal exchanges are those that target business across numerous industries, such as an office supplies exchange. Vertical exchanges are those that target business within a specific industry throughout the supply chain, such as a health care industry exchange. As trading exchanges evolve, they progress towards a medium through which eprocurement, supply-chain management, and customer relationship management are conducted.

Some exchanges, such as Covisint, have evolved into SaaS providers, offering suites of applications over the internet (the cloud), which in the case of trading exchanges make good platforms for collaboration.

The growth of the online auction industry sparked by consumer-to-consumer (C2C) giant eBay has resulted in increased awareness of auctioning applications. The business-to-business (B2B) community has started using auctioning techniques in the eprocurement process as an efficient means of executing transactions for many types of goods and services. B2B transactions have commonly been carried out through the use of reverse auctions, and as the industry and technologies develop, many of the trading exchanges are facilitating auctioning processes.

The auctioning process employs numerous technologies to operate efficiently and effectively. For all auction participants to be treated fairly, it is essential that auction policies are provided and that bidders are kept up-to-date throughout the auction period. Auctions in the future are predicted to increase the use of dynamic pricing in business, possibly in both B2B and business-to-consumer (B2C) transactions.

Key Terms

Dutch auction (p. 187)

dynamic pricing (p. 191)

English auction (p. 187)

horizontal trading exchange (p. 178)

maverick buying (p. 177)

private exchange (p. 178)

public exchange (p. 179)

request for proposals (RFP) (p. 188)

reverse auction (p. 188)

sealed-bid auction (p. 188).

vertical trading exchange (p. 178)

Vickrey auction (p. 188)

web services (p. 184)

Yankee auction (p. 187)

MyEbusinessLab Tools for Online Learning

To help you master the material in this chapter and stay up to date with new developments in ebusiness, visit the MyEBusinessLab at www.pearsoned.ca/myebusinesslab. Resources include the following:

- **Pre- and Post-Test Questions**
- **Additional Chapter Questions**
- **Author Blog**
- **Recommended Readings**
- **Commentaries on Current Trends**
- **Additional Topics in Ebusiness**
- **Internet Exercises**
- **Glossary Flashcards**

Endnotes

1. T. Wilson, "E-procurement Revisited—More Than Cheap Supplies,"*Internetweek* (April 23, 2001).

2. W. Atkinson, "Web Ordering, Auctions Will Play Limited Role,"*Purchasing* (April 5, 2001).

3. B. Gates with C. Hemingway, *Business @ The Speed of Thought: Using a Digital Nervous System* (New York: Warner Books, 1999).

4. B. Gates with C. Hemingway, *Business @ The Speed of Thought: Using a Digital Nervous System* (New York: Warner Books, 1999).

5. R. Handfield, "E-procurement and the Purchasing Process," Hot Topics, Supply Chain Resource Consortium, NC State University, October 22, 2003, http://scm.ncsu.edu/public/hot/hot031022.html, accessed November 20, 2004.

6. H. Harreld, "Optimizing Supplier Selection,"*InfoWorld* (November 16, 2001).

7. J. Geriant, "Drug Company Triples Cost Savings via E-procurement,"*Supply Management* (March 15, 2001).

8. "E-procurement Savings,"*Controller's Report*, (April 2001).

9. "E-procurement Saves,"*Internetweek* (April 2, 2001).

10. B. Gates with C. Hemingway, *Business @ The Speed of Thought: Using a Digital Nervous System* (New York: Warner Books, 1999), 49.

11. "eMarketplaces Boost B2B Trade," Forrester Research (February 2000).

12. J. Burke, "Is GE the Last Internet Company?"*Red Herring* (December 15, 2000), 55.

13. J. Burke, "Is GE the Last Internet Company?"*Red Herring* (December 15, 2000), 55.

14. Vendio Services Inc., website, www.vendio.com, accessed April 20, 2004.

15. Vendio Services Inc., website, www.vendio.com, accessed April 20, 2004.

16. D. Wyld, *The Auction Model: How the Public Sector Can Leverage the Power of E-Commerce through Dynamic Pricing* (Southeastern Louisiana University: November 2000).

17. M. Kumar and S. Feldman, *Internet Auctions*, Iac report (IBM T.J. Watson Research Centre: November 1998).

18. D. Wyld, *The Auction Model: How the Public Sector Can Leverage the Power of E-Commerce through Dynamic Pricing* (Southeastern Louisiana University: November 2000).

19. D. Wyld, *The Auction Model: How the Public Sector Can Leverage the Power of E-Commerce through Dynamic Pricing* (Southeastern Louisiana University: November 2000).

20. W. Atkinson, "IT Firm Uses Reverse Auction for Big Contract Labor Buy,"*Purchasing* (December 22, 2000).

21. D. Wyld, *The Auction Model: How the Public Sector Can Leverage the Power of E-Commerce through Dynamic Pricing* (Southeastern Louisiana University: November 2000).

22. M. Sawhney, "Making New Markets: Sellers Need to Better Understand Buyers to Achieve the Promise of the Net Economy,"*Business 2.0* (May 1999).

Chapter 9
Customer Relationship Management

Learning Objectives

When you complete this chapter you should be able to:

1   Describe the process of customer relationship management (CRM) and explain its relevance to ebusiness.

2   Identify the sources of data for CRM and how that data can be turned into information.

3   Outline the goals of CRM and how technology helps to achieve those goals.

4   Name and describe the core internet-enabled CRM technologies.

5   Describe how CRM fits into systems integration.

6   Identify the issues that can arise during CRM implementation and how they may be addressed.

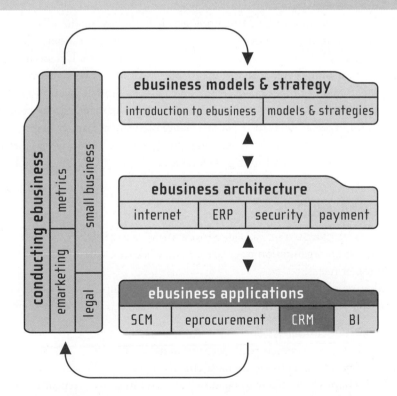

INTRODUCTION

EBUSINESS, WITH ITS NEED FOR SPEED IN MEETING—EVEN ANTICIPATING—THE WISHES OF customers, has increased the demand for a customer-centric approach to business. The key to finding out what customers want, developing relationships with them, and managing those relationships lies in the careful application of appropriate technologies.

Customer relationship management (CRM) in an ebusiness context is the use of technology to establish, develop, maintain, and optimize relationships with customers by focusing on the understanding of customers' needs and desires.[1] Besides technology, CRM also necessarily involves business processes, human resources, and strategies to enable businesses to focus on customers to deliver better profitability. CRM technologies allow customer information to be gathered through a single point and then used throughout an organization to improve the relationship with customers (either businesses or end consumers).

CRM has been adopted by organizations large and small, online and offline. For example, Canadian Tire Corporation adopted some of Blue Martini Software's CRM applications to better serve and interact with customers, both online and through its call centre. Online customers are able to benefit from Canadian Tire's loyalty program, Canadian Tire Money, and the company can track and understand its customers' online shopping habits using the CRM software. In addition, the online store can customize prices based on the shopper's postal code, since prices at each store vary because each store's independent franchise owner can set its own prices. This enables customers to see prices that correspond with the prices at their local stores. Offline customers who phone the Canadian Tire call centre are better served because customer service representatives (CSRs) are automatically provided with account histories and information on the customers. The application of CRM technologies is helping Canadian Tire retain its competitive position in the retail market for automotive, sports, and home products.

Although CRM is a relatively simple concept, successfully carrying out a CRM implementation and developing the appropriate attitudes with employees can be very challenging. Similar to other major technology implementations such as ERP systems and eprocurement systems, changes required in business processes are always a challenge. While the basic idea of focusing on the customer has existed since business began, CRM offers a revolutionary means of fully understanding, predicting, and responding to customers and potential customers. See the Estrategy box for an example of CRM by an online retailer.

THE CRM PROCESS

CRM MUST INCLUDE THE MAJOR FUNCTIONAL AREAS (E.G., MARKETING, SALES, service) across an organization to create a framework that will allow employees to better fulfill customer needs.

Marketing can use CRM to establish new relationships as well as develop and optimize existing relationships through a better understanding of questions such as:

Who are our customers?
What do these customers really want from us?
What advertising methods are most effective?
Which channels are likely to be most successful in gaining repeat business?

Estrategy

eBags Focuses on the Customer

eBags is an online retailer of bags, luggage, and travel accessories based in Denver, Colorado, which sells in both the United States and the United Kingdom. The company's management feels that the key to maximizing profitability is understanding the customer and designing advertising campaigns and websites based on customers' needs. When the corporate website was redesigned, it included an extensive customer interface that features its loyalty program and various aspects of customer interests, such as setting up an account, managing that account, communicating with the company and help with shopping.

eBags decided that a customer loyalty program was required to retain existing customers and chose KANA e-Marketing for its program. As well as focusing on the loyalty program, eBags is integrating its front-end website and its back-end applications (J.D. Edwards ERP and Oracle databases) with the KANA CRM applications. Other information sources such as email, live online chat, and telephone conversations are also being captured to add to the information eBags possesses about customer behaviour.

The president and CEO of eBags, Jon Nordmark, described the importance of the CRM initiative as follows:

> Conversion rates are the best measure of customer satisfaction. Improving those rates means making continuous improvements on click-throughs on emails, getting more browsing customers to put items in their shopping carts, and getting more shopping carts all the way to the order desk.

The CRM application allows eBags to more quickly analyze the customer information it gathers, up to five times as fast as previous analytical tools, which can save the company numerous lost opportunities.

Once the website redesign and customer analysis techniques were in place, eBags began to employ email marketing and campaign management using its CRM application. By capturing all data related to the campaigns, including response rates, buy rates, and customer analysis, as well as using web analytics on the site, eBags has been able to determine behavioural patterns. For example, eBags has found that it only gets 9 percent of all shoppers to actually place items into their shopping carts, but of those 9 percent there is a 40 percent conversion rate to sale. eBags was a pioneer of web analytics, using Omniture to test how effective its web images were for selling:

it discovered that 20 percent more click-throughs came from lifestyle images featuring its products than from images of the products alone.

eBags has learned a number of important facts about its customers through the use of technology, such as how its email ad campaigns work. The analysis of data has led eBags to conclude that customers are much more likely to buy items placed at the beginning or end of an email ad. This information allows eBags to design more profitable campaigns by placing high-margin items at the beginning and end of email campaign messages.

eBags didn't stand still after successfully employing its CRM application; in fact, Nordmark stated that he wanted the company to link its databases and share information extensively with those of its suppliers and partners. Since the eBags system is already automated, Nordmark argues that collaboration is simply the next logical step.

Looking to expand its online presence and brand image, eBags has partnered with notable companies such as Amazon.com and AAA. The partnership with AAA offers members discounts on eBags products at the AAA travel store. Through a partnership with Amazon, eBags is able to offer its products to even more potential customers. The partnership with Amazon, however, is somewhat different. Instead of sending customers directly to the eBags site, eBags merely acts as a distribution partner for Amazon.

eBags
www.ebags.com

Questions

1. What possible advantage could eBags see in sharing its CRM data with suppliers and partners?

2. Do partnerships such as the one with AAA complicate the CRM process and data capture? How?

3. From a CRM perspective, which information do you think eBags would value the most?

Sources: www.ebags.com; "eBags Learns That Lifestyle Images Work Better Than Product Images," *Internet Retailer.com*, August 4, 2005, www.internetretailer.com/dailyNews.asp?id=15692; T. P. Moore, "Web Retailers Try to Keep Shopping Carts Moving Along," *Denver Business Journal*, December 8 2006, www.bizjournals.com/denver/stories/2006/12/11/story15.html.

In addition, marketing can better develop and manage campaigns by using centralized customer data, rather than the piecemeal information that is often used in the absence of an organized CRM process. The concept of emarketing is explored more fully in chapter 11.

The sales area will benefit from CRM by providing sales representatives with better information that they can use to up-sell or cross-sell products and services. **Up-selling** is the process of encouraging customers to purchase higher-priced products or services. **Cross-selling** is the process of encouraging customers to purchase complementary or additional products or services from the firm. If a business customer phones a salesperson and the CRM application can automatically provide the customer's purchase history, credit details, and other information, the salesperson may be able to generate more sales dollars than would be possible without the information. If the salesperson can up-sell a customer from a mid-level product to a higher-quality product, sales will increase, and the customer will have a better product offering. The salesperson may also be able to cross-sell by providing customers with information regarding optional equipment that is available or details of how products can be combined to enhance their capabilities. In advanced systems, these selling opportunities may even be scripted and provide additional details the customer may wish to know, such as how the product compares with that of the competition.

The customer service area of many businesses also offers the opportunity to become involved in selling while providing valuable customer service. For example, when a bank customer phones looking for information on current interest rates, a CSR can see that the customer has outstanding credit card debts for the past few months but has a strong credit rating. A scripted discussion may appear on-screen that guides the CSR through the process of "selling" the customer debt services by consolidating high-interest credit cards into a personal loan. This situation essentially can turn a service-based interaction into a selling opportunity.

An illustration of the CRM process will provide a clearer understanding of the processes and technologies involved in CRM. Figure 9.1 shows the core components of CRM and outlines the integration of internal departments. Integration of internal processes across the organization must include all potential areas that may directly or indirectly impact the customer. For example, sales would be an obvious area to include in CRM, but research and development (R & D) may be another important integration point. Information on customer feedback needs to be linked to the design process, while information about R & D relating to new products needs to be communicated to sales and marketing internally, and selectively to customers.

The process of CRM can be described as data capture, data analysis, strategic decision making, and implementation (see figure 9.2).

Data Capture

The first stage, data capture, occurs from each of the touch points in figure 9.1, including online sources (e.g., web forms, email), offline sources (e.g., warranty registration cards), and back-office data integration. Data are stored in a data warehouse and will generally be formatted and modified to suit the particular requirements of the organization by removing unnecessary data elements and adding any necessary data descriptions. A **data warehouse** is a central data repository utilized to organize, store, analyze, and report upon data for decision-making purposes.

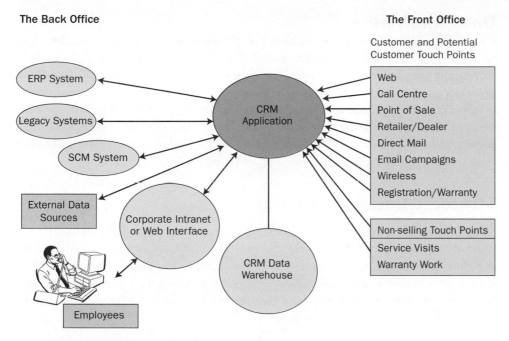

Figure 9.1 CRM integration

CRM requires integration of customer data and access to the CRM application to occur seamlessly across multiple systems.

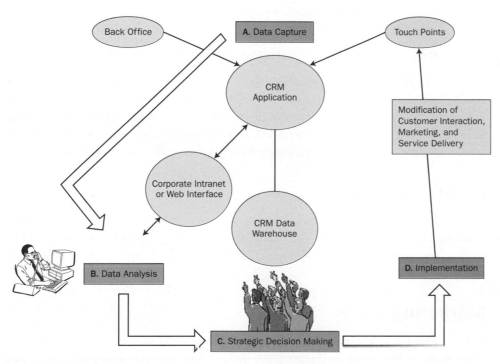

Figure 9.2 The CRM process

The CRM process is a cycle that begins and ends with customer touch points.

Data Analysis

CRM applications offer a number of tools to analyze and understand customer data. The second step of the CRM process, data analysis, involves the use of CRM applications to explore the data to identify relevant customer information. Some organizations refer to this component of CRM as **customer intelligence**. The data analysis stage requires the involvement of individuals who have a strong understanding of the organization's business strategy and the industry. This analysis may be carried out by any of sales, marketing, service, or other personnel, but collaboration across departments will often lead to the discovery of important factors that may not otherwise have been learned.

Strategic Decision Making

The information resulting from the data analysis stage may lead to the identification of areas where management should make changes. The management team would compare any planned initiatives to corporate strategy. For example, marketing analysis may highlight an opportunity to sell a new upscale product, but management's strategic objective may be to focus on cost-effectiveness. Therefore, the marketing opportunity may be dismissed in favour of a cost-reduction measure.

Implementation

Implementation is a critical stage, where objectives must be understood and outcomes predicted. Predicted outcomes should be measurable. Cross-departmental teams are often necessary to effectively implement change.

CRM vs. Business Intelligence

While CRM makes use of data warehousing technology and data analysis techniques, it is not the same as business intelligence (BI). CRM data may be used within a BI application but would only form one component of the system. As illustrated in figure 9.3, business intelligence is broader in scope than CRM. As technologies continue to converge, CRM applications are becoming offerings within BI applications. BI is examined in chapter 10.

GOALS OF CRM

THE GOALS OF CRM ARE MANY AND CAN BE ORGANIZED INTO A NUMBER OF KEY AREAS, SUCH as marketing, sales, and service. The overall goal of any CRM implementation should be to improve customer relationships by providing better service, improved sales efforts, and reduced marketing costs.

Marketing Goals

The goals for CRM in the marketing area are extensive and in many cases overlap with other areas. Some of the marketing goals include improved marketing planning, sales forecasting, competitor intelligence (e.g., asking customers about their experience with competitors), trend analysis, and performance analysis.

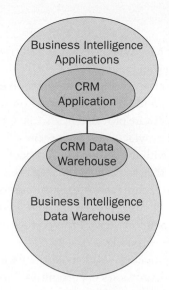

Figure 9.3 CRM and BI

CRM overlaps with BI but has a different focus and narrower scope.

Sales Goals

In the sales area, CRM strategies aim to increase efficiency, improve customer interaction and service, and simplify the sales process. In addition, sales goals include the redirection of sales to the most efficient and effective selling channels (e.g., telesales, internet sales, etc.).

CRM efforts have developed naturally from some firms' efforts in the area of **sales force automation (SFA)**, the process of simplifying sales in the field and the integration of sales activity into the corporate information structure. CRM is a much more encompassing strategy than SFA, but the two share some common goals. SFA efforts began with simplistic tools such as contact managers, and later emerged into sophisticated technologies to track leads, integrate databases, and share information with back-end systems. Some of the leading CRM application providers have evolved from being SFA providers in the past.

sales force automation (SFA): The process of simplifying sales in the field and the integration of sales activity into the corporate information structure.

Service Goals

Service departments and CSRs have the capability, through the use of technology, of becoming effective sales contacts by developing an enhanced understanding of customer needs. As with other areas in the organization, customer service needs to examine its role as a customer touch point and learn which service methods are most effective for particular customer groups. (See the Canadian Snapshots box for a look at customer service goals at Hydro-Québec.)

CRM METRICS

CRM involves gathering large volumes of data for analysis to better understand customers. The large volumes of data, however, will lead to storage capacity problems and result in slow response times if unnecessary data are not purged from the system. CRM metrics are discussed in Chapter 12.

SOCIAL CRM

CRM HAS BECOME MUCH MORE POWERFUL WITH THE INCREASING USE OF SOCIAL media, such as Facebook, Twitter, and LinkedIn. Facebook is often used for CRM because of its extensive penetration into the community at large. To employ social CRM, a company sets up its own Facebook profile (or profiles based on segments or product lines of the company). It then installs software provided by a social CRM provider, such as Oracle or Cisco. Most of the big CRM providers now offer social CRM tools.

Social CRM tools interact with the activity on Facebook and provide an interface for company managers to monitor that activity and manage the customer-related aspects of it. For example, Facebook allows visitors to write on the corporate wall, and the company can respond to those comments. It also provides for "like" buttons, which a company can monitor and analyze from the point of view of the profiles of those liking or unliking a particular element in the Facebook profile.

Social CRM software will provide metrics about the Facebook activity of a company and also analyze its fanbase to identify sales opportunities. Most importantly, social CRM provides an opportunity for a company to interact with its customer base and include their views for consideration by its decision teams.

While all of these things are possible, every company will not find it worthwhile to implement all of them. Therefore, they need to develop a strategy that responds to their corporate marketing objectives and is consistent with their corporate strategic plans.

The data capture process described earlier is simplified by technology that can easily gather data from customers and prospects. Social CRM accomplishes this objective well. Also, information typed into online forms or through email can be automatically moved to the data warehouse through automated tools.

Collecting information about customer behaviours is actually easier online than in a traditional bricks-and-mortar retail business. The latter may never realize that potential

> **Social CRM:** The use of social media in deploying Customer Relationship Management.

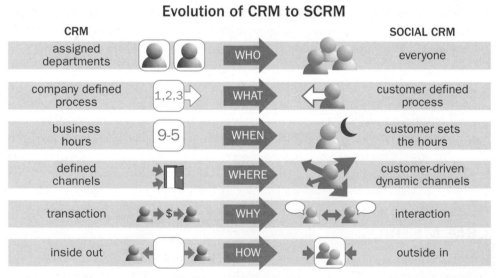

Figure 9.4 Evolution of CRM to social CRM

Source: © 2010 Chess Media Group.

Hydro-Québec Improves Customer Service

Hydro-Québec is one of Canada's largest providers of energy, with more than 3.5 million customers throughout North America. With the deregulation of the energy markets, Hydro-Québec has decided to adopt a proactive strategy to deal with customer service and relationship management.

According to Hydro-Québec's vision statement, "Customers are the reason we are in business and we must show them that, at Hydro-Québec, the customer comes first. Whether in Quebec or on international markets, we want to satisfy our customers by supplying energy products and services of a quality that meets their needs at competitive prices." While numerous companies may have statements similar to this, Hydro-Québec has taken action by adopting Siebel (now owned by Oracle) applications to assist in CRM.

Hydro-Québec adopted Siebel Sales to improve relationships with corporate customers and improve information sharing among sales and service staff. Realizing that deregulation might bring substantial competition, the company began implementing its CRM strategy with corporate customers, who make up a large portion of sales and offer a stronger opportunity for relationship development than residential customers.

Siebel Sales allows company representatives to consolidate and share customer information in a manner that was never before possible. Previous attempts to automate the system based on periodic updates resulted in little success due to missing information and lack of timeliness. The adoption of CRM has allowed employees to work more successfully as a team, and management claims that customer service has been improved with more accurate and up-to-date information available.

Sales contact in the past had been primarily in person, and Hydro-Québec realized that customers were beginning to demand more personalized and timely service. The company is improving on its CRM strategy by adopting additional products from Siebel, including Siebel eChannel and Siebel Handheld. Siebel eChannel allows customers to communicate with the company by internet, email, and cellular channels while continuing to capture data and provide seamless customer service. Siebel Handheld is an application that lends support to sales staff so they may interact with the CRM application anytime, anywhere.

Hydro-Québec's implementation of Siebel applications is being integrated with both its back-end ERP system (Oracle) and its front-end applications, allowing efficient transfer of information. One of the key selling points of the Siebel applications to Hydro-Québec was the integration of French-language support that was well designed and reduced requirements for translation.

The benefits of CRM at Hydro-Québec include improved customer service, enhanced information sharing and team selling, faster sales cycles, and an increase in customer retention rates.

Hydro-Québec
www.hydroquebec.com
Siebel Systems
www.oracle.com/siebel

Questions

1. Should deregulation have been the motivator for Hydro-Québec to get involved in CRM?

2. What types of communication are likely to take place through Siebel eChannel with corporate customers? How is this more efficient?

3. Will CRM assist Hydro-Québec in any way to develop relationships with residential customers? How?

Sources: www.hydro.qc.ca; www.oracle.com/applications/crm/siebel/index.html.

customers were in the store but couldn't find the product they were looking for, but online stores can find this out through click-stream analysis, log-file analysis, and efficient feedback systems. Web analytics have also been used to track customer behaviour online in order to provide hot leads to salespeople interacting with those customers. For example, web analytics that are tied to lead-tracking software can tell when people click on a promotion and the depth of their investigation so that sales personnel have information on which prospects are most ready to buy.[2]

Online Contact Management

Internet-based contacts can be a valuable resource for developing customer relationships. It is common, for example, for individuals to be contacted by salespeople after registering online for free demos and product white papers. The CRM systems at these businesses were designed to capture the information needed on prospective buyers so that a salesperson could later follow up with them. Some studies have indicated that personal follow-up with such contacts has resulted in a 20 to 37 percent increase in sales. The internet can be a tremendous means of gathering information on prospects, but it is necessary to use that information effectively to generate sales.

Online Marketing Campaigns

CRM analyses should lead to the ability to create targeted online marketing campaigns by better understanding who the online customers are, how their needs may differ, and what predictors of buying are relevant. As businesses move to an online sales channel, historic information regarding customer segments and buying patterns may need to be completely reevaluated. Customers making use of internet technologies for purchasing may have different demographics, and new prospects may be found who would not have been identified through traditional campaigns.

Email Campaigns The use of email for sales is a controversial but important area for ebusinesses to consider. Sending a large volume of general-interest emails will likely result in negative attitudes by customers; however, targeted email can be very beneficial. Past customers are known to be those who are most likely to buy again, so email offers to existing customers, if done appropriately, can result in additional sales. The use of email in online marketing is discussed more fully in chapter 11.

CRM applications such as those offered by Oracle's Siebel Systems include advanced tools for creating, managing, and analyzing email campaigns. To benefit from experience, it is essential that email campaigns be carefully monitored. Details of sales arising from email campaigns should be used to evaluate campaign success.

Real-Time Chat The internet brings a number of technologies to the table to create relationships with customers or potential customers, an important one being the use of chat technologies. A number of service providers are available that can integrate live chat into a website so that a user can ask to chat immediately with a human being. For example, HumanClick Ltd. provides chat applications that can be used to provide improved customer service on a website. In addition, social CRM, through such facilities as the chat function in Facebook, provides this resource.

Chat functions are similar to instant messaging (IM), which has become extremely popular, especially with younger people. The potential business applications of this technology are impressive. A prospective customer can get information immediately from a sales representative, for instance, rather than having to dial a toll-free number (potentially having to go offline to do so). Many "browsers" would not go the extra step to phone with a question, but the live chat session makes the inquiry convenient and hassle free, potentially leading to new business. Existing customers can also utilize real-time chat or IM for assistance with finding specific product information or to learn about special offers to existing customers.

Advanced technologies also allow chat sessions to be interactive, with the support person actually guiding the user through the web, giving detailed advice on where to find something and effectively taking the customer to the site they are looking for.

Voice over Internet Protocol Similar to real-time chat sessions in its utility, **Voice over Internet Protocol (VoIP)** is an application that can enhance service to customers and prospects. VoIP is an internet telephony protocol that relays voice signals across the internet, whether in a computer-to-phone call or a computer-to-computer call. VoIP allows users to phone a customer service representative through the internet by clicking on a "Phone us now" button on a website. As broadband technologies continue to improve, the use of VoIP is likely to increase, allowing users a convenient, low-cost method of connecting with businesses to receive service.

Voice over Internet Protocol (VoIP): A set of protocols for carrying voice signals/telephone calls over the internet.

Intelligent Agents Also known as "web bots" or "bots" (from "robots"), **intelligent agents** are automated tools that can help users find products or information throughout a site and can contribute to up-selling and cross-selling of products. For example, if a truck owner is searching a supplier's site for a needed part and has difficulty identifying the specific part required, an intelligent agent could pull information about the customer's existing truck, past buying patterns, and other details to select web content that may be useful to the customer. The intelligent agent may come back with suggestions that might work for the customer, including higher-quality products or supplemental items that can be purchased. Intelligent agents have been found to increase the quality and efficiency of the decision that the end user ultimately makes.[3]

intelligent agent: An automated tool that can help users find products or information throughout a site and can contribute to up-selling and cross-selling of products.

Email Management The volume of email requests sent to many organizations with a successful web presence quickly outpaces the capability of the organization to respond. An effective CRM strategy would require that email requests be handled in a very reasonable period of time. User and customer expectations are leading to faster and faster response times. Email management technologies are available to help deal with the mass of emails that are sure to come with growth.

Email represents one of the many customer/prospect touch points discussed earlier and, as such, is a form of data that must be captured. Leading CRM providers' applications integrate email data into the CRM applications so that call centre staff who later receive contact from a customer can review former correspondence, thus remaining up to date with all business/customer information.

Incoming email can be sorted and redirected to appropriate individuals by applications that seek out keywords in the email and identify those within the organization who can address the concern or question. In addition, many applications can put together draft responses to questions based on predefined templates (or FAQs), which employees need only review and edit prior to responding to the customer or prospect. Other features such as auto-acknowledgement of requests, statistical analysis, and standard email system integration are also available.

Customer Self-service

As a means to reduce costs and simplify service, customer self-service has become a normal part of the business landscape in recent years. It is essentially the application of technologies that allow customers to define their problems and find solutions to them. Allowing those customers who are content to service themselves to do so also can allow the business to focus its time on those customers who wish to have personal (person-to-person) service.

Internet-enabled CRM is an important area of CRM that includes numerous tools and applications to better serve the customer. (See the New Business Models box to see how The Outback Steakhouse is coping with vast changes in the CRM area.) Ranging from simple tools such as email applications to complex integrated systems, internet-enabled CRM is growing in importance and will continue to develop over the next several years.

TECHNOLOGIES AND INTEGRATION

MANY OF THE TECHNOLOGIES DISCUSSED IN THIS BOOK ARE USED TO ALLOW CRM applications to operate in an integrated fashion. Businesses are investing heavily in the development of integrated systems, and CRM efforts require that a number of integration points be considered. To develop customer relationships, it is necessary to capture, process, and share information across the enterprise. The information may originate in the ERP system, the SCM application, within legacy systems, or be drawn from external data sources.

The ERP system is the cornerstone source for data on the internal side of the business. For example, all current information related to the customer (e.g., orders placed, orders in production, orders being shipped) should be up to date within the ERP system. These data need to be available to the CRM system so salespeople or CSRs can discuss issues in a current fashion at the various touch points they deal with. The integration of the CRM application and ERP system is critical, and its implementation will vary depending on the particular systems employed.

The integration of data from the supply chain will also be important in successful CRM applications. For customers to gain access to information regarding expected delivery dates or other factors, the CRM application must be interfaced with the SCM system. Much of the data within the CRM system will also be useful for SCM processes such as forecasting and demand analysis. In order for the entire value chain to operate effectively, it is essential that internal and external data be integrated.

The use of external data sources complicates the process of data integration. As more companies integrate their systems with each other, the intricacies of each ERP system and other applications can create major roadblocks to data sharing. Some of the tools used to overcome these difficulties are discussed in the next section.

The integration of data must be carried out as a critical component of developing a CRM strategy. Identification of relevant data sources must be followed by developing an understanding of the technologies to be employed, and by creating data structures that will allow the data to be easily analyzed. The complexity of the data must not be allowed to encroach on the usefulness of the information that can be obtained through analysis.

IMPLEMENTING CRM

IMPLEMENTATION OF CRM IS A PROJECT THAT REQUIRES PLANNING SIMILAR TO other major technology projects, such as ERP, but also requires managers to deal with a number of implementation concerns. The implementation process may take from several months to several years to complete, and will progress through a number of stages as the "learning curve" takes place.

Social Media at the Outback Steakhouse

The Outback Steakhouse is a popular restaurant and one of its most popular products is something called the Bloomin' Onion. A large onion cut to resemble a flower and then covered in egg batter and deep fried, the dish represents a tasty appetiser good for dipping.

The Outback has been experiencing a reduction of business because of the recession, and wanted to find ways to encourage its customers to come out more often. However, it couldn't afford advertising, and after some careful strategising and planning, landed on an unusual way to reach out to their customers. They decided to use Facebook—not unusual in itself—and combine it with the Bloomin' Onion to make an ad hoc marketing package.

They created a Facebook application offering a free coupon for a Bloomin' Onion in exchange for the email address and zip code of the potential customer. With this information, Outback was able to contact the customer, providing directions to their nearest Outback restaurant. The Facebook application also provided a "share with friends" button, thus spreading the reach of its campaign at no cost.

The Outback had the application developed using a Microsoft cloud platform under development, thus avoiding heavy development costs. Their objective was to devise a low-cost means of reaching out for more traffic to their restaurants. The company felt sure that after the customers got a taste of the Bloomin' Onion, they would be hooked, buying other products and coming back to the restaurant again.

During the first few weeks of the campaign, 670,000 coupons were distributed, considerably more than the original goal of 500,000. Prior to the advent of these Microsoft toolkits for developing Facebook apps, it would have been much more difficult for Outback to create and launch the promotion so quickly.

This is a good example of Microsoft's platform-as-a-service (PAAS) initiative, in which Microsoft provides the tools, and the customer creates the apps. They felt that the cloud would be a useful way to move ahead with the project. The cloud, particularly a platform-as-a-service, offers stability in its basic platform, but allows the customers to develop custom apps. There is also a greater chance of the apps meeting the customer needs using the cloud.

The Outback Steakhouse
www.outback.com

Questions

1. What are the advantages of a Facebook promotional campaign such as that used by Outback compared to a traditional marketing campaign?

2. Would it be possible to do the same thing without the cloud toolkits supplied by Microsoft?

Source: C. Babcock, "Microsoft Pushes Platform As A Service In Cloud," *InformationWeek*, November 8, 2010, www.informationweek.com/story/showArticle.jhtml?articleID=228200447

Implementation Concerns

Many of the implementation concerns related to CRM projects are similar to those that arise in ERP projects and can result in very expensive, failed projects. It is important when undertaking such an implementation to consider the political, cultural, and technological concerns that are likely to arise as the project progresses. As with ERP implementations, technology is important, but it is critical that business strategies, processes, and people considerations drive the implementation.

Political and Cultural Concerns Political and cultural concerns can get any technology project into trouble as employees struggle with changes in responsibilities and processes. Team-based approaches with strong buy-in from management tend to reduce the concerns in this area, but they will still invariably arise. For example, CRM implementation will require various departments such as sales, service, and marketing to review their data requirements, processes, and customer touch points to plan for the implementation. As these and other topics are considered, the "ownership" of customer touch points is likely to become an issue, necessitating management to deal with the changes that are inherent in developing a true customer-centric approach.

CRM implementation will also require a number of employees to adjust their responsibilities when dealing with customers. For example, CSRs may now become responsible for selling products or services, as described earlier in the chapter. This change alone may require the development of new compensation arrangements within the firm, whereby the traditional "salesperson" is no longer the only employee receiving commissions or performance bonuses based on sales. These types of cultural changes are likely to cause difficulties as the CRM strategy is adopted, but can also be valuable learning tools for adept managers who identify means by which customer relationships can be improved throughout the enterprise.

Technological Concerns Technological concerns for a CRM implementation project focus on integration with existing technologies and planning for new technologies. As discussed earlier in this chapter, a CRM system should ideally be integrated with ERP and other applications to be an effective tool. CRM applications vary a great deal in structure, ranging from the typical old client-server approaches to cloud applications.

Many of the linkages required to integrate CRM will be based on enterprise application integration (EAI) tools such as middleware. Middleware is software that serves to link together or communicate between two separate and different programs. In addition to middleware, XML is a language that is being used to simplify the integration of technologies by permitting applications to read and understand its standardized format. Despite the capabilities of middleware, EAI, and XML to allow organizations to integrate systems, integration can be quite complex. For example, a 2004 study of 198 organizations in the United States, Europe, and Australia that had implemented enterprise software (ES) found that 42 percent of the organizations had realized no or limited integration with the software. In addition, fewer than 30 percent of the organizations had actually managed to integrate information exchange with their suppliers or customers.[4]

CRM integration needs to focus on the numerous touch points and processes involved in CRM. Customer contacts that occur, for example, at a wholesale outlet or via a website should enable data from the customer to be captured and stored in the data warehouse. In addition, call centres need access to integrated customer data that may require the business to adopt computer telephony integration. For example, Genesys Conferencing integrated its salesforce.com software with the Avaya contact centre so that if a customer were to call the contact centre, a screen pop-up with the relevant customer's information on it would appear automatically.[5]

computer telephony integration (CTI): A technology that allows telephone systems to integrate with computer systems to aid in customer service and data capture.

Computer telephony integration (CTI) is a technology that allows telephone systems to integrate with computer systems to aid in customer service and data capture. An example of CTI in action would be a customer service request coming in by phone. As the phone system recognizes the caller (through caller identification), the call is redirected to an appropriate CSR within seconds, and information is pulled from the CRM system related to the customer and output to the CSR's computer screen. Without any demands being placed on the CSR, the customer is now ready to be serviced by a knowledgeable employee who has a great deal of information related to the customer. This information can be used to provide service and potentially to sell products or services that the customer is likely to buy, based on the system's analysis.

Technological concerns will vary in complexity and cost but must be considered in relation to the implementation project's objectives. The critical stages of implementation for technologies include the CRM application selection stage and integration stage. CRM application selection will dictate how the project proceeds and the capabilities of the system for integration. Once again, the use of cross-functional teams at the planning stage is critical to allow the best application to be chosen for the organization.

Implementation Stages

The implementation of CRM will evolve through a number of stages over the term of the project. Some implementations will end up with only basic functionality, while others will evolve into advanced systems that are used extensively throughout the organization. Various methodologies exist, but most CRM implementations will progress through the following stages: planning, process redesign, integration, education, analysis, and change implementation.

Planning The planning phase of CRM adoption and implementation is an important foundation to the entire project. Setting the stage for the remainder of the implementation, planning will address such areas as needs analysis, software selection, project responsibilities, and project time lines. The planning phase may consider some preliminary requirements for process change and will evaluate and provide input into the CRM strategy.

The planning process should be carried out by a cross-functional team of employees (and consultants) to establish input from the entire enterprise. As discussed earlier, the team approach will allow concerns of various departments to be raised early in the process. Otherwise, the system created may not be appropriate for or acceptable to the end users. Such was the case where a large brokerage with a number of independent financial advisors implemented a system without user input. They already had their own CRM systems in place, and did not derive any tangible benefit from switching, so the system was not widely adopted. The brokerage eventually had to get rid of the system it had implemented and restart CRM from the planning phase, this time involving all the stakeholders.[6]

It is also important to have consultants involved at the planning process so that the project goals and time line are reviewed for reasonableness. Consultants will also be able to offer important advice as to how departments can plan for the implementation and what process revisions are likely to be required.

Process Redesign Business processes are likely to change as the CRM implementation project moves forward, accommodating technological requirements and revised employee/departmental responsibilities. Process redesign and business process reengineering (BPR) will occur throughout the implementation of CRM and often afterwards as well, but should be planned early in the implementation process. One large European telecommunications firm found a number of problems with poor-quality data in its CRM systems. Part of the data-entry problem resulted from the CSRs in the call centres, who were given incentives based on the number of calls they made rather than on care in data entry. The training and employee performance assessments for the CSRs had to be adjusted.[7]

Early planning for BPR will allow employees and their departments time to consider and provide feedback on the proposed changes. Some process changes may be dictated by

Global CRM at Open Text

Businesses need fast and reliable means of communication, and Open Text is a world leader in that area. In 2010, Open Text purchased Streamserve Inc. and then integrated it into its larger organization. Open Text works under alliances with major application vendors, systems integrators, and ebusiness providers such as IBM, SAP, and Oracle. The company is an established innovator in the enterprise business communication (EBC) market, with more than 4000 customers around the globe. Open Text's approach enables their customers to reduce communications costs and increase their ROI from enterprise business applications. The Open Text solutions also make all of their customers' printed and electronic output more personalized and customer focused.

Since 1995, the company has sold its solution in over 100 countries globally.

Salesforce.com is the market and technology leader in on-demand CRM. Salesforce customers include 11,000 companies of all sizes, in all industries, and in many locations around the world. Open Text selected salesforce.com for its global CRM.

In making the selection, Open Text was focused on its competitive position, and felt a need to stay ahead of the competition. Sales personnel had come to rely on CRM systems in formulating their strategy, therefore they could not wait for long periods of time for new systems to be started up. A system like salesforce has the experience and acumen to have its CRM system in operation on a timely basis. Moreover, the company knew from its prior research that the salesforce product had a strong track record of customization without a need to drastically alter basic infrastructure. The ability to customize painlessly would mean a lot to Open Text as it continued to grow and expand.

StreamServe began to investigate CRM solutions in order to increase demand for its business communication management (BCM) technology in Europe and the United States and in emerging regions such as Eastern Europe and Asia. In making their decision, Open Text found that salesforce had numerous advantages that would be of great benefit to it now and in the future. They determined that the product enables fast implementation, offers scalable architecture and state-of-the-art functionality in addition to its strong integration and customization capabilities.

Open Text already was running Microsoft's ERP system, so which had to be integrated with salesforce in addition to its legacy systems. Nevertheless, implementation was completed on schedule in just 30 days.

Before making a final decision, Open Text took the opportunity to include several of its employees in the decision process. They exposed them to the product, and provided them with the opportunity to observe and test its functionality. The feedback was extremely positive and enhanced the selection team's understanding of the functionality of salesforce.

StreamServe
www.streamserve.com

Questions

1. Why would Open Text have considered that a Global CRM system would help in meeting its objectives?

2. What considerations would Open Text have had to consider that would be unique to a global CRM implementation?

Source: "StreamServe Implements salesforce.com for Global CRM," www.salesforce.com/ap/company/news-press/press-releases/2004/08/040823.jsp.

---

the CRM application that is chosen, but others will be necessitated to achieve the strategic goals of the CRM implementation. Feedback and discussion of the process redesign will allow employees to provide input into the process and will often result in suggested improvements that improve the overall implementation.

Integration The implementation project's technological aspects will focus on integration of data once the CRM application has been installed. Relating to the goals established in the planning process, the implementation team will work towards integrating any systems required for project success. This integration stage will often continue to evolve as further stages of the implementation take place. Future investments in integration will occur once management and employees buy into the CRM system and begin to demand more capabilities from it.

An integration headache that occurred with the same European telecommunications firm discussed above came about when the legacy customer database systems were integrated into one system. It was found that not all the customers in the various databases had unique addresses, or names, so that when the systems were combined, the identification of customers became troublesome.[8]

Education The implementation of any new technology involves a learning curve and an educational process. For CRM implementations, the educational process will involve both technology training and CRM-focused learning. In addition to basic navigation and introductory training, there will be a need for training for advanced queries for those users who will be responsible for the more advanced analytical aspects of the CRM application.

CRM-focused learning sessions should be provided to all employees who will interact with customers to implement a common strategy of customer contact. The CRM strategy's goals can only be achieved if employees are aware of the requirements and understand the customer-centric approach being adopted. The learning sessions also serve to inform and educate staff on the process revisions adopted so that customer touch points have common service levels.

Analysis The analysis stage of CRM implementation comes once the implementation has reached a stage where data are collected and the CRM application can begin to provide useful information. An interesting analysis of the stages of growth for CRM was written by Ronald Swift, who outlines the stages as reporting, analyzing, and predicting.[9]

Reporting The reporting stage of analysis is characterized by the use of pre-configured reports and queries on the data. In this initial phase of implementation, users become familiar with the system by developing an understanding of the customer, what products and services sell in particular areas, and other basic analysis. The reporting phase is primarily historical in focus, with the limited use of ad hoc querying.

Analyzing The analyzing stage is a step up from reporting, whereby managers and users begin to ask questions about why events are occurring. This stage of implementation begins to truly develop a CRM mentality, whereby users ask what the causes of specific events and trends have been. Analyzing data may look more specifically at understanding why particular product lines did not meet targets, why a marketing campaign was so successful, or other similar kinds of questions. The analyzing stage of implementation is one that will proceed concurrently with other activities, such as education and process redesign.

Predicting The final stage of the analysis phase of a CRM implementation is the predicting phase, in which the business begins to truly capitalize on the CRM initiative by utilizing the data for strategic purposes. In the predicting phase, businesses begin to set marketing strategy, service goals, and modify touch points based on analysis from the CRM system. For example, the marketing and sales departments may perform analysis to identify which customers are most at risk of going to alternative suppliers, and carry out proactive relationship measures to retain them. In this phase of CRM implementation, users are very familiar with the system and have developed an appreciation for the value of CRM.

The time that individual businesses will spend at each stage will vary and, despite large investments, those who don't spend adequately on education and change management efforts will never progress to the predicting stage of analysis.

Change Implementation The change implementation stage of CRM implementation is the point at which businesses begin to capitalize on their investments. This will normally occur after the business has been able to reach either the analyzing or predicting phases, described above, and truly understands its customers.

At this stage, businesses will focus on efforts such as redesigning processes after successful or unsuccessful efforts have been evaluated. For example, a company may run an internet-based advertising campaign based on CRM analysis, which has identified a target group likely to buy through this channel. If this campaign is successful, the company may continue with this strategy by modifying processes that strengthen and support the use of this channel by specific groups, such as creating targeted websites. Change implementation should further enhance relationships with customers by making it easier for them to deal with the company through the channel of their choice.

CHAPTER SUMMARY

Customer relationship management (CRM) in an ebusiness context is the use of technology to establish, develop, maintain, and optimize relationships with customers by focusing on the understanding of customers' needs and desires.

The key functional areas for CRM include marketing, sales, and service. The customer service area of many businesses also offers the opportunity to become involved in selling, while providing valuable customer service. The process of CRM can be described as data capture, data analysis, strategic decision making, and implementation.

CRM applications offer numerous tools to analyze and understand customer data. Data analysis is the use of CRM applications to explore the data to identify relevant customer information. Some organizations refer to this component of CRM as customer intelligence.

While CRM makes use of data warehousing technology and data analysis techniques, it is not the same as business intelligence (BI). As technologies continue to converge, CRM applications are becoming offerings within BI applications. The overall goal of any CRM implementation should be to improve customer relationships by providing better service, improved sales efforts, and reduced marketing costs.

In the sales area, CRM strategies aim to improve the sales process by increasing efficiency, improving customer interaction and service, and simplifying the process for salespeople. In the service area, CRM strategies can strengthen and develop the customer relationship from the date of original sale.

Social CRM allows businesses to efficiently gather and distribute customer data, as well as provide a new medium for communication with customers.

Leading CRM providers' applications integrate email and social media data into the CRM applications so that call centre staff who later are contacted by a customer can review correspondence and social media activity to remain up to date with customer attitudes and habits. This ability to integrate data to assist customer service is a major development for companies in the ebusiness arena.

The critical stages of implementation for technologies include the CRM application selection stage and integration stage. The implementation project's technological aspects will focus on integration of data once the CRM application has been installed. For CRM implementations, the educational process will involve both technology training and CRM-focused learning. To implement a common strategy of customer contact, CRM-focused learning sessions should be provided to all employees who will interact with customers.

Key Terms

computer telephony integration (CTI) (p. 208)

cross-selling (p. 198)

customer intelligence (p. 200)

data warehouse (p. 198)

intelligent agent (p. 205)

sales force automation (p. 201)

social CRM (p. 202)

up-selling (p. 198)

Voice over Internet Protocol (VoIP) (p. 205)

MyEbusinessLab Tools for Online Learning

To help you master the material in this chapter and stay up to date with new developments in ebusiness, visit the MyEBusinessLab at www.pearsoned.ca/myebusinesslab. Resources include the following:

- **Pre- and Post-Test Questions**
- **Additional Chapter Questions**
- **Author Blog**
- **Recommended Readings**
- **Commentaries on Current Trends**
- **Additional Topics in Ebusiness**
- **Internet Exercises**
- **Glossary Flashcards**

Endnotes

1. T. Fox and S. Stead, "Customer Relationship Management: Delivering the Benefits" (white paper, CRM [UK] Ltd., and SECOR Consulting Ltd., 2001).

2. M. Lager, "Shoppers and Buyers: Divide, and Conquer Both." *Customer Relationship Management* 10, no. 9 (September 2006), 14.

3. G. Häubl and K. B. Murray, "Double Agents." *MIT Sloan Management Review* 47, no. 3 (Spring 2006).

4. T. H. Davenport, J. G. Harris, and S. Cantrell. "Enterprise Systems and Ongoing Process Change,"*Business Process Management Journal* 10, no. 1 (2004), 16–26.

5. salesforce.com, "Genesys Conferencing Utilizes Salesforce for Global Follow-the-Sun Support Operations," news release, January 25, 2007.

6. B. Goldenberg. "Conquering Your 2 Biggest CRM Challenges,"*Sales and Marketing Management* (March 26, 2007), 35.

7. A. Reid and M. Caterall, "Invisible Data Quality Issues in a CRM Implementation,"*Journal of Database Marketing and Customer Strategy Management* 12, no. 4 (2005), 305–314.

8. R. Swift, "The Stages of Growth for CRM and Data Warehousing,"*DM Review* (September 2000).

9. Christopher J. Bucholtz, "Industries Geared for Social CRM Success,"*CRM Buyer*, October 21, 2010, www.crmbuyer.com/story/71077.html?wlc=1287748111, accessed October 27, 2010.

Chapter 10

Business Intelligence

Learning Objectives

When you complete this chapter you should be able to:

1 Compare and contrast how business intelligence (BI) and enterprise resource planning (ERP) systems handle data.

2 Describe the benefits of BI systems.

3 Name and describe the major functions of BI systems.

4 Explain the types of technologies and solutions used in BI systems.

5 Discuss the implementation of BI systems and the stages it needs to follow.

6 Describe how businesses can use data warehouses and data marts within the BI infrastructure.

7 Describe critical success factors and emerging trends in the field of BI.

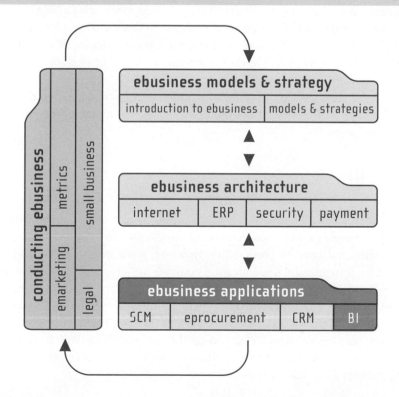

INTRODUCTION

GLOBALLY, CORPORATIONS ARE STRUGGLING TO KEEP PACE IN THE "INFORMATION economy," and the rapid growth of the internet and related technologies is strengthening the demand for data management strategies. Business intelligence (BI) involves the use of computer techniques to analyse a wide array of data so as to convert those data into useful information that can be used to enhance decision making. Accordingly, BI has emerged as a powerful tool that enables businesses to capture, analyze, interpret, and report on data—thus creating valuable information for the enterprise.

Implementing BI remains one of the top technology initiatives in many enterprises. Massive investments in ERP and CRM systems, along with data storage capacities generally, have resulted in huge data storage mechanisms. However, these increases in data volumes don't do a business much good if executives can't extract meaningful information from them. BI supports the analysis of data from any source (internal or external) to provide valuable information for making operating, tactical, or strategic decisions.

The concepts of BI are not entirely new and have emerged from data-mining techniques, decision support systems, data warehousing, knowledge management, and other business tools that have been used for many years. BI differs from these other tools in that it is a completely integrated approach to data management and has been made possible by advances in technology such as the internet, ERP, and database systems. BI tools are provided by a number of software companies. The top five companies are SAS Institute, SAP, IBM, Oracle, and MicroStrategy, not necessarily in that order.

BI applications can be closely related to CRM strategies, as discussed in chapter 9, because BI is often used for extended analysis of data gathered by CRM systems. For example, a company may use BI tools to identify customer segments that are highly profitable and develop strategies to ensure that it retains those customers (a CRM activity). BI is more comprehensive than CRM, however, because it deals with a wider variety of data. For example, a business analyst may use BI applications to identify potential operating problems based on historical data in the system and deploy additional service and upkeep in that area (an operating activity). Essentially, BI can be used any time an organization wants to better understand its data to improve decision making. See the Canadian Snapshots box for a discussion of the use of BI technology at the Ontario Lottery and Gaming Corporation.

ERP VS. BI

BI HAS EVOLVED FROM PREVIOUS DATA MANAGEMENT SYSTEMS SUCH AS DATA warehousing, although BI employs data warehousing as part of its data analysis arsenal. As businesses struggle to gain a competitive advantage, BI offers the potential to improve decision making and improve profitability. However, many organizations have invested heavily in ERP systems, which are meant to provide an integrated data environment—raising a question of why BI is necessary.

The main reason ERP systems do not provide the analysis offered by BI systems is that they were devised as transaction-processing systems. While they do enable the reporting of those data, they are not heavily focused on the analysis of the data. In addition, they only contain the data arising from transactions, while BI draws data from diverse sources, including industry data, news reports and trade journals.

SAS Institute
www.sas.com

SAP
www.sap.com

IBM
www.ibm.com

Oracle
www.oracle.com

MicroStrategy
www.microstrategy.com

The Ontario Lottery Uses BI to Fight Fraud

A few years ago, the provincial ombudsman criticized the Ontario Lottery and Gaming Corporation (OLG) for not doing enough to stop retailers from selling hundreds of millions of dollars of tickets a year by fraudulently cashing in on winning numbers. The OLG was aware of this fraudulent practice but had always had difficulty dealing with it. Many people buy lottery tickets; the OLG handles some 1.2 billion lottery transactions a year and has a tremendous repository of data, consisting of some 12 billion transactions since 1999.

In trying to deal with the possibility of fraud, the OLG had to try to analyze these transactions, which it did by using simple query tools, Excel spreadsheets, and manual scanning. To complicate matters, for security reasons, lottery commissions around the world had a strategy of separating rather than uniting transaction data. As a result of this basic system, it would often take the OLG months to do a single investigation. It was only in very recent years that BI has become affordable for the OLG. The cost of hardware, software, and advisory services for the tool was estimated at $1.7 million.

After the public criticism of its inability to detect the frauds, the OLG decided to turn to BI. Its new tool, named Data Analysis and Retrieval Technology (DART), is built around a high-end database and can handle vast amounts of data, looking for suspicious patterns. In fact, shortly after the OLG adopted this system, patterns were flagged around the launch of a Poker Lottery game; from these patterns, the OLG realized that retailers were paying out winners without verifying the numbers at their lottery terminals. In addition, information gathered by using DART helped the Ontario Provincial Police charge a former retailer and two relatives with wrongly getting the corporation to pay out a $12.3 million prize.

With the use of DART, the OLG can tear through its entire database in a matter of two or three minutes. DART can help the OLG determine where and when each ticket was bought, whether other lottery games were played at the same time, and where and when the winner was checked. Incredibly, DART can also check on what the store owner was doing at the terminal in the minutes before and after a transaction. When a winner claimant shows up with a story, the corporation can check the story against the data, which provides an effective preventive check in preventing fraud.

DART does more than just show the history of a ticket. It can also track down evidence that a player regularly uses the same series of numbers to help verify the claim. It can also show whether a winning claimant has a relationship with a retailer or OLG staffer. And it can also show a retailer's access to the lottery terminal for the five minutes on either side of a transaction to highlight any suspicious activity.

The OLG feels that DART is so good, it may be able to sell the tool to other lottery corporations.

Ontario Lottery and Gaming Corporation
www.olg.ca

Questions

1. What other possible uses could the DART tool be used for?

2. Is using a tool such as DART a good way to prevent and control fraud?

Source: H. Solomon, "Ontario Lottery Turns to BI to Fight Fraud," by *ComputerWorld Canada*, November 24, 2010, www.itworldcanada.com/news/ontario-lottery-turns-to-bi-to-fight-fraud/142009.

While ERP systems have succeeded in integrating the transaction systems of business, they have been unable to satisfy all of the information needs—leaving a place for BI strategies.

ERP limitations in the intelligence area include the difficulty in incorporating additional data. Reporting and analysis requirements today reach far beyond the basic debits and credits in the accounting system; they demand information on competitors, ecommerce statistics, and the supply-chain data that are often not found within the ERP system. It is conceivable that ERP systems could be modified to include other data needs, but due to the reasons already cited, an external data warehouse is a superior solution.

Although business changes at a rapid pace, it can be important to carry out analysis over numerous years to identify important trends. Maintaining several years of data within any environment can be difficult, and within ERP huge storage capabilities would be required that can be reduced by adopting BI. With BI systems the data can be "cleaned" and stored in more efficient formats than is possible with ERP.

Several years ago, ERP vendors recognized the weaknesses of their systems for business analysis and introduced their own BI applications to enhance their ERP systems. SAP, for example, introduced Business Warehouse (BW) to enhance its ERP and CRM offerings. SAP also incorporated SAP BW into its product offering known as Strategic Enterprise Management (SEM), which allows users to integrate ERP data with BW data in a process-oriented and strategic manner for analysis.[1]

In addition to offerings from ERP vendors, numerous BI application providers have created customized interfaces to simplify the data extraction process from ERP systems. For example, Cognos has an extraction application designed to simplify the process of gathering data from an SAP ERP system. Other leading BI providers have similar applications for various ERP systems. See the Estrategy box for an example of how BI contributes to a business over and above the contribution of ERP.

BENEFITS OF BI

SOME OF THE KEY BENEFITS OF BI INCLUDE CONTINUOUS RATHER THAN PERIODIC management, improved management of diverse business functions, improved collaboration, and improved understanding of customers.[2]

Continuous Rather Than Periodic Management

Traditionally, managers have had to manage operations based on periodic reports produced weekly, monthly, or quarterly. This approach has been likened to driving a car while looking in the rearview mirror. BI gives managers an opportunity to manage based on a continuous flow of information that is current and accurate. In addition, the information can be correlated with other data at any time. BI can contribute new insights on business performance to managers and improve their understanding of business operations, reduce delays in decision processes, and help them respond quickly to changes in market conditions.

Improved Management of Diverse Business Functions

A simple BI architecture can help businesses monitor different functions—including marketing, HR, and finance—at the same time. Marketing managers can use the data to analyze which products are profitable and which should be eliminated. These managers can also adjust sales strategy by tracking a product's life cycle. For human resource managers, BI can use metrics and criteria to help identify highest-quality employees, reduce employee turnover, and measure the effectiveness of training programs. Finance managers can get a clear view of the company's financial performance, analyze current financial conditions, and undertake financial forecasts.

Kansai Paint Singapore Goes Global

Kansai Paint Company Ltd. (KPC) is a major manufacturer, marketer, and technical service centre for paint customers in Asia. KPC has a network of factories and offices across the Asia Pacific region. It offers a spectrum of products including decorative paints, auto refinishes, and industrial, marine, and protective coatings.

KPCs Singapore (KPS) wanted to expand from being a Southeast Asian company to having a worldwide presence. To enhance its competitive position, KPS adopted the Lawson M3 ERP system. KPS selected M3 ERP technology because it was designed for its specific industry, supported international trade, and was priced attractively for a medium company with complex operations but limited resources.

Lawson's M3 ERP delivered considerable value to KPS. However, an ERP system could not satisfy all of KPS's data management needs. KPS knew that to compete globally, it had to streamline its business processes and improve efficiency. It concluded that BI could integrate reporting systems, and help reduce costs and increase revenues by supporting marketing and sales opportunities. BI could also help the company manage large-scale stock supplies for projects involving both established and newly built plants.

Thus, KPS added Lawson's BI functionality to its ERP infrastructure to support the management of customer portfolios, inventory, and transaction processing. The BI solution is easily and flexibly deployed for generating a rapid return on investment. It can be tailored to help meet the needs of companies, departments, and individuals. In addition, its user-friendly design encourages better user adoption, which helps enable effective deployment of resources, enforcement of standards and regulations, and rapid response to change.

KPS's upgraded portfolio of applications will cover its entire business operation, including financials, sales processing, warehousing, purchasing and procurement, manufacturing, and shop floor, as well as the management and review of control reports. By centralizing and automating its systems across all departments, KPS can now make decisions more quickly and concentrate on keeping pace with changing market demands. It can focus on staying competitive with more effective management of orders across its spectrum of products. The application will also help the company improve its vision into the management of contractual terms and conditions, handling invoicing and settlement, and generating comprehensive reports for all areas of its business activities.

Kansai Paint Company
www.kansai.co.jp/global_site
Kansai Paint Singapore
www.kansaipaint.com.sg

Questions

1. What benefits will the BI implementation provide to KPS that would not have been available in the ERP system?

2. How will KPS use BI to support its business strategy?

3. What difficulties might KPC and KPS encounter in the future?

Source: "Kansai Paint Singapore Selects Lawson Business Intelligence," www.lawson.com/WCW.nsf/pub/new_13E748, accessed January 22, 2007.

Improved Collaboration

BI enables different divisions to share common data resources, which can produce a collaborative work culture among employees. Working on the same databases helps the company to more easily make consistent decisions in a shorter period of time. Instead of communicating with each other by submitting department reports monthly, departments can see the company's strategy and development through the information made available by the BI system.

Improved Understanding of Customers

BI solutions enable businesses to monitor customers' purchasing behaviours. Data warehouses gather information on customers' behaviours. Then BI solutions help businesses to classify and analyze this information according to a variety of criteria. This analysis leads to a better understanding of customers' reactions to prices, products, and promotions, and it can lead to action plans to meet or exceed their expectations.

BI FUNCTIONS

A NUMBER OF FUNCTIONS HAVE EMERGED AS BI SOLUTIONS CONTINUE TO EVOLVE and business needs for reporting and analysis change. BI tools should be considered an extension of the power of the ERP system and focus on data integration and organization, data analysis, performance analysis, information dissemination, and collaboration (see figure 10.1).[3]

Data Integration and Organization

A BI application performs a key function of integrating and organizing all data considered relevant for managing the enterprise. The sources of data for BI can be numerous, including both internal and external data sources. Internal data sources can include ERP systems, CRM systems, eprocurement systems, legacy systems, and call centres. External data sources can include supply-chain partners, industry information regarding competitors, or other external information such as economic indicators (see figure 10.2). The BI application serves to integrate all of these data sources in a manner optimized for reporting and analysis.

A data warehouse is a central data repository used to organize, store, analyze, and report on data for decision-making purposes. Essentially, a data warehouse is a system that exists outside the online transaction-processing (OLTP) system or ERP, and is dedicated to the analytical aspects of the organization. An **online transaction-processing (OLTP) system** is a program that facilitates and manages transaction-oriented applications, typically for data entry and retrieval transactions across a network. In some organizations,

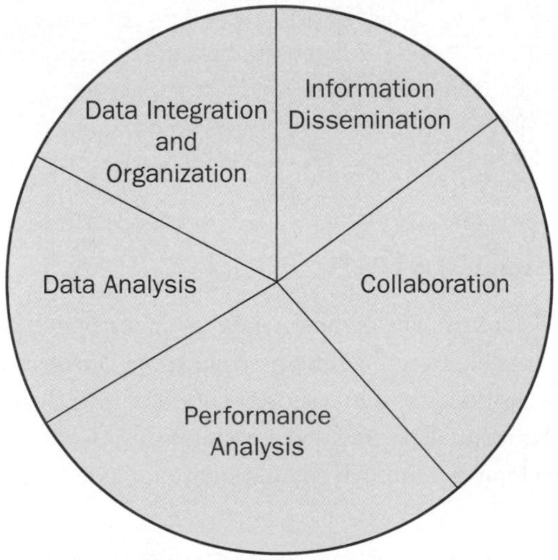

online transaction-processing (OLTP) system: A program that facilitates and manages transaction-oriented applications, typically for data entry and retrieval transactions across a network.

Figure 10.1 Business intelligence functions

The tools of BI can be used to focus on data integration and organization, data analysis, performance analysis, information dissemination, and collaboration.

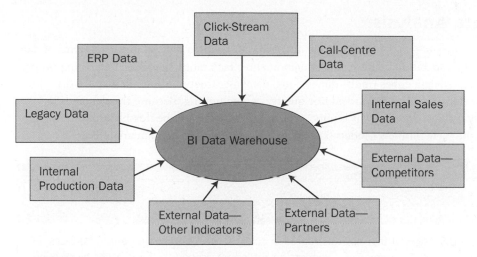

Figure 10.2 Data sources for business intelligence

Numerous data sources contribute to the BI data warehouse, including internal and external sources.

data warehouses are also divided into smaller, dedicated databases known as data marts. BI solution providers structure their warehousing solutions in a variety of ways, with some solutions focusing on data marts and others focusing more specifically on the larger data warehouse. For example, a store that uses a data warehouse to support its sales strategy may wish to get answers to questions such as: Who are my best customers? What are my customers' favourite brands or designs? How do they feel about our service? What are acceptable prices to customers for various products? When customers bought a particular product on a particular day of the week, what else did they buy? Using its data warehouse to obtain answers to these questions can help the store develop insights into customers' purchasing behaviour and thereby help it set its future sales strategy.[4]

Whether the BI system is based upon a data mart or data warehouse is of little significance when considering the importance of BI. In either case, the data in the system will be structured around metadata. **Metadata** is a structured definition of data—it is data about data. For example, a number of data tables within an ERP system may be consolidated with ecommerce data into a single table when the data is extracted. The extraction process would involve the movement of the data and may also remove unnecessary fields and combine other fields. The changes and combinations of the data may then be described by metadata so that an end user or data warehouse administrator can better understand where the data originated and how it has been formed.[5]

metadata: A structured definition of data; it is data about data.

The integration of data occurs through a number of methods, as the data warehouse consolidates data from numerous sources. **Extraction, transformation, and loading (ETL)** is the process of gathering data from a system, such as an ERP system, which can be simplified and stored within the data warehouse. Many sources of data will require ETL so that data from systems such as ERP and legacy systems can be combined into a common database. The frequency with which ETL will occur within a given organization will depend upon the industry and the type of reporting environment desired. If management wishes to have very up-to-date information, ETL could occur daily; if the reporting is for several past periods, weekly or monthly, it may be acceptable for ETL to occur less frequently. Most ebusinesses would require frequent updates of data to stay on top of crucial trends and performance indicators necessary to manage the business.

extraction, transformation, and loading (ETL): The process of gathering data from a system, such as an ERP system, which can be simplified and stored within the data warehouse.

Data Analysis

data cube: A multi-dimensional database structure that allows quick drill-down and reformatting of data.

The many users of BI applications in organizations have diverse needs in terms of data analysis capabilities. The levels of data analysis may range from basic reporting on pre-configured **data cubes** (multi-dimensional database structures that allow quick drill-down and reformatting of data) to ad hoc queries or data mining. Because the demands for data analysis range drastically, it is important that BI applications be flexible and user-friendly. See the New Business Models box for an example of BI-based data analysis.

New Business Models
U.S. Bank Extends BI to Customers

U.S. Bank is a regional player in the U.S. Midwest that has taken an innovative approach to the use of its BI system. The system, called ScoreBoard, is used for analyzing spending patterns among the customers and determining revenue trends. The innovation was that US bank decided to add the customers themselves to the users of the system.

Management of the bank felt that by including the customers, they would be able to gain insight into their thinking, why they are spending on certain products, why they are spending more or less and what their expectations are. Management would also be able to share their own insights with their customers. The project was under the direction of the payment services division, which handles corporate cards and merchant processing for about 1 million small business customers. After gaining some feedback, they found that small business owners want to focus on their business, whether it be selling goods or providing services and do not like having to look after financial management, although they recognize the necessity of that activity.

While it is not uncommon for companies to share certain data with their customers, usually through their CRM systems, the ScoreBoard application includes industry data aggregated from the Visa network and broken down by state, month, quarter, and year for more than 120 industries. U.S. Bank felt that this data would appeal to small business owners, who can use the data to analyze their companies relative to the industry and perhaps also see how others in the industry are addressing industry-wide issues.

For example the application would allow customers to observe how other restaurants are doing in order to compare with their own performance.

Inclusion of industry data in analytical tools is a significant difference between conventional CRM systems and BI. Traditional BI systems tend to be made available only to employees, and research indicates that generally not more than 25 percent of them actually gain access. The problem

is rooted in costly licenses and complicated interfaces. BI vendors have tried to respond to these issues by devising new approaches to licensing, using web-based delivery and developing user-friendly dashboards and attractive data visualizations.

U.S. Bank sent out RFPs for the new system to eight potential suppliers, including Information Builders, which already supplied some of U.S. Bank's existing systems, particularly an old corporate card system that continues to serve millions of customers. U.S. Bank ended up choosing Information Builders because it seemed to provide the best value for the money.

The customers' ability to use ScoreBoard for tracking business card expenditures and merchant processing transactions was launched in May. After working out the bugs, the bank started marketing the card-expenditure ScoreBoard in July, and in October it surpassed the 100,000-customer milestone.

The latest step took place when the bank enabled its small business customers to enter cash and check income to the merchant processing platform. With that information, the customers could analyze their total revenue stream, not just credit card transactions processed by U.S. Bank.

Normally, customer turnover in the company's business is as much as 20% per year, but the company feels that the new application will increase customer retention, thus reducing this rate and saving revenue.

Questions

1. How will the new analysis tools help the bank in doing its core business of banking?
2. Will the new BI system help U.S. Bank to upsell and cross-sell products?

Source: D. Henschen, "US Bank Takes BI Beyond Employees," InformationWeek, November 4, 2010, www.informationweek.com/news/228200454.

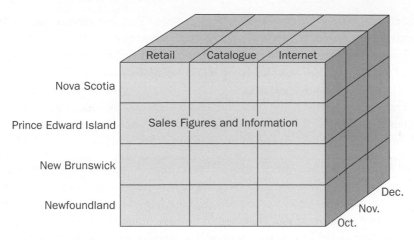

Figure 10.3 Illustration of a data cube

This illustration shows how a data cube could structure data for an Atlantic Canadian company selling via different channels to allow drill-down and data analysis in a structured format.

Many BI applications make use of data cubes. Essentially, a data cube packages data into a cube-like format that has data elements as blocks and data fields within each block (see figure 10.3). If a user performs an analysis on sales in the Atlantic Canada region, the user will be able to quickly drill down and receive information regarding each province within the region or by sales channel. While data cubes are a common format for data warehouses, some critics feel that they lack flexibility and reduce the ability of users to create custom reports. Other, more advanced design formats for data warehouses include star and snowflake schemas.

BI allows users to have access to reports and information that previously resided only in the information systems group. By moving data access directly to users, businesses reduce the demands on information systems for routine reporting needs and allow users to more quickly analyze data in the fashion they want. Information systems staff can focus their attention on the appropriate hardware, software, and integration issues for which their expertise is required. The types of data analysis and reporting required range from standard reports through to data mining (see figure 10.4).[6]

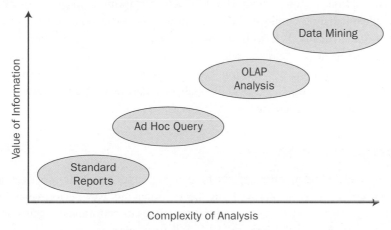

Figure 10.4 Data analysis and reporting methods

The value of BI increases as the complexity of the level of analysis increases beyond standard reporting.

Standard Reports   Users commonly want to access standard reports, such as income statements and inventory lists, which may be available within the ERP system as well as the BI system. The system should provide numerous standard reports for users, to reduce the need for ad hoc queries and ERP-based reporting. Many standard reports are provided with purchased BI software applications. Custom-designed systems will require programmers to create the standard report lists. Standard reports may provide useful general information but are of low value to focused decision making, since they tend to lack the detail needed for specific decisions and often necessitate further analysis.

Ad Hoc Query   **Ad hoc query** is the ability for users to generate any type of query or report they wish within the system. To carry out ad hoc queries, users will require sufficient understanding of the data structure, and may require additional training with the BI system. The purpose of ad hoc query is to allow users who have limited understanding of programming languages to create custom reports using the querying capabilities of the BI system.

OLAP Analysis   **Online analytical processing (OLAP)** provides the ability for users to perform detailed, summary, or trend analysis on data and allows for drill-down into that data. Most users will be familiar with drill-down, as it works in a similar manner to the hypertext format of the internet (in fact, some of the BI application providers use HTML as the interface). The OLAP-enabling technology is designed to create ease of use, flexibility, and improved performance in the system by simplifying data structures and organizing standard data elements into data cubes. OLAP is carried out in numerous ways by different BI solutions, including client-side OLAP, relational OLAP (ROLAP), multi-dimensional OLAP (MOLAP), and other hybrid forms of the technology, but these technologies are outside the scope of this book.[7]

Data Mining   Data analysis techniques such as data mining can have a drastic impact on transactional system performance and are, therefore, best suited to BI. **Data mining** is the analysis of data for relationships that may not have previously been known. For example, data mining of sales data at a sports retailer may reveal that customers who buy particular golfing equipment are likely to buy a specific type of hockey equipment in the fall or winter. Discovery of information from data mining can be useful within many areas of the business, from customer analysis to production planning and cost control.

The level of analysis employed by users will vary with their skill levels, both technologically and analytically. While the technology will allow nearly unlimited analysis of data, users need to understand the relevance of reports and output if the technology is to have any impact on decision making. For this reason, business analysts within various departments are becoming valuable individuals who can identify important information for management decision making.

Performance Analysis

Performance analysis and monitoring have become important in measuring success as well as evaluating prior decisions to improve future decision making. **Key performance indicators (KPIs)** are important standards that a company measures its performance against in relation to goals, competitors, and the industry. KPIs will vary substantially by industry and firm, depending upon the products or services offered and the corporate strategy. Some common

Fighting Terrorism with BI Software

Since the World Trade Center attacks of 2001, the war against terror and the prevention of future attacks have become increasingly important. Security has been tightened substantially around the world, and immense efforts are undertaken to identify potential terrorists long before they can do any harm. Information technology, and data-mining systems in particular, is playing an increasing role in this effort. The approach is similar to how companies link internal and external databases to identify new opportunities or to anticipate potential problems.

By linking government databases from various sources, for example, immigration and law enforcement, data-mining techniques can be employed to identify "persons of interest." The federal government in the United States has introduced a system that could be used to make air travel more secure. The program requires all airlines to electronically submit passenger information to the U.S. government before a flight. The information demanded by the government is quite comprehensive and has been subject to a heated privacy debate: In addition to name, nationality, and age of the passenger, additional information, such as credit card number, telephone number, and even the type of meal, is among the data requested. This information is cross-referenced with government databases as well as external sources such as credit card databases. Instead of only matching passenger data with "wanted lists," the data is analyzed to find potential terrorists, even if they do not appear suspicious on the surface.

According to the U.S. government, every passenger would be assigned a colour, depending on the "score" determined by the system. Green means that no further checks are required. Yellow means that additional screening is necessary. If a passenger is flagged as red, he or she will not be permitted to board a flight. The announcement of the program has sparked substantial controversy, both by privacy groups and by foreign governments. Groups such as the American Civil Liberties Union in the United States claim that the program is too intrusive and violates individual rights. The European Union has strong reservations about the system, since privacy laws in Europe do not permit such extensive sharing of data, especially with a foreign government. The scope of the system is still subject to a fierce debate. Supporters of the system argue that the threat of terrorism is more important than privacy concerns and that every available technology should be used to identify suspects. Others are more cautious and only want the system to match passenger data with lists of known suspects.

No matter what the ultimate capabilities of the system, it does give an interesting look into the future. Will BI software be used to identify potential criminals before they ever commit a crime?

U.S. Transportation Security Administration
www.tsa.gov

Questions

1. What other government uses can you see for data-mining systems?

2. What are the implications of using data-mining technologies to prevent terrorism? What are the benefits? What are the dangers?

3. Do you think Canada should introduce laws that govern the use of data mining by the private sector and the government?

Sources: Wired; American Civil Liberties Union; U.S. Transportation Security Administration.

---

examples of KPIs include market share percentages, revenue growth, and quality deviations. In many cases, KPIs are linked to a **scorecard**, which is a multi-dimensional measurement tool aimed at capturing a variety of performance indicators. The well-known **balanced scorecard** developed by Robert Kaplan and David Norton is a means to reduce the limitations of the traditional performance measures used in business, which tend to be too heavily loaded towards financial indicators.[8] As discussed in more detail in chapter 12, this scorecard includes performance metrics on customers, internal processes, learning and growth, and financial performance.

scorecard: A multi-dimensional measurement tool aimed at capturing a variety of key performance indicators.

balanced scorecard: A scorecard that includes performance indicators related to accounting and finance, human resources, internal processes, and customers.

The use of KPIs and/or scorecards for performance measurement and analysis require the capture of large volumes of data. BI and data-warehousing technologies aim to capture data for decision making and performance analysis and, therefore, are well suited to be combined into KPI monitoring or scorecard creation. BI applications can be configured to automatically notify individuals of specific changes in KPIs or other indicators deemed important by management.

Several BI and data-warehousing vendors have configured their applications to easily support the use of both KPIs and scorecard analysis. SAP's Strategic Enterprise Management suite and Cognos's Visualizer products both use colour-coded information (green, yellow, red) to allow users to quickly identify indicators that are operating within or outside predefined or historical limits. As technology improves, users continue to find more and more information at their fingertips for decision making, and BI provides the perfect environment for performance analysis.

One company that has achieved success in employing BI technology for performance analysis is Grand & Toy. Toronto-based Grand & Toy is one of the largest office supplies companies in Canada. Recognizing the need for improved information management at the company, management set out to establish a data-warehousing system as they moved away from the use of mainframe technology and standardized reports. Speaking of historical decision making, the director of marketing commented, "Profitability analysis was based on a combination of dated information, educated guesses, and opinion." The weak reporting system and data were unable to even distinguish retail from commercial sales or easily identify increases in sales attributable to promotions or discount prices.

Grand & Toy selected Cognos PowerPlay and Cognos Impromptu to create its BI applications. The system was built upon a new data warehouse, and numerous reporting capabilities from standard reports to OLAP analysis are now available. The implementation team created customized reports for product profitability analysis and customer analysis that can be monitored easily by the merchandising and sales departments. Analysts can report on products by dimensions such as location, promotion type, stock-keeping unit (SKU), and weekly sales. Customer analysis is similarly powerful. Grand & Toy has recognized gains in both its gross margin on products and overall profitability, which it attributes to improved decision making based on BI technology.

Information Dissemination

Communicating information to users and partners on a timely basis is critical in facilitating decision making at key points in the process. Information dissemination tools exist that integrate closely with BI applications to carry out this function. For example, MicroStrategy's Narrowcast Server is an application dedicated to delivering the right information to the right user in a personalized format and on a timely basis.[9] The growth in technological tools means that information must now be disseminated in numerous formats, from email to cellphones, PDAs, and pagers.

The dissemination of information can be configured to meet a number of different criteria. For example, a production manager may wish to receive notification of changes in demand above a specified limit. Furthermore, he or she may want to receive the information using wireless technology, so that setup or other necessary modifications on the shop floor can be planned or even commence immediately. Partners of the supply chain may wish to be notified immediately of any changes in production or delivery schedules so that customers can be updated or orders can be revised to reflect the change in circumstances.

The application of intelligence technologies to ongoing operations has limitless potential, as managers increasingly require up-to-date information to make important decisions.

Collaboration

The management of organizations has progressed to the point where focusing on only one enterprise limits the ability to reduce costs and increase sales. Supply-chain management, eprocurement, and customer relationship management all require that data and information be shared among members of the entire supply chain. While some of the information to be shared can be facilitated by ERP systems, BI and data-warehousing applications provide businesses with the opportunity to share and collaborate on information useful for decision making.

During 2001, Home Depot began sharing detailed data with some of its suppliers, in an attempt to increase sales and efficiency within the supply chain. Home Depot is marrying information regarding employees, inventory, and sales to allow its major suppliers, such as Georgia-Pacific Corp., to better understand operations at the shop floor level.[10] This form of collaboration in the analysis and interpretation of data has continued to grow as new technologies simplify the process, and will continue to blossom as the successful outcomes increase profitability.

Home Depot
www.homedepot.ca

Collaboration can occur in any aspect of inter-enterprise management and should result in value to all enterprises involved. Retailers and dealers can share detailed information with manufacturers and wholesalers (and vice versa) so that analysis of correlation among variables, such as production costs and rush orders, or retail sales trends and manufacturing overtime costs, can be carried out. As businesses learn to embrace collaboration, numerous benefits should be achieved, leading to improved customer satisfaction and supply-chain efficiency.

TECHNOLOGIES OF BI

To FULLY APPRECIATE THE VALUE OF BI APPLICATIONS, IT IS NECESSARY TO CONSIDER the technologies that underlie the user interface. While many vendors have accomplished the goal of simplifying the ease of use of their technologies, it is important to understand the core and enabling technologies employed for the full potential of BI to be obtained. The major technological components of BI architecture can be described as core technologies, enabling technologies, and solutions.[11] Figure 10.5 illustrates these technological components.

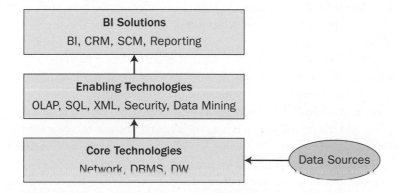

Figure 10.5 Business intelligence architecture
The BI architecture includes core technologies, enabling technologies, and solutions that allow the transformation of data into valuable information for management.

Core Technologies

Core technologies are those that provide the basic infrastructure for BI. Included in this category are basic networking technologies that facilitate the entire system, as well as database management systems (DBMSs) and the data-warehousing technology. Core technologies create the operating environment within which BI operates, and their design and structure will have a significant impact on the success or failure of BI initiatives. In most companies the existing networking infrastructure will be utilized for BI, since local area networks (LANs), intranets, or other networking technologies will already be in place.

The use of internet technologies and protocols such as TCP/IP has significantly reduced the complexity of linking numerous systems. BI implementations where the application chosen uses an HTML interface (such as the MicroStrategy example provided earlier) can capitalize on internet technology when dealing with integration issues.

The networking design of a company has a substantial impact on performance in the BI environment as well as on transactional or ERP applications. The number of network servers, their ability to distribute workloads, and the overall size of a network are all factors that will affect network performance. Numerous networking technologies such as routers, firewalls, and even operating systems will also need to be evaluated, as the deployment of BI and any other corporate applications can cause substantial increases in network traffic, that is, the number of messages sent back and forth by the applications when attempting to satisfy users' requests for information. Unless the architecture of the system and the system components themselves can handle such traffic demands, the entire system can come to a crawl, hampering not just BI but other business operations as well. The concept of network design and management is a large area and is examined in numerous other texts. The key here is to understand that, as a core technology for BI, networking can have a dramatic impact on performance, flexibility, and integration.

The type of core technology chosen for the company's databases can vary as well and will be based on numerous factors. The most common form of database is the relational database. A **relational database** is a database that uses numerous tables and can relate fields or tables to one another, and can easily be reorganized or extended.

To understand how a relational database can reduce data duplication, let's look at a typical sales transaction. A customer order transaction for a specific quantity of inventory items could be recorded by an order entry clerk with all fields necessary, including date, customer, customer information (address, contact, etc.), purchase order number, inventory items ordered (item number, description, location, etc.), quantities, and numerous other details necessary for an organization to record and track sales. Under a traditional transactions based system, when another sale takes place, several of the data fields that have already been recorded, including customer address and inventory descriptions, would be duplicated, resulting in additional data to store, back up, and manage. If some of the same information is used in the payroll system to track commission sales, that information could be duplicated as well, and if the information in the sales system and the payroll system is not synchronized, the two sets of information could become inconsistent. The relational database would reduce this duplication of data by storing different types of data within separate tables. Information that is relatively fixed in nature, like customer name and addresses can then just be referred to when recording subsequent transactions and not re-entered (see figure 10.6). The customer number could be used as a relational field, meaning it could be used to access the name and address without re-entering them. Similarly, an inventory number could be used as a relational field that relates to the inventory

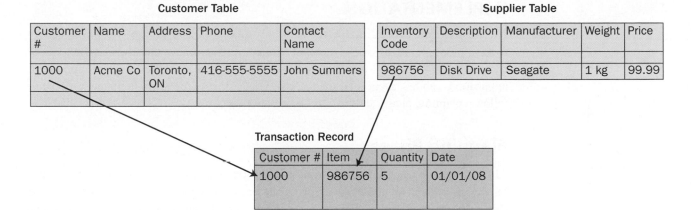

Customer Table						Supplier Table				
Customer #	Name	Address	Phone	Contact Name		Inventory Code	Description	Manufacturer	Weight	Price
1000	Acme Co	Toronto, ON	416-555-5555	John Summers		986756	Disk Drive	Seagate	1 kg	99.99

Transaction Record

Customer #	Item	Quantity	Date
1000	986756	5	01/01/08

Figure 10.6 Relational databases

The use of relational databases reduces data redundancy, inconsistency, and errors by minimizing duplication and the amount of information that needs to be entered into a system. The system can link order information to other fields in the inventory and customer tables as necessary to get other needed information, such as price or shipping addresses.

table for details of description, size, weight, and so on. Since re-entry of data is usually a source of errors, this approach would also result in more accurate data.

Microsoft Access represents a common example of a relational database. The use of database technologies such as a relational database management system (RDBMS) provides a data warehouse with the flexibility to add additional data sources in the future, and redefine the structure of the data if necessary. The data warehouse structure will also be designed so as to reduce the amount of replication of data within the database.

Enabling Technologies

Enabling technologies are technologies that enable BI applications to interact and perform tasks within the core technologies, such as the data warehouse. Some of the key enabling technologies for data warehousing and BI are OLAP, Structured Query Language (SQL), XML, security, messaging/workflow systems, and data-mining technologies. The enablers for BI essentially allow either a BI user or a specific BI solution to carry out tasks of reporting, analysis, or modelling within the system.

enabling technologies: Technologies that enable BI applications to interact and perform tasks within the core technologies, such as the data warehouse.

BI Solutions

BI solutions are technologies that enable the reporting and analysis of data at the client or user end of the process. The focus in this chapter has been on BI applications, but, as discussed earlier, reporting and analysis may take place within other specialized applications as well. CRM and supply-chain management technologies may be integrated into or operated separately from the BI application and, as such, may also share data warehouses or data marts.

The BI solution chosen does not have to be vendor specific. Several companies have adopted products from more than one vendor to suit their particular needs most effectively. Once again, internet and networking technologies, application programming interfaces, and other technologies can allow numerous systems to be tied together to best accomplish corporate goals.

IMPLEMENTATION

IMPLEMENTATION OF A BI INITIATIVE REQUIRES MANY COMMON IT PROJECT MANAGEMENT tools to be employed, as well as numerous BI-specific concepts. As with ERP, the focus of the implementation of BI is on business issues and on understanding which technological applications can best support business needs. The basic structure of an implementation will follow a planning phase, architecture design, and execution.

Planning Phase

The planning phase of BI implementation must first focus on establishing reasonable goals for the project and aligning BI goals with corporate goals and strategy. It is essential that this phase clearly identify what areas of concern the BI implementation is attempting to address, so that the system is designed appropriately and so that the success of the project can later be determined.

The goals established will assist the project team in defining the scope of the project. As described earlier in this chapter, BI initiatives rely upon data warehouses and data marts. The choice of departmentalized data marts vs. deployment of a corporate-wide data warehouse will impact the scope of the project and all implementation phases dramatically. The selection of a major data warehouse does not prohibit the utilization of data marts by departments at a later date; it does, however, call for specific database design and integration tools to be employed. Similarly, the development of a BI initiative that attempts to allow departments to implement data marts that will later be integrated does not prevent the company from developing a corporate-wide BI strategy. This method, however, does require that the individual data mart projects be carried out in unison with strong communication ties, so that roadblocks don't develop later (e.g., by using different metadata definitions within each data mart for similar data elements).

The planning phase of BI implementation must also consider specific success factors required for BI. The analysis of industry practices and technological requirements for success will help to prevent the investment of time and money into a project that later needs to be abandoned.

Critical Success Factors for BI To be successful, BI applications, similar to other technological tools, must meet a number of requirements. The critical success factors for BI include ease of use, scalability, flexibility, performance, data quality, and security.

Ease of Use The growth in use of the internet came with the rise of the World Wide Web's graphical interface; similarly, BI technologies will grow in value as they become easier to use. Much of the same data being used in BI applications today has been available for decades, but it was locked within legacy systems. In the mainframe environment, querying data for ad hoc reports involved a detailed understanding of the data structure within the system, as well as an ability to program in a query language. For these reasons, reporting was an expensive task and often took extended periods of time.

Several advances have been made already in improving ease of use of BI tools. The adoption of HTML or weblike interfaces has improved the ability of most users to navigate and find reports. Ad hoc queries can be carried out by most users with little input from information systems staff, thus reducing costs and time to carry out reporting.

Fannie Mae, one of the largest financial institutions in the world, has adopted data warehousing and BI technologies to allow its employees to more easily create reports. Historical data in the financial industry is critical for long-term analysis, and Fannie Mae maintains large volumes of data back to 1979. In addition to its own data, Fannie Mae stores data from more than 70 external sources. In the past, a report requiring access to historical data could take weeks and require several programmers. The mainframe backup system was used to restore data from tapes where programmers would then need to consolidate and query the data to produce the requested reports. Today, Fannie Mae employees can access historical reports directly through their SAS Institute system (a BI provider) within minutes, thus reducing the time for analysis and increasing customer satisfaction.[12]

Fannie Mae
www.fanniemae.com

Ease of use will continue to develop as users request additional functionality and the volume of data increases. The conversion of data from complex ERP systems into data warehouse information supplemented by metadata descriptions will assist users to better understand the reports and data they analyze as systems begin to provide additional help functions. High-level analysis and data mining, however, have a limited ability to become easier. While performing data mining can be simplified by technology, the interpretation and understanding of the results is left to the user.

BI applications have simplified reporting and data analysis through web interfaces and must continue to improve value through ease of use. For example, standard reports should be easy to create and share with other users, tools such as wizards should be included to assist users to build custom reports, and advanced users should be able to share interpretations of data with the user community in a simple manner.

Scalability

Companies must ensure that the system they implement is extremely scalable. This capability is partially determined by the approaches followed in the implementation phase as well as the configuration of the system, but needs to remain a priority. The volume of data that an organization captures can grow rapidly as the value of BI is realized throughout the enterprise. Scalability and performance are similar and interrelated, but not the same. **Scalability** is the ability of a system to maintain a set rate of performance as the number of users or volume of usage increases.

scalability: The ability of a system to maintain a set rate of performance as the number of users or volume of usage increases.

Many data-warehousing/BI projects integrate data from ERP and legacy systems from the outset. This scenario can result in a relatively predictable volume of data that can be used for reporting and analysis. Once the value of BI is discovered, however, many users begin to request that additional data from ecommerce transactions, click-stream data, and external sources be captured as well to increase the usefulness of BI for decision making throughout the firm.

Hardware and software implications must be considered when evaluating the scalability of a BI solution. An obvious hardware issue is hard disk capacity, which can easily reach into the terabytes as data capture grows. In addition, the scalability of hardware performance should be considered as the potential increase in the number of users could bring the speed of the server to a standstill. The hardware selection will likely not be driven by distant future demands on the system, but it is important to be thinking at least a couple of years ahead to avoid wasted capital investments.

Software issues range from operating system selection to BI application selection. As the BI application is chosen, it is important that the entire environment be considered so as to simplify integration and improve compatibility. Other software concerns will include database selection and the use of customized ETL tools. Throughout software evaluation, it is crucial that planned and future demands be considered carefully.

Flexibility The flexibility of the BI system may be put to the test as the adoption of the technology throughout the firm grows. Varying data sources will often place demands on BI applications, and software and hardware selection must consider the need for flexibility. The number of known data sources at the beginning of implementation will often necessitate specific technology choices, but businesses must plan ahead for potential external sources of data, such as web-based data or partner data.

The BI system should also be flexible in allowing multiple data models within large enterprises. Advanced users and data-warehousing specialists often disagree on the "best" models to be used for the database design, and flexibility in this regard can be very important. Some data warehouses are constructed so that data is standardized within the warehouse, and then data marts are utilized to test alternative models.[13]

Performance Fast and accurate access to information will increase the value and use of BI applications. As with scalability and system selection, performance must be evaluated on an ongoing basis to ensure user satisfaction. Performance can be seriously hindered within a data warehouse by numerous data-mining or large-scale analyses. If data mining is to be a common occurrence, policies should be established to control the impact on performance, and alternative system designs should be evaluated.

Performance may also be affected by the chosen update frequency for the data warehouse. Frequent updates can hinder system performance; however, they result in more up-to-date information. A balance needs to be established in this circumstance.

Data Quality A data warehouse is designed to enable users to gain information and knowledge from data. If the data are of high quality, meaning that they are complete, current, accurate, and authorized, then the BI system can provide useful analyses. However, if the data are of poor quality, then many of the potential benefits of BI are compromised. One reason that companies may have data quality problems is that they obtain much of their data from external sources such as suppliers, contract manufacturers, agents, distributors, retailers, and consumers, who may not have data quality programs in place. Another problem is created when companies have global operations with varying standards of attention to data quality. In addition, many companies grow through mergers and acquisitions, whereby they acquire entities whose data are of poor quality. As a result of these factors, even well-designed BI systems will perform suboptimally unless a data quality program is established and enforced. A data quality program ensures that consistent data quality/integrity standards are developed and applied throughout the organization and at interfaces with external data sources to achieve data quality goals. A dedicated data quality team, established accountability for data quality, communication of data quality objectives and standards, auditability provisions, and continuous monitoring contribute to compliance with data quality standards and data quality goal achievement.

Security A data warehouse is designed to allow users to gain information and knowledge from data. However, the presence of confidential data in the system necessitates that an appropriate level of security be in place. The security level can range from all users having full access to read, write, and change data records (not reasonable) to only one "superuser" having complete access to the system (not practical). Within this range, each business will need to evaluate the objectives of its data-warehousing/BI strategy and consider the implications of security on the rest of the implementation.

In examining BI objectives, the business must keep in mind that users with higher decision-making potential should have greater access to information. Despite the ease of giving all users access to the data, it is not reasonable to allow a payables clerk to examine the payroll records for the entire company or to "borrow" corporate knowledge for personal gain. As such, the data warehouse needs to be designed with some reasonable security controls over data access to prevent misuse of data.

Consultants in the field of data warehousing have seen a significant impact on performance caused by inappropriately designed security measures. One consultant has observed a 20 to 500 percent increase in query run times as a result of a security implementation.[14] This indicates that, although general database design is important, security system design is also important for both authorization and performance purposes.

One of the key decisions in establishing the security framework is deciding whether the security should be built into the BI application or directly into the database (see figure 10.7). The security design will be affected by several factors, including the number of users, the number of applications with data access, and the operating environment. If open database connectivity (ODBC) is available from the data warehouse, it will be necessary for security to be built at the database level to ensure protection of data access from other connected databases.

Designing security for a data warehouse can be difficult, since user access in this environment is much different from the objectives of security in the transactional (ERP) environment. Within the financial environment, the user's role is clearly defined and the requirement for access outside of the functional area is rarely necessary. In the data warehouse environment, some users will be limited to their functional area while others will need the ability to analyze and report upon company-wide data. Numerous security types can be established, but the increase in types leads to increased complexity and upkeep.

In addition to the design of security for employees, it will be necessary to determine what type of access is required for outside users. Some BI proponents argue that sharing specific information with customers, suppliers, and partners has tremendous value from a complete supply-chain and relationship perspective. Opponents argue that other methods of overcoming the lack of digital communication can be more successful and less costly. Each organization must decide which approach to information sharing it prefers to take. If outside users will access information, additional security concerns need to be addressed.

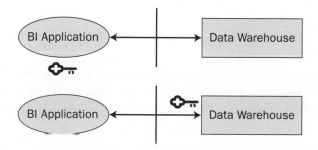

Figure 10.7 Two major approaches to security in data warehousing

Data warehouse security can be established at the application or database level, with the appropriate design depending on many other factors within the organization.

In most circumstances, outside users will be able to access only information regarding their own relationship with the business. Basic or summarized information regarding supply and demand may also be shared in some organizations. The feeling of many in this regard is that more information leads to better knowledge, which then leads to improved decision making.

The complexity of security and its potential impact on data warehouse performance suggests that security is not an issue to take lightly. To facilitate implementation in an efficient manner, security should be designed along with the data warehouse. Building both the security framework and the data warehouse format at the same time may allow for both to develop more efficiently, since database design affects security and security affects database design. Despite the importance of designing security and the data warehouse concurrently, consultants point out that rarely are security issues addressed until the later stages of an implementation, leading to greater complexity, time, and costs.[15]

Architecture Design

The design of a system for BI applications is considered at the initial planning phase of the implementation, but will need to be revised into achievable project requirements at the architecture design stage. Two critical elements that need to be determined are database design and system architecture.[16]

Database design is tied in part to the outcomes and analysis methods to be employed. However, the database design is also closely tied to the vendor applications chosen, meaning that the architecture design stage will be carried out in concert with software selection and consultant recommendations. The database type and structure can be affected by the vendor's OLAP type and may also vary depending on whether the implementation uses a data warehouse or data mart approach. The design of the database in this phase of implementation also needs to take into account the concerns about security design described earlier.

System architecture is a second critical issue to consider because the system will affect several functions and abilities (flexibility, performance, scalability, etc.). The architecture decisions will also be linked to such factors as software application choice, number of users, hardware selection, and existing corporate infrastructure. One of the considerations to be made at this point will be whether to use a two-tier or three-tier access design for the data warehouse/data mart (see figure 10.8). Two-tier structures are simpler and often less costly, but if the number of users is high, performance can easily degrade. A three-tier structure allows the servers within the system to balance the load of user requests and is also required for some specific vendor products.

Execution

In the execution phase of BI implementation, numerous common management techniques come into play. Top management commitment needs to exist throughout the project to ensure adequate resources are dedicated and to gain employee buy-in. In addition, a team approach to the entire project is necessary to allow departmental input and evaluation of the project planning and implementation.

Project management techniques should be embraced throughout the implementation so that costs, human resources, and consultants are controlled in a reasonable fashion. Use of project management techniques will assist the project to maintain reasonable timelines and also allow for evaluation of success at critical stages of the implementation.

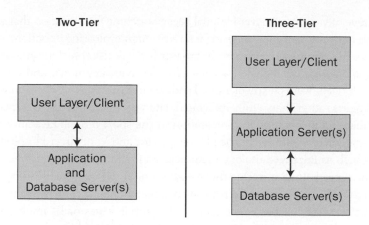

Figure 10.8 Two-tier and three-tier data warehouse structures

Two-tier and three-tier structures for data warehouse design can impact system performance dramatically. The three-tier structure is more easily scaled as the number of users grows.

The implementation of any new technology will also require management to plan its approach to the implementation; that is, they must engage in "change management." The implementation of BI can create tensions among departments over data ownership issues and user frustration with new applications. Management must ensure that issues of data ownership are addressed to allow the project to be implemented successfully. In addition, the later stages of the implementation should involve strong commitments to training, since users will be employing new technologies in their work.

Training will allow users to develop an appreciation for the BI applications, and can also provide top-level users with guidance on analytical approaches. The importance of training is to allow users to truly take the onus for reporting and analysis off the information systems department. Appropriate training will also allow top-level users to understand the impact of data mining and other complex queries on system performance.

During the execution phase of implementation, the business should ensure that it has given consideration to the goals and outcomes defined at the planning stage. Return on investment (ROI) is a common tool used to evaluate business investments, and many companies have employed ROI as a basis to measure BI implementation success. A study by International Data Corporation found that the overall ROI on data-warehousing/BI initiatives among 62 large organizations was 41 percent, with payback periods ranging from 2 to 3 years.[17] While ROI is a difficult measure to quantify, it can be used as an overall assessment of the project. Other metrics should also be employed to help assess a project's outcomes, such as query response time, number of users actively using the system, and analyses of important information discovered. Each organization needs to assess the metrics according to their objectives to determine an appropriate mix of financial and operational measures.

One organization that has successfully implemented a BI solution and measured its success with primarily non-financial measures is the Vancouver Hospital and Health Services Centre. The Vancouver Hospital is the second largest in Canada and manages more than 37,000 acute-care and 81,000 emergency visits per year, in addition to a growing number of surgeries and other medical services. Like other hospitals in Canada, Vancouver Hospital has increasingly found it difficult to keep up with demand for many of its services, leading to long patient wait times and issues with employee scheduling. Having collected data from numerous sources for several years, Vancouver Hospital began searching for a solution that would allow it to improve its decision making and patient service. After evaluating its options, the hospital chose Cognos BI as its solution provider for browser-based decision-making and analysis tools.

The implementation included a team of executives, key users, and consultants to ensure that all needs were clearly identified and communicated. The decision was made to utilize data marts rather than a fully integrated data warehouse because the specific objectives identified did not require full integration in the short term. The solution was built around the parameters outlined at the planning stage, and Vancouver Hospital wanted to use metrics such as improved use of patient beds and reductions in wait times for surgery to determine success. In monitoring the overall hospital services, the BI solution employs the balanced scorecard approach to performance measurement. The Vancouver Hospital implementation team has been successful at the initial stages of BI implementation by following logical, business-oriented strategies and working in a team environment.

Maintenance and Change Management

It is important to recognize that the design and implementation of a BI system must be revised as new user requirements and new technologies come along. As technologies such as ERP systems, databases, and the internet continue to evolve, BI, including the company's specific implementation of BI, will need to keep pace if it is to continue to provide value to the firm. Flexible systems are needed to enable the BI implementation to adapt as the organization's needs change. For example, an organization may develop new lines of business or acquire business units to extend existing lines of business or create new ones. The company's BI systems will need to be modified to incorporate such changes quickly and effectively, and new business units that have not previously used BI will need to learn how to take advantage of this technology.

EXTENSIONS OF TRADITIONAL BI

The increased use of data analysis tools in business decisions has led BI vendors to work on implementing new technologies for a broad range of BI applications. Key new developments in BI applications are BI on mobile devices, enhanced search capabilities, real-time BI and cloud computing.

BI on Mobile Devices

Many modern business systems are now available through mobile devices, such as smartphones and iPads. With this capability, users can analyze data any time and anywhere, making analyses available on a timely, secure, and personalized basis. Encryption and compression are used to protect the information and make it usable on a small device.

Enhanced Search Capabilities

BI systems have been designed to deal with structured information contained in databases and tables. However, organizations also capture great volumes of unstructured information, such as emails, memos, documents, telephone records, contracts, and customer responses to surveys.

Enterprises often benefit from the structured and unstructured data in their data warehouses by integrating BI with a search engine such as Google. The application obtains search results and ranks them based on the priorities derived from a synopsis of users' previous reports, analyses, and dashboards in the organization's system.[18] This application combines data integration technology with search engine technology to provide more information than general keyword searching is able to do.

Real-Time BI

The action time horizon of decisions based on BI depends on three components: the time required to capture business transaction data for analysis, the time required to analyze this data and deliver the results to the user, and the time for the user to make a decision and take action. Different events need different action times depending on specific user requirements. Traditionally, decision makers relied on BI applied to historical data that was weeks or months old. However, the action and reaction times for many decisions are being compressed into increasingly shorter time frames. Enterprises are seeking to implement real-time BI to increase the speed and efficiency of short-term tasks such as data integration, data reporting, performance management, and automated actions. In response, many BI solutions are being improved to offer real-time or near-real-time information.[19]

One issue that can arise with real-time BI is that some information streams may not be synchronized with other information streams and thus may portray a misleading picture of the context in which the information is being gathered. Another issue is that real-time information may contain volatility that could lead to erratic decisions if the information is not assessed in light of longer-term trends. Also, many decisions take time to be implemented, and they may need time for their consequences to be evident; thus, real-time information may not be useful until sufficient time has passed to permit valid assessments of such decisions.

BI in the Cloud

Cloud computing, in the form of software as a service (SaaS), was introduced in earlier chapters. Several BI providers now operate as SaaS providers, offering their BI solution on their own servers on a rental basis.

In Canada, many SaaS BI providers are resident in the United States and are therefore subject to the U.S. PATRIOT Act, which requires that data resident in the United States be available for analysis by government employees. Canadian companies are also subject to the Privacy Act in Canada and are therefore required to limit the availability of data. Essentially, many companies maintain that the provisions of the PATRIOT Act cause them to violate the provisions of the Privacy Act. This factor has served to limit the usage of BI in Canada.

CHAPTER SUMMARY

The growth in the information economy has led to the need for a much more sophisticated understanding of business processes, statistics, financial information, and other "information based on data." Business intelligence (BI) is the environment that supports analysis of data from any source (internal or external) to provide valuable information for making operating, tactical, or strategic decisions.

The primary enabling technologies of BI systems are data warehouses and data marts. Data warehouses are repositories of data that have been designed and optimized for analysis and enquiry rather than transaction processing. Data marts are similar to data warehouses but are designed to satisfy the needs of a specific user group within the organization. Implementations of BI applications may make use of both data warehouses and data marts and can take several different forms.

The analysis of data can be carried out in numerous ways with BI systems. Data mining is a common technique used in BI, where the analyst attempts to discover important trends or information within the data. In addition to advanced analysis forms such as data mining, BI can be used to monitor key metrics for the organization—often called key performance indicators (KPIs). Many organizations also employ BI to gather information to create scorecards, tools that monitor numerous financial and non-financial KPIs important to the industry.

The implementation of a BI system is a complex task requiring sophisticated project management. The design of the system will be driven by the desired outcomes, software applications chosen, data warehouse/mart design, and several other factors. Similar to other technology projects, it is crucial to have management buy-in, team support, and a strong focus on the business processes involved.

The critical success factors for BI include ease of use, scalability, flexibility, performance, data quality, and security. For the application to be useful and meet the objectives established, it is critical that the implementation and software selection carefully consider these factors. The cost and time required for successful BI implementations can be substantial, so it is necessary to put comparably substantial time into the planning process. In addition, as technology advances and business strategies evolve, it will be necessary to modify BI implementations or roll them out to new business units.

More recent trends such as BI on mobile devices, enhanced search capabilities, real-time BI and cloud computing have been introducing new opportunities for and benefits from BI.

Key Terms

ad hoc query (p. 224)

balanced scorecard (p. 225)

core technologies (p. 228)

data cube (p. 222)

data mining (p. 224)

enabling technologies (p. 229)

extraction, transformation, and loading (ETL) (p. 221)

key performance indicators (KPIs) (p. 224)

metadata (p. 221)

online analytical processing (OLAP) (p. 224)

online transaction-processing (OLTP) system (p. 220)

relational database (p. 228)

scalability (p. 231)

scorecard (p. 225)

MyEbusinessLab | Tools for Online Learning

To help you master the material in this chapter and stay up to date with new developments in ebusiness, visit the MyEBusinessLab at www.pearsoned.ca/myebusinesslab. Resources include the following:

- **Pre- and Post-Test Questions**
- **Additional Chapter Questions**
- **Author Blog**
- **Recommended Readings**
- **Commentaries on Current Trends**
- **Additional Topics in Ebusiness**
- **Internet Exercises**
- **Glossary Flashcards**

Endnotes

1. SAP website, www.sap.com.
2. Cognos website, www.cognos.com/solutions/, accessed February 12, 2007.
3. R. Kalakota and M. Robinson, *e-Business 2.0: Roadmap for Success* (Toronto: Addison-Wesley, 2001).
4. www.b-eye-network.com/view/2841, accessed March 2, 2007.
5. J. Wu, "What Is This Data? End User Presentation of Meta Data,"*DM Review* (October 2000).
6. J. Wu, "User Requirements for Enterprise Query and Reporting,"*DM Review* (April 2000).
7. R. Kalakota and M. Robinson, *e-Business 2.0: Roadmap for Success* (Toronto: Addison-Wesley, 2001).
8. J. Oliveira, "The Balanced Scorecard: An Integrative Approach to Performance Evaluation,"*Healthcare Financial Management* (May 2001).
9. MicroStrategy website, www.microstrategy.com/Software/Products/Narrowcast_Server, accessed November 25, 2004.
10. P. MacDougall, "Companies That Dare to Share Information Are Cashing In on New Opportunities, "*InformationWeek* (May 2001).
11. R. Kalakota and M. Robinson, *e-Business 2.0: Roadmap for Success* (Toronto: Addison-Wesley, 2001).
12. J. Ryan, "Cost-Effective Performance, Smarter Decision Support—Alpha Brings It Home to Fannie Mae," Techguide.com.
13. C. Kelley, "Stars and Snowflakes: Do You See a Snow Storm or Constellation Coming Your Way?"*Data Warehousing* (February 2001).
14. C. Silbernagel, "Data Security: Protecting the Warehouse from Within,"*DM Review* (June 1999).
15. J. Cunningham, "Data Warehousing: A Security Perspective,"*DM Review* (November 2000).
16. B. Love and M. Burwen, *Business Intelligence and Data Warehousing: Crossing the Millennium* (Palo Alto, CA: Palo Alto Management Group, February 1999).
17. J. Ryan, "A Practical Guide to Getting Started with Data Warehousing," Techguide.com.
18. www.baselinemag.com/article2/0,1540,2062322,00.asp, accessed March 6, 2007.
19. www.dmreview.com/article_sub.cfm?articleId=1009281, accessed March 6, 2007.

PART 3 CASE STUDY
NTUITIVE

Mark Orlan, Ntuitive Inc.'s CEO and major shareholder, is making a presentation to a potential client, the marketing manager at a major airlines:

"The market research industry is a huge industry, and a very labour-intensive one. We all have experienced surveys of one kind or another. We have all filled out an online survey at one point or another. Not only is it labour-intensive to design the survey and gather the data, but what happens to that data after it is collected? Do you need a database expert, a programmer, a statistician to get at your data? We bring market research out of the back office, reduce the mystery, put the results in the hands of typical business managers. You don't have to be a statistician or a PhD to collect, analyze, or use the information. . . . Business intelligence is still not well understood, but after you see our live demo, I'm sure you will see the contribution that our company can make to your customer relationship management, and in particular your customer loyalty program."

Ntuitive is a small technology company, which has been in business since 2000. The company has few employees, yet it has a roster of very well-known Fortune 500 companies as clients, including Canadian Tire, GE, Timberland, Sprint, and Benjamin Moore. In developing its Nvision product, the company teamed up with Cognos Inc. and then when Cognos was purchased by IBM in 2009, Ntuitive went with them and is now a part of IBM.

Ntuitive initially did contract programming work, but that changed when it was asked to develop software to collect information by News Marketing Canada. The company sent people out across Canada to gather information on behalf of customers. For example, it was hired by Wrigley's to gather information about how Walmart managed Wrigley's products. News Marketing employees would check out where the product was in the store, what the stock levels were, all sorts of information that would help Wrigley's manage its sales. The information would be recorded on paper surveys and then typed into spreadsheets for analysis purposes. This was a very time-consuming, labour-intensive process. Ntuitive developed an improved collection mechanism for News Marketing Canada using voice response technology, and licensed it to this and other companies that needed to collect information to support their marketing and sales activities.

According to Orlan, "Over the next few years, we said, 'Why don't we genericize and web-enable this process?' So we built a web interface to be able to design, collect and analyze survey information, including unstructured information. However, the back end was still a problem. For example, News Marketing Canada was relying on 20 programmers to produce custom reports for every client. The programmers were coding database extraction routines [for] all of the required reports."

"We said, 'Why don't we integrate reporting tools into our solution set?' So we became a Cognos partner to take advantage of the reporting tools that the company provided as part of its Business Intelligence software suite. We knew Cognos was the market leader, so we focused on working with them, [and] developed expertise that led to our most recent version of our main product, NVision.

"In summary, we saw an opportunity to be able to collect information and report on that information right away. Take out the customization, take out the programming—automate the integration between data collection and reporting. We can collect any kind of information, any questions and answers, and report on that right away.

"NVision is enterprise scale. We do all the hosting. It automates the complete lifecycle, everything from survey design, to data collection, to analysis. If you don't already have a survey designed, we can help you design one with our Design Studio. We'll work through a scenario with you, we'll build a survey and actually key in all the questions [and] the response options without any programming. It's a web-form type of interface.

"Then we link in the appropriate data-capture engines, web forms, voice response, and/or kiosk. The same survey can be administered over these various channels. Once the information is collected we build cubes. Cognos and the other BI system suppliers use this cube or data mart concept. Then we can produce analytical reports off that data mart. In other words, you can build any survey, publish it to the web, collect the data, push a button to build a cube, and access reports right away. That whole cycle is very quick. And you can change the survey and reports on the fly.

"Here's one example of a project we did for Liberty Travel, a travel company in the Northeast U.S. with over 200 locations. We help them set up a mechanism to invite people who come in for a travel booking to participate in the survey. The agent logs the customer's email address and some other booking information about them. Within three days they get an email in their inbox saying please fill out our survey and tell us how we did. Tell us about the service experienced in the store. Another option is for customers to pick up printed invitations in the stores themselves. So people just browsing around the store can pick up a survey invitation go to the website or call a 1-800 number and respond to the same survey by keying in the responses on the telephone keypad. The data is collected and is reported on right away.

"We helped another company gauge its customers' reaction to changes it made to its website. They emailed 30 000 people in one blast and within two hours got about 5000 responses back. They didn't even offer any incentives and still got a tremendous response. However, we often find that incentives are needed, and we can build incentives into the process to make it fun for people to fill out surveys or to choose one survey over another.

"We can put in any kind of question and answer in our survey. All the branding is done very easily. Drop-down boxes can be custom defined. Open-ended text can be utilized—we can pull in key words and put them in context and analyze open-ended text without having to browse through thousands of responses.

"As for output, you can get graphs, charts, and tables. You can drill down. You can modify reports instantly by just dragging and dropping. It's a very dynamic environment. And the system integrates with Microsoft Office Suite, including PowerPoint.

"Companies talk about customer satisfaction and that's great. What if the customer is dissatisfied? What do we do with that? How can we be proactive with the knowledge that we learn from the survey? We plotted some information about customer satisfaction ratings on a survey over a number of weeks and saw the satisfaction was dropping. Then, a few weeks later the sales started dropping—about three weeks later. Management had some serious work to do to reverse the situation. But fortunately for them, they caught the trend early and were able to take corrective action.

"If you take a dashboard and build thresholds in, then an executive can log in and see right away if he's below a threshold."

After Mark finished the presentation, he turned to the marketing manager and asked him what he thought. The marketing manager replied, "I love the concept. But I don't know if I can make a deal. I have to check with our IT department whether your software is compatible with our systems and whether they will support it if I license it. Also, even though it looks simple to use and all, I'm not sure I have the time to play with it and get comfortable with the design process and so on quickly enough for the upcoming survey that we need to do. Once that survey is done, my budget is used up for the year, so I couldn't do something with you for several months. Let me talk to the IT folks and get back to you in a couple of days."

Mark returned to the office. This was the third presentation this month, and he wasn't sure that the marketing manager was persuaded to try NVision enough to take on the IT department if their answers were ambiguous or unsupportive.

Mark also thought that he hadn't emphasized the cost–benefit as strongly as he might have. His software reduced the cost of gathering and reporting information to less than $1 per respondent from an industry average ranging from $20 to $80 per respondent. Even hosted web surveys cost $5 per respondent due to the labour involved in handling and analyzing the data after the survey was collected. NVision eliminated most of those costs. On the other hand, those cost savings would not matter very much to the IT department. It was concerned about a whole slew of other issues.

Questions for Discussion

1. What are some examples of analyses that could benefit from a system like NVision?
2. What issues does this type of BI raise? How should they be addressed?
3. Is software licensing the best way to sell NVision? What other options could Mark consider?
4. How should Mark respond if the IT department is not supportive?

Source

Interview with Mark Orlan, CEO, Ntuitive Inc.

Chapter 11

Emarketing and Advertising

Learning Objectives

When you complete this chapter you should be able to:

1   Describe how emarketing and online advertising tools fit into the strategy of a business.

2   Describe the emarketing strategy process and its components.

3   Describe the types of online research tools available to an ebusiness and how they can be applied to understand user behaviour.

4   Discuss the implementation process for an emarketing strategy and identify common marketing tactics.

5   List and describe the major online advertising tools available to an ebusiness.

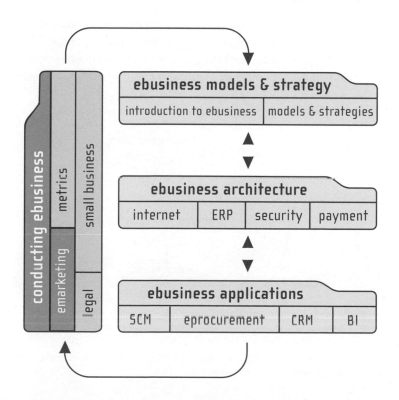

INTRODUCTION

THE CONCEPT OF EMARKETING HAS GONE THROUGH A RAPID CYCLE OF DEVELOPMENT over the past few years—from introduction to craze, decline, and stabilization. Initially, the promise of global markets, unlimited customers, and an improved communication medium led many to the conclusion that internet marketing and online tools would guarantee global exposure, rapid growth, and business success. The potential of emarketing was perhaps misunderstood in these initial stages, and more recently the development of the internet's use for marketing purposes has settled into a more reasonable approach: the internet represents one important component of an overall marketing strategy.

Emarketing is the utilization of internet and electronic technologies to assist in the creation, implementation, and evaluation of marketing strategy. This chapter will review emarketing concepts such as online research, internet advertising technologies, and online consumer behaviour, with reference to the emarketing strategy process outlined in figure 11.1. The emarketing process progresses through a cycle similar to other business initiatives. The flexibility of the internet, however, allows for the strategy to be fluid in nature, although numerous changes can still be costly and result in poorer-than-expected performance.

The concept of emarketing is closely related to customer relationship management (CRM) but is a broader concept that businesses need to consider (see figure 11.2). CRM and business intelligence (BI) are tools that may be used throughout the emarketing process, primarily to gather and analyze the data needed to formulate and execute marketing strategies. The CRM application may also be the tool used to evaluate the success of marketing campaigns.

> **emarketing:** The utilization of internet and electronic technologies to assist in the creation, implementation, and evaluation of marketing strategy.

Online Branding

Ask any individual to name companies that come to mind when they think of the internet, and you are likely to hear Amazon.com as one of the responses. That is because Amazon has developed a successful marketing strategy that incorporates online, print, and other advertising methods to successfully identify its brand as the leading online provider

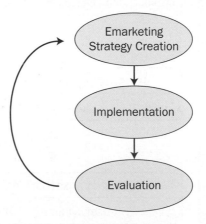

Figure 11.1 The Emarketing Strategy Process

The emarketing strategy process includes strategy creation, implementation, evaluation and revision—all within the larger context of overall business strategy.

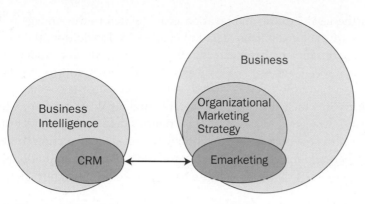

Figure 11.2 The Relationship Between Emarketing and CRM

The relationship between emarketing and CRM can be close in firms pursuing both strategies, but each is a unique aspect of ebusiness.

of books, CDs, and many other products. Internet startups like Amazon focused initially on the emarketing components of their marketing strategy, while brick-and-mortar competitors like Barnes & Noble stuck to more traditional marketing tactics. As the brand recognition of Amazon rose, Barnes & Noble developed more of an emarketing strategy, while at the same time, Amazon branched out into more traditional media to continue to capitalize on its brand recognition. This example of the development of the online book industry illustrates an important point—whether a company originates as a bricks-and-mortar firm or an internet startup, emarketing must form an important component of its overall business and marketing strategy.

An important focus of emarketing is brand creation and brand reinforcement. A **brand** is a name, term, sign, symbol, design, or combination of these attributes that is used to differentiate a product or service from its competitors. Emarketing can help create brand awareness that can attract visitors to an ebusiness website and potentially convert them to buyers. There is controversy about the degree of importance that should be attributed to online brands, given the opportunities to send traffic to various sites through rating services, banner ads, and comparison shopping sites. Yet many analysts believe that branding of online businesses is critical due to their lack of physical presence, their remoteness from customers, and customers' need to trust the parties they do business with. A strong brand can build customer confidence, loyalty, and satisfaction, and, in the long run, it can help an ebusiness reduce its marketing costs, improve its margins, and extend the developed brand to new products and services. Developing a strong brand requires the following: an understanding of the target customer and key leverage points in the customer's ebusiness experience; competitor monitoring; a compelling communication program with regular feedback systems; and consistent, reliable product delivery and service performance.

brand: A name, term, sign, symbol, design, or combination of these attributes that is used to differentiate a product or service from its competitors.

STRATEGY CREATION

THE CREATION OF AN EMARKETING STRATEGY REQUIRES THE USE OF BOTH TRADITIONAL and online tools. As with any other strategic plan, the development of an emarketing strategy requires an analysis of competition and other environmental factors. One of the major areas of concern at the strategy creation stage is evaluation of the environment in terms of the legal, ethical, and taxation issues related to the strategy to be devised. These topics are explored in more detail in chapter 13. In addition, the firm may carry out market opportunity analyses such as a PEST analysis, which considers the political, environmental, social, and technological aspects of the environment in which an ebusiness operates; a Porter Five Forces analysis, which considers the competitive landscape in the industry in which the ebusiness operates; and a SWOT analysis, which considers the entity's strengths, weaknesses, opportunities, and threats to identify potential areas of focus. It is essential during the formulation of the emarketing strategy that the relationship between the emarketing strategy and the overall organizational strategy be thoroughly considered, to ensure consistency and to achieve synergies that can benefit the business.

market segment: A group of customers who share common needs and/or characteristics that the selling firm may be able to satisfy.

The research process should provide management with the information necessary to define the segments in their market. A **market segment** is a group of customers who share common needs and/or characteristics the selling firm may be able to satisfy. The primary methods of market segmentation include demographics, geography, psychographics, and behaviour.[1] With the growth of social networks, new techniques for identifying segments are being developed based on understanding buzz and sentiment, influencers and opinion leaders and locations of key conversations. An understanding of psychographics and user behaviour, combined with demographic information and geographic analysis, provides the information needed to create numerous market segments, which in the past would have taken much more extensive research to gather. Developing an understanding of the market segments that exist helps the business identify its target markets and implement its marketing strategy.

The internet opens up a strong channel for the development of strategy and is a crucial component of successful emarketing plans. It is important, however, that firms carefully evaluate their strategies in the context of both traditional customers and online customers, as each group may have differing interests and attitudes. One of the frequently cited examples of innovative multi-channel strategies is the U.S. Super Bowl. Because of the intense interest in this sporting event and the high cost of advertising associated with the event (e.g., $3 million for a 30-second spot in 2009), marketers use the event to spur the creation and implementation of innovative ways of leveraging their advertising budgets to maximum effect. In 2009, Super Bowl advertisers used various combinations of interactive TV ads, web search strategies, special purpose websites with interactive content, contests, games and other promotions, mobile phone applications, and social networking campaigns before, during and after the event to generate interest in the products and services being advertised.[2] The processes used for such strategy creation include online research, user behaviour analysis, and advertising planning.

Online Research

The internet offers a particularly valuable opportunity to carry out research to develop marketing strategies. An abundance of information is available dealing with demographic trends, social and cultural climates, competition, industry statistics, technological innovation, economics, legal data, and political environments.[3] The sources for these types of data are many, and much information can be obtained for free, while other information will be fee-based. These data sources are forms of secondary data that are useful in carrying out the environmental and market opportunity analyses in the strategy creation stage.

Secondary data are data that have not been developed specifically for the task at hand, but that may be useful for decision making. The abundance of secondary data on the internet provides marketers with information that can be used in crafting a strategy, but it needs to be used cautiously. For example, the Canadian government's Industry Canada site, www.ic.gc.ca, provides a great deal of information that originates from reliable sources such as Statistics Canada. Many of the research firms, such as Forrester Research and Gartner Group, also provide access to some of their research online. However, many other databases and surveys exist online that have been created using unknown and often questionable practices that should not be relied upon without careful review. The key to the use of secondary data is to examine the reliability of the source and ensure that the use of the data within a specific context doesn't reduce its reliability.

The strategy creation stage in most organizations will also lead marketers to gather primary data. **Primary data** is information that is gathered in an effort to better make a particular decision. Typically, primary data will be of a more specific nature than secondary data, and since it is proprietary will often be more expensive to gather. Many businesses gather primary data on an ongoing basis to assist in evaluation of, and future planning for, their emarketing strategies. For example, some online retailers ask customers to complete a satisfaction survey after each experience they have with the company. Some of the common methods of gathering primary data online include surveys, experiments, focus groups, and observation.[4]

Surveys Surveys can be conducted online either through the use of email or web-based methods. Early users of online surveys used email extensively; however, the use of email technologies requires the surveyors to develop means of capturing the data in a database for analysis, which can be more difficult than with internet technologies such as forms. In addition, the growth of spam has led to a reduction in the use of email by legitimate businesses for this purpose. It is now considered essential to gain the advance approval of recipients before sending them unsolicited emails. Researchers still use email to reach users for their research, but often the email now directs users to a website to complete the survey.

The process of collecting data through the internet is relatively simple with the use of modern technologies. Users simply enter the responses into a survey form, and upon clicking "Submit" the responses can be loaded into a database in a form configured by the data collector. Surveys can be designed and hosted on the internet using readily available software applications, which significantly reduce the cost of research compared to the use of paper. In addition, many researchers are finding that the response rates to email and internet research are very similar to paper surveys.

The use of online surveys allows for significant reductions in time for data collection and analysis. If the data input is automated, the need for data entry and error checking is reduced. Users tend to respond to email and web-based surveys either very quickly or not at all. The flexibility of design for online surveys also simplifies the completion process for users. Question formats can be customized to responses given in previous questions, and the use of drop-down boxes, radio buttons, and other online tools can make surveys very user friendly.

secondary data: Data that have not been developed specifically for the task at hand, but that may be useful for decision making.

primary data: Information that is gathered in an effort to better make a specific decision.

Experiments Online experiments are research methods that attempt to determine a cause-and-effect relationship by exposing participants to different stimuli.[5] A researcher may, for example, design different versions of websites and measure visitors' responses to them such as willingness to provide personal information, time spent exploring the site and even purchases made. This type of experimentation provides the marketing researcher with a better understanding of the effectiveness of various designs and various advertising formats.

Focus Groups The use of online focus groups has emerged as a successful application of internet technology. The ability to reach disparate areas at a low cost is one of the major advantages of the internet for conducting focus groups. Popular web technologies such as chat rooms and collaboration tools allow a focus-group leader to carry out effective research at a reasonable cost. Participants in online focus groups can provide feedback based on their analysis of a business's online presence, and formats can be set up in which they are less likely to be influenced by the comments of others.

Critics of online focus groups claim that technology gets in the way of important face-to-face discussion. For many who have conducted focus groups in person, much of the value obtained is the interpretation of actions and facial expressions that often accompany participant feedback. Some critics are also concerned with an inability to confirm the identity of participants; however, technology solutions can be used to overcome this problem if desired.

Observation The use of observation in understanding user behaviour online is very valuable. The internet provides an excellent medium for monitoring user behaviour through such technologies as click-stream analysis. Click-stream analysis forms an important component of CRM strategy, as well as website design and emarketing strategy. The primary importance of observation online is to understand how users navigate websites and then utilize that information to improve the likelihood that users will change their behaviour in a favourable manner, such as staying on the site longer or increasing the likelihood of a purchase. Click-stream analysis is also an important input into ebusiness performance measurement (metrics), as is discussed in chapter 12.

User Behaviour Analysis

The data collection methods we have just discussed provide data for use in user behaviour analysis as well as for other primary data collection. Online user behaviour includes search methods, types of internet usage, shopping patterns, email usage, and conversations via social networks. The understanding of online user behaviour is extremely important to organizations, whether they sell products and services online or not. The value of understanding user behaviour, in addition to demographic and geographic information, is the enhanced ability to create effective marketing and advertising strategies. If a particular user is very unlikely to buy a product online but commonly seeks information through the internet, a strategy may be to offer specific discounts for the first online purchase. The key to understanding whether this is a valid strategy is to better understand user behaviour.

Tracking of user behaviour is a technique that emarketers commonly use. For example, a person who visited Amazon's Zappos.com site and viewed, but didn't buy, a pair of shoes reported being offered ads for those shoes and even discount coupons for the shoes on various other websites that she visited. She felt she was being followed by shoe ads; and, in fact, she was, because marketing agents acting on behalf of the Zappos.com site had tracked the fact that the customer was interested in the shoes but did not buy them and therefore considered her as a target for **remarketing** (also called retargeting)—a process whereby a user who leaves an item in a shopping cart has a cookie placed on his or her computer that can be read by marketing software on other sites that can dynamically compose advertising or special offers designed to persuade the user to reconsider the purchase. Online remarketing is controversial because many people view it as an infringement of their privacy. Some marketing agencies (e.g., Criteo.com, TellApart.com) defend this approach by arguing that ultimately the users will benefit by being served with more personalized and more relevant ads and offers. They also permit users to opt out of their remarketing programs. Others offer users incentives for providing access to their behavioural data in the form of discounts on purchases as well as the ability to access their data to ensure it is accurate. Still others argue that remarketing is not a breach of privacy because the target is identified by a cookie that is not linked to a person's identity. Chapter 13 discusses privacy issues associated with online tracking and user behaviour analysis in more detail. See the Ebusiness in Global Perspective box for an example of how a company uses behavioural data to expand its existing web marketing efforts to mobile devices.

To better understand user behaviour, companies also may be able to rely on secondary data. For example, much research is being carried out regarding the success rates of banner ads in capturing the attention of web users. This type of data may not specifically be designed for a particular company's products but can often be generalized to many different industries. The findings from secondary data analysis may also assist companies in developing the appropriate primary data research tools. Chapter 12 discusses user behaviour analysis in more detail for assessing the performance of an emarketing strategy or evaluating the overall performance of an ebusiness.

remarketing (or retargeting): The process of tracking customers who don't complete a purchase by placing cookies on their computer to make it possible to make repeat offers for the abandoned item on other websites that the customers visit.

Ebusiness in Global Perspective

Apple Fine-Tunes Mobile Ads

Apple is preparing for a showdown with Google. Both companies see the advertising potential of mobile devices that have hitherto been free of the online advertising fever that has swept the rest of the internet. Now, as smartphones and tablets with web-browsing capabilities paralleling those of laptop and desktop computers are becoming ubiquitous, mobile devices are becoming an attractive new territory for running ads. In mid-2010, Apple started placing ads in iPhone applications for the first time. Google is not willing to give up this advertising territory. Not only did advertising

revenue make it the giant that it is today, they still represent its main source fo revenue.

With its iTunes, iBooks, and App Store websites, Apple has access to information on the habits of 150 million users. It can study what books, music, videos, TV shows, and software apps have been downloaded and track users' various related activities, behaviours, and locations. Combined, these factors enable Apple to create user profiles and then send promotional messages to their mobile devices and integrate such messages into apps created for

>

the mobile devices. More than 5 billion apps have been downloaded already.

Google is rolling out its own mobile ad strategy for the Android mobile operating system platform. It purchased the mobile ad network AdMob and has access to a wealth of information on how people use web search, email, and software on the Android platform.

Apple
www.apple.com

Google
www.google.com

Questions

1. Who has the upper hand in the battle for mobile ad revenues: Apple or Google? Why?

2. What are the risks to mobile device users from mobile ad strategies being pursued by companies such as Apple and Google?

3. What benefits do mobile ad strategies have for users?

Source: A. Satariano, "Apple Studies Downloads to Fine-Tune Mobile Ads," *Globe and Mail*, July 7, 2010, B8, www.businessweek.com/news/2010-07-06/apple-studies-user-downloads-to-fine-tune-mobile-ads.html.

Advertising Planning

One of the major planning components that will take place once the target markets have been identified is advertising and communication planning. Numerous advertising possibilities exist through the internet, traditional media, and wireless applications, and the business will have to tie the planning to each of the specific target markets identified at this stage. The target markets chosen will affect whether the advertising strategy is mass marketing, niche, or multi-segment, which in turn determine the types of advertising methods to choose from. Advertising options and technologies are discussed in more detail later in the chapter.

The strategy creation stage should conclude with a comprehensive emarketing plan. The plan should include budgets and outcome measurements so that the campaign can be analyzed. If the business is involved in CRM, the planning phase will incorporate the CRM application into the overall plan of action as well. Often the strategy creation stage will necessitate outsourcing to be organized, and may also require changes to internal processes as emarketing and CRM applications are integrated within the enterprise. The emarketing strategy must be coordinated with all other marketing efforts and evaluated with regard to overall corporate strategy prior to implementation.

IMPLEMENTATION

IMPLEMENTATION OF AN EMARKETING STRATEGY IS A STAGE OF BOTH EXECUTION and preparation for evaluation. The strategy must be put into place, but at the same time emarketing allows the collection of data to occur during implementation and after the strategy is implemented. Since the emarketing process can occur rapidly and is flexible in nature, it may be possible for changes to be made during a campaign as well, based upon preliminary analysis.

The internet's flexibility allows businesses to move from implementation back to strategy creation relatively quickly. For example, Chapters Indigo may decide to reorganize its website, focusing first on the ebusiness books category, to improve the ease of use and improve its branding effects. After preliminary evaluation, however, the company may find that the changes reduced the time spent on the site while not improving the purchases-to-visitors ratio. In this case, the company may decide to re-evaluate the site revisions and branding strategy prior to moving the new design into other areas of its site. Similarly, organizations conducting promotions through banner ads may decide to abandon banner changes if the click-through rates fall during the campaign.

The implementation of a marketing strategy will focus on a number of interrelated components within each target market. The strategy developed will include plans of action for website design, making the website visible on the web, online advertising, affiliate programs, partnerships, promotions, public relations, and pricing. To examine the complex task of emarketing implementation, we will examine these components below as each will have an impact on overall success.

Website Design

The concept of website design has developed very rapidly during the tremendous growth of the internet from the mid-1990s through to the early 2000s. The basic phases of site design that have occurred include the brochureware, interactive, and personalization phases.[6] Early site design was essentially the digitization of existing marketing materials— a phase known as the **brochureware phase** of the internet. The brochureware phase was the most logical step at the time, since it was cost-effective and the use of the internet for commercial purposes was in early development. This phase of site design lasted only briefly, for the online innovators quickly learned that the interactive medium of the internet offered much more dynamic and powerful opportunities.

Website innovators began to create sites that were more interactive than early sites and offered two-way communication. Many of the sites in this **interactive phase** began collecting information through email and online forms and established the ability to conduct ecommerce transactions. The interactive phase of the internet site design has progressed from simple form-based ecommerce transactions over insecure connections to sophisticated shopping cart transactions over secure networks. Many businesses continue to work within the interactive phase.

The improvement in web programming and site design software, along with a desire to move to "one-to-one" marketing strategies, has led many businesses to the personalization phase of the internet. The **personalization phase** develops one-to-one marketing techniques through the use of cookies and other tracking tools. The personalization of websites allows marketers to tailor the site to the specific wants of the user in an attempt to both improve the chances of making a sale and to improve the relationship with the customer. For example, Yahoo! offers its users the ability to create a My Yahoo! customized page where the user can specify preferred sources for information about the news, entertainment, weather, stock portfolios, and so on.

The personalization of websites allows users to see advertising and information closer to their preferences, which increases the likelihood they will stay on a site—known as **site stickiness**. In addition, the personalization allows the business to create more appropriate, targeted ads for users based on historic transactions combined with preferences.

Personalization has resulted in mixed feedback from users over its adoption by businesses. The key concern over personalization is whether users can truly control what they see. In many instances users would prefer to block most advertising and simply focus on information relevant to their internet usage. However, sites such as My American Express were designed to allow for improved marketing efforts and to increase site stickiness.

brochureware phase: An early stage of the internet's development, in which commercial enterprises primarily put existing marketing brochures in digital format.

interactive phase: A stage of the internet's development in which websites began to allow two-way communication through email and web forms.

personalization phase: A stage in the internet's development in which websites began to develop one-to-one marketing techniques through the use of cookies and other tracking tools.

site stickiness: A term describing the likelihood that users will stay on a particular website, and the amount of time they will spend there.

Online retailers such as Chapters Indigo and Amazon.com have carried out other personalization efforts. The booksellers have attempted to personalize websites through the use of cookies and user registrations to allow for customized webpages based on users' transaction histories. The difficulty in employing automated tools for personalization is in understanding what preferences truly are. A user who enjoyed reading about golfing and hiking would be happy to see suggestions for reading in this area upon returning to a bookseller's site. However, users complained that booksellers' websites would often tailor the pages with advertising for extended periods of time for items purchased as a one-time event. If, for example, a father purchased a child's friend a Pokémon book for a birthday gift and was inundated with ads for related products for months afterwards, neither the retailer nor consumer would benefit.[7] Personalization offers the potential to improve marketing efforts but must be used carefully.

Designing to Appeal to Visitors Many aspects of website design are based on demographic, cultural, and technological considerations. The nuances of multimedia design, fonts, colour schemes, templates, and other website design issues all need to be considered in order to portray an image of professionalism and encourage users to fully utilize the features of the site.

Designing to Gain Trust The design of a website can affect visitors' assessments of the trustworthiness of the website. This is particularly important to help convert a visitor into a customer. Visitors place more trust in websites that are easy to navigate, prominently display contact information such as telephone numbers of key company contacts, customer testimonials reflecting satisfaction with the company's products and services, company history, physical location address and photo, logos from well-known business partners and trust marks and seals attached to privacy, security and processing integrity commitments. These will be discussed later in this chapter under the heading of "Public Relations."

Making a Website Visible on the Web

The web is large and widespread; simply launching a new website does not provide any assurance that people will find it. Numerous considerations, including the following, must be kept in mind to ensure that a website is visible:

- obtaining a good domain name
- metatags
- registration with search engines
- launching an ebusiness marketing program

Obtaining a Good Domain Name The internet offers the opportunity for businesses to adopt and use domain names in numerous formats. The selection of a domain name may not seem to be the most critical area of emarketing but, as with product-naming decisions, can be very important to branding. A domain name is portable from one server to another, so the possession of a domain name adds stability to the name of a site. The IP address, however, changes from time to time. It is generally desirable to have a domain name that is similar to the business name, but this is not always possible because many names have been taken by others.

The first domain names to be taken tended to be those with a short descriptor and the .com extension (e.g., Buy.com) to aid in ease of recall. Numerous domain names have been acquired by businesses, sometimes for substantial sums, after the value of their "brand" was recognized. For example, the Business.com domain was purchased for US$7 million to capitalize on the easy-to-remember name. Many factors must be considered when looking into domain name usage, such as competing names, spelling errors, and anti-company sites.

The use of a domain name that is also held by other businesses or internet users with different extensions can be a risky endeavour. For example, a politician in Nova Scotia registered a domain of his own name with the .net extension prior to an election. He was soon embarrassed to discover that the .com extension with the same domain name (where many constituents ended up in error) was a self-promoting porn star—not exactly the kind of publicity he was looking for. Several businesses have run into difficulties with similar scenarios, and for this reason it is often important to register more than one name and attempt to control other similar names.

The ease of registering domain names results in the ability of individuals to capture potentially valuable sites—a practice known as cybersquatting. **Cybersquatting** involves registering a domain name with the intention of using the name for financial gain, without legal right to its use. This concept has become problematic, and its legality is addressed in chapter 13.

cybersquatting: Registering a domain name with the intention to use the name for financial gain without legal rights to its use.

Despite popular misconception, however, there is some control over cybersquatting. If a company owns a copyright to a name, such as Loblaws, it is very difficult for another company to obtain that domain name. Various national and international committees have been set up to control the distribution of domain names.

When registering a domain name, it is desirable for a business to plan ahead for misspellings and anti-business sites. An example of a company that did not plan for its web presence is Nissan Motors. North Carolina–based Nissan Computer Corporation registered the domain www.nissan.com in 1994 but didn't consider registering variations on its name. As a result, www.nissanauto.com and www.nissaneurope.com were acquired by an online quote website. Nissan Motors has not been successful in several appeals to acquire the nissan.com domain name and has had to settle for www.nissanmotors.com and www.nissanusa.com. The registration of multiple domain names should always be considered when misspellings are likely. In addition to misspellings, some businesses have taken proactive measures to register various "___sucks.com" domains and other anti-business sites that may damage their brand image on the web.

Metatags To find sites of interest, search engines use algorithms that include analyses of the words used on websites. Thus, it is important that the most critical words, those that most likely would be the search terms that users would enter into a search engine when searching for the types of goods or services that the site offers, be strategically located at or near the top of the website's main pages, or within metatags. For example, one of the metatag lines on the site for the *Globe and Mail* newspaper is as follows:

> META NAME="Keywords" CONTENT="canadian news, national newspaper, daily news, breaking news, political news, world news, canadian business news, canadian newspapers online, international news, report on business, national news, canadian sports, travel information, globe and mail, globe & mail"

This metatag line enables search engines to find the site if any of these search terms are used.

Registration with Search Engines One of the major means of driving traffic to a website is through search engine registration. Using search engines to identify sites of interest is one of the primary means by which users find sites that they are not already familiar with; therefore, being registered with search engines is critical if a website is to be found. In addition to being listed, it is important that sites also show up high on the list of search results—a fact that requires different tactics with many of the different search engines. For example, registration with the Yahoo.com search engine will make the site show up on searches in the United States and other countries which use that site. If the sole intent is to do business in Canada, then registration with Yahoo.ca is needed. Similar reasoning applies to doing business in Europe and Asia.

search engine optimization (SEO): A field that specializes in driving traffic from search engines to websites.

Search Engine Optimization (SEO) Search engines use complex algorithms to decide where a website will rank in the list of results delivered in response to a search term entered by a user. These algorithms take into account key words embedded in the metatags, headings and text of the website, content that relates to those key words, and links to the website's URL from other websites. The higher a website scores on all these factors, the higher its rank. This is important because it is generally thought that search engine users focus on the first few results on the first page of the list of results delivered. By paying attention to the ways that search engines rank websites, website designers can influence a website's ranking. The ranking will in turn drive traffic to the website, and some of that traffic will be "converted" from simply visiting the website to purchasing the products and services offered by the website. Search engine optimization (SEO) has become an internet marketing field that specializes in driving traffic from search engines to websites. The goal is to take actions that will result in a target website being ranked high in the list of results obtained by a search engine when users enter search terms so that its URL is displayed prominently in the list of search results.

SEO tactics include identifying relevant key words and adding these key words to the website in strategically effective locations, such as the metatags section of the web's code. However, metatags are not the only part of a web site that search engines analyze to index websites. Search engines are also beginning to read audio, video, and image files; thus, SEO tactics also include developing website content with an understanding of how search engines will use the content to rank a website. Other tactics include negotiating paid sponsorships, whereby a company buys a listing in a prominent section of the search results, identified by terms such as "Sponsored Links." This is usually done by bidding on relevant key words on sites such as Google's AdWords. SEO is such an important aspect of marketing today that courses in the subject are being offered, as are jobs with titles such as SEO director, manager, architect, or specialist.[8,9]

ONLINE ADVERTISING

THE EVOLUTION OF WEBSITE DESIGN AND ONLINE TECHNOLOGIES HAS LED TO TREMENDOUS improvements in the capabilities for online advertising. The understanding that online media are unique and require innovative approaches has led to the development of creative new means to capture attention, create brand strength, and modify payment methods in the advertising area. In this section the common forms of online advertising, including classified

In the fall of 2010, Yellow Pages Group Co. announced the launch of a new online advertising and marketing company to be known as Mediative. This move was an attempt by the Montreal-based company to address a major weakness in its business strategy.

Yellow Pages is known for the print directories that have been the mainstay of its business model for decades. But times have changed. Print advertising such as that offered through the Yellow Pages books is under pressure. Television is the most popular medium for advertisers. Print media such as newspapers and magazines are in second place. However, the web is slated to overtake print media as an advertising channel by 2012 or soon thereafter.

Also, more than 90 percent of Yellow Pages revenues come from local ads, but with the global reach of the Web, national advertisers are not drawn to local advertising such as that offered by Yellow Pages. Instead, they are seeking national and international coverage ads.

Mediative will advertise on well-known websites and search engine websites such as Google and Bing, as well as Facebook and other social networking sites. Mediative will provide a service that will enable companies and agencies to bid on ads and track what they spend and how much activity results from their advertising expenditures.

**Yellow Pages Group
360.yellowpages.ca/en**

Questions

1. What is the major weakness that Yellow Pages is attempting to address?

2. Are there any advantages to local ads that are the company's strength?

3. What additional improvements can Yellow Pages make in its strategy?

Sources: S. Krashinsky, "Yellow Pages Launches Unit to Expand Web Business," *Globe and Mail*, October 26, 2010, www.ctv.ca/generic/generated/static/business/article1772320.html; S. Houpt, "Web Ads May Surpass Print, Ending an Era," *Globe and Mail*, December 7, 2010.

advertising, display advertising, search engine marketing, in-text advertising, email advertising, affiliate programs, partnerships, promotions and public relations are discussed.

Classified Advertising

Online classified advertising is a form of advertising that has existed since the inception of the internet. Classified ads group advertisers under headings representing the categories of goods or services being offered. In fact, the early web directories could be seen as a form of classified advertising for websites to enable internet users to find them easily and rapidly. Today, web-based classified advertising is an important channel for both online and offline providers of goods and services to reach their target audiences. Advantages of web-based classified advertising are its low cost, broad reach and better searchability compared to traditional paper-based classified ads in newspapers and directories such as the Yellow Pages. The most popular classified ad sites are craigslist, yellow pages and kijiji (a subsidiary of eBay), although there are many, many classified ad sites on the web. See the Canadian Snapshots box for an example of a well-known company seeking to transition from a business model based on the provision of paper-based classified advertising services to an internet-based business model.

Display Advertising

Display advertising was a mainstay of online advertising for many years in the form of banner ads, buttons, interstitials, superstitials and other methods of associating companies with elements on a displayed web page. Display advertising has grown and changed over time, although new advertising methods such as search engine marketing, relationship marketing and online promotion are becoming popular alternatives.

Banners The first banner ad on the web appeared on the HotWired site in 1994. Banner ads are graphical images, which may include interactive applications such as those described later in this chapter, that appear on websites to attract users to click-through to other websites or sections of the present website. Buttons are similar to banners and could be used to submit data on webpages or as a means of clicking through to another webpage. Businesses can charge other sites through various arrangements to host banners and buttons on their pages that can link users to other organizations. Banner advertising is a widely used form of online advertising, despite criticisms that it is a relatively ineffective selling tool. Critics of banner advertising cite surveys of web surfers who report that they ignore banner ads altogether and low click-through rates of less than 1 percent as proof of the ineffectiveness of banners. However, some researchers have claimed that exposure to banner ads online can significantly improve brand image and brand perception that may result in visits to a company's website and sales at a later date.[10] Proponents of banner ads argue that the fault with low click-through rates may lie in poor design of banner ads or weaknesses in company offerings and reputation rather than in the value of banner ads as an advertising approach. When ads are customized based on criteria such as location, content of web pages visited, or search engine key words, click-through rates can increase dramatically, and this has led to the tremendous growth of search engine marketing, as described later in this section.[11] Google, Yahoo!, and others have developed ad exchange systems that give marketers the ability to target ads to focused subsets of web users.[12]

The widespread use of banner ads has led to the development of standard sizes and formats for banners. The Coalition for Advertising Supported Information and Entertainment (CASIE), a joint effort of the Association of National Advertisers and the American Association of Advertising Agencies, in conjunction with the Interactive Advertising Bureau, developed the Universal Ad Package, which contains standard dimensions that more easily allow website designers to integrate banners and allow users to readily identify them.[13] As the technologies used in banner advertising have advanced, new standard formats have been developed that are better suited to interactivity, animation, and multimedia tools within banners as well.

Banners are easily created using software applications. Many banners are designed and stored as animated GIFs. **Animated graphic interchange format (GIF)** is a file format that consists of a series of frames that are shown in a particular sequence. The animation attempts to both capture the user's eye and deliver a more complete message than can be delivered within a single banner's image size.

Other banners also have the ability to select specific sections of a target site using drop-down boxes and other interactive applications. Higher-quality banners can be produced in HTML formats, or by using Flash technology to create so-called "rich media" that include dynamic motion. Some industry observers have recorded major improvements in click-through rates based on the usage of these forms of rich media in banners.[14]

The cost of banner advertising varies dramatically, depending on the location of the advertisement, the host company, and any barter deals that are in place. Costs of advertising are often measured in **cost per thousand (CPM)** impressions. Charges are set for

animated graphic interchange format (GIF): A file format that consists of a series of frames that are shown in a particular sequence.

cost per thousand (CPM): A standard measure of impressions in online advertising. Charges are set for each thousand users who visit a site or see an advertisement.

each thousand users who visit the site or see an advertisement. The range in costs can be from less than US$10 to US$100 CPM, and on premium, targeted sites the costs may even exceed these amounts. The CPM for online advertising is often compared with traditional media costs, but marketers must be careful to ensure that the rates are compared based on media-specific terms. For example, the ability to use targeted marketing online is much higher than through broadcast media such as television. Running an advertisement during a prime-time television show is expensive, and results in only limited targeting due to the wide demographic bases on television. On the other hand, the use of banner ads would allow the ad to appear on websites specifically targeted to audiences and often related to products that users are searching for.

Banner ads are often run on websites through bartering arrangements. The trading between sites of banners often allows for sites to cooperatively increase traffic and reduces the cash cost of emarketing. The barter of banners and other advertising has resulted in difficulties in measuring the size of the online advertising market, and also has caused complexities in accounting for the costs and revenues associated with online advertising.

Interstitials The use of interstitials is another common form of online advertising that has been used by many businesses. **Interstitials** are web-based windows that pop up as a user enters an internet site, aiming to catch the user's attention. These pop-up boxes, also known as **daughter windows**, commonly promote a specific product of a site or aim to gather survey data (see figure 11.3). The requirement for users to pay attention to an interstitial—either to use it or to close it—is one factor that proponents of interstitials claim as part of their effectiveness. This same factor is what annoys many internet users—the requirement to click and close boxes to which they do not wish to pay attention. Interstitials are now facing

Interactive Advertising Bureau
www.iab.net

interstitial: A Web-based window that pops up as a user enters an internet site, aiming to catch the user's attention.

daughter window: Another name for inter-stitial or pop-up window.

Unicast by Viewpoint
www.unicast.com

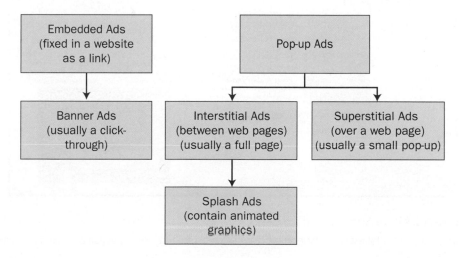

Figure 11.3 Basic Types of Website Advertisements

a period of turmoil, as advertisers find them powerful, but often visitors to websites do not want them, and various companies are offering tools that embed in a web browser and block any pop-ups from being displayed. While the fact remains that using pop-ups is one of the best means of increasing traffic to a website, retaining that traffic depends on other factors, such as website design, content, and interest to users. Planned use of interstitials allows advertisers to get attention; the key is to find a balance between use and overuse.

superstitial: An internet advertisement spot that loads into a user's browser while the internet connection is idle and then launches as a daughter window, showing a short, TV-like advertisement.

Superstitials The rise of internet advertising led one innovative company, Unicast, to create an advertising format tailored to the web: superstitials. **Superstitials** are internet advertisement spots that load into a user's browser while the internet connection is idle and then launch as a daughter window showing a short, TV-like advertisement. Superstitials have demonstrated performance equivalent to television ads in terms of recall, communication, and persuasion.[15]

Unicast created the superstitial format to provide advertisers with an improved medium over banner ads and interstitials. The benefit from a user perspective is that the ads do not use up bandwidth while you are attempting to use your internet connection (see figure 11.4). Hundreds of major companies, including Coca-Cola, NBC, and Kia, have adopted the use of superstitials in their online advertising initiatives. The format not only offers a broadcasting capability but also allows interactivity and direct links to purchasing products—an ability promised but not widely delivered by webTV for the past several years. Samples of superstitials can be viewed at www.unicast.com.

Multimedia The internet provides a dynamic medium through which advertising can take on a multimedia approach relatively easily. Several technologies such as Shockwave,

Figure 11.4 The Superstitial Process

Unicast's superstitial format is an efficient process designed to minimize user disruption and maximize advertiser effectiveness.

Source: Reproduced with permission of Yahoo! Inc. © 2011 by Yahoo! Inc. YAHOO! and the YAHOO! logo are registered trademarks of Yahoo! Inc.

Java, and Flash provide the capability to integrate animation, sound, and interactivity into webpage design. For example, Disney's internet presence makes use of Flash to build sound and pop-up boxes into its site in numerous places.

The use of multimedia and advanced software on websites has led to some criticism in the past. Multimedia results in increased transfer of data between the web server and the user's computer, and also requires the user to have specific plug-ins installed on his or her system. The increased transfer of data requires advertisers to consider their strategy carefully, as some internet users may easily become frustrated with slow-loading graphics. The use of multimedia, therefore, requires the consideration of segmenting dial-up vs. broadband internet users, and may require an alternate website design. This is commonly seen on corporate sites where users may select, for example, Flash-enabled or non-Flash sites.

RSA
www.rsa.com

Multimedia tools are also useful in providing service and information related to the company. For example, RSA, the Security Division of EMC, offers numerous Flash demonstrations that explain security applications and concurrently promote the RSA brand. The use of demonstrations and other information online takes advantage of the unique aspects of the internet by allowing users to interactively move from a demonstration to additional product details or to purchase the product.

Disney
www.disney.go.com

Advertisements are being streamed directly into predetermined spots in video games via the internet. For example, Fight Night Round 3 from EA Sports shows advertising banners in the background that can be changed based on the advertisements placed by online advertising agents or brokered through online advertising exchanges which match up available advertising spots with advertisers who want to use them.[16]

Interactive Tools The creation of interactive tools is leading internet innovators to develop multiple new formats for advertising online. Interactive ads provide advertisers with numerous capabilities such as branding, interactive selling, and other advertising techniques by using technology that seemingly floats ads over the existing web browser. Interactive advertisements allow marketers to carry out targeted marketing and branding techniques in numerous formats. For example, Yahoo!'s website displays an interactive advertisement of a new movie that, when clicked, plays the trailer of the movie.

Ad Engines Some companies find it difficult or costly to create and update online ads. An ad engine is software that can build or update a display ad automatically by searching for information on the internet such as photos, reviews, customer testimonials and other text. The developer of this service is targeting small businesses who would like to establish an internet presence easily and inexpensively.[17]

Adware One of the problems associated with online advertising is that consumers are beginning to find some of the techniques used intrusive. One of the worst offenders in this regard is adware that installs itself on a user's computer and generates pop-up ads, sometimes to the chagrin of not only the user but the very companies whose products and services are being advertised. For example, one software downloading site downloads at least 16 adware applications with each software download. The adware producer pays the software downloading site 30 cents per adware application downloaded. It in turn collects payments from brokers who channel ads through the adware. These brokers in turn act as agents for other brokers, and so on, creating a chain that can be difficult to trace.[18] Tools are available to block most unwanted adware, as discussed in chapter 5.

Search Engine Marketing

Just as display advertising was beginning to lose its momentum, search engine marketing, also called search ad marketing, created a boom in online advertising. Google is the search engine that is most closely associated with this type of advertising and Google's phenomenal growth is largely due to its success at developing this type of marketing. When a web user keys in a search term into Google, a list of search results is produced based on the algorithms used to match the search term and web content that relates to that search term. The results are displayed on the left-hand side of the screen and can go on for many pages. At the same time, related sponsored ads (discreetly identified as such) are listed at the very top of the screen preceding the search results and on the right-hand side of the display. These ads contain links to websites and web content that advertisers hope Google users will respond to when seeing the results of their search query. While many users do not click on those ads, many more click on the sponsored ads than click on banners and other less customized display ads.

Advertisers bid on key words that will be associated with the links that they will pay to sponsor. They pay a fee for displaying an ad and an additional fee when a user clicks on the sponsored ad. Depending on the demand for certain key words, the cost for sponsoring a key word can range from dollars to pennies per display. Some marketers bid on easily linkable key words (e.g., the key word "Oscars" for Coca-Cola) but others bid on unlikely combinations to attract new customers (e.g., the key word "platypus" for Honda). The search ad associated with "platypus" invited the user to see the platypus in Honda's Element vehicle. Clicking on the link took the user to a website that displayed ads for the Element and a related game. Each click cost between 10 and 15 cents. For another campaign, Honda purchased several thousand search terms related to the Super Bowl and generated 3.5 million impressions from Yahoo! and Google the day after the Super Bowl.[19] Google's AdWords site provides tools for marketers to bid on and manage the related marketing program.

An offshoot of search ad marketing is Google's Gmail service. In exchange for the benefits of using the service, users grant Google the right to scan their emails for key words so that it can display sponsored ads similar to those on Google's search website.

As will be discussed in chapter 12, search ads are popular because they provide easy metrics to calculate, and this, in turn, leads to more efficient auction-based pricing of key word purchases. This type of advertising has become such big business that many companies have been established to act as intermediaries between the search engines and companies seeking to place search ads. In addition, SEO, described earlier, has become a recognized service designed to boost a company's ranking in various search engines' results displays so that its website and search ad appear closer to the top of the list than they might otherwise appear. Marketing agencies such as Omnicom Media Group and ValueClick can help companies optimize their web sites for various search engines, identify relevant key words to bid on, help place bids at various times to coordinate with company events such as new product launches, promotions and other events, track the success of ad placements and suggest changes and improvements.

As happened with display advertising, however, the momentum appears to be shifting away from search engine marketing and towards social network marketing. Facebook is the company that is most closely associated with the development of this type of marketing, as will be discussed later in this chapter, and is therefore a beneficiary of this changing tide.

Click Fraud One of the problems associated with both display ads and search ads is sites that generate false click-through counts to obtain payment from marketers under false pretences. This issue is discussed in chapters 5 and 12.

In-Text Advertising

When Forbes online first came out with in-text ads in 2004, it created an outcry that led to the cancellation of the practice. Today, however, in-text advertising is back in favour. In-text advertising pops up in small windows when a reader moves a cursor over highlighted, double-underlined words in a story. Pausing over a link produces a bubble containing written ads, voiceover, or video. In-text marketing companies scan web pages of online news sites and magazines and choose words they consider relevant to the products being marketed based on their location on the page and the content of the story. Publishers are paid by the marketing companies based on how many times readers scroll over a word. Advertisers pay the marketers on a pay-per-click basis.

It appears that in-text ads result in much higher click-through rates than banner ads. However, they are controversial. Some journalists believe that they blur the dividing line between news and advertising.[20]

Email Advertising

Email is an important vehicle for corporate advertising and marketing campaigns, but it should be used very carefully. The overuse of the ability to send unsolicited email has led to consumer revolt in several instances, and can also result in legal problems in some locations. Sending out mass unsolicited email is known as spamming; **spam** is the name given to unsolicited email sent in an attempt to gain commercial advantage. The rising problem with spam was created by the relative ease of gathering large numbers of email addresses over the internet through newsgroups, chat sites, and other websites. Many ISPs and online email services (e.g., Windows Hotmail, Yahoo!) now provide some protection against spam by blocking largely distributed emails and attempting to shield users from the disruptions caused by spam. Despite these efforts, users still often receive spam offering numerous products and services (see figure 11.5).

spam: Unsolicited email sent in an attempt to gain commercial advantage.

To utilize email advertising, marketers need to be careful not to be mistaken for spam. The use of email advertising is commonly carried out through permission marketing. Permission marketing occurs when users are given the choice to receive email offers and advertising (e.g., when registering on a website for the first time), or agree to receive offers related to computer products. Permission marketing is evident on many sites, and allows users to select the types of advertising that they are willing to receive. Opt-in email campaigns reportedly have double the response rate of spam email campaigns. In addition, opt-in emailers have a more sustainable business model that ISPs will not seek to shut down.[21] This type of marketing helps marketers target potential customers, but because users must opt-in first it results in much less reach.

Some advertisers have heralded email marketing as a powerful tool. To undertake email marketing that is not confused with spam, several points should be kept in mind:[22]

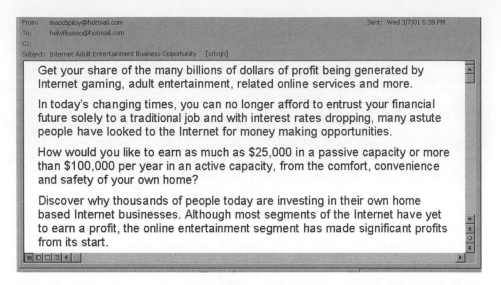

From: maocbpiioy@hotmail.com
To: fwkvfksooo@hotmail.com
Cc:
Subject: Internet Adult Entertainment Business Opportunity   [xrlxqn]
Sent: Wed 3/7/01 5:39 PM

Get your share of the many billions of dollars of profit being generated by Internet gaming, adult entertainment, related online services and more.

In today's changing times, you can no longer afford to entrust your financial future solely to a traditional job and with interest rates dropping, many astute people have looked to the Internet for money making opportunities.

How would you like to earn as much as $25,000 in a passive capacity or more than $100,000 per year in an active capacity, from the comfort, convenience and safety of your own home?

Discover why thousands of people today are investing in their own home based Internet businesses. Although most segments of the Internet have yet to earn a profit, the online entertainment segment has made significant profits from its start.

Figure 11.5 Example of a Spam "Business Opportunity"

Spam offers continue to spread through email, disrupting users and weakening the effectiveness of email marketing.

1. Customers should have opted in to receiving the email and have the ability to opt-out at any time. The spam example in figure 11.5 contained an unsubscribe option; however, repeated attempts to be removed from the list failed, and attempts to contact the "spammer" were unsuccessful.

2. Email is not the same medium as direct-mail advertising and should not be treated the same. The design of email campaigns needs to be carried out differently from mail ads, which are often long, with various typefaces and "free" offers. Similar email campaigns have a lower success rate, as users become frustrated with the volume of advertising material they receive. Another difficulty with the design of email campaigns is the incompatibility of various email applications. The formatting of an email due to word-wrap and other functions can be altered by each recipient's software, resulting in an unprofessional appearance if design is not carefully planned.

3. Giving *away* information can be a powerful form of email marketing. Many businesses offer electronic newsletters or information services that provide a great opportunity to build brand image and also sell products and services. For example, Air Canada offers email notification of discount fares on selected destinations to users who have opted to receive the information. The provision of this service allows Air Canada to tout its brand and sell off discount flights to customers.

4. Email marketing is a learning process. It is important that organizations use the information they have gleaned from other sources such as previous campaigns, CRM, and/or BI initiatives to improve their marketing campaigns. For example, the identification of target markets and preferences of opt-in customers may allow marketers to develop specific campaigns and use trial-and-error methods. It is important that the trial-and-error attempts do not tarnish the brand or lead to categorization of a marketer as a spammer, but are used to determine what campaigns have been most effective for click-through or sales increases.

5. Ensure adequate resources for ecampaigns. To carry out ecampaigns, human resources, technology, and financial resources are required. Organizations must balance the commitment of resources towards email campaigns, and may wish to look at outsourcing as an option to reduce the human and technology resources required in-house.

6. Email isn't free. Despite the ease with which we are able to click "send," email campaigns can become costly. The use of email for advertising will require extensive upkeep of lists and integration with other applications and may also demand investments in design. For example, as discussed earlier, the use of various email applications by users will require that design is carefully carried out—a job often requiring outsourcing.

7. Always look ahead. The use of wireless technologies, smartphones and tablets, and voice email access will offer advertisers new opportunities to apply email advertising across a variety of media. Shifts in demand and demographics will continue to impact advertisers for the foreseeable future—necessitating forward-looking plans.

Promotions

The use of promotions is an important aspect of emarketing and advertising. Promotional tools such as coupons, discounts, contests, points programs, and demos/free trials are all easily employed over the internet. Several online companies provide tools to create these types of promotions or provide the services for a fee. For example, Vancouver-based Splashdot.com helps organizations convert website visitors into paying customers by enabling their websites to interact with visitors through contests, loyalty programs and promotions. The company's first client was B.C. Lottery Corporation, which implemented a contest that encouraged people to dream of what they would do if they won a lottery and to share these dreams on the B.C. Lottery website. The idea was to encourage visitors to make repeat visits, spend more time on the site and entice them to purchase lottery tickets.[23] In addition to using webpages to provide these promotional tools, it is possible to integrate promotions into email campaigns. For example, a targeted and timely advertisement by an optical care provider reminds customers that it is time to replace their disposable contact lenses, and offers a discount at the same time. The email ad also attempts to establish new business by providing compensation for referring a friend to the company.

A large number of companies offer points programs and customer loyalty programs online. These programs range from the more traditional airline miles/points to online cash, such as PayPal points. Bricks-and-mortar companies that have loyalty programs have also begun to move their programs online to increase usage and move their online strategies forward. The theory behind games, contests and loyalty programs is that these activities draw customers into a voluntary relationship with the company. That could be especially important to permission-based marketing if "do not track" legislation is introduced in Canada, as is being contemplated in the US.[24] See the New Business Models box for an example of a company that has combined traditional coupon marketing with social networking.

The web has many locations where users can access free trials and demos. Perhaps most common are software demos that can be downloaded at sites such as CNET's Download.com. The provision of software demos provides many software businesses with a powerful avenue to display their products and allow users to ensure that they are satisfied with the products prior to purchase. However, as described earlier, many software

New Business Models

Social Shopping with Groupon

Launched in November 2008 in Chicago, Groupon calls itself a collective-buying platform that features daily deals for things to do, eat, see, and buy in more than 40 countries. By promising businesses a minimum number of customers, Groupon can offer deals that aren't available elsewhere.

Groupon sells coupons for deeply discounted products and services to its subscribers, who then have a period of time, such as a year, to use those coupons to purchase the products and services from the supplier at the discounted prices.

At the end of 2010, Groupon's revenues were in the $50 million per month range, and the company had roughly 50 percent gross margins, making it one of the fastest-growing companies on record and drawing a valuation of $6 billion from Google, which Groupon turned down, reminiscent of Facebook's refusal to accept a multi-billion-dollar offer from Yahoo!.

Interestingly, in mid-2010, another social shopping website, Woot.com, agreed to be acquired by Amazon Inc. for about $110 million. Woot's business model was admittedly different from Groupon's (i.e., Woot.com offered a limited quantity of one product at a special price per day). But the difference in valuations is nevertheless striking.

Many enthusiastic supporters have called Groupon a runaway success, but an article on TechCrunch.com identified some potential problems with Groupon's business model. It needs a lot of salespeople on staff for each market it handles, and there are no barriers to entry or switching costs for either buyers or sellers. Business models that rely on this approach have difficulties sustaining their profit margins and become less attractive as time passes.

Groupon
www.groupon.com

Questions

1. Why has Groupon been so successful so quickly? What advantages does Groupon provide to marketers over a website such as Woot?

2. What can Groupon do to avoid having its margins crushed by competitors?

3. Why do you think Groupon didn't accept Google's offer? Was it the right decision? Why?

Sources: www.groupon.com; http://techcrunch.com/2010/10/17/why-groupon-is-no-ebay/.

---

downloading sites earn revenues by downloading adware and spyware at the same time as the software or demo.

Companies also use chat communities to promote their products. For example, Johnson & Johnson uses teen chat communities as an avenue to provide trials of its Clean & Clear skin-care products. The company provides teenage girls with the opportunity to send their friends electronic postcards that offer samples of Clean & Clear.[25] While tangible products require either physical shipment or customer pickup, the internet provides the opportunity to target customers and profile these products at a reasonable cost. As will be discussed in the next section, the use of social media such as chat communities and social networks is one of the most important recent developments in emarketing.

ALLIANCES AND PARTNERSHIPS

THE INTERNET OFFERS UNIQUE CAPABILITIES FOR COMPANIES TO ENTER INTO alliances to support their emarketing strategy through affiliate programs and partnerships.

Affiliate Programs

The use of affiliate programs as part of a strategy to increase website traffic and sales has become a common component of emarketing strategy. Popularized first by CDnow,

affiliate programs are agreements between website operators whereby delivery of customers or prospective customers to another company's site results in compensation becoming due. CDnow owners became interested in the concept of affiliate programs when the company was at an expensive stage of its life cycle and the cost of banner ads seemed risky. CDnow's affiliate program grew to over 250,000 members and provided it with a major source of customer acquisition.[26]

Many companies have created affiliate programs in an attempt to increase traffic to, and sales on, their websites. For example, Chapters Indigo offers an affiliate program that nearly any site can join and earn commissions of 5 to 20 percent for click-throughs that lead to sales. The affiliate program becomes operational as soon an internet user clicks on a banner ad or button at an affiliate site and is redirected to another site (e.g., Chapters Indigo). When the user arrives at the destination site, the affiliate's referring address is tracked so that if the user purchases a product, the affiliate will be eligible to receive the commission they are due. The ease of joining and potential for commissions makes affiliate programs attractive. Chapters Indigo provides numerous helpful tools such as pre-designed banner ads and custom HTML codes that allow even novice web designers to integrate the affiliate program. The concept is similar for many of these programs but payment amounts can differ.

For affiliate program providers, one of the major benefits of these programs is that the cost of acquiring customers is paid only if the user actually purchases something. In addition, the affiliate program gains a new customer who may come back to the site directly on the second visit (either through brand recall or email advertising), which results in only paying the affiliate commission once.

> **affiliate program:** An agreement between website operators whereby delivery of customers or prospective customers to another company's site results in compensation becoming due.

Partnerships

Online partnerships can be used to create increased traffic or to target specific products and services to a market segment. For example, eBay and Sympatico have formed a partnership in Canada that allows eBay to improve its user base by increasing its use on the popular Sympatico service. Other prominent partnerships have been formed that allow businesses to work together and capitalize on each other's strengths. For example, Amazon and Toys "R" Us formed a partnership in which Amazon used its existing technologies and ecommerce capabilities to facilitate online transactions with Toys "R" Us.[27] Partnerships can allow businesses to benefit in a number of ways in the online world.

PUBLIC RELATIONS

Public relations is the activity of creating goodwill or a positive company image. Typically, public relations objectives are to reach a wider audience than advertising—targeting shareholders, employees, communities, the media, and the public. As an efficient and effective communication tool, the internet offers numerous methods for satisfying a company's public relations strategy. A review of most corporate websites will reveal a news or press release section whereby current information can be disseminated easily and cost effectively. In addition, online delivery of information such as annual reports and shareholder information allows for the integration of multimedia and internet enhancements, along with additional details that cannot be as easily delivered in print.

The proliferation of internet sites, online magazines, news services, and industry organizations offers tremendous potential for public relations online. Many companies encourage employees to become involved in writing articles for publication on the internet (and in print) in order to portray an image of excellence and industry leadership. In addition, publication on the internet is often accompanied by a link to the writer's or employer's website. The combination of published material and interactivity may lead to improved brand image, increased website traffic, and perhaps increased sales.

A key objective of public relations is to instill trust in an ecommerce site. Trust can allay market participants' fears about the riskiness of conducting business on the internet. These fears have declined significantly in recent years, as major internet sites have become widely known and trusted, but a cautious attitude still exists about sites that are not well known. Such fears stem from the lack of physical presence for many entities involved in ecommerce; the anonymity of many internet users; widespread outsourcing of various ecommerce functions, which creates a complex web of relationships; and demonstrated vulnerabilities of some ecommerce sites to security, availability, integrity, confidentiality and privacy abuses. Those fears can relate to the internet as a whole, as well as to specific concerns about particular ecommerce sites or participants in an online marketplace.

A number of mechanisms can help reduce such concerns and signal that an ecommerce entity or individual participant is trustworthy. Interestingly, a website's design and look have been found to be among the most important factors associated with a website's credibility, despite the fact that fraudsters can create professional-looking sites to deceive their victims.[28] Credit card guarantees discussed in chapter 6 contribute to trust in ecommerce. Two mechanisms that are particularly noteworthy, because they provide external evidence about a site's trustworthiness, are trustmarks or "seals of approval" and online feedback mechanisms, also called "digitized word of mouth."

Trustmarks, Service Marks, and Seals

trustmark, service mark, or seal: A graphic representation similar to a logo that is placed on websites to indicate that the entity complies with certain recommended ecommerce practices and is therefore a trustworthy business partner.

Many sites use trustmarks, service marks, or seals to convey a positive company image and help overcome customers' fears that a seller may not fulfill its commitments to them, that the system may not be available when needed (for example, an online brokerage site) security or confidentiality of their data may be compromised (for example, credit card numbers or sensitive customer lists), or that their personal information will be misused. **Trustmarks, service marks, or seals** are graphic representations similar to logos that are placed on websites to indicate that the entity complies with certain recommended ecommerce practices and is therefore a trustworthy business partner. Due to the graphic nature of the web, there are many such marks, seals, or logos on the internet with a variety of meanings that are often not clear to customers. For example, the WebTrust seal is a service mark which is intended to be more authoritative than a registered trademark or logo; however, this distinction would not be visible to customers viewing the graphic image. We will consider several programs designed to label ecommerce sites as being trustworthy—TRUSTe, BBBOnLine (both Reliability and Privacy), and WebTrust, although the last is primarily used in connection with independent assessments of the systems employed by certificate authorities to issue digital certificates, which are discussed in chapter 5. Figure 11.6 illustrates the trustmarks, service marks, and seals associated with these programs.

Figure 11.6 Trustmarks, Service Marks, and Seals

Trustmarks, service marks, and seals are graphic symbols used to represent authoritative sources that testify to the trustworthiness of an ecommerce site.

Sources: TRUSTe and the seal are trademarks of TRUSTe; BBBOnLine logos reprinted with the permission of the Council of Better Business Bureaus, Inc., Copyright 2007. Council of Better Business Bureaus, Inc., 4200 Wilson Blvd., Arlington, VA 22203. World Wide Web: www.bbb.org; WebTrust logo reprinted courtesy of The Canadian Institute of Chartered Accountants.

TRUSTe The TRUSTe seal was developed by TRUSTe.org to indicate that an entity follows privacy principles that comply with the fair information practice principles approved by the U.S. Federal Trade Commission. In particular, the entity must clearly disclose on its website its collection and use practices regarding personally identifiable information (PII). Users must be given choice and consent over how their personal information is used and shared. Finally, access and data security measures should be in place to safeguard and update PII. Websites that display the TRUSTe privacy seal must agree to comply with ongoing TRUSTe oversight and its dispute resolution process. TRUSTe monitors licensees to ensure compliance with their stated privacy practices and TRUSTe program requirements. The oversight process includes periodic website review, "seeding," and online community monitoring. Seeding involves signing up on an ecommerce site under a dummy user ID that is solely used for that purpose, and explicitly opting out of any sharing of personal information by the company. By monitoring whether the dummy user ID receives unwarranted email, it is possible to determine whether the entity honoured the user's request.

BBBOnLine BBBOnLine is an arm of the Better Business Bureau (BBB) that is devoted to websites. The BBB Accredited Business Seal indicates that a company is BBB accredited, commits to adhere to the BBB Code of Business Practices, including its online standard, has been in business for more than a year, respects the privacy and email preferences of its visitors and commits to work with its customers and BBB to resolve disputes. To be accredited by BBB, a business or organization affirms that it meets and will abide by The BBB Code of Business Practices which represents sound advertising, selling and customer services practices designed to enhance customer trust and confidence in business.

WebTrust The WebTrust service mark was developed by the American Institute of Certified Public Accountants (AICPA) and the Canadian Institute of Chartered Accountants (CICA) to provide assurance on ecommerce system security, availability, processing integrity, and privacy. Security means that the system is protected against unauthorized access (both physical and logical). Availability means that the system is available for operation and use as committed or agreed. Processing integrity means that system processing is complete, accurate, timely, and authorized. Privacy means that personal information obtained as a result of ecommerce is collected, used, disclosed, and retained as committed or agreed.

Epinions
www.epinions.com

Elance
www.elance.com

Slashdot
www.slashdot.org

TRUSTe
www.truste.org

BBB*OnLine*
www.bbbonline.org

A WebTrust service mark on a website means that the site has been certified by authorized CA/CPA WebTrust licensees, that adequate disclosure of the company's business practices is provided, and that these practices have been audited against the stringent criteria established by the AICPA and CICA.

Digitized Word of Mouth

It is generally believed that word of mouth is one of the most powerful promotion methods. The internet offers important new possibilities for **digitized word of mouth** advertising and promotion, and for building trust in ecommerce sites through formal online feedback mechanisms. Perhaps the best-known example of such feedback mechanisms is eBay's buyer and seller ratings following a transaction. Such ratings help establish buyer and seller reputations on eBay for repeat business activity. Other examples include Epinions Inc., which provides an online forum for users to write reviews about products and services, and for others to rate the usefulness of those reviews. At Elance Inc., a professional services marketplace that helps buyers/contractors requiring services match up with freelancers offering services, contractors rate their satisfaction with subcontractors. Slashdot is an online discussion board owned by the Open Source Technology Group, where postings are prioritized according to ratings they receive from readers.

Online feedback systems can help promote ecommerce activity on a particular site, as well as the broader ecommerce community. Creating opportunities for digital word of mouth can be an important trust-building tactic for many ecommerce sites, especially online marketplaces and exchanges that might otherwise be viewed as too risky for transacting business. However, to be effective, the site needs to attract a sufficient number of participants to neutralize attempts by some users to manipulate the feedback mechanism.[29] In this regard, one approach has been the creation of artificial word of mouth by marketers seeking to leverage the power of this promotional device. For example, marketers have started to pay bloggers (authors of **blogs**, which are websites containing personal or corporate posts available to be read by web surfers) to promote certain products in their blogs, thereby creating word of mouth for those products. Another approach is the recruiting of volunteer "buzz agents" to create word of mouth through a variety of online and offline activities. BzzAgent Inc. has more than 750,000 volunteers spreading word of mouth about products ranging from TV shows to consumer products. One concern that has been expressed by critics of this type of marketing is that the volunteers and the marketers who recruit them to "manufacture" word of mouth using a variety of covert techniques are abusing the trust that their acquaintances place in them.[30]

Collaborative Filtering One of the earliest and still widely used forms of digital word of mouth, collaborative filtering makes recommendations to a customer based on what other customers purchased. For example, when a shopper selects a book at Amazon.com and adds it to his or her shopping cart, Amazon recommends other books purchased by users who purchased the same book. Another example is a website with a product comparison feature that reports what actions most users of the product comparison feature took next (i.e., they bought item A or item B).

Customer Reviews Many ecommerce sites have recognized the importance of social marketing and word of mouth and have added customer reviews to their product listings.

For example, TripAdvisor.com provides customer ratings that make the site a valued destination for travellers. Hotels and other travel service providers appear to take customer reviews on this site very seriously and are quick to respond to negative comments because they recognize their impact on other customers' travel choices.

Social Networks The most significant development of the past few years in the marketing area is the growth of social networking sites such as Facebook, Twitter, YouTube, and Flickr. Marketing and advertising to members of social networks is still in its early stages but is gaining momentum. Many consumers consider social media to be more reliable and more credible or trustworthy than advertising.[31] Thus, some commentators believe that social network marketing will supplant search engine marketing and Facebook will surpass Google as the most effective business model on the web. Whereas Google relies on revenue from search ads, social networks can benefit from the tendency of most consumers to turn to user reviews and recommendations when deciding what and where to buy.

PRICING

ESTABLISHING PRICES THAT MAXIMIZE PROFITABILITY IS A DIFFICULT TASK FOR businesses. The internet offers a new medium within which businesses must establish pricing policies that capture potential sales and maximize profits. The traditional practices of establishing prices that remained in effect for extended periods, however, are no longer necessary. The internet offers the capability of changing prices relatively rapidly and offering varying prices to customer segments.

Many companies have been concerned about how to deal with pricing between online vs. offline sales channels. The online channels originally were expected to become extremely competitive based on price, but the low prices charged by many pure-play competitors forced them out of business. The establishment of multi-channel pricing requires a focus on customer segments and can also create additional complexity within an organization—the dreaded channel conflict that can confuse and frustrate customers and drive away distribution partners. Prices online have not fallen as drastically as some pundits had predicted and, in fact, some online companies claim to use higher prices in their online channel because of the convenience, additional services, and appropriate segmentation. In contrast to claims regarding the importance of low prices on the internet, a McKinsey study found that most online buyers actually do very little shopping around, and many tend to return to sites used in the past—suggesting that brand may be as important as pricing.[32]

Low prices may not be the most important factor online, but a solid pricing strategy can lead to substantially improved profitability and market share. For example, some B2B sellers have indicated that they segment customers by the extent to which the customer conducts business with them. Those customers who carry out the majority of their purchases with the seller receive improved pricing, while those who use the seller only as an alternate means of supply may pay a premium price. This form of segmentation led an electronic components company to charge a premium of up to 20 percent to some customers, with little impact on volumes sold.[33]

The internet provides an opportunity for ebusinesses to conduct test pricing and price-related research in an effort to optimize prices. The difficult aspect of altering prices, however, is to do it in a fair manner. As part of a price test, Amazon offered potential customers discounts that ranged from 30 to 40 percent but was criticized when existing consumers became aware of these actions. The bad publicity associated with such research requires that companies carefully consider any test pricing strategies they plan to carry out. Ebusinesses may also optimize prices by making adjustments related to supply and demand on an ongoing basis. The adjustment of prices online can be much simpler than in the traditional sales channels, where price lists, signage, and multiple sales channel firms may all need to be updated with regard to changes. The previous section on promotions discusses coupons and discounts that represent a form of emarketing through price adjustments. Although eBay is the world's best-known auction site, auction-based pricing is a viable, but underutilized, option for many companies to maximize revenues. See the Estrategy box for an example of how one company created flexible auction-like pricing as part of its emarketing strategy.

One of the most interesting pricing strategies on the internet is the use of free services to attract customers who can then become a source of advertising revenues or who can be upgraded from basic to premium services. All the major portals, such as Yahoo! and MSN, provide free services in return for the right to display ads. Google is the best-known example of this pricing approach, giving away free search services and email services for the right to show the user an ad.

A strategy some companies are following is to provide a basic service for free and a premium service for a fee. For example, the *Wall Street Journal* follows this type of pricing approach. Skype gives away computer-to-computer internet calling but charges for calls from computer to telephone. Amazon gives free shipping but charges for the goods purchased.

Estrategy

Emarketing and Pricing Strategies

When West Coast Golf Online (WCGO) allowed customers to haggle, its annual revenues increased 685 percent.

WCGO was uncompetitive because the prices listed on its website were fixed. In contrast, its competitors who sold much of the same merchandise engaged in bargaining and haggling with their customers. WCGO reviewed its marketing strategy and concluded that its revenue model was unsustainable. It replaced its fixed price sales approach with one based on haggling. It added a "Make An Offer" button to enable customers to propose a price for each item of interest and recorded the lowest price that it would accept in its database. When a customer made an offer, the system would compare it to the minimum acceptable price and if it was higher, it would accept the purchase, but if it was lower it would respond "We are sorry, your bid is lower than we can sell the item for. Please try another bid or another product."

At first glance, it appeared that they were emulating Priceline's successful "Name Your Price" model. But this turned out not to be the case.

West Coast Golf Online
www.westcostgolfonline.com

Questions

1. Does the increase in revenues impress you? Why?

2. Can you see any disadvantages in the haggling approach implemented by WCGO?

3. What other options could WCGO consider in place of the haggling system it implemented?

Sources: Harvey Schachter, "E-marketing: Let Them Haggle," The Globe and Mail, September 1, 2008.

EVALUATION

The ability to modify or refine marketing campaigns is simplified online and can occur several times per week or even per day. Staples assesses its online marketing campaigns by the hour, according to a number of key metrics. If those metrics indicate that a particular strategy is not working, the marketing campaign is quickly revised. In addition, Staples adjusts the allocations of its marketing budget on a weekly basis to focus on the most crucial elements within a set dollar budget.[34] The development and understanding of key metrics can help businesses adjust emarketing strategies in internet time. The metrics to be used will vary drastically by industry and the particular strategy being pursued. Thus, in developing the emarketing strategy, a business should determine which metrics are relevant and ensure that an appropriate measurement process exists to evaluate the success of strategy implementation. Chapter 12 contains an in-depth discussion of various metrics that can be used to assess the performance of ecommerce sites.

CHAPTER SUMMARY

Emarketing is an important component of the overall marketing and business strategy of ebusinesses. While many dot-com businesses have failed, spending on online advertising continues to grow. Thus, the importance of having an emarketing and advertising strategy should not be underestimated. The emarketing process includes strategy creation, implementation, and evaluation.

An emarketing strategy is developed at the strategy creation phase, when research is carried out, target markets are identified, and a strategy is devised. Secondary research information may be gathered through the internet as well as other methods, while ebusinesses may also engage in primary research. Primary research may be carried out through surveys, experiments, focus groups, and observation.

Any business, including an ebusiness, must aim to use the data it has gathered to segment the market and identify target markets. The unique aspect of emarketing is that targeted marketing is often more easily conducted online than through offline businesses.

The emarketing and advertising strategy should be implemented in a fluid manner to capitalize on the capabilities of the internet. If implemented and carefully monitored, the strategy can be revised midstream to better meet the needs of customers. Implementation includes website design, enhancing visibility of the website on the web and online advertising and promotion.

Advertising online has changed dramatically as software and hardware improvements have been made. While simple banner ads are still commonly used, the internet now allows advertisements to take on a television-like quality with multimedia and interactivity added in. Many advertising tools such as email require careful monitoring, design, and execution to be effective—often requiring trial-and-error or outsourcing. Search engine advertising and in-text advertising are dominant advertising tools that have created an industry around placing links leading to a company's website. Social marketing is still in its infancy but is thought to be the next big development in emarketing.

Alliances, affiliate programs and partnerships can be used to increase website traffic and sales. They can also help create a competitive advantage by creating barriers to entry to competitors lacking such alliances, affiliations and partnerships.

Public relations activities are increasingly necessary due to the proliferation of internet sites. A key objective of such activities is to build trust. Trustmarks, service marks, and seals can help convey a positive company image, but they are still not well understood in the marketplace. Digitized word of mouth is a powerful tool for promoting a company and its products and services. The explosion of social networking sites, media and tools is making digital word of mouth an essential component of an emarketing strategy.

Online pricing strategies can be made flexible through the addition of auctions and various promotions. Through the provision of free services, many entities can capture subscribers who they can monetize via advertising revenues or upgrade to premium services.

Emarketing and advertising strategies must be evaluated on an ongoing basis to ensure that the desired outcomes are being achieved. In addition, the fit of the emarketing strategy within the general marketing strategy and overall business strategy must be kept in mind as online and offline operations continue to converge. Suitable metrics should be developed and used continuously to evaluate and adjust emarketing and advertising strategies and tactics on an ongoing basis.

Key Terms

affiliate program (p. 265)

animated graphic interchange format (GIF) (p. 256)

blog (p. 268)

brand (p. 245)

brochureware phase (p. 251)

cost per thousand (CPM) (p. 256)

cybersquatting (p. 253)

daughter window (p. 257)

digitized word of mouth (p. 268)

emarketing (p. 244)

interactive phase (p. 251)

interstitial (p. 257)

market segment (p. 246)

personalization phase (p. 251)

primary data (p. 247)

remarketing (or retargeting) (p. 249)

search engine optimization (SEO) (p. 254)

secondary data (p. 247)

site stickiness (p. 251)

spam (p. 261)

superstitial (p. 258)

trustmark, service mark, or seal (p. 266)

MyEbusinessLab | Tools for Online Learning

To help you master the material in this chapter and stay up to date with new developments in ebusiness, visit the MyEBusinessLab at www.pearsoned.ca/myebusinesslab. Resources include the following:

- Pre- and Post-Test Questions
- Additional Chapter Questions
- Author Blog
- Recommended Readings
- Commentaries on Current Trends
- Additional Topics in Ebusiness
- Internet Exercises
- Glossary Flashcards

Endnotes

1. J. Strauss and R. Frost, *Marketing on the Internet: Principles of Online Marketing* (Upper Saddle River, NJ: Prentice Hall, 1999).

2. E. Steel, "Labatt Brews Up Interactive Super Bowl Ads," *Globe and Mail*, January 28, 2009, B7, B11.

3. J. Strauss and R. Frost, *Prentice Hall's e-Marketing Guide* (Upper Saddle River, NJ: Prentice Hall, 2001).

4. J. Strauss and R. Frost, *Marketing on the Internet: Principles of Online Marketing* (Upper Saddle River, NJ: Prentice Hall, 1999).

5. J. Strauss and R. Frost, *Marketing on the Internet: Principles of Online Marketing* (Upper Saddle River, NJ: Prentice Hall, 1999).

6. Adapted from W. Hanson, *Principles of Internet Marketing* (Cincinnati, OH: South-Western College Publishing, 2000).

7. M. Hicks, "Getting Personal: E-biz Firms Search for Better Ways to Customize Content," eWEEK (October 2, 2000).

8. "Wake Up Your Website," *Globe and Mail*, November 2007, 35.

9. P.R. Olsen, "A Future in Directing Online Traffic," *New York Times*, January 11, 2009, BU10.

10. R. Briggs and N. Hollis, "Advertising on the Web: Is There Response Before Clickthrough?" *Journal of Advertising Research* (March/April 1997).

11. R.D. Hof, "So Many Ads, So Few Clicks," *BusinessWeek,* November 12, 2007, 38.

12. "Google's Key Source of Revenue Slows," *Globe and Mail*, July 16, 2010, B8.

13. Interactive Advertising Bureau website, www.iab.net/comm/adsizes.asp, accessed April 28, 2004.

14. L. Hughes, "Rich Media Spicing Up Online Buying Choices," *Advertising Age* (February 2001).

15. Harris Interactive, marketing study (June 2001); Unicast website, www.unicast.com/research/pdfs/effectiveness_of_superstitial_relative_to_tv.pdf, accessed April 28, 2004 [link no longer active].

16. "Do Gamers Actually Notice Ads? Proof Is at Hand," *Globe and Mail,* June 3, 2008.

17. "An Ad Engine to Put 'Mad Men' Out of Business," *New York Times,* May 23, 2010, BU4.

18. B. Grow and B. Helm, "Your Ad Here. And Here. And Here," *BusinessWeek*, April 24, 2006, 36.

19. J. Fine, "Rise of the Lowly Search Ad," *BusinessWeek*, April 24, 2006, 24.

20. C. Holahan, "Pitching Between the Lines," *BusinessWeek,* December 3, 2007, 60.

21. M. Patriquin, "Got Corp. Avoids Dreaded Spam Label Through 'Opt-in' Ads," *Globe and Mail*, May 19, 2005, B13.

22. N. Wreden, "Mapping the Frontiers of E-mail Marketing," *Harvard Management Communication Letter* (September 1999).

23. P. Kennedy, "Part people make a splash on the Web," *Globe and Mail,* May 11, 2005, B4.

24. "FTC bacls dp-not-track system for Web," *Globe and Mail,* December 2, 2010.

25. D. Kenny and J. Marshall, "Contextual Marketing: The Real Business of the Internet," *Harvard Business Review* (November/December 2000).

26. D. Hoffman and T. Novak, "How to Acquire Customers on the Web," *Harvard Business Review* (May/June 2000).

27. Amazon.com website, www.amazon.com, accessed April 28, 2004.

28. B.J. Fogg, et al., "How Do People Evaluate a Web Site's Credibility? Results from a Large Study" (research report, November 11, 2002), www.consumerwebwatch.org/news/report3_credibilityresearch/stanfordPTL.pdf, accessed November 29, 2004.

29. C. Dellarocas, "The Digitization of Word of Mouth: Promise and Challenges of Online Feedback Mechanisms," *Management Science* (October 2003).

30. R. Walker, "The Corporate Manufacture of Word of Mouth," *New York Times Magazine* (December 5, 2004): 69–75, 104, 130–131.

31. "Social Media Is a Credible Means," *Globe and Mail*, April 10, 2009, B5.

32. W. Baker et al., "Price Smarter on the Net," *Harvard Business Review* (February 2001).

33. W. Baker et al., "Price Smarter on the Net," *Harvard Business Review* (February 2001).

34. N. Aufreiter, et al., "Marketing Rules: What Sets Winners Apart? More Than Anything Else, It's Lightning Fast Marketing," *Harvard Business Review* (February 2001).

Chapter 12

Metrics for Performance Measurement in Ecommerce

Learning Objectives

When you complete this chapter you should be able to:

1 Explain the benefits that metrics provide to an ebusiness.

2 Identify and describe the importance of the major types of metrics.

3 Explain how traffic metrics can help an ebusiness assess its internal processes.

4 Explain how marketing-oriented metrics can help an ebusiness plan its marketing efforts.

5 Identify the major types of financial and other performance metrics.

6 Describe the major sources of information for creating performance metrics.

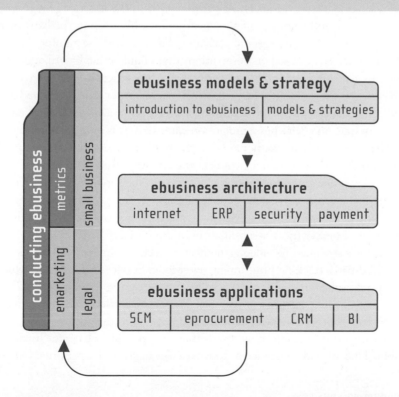

INTRODUCTION

THE FOCUS OF THIS CHAPTER IS MEASUREMENT OF EBUSINESS PERFORMANCE. There are a great many metrics that can be used to measure ebusiness performance, ranging from the number of hits on a website, to the proportion of customer visits that result in a sale, and ultimately, to the profitability of ebusiness activities. One of the great benefits of the internet is that it enables tracking and measurement of business activity. In this chapter we will consider the benefits provided by well-designed metrics, what aspects of ecommerce can be measured, and the sources of information for such measurements.

BENEFITS OF METRICS

MANAGEMENT AND MEASUREMENT GO HAND IN HAND. COMMONLY HEARD expressions in business are, "If you don't measure it, you can't manage it" and "If you don't measure it, it doesn't get done."

Metrics can help an entity to better understand its business model—to understand the customer base and thereby better target the content of the ecommerce website; to better handle promotions and discounts, product placements, up-selling and cross-selling; and to better manage price points. Metrics can also provide guidance to the personnel who are assigned the responsibility for achieving strategic objectives.

Metrics act as an incentive to motivate certain types of performance. We all pay attention to the things for which we know we are going to be held accountable. For example, if you are given marks for a task in a course, then you're more likely to do that task than an optional task for which there are no marks assigned. If a sales agent is paid a higher commission for certain types of sales than others, then the agent is more likely to focus on generating the high-commission sales.

Metrics provide a basis for analyzing performance. In the absence of metrics, performance assessment would be based simply on end results, like cash in the bank, with little insight into the nature of the specific activities that led to those results. Any detailed analysis would have to be based on observations that could be haphazard and subjective, resulting in poorly supported and biased performance assessments. Also, they could focus unduly on easily observed or surface aspects of behaviour, rather than on desired outcomes. For example, metrics can be used to determine whether promotion campaigns are actually working. Every time an entity has a promotion campaign, it is giving something of value away in order to attract business, hoping that the new business attracted will pay for the promotion. Simply observing that a great deal of effort went into planning and organizing a series of weekly promotions does not provide any information about the effectiveness of that activity. If the entity doesn't keep track of the outcomes of promotions in terms of increased traffic or revenue, it will never know whether its promotions add value.

For example, Massive Inc. is a subsidiary of Microsoft Corp. that provides an ad delivery system for ads streamed to video game players. Massive Inc. submitted its ads to an audit by a third-party tracking firm, Interactive Media Services Group Ltd., which helps companies track web traffic and email activity. By measuring users' responses to online ads, such audits may help advertisers overcome one of the barriers to the growth of online advertising: proof that web users actually see and respond to the ads.[1]

Another important benefit of metrics is that they provide a basis for holding people accountable. They provide guidance as to what tasks ought to be performed, motivation

Interactive Media Services
www.imservicesgroup.com

to do those tasks, and, subsequently, a standard against which performance can be evaluated and rewarded and non-performance can be addressed.

ALIGNING METRICS WITH BUSINESS OBJECTIVES

MEASUREMENT SHOULD RELATE PERFORMANCE TO OBJECTIVES. IF AN ENTITY HAS set objectives and knows how to measure them, then this is an indication that it knows how to link its activities to its business objectives. This way, the metrics can be helpful in achieving strategic objectives; they enable the actions required to meet objectives to be identified. For example, if an ebusiness wishes to grow its customer base, then it can establish a metric of traffic volume for its ecommerce site, such as the number of visits per week during a campaign to attract customers. Such a metric immediately focuses attention on bringing traffic to the website, and personnel will be focused on tactics to achieve this objective. The effectiveness of chosen tactics will be assessed by the number of actual visits per week, thus relating the activities to the objectives.

An ebusiness may have different objectives at different times in its life. For example, maximizing traffic might be an objective early on when an ebusiness is trying to get established and it just wants to get attention from potential shoppers. However, maximizing traffic may not necessarily lead to maximum profit; in fact, it may lead to losses, because there might be significant advertising and marketing costs associated with generating that traffic. But during the business startup phase, maximizing traffic may be a legitimate objective, and the costs involved may be considered an investment for the future.

Although traffic is definitely a key metric for ecommerce, even more important is the conversion of traffic into customers. By "customer" we mean an entity that fulfills the main objective for the site, which could be content consumption, lead generation, sales, or customer support. For example, for sites that provide content, traffic alone might be an insufficient measure of content consumption. Instead, the average length of visits, the average number of page views per visitor, and net subscriptions (new subscribers minus cancellations) could be useful metrics. For lead-generation sites, useful metrics might be white paper downloads, number of opt-ins for future email contact, and average length of visits.

For a product sales site, maximizing revenue could be the main objective. Maximizing revenue is not the same as maximizing traffic, because maximizing traffic is focused on getting visitors to a site, whereas maximizing revenue is focused on selling products and services by converting visitors into buyers. For example, generating traffic but not having the products that customers want in stock would not help generate revenue. So having a revenue-maximizing objective would focus attention on products and services as well as traffic. Revenue-related metrics such as sales per visitor rate the website's success in converting visitors to buyers.

Increasing market share is different from maximizing sales because it involves competition more completely. Metrics of market share by definition involve competing with others, trying to take some of their business. That is a very different objective than simply creating sales. For example, an entity can attempt to generate sales through advertising, which might increase the size of the sales pie, but some of the increase may go to competitors, leaving the entity's share of the pie with little or no increase.

Minimizing transaction costs is an objective that is aimed at reducing the costs of doing business. At the startup phase of a business or launch of a particular product or service, it might be beneficial to provide a significant level of support to customers through dedicated call centre support and so on. But that support translates into significant transaction costs. Over time, the objective would be to minimize those costs by reducing the number of people in support functions or keeping the same number of people but putting through much more business activity. A metric such as cost per visitor would focus attention on transaction costs.

Maximizing return on investment (ROI) deals with earnings relative to the investment incurred to start the ecommerce activity, including site-development costs. That could be an important objective as an ebusiness matures. During the dot-com bubble the conventional wisdom was that entities were supposed to spend a lot of money maximizing traffic and sales, without worrying about ROI. Huge sums of money were spent on developing ecommerce sites and on advertising to attract customers to ebusinesses that never generated a return on the huge investments made. Metrics that recognize expenditures on ecommerce sites as investments will focus on return rather than income alone. A marginal income stream could satisfy revenue and expense metrics but might not satisfy requirements based on ROI.

In summary, objectives must be linked to strategy and must be specific. If they are vague, it will be difficult to establish metrics for assessing their level of achievement. And if an entity doesn't know how to measure an objective, then it won't know how to deliver it.

LIMITATIONS OF METRICS

ALTHOUGH METRICS CAN HELP A BUSINESS ACHIEVE ITS STRATEGIC OBJECTIVES BY guiding, motivating, and holding personnel accountable for their actions, metrics also have limitations that should be recognized. For example, when strategies change rapidly, as is the case for many startups, metrics can quickly become irrelevant or even misleading. Some measures may be ambiguous or susceptible to faulty analysis and interpretation. For example, website stickiness may be good in some circumstances and bad in others.

Also, it is important to recognize that measurement can be costly, consuming money and the time of key personnel.

Online measures are vulnerable to tampering by insiders or outsiders, and therefore the data sources should be safeguarded against unauthorized access. A case in point is Air Canada's contention that certain WestJet executives accessed and used performance measures posted on Air Canada's intranet to gain an unfair competitive advantage over Air Canada on certain routes.[2]

Soft metrics are sometimes not as well accepted as hard data, but may be as important. Hard data may reflect attributes that are easy to measure, rather than the most important attributes. Some metrics may need to be subjective; for example, supervisors' ratings of their employees, visitors' ratings of their overall experience on a website, and so on.

Click Fraud

As mentioned in chapter 11, one of the problems associated with both display ads and search ads is click fraud—fraudulent sites generating false data to generate metrics for which they can extract payment from marketers under false pretences. A person, an automated script, or a computer program may imitate a legitimate user of a web browser clicking on an ad for the purpose of generating a charge per click without having actual interest in the target of the ad's link.[3] It could be a competitor seeking to use up a target company's advertising budget by repeatedly clicking on an ad. Another way that a competitor can attack a target company is by repeatedly loading a website into a browser but not clicking on it. This eventually can cause a search engine to discard that website, making it invisible to potential customers unless they type the URL into their browser or connect via some other link. In another type of click fraud, a company that has a link posted on its website seeks to maximize its own share of the pay-per-click revenues by clicking its own posted link.

Click fraud is the subject of some controversy and increasing litigation due to the fact that advertising networks can benefit from such frauds by collecting fees for clicks that they have been able to generate even if the clicks are not from legitimate customers or potential customers. Estimates of the amount of fraudulent clicking run from 10 to 50 percent.[4] Companies like Google, Yahoo!, and MSN that generate the ads that companies pay for and calculate the amounts owed and owing assert that they have the click fraud risk under control and that they detect and do not charge for fraudulent clicks. However, it is advisable for companies that pay for such advertising to obtain detailed breakdowns of the source and timing of the clicks that they are billed for to ensure that they are not paying for fraudulent clicks or to obtain assurance that the agencies that place pay per click ads on their behalf have effective monitoring programs in place to limit their customers' exposure to click fraud.

WHAT TO MEASURE

Now that we have considered the value of measuring performance, let's consider what aspects should be measured. There is much that is still not well understood about various metrics, and the metrics that are "in" one day may be "out" another. Nevertheless, several broad categories of measurements should be considered for use in assessing performance of ecommerce units:

- traffic and site usage metrics
- social network metrics
- marketing metrics
- financial metrics
- other performance metrics
- multi-dimensional scorecards

Traffic and Site Usage Metrics

Traffic Metrics   The earliest form of online business measurement is related to traffic measurement. While such measures can be very crude, they can provide a surprising amount of useful information about traffic volumes, site usage, sources of traffic, and visitor attributes.

Traffic is the most basic unit that financial backers, advertisers, and affiliates look for. In the early days of ebusiness, companies spent any amount necessary to generate interest in, or traffic on, their sites, because this translated into financial support, share price growth, and so on. The number of "users" is a basic but important traffic metric that is referred to in the Estrategy box.

Site traffic analysis can help determine the volume of traffic on a website, as well as which sections of a website are visited, when they are visited, by whom they are visited, and where the visitors came from. Traffic volume can be measured in a variety of ways: hits; page views; ad views, ad impressions, or banner impressions; visits; and unique visitors.

Hits

hit: A single download of any information from a website.

Hits   The oldest traffic metric involves measuring hits. A **hit** is counted any time that something is requested from the web server. It can be a page, a picture, or just a link to another location. Anytime that you click on a page, that would be called a hit. A hit is a very broad piece of information. When somebody creates a hit, you don't know what they looked at and what they saw. Also, a single webpage can account for a dozen hits if it has many photos, while a text-only page could generate just a single hit. As a result, the relevance of hits for measuring traffic on a website has been questioned, and alternative measures of traffic volume have been widely adopted.

page view: A single download of an entire page of information.

Page Views   The next type of information that is used is a **page view**, which occurs when an entire page of information is downloaded. That would be considered more valuable, because all of the information that is displayed on that page would be viewed, or at least presumed to be viewed, by the user.

ad views: A measure of the number of times a page with a banner ad or another advertisement is viewed during a period of time.

Ad Views, Ad Impressions, and Banner Impressions   **Ad views**, ad impressions, and banner impressions are a more focused measure of the number of times a page with a banner ad or other advertisement is viewed during a period of time. This measure would be particularly useful to advertisers who pay for a specified number of such views as part of a marketing campaign.

visit: A collection of webpages a visitor views in a time period while on a website.

Visits   A **visit** is not just a single page view, it's a whole collection of pages that are viewed by a single user during a period of time—usually 30 minutes. By gathering all of those pages into one unit, called a visit, that is identified with a particular user, an entity can get better information than by looking at thousands of potentially unrelated hits.

Unique Visitors   The number of non-repeating visitors in a specific time frame measures the volume of activity in terms of purported individuals, although it is really computers (i.e., IP addresses) rather than individuals that are counted in this type of analysis (i.e., many individuals may share a single computer or a single IP address).

Traffic analysis tools normally rely on the IP address to group various hits and attribute them to the same user. However, proxies and "floating" IP addresses make this method inaccurate. Since it is possible to store the content of a cookie in the log file, some tools allow for more precise tracking by assigning a unique ID in the cookie, then dumping the cookie content to the log file at every hit, thereby being able to more accurately track the user session.

user: A visitor who registers on a website by providing at least their email address.

Users   Websites often want to count the number of individuals who register on a website by providing at least their email address; this is called the user count. This metric is more conservative than the tally of unique visitors since some visitors may not wish to provide any personal information to a site. However, this metric may overstate the actual number of active users because some users who initially register on a website may later decide to opt out of a website because they don't like the service or don't want to provide the information requested from them to enable the service.

Time   With the advent of applications that deliver content such as music and video to users without requiring them to click numerous buttons or banners or scroll through pages, a preferred metric representing engagement with a website is the amount of time a user spends on it. This metric may result in different rankings of websites. For example, search sites such as Google do not consume much user time, whereas game sites such as Electronic Arts and sports and entertainment sites such as AOL Sports do.[5]

time: A measure of a visitor's engagement with a website.

Search Engine Ranking   Search engines rank websites according to their estimated relevance to various search terms or key words. The more relevant the website is to a search term, the closer it is to the top of the list of search results displayed by the search engine and the more likely it is to be clicked by the user who entered the search term into the search engine. One of the factors used to determine a website's relevance is the number of links associated with the search terms that point to a particular website. The more such links, the higher the ranking of a web site. The search engine rank can therefore be viewed as a metric of potential traffic that could be generated by a website.

search engine ranking: A measure of closeness to the top of the list of links returned by a search engine.

Estrategy

Mint.com Measures "Users"

Mint.com is a highly rated online personal finance service that offers its users a data organization and analysis service. Mint users enter basic information about their bank accounts and Mint organizes and analyzes the information to produce a customized budget as well as related financial advice such as whether the user should consolidate certain accounts to reduce interest charges, how the user should invest excess cash to earn a return on available funds, and so on. Mint's website promises that all financial advice offered is unbiased. The service is free to users. Mint earns brokerage fees from partners whose products and services are purchased by users.

On January 28, 2009, Intuit wrote a letter to Aaron Patzer, CEO of Mint Software Inc., challenging some user statistics cited by Mint.com in various media channels. The letter focussed on a claim by Mint.com that as of January 26, 2008 it had more than 850,000 users and they were growing at a rate of over 3,000 users per day.

Intuit saw the increasing growth in Mint's user base as a threat, especially if it was not true. In the U.S. advertising claims must be supported by evidence before used in advertising. Therefore, Intuit challenged Mint to substantiate the number of "users" it claimed to have.

Intuit appeared to threaten legal action unless Mint responded by February 6, 2009.

Mint.com replied that it considers anyone who filled in an email address, zip code, and password to be a "user," regardless of whether that person actually linked a bank account to a Mint user name. This definition of user may overstate the number of people who actually use Mint.com on a day-to-day basis because, after registering, some new members would balk at providing their bank account information. However, they would still be counted as new members.

Aaron Patzer defended Mint.com's method of counting users, noting that over 70 percent of registered users have, in fact, linked at least one bank account to Mint.com, with most of them linking five or six financial accounts. He also noted that "members" who didn't link their bank accounts to Mint.com would nevertheless still receive regular offers

>

from Mint.com's partners, making their inclusion in the user count legitimate.

After receiving this response, Intuit retorted that using Mint.com's approach to measure users Quicken Online had more than 650,000 users and had been adding approximately 45,000 new users each week since January 2009.

Mint
www.mint.com

Intuit
www.intuit.com

Questions

1. Why did Mint.com report the number of users on their ecommerce website? Is this a useful metric? What other metrics might be useful?

2. Why did Intuit challenge Mint.com's claims?

3. What can we learn from the two sets of measures?

Sources: http://techcrunch.com/2009/02/19/quicken-online-cant-believe-mint-is-doing-so-well-sends-threatening-letter/, accessed January 3, 2011; http://techcrunch.com/2009/09/13/intuit-to-acquire-former-techcrunch50-winner-mint-for-170-million/, accessed January 3, 2011.

Site Usage Metrics   Traffic is a general indicator of a site's potential; however, to obtain meaningful insights, the analysis must get deeper. Site usage metrics help an ebusiness assess the effectiveness of its ecommerce website. The "Marketer's Common Sense Guide to Emetrics"[6] uses the analogy of the leaky bucket to describe the sales losses that result from a poorly designed website. Website traffic is like water that fills a bucket. Website design problems are like holes that permit visitors to escape without fulfilling the sales objectives of the website. Site usage analysis can help trace the losses at various points in the pathways through the website from entry point to exit, and help eliminate the holes that permit "leaks" instead of converting visitors into buyers.

Site usage can be analyzed spatially or temporally. Spatial usage analysis can identify visitor behaviour according to the following:

- top entry pages—pages most commonly entered
- top exit pages—pages most commonly exited from (exit pages can represent leakage from a website, indicating premature exit by visitors)

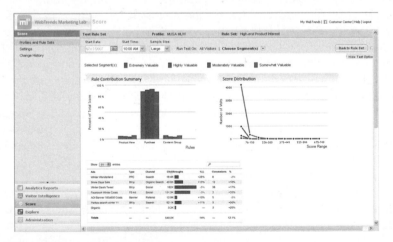

Figure 12.1 WebTrends dashboard

Illustration of a WebTrends dashboard.

Source: WebTrends website, www.webtrends.com, accessed May 2004. © 1995 WebTrends from NetIQ Corp.

- most-visited pages—pages most frequently visited
- least-visited pages—pages least visited
- single-visit pages—pages only visited once (these may represent trouble spots in the website)
- paths within site—most common paths taken by visitors (these may represent design problems if the most common path does not lead to successful completion of an ecommerce transaction or other site objective)

Temporal site usage analysis can identify traffic by month, week, day of week, and hour of day. Such breakdowns can be useful to correlate with the timing of promotions or website changes to determine their efficacy. In fact, most traffic measurements should be reported for a specified and consistent time period to ensure comparability of metrics.

Social Network Metrics

With the dramatic rise in the use and importance of social networking, new metrics are being developed to reflect activity on social networking websites to complement traffic metrics and marketing metrics (as discussed in the Canadian Snapshots box). The field of social metrics is still evolving, but research into social marketing analytics conducted by Web Analytics Demystified and Altimeter Group identifies four business objectives, related key performance indicators (KPIs) and metrics for those KPIs, as summarized in figure 12.2.

social networking website: A website that enables subscribers to link with other subscribers to share personal, professional or commercial interests.

Dialogue   A business can create a dialogue with its customers and potential customers by producing content to engage an audience and attract contributors. Awareness and word of mouth can be built through conversations, and the promotion and endorsement of these conversations can occur through blogs, communities, or social networks such as Facebook and Twitter. Metrics for this business objective include share of voice, audience engagement, and conversation reach.

conversation: Interactive messages that flow through email, blogs and social networks.

Advocacy   A business can attract the support of individuals who have no official connection to the entity or brand and get them to act as ambassadors for the company or its products by encouraging word of mouth activity, promoting and endorsing conversations shared by individuals, developing relationships with influential individuals who have an affinity towards the company or its offerings, and nurturing existing relationships with customers. Such advocacy enables a business to extend its reach beyond its immediate circles of influence. Metrics for this business objective include active advocates, advocate influence, and advocacy impact.

Support   Social media channels can be used to enable customers to support each other directly or for the company to use the same channels to support customers. Metrics for this business objective include issue resolution rate, resolution time, and satisfaction score.

Innovation   The knowledge base created by social networks such as Facebook, Twitter, and other channels can contain valuable information that can be mined for insights and ideas to promote innovation of a company's products and service offerings. Metrics for this business objective include topic trends, sentiment ratio, and idea impact.

sentiment: Measure of positive or negative comments about a website, product or topic.

Business Objectives	Key Performance Indicator	Components of Potential Metrics
Dialog	Share of Voice	Brand Mentions divided by Total Mentions (Brand + Competitor A, B, C...n)
	Audience Engagement	Comments + Shares + Trackbacks divided by Total Views
	Conversation Reach	Total People Participating divided by Total Audience Exposure
Advocacy	Active Advocates	# of Active Advocates (within past 30 days) divided by Total Advocates
	Advocate Influence	Unique Advocate's Influence divided by Total Advocate Influence
	Advocacy Impact	Number of Advocacy Driven Conversions divided by Total Volume of Advocacy Traffic
Support	Resolution Rate	Total # Issues Resolved Satisfactorily divided by Total # Service Issues
	Resolution Time	Total Inquiry Response Time divided by Total # Service Inquiries
	Satisfaction Score	Customer Feedback (input A, B, C...n) divided by All Customer Feedback
Innovation	Topic Trends	# of Specific Topic Mentions divided by All Topic Mentions
	Sentiment Ratio	Positive : Neutral : Negative Brand Mentions divided by All Brand Mentions
	Idea Impact	# of Positive Conversations, Shares, Mentions divided by Total Idea Conversations, Shares, Mentions

Figure 12.2 Social network metrics

Source: Jeremiah Owyang and John Lovett, "Social Marketing Analytics: A New Framework For Measuring Results In Social Media," April 22, 2010. © Altimeter Group. Used with permission.

New Business Models
Using Metrics for Social Networks

Toronto-based Sysomos started as a research project at the University in Toronto in 2006. Today, the company offers social media monitoring and analytics products that give corporations, marketers, public relations agencies, and advertisers information to support business and strategic decisions. Through the use of contextual text analytics and data-mining technology, Sysomos collects billions of social media conversations from blogs, Twitter, social networks, messages, boards, wikis, and a growing number of major news sources. Sysomos's technology features the following:

A comprehensive and spam-free archive, featuring billions of conversations dating back to 2006

Continually updated content from blogs, social networks, micro-blogging services, wikis, message boards, video sharing sites, and news sources

Geography and demographic (age, gender, profession) information

Automated sentiment metrics to assess whether conversations are positive, negative, or neutral

>

Text analytics identifying key themes, emerging topics, and trends

Measurable metrics about popularity, geographic/demographics, and authority

The ability to drill down into demographics and conversation topics

The ability to compare reach, share of voice, and brand impact against competitors

Sysomos has an impressive customer list that includes many well-known companies whose logos are prominently displayed on its website.

In mid-2010, Sysomos was acquired by Marketwire, whose services include press release distribution, media contact management, multimedia, media monitoring services, and other related services. Marketwire wanted to integrate Sysomos's social analytics tools into its offerings.

Sysomos
www.sysomos.com

Marketwire
www.marketwire.com

Questions

1. What are the strengths and weaknesses of the metrics offered by Sysomos?

2. How can social metrics be used to support ebusiness strategy?

3. Why would a company like Marketwire be interested in Sysomos?

Sources: www.sysomos.com; www.marketwire.com.

Marketing Metrics

The purpose of marketing measurement is to help market an entity's products and/or services better. With the advent of customer relationship management (CRM) systems, collaborative filtering, and personalization tools, sophisticated customer-focused methods have been developed for gathering important marketing information. We will discuss marketing measurement related to the following topics:

- click-through (pay-per-action and pay-per-call)
- conversion rate
- referrer analysis
- location analysis
- customer profile analysis
- shopping basket analysis

Click-Through Rate   One of the goals of marketing and advertising is to attract as many "eyeballs" as possible to view a target message such as a banner ad. However, attracting viewers is not necessarily effective at converting them to customers of a company's products and services. In the early days of ecommerce, banner ads were the main form of online advertising and advertisers paid websites for the number of banners viewed by website visitors. It was difficult to establish a relationship between the display ads such as banners and the outcome sought—clicking on the banner, visiting the advertised website (click-through), and purchasing goods and services offered by the companies doing the advertising. As online measurement technologies improved, metrics based on the number of banner ads displayed have lost some of their appeal, in favour of metrics based on actual click-throughs—that is, the proportion of visitors who click a banner or button to get to the advertised website after being shown a display such as a banner ad. Click-through rates have been declining over the years as the novelty of web ads has worn off, especially among sophisticated web users, such as members of social networking sites. The average click-through rate of standard banner ads across the whole web is less than one-fifth of 1 percent.[7] This rate can, however, be dramatically improved through personalization and customization of displays based on characteristics of users.

An extension of the click-through rate, **pay-per-action**, involves measuring and rewarding actions that result from click-throughs rather than the number of click-throughs themselves. For example, **pay-per-call** measures and rewards the number of calls placed by visitors during a specific time frame in an attempt to assess the effectiveness of advertising on a website. In a pay-per-call approach, rights to key words such as "Vancouver lawyers" are auctioned, as in a pay-per-click approach, but instead of clicking on a link leading to the advertiser's website, the user is directed by the ad to make a telephone call to the advertising company, using a special number supplied on the website, or to leave his or her contact information to get a return call from the merchant. The advertiser pays for each call as it would for each click on the link in a pay-per-click system. Naturally, the amount paid per call would probably be significantly higher than the amount paid per click on a link. This approach is particularly beneficial for small local service businesses.[8]

pay-per-action: Measures and rewards actions that result from click-throughs rather than the number of click-throughs themselves.

pay-per-call: Measures and rewards the number of calls placed by visitors during a specific time frame.

conversion rate: Proportion of click-throughs that actually result in the purchase of goods or services.

Conversion Rate

A click-through may not result in a sale. The conversion rate is the proportion of click-throughs that actually result in the purchase of goods or services. Many factors go into determining this rate, including the design of the website, the quality of the product or service being offered, the degree of trust that the website can instill in the visitor, especially a first-time visitor, and the promotions used to entice the visitor to purchase an item (e.g., discounts or coupons).

Referrer Analysis

Web server log files contain information about a visitor's previous URL. Referrer information can also be purchased from infomediaries such as DoubleClick. From this information, it is possible to determine where traffic is coming from and thereby measure the effectiveness of advertising campaigns. If an entity is advertising on a website but not receiving traffic from it, then the advertising expenditure may not be effective. Conversely, if the traffic is coming from places where the entity is not advertising, then it should consider what factors may be responsible for attracting that traffic.

Location Analysis

Location analysis involves a breakdown of customer behaviour by geographical origin. Location analysis has great importance for marketing, since some promotions campaigns and advertising have regional, national, or international reach. Location metrics can also help assess the performance of managers of different geographical regions and the effectiveness of local marketing efforts in generating traffic and revenues. In the absence of explicit data, rough location can be inferred by IP address; however, proxies pose a severe limitation to this method. Increasingly, user surveys or visitor registration are used to obtain information such as location and, of course, purchasers provide their location as part of their shipping information.

Customer Profile Analysis

Customer profile analysis involves a breakdown of visitor behaviour by profile attributes. Such analysis focuses on analyzing user behaviour relative to the actions taken by an ebusiness to attract visitors and to persuade them to purchase goods and services, provide information, or otherwise contribute to the objectives established for an ecommerce website. As we have already noted, the internet allows real-time or quasi-real-time sampling of a target audience. New visitors come in to an ebusiness website as "anonymous," but are immediately profiled based on their actions. Every action is recorded in the web server log file. By interacting with the ecommerce site, visitors provide information that can be used to form "user profiles," which in turn can be used for marketing purposes, such as selecting what products to display, and so on.

The entity's marketing efforts can be significantly aided by creating a profile of the typical user or classes of users, by tracking attributes such as age, gender, household income, average purchase, total purchases, and so on. Customer profile data can be derived from data provided by customers explicitly and also from the implications of the customer's attributes or behaviour. Explicit information is given by the user when subscribing to a service, making a purchase, completing a survey form, and so on—for example, name, address, and marital status. Implicit information can be inferred from the user's actions and/or purchase history, for example, favourite colour, age group, or preferred topics. Such inferences may require the use of data-mining tools to identify key patterns of interest to the entity. For example, if a customer buys three red shirts and only one blue shirt, the implicit information is that the customer prefers the colour red to blue. A system may not have explicit gender information about a customer. However, if the customer purchased male fashions, then the system could conclude that the customer is male. These types of inferences are obviously fraught with all kinds of limitations, but nevertheless, data-mining tools attempt to make such inferences.

User profile analysis can help an entity assess whether it is reaching its target audience, and thereby evaluate the efficacy of its marketing campaigns.

Shopping Basket Analysis   Shopping basket analysis involves a breakdown of the items purchased in a sample transaction. Shopping basket analysis can help develop an understanding of customers' purchasing behaviour and customers' value reasoning. Itemsets are sets of items that appear together in many transactions. Knowledge of itemsets and their frequency can be used to improve product placement or for cross-sell and up-sell. For example, by using shopping basket analysis, a company may offer a recommendation to a customer, such as, "Customers who purchased X also purchased Y," which you see on Amazon.com. Shopping basket analysis can help an entity assess and predict product demand and, thereby, the efficacy of its marketing campaigns.

Financial Metrics

Financial metrics track revenues, expenses, return on investment, and shareholder value creation.

Revenues   Revenue streams in a typical ebusiness include the sales revenue from products and services, advertising revenue (e.g., $3 CPM), affiliate commission (e.g., 15 percent of an order generated for an affiliated site via a click-through or other referral), and database marketing (e.g., customer name sales to others for $10 to $1000 per name).

Sales analysis involves a breakdown of revenue streams per period, product category, referrer, time of day, etc. Sales analysis can be extended to identify top-selling products, least-selling products, and product margins. It can also include a breakdown of sales by shopper profile, demographics, geographical location, etc. Advanced sales analytics can involve analysis of product clusters, purchase patterns, shopping basket analysis, and the prediction of future sales based on the patterns observed.

Expenses   Expense metrics include fixed costs, operating costs, and marketing costs. Fixed costs include infrastructure costs and operating costs. Infrastructure costs include store development (e.g., $250,000–$1 million), catalogue development (e.g., $5–$10 per stock-keeping unit, or SKU), store hosting services (e.g., $50,000–$200,000 per year). In addition, credit card companies typically require a merchant account deposit that can range from $10,000–$50,000. Although it is not really a cost, it nevertheless requires a cash outflow.

Operating costs include site maintenance, advertising/promotion, marketing, and operations. Variable costs include product/service costs, per-unit licensing costs, commissions on click-through sales, etc., and distribution costs for non-electronic goods or services.

Return on Investment (ROI)   ROI is calculated as (revenues − expenses)/assets. A strength of this metric is that it combines three key financial measures into a single composite metric. A weakness is that it omits non-financial measures such as customer service, operational quality, and innovation. Calculating ROI is simple; however, deciding what numbers to quantify can be difficult. The difficulties arise when economic benefits of ebusiness endeavours are intangibles such as customer service, competitiveness, communications, and content management. These softer benefits (intangibles) are much harder to measure, but some firms are working on ways to factor intangible benefits into their analyses of ecommerce initiatives to create a more effective and accurate measure of payback; for example, they might conduct customer satisfaction surveys either directly or over the internet to learn how customers are interacting with their systems.

Other Performance Metrics

Other performance metrics can be used to assess the performance of internal ebusiness units, as well as the performance of ebusiness partners ranging from IT service providers such as ISPs and website hosting services to other outsourcing-service providers such as transaction-processing services, logistics service providers, payment processors, and others. For example, performance metrics may relate to network availability, system response time, transaction-processing accuracy, transaction-processing timeliness, responsiveness to requests for system changes, help-desk effectiveness, security-incident handling, customer satisfaction, degree of innovation, and so on. Typically, such metrics are embedded in service level agreements that define performance criteria tailored to the services being provided, as well as penalties for non-performance.

Multi-Dimensional Scorecards

Multi-dimensional scorecards bring several metrics together to create a multi-dimensional measure of performance. Such scorecards can be created externally or they can be created internally using approaches such as the balanced scorecard.

Internal Scorecard   The best-known prescription for internal scorecard creation is the balanced scorecard format developed by Robert Kaplan and David Norton. They created the format out of a concern that business managers were overly focused on financial metrics and were insufficiently motivated or guided by other performance metrics, such

Financial Metrics	Customer Metrics	Internal Process Metrics	Learning and Growth Metrics
• Online revenue per customer	• Level of service delivery	• Availability of systems	• Staff productivity & morale
• Cost per online customer	• Satisfaction of existing customers	• Volume of transactions processed	• # of staff trained in new services
• Cost-efficiency of ebusiness processes	• # of new customers reached	• # of errors	• Value delivery peremployee

Figure 12.3 Example of a balanced scorecard for an ebusiness

A balanced scorecard assesses financial and non-financial metrics.

as customer satisfaction, that would determine the entity's long-term success.[9] While financial metrics are important, they represent the financial results of marketing operations and other actions taken that should also be measured and assessed. A good set of metrics should incorporate measures of those actions rather than ignore them. Kaplan and Norton created a scorecard with four major sections: customer, internal process, learning and growth, and financial performance. The idea is that a small number of metrics must be identified in each of these four areas to guide and motivate managers to focus on long-term drivers of business success.

Customer-oriented metrics include market share, traffic analysis, shopping analysis, acquisition cost, awareness, and satisfaction/loyalty. Internal process metrics include innovation, efficiency, effectiveness and economy of ebusiness operations, and system reliability. Learning and growth metrics address employee capabilities and motivation. Financial metrics focus on revenues, expenses, and ROI.

In summary, the balanced scorecard approach involves taking measurements in four different areas rather than focusing solely on financial performance measures, as illustrated in figure 12.3.

Since it is not solely financial, a balanced scorecard gives a balanced perspective on the actions required to achieve strategic objectives. The main differences between scorecards used by different entities are the metrics that are selected in each of the four categories and how well those metrics align with the entity's strategic objectives—in other words, how well they guide and motivate personnel to take specific actions that will lead to achievement of those objectives.

External Scorecards Numerous organizations provide scorecard services on the internet. For example, a scorecard from Watchfire GómezPro (acquired by IBM in 2007) considered 150 or more different variables to arrive at a rating of an ecommerce website's quality. To create the quality criteria, Watchfire GómezPro first reviewed all of the features and services delivered online (and to some degree offline) across an industry. While practices can vary across industries, Watchfire GómezPro typically identified criteria in at least four categories:

1. Ease of use—demonstrations of functionality; simplicity of account opening and transaction process; consistency of design and navigation; adherence to proper user

interaction principles; integration of data providing efficient access to information commonly accessed by consumers.

2. Customer confidence—availability, depth, and breadth of customer service options, including phone, email, and branch locations; privacy policies, service guarantees, fees, and explanations of fees.

3. Online resources—availability of applications for specific products; ability to look up account information for each product; ability to transact in each product online.

4. Relationship services—online help, tutorials, glossary, and FAQs; advice; personalization of data; ability to customize a site; reuse of customer data to facilitate future transactions; support of business and personal needs such as tax reporting or repeated buying.

Unlike services such as BizRate that base their ratings on consumer feedback, Watchfire GómezPro relied on its analysts to assess the various features of each website and make the decisions on each of the criteria. The company believed its experts had the capabilities to "define the elements of quality in the internet delivery of services." Watchfire GómezPro's methodology was exactly the opposite of BizRate's, which uses consumer surveys to compile ratings. The overall result of the rating process was a scorecard, with each website given a ranking between 1 and 10, with 1 being the lowest and 10 the highest. Watchfire GómezPro claimed that it was able to maintain objectivity across firms and create comparable rankings by making metrics objective and unambiguous; for example, a site either offers Saturday telephone customer service or it does not. The rankings were posted on the Watchfire GómezPro website, and high-scoring companies also often posted their rankings prominently on their website. Since being acquired by IBM in 2007, the company has discontinued this rating service.

Canadian Snapshots

Using Metrics to Rate Egovernment Maturity

According to a research study by global management consulting firm Accenture Ltd. (released May 4, 2004), Canada ranked number 1 out of 22 countries in egovernment maturity for the fourth consecutive year. The study found Canadian egovernment practices ranked first in all categories, including service breadth, service depth, and customer relationship management (CRM), earning 80 percent out of a possible score of 100—13 percent better than its closest challengers Singapore and the United States.

Accenture's study examined the egovernment practices of 22 countries, including Canada, Australia, the United States, the United Kingdom, Singapore, Brazil, France, and Germany.

Accenture researchers in the countries used the internet to obtain access to 201 services that national governments typically provide in the human services, justice and public safety, revenue, defence, education, transport and motor vehicles, regulation and democracy, procurement, and postal sectors. The researchers focused on the functionality, quality, and maturity of services offered. Services were categorized into three levels—publish, interact, and transact—reflecting the level of service maturity. Services also were evaluated on the basis of the extent to which the government used CRM to manage its customer (citizen and business) interactions. Scores in these areas were combined, with 70 percent weighting allocated to service maturity and 30 percent weighting to CRM, to derive an overall rating for the maturity of egovernment services.

In addition, telephone interviews were conducted with senior executives in agencies with customer-facing

>

responsibilities for welfare, immigration, revenue, licensing, and employment services in a subset of the target countries. This research was supplemented with information about the egovernment environment in each of the countries, including details about the country's egovernment program, recent political and legal developments related to egovernment, and other details about the processes being used to implement egovernment.

According to Graeme Gordon, an Ottawa-based partner with Accenture's government practice in Canada, the nation has earned its top spot based on the fact that its egovernment vision is predicated on customer centricity and a "whole of government" approach, which incorporates the different levels of government to deliver the best possible service to the user community.

"Canada's action plan is built on a solid foundation of fact based on the known information from the customer base," Gordon said. "It regularly surveys citizens and businesses for indications of attitudes and needs, and the processes [Canada] has appear to be the most extensive compared to other countries in the survey, in terms of gathering and understanding the needs of the citizens."

Canada also actively markets its egovernment services. It advertises on TV and radio, and it places ads in airline magazines and newspapers to get citizens to use the Government of Canada site.

However, despite Canada's leading role in egovernance, the study found that advances in maturity on the whole are slowing down around the globe and even countries like Canada—with the most advanced egovernment practices—have a long way to go to achieve dramatic results.

Government of Canada
www.canada.gc.ca

Questions

1. Should the Canadian government be spending tax dollars on external consultants to evaluate egovernment services? Why?

2. What are the strengths and weaknesses of the scorecard used to evaluate egovernment maturity?

3. How can metrics be used to address the finding that advances in egovernment maturity are slowing down?

Sources: C. Suppa, "Study: Canadian Egov Maturity Ranks First Globally," Industry Standard, May 5, 2004, www.thestandard.com/article.php?story=20040505163338275, accessed May 25, 2004; "The Government Executive Series: eGovernment Leadership: High Performance, Maximum Value" (research paper); "eGovernment Leadership: Engaging the Customer Study" (news release), www.sagepub.co.uk/resources/heeks/MEgovOnlineApp%20Refs%20edit.doc, accessed September 20, 2007; E. Chabrow, "Canada Is Still No. 1 in Egovernment Rankings,"*InformationWeek* (May 6, 2004).

SOURCES OF INFORMATION

Users browsing a website, users clicking on banner ads, users interacting with surveys; and shoppers making product selections, shoppers making purchases, shoppers contacting customer service—all these customer activities can be tracked and analyzed to better understand customer behaviour and align the design of the ebusiness with customer behaviour. The data for all the analyses discussed in this chapter are available from four main sources. The most obvious source is user-stored data found in cookies and electronic wallets. The next most-used source is the data found in web server log files. A third key source is the transaction databases that record information about sales. A fourth source is the user profile databases created by the entity or infomediaries.

Click-Stream Analysis

Click-stream analysis is a method by which a user's path through a website can be tracked and analyzed. The key here is to analyze the data to identify important trends, such as difficulty in finding specific sites or information, searches that yielded no results, or constant "back" movement through the site. By analyzing click-stream data, an ebusiness can identify website design errors, which can be corrected before other customers run into

click-stream analysis: A method by which a user's path through a website can be tracked and analyzed.

them. In other circumstances, click-stream analysis may be correlated with other factors about the customer, such as personal demographics or industry of employment, that may lead to the discovery of trends related to specific target markets. For example, the correlation of user registration data (such as industry type) or other, offline information with click-stream analysis may lead an organization to the conclusion that its website is not organized in a manner well suited to particular industries. The site could then be reworked to better suit specific industries, or a specialized design could be developed to address this problem.

Cookies

cookie: A small text file stored by a website on an individual computer that allows the site to track the movements of a visitor.

Click-stream data is enabled by a number of technologies. **Cookies** are small text files stored by a website on individual computers that allow the site to track the movements of a visitor. Cookies are often added to an individual's computer the first time that a site is visited and can track a great deal of information, such as time spent on a site, passwords, shopping cart information, preferences, and the most recent site visited.

The use of cookies can personalize a website, by remembering the user's profile and organizing the website's presentation. Privacy concerns have often been raised about cookies; however, many people are satisfied that they are not harmful and do not invade privacy. The primary concern over cookies is the fact that they are stored on the user's computer and can potentially provide information regarding other sites visited, preferences, and shopping habits. However, information in a cookie is not generally readable by anyone except the entity that placed it there; it is typically numbers and letters that would mean nothing to anyone except when it is combined with the information that is already stored on the web server side. The use of cookies as an online technology has become standard practice but will continue to evolve as privacy concerns are worked out.

The privacy concerns tend to relate to the use of cookies to analyze the user's shopping habits and create targeted marketing. For example, after searching for several books related to golfing on Chapters Indigo's website, a user may notice that the banner ads on the site are for several golf-related products and that featured books the next time the user visits the site are golf related. The personalization of websites by this means can be beneficial to the user, but to some it is too intrusive to be acceptable. Privacy concerns are considered more fully in chapter 13.

It is important to note that data stored in a cookie can be easily erased by the user, or the user can decide not to accept cookies at all. Therefore, cookies are often used to store non-critical data such as personalization for anonymous users, log-in information (log-in name only, not password), the date the user last logged on, and so forth.

Electronic Wallets

electronic wallet: A file that securely stores a user's information, such as name, address, credit card number, and ship-to address, for frequent use in executing ecommerce transactions.

Electronic wallets are a more elaborate version of cookies, because a cookie may only have two or three items of information, whereas a wallet could contain quite a bit more information. Electronic wallets initially provided a more secure method to transmit credit card information over the internet, but have evolved to more general uses as well. An electronic wallet could contain the user's credit card number, name, address, ship-to address, and so forth. Having that information available in an electronic wallet would be particularly useful for a frequent shopper, because it would eliminate the necessity of having to retype that information each and every time the user wanted to buy something. Also, wallet information could be kept very secure at a specially designated storage location that is neither at the online store nor on the user's own computer (where it could be perhaps read by someone who has access to the computer). The use of an authority for storing digital wallets can provide both security and convenience when shopping.

Several different versions of wallets are competing to become the standard. In the end there may be two or three different types of wallets. Some may be stored locally on the user's computer, whereas others, particularly ones involving financial transactions, might be stored at the bank. For example, a user's wallet could be stored at the Royal Bank in a database. If the user were shopping at Chapters Indigo, then, instead of Chapters Indigo requiring the user to type in a list of information, it would ask the user for his or her key. Chapters Indigo would use that secret key to contact the bank, which would in turn use it to process the payment transaction, and then transmit payment directly from the Royal Bank to Chapters and deduct the amount from the user's account. Encryption techniques would make sure that users can send the key but can't read the key.

Web Server Log Files

Log files contain details of every action that has occurred on a website, and they are some of the most widely used data sources for traffic analysis. Web server log files are text files stored on a web server. Every line represents a hit containing the following information: HTTP request, date, time, operating system, browser type, and referrer URL. The referrer URL is the source that that request came from. This information is very useful. With just this little information an entity can determine where a visitor came from, whether it was a referral from a banner ad or another advertising vendor. Other information that can be retrieved from the log includes, for example, which browsers people are using (Internet Explorer, Netscape, Firefox, etc.), or which operating systems people are using (Macintosh, Windows, Unix, Linux, etc.).

log file: A file stored on a web server containing details of every action that has occurred.

Log file analysis is the process of analyzing information regarding the movements of users throughout a site based upon data captured in server log files, and can be carried out by a number of means, including basic database techniques or advanced internet-based products such as those offered by WebTrends (see figure 12.1 on page 282 for an illustration of a sample WebTrends display).

log file analysis: The process of analyzing information regarding the movements of users throughout a site based upon data captured in server log files.

Log files are often used for other purposes, not just for performance analysis. Log files are often used to recover from a system failure. If a server crashes while processing a transaction, the log file can be used to reprocess the transaction or at least to get the system back to the state it was in before it crashed.

Web Bugs

Web bugs (also known as **clear GIFs**) are image files embedded into a webpage that can track user movements without the user knowing. Essentially, web bugs are clear images, or images that blend in with the background of a page you are viewing. The web bug sends information to a server (belonging to the company itself or an advertising firm) each time you request a new page and thus tracks your movements. This allows the analyzing

web bug (clear GIF): An image file embedded in a webpage that can track user movements without the user's knowledge.

firm to understand your movements throughout the site and is one method of capturing click-stream data.

Transaction Databases

A transaction database is an accounting data file that keeps track of items that were sold, the quantity, the means of settlement, the terms, the date, and so on. This type of information can be useful for understanding shopper behaviour. However, the richness of the information contained in such a database is implementation-specific. As in the case of user profile data, there will be explicit data reflecting the transaction and implicit data inferred by analysis of the user's behaviour. Such inferences may require the use of business intelligence or data-mining tools to identify key patterns of interest to the entity.

User Profile Databases

The user profile database contains information about visitors and shoppers. (There are many more visitors than there are shoppers.) The database can contain explicit data provided by users; for example, these data might include information about their address, their name, or their age, if they answered requests for this information on forms or provided information in their electronic wallet. The database could also have implicit data, data that is inferred by analysis of user characteristics, as described previously. Such inferences may require the use of data-mining tools to identify key patterns of interest to the entity.

Social Media and Networks

social media: blogs, opinion sites, chat rooms, photo, music, video and game sharing sites and other sites promoting social interaction

Social media includes blogs, opinion sites, chat rooms, photo, music, video and game sharing sites and other sites promoting social interaction. The best-known social networking websites are Facebook, Twitter, and Digg, but there are many others, including many outside North America. These media contain an enormous number of continuous interactions and conversations that can be mined to extract a wealth of information on the topics of the conversations, the location of conversations of interest, the sentiment (positive/neutral/negative) expressed in the conversation of interest, the **influencers** (influential individuals or websites) affecting the conversations, the media involved (blog, video, etc.), and the trends in all of these over time. The use of data-capture, data-mining, and text-analysis tools may be required to handle the information spun off by social media and social networking websites. Infomediaries may be another alternative for obtaining access to the constant stream of data generated by social media and social networking websites and to derive meaningful information from them.

influencer: individual or website that is at the hub of conversations

Infomediaries

Infomediaries are organizations that monitor, analyze, and report on web activity for a fee. There are numerous organizations that track important metrics ranging from traffic on the web to ebusiness performance to industry performance to financial reports. The best-known web analysis entities are Coremetrics (IBM), Google, Omniture (Adobe) WebTrends, and Yahoo!. Market research is provided by organizations such as BizRate, comScore, Nielsen/NetRatings. Analyst reports are available from market research entities such as Forrester Research, Jupitermedia Corporation, Aberdeen Group, Frost & Sullivan, and IDC. Finally, financial information is available from EDGAR Online Inc., Standard & Poor's, and other providers.

Ebusiness in Global Perspective

NPR Online

During the summer of 2004, National Public Radio (NPR) began receiving email messages from customers saying that they wanted podcasts. It also found that the term "podcast" was one of the most-searched terms on its website, NPR.org. By August 31 of that year, NPR had launched podcasts on its site.

Within six days of the launch, NPR's "Story of the Day" podcast reached the number 1 spot on iTunes for most downloaded podcast. By the end of November, the company's podcasts held down 11 spots on the iTunes Top 100—more than any other media outlet.

NPR is providing its own content but is also hosting podcasts for member stations, and selling and splitting underwriting revenues with them. The company saw this as a chance to find a new business model for working with stations. Previously, NPR's income was split evenly from fees paid for content by member stations. Podcasting gave NPR a new model for selling underwriting, and sharing the proceeds with stations.

The most popular NPR podcasts have been "best of"-type offerings, such as NPR Movies, NPR Technology, and NPR Music, which take content from various radio shows on the same topic. That makes it easier to sell to underwriters interested in a particular topic.

NPR believes that shorter content has been more popular than longer content, perhaps because people listening to podcasts are multi-tasking and don't have the attention for long-form content. A case in point is the "Story of the Day" podcast, which runs from four to eight minutes.

One media observer said that media companies usually make the fundamental mistake of looking at things as the adjunct to the core product that they're providing, and not as a fundamental shift in the way that they are creating media itself. The appeal of podcasting appears to be that it is a unique, independent niche-programming method that differs considerably from mainstream programming.

The Challenges of Podcasting

Several issues must be dealt with before a podcasting line of business can be relied on to make money. First, anyone who sells advertising usually has to have metrics on the audience, such as who is listening, how often, and the demographics of the listeners. The problem with podcasts is that there is currently no way to track who actually listens to them. Just because someone subscribes to a podcast doesn't mean he or she actually downloads it or listens to it.

NPR hopes to get listener information when technology companies can solve the metrics issue, as long as it doesn't invade personal privacy.

There is also bandwidth cost to consider. The more popular a podcast, the more it costs to support downloads. Since NPR.org had already been serving streaming audio for some time, it could negotiate good bandwidth deals with vendors.

Another issue is the intrusiveness of ads on podcasts, which is a medium born in part out of people's frustration with the ad saturation of broadcast radio. Most podcasts have toned down the commercialism, and tried to use more low-key sponsorships and spots voiced by the host. NPR had an advantage in this respect because it was already used to using less intrusive ads in its radio and web programming.

NPR's research indicated that listeners wanted something different than was offered by mainstream media. They wanted interesting advertising and to be involved in the process.

National Public Radio (NPR)
www.npr.org

Questions

1. What metrics were involved in launching the podcasting initiative of NPR.org?

2. What metrics could be used to gauge the success of NPR.org's podcasting business?

Sources: www.npr.org; M. Glaser, "Will NPR's Podcasts Birth a New Business Model for Public Radio?" Online Journalism Review, November 29, 2005, www.ojr.org/ojr/stories/051129glaser/index.cfm, accessed July 4, 2007.

CHAPTER SUMMARY

The internet enables an unprecedented degree of activity measurement. Ebusiness performance can be measured in several ways, ranging from measures of traffic on an ecommerce site, to measures of customer behaviour, and ultimately, to measures of ebusiness effectiveness.

Performance metrics linked to specific objectives can help management achieve its strategic objectives by providing guidance, motivating performance, analyzing outcomes, and holding personnel accountable for their actions. However, metrics must be synchronized with business realities, should be unambiguous, and should involve a reasonable cost. Click fraud represents a challenge to the use of metrics.

Metrics used to assess performance of ecommerce websites fall into six main categories: traffic and site usage metrics, social network metrics, marketing metrics, financial metrics, other performance metrics, and multi-dimensional scorecards. Traffic metrics can be based on hits, page views, ad views, visits, visitors, users, time spent and search engine rank. Site usage metrics can be spatial and temporal measures of traffic in various sections of an ecommerce website.

Social networks lend themselves to measures of the nature and amount of dialogue, advocacy, customer support and innovation. Metrics include share of voice, audience engagement, conversation reach, satisfaction and sentiment, as well as influence, reach and impact.

Marketing success metrics such as the click-through rate and conversion rate are widely used as are metrics that provide information about sources of visits, visitor shopping behaviour, user profiles, and product purchase patterns.

Financial metrics provide information about revenues, expenses, and return on investment. Other performance metrics measure website availability, processing integrity, service quality, and so on. Multi-dimensional scorecards attempt to bring a number of metrics together for use in performance assessment to prevent the excessive focus on one particular category of metrics.

There are many sources of information for metrics, including click-stream analysis, cookies, electronic wallets, web server log files, web bugs, transaction databases, user profile databases, social media and networks and infomediaries.

Key Terms

ad views (p. 280)

click-stream analysis (p. 291)

click fraud (p. 278)

click-through rate (p. 285)

conversation (p. 283)

conversion rate (p. 286)

cookie (p. 292)

electronic wallet (p. 292)

hit (p. 280)

influencer (p. 294)

log file (p. 293)

log file analysis (p. 293)

page view (p. 280)

pay-per-action (p. 286)

pay-per-call (p. 286)

search engine ranking (p. 281)

sentiment (p. 283)

social media (p. 294)

social networking website (p. 283)

time (p. 281)

user (p. 280)

visit (p. 280)

web bug (clear GIF) (p. 293)

MyEbusinessLab — Tools for Online Learning

To help you master the material in this chapter and stay up to date with new developments in ebusiness, visit the MyEBusinessLab at www.pearsoned.ca/myebusinesslab. Resources include the following:

- **Pre- and Post-Test Questions**
- **Additional Chapter Questions**
- **Author Blog**
- **Recommended Readings**
- **Commentaries on Current Trends**
- **Additional Topics in Ebusiness**
- **Internet Exercises**
- **Glossary Flashcards**

Endnotes

1. "Do Gamers Actually Notice Ads? Proof Is at Hand," *Globe and Mail*, June 3, 2008.

2. D. Paddon, "Air Canada Suit Adds WestJet CEO Clive Beddoe, Others as Defendants in Suit," www.cp.org/english/online/full/Business/041105/b1105122A.html [link no longer active], accessed December 5, 2004.

3. www.businessweek.com/magazine/content/06_40/b4003001.htm.

4. C.C. Mann, "How Click Fraud Could Swallow the Internet," Wired 14.01, January 2006, www.wired.com/wired/archive/14.01/fraud.html.

5. J. Fine, "Rankings: A New Web Order," *BusinessWeek*, July 30, 2007, 22

6. B. Eisenberg and J. Novo, "The Marketer's Common Sense Guide to E-Metrics" (white paper), http://download.netiq.com/CMS/WHITEPAPER/NetIQ_WP_WRC_MarketersGuidetoEMetrics.pdf, accessed May 9, 2004.

7. R.D. Hof, "So Many Ads, So Few Clicks," *BusinessWeek*, November 12, 2007, 38.

8. D. Koenig, "Pay-per-Call Advertising Gets Kudos for Luring Web Surfers," *Globe and Mail*, September 8, 2005, B15.

9. R. Kaplan and D. Norton. "The Balanced Scorecard—Measures That Drive Performance," *Harvard Business Review* (January–February 1992): 71–79.

Chapter 13

Privacy, Legal, and Taxation Issues in Ecommerce

Learning Objectives

When you complete this chapter you should be able to:

1 Explain the importance of law in the context of ebusiness and ecommerce.

2 Identify and describe the major issues surrounding internet privacy and solutions and technologies that have been proposed to address them.

3 Discuss how organizations can comply with privacy legislation.

4 Describe how intellectual property issues impact ecommerce.

5 Identify the major legal issues that companies need to be concerned with on the internet and solutions that have been proposed to address them.

6 Discuss the taxation issues that ecommerce has created.

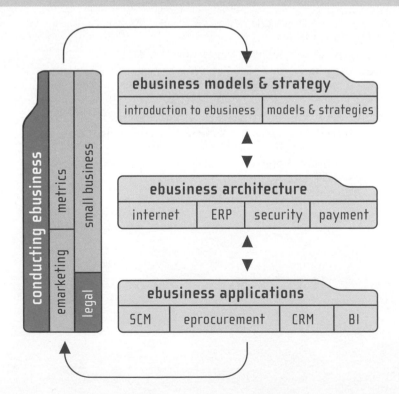

INTRODUCTION

THE RAPID GROWTH IN ECOMMERCE AND THE INCREASE IN GLOBALIZATION OVER THE PAST several years have given rise to several new issues in the areas of law and taxation. The legal and tax systems of Canada and most countries worldwide were not designed for the complications of commerce conducted through electronic means. While the existing legal system had previously addressed many issues similar to those raised by ecommerce, the legislation and legal infrastructure have numerous areas where the concerns over ecommerce are not well addressed. Substantial effort has been directed to legal and taxation issues related to ecommerce in the past few years, and progress has been made; however, there remains a great deal of change to be made in the future. This chapter will review the issues, progress, and remaining challenges of the law and ecommerce.

The concerns over ecommerce legal issues were perhaps brought to the forefront by the Napster situation, although it focused on only one major area of concern—intellectual property. The Napster service was essentially brought to a halt by the rulings of the court system, which stated that the music-copying application violated the intellectual property rights of musical artists and other copyright owners by allowing the illegal copying of MP3 files. As an important and developing area, intellectual property issues such as copyright, trademarks, domain names, and patents are all being addressed by the legal systems within countries worldwide.

The improvements in technology and ecommerce applications have given rise to serious concerns over privacy on the internet. The tracking of users and potential identification of individuals through technology threatens the right to privacy of all internet users, and thus is a growing area of importance. The Canadian federal government has also addressed the issue of privacy through comprehensive legislation, as discussed in more detail below. Other countries and international organizations are also monitoring issues with regards to privacy, and many have adopted similar legislation and guidelines that both consumers and businesses need to be aware of.

The legal system is also addressing numerous other issues with regard to ecommerce. Some of the principal concerns are in relation to jurisdictional issues, which also impact taxation. In addition, electronic contracts, enforcement, liability, and unfair competition issues all arise as the use of the internet and globalization of commerce change the competitive landscape of business. These issues will be discussed throughout this chapter with an aim to highlight areas of importance for management of ebusinesses—in specific cases, it is important to consult professional legal counsel.

INTERNET PRIVACY

THE CONCERNS OVER PRIVACY HAVE GROWN IMMENSELY AS ECOMMERCE HAS DEVELOPED AND consumers and businesses have found themselves providing a growing amount of information to often-unknown sources. The major concerns in this regard are wide-ranging, since many types of private information could impact employment, personal finances, and other aspects of life. For example, medical information is a key privacy concern. Imagine if an individual's medical records became available to a potential employer when that individual had a serious illness—the individual could be turned down for a job based on what should be confidential information. In less serious cases of privacy infringement, advertisers may gather details about an individual and flood that person with ads and other information—a major annoyance. Despite the severity of the issue, two things are certain—individuals have a right to privacy, and the internet has changed the landscape in which privacy must be protected.

Information of a personal nature can be gathered through numerous means over the internet. For example, while surfing the web, users' movements can be tracked by the use of cookies, web bugs, and other tracking tools, as described earlier in this book. Other data/information can be collected or revealed about an individual through chat groups, news boards, or email. The number of potential sources of information available makes it quite possible that a person's privacy can be inappropriately handled through the internet. The ability of online businesses to gather data has also been complicated by the issue of merging the online data with offline data, as was the case with DoubleClick. DoubleClick was essentially given the approval to merge data—with the exception of medical and financial information—as long as users are made aware of the use and have the ability to opt-out.

The increasing concerns over privacy have led to the development of legislation within Canada and abroad. The Canadian government developed the Personal Information Protection and Electronic Documents Act (originally Bill C-54, and later introduced and approved as Bill C-6) as a component of Canada's ecommerce strategy. The strategy recognized that one important component of assisting Canada to become a world leader in ecommerce was to instill confidence in the internet through legislation and other means.[1] The **Personal Information Protection and Electronic Documents Act (PIPEDA)**, which came into full effect on January 1, 2004, provides privacy protection for personal information.

PIPEDA is federal legislation that applied initially to federally regulated organizations, including airlines, banks, telephone companies, and broadcasting companies. In addition, all businesses in Nunavut, the Yukon, and the Northwest Territories were subject to the act as of January 1, 2001. The second phase of implementation for PIPEDA took effect on January 1, 2002, when all organizations that collect, use, or disclose personal health information come under the legislation. The final phase of implementation was January 1, 2004, when the act became applicable to all commercial activity,[2] unless a firm is operating in a province that has passed privacy legislation that is substantially similar to the federal legislation—an attempt by the federal government to encourage harmonization within Canada. The standards for assessing substantial similarity were established by the privacy commissioner of Canada. As of January 2004, British Columbia, Alberta, and Quebec had all passed provincial private-sector privacy legislation, and by November 2004 all three had been reviewed and deemed to be substantially similar by the federal privacy commissioner. Ontario has passed the Personal Health Information Protection Act, which was declared substantially similar to PIPEDA by the federal privacy commissioner in November 2005. However, Ontario has yet to pass privacy legislation that would govern the private sector in Ontario, so PIPEDA still applies to most Ontario-based ecommerce websites.

PIPEDA is designed to protect any personal information that is collected, used, or disclosed within the private sector. The privacy rights of Canadians with regard to the personal information collected, used, or disclosed by federal governmental organizations are protected by the Privacy Act (1983). Most of the provinces have similar legislation in effect with regard to provincial government organizations. **Personal information** is defined within the act as information that could identify an individual and could

PIPEDA on the Web
www.priv.gc.ca

Personal Information Protection and Electronic Documents Act (PIPEDA): Canadian legislation that has provided privacy protection for personal information since coming into full effect on January 1, 2004.

personal information: Information that could identify an individual and could potentially be used to discriminate against that person or invade his or her privacy.

potentially be used to discriminate against that person or invade his or her privacy, such as the following:

- name, age, weight, and height
- medical records
- income, purchases, and spending habits
- race, ethnic origin, and colour
- blood type, DNA code, and fingerprints
- marital status and religion
- education
- home address and phone number[3]

The definition of personal information covers each of these specific items to ensure that individuals' privacy is respected and not used inappropriately. The misuse of this information can lead to inappropriate business practices, identity theft, and discrimination, and is therefore of critical importance.

The privacy principles within PIPEDA were based upon the 1996 standards established by the Canadian Standards Association (CSA) in its Model Code for the Protection of Personal Information. This code, similar to the subsequent legislation, established the rights of individuals to access personal information about themselves held by organizations, and to have that information corrected if it is incorrect.

The 10 principles included in the CSA code are as follows:

1. *Accountability*—Organizations are responsible for all personal information under their control and shall establish procedures to ensure that the organization complies with all of the 10 principles.
2. *Identifying purposes*—Organizations will identify the purpose for which they are collecting personal information to individuals prior to or at the time that the information is collected.
3. *Consent*—The individual must give consent to the collection, use, or disclosure of their personal information.
4. *Limiting collection*—All information must be collected by fair and legal means and should be limited to information deemed necessary by the organization for the purposes outlined to the individual.
5. *Limiting use, disclosure, and retention*—The use of personal information should be limited to the purposes outlined to the individual at the time of collection unless further consent is obtained and information should only be retained for as long as deemed necessary by the terms outlined.
6. *Accuracy*—Organizations shall keep personal information accurate, complete, and up-to-date.
7. *Safeguards*—Appropriate security and internal controls should be in place to protect personal information.
8. *Openness*—Organizations should make their policies readily available to individuals with regard to the handling of personal information.
9. *Individual access*—Individuals have the right to request whether information about them exists and to request the ability to review that information and challenge its accuracy and completeness.

10. *Challenging compliance*—Individuals are able to address their concerns over compliance with the above principles to a designated individual or individuals. In the Canadian context this principle now leads ultimately to the privacy commissioner, who has the right to investigate concerns where individuals do not receive satisfaction from the company or organization itself.[4]

The principles set out in the CSA code are, of course, only a set of guidelines that can be interpreted differently by different organizations and individuals. The PIPEDA legislation was intended to give the privacy commissioner the authority to handle complaints related to privacy when individuals are not satisfied with the outcome of their discussions with an organization. One recent example of the type of dispute over interpretation that can arise with the legislation involved a 2009 PIPEDA investigation of an online discount air ticket seller. The ecommerce site required all ticket purchasers to provide their exact month and year of birth for the purpose of providing an insurance quote that the purchaser could opt to purchase, in addition to the ticket itself. Although the insurance purchase was optional, it was impossible to purchase a ticket without providing the exact month and year of birth. A purchaser who provided the information but declined the optional insurance subsequently found this personal information included on an e-mail confirming her ticket purchase. When she complained to the air ticket seller, she was told that this information had to be collected as the seller was required by law to make an offer of insurance purchase to the customer. The complainant was not satisfied and made a complaint under PIPEDA to the federal privacy commissioner's office. Upon investigation, it was determined that it was not necessary to obtain exact month and year of birth information and that less detailed age information would suffice to meet the legal obligations that had been identified by the business. This decision focused on the fourth principle: limiting collection, specifically allowing an organization to collect only information that is necessary for the purposes outlined. In addition, the investigation also identified that the business did not have a privacy policy, which was also deemed a violation of principle four. This case illustrates how privacy issues can be an ongoing concern for business even when they are making an effort to be privacy compliant.[5]

Canadian Snapshots

Canada's Privacy Commissioner vs. Facebook

In mid-2009, Canada's privacy commissioner, Jennifer Stoddart, ruled that Facebook had failed to adequately respond to certain allegations about its practices that contravened federal privacy law. Stoddart gave Facebook a month to address concerns in four areas:

Limits on disclosure of information to add-in programs to that necessary for the add-in programs to function. (Users of add-in programs were required to share all their information except for contact information if they wanted to use one of Facebook's 350,000 add-in programs, such as Mafia Wars, a game with millions of users around the world.)

Better disclosure, transparency, and protection related to activating and deleting accounts.

Better handling of accounts of deceased users.

Limits on the collection of personal information of non-users.

The privacy commissioner was responding to a complaint against the company brought in May 2008 by the Canadian Internet Policy and Public Interest Clinic (CIPPIC). Canada's privacy commissioner was the first regulator to investigate Facebook's privacy practices. The report issued by the Elizabeth Denham, assistant privacy commissioner of Canada, was hailed as a comprehensive, high-quality

>

investigation. Although the privacy commissioner's jurisdiction was limited to Canada, the ruling would have a global impact because of Facebook's global operations.

The settlement reached at the time seemed to have brought the matter to a close, but in May 2010, Facebook introduced several changes to make it easier for companies to access customer information and track their internet activity and harder for Facebook users to protect their data. These changes drew criticism from privacy advocates in Canada, Europe, and the United States. Mark Zuckerberg denied that these changes were intentional, stating that the intention was to give users lots of granular controls, which unintentionally made it confusing and more difficult to manage privacy settings. He promised to introduce simpler privacy controls.

Since then, a new privacy concern has come to light in the form of the Like button. Initially, the Like button was available only to Facebook users who clicked the button to share with friends their opinions about pictures, videos and other information. Facebook then offered the Like button to outside websites, exposing some users' likes without their awareness or consent.

One analyst warned that if Facebook doesn't focus all its efforts on securing its users' personal information, it risks becoming obsolete. Others, however, point out that being online in almost any way involves a loss of privacy and hence a potential risk.

Office of the Privacy Commissioner of Canada
www.priv.gc.ca

Questions

1. Why are regulators around the world so concerned about internet privacy issues in general and, in particular, privacy practices of social networking sites? Is it a contradiction to harp on privacy issues at social networking sites such as Facebook that are designed for the express purpose of sharing personal information?

2. Are social networking sites truly concerned about their users' privacy, or are they playing cat and mouse with regulators by continuously inventing new technologies aimed at helping advertisers and other paying customers access Facebook users' data?

3. Can adequate privacy protections be provided on social networking sites? How?

Sources: K. Bardeesy, "Profit vs. Privacy: Ottawa Takes on Social Media Giant for Violating Canada's Laws," *Globe and Mail*, July 17, 2009, A1, A4; M. Ingram, "Welcome to the Social Network, Where Your Privacy Has to Be Flexible," *Globe and Mail*, July 17, 2009, A1, A4; O. El Akkad and J. McNish, "Facebook Backs Down," *Globe and Mail*, May 26, 2010; J. McNish, "Facebook's 'Like' Button Raises Privacy Concerns," *Globe and Mail*, September 23, 2010; Assistant Privacy Commissioner of Canada, *Report of Findings into the Complaint Filed by the Canadian Internet Policy and Public Interest Clinic (CIPPIC) Against Facebook Inc. Under the Personal Information Protection and Electronic Documents Act by Elizabeth Denham*, July 16, 2009, www.priv.gc.ca/cf-dc/2009/2009_008_0716_e.cfm.

Establishing a Privacy Policy

The enactment of PIPEDA has led to the need for all businesses and organizations to establish a privacy policy that can be disclosed and communicated to internet users and customers. To comply with the principles in the act and to provide customers with relevant information, the webpages of many businesses now include a "Privacy Policy" link that leads to a full disclosure of the company's policy. For example, Bell Canada would have had to comply with PIPEDA and establish a privacy policy and other disclosures on its website, as shown in figure 13.1, prior to January 1, 2001, because it is a federally regulated organization. (Since 2004 PIPEDA has applied to all businesses engaged in commercial activity in Canada.) Included in the privacy policy is a discussion of the types of information collected by Bell, the companies that may share the information (related parties), and an opt-out clause to prevent sharing with other subsidiary firms. The privacy policy also discusses the company's use of cookies, observes that it fully complies with PIPEDA, and discloses how customers may direct their concerns both inside and outside the company (e.g., the privacy commissioner's office).

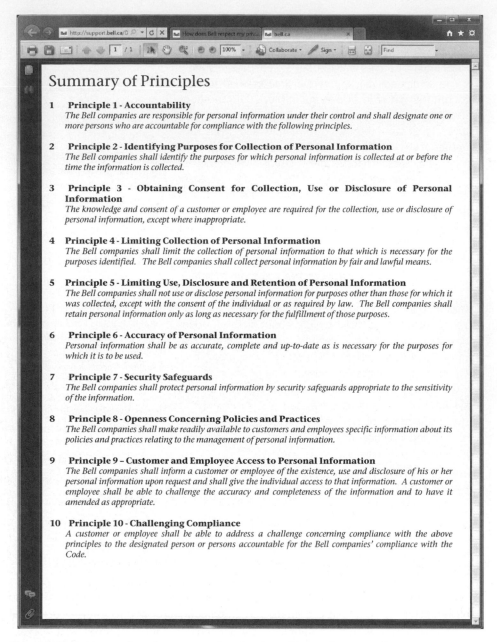

Figure 13.1 Example of an organization's online privacy policy

Bell's website includes detailed information about its privacy policy to users and discusses the means by which users may address their complaints or concerns.

Source: Bell's Privacy Principles extracted from Bell's Code of Fair Information Practices. Courtesy BCE IP Group.

Other Privacy Legislation

The development of legislation in Canada and other countries has been somewhat pressured by the lead taken with regard to privacy in Europe. The European Union's Privacy Directive went into effect in 1998 and established relatively strong privacy regulations for members of the European Union (EU). In addition, the legislation restricts the flow of personal information outside the EU by permitting its transfer only to countries that provide an "adequate" level of privacy protection.

Prior to the enactment of PIPEDA, Canada had little protection for privacy. However, once PIPEDA was passed, the EU approved the federal legislation as "adequate" for the purposes of transferring personal information held by EU-governed organizations to Canada-based organizations governed by PIPEDA. However, other countries, such as the United States, were primarily using policies of self-regulation or sector-specific legislation. The EU's approach led to extended negotiations with the United States and many other countries to establish what has become known as the "safe harbour" agreement.[6] Agreed upon in July 2000, the safe harbour provisions allow for specific companies to be certified as complying with the EU requirements by becoming voluntarily compliant. This will permit U.S. businesses to obtain personal information from EU businesses and effectively conduct business in EU nations.

A new legislative initiative on the horizon in the United States is a "do not track" registry. This initiative is a response to complaints about the extensive use of online tracking for behavioural targeting purposes by advertisers, as discussed in chapters 11 and 12. Analogous to the "do not call" registry that exists for telemarketing, the "do not track" registry would enable users who wanted to opt out of all marketing programs to register on a specified website. Marketers would be required to check the registry and remove potential targets from their marketing programs or face penalties. A bill has not been introduced yet, but hearings have been held about this matter.

Another major issue of concern in the privacy area is the protection of privacy for children. The internet is an open network, and many children have become avid users. While children can often learn to use the internet quite quickly, they are less likely to understand the risks and concerns over privacy protection than adults are. The U.S. government passed the Children's Online Privacy Protection Act, which established privacy requirements for websites that target children. The Children's Online Privacy Protection Act applies not only to U.S. sites but to any website that is perceived to be targeting U.S. children and, therefore, can have wide-reaching effects on the operation of any website in Canada or elsewhere. For example, a toy company established in Canada may decide to sell into the United States to expand its market. If that company's website could conceivably be used by children and aims to sell to that market, the company must be aware of the Children's Online Privacy Protection Act and its implications on information collection and use. The growth in concerns over privacy protection will continue to give rise to legislation and policies that businesses must consider as they operate outside their own country's boundaries through the internet.

Privacy and Wireless Devices

The increasing use of wireless technologies is bringing additional privacy concerns to the forefront. Users of cellphones, personal digital assistants (PDAs), and other wireless devices may be subject to all of the concerns over internet privacy but may also be subject to additional concerns. The use of wireless technology can potentially allow a user's exact location and movements to be tracked, in addition to websites visited, telephone calls placed, and other information transferred. These issues are of critical importance, as an individual's location and activities are very private information that needs to be protected from misuse.

The use of wireless technologies also brings with it concerns over security. The security of internet access through telephone, cable, and other access methods has been developing for several years, and just as users are beginning to feel comfortable with these systems, wireless has added a new dimension. Consider the use of a PDA to conduct financial transactions through a bank—requiring the user's password and other personal information to be transmitted. This information now travels through the airwaves, and therefore can be much more susceptible to theft or misuse if appropriate security mechanisms are not in place.

The risks of misuse of wireless technologies and infringement of privacy need to be balanced with what may be considered useful to the individual. For example, some advertisers hope to be able to deliver discounts to wireless devices in the appropriate location, such as in a specific mall. If a wireless user walks into the West Edmonton Mall and receives a list of discounts for various stores in the mall, the advertiser has potentially delivered a valuable service. On the other hand, that delivery indicates that the individual's movements are being tracked by at least one organization (the wireless service provider) and the information could be passed to advertisers or other organizations, potentially compromising the individual's privacy and freedom of movement. These types of privacy concerns will continue to evolve but represent important issues for individual consumers to investigate fully and for organizations to develop policies around.

Privacy and Technologies

The concerns over privacy on the internet have stimulated some entrepreneurs to develop software and applications designed to assist users to avoid privacy issues. David Sobel, then general counsel for the Washington DC-based Electronic Privacy Information Center (and now senior counsel for the Electronic Frontier Foundation), stated, "Technologies that facilitate anonymous use of the internet are really critical to the survival of the internet as an open and democratic forum."[7] The technologies that can be used to protect an individual's privacy online are many, but most attempt to accomplish a similar goal—to make the user an anonymous web surfer.

Software programs that can reduce privacy issues include solutions provided by Anonymizer, SafeWeb (owned by Symantec), IDzap, Somebody, and several others. Such solutions are geared towards allowing users of internet service providers to surf anonymously, by removing information regarding the user's IP address and other identifying information. The software scans all outgoing communications for sensitive or identifiable information to prevent its release without user consent. Users can also release information to trusted parties by asking to unmask some information to complete a purchase or fill out a particular form online. Tor Hidden Services is an open source, free, technology designed to conceal the origins and destinations of data and hence the identity of senders and recipients. The communication is encrypted during transit but its traffic route is not only unknown, but unknowable.[8] See the New Business Models box for a discussion of the privacy protection issue and some of the concerns it raises.

The use of technologies to protect privacy can take numerous forms. Some applications allow users to control cookies and web bugs while surfing the internet. Other programs, such as Webwasher and AdSubtract, can be used to block out banner ads to reduce

Electronic Privacy Information Center
www.epic.org

the amount of advertising one is subjected to. The growing concern over advertising and privacy has led a relatively small percentage of people to sign up for services such as these.

The technological tools that are designed to protect privacy don't come without their costs and complications. Many of these tools can impede the speed of web usage, since information must pass through a specific server and be rerouted to the user. In addition, the tools can require service fees to be paid depending upon the services selected. Cookie management applications can result in the inability to use certain websites altogether, and may limit the capability to use personalization tools and other aspects of some websites. You can see the impact of cookie management by altering the settings within your web browser to "Do not accept cookies" or "Confirm cookies" and surfing through some websites. The disadvantages of privacy protection tools, as described here, are why privacy advocates are pushing for stronger legislative controls to automatically protect users' privacy.

New Business Models
Privacy Fighting at Anonymizer

The technologies of the internet bring both positive and negative changes to the world. One of the most serious concerns in recent history has been the protection of privacy and the rights of individuals to use the web without being tracked and monitored. One of the leading applications for protecting one's privacy online is Anonymizer, Inc.

The ability for employers to track employee use of the internet while at work is an issue that has led to much debate. With no clear legal ruling on the issue, companies like Anonymizer have developed a business model that aids web users in "masking" their identity from employers, governments, ISPs, and even the websites they visit. Anonymizer essentially masks a web surfer's IP address and allows surfers to visit sites that may be banned or controversial.

The use of anonymous surfing technologies has led to concerns by those who seek to protect specific groups from material on the internet. Few would disagree with schools aiming to block children from reaching pornographic material online, but tools like Anonymizer can allow web-savvy students to circumvent the protective controls if those sites themselves are not blocked. Anonymizer has a variety of services, including private surfing, email, chat, and telephony, with the fee for service depending upon the options chosen. Some of its competitors offer similar services—some for free.

Other uses of monitoring and blocking tools online are much more controversial. Many countries and governments severely restrict the use of the internet for citizens and monitor their usage. For example, Saudi Arabia restricts its citizens from accessing material that is pornographic or contrary to the state system by routing all internet traffic through a central server with filter mechanisms. Other countries such as China severely restrict internet use by requiring ISPs to block sites of Western media, Taiwan and Hong Kong newspapers, and human rights groups. From a Western perspective these practices seem questionable, but tools like Anonymizer can allow web users in these countries to circumvent the rules—at least until the government catches up.

The use of Anonymizer and other applications like it (such as SafeWeb) has created much concern for governments in some countries. Essentially, Anonymizer makes it appear to government filters that the user is visiting the IP address of Anonymizer, even if the user actually accesses pornography or other banned materials. Anonymizer simply encrypts the material and uses a framing mechanism to display the user's destination. Attempting to prevent use of this tool, governments have attempted to block access to Anonymizer's IP address. Anonymizer, however, feels that the internet should be an open forum, and to allow users to continue to use its services, it cycles through various domain names and IP addresses so that users effectively stay one step ahead of their governments.

Some governments and employers are likely very upset with applications like Anonymizer, since their ability to control and monitor use of the internet is diminished. Privacy advocates, however, congratulate such services on protecting the rights of individuals and keeping the internet an open medium.

>

INTELLECTUAL PROPERTY

THE ENVIRONMENT OF THE INTERNET, FULL OF "FREE" RESOURCES AND SHARED INFORMATION, has led to a great deal of confusion and controversy surrounding intellectual property. **Intellectual property** is a creation of the mind such as an invention, artistic work, symbol, name, image, or design used in commerce. Intellectual property can be divided into two primary categories—copyright and industrial property. **Copyright** includes literary and artistic works such as books, poems, films, and musical works. **Industrial property** includes patents, trademarks, and other industrial designs.[9] Most countries have dealt with intellectual property law for many years and established laws that have become well interpreted. The internet has changed the circumstances by complicating the issues around intellectual property. See the Estrategy box for a strategy by an internet startup to aid businesses in addressing intellectual property issues.

The issues surrounding intellectual property on the internet have a much wider range than just illegal copying of music files. In fact, there are issues with regard to patents, trademarks, books, and most other forms of intellectual property—both copyright and industrial property.

intellectual property: A creation of the mind such as an invention, artistic work, symbol, name, image, or design used in commerce.

copyright: A category of intellectual property that includes literary and artistic works such as books, poems, films, and musical works.

industrial property: A category of intellectual property that includes patents, trademarks, and other industrial designs.

Trademarks

trademark: A distinguishable feature such as a word, symbol, picture, logo, or design that can be used to identify the products or services of a specific individual or organization.

A **trademark** is a distinguishable feature such as a word, symbol, picture, logo, or design that can be used to identify the products or services of a specific individual or organization. A trademark provides the owner with the exclusive right to use the mark within the jurisdiction of the appropriate governing body.[10] Trademark legislation provides relief to the owner of a trademark where someone has infringed upon the owner's exclusive right to use the mark by using a trademark in a manner that is likely to lead to confusion as to the source of the associated goods or services (i.e., members of the public will believe that the goods of the infringer emanate from the owner of the trademark).

Trademark issues can arise in many ways online. A major area where trademark issues arise is in relation to domain names, which will be discussed further in the following section. In addition to trademark infringements from metatag and domain name use, the legal community has recently demonstrated that trademark use for content or product promotion purposes is also inappropriate.

The issues surrounding trademark law are complex, but some scenarios have demonstrated that many of the traditional rules continue to apply online. A small Canadian software developer from Waterloo, Ontario, Pro-C Ltd., filed a lawsuit against U.S. retail giant Computer City for trademark infringement. Pro-C had registered a domain name (www.wingen.com) and owned a registered trademark in both the United States and Canada (WINGEN). In 1997, Computer City launched a new computer product named "Wingen." The product was offered for sale in the company's stores in the United States and through its website, www.computercity.com. No sales were actually made in Canada. The case turned on what constitutes "use" in Canada.

Since a Canadian trademark registration confers the exclusive right to use the mark in Canada in respect of the associated wares and services, if Computer City was deemed to be using the mark in Canada, then there would be infringement. At trial, the judge departed from the current state of the law as to what constitutes "use" in Canada and stated that "the determination of use in Canada requires a 'holistic approach.'" The trial judge disregarded the language in the Trade-marks Act, which states that there must be use in Canada. The trial judge found Computer City liable for trademark infringement and awarded damages of approximately $1,250,000.

The case was successfully appealed. The Court of Appeal of Ontario overturned the trial decision[11] and noted that infringement in Canada is dependent upon "use" of the registered trademark as that term is defined in the Trade-marks Act. Particularly, the Court of Appeal held that Computer City's passive website could not constitute use in association with wares, because no transfer of ownership was possible through that medium. The mere access by Canadians to a trademark on a website does not necessarily constitute use of that trademark in Canada; there has to be actual commercial activity in Canada.

The ruling indicates that trademark infringement online is as serious as through traditional channels. The jurisdiction of the case was also dealt with, since the Canadian court ruled that the web-based advertising was sufficient to allow a Canadian court the authority to rule.[12] (Jurisdictional issues are discussed further later in this chapter.) The Pro-C case indicates that trademark infringement is a serious matter and that all companies dealing online must take sufficient measures to ensure that they are not inappropriately using trademarks registered in any country to which they could potentially be selling.

Domain Names

The growth in ecommerce and internet startups has led to the registration of many domain names. The original primary domain name extensions established in 1985—.com, .edu, .gov, .mil, .net, and .org—have been heavily used, and a demand emerged for additional extensions. An announcement by ICANN in 2000 resulted in the addition of several new primary domain names: .aero, .biz, .coop, .info, .museum, .name, and .pro. These were intended to increase the ability of organizations to select names related to their business or activity.

Domain names are controlled internationally by InterNIC, which is organized under the U.S. Department of Commerce and it allocates domain name registration for the .com, .org, and .edu domain names. InterNIC also licenses various other organizations around the world to provide these domain names. For example, in Canada, domain names can be purchased from A Technology Inc., Tucows Inc., and ZiD.com, among others. These organizations also provide the .ca domain name for Canadian companies.

InterNIC
www.internic.net

Tucows
http://about.tucows.com

ZiD
www.webhosting-canada.com

A domain name takes a user to a particular IP address, and is, in fact, just a simple way of naming a web server location, in an easy-to-remember format. For example, the domain name for the *Globe and Mail* newspaper is **www.theglobeandmail.com**, and the IP address for that web server is 199.246.67.250. The website can be accessed by entering http://www.theglobeandmail.com or by entering http://199.246.67.250. The domain name is much easier to remember.

Controversies over domain name use have become commonplace over the past several years. The phenomenon of cybersquatting, registering a domain name and using it in bad faith, has caused numerous legal disputes and given rise to both legislation and dispute resolution mechanisms within North America and internationally. The huge number of registrations of the leading domains (such as .com, .net, .org, and .ca) in Canada has led to increased competition and controversy over domain name policies.

The legal system's early attempts to deal with domain name disputes made use of trademark law in a major portion of the decisions made. The use of trademark law to deal with domain disputes, however, has resulted in many complications, since the two concepts may be closely related but are quite distinct. Trademarks are limited in availability, and not all words or marks are available to be registered—this is the key difference between trademarks and domain names. Domain names are by nature unique, can only be held by one owner, and do not need to conform to trademark legislation, as they can take any form (subject to the registrar's rules for length, characters allowed, etc.). For example, surnames such as Smith and general descriptive words such as coffee are not able to be registered as trademarks under the Canadian Trade-marks Act; however, an individual or organization could register the associated domain names—smith.com, smith.ca, coffee.com, coffee.ca, and so on. This distinction made it difficult for the legal system to apply trademark law in settling all domain name issues.

The complications in dealing with domain name disputes gave rise to new legislation in the United States to reduce the difficulty in settling them. A famous case took place in 1994, when a young technology writer noticed that the domain name mcdonalds.com hadn't been registered. When McDonald's Restaurants wanted to register it, it was, of course, taken, and so a legal battle ensued. After much expense, the dispute was settled by McDonald's giving a donation to a charity. After this high-profile case, much better control was exerted over domain name distribution, and now, companies that have trademarked names, such as McDonald's, have priority rights to domain names using those names.

The first piece of legislation to address the issue was the Trademark Dilution Act, which aimed to reduce the requirements of proving that a domain name infringed on a trademark. Prior to this act, a complainant would need to prove that the domain name was using a trademark for commercial purposes and the use was in competition with the trademark owner. This did not adequately allow trademark owners to recover domain names where the use of the domain was not in competition with the owner. For example, under these rules it would be possible to register cokeclassic.com as a domain and use the website to sell t-shirts without "infringing" on the trademark, since the company would not be in competition with Coca-Cola. Noting that this type of use could inhibit the growth of ecommerce and is contrary to the intention of trademark law, the U.S. government enacted the Trademark Dilution Act, effectively removing the requirement to show that the domain holder was in competition with the trademark owner.

The U.S. Congress later enacted a second piece of legislation to further reduce the requirements for trademark holders to prove infringement—the **Anticybersquatting Consumer Protection Act (ACPA)**. The ACPA reduces the trademark holder requirements to simply demonstrating that a domain name has been registered in bad faith and that it has been used in an attempt to make a profit.

The Canadian legal system has not made any specific amendments or enacted new legislation. The domain dispute process has been partially assisted by the establishment of dispute resolution mechanisms. The most influential domain name registrar is the **Internet Corporation for Assigned Names and Numbers (ICANN)**, which controls many of the top-level domains. ICANN is a not-for-profit organization that describes its own responsibilities as "Internet Protocol (IP) address space allocation, protocol identifier assignment, generic and country code domain name system management, and root server system management functions."[13] These services were originally performed under U.S. government contract by the Internet Assigned Numbers Authority (IANA) and other entities.

The Uniform Domain Name Dispute Resolution Policy (UDRP), established by ICANN, only applies to top-level domain names (.com, .org, .gov, .bus, etc.). It functions primarily as a written arbitration system, and has in many cases provided a lower-cost, quicker alternative to court proceedings in blatant cybersquatting situations. However, various aspects of the UDRP have been criticized since it was implemented. The Canadian Internet Registration Authority (CIRA) has also developed a dispute resolution procedure for alleged cases of cybersquatting involving .ca domain names. The **Canadian Internet Registration Authority (CIRA)** is a not-for-profit Canadian corporation that is responsible for operating the .ca internet country code top-level domain. The .ca domain name dispute procedure was developed after the UDRP, and CIRA attempted to address many of the perceived shortcomings with the UDRP during development of the .ca policy.

Metatags

The dispute between former rivals Chapters Online Inc. and Indigo Online Inc. provides a good example of the types of issues that can arise on the internet as competitors strive to gain a captive audience. Chapters had inserted the term "Indigo" within its metatags on its website so that users searching for that term would see the Chapters website listed. As discussed in previous chapters, metatags are sets of keywords in the source code of a HyperText Markup Language (HTML) page that help search engines to categorize websites. Once Indigo discovered that Chapters had used its trademarked name in the metatags, it threatened to sue, and Chapters quickly removed the term from its website. Ironically, these two companies merged in 2001 and combined their affiliate programs and advertising efforts. The issue of metatags has not been completely dealt with in all courts of law, but indications can be drawn from cases completed to date. It appears that the use of any trademarked name in an attempt to draw traffic to a site for commercial purposes is inappropriate. The U.S. court system has ruled on several occasions that use of a trademark within metatags for commercial purposes is trademark infringement.

Some cases have begun to provide guidance as to what is acceptable use of trademarks in metatags within Canada and abroad. For example, in early 2001 a British Columbia court ruled that the use of the trademarked names "British Columbia Automobile Association" within the metatags of a criticism and protest site did not constitute

Anticybersquatting Consumer Protection Act (ACPA): U.S. legislation that requires a trademark holder to simply demonstrate that a domain name has been registered in bad faith and that it has been used in an attempt to make a profit.

Internet Corporation for Assigned Names and Numbers (ICANN): A domain name registrar that holds control over the primary top-level domains.

CIRA
www.cira.ca

Canadian Internet Registration Authority (CIRA): A not-for-profit Canadian corporation that is responsible for operating the .ca internet country code top-level domain.

copyright infringement. Also at issue in the case was the use of the letters BCAA within the domain name of BCAAonstrike.com (not in operation now). The union in the case had been on strike and had established websites to provide public information related to their concerns. The court found that the use of the trademarked terms did not infringe on copyright, primarily based upon three key factors:

1. The domain name was not identical to the trademark and should not create confusion.
2. The union was providing public information and not competing with the BCAA and, therefore, not attempting to take business directly from the trademark owner.
3. The union's site displayed a disclaimer that clearly indicated that the site was not a BCAA site, and the court liked that the disclaimer clearly removed any confusion over the identity of the site owner.[14]

This case appears to give website owners, social activists, and critics the right to use trademarks to attract visitors, as long as the public is not confused as to who the owner is and the content of the site is not defamatory in nature. The right of free speech has been upheld here and provides some guidance for the future.

The British Columbia Automobile Association case has been applied in at least one other case (BC v. Canada Domain Name Exchange Corporation). Thus, the results of this case would appear to provide some guidance to commercial enterprises. The use of a domain name that causes confusion, use of a trademark to lure business away from a competitor, and lack of a disclaimer for discussion of a trademark are all risk factors for commercial enterprises. In general, domain names should not be closely related to another's trademark (as will be discussed shortly), and metatags should not include the trademark of another firm where the nature of the website in question is commercial.

COPYRIGHT

COPYRIGHT IS ONE OF THE IMPORTANT ISSUES IN LAW WITH REGARD TO DIGITAL MEDIA and the use of the internet. Copyright law is designed to protect many different things, such as books, computer programs, music, website content, art, and movies. While it is often assumed that copyright protects ideas, it aims only to protect the embodiment of ideas—that is, their form and presentation. The major means by which copyright can be violated include plagiarism, piracy, bootlegging, and counterfeiting.[15] Each of these violations results in the inappropriate use of another's work for commercial or other purposes. The Canadian Snapshots box gives an example of copyright infringement on the internet.

The Canadian Copyright Act was first written in 1921 and changed substantially in 1988. The increased concern over copyright due to technologies such as photocopiers, fax machines, and computers led to the modifications to the act in 1988. The Copyright Act has been the subject of a few attempted legislative amendments in recent years. Since 2007 two separate bills intending to amend the Copyright Act died on the order paper once Parliament was dissolved. In June 2010 the sitting government brought another bill forward, intending to amend the Copyright Act. At this writing, this bill has not yet been passed into law and, in a minority government situation, it is quite possible that Parliament could be dissolved once again before the bill is passed. Nonetheless, the most recent bill was introduced as a high-profile legislative initiative by the government's Minister of Industry. It attempts to address a number of copyright related issues that have developed with the emergence of the internet, including technological protection measures, recording and subsequent utilization of copyrighted material, international harmonization, and clarifying the roles and responsibilities of internet service providers and search engines with regard to copyright matters.[16]

The Copyright Act provides copyright owners with the "sole and exclusive right to reproduce, perform, or publish a work." In general, any original creation is afforded protection under the act, and that protection lasts for 50 years after the death of the final author or creator. Canadian laws provide protection in over 140 countries worldwide, as well as through the application of international agreements. The following sections describe a number of areas where copyright law has evolved to recognize the nature of technology and dissemination of material via the internet.

Digital Music Sharing

The complexity of copyright law was brought to the forefront in the Napster case. The creation of a technology that could easily allow millions of individuals to share and distribute copyrighted music files over the internet led to lawsuits that had far-reaching effects on the music industry and many others. The major defence offered in the Napster case was that the software did not result in Napster actually distributing the music files; it merely helped music lovers to find each other. The opponents contended that the Napster application provided a tool that used the internet to distribute copyrighted material and, therefore, facilitated inappropriate activities online. The importance of the Napster case has been to bring attention to the issues of copyright online and to encourage the legal community and governments to revisit legislation that was primarily written prior to the internet.

Napster was eventually shut down as a free file-swapping service. New companies quickly filled the vacuum created by Napster's demise in the belief that the next generation of peer-to-peer networks could surmount the copyright challenges involved. However, these companies (Kazaa, Gnutella, etc.) were also successfully sued, indicating a clear preference by courts to find that file sharing on the net violates copyright if it is readily apparent that the technology is primarily used for infringing purposes, and the technology provider is aware of, and even encourages (implicitly or explicitly) such use.

In some circumstances, industry organizations such as the Recording Industry Association of America (RIAA) even resorted to identifying and launching lawsuits against individual's allegedly downloading files in violation of copyright. The Canadian Recording Industry Association (CRIA) also attempted something similar but was largely unsuccessful in convincing Canadian Courts that there was a prima facie infringement under Canadian law. The RIAA, although more successful with this initiative than the CRIA, has also moved away from this strategy in recent years as a result of legislative and judicial developments that assisted the industry.

Recording Industry Association of America (RIAA)
www.riaa.com

Collectives

As set out on the Copyright Board of Canada website, a collective is an organization that administers the common rights of several copyright owners (e.g., rights in music). The collective acts for its members to grant permission to use the members' works, and sets the

Copyright Board of Canada
www.cb-cda.gc.ca/new-e.html

conditions for that use. Collective administration is widespread in Canada, particularly for music performance rights and the like.

In Canada there exists a procedure whereby a collective can file with the Copyright Board a proposed tariff of all royalties to be collected in respect of use of its copyright material. The board will consider the proposed tariffs and objections and, after it has completed its inquiry, certify the approved tariff, publish its decision, and provide reasons in support of it. The board has established tariffs for a number of different media. For example, recently the board decided that a ring tone (e.g., a small clip of a musical work created from a recognizable and distinct element of a song) is sufficient to warrant protection under copyright, and has established tariffs in respect of use of ring tones payable by the users thereof.

The Copyright Board has also set tariffs for use of music in fitness studios, hotels, and retail stores. Collectives are a powerful tool to allow copyright owners to be compensated justly from otherwise unauthorized use of copyright material.

Media Neutrality

Recent case law has recognized the concept of media neutrality in copyright. Section 3(1) of the Copyright Act provides the owner with the exclusive right to produce or reproduce a work in any material form whatever. The Supreme Court of Canada recently confirmed that, regardless of the media by which copyright material is presented, copyright protection applies. In Robertson v. Thomson Corp S.C.J. No. 43, the plaintiff was a freelance author who wrote two articles that were published in the *Globe and Mail* newspaper. Subsequently, the articles were reproduced in online databases and CD-ROMs. In 2006 the Supreme Court of Canada confirmed that, although newspaper producers have copyright in their newspapers as compilations or collective works, and thereby hold the right to publish a substantial part thereof, the reproduction of articles in online databases was not covered by that right.

The issues that can arise with respect to copyright online are many and can include piracy, plagiarism, linking concerns, and even website framing issues (discussed below). The piracy and plagiarism concerns are similar in many ways to the copyright issues that have existed since the creation of the printing press—protected materials being copied and misused without the owner's permission. These issues have become much more serious, however, with the evolution of the internet, where material is considered free.

Deep Linking

deep linking: The creation of a link on one website to a specific part or page (not the homepage) of another website.

The concept of deep linking is one that has caused difficulty for businesses and the courts in applying existing copyright law. **Deep linking** is the creation of a link on one website to a specific part or page (not the home page) of another website. The concern over deep linking is understandable, since huge investments in web design have been made by businesses in relation to advertising, customer relationship management, and business intelligence efforts.

Deep linking can effectively wipe out the effectiveness of these efforts by moving users directly to a specific part of a website. Deep linking has been considered by various courts in different jurisdictions. Unfortunately, the results of the decisions have created uncertainty. It appeared that courts in the United States were coalescing around a position that it was legally acceptable to engage in deep linking provided that the source of the deep-linked page or part was effectively acknowledged. However, in the EU, a variety of European courts have taken positions that both support and contradict (i.e., deep linking is not appropriate in any manner without proper consent) the position of most U.S. courts.

A young Canadian ebusiness owner, Jean-Pierre Bazinet, has experienced first-hand the difficulties that can arise through the issue of copyright and deep linking. Bazinet's website, Movie-List.com, provides information about movies and links to trailers and promotional information online. In 1999 Bazinet received a request from Universal Pictures to remove all copyrighted materials from his site and later to remove all "deep links" to trailers, with the threat of legal action.[17] Having little ability to fight the case in court, Movie-List.com removed all links to Universal's trailers but left the issue in an overall state of confusion. Linking is one of the major applications of the internet; however, its use must be related back to issues of copyright concerns.

The issue of deep linking is one that may or may not continue to cause difficulties within the legal system. In considering the issues that deep linking causes, it is interesting to think of how links are established by search engines. The issue of deep linking and some out-of-court settlements seem to indicate that it may be inappropriate; however, search engines also direct individuals to specific sites below the corporate home page of sites. This would seemingly be a similar concern, since many search engines create their own database of sites without the permission of the content owners, due to the use of spiders and other web-crawling tools.

Databases

Copyright issues have been raised with respect to databases, a vital component of many ebusinesses. The concern over databases is in determining whether they are original or not—because databases determined not to be original are not protected by copyright. For example, a Canadian court ruled that Yellow Pages telephone listings were not protected by Canadian copyright laws because they did not meet the criteria of originality required for protection.[18] Organizations such as the World Intellectual Property Organization (WIPO) have called for extending the scope of protection for databases internationally, since they are the lifeblood of many organizations despite the "originality" aspect. The cost to develop and gather the data can be substantial, and often the benefits obtained from the data are only realized after extensive data analysis. The issues around database protection continue to develop as ecommerce grows and the legal community and court systems address the concerns that arise.

Website Framing

The issue of website framing is an area that has resulted in lawsuits. **Website framing** is the use of HTML and browser technology to split a page into segments, which is useful for facilitating ease of use and building impressive websites. The issue that can arise with regard to copyright and website framing occurs when one site links the material or webpages of another organization into its own frame. For example, figure 13.2 illustrates how a page might be framed with material from another company that could result in copyright issues.

website framing: The use of HTML and browser technology to split a page into segments, which is useful for facilitating ease of use and building impressive websites.

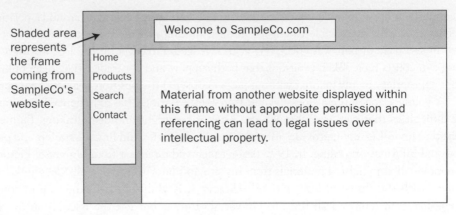

Figure 13.2 Illustration of website framing

The display of information in a website frame can lead to legal issues. Designers need to be fully aware of copyright concerns in this regard.

The website framing issue arose in a case between Imax Corporation and Showmax Inc. of Montreal that was decided in early 2000. The issues in this case involved both offline copyright and trademark concerns as well as online issues related to framing and linking. In its arguments, IMAX stated:

> The defendant's internet website uses linking and framing technology such that viewers of the Showmax website see the IMAX mark juxtaposed with the SHOWMAX mark in a manner likely to foster the mistaken belief that the two companies are related.

The use of framing was resulting in confusion for consumers that the two companies may be related, and therefore the issue of trademark had some validity for the court. In addition, the reproduction of materials created by IMAX on the Showmax site resulted in a reasonable argument that Showmax was infringing on the copyright materials of IMAX under the Copyright Act. The court ruled in favour of IMAX, stating that, although no measurable profits or costs could be determined, the use of IMAX materials by Showmax was inappropriate.

Website designers must take the website framing issue into consideration, as the increasing concerns over copyright issues can result in costly legal battles and negative publicity. In designing any framed sites in particular, it is preferred that any materials not owned by the organization be opened within a new browser window so that users are clearly aware that the material is from another location. If the material is to be viewed within a frame, it may be best to seek permission from the copyright owner to avoid concerns. The framing of copyrighted or trademarked materials may not cause difficulties if it is evident to users that the material comes from another source; however, caution should be taken in judging what "evident to users" might mean, since a court may have the final decision.

Since the invention of the printing press, the legal system has attempted to deal with issues of copyright infringement. The internet may have reduced the difficulty with which copyright is violated, but it has not simplified the methods for dealing with the problem. The increased efforts to deal with copyright issues in many countries, and the recognition that international standards are increasingly necessary, will help in the ongoing development of workable copyright solutions.

Patents

Patents are documents issued by the government that grant an inventor or patent owner the right to make and use an invention for 20 years after the patent is filed.[19] The issue of patents has recently become a concern for ecommerce and ebusiness because "processes" are covered as inventions that may be protected by patents. They are referred to as business method patents. Business method patents have been recognized in the United States but not in Canada, although many business method patent applications are pending in the hope that they will be. One of the most recognized examples of a business method patent is Amazon.com's 1-Click process of its online purchasing system, which allows users to easily make purchases by speeding up the checkout process. This process was patented by Amazon in 1999, and in late 1999 the company filed suit against Barnes & Noble for infringing upon its patent through the use of "Express Lane" technology. Amazon claimed that Express Lane was copying its patented process and therefore it was illegal. Both parties claimed success at various points of the legal dispute, with Amazon winning an initial injunction and Barnes & Noble successfully overturning it on appeal. The parties eventually settled the lawsuit just before it went to trial without disclosing the terms of settlement. Ongoing issues such as the 1-Click patent process are very important to businesses that seek to maintain a competitive advantage in the online world.

patent: A document issued by the government that grants an inventor or a patent owner the right to make and use an invention for 20 years after the patent is filed.

Open Sourcing

Open sourcing was popularized by Linus Torvalds, a Finnish programmer who created Linux, an operating system intended to be shared and improved through a collaborative and open process by interested programmers around the world. Other examples of well-known open source products are the Apache HTTP Server, the e-commerce platform osCommerce, and the internet browser Mozilla Firefox.

Open sourcing has become an important channel for creating intellectual property. Open sourcing implies open rights to any party to study, use and modify a piece of intellectual property such as software and allows for tremendous flexibility of usage and rapidity in the spreading of applications. Open sourcing is an extremely effective collaboration mechanism for the development of both internet and information standards. The concept has attracted some of the best programmers on the internet and has resulted in a highly rated collection of royalty-free software that can be used by anyone who wishes to do so, providing they respect the terms under which the open source software is made available to them.

Open source software can be protected like other intellectual property in order to prevent its misuse; for example, taking royalty-free code and charging others who are unaware of its origin for using it. Thus, adopters of open source software must acknowledge the source of the software and respect the terms under which the open source software is made available to them or risk legal action that could put them out of business.

JURISDICTION

THE ISSUE OF JURISDICTION ARISES ON NUMEROUS OCCASIONS ON THE INTERNET—THE global medium of communication and ecommerce. Many of the areas of law already discussed in this chapter (e.g., copyright, trademark, and privacy) as well as econtracts can be of concern. WIPO categorizes the major complexities of jurisdiction into three main issues:

- the jurisdiction within which to adjudicate a dispute at a particular location, known as the forum
- the appropriate law applicable to the dispute (also known as choice of law)
- the recognition and enforcement of judgments within foreign jurisdictions[20]

The complications that arise due to these issues have been seen on numerous occasions in courts in Canada, the United States, and elsewhere throughout the world.

The jurisdictional issues call into question many business practices as well as actions of individuals online. For example, individuals who create personal websites could be at odds with issues of obscenity, hate speech, or slander worldwide if appropriate jurisdictional issues are not in place and enforced. The United States has much stronger protection of free speech than many countries, which complicates many matters. Their constitution prevents the courts from rendering a verdict on many issues that other countries would consider inappropriate. In addition to individual websites, businesses must be concerned with jurisdictional issues that can question the practices carried out online.

Perhaps the best-known issue with regard to free speech was the case involving Yahoo! France and the sale of Nazi memorabilia within its auctions. In late 2000, a French court ordered the company to block access within France to Nazi materials. In early 2001, the company eliminated the sale of all such memorabilia worldwide but also elected to pursue legal action in the U.S. court system to overrule the French courts. Yahoo! obtained a court order in the United States stipulating that the French court had no jurisdiction over U.S.-based servers, and that Yahoo! had no legal obligation to remove Nazi memorabilia from its U.S. website. However, in a subsequent appeal, the original decision was vacated, as it was concluded that California courts had no jurisdiction over the French organizations involved in the litigation. The case demonstrates the complexity of jurisdictional matters and the difficult balance to be made over the internet, as various international laws, customs, and business practices result in disputes. It also highlights an area in which the development of international agreements may be beneficial to both businesses and governments.

In attempting to deal with the issues over jurisdiction, the courts in the United States and Canada have applied a standard that has become known as the passive versus active test. The **passive versus active test** attempts to place the website of an online business along a continuum based upon the interactivity of the website to determine if operations within a jurisdiction were planned. The test could determine, for instance, that a Canadian firm's website that provided information about its products and manufacturing process was "passive" and, therefore, would not give a U.S. court the right to govern the issue. A website that resulted in online sales within an area, and that gathered personal information to complete the transaction, however, would have been ruled to be "active," and courts within the reach of the website (globally) could attempt to claim jurisdiction. However, the grey area between active and passive was the subject of much debate, and courts used different approaches from one case to another when making a decision. In addition, the test created unproductive incentives for website operators to limit interactivity at a time when increasing ecommerce activity (likely to be considered "active") was becoming the norm.

passive versus active test: A standard that attempts to place the website of an online business along a continuum, based on the interactivity of the website, to determine if operations within a jurisdiction were planned.

Betfair

Called the eBay for gamblers, Betfair.com is a betting exchange that offers thousands of betting events per week, including horse racing and other sports as well as casino games. Internet gambling is a multi-billion-dollar industry. It offers new forms of betting, accessibility, and liquidity. It also offers temptation that some people cannot resist as well as new opportunities for cheaters.

Although gambling is viewed as being immoral in some communities and is illegal in many jurisdictions, it is legal in many others. Gambling ranges from bingo, to lotteries, to casinos, to betting on sports and horse racing. Some gambling activities are private, some are regulated, and some are government sponsored, such as provincial lotteries in Canada.

In 2006 and 2007, the U.S. government took aggressive action against online gambling companies by making it illegal for banks and credit card companies to settle payments on online gambling sites and arresting executives of online gambling companies in or travelling through the United States. The U.S. opposition to online gambling is based on concerns that it is too easy for minors to gamble online and for criminals and terrorists to use Web gambling to launder money. The British government has criticized the U.S. position on internet gambling, and some U.S. lawmakers are attempting to reverse the U.S. position on online gambling.

Betfair is licensed in the United Kingdom, where online gambling is legal and regulated. Betfair has 2 million customers in 80 countries who bet against each other (in contrast with traditional betting against the house). At any given time, Betfair's customers have several hundred million dollars on account with Betfair, and it handles millions of transactions each day—more than the London and New York stock exchanges combined. Betfair takes 2 to 5 percent commission on winning bets.

Betfair's founders, Andrew Black and Edward Wray, emphasize transparency. With backgrounds in the stock market and investment banking, they wanted to transplant the fundamentals of investment banking to sports.

According to one Betfair managing director, the company can identify every bet ever placed, from what funds, and where those funds are going. It is a complete audit trail, and the company is willing to share it with the sports governing bodies. Many sports governing bodies have not accepted this offer, but Betfair has agreements with a large number of sports governing bodies, promising to share real-time information on unusual betting activity. In fact, over the past several years, it has noticed dozens of cases of suspicious betting activity, leading to investigations in horse racing, soccer, and tennis.

Betfair
www.betfair.com

Questions

1. Should online gambling be allowed? Should online gambling be regulated or state run, as the provincial lotteries and casinos in various Canadian provinces?

2. Is it appropriate for the United States to prosecute executives of online gambling companies? What if those companies operate outside the United States?

3. What are the risks to users of gambling sites such as Betfair? How do they compare with the risks of sites such as eBay or online brokers such as TD Waterhouse?

Source: J. Drape, "Web Site Puts Focus on Fix in Sports Bets," *New York Times*, May 25, 2008, 1, 11; L. Woellert, "A Web Gambling Fight Could Harm Free Trade," *BusinessWeek*, August 13, 2007, 43; J. Wardell, "U.S. Probe Hits Shares in Online Gambling Firms," *Globe and Mail*, January 23, 2007, B11; S. Stewart, "Uncle Sam Nabs Net Millionaires," *Globe and Mail*, January 17, 2007, B1; www.youtube.com/watch?v=d05joU_FSYo.

The difficulties with the passive versus active test meant that, after some early judicial acceptance of the test, it eventually gave way to other considerations in subsequent court decisions. Michael Geist, an expert on internet law and an early critic of the passive versus active test, favours the "targeting test." With the targeting test, a greater focus is placed on identifying the jurisdictions a website operator intends to be active in, taking into consideration a variety of factors (e.g., technology employed, online contracts used by the website operator, and knowledge of the intended target).[21] Although the "targeting test" has gained greater acceptance, the application of the test has not always been uniform. Due to the challenges of addressing jurisdiction, there have been increasing calls for international co-operation in this judicial area.

The uncertainty over the application of law and jurisdiction will become a major threat to electronic commerce if it is not handled in the near future. Some countries, such as the United States, have even created legislation that claims to provide rights to govern internationally. Notably, the Children's Online Privacy Protection Act is written to apply both to U.S. websites and any website in the world where a firm is targeting children from the United States. Many other cases have resulted in countries claiming jurisdiction over issues in foreign states—and with little concern for the passive versus active test. The Alberta Securities Commission took legal action against the World Stock Exchange (of Antigua/Cayman Islands), an online exchange, in a Canadian court after it was ruled that the impact of the website substantially impacted Alberta.

The issues over jurisdiction continue to complicate ecommerce transactions, but some steps may assist businesses in addressing jurisdiction. For example, many companies now include "choice of laws" clauses within their contracts to allow trading partners to agree in writing to the legal jurisdiction. This practice is common among B2B partners but should be used carefully when dealing with B2C customers. Simply including the forum for jurisdiction in an econtract is subject to the same constraints that apply to other econtract issues (discussed below). In the case of Mendoza v. AOL, a U.S. court ruled that AOL's move to dismiss a case brought against the company in a state outside of Virginia, which the agreement specified, was overruled. The judge found that "it would be unfair and unreasonable because the clause in question was not negotiated at arm's length, was contained in a standard form contract, and was not readily identifiable by the plaintiff due to the small text and location of the clause at the conclusion of the agreement."[22]

Individuals must also ensure that they are aware of the legal issues they may encounter by dealing with companies in certain countries or making agreements to adhere to another area's laws. Signing an agreement that the choice of laws is in Texas, for instance, may require an individual to incur travel costs and excessive legal costs to address legal issues. Addressing these types of concerns for both businesses and individuals is of extreme importance to the future growth of online business. For now, the passive versus active test is still common, but as additional cases are reviewed the jurisdictional issues are likely to evolve to a more complex analysis.

In fact, recent case law has established that a foreign judgment is enforceable in Canada if there is a real and substantial connection between the foreign jurisdiction and the defendant or the cause of action. For example, in Disney Enterprises Inc. v. Click Enterprises Inc., (2006) 49 CPR (4th) 87 (Ontario Sup Ct Jus), the plaintiffs were U.S. movie studios that obtained a judgment from a New York court for damages related to copyright infringement. The defendants were based in Ontario and offered memberships that gave customers the technology necessary to download and copy the plaintiff's films. The defendants took the position that the New York court had no jurisdiction over them in Ontario. The court stated that the New York court could exercise jurisdiction over this Ontario defendant, as the necessary connection to the jurisdiction was present. The court was of the view that the approach to be taken with the internet should be flexible, and that either the country of transmission or the country of reception of internet communications may take jurisdiction. In this case, it was reasonable and fair for the court of New York to take jurisdiction, and the connection test was satisfied as the defendants used the internet to access the United States, provided memberships to residents of New York, and had contracted with service providers in the United States to process payments of members.

ECONTRACTS

To conduct business effectively, it is necessary for contracts to be completed in an appropriate manner. The completion of contracts has evolved extensively from the original "handshake" approach to "pen and paper" and now "electronic contracts," or "econtracts." The issue for ecommerce with respect to contracting is the need for recognition of electronic contracts, to ensure enforceability equal to that of more traditional contracting approaches. The governments of many countries, including Canada, have responded to the need for recognition of electronic contracts and created legislation. For example, in Canada PIPEDA gives legitimacy to econtracts as described below:

> The purpose of this Part [of the Act] is to provide for the use of electronic alternatives in the manner provided . . . where federal laws contemplate the use of paper to record or communicate information or transactions.[23]

An econtract must fulfill the legal requirements of a contract, namely offer, acceptance, and consideration. The Canadian courts generally recognize that, if the parties clearly intend to enter into a contract through email or web-based submissions, their communication of offer and acceptance will produce an enforceable agreement. To constitute a valid offer on a website, the website must contain all the material terms and applicable conditions of the econtract and the steps required to enter into it. An offer made by electronic means may be seen to imply an authorization to communicate the acceptance by electronic means as well. Electronic offers should specify the method(s) of acceptance, and when and where the econtract will be deemed to be formed.

Many of the provinces have also enacted legislation to address these issues at the provincial level as well. The recognition of econtracts through legislation allows the court system to deal more appropriately with electronic contracts than was previously possible.

The United Nations Commission on International Trade Law (UNCITRAL) developed the Model Law on Electronic Commerce in 1996 to address issues such as econtracting. The UNCITRAL Model Law attempts to guide governments in creating legislation that will stimulate international trade and lead to a harmonization of legal systems. The econtract issue concerns such factors as the form of communication, acknowledgement of receipt, and acknowledgement of acceptance.[24] As with paper-based contracts, it is necessary for econtracts to be recognized as fluid mechanisms that can be received but unsigned at stages of the negotiations. Efforts of international organizations such as the United Nations have assisted in stimulating many countries to address these issues.

United Nations Commission on International Trade Law (UNCITRAL)
www.uncitral.org

The creation of ecommerce legislation has led to litigation over contract issues throughout the world. As a leader in ecommerce and as a litigious country, the United States has addressed many of the concerns over contracting in its court systems. According to Michael Geist, two issues arising from U.S. court rulings are key to properly dealing with econtracts:

1. *Form of assent*—It is necessary for users to indicate by some active means that they agree to the terms and conditions found within the contract. This issue calls into

question many of the standard-form contracts that we see every day, since in the online world assent is increasingly difficult to prove.

2. *Reasonableness of contract terms*—The court systems are as likely to rule that a contract is invalid in the online world as they are in the offline world if the terms are not reasonable. The Mendoza v. AOL case mentioned earlier was an example where the court ruled that expecting a customer to come to a specific state to deal with a complaint was unreasonable.[25]

shrink-wrap agreement: An agreement printed on the outside of shrink-wrapped software packaging which says that the use of the software product is subject to license terms.

Shrink-wrap agreements are agreements printed on the outside of shrink-wrapped software packaging which say that the use of the software product is subject to license terms. According to Canadian law, to be enforceable, the existence of license terms must be indicated clearly on the outside of the software package. It is sufficient that the purchaser is made aware of the fact that the software is subject to a license before the purchase, however it is not necessary for the customer to be made aware of all the terms of the license agreement. To be valid, the customer must be given a real opportunity to accept or reject the terms (i.e., return the product), once they have had an opportunity to review them (i.e., after opening the product).

click-wrap agreement: The online equivalent of a standard agreement included in shrink-wrapped software bought in physical locations.

Click-wrap agreements are the online equivalent of the standard agreements included within the shrink-wrap of software bought in physical locations. Under Canadian law, a licensee is bound by all the terms of a license contract if, at the moment of acceptance, the licensee had actual knowledge of the existence of the contract. The click-wrap procedure addresses the issue of form of assent by allowing software to be downloaded only after the licensee has seen the licensing contract; i.e., the etailer requires potential licensees to scroll through the terms of contracts and click on "I Agree" or some similar button to ensure that the form of assent criteria is being met. In such cases the enforceability of click-wrap licenses is generally not an issue. However, if an etailer fails to provide such features, they may be unable to enforce their econtract. For example, in Ticketmaster v. Tickets.com, a U.S. court concluded that the terms in the contract could not be enforced, since users were not required to click "I Agree" to acknowledge reading the terms.[26] This issue requires website designers to clearly provide the terms of a contract and acknowledgement by the user through an active mechanism such as a button or link.

TAXATION

INTERNET TAXATION IS ANOTHER AREA OF ECOMMERCE AND EBUSINESS THAT IS COMPLEX and has caused considerable difficulty for the legal system and legislators. The issues encompass both income taxation and sales taxes, the two major forms of taxation. The complexity of taxation in the bricks-and-mortar world is more than enough for lawyers, accountants, and legislators to deal with—adding the internet to the mix has given rise to numerous issues that need to be addressed.

permanent establishment: A term in Canadian law and in international tax treaties that is used to determine where a business is located for tax purposes.

physical presence: A term for a test under U.S. law and internationally that is used to determine whether a business has a permanent establishment in a jurisdiction and hence considered to be subject to taxation in that jurisdiction.

The issue of jurisdiction as discussed earlier also causes problems for taxation in the global economy. One of the major issues focuses on where a business is located for tax purposes—known as **permanent establishment** in Canada or **physical presence** in the United States. The permanent establishment of an online company can be very difficult to determine, since it could be the location of the vendor's head office, the location

The Taxman Cometh

Amazon.com Inc. recently stated that it is taking a stand for free speech by fighting a request from the state of North Carolina tax authorities for information on people who have bought about 50 million items since 2003.

North Carolina requires residents to pay taxes on online purchases if buying the same item in a store would result in a sales tax. Out-of-state retailers cannot be forced to collect this tax if they have no physical presence in the state. However, state officials argued that Amazon had a physical presence in the state by virtue of the fact that North Carolina residents used their blogs to post links to Amazon's website to promote Web shopping deals and offer coupons. Therefore, it should collect and remit sales taxes on behalf of North Carolina.

Amazon responded by cutting off business relationships with such affiliates and then filed a federal lawsuit in Seattle, where it has its headquarters, asking the court to find North Carolina's request for information unconstitutional on the grounds that disclosing the names and addresses of buyers, as requested, would harm customers who bought controversial books or movies by intruding on their right to purchase books, movies, and music free from such intrusion.

In a separate case, the Canadian Revenue Agency (CRA) requested eBay to turn over the names, addresses, phone numbers, and email addresses of all high-volume sellers on eBay. The CRA wanted to find out whether those individuals or companies reported the income they made from online sales.

The company argued that it did not have access to the records because eBay Canada is a subsidiary of eBay Inc., and all the information requested by CRA was stored in computers outside Canada.

Amazon.com Inc.
www.amazon.com

eBay Inc.
www.ebay.com

Questions

1. Is Amazon's stand defensible? Is eBay's stand defensible?

2. Should states such as North Carolina, where Amazon does not have a physical presence but has affiliates who utilize Amazon's website to sell goods or services, be entitled to collect sales taxes?

3. Should companies such as Amazon.com and eBay.com be required to hand over information to government tax agencies to support their investigations? What about non-tax investigations?

Source: "Amazon Fights State's Request for Customer Data," *Globe and Mail*, April 21, 2010, B10; P. Waldie, "Taxman Goes Browsing on eBay," *Globe and Mail*, September 27, 2007, B1, B8.

of the website's ISP, the physical location of the server, or some other location such as the branch closest to the customer. This difficulty in establishing jurisdiction results in extreme difficulties in determining the appropriateness of collecting income taxes, and can also add complications to the subject of sales taxation.

The Canadian sales tax system has a number of mechanisms in place to encourage compliance, but the concept of self-assessment is likely to fail in the online world equally as it has in the offline world. Sales taxes are supposed to be paid in the province where the good is consumed—the complexity arises, of course, when the vendor and customer reside in different locations. Assume that a student from Winnipeg goes online to purchase a new computer system from a New Brunswick business. The transaction should result in Manitoba sales tax being applied; however, the New Brunswick business is not likely registered as a tax collector for Manitoba. The student should self-assess the sales tax but there is very little likelihood that the transaction will be investigated by Manitoba and, therefore, collection is unknown. The complexity of this transaction grows if a foreign country is added into the scenario and issues of federal taxes and customs duties arise. These jurisdictional issues will continue to cause difficulties in the Canadian and international systems until increased harmonization occurs.

The risks of tax revenue declines as identified above have led some governments to take action, but whether the actions taken are appropriate is another question. For example, British Columbia amended its legislation in March 2000 to require "persons located outside the province that in the ordinary course of business solicit persons in British Columbia for orders to purchase tangible personal property"[27] to register and collect sales tax for the province. Some analysts claim that the legislation would not be able to force out-of-province businesses to register, since the B.C. courts don't have jurisdiction, but the intention is still controversial. While this legislation may benefit the province's tax collection, it could discourage electronic commerce. If every Canadian province and territory followed suit, online businesses would need to register and periodically file 13 sales tax forms. If each of the states in the United States follows suit, businesses could be required to register in over 60 separate jurisdictions. Estimates of international taxation systems reach nearly 7500—any requirements to conform to this number of systems would simply fail, but the number illustrates the extent of the problem.[28] Harmonization sounds like a simple solution to this problem, but encouraging international and even provincial governments to reach a consensus on appropriate taxation methods is unlikely to occur quickly.

The United States has developed legislation to impose a moratorium on internet taxation—the Internet Tax Freedom Act. This legislation does not remove online sales taxes; it simply provides that no new internet-based sales taxes be developed that could slow the growth of ecommerce. The act also created ongoing committees that will continue to review the issue of internet taxation and make recommendations to the U.S. Congress.[29] The issue of taxation will continue to develop over time, since the existing legislation in most countries is unclear on internet transactions.

The issue of the type of income is another that ecommerce has brought attention to. The digitization of products calls into question whether the sale is a product or a service. The purchase of a software package in a retail store would clearly be a product but downloading that same software from an online store is less clear—is it now a product or a service? The distinction may seem unimportant, but in many jurisdictions the tax laws vary between the two, and therefore it is necessary to make a choice. For items such as music, the issue over the digital delivery leads to confusion over the type of revenue earned—is it sales, license fees, or royalties? The issue of product type, like many other tax and legal issues, is one where experts need to be consulted.

The taxation issues on the internet must be addressed by legislators and the legal system. To reduce uncertainty and encourage compliance, the system needs to be understandable and, where possible, harmonized. The lack of appropriate standards may encourage non-compliance (deliberate or not), and the development of inappropriate regulations may only lead to hasty decisions and more complexity. The evolution of taxation on the internet may take several years but one thing is for sure—we will all continue to pay taxes in some form or another, but where?

CHAPTER SUMMARY

The internet's global reach has created numerous legal issues for ebusinesses to be aware of. In addition, the power of technology to capture and analyze data has caused concern over individuals' right to privacy. These developing issues require the attention of managers of ebusinesses to ensure that appropriate actions are taken to mitigate risks and operate in a socially responsible manner.

Privacy can be compromised through the inappropriate use of personal information about an individual. The gathering of personal information in Canada has come under the scope of new legislation known as the Personal Information Protection and Electronic Documents Act (PIPEDA). This legislation aims to protect individuals' rights to privacy and stimulate the growth of ecommerce. To comply with the act, businesses must inform users of the information they collect and its purpose—often done through a privacy policy on the company's website.

The ease of use of the internet has also resulted in ease of theft of copyright materials, trademarks, and patents. The concerns over intellectual property require organizations to consider their own use of others' material as well as the protection of intangible assets owned. Activities such as linking to other sites and website design have resulted in legal cases due to inappropriate use of copyright materials, requiring managers to give thought to the legal implications of various activities.

The many disputes over trademarks and domain names have led to the establishment of processes known as dispute resolution mechanisms. While trademarks are unique in many ways, they differ from domain names in that they cannot be general in nature. The unique aspect of domain names has led to court cases, where outcomes can be unpredictable.

The taxation of online transactions is closely related to the issue of jurisdiction on the internet. Determining where a company is located is complex in the internet age and creates uncertainty over which laws apply and what taxation mechanisms should be in place. Ebusinesses must examine their operations and, through legal and governmental consultation, ensure that they are complying with the appropriate rules and regulations in order to limit their risk.

Key Terms

Anticybersquatting Consumer Protection Act (ACPA) (p. 311)

Canadian Internet Registration Authority (CIRA) (p. 311)

click-wrap agreement (p. 322)

copyright (p. 308)

deep linking (p. 314)

industrial property (p. 308)

intellectual property (p. 308)

Internet Corporation for Assigned Names and Numbers (ICANN) (p. 311)

passive versus active test (p. 318)

patent (p. 317)

permanent establishment (p. 322)

personal information (p. 300)

Personal Information Protection and Electronic Documents Act (PIPEDA) (p. 300)

physical presence (p. 322)

shrink-wrap agreement (p. 322)

trademark (p. 308)

website framing (p. 315)

To help you master the material in this chapter and stay up to date with new developments in ebusiness, visit the MyEBusinessLab at www.pearsoned.ca/myebusinesslab. Resources include the following:

- Pre- and Post-Test Questions
- Additional Chapter Questions
- Author Blog
- Recommended Readings
- Commentaries on Current Trends
- Additional Topics in Ebusiness
- Internet Exercises
- Glossary Flashcards

Endnotes

1. Electronic Commerce Branch, Industry Canada, http://e-com.ic.gc.ca/english/strat/index.html, accessed May 9, 2004.

2. Office of the Privacy Commissioner of Canada, "Privacy Legislation in Canada," www.privcom.gc.ca/legislation/index_e.asp, accessed May 9, 2004.

3. Office of the Privacy Commissioner of Canada, "Frequently Asked Questions," www.privcom.gc.ca/faq/faq_01_e.asp#004, accessed December 6, 2004.

4. Office of the Privacy Commissioner of Canada, "Privacy Legislation in Canada" (fact sheet), www.privcom.gc.ca/fs-fi/fs2001-02_e.asp, accessed May 9, 2004 [link no longer active].

5. "Findings Under the Personal Information and Electronic Documents Act (PIPEDA)—Case Summary 2009-006—Airline Ticket Seller Was Mistaken In Its Collection of Exact Age Information," www.priv.gc.ca/cf-dc/2009/2009_006_0324_e.cfm, accessed August 18, 2010.

6. World Intellectual Property Organization, "Primer on Electronic Commerce and Intellectual Property Issues," www.WIPO.int, accessed May 9, 2004.

7. "Privacy Fears Heightened," *Globe and Mail*, March 18, 2001.

8. V. Heffernan, "Granting Anonymity," *New York Times Magazine*, September 19, 2010, 18–20.

9. World Intellectual Property Organization, "Primer on Electronic Commerce and Intellectual Property Issues," www.WIPO.int, accessed May 9, 2004.

10. L.E. Harris, *Canadian Copyright Law*, 3rd ed. (Toronto: McGraw Hill Ryerson, 2001).

11. Pro-C Limited v. Computer City [2001] 14 C.P.R. 4th.

12. M. Geist, "Trademark Confusion Creeps into Web Site Content," Globe and Mail, September 7, 2000.

13. Internet Corporation for Assigned Names and Numbers (ICANN), www.icann.org/tr/english.html, accessed May 9, 2004.

14. M. Geist, "B.C. Court Shores Up Protection for Anticorporate Protest Sites," *Globe and Mail*, February 15, 2001.

15. L.E. Harris, *Canadian Copyright Law*, 3rd ed. (Toronto: McGraw Hill Ryerson, 2001).

16. Government of Canada "Balanced Copyright," www.ic.gc.ca/eic/site/crp-prda.nsf/eng/home, accessed August 18, 2010.

17. C. Kaplan, "Is Linking Always Legal? The Experts Aren't Sure,"*New York Times*, August 6, 1999.

18. L.E. Harris, *Canadian Copyright Law*, 3rd ed. (Toronto: McGraw Hill Ryerson, 2001), 20.

19. L.E. Harris, *Canadian Copyright Law*, 3rd ed. (Toronto: McGraw Hill Ryerson, 2001), 3.

20. World Intellectual Property Organization, "Primer on Electronic Commerce and Intellectual Property Issues," www.WIPO.int, accessed May 9, 2004.

21. M. Geist, "E-commerce and Jurisdiction" (slide show presented at the Regional Expert Conference on Harmonized Development of Legal and Regulatory Systems for E-commerce, July 8, 2004, Bangkok, Thailand), www.unescap.org/tid/projects/ecom04_s6geist.pdf, accessed November 15, 2006.

22. M. Geist, "All Electronic Contracts Are Not Created Equal,"*Globe and Mail*, May 25, 2001.

23. Personal Information Protection and Electronic Documents Act, Statutes of Canada 2000, c. 5 s. 32.

24. United Nations Commission on International Trade Law, "Model Law on Electronic Commerce," United Nations, 1996.

25. M. Geist, "All Electronic Contracts Are Not Created Equal,"*Globe and Mail*, May 25, 2001.

26. M. Geist, "All Electronic Contracts Are Not Created Equal,"*Globe and Mail*, May 25, 2001.

27. R. Lewandowski, "The Net Tax Nightmare," CA Magazine (March 2001): 21.

28. H.M. Deitel, et al., *E-Business & E-Commerce for Managers* (Upper Saddle River, NJ: Prentice Hall, 2000), 326.

29. H.M. Deitel, et al., *E-Business & E-Commerce for Managers* (Upper Saddle River, NJ: Prentice Hall, 2000), 326.

Chapter 14
Ecommerce and Small Business

Learning Objectives

When you complete this chapter you should be able to:

1   Explain how ecommerce can be an opportunity for small businesses.

2   Discuss the development of estrategy for small business ecommerce.

3   Explain how a small business can establish an ecommerce presence.

4   Identify and describe some of the useful services and sources of information on the internet for small businesses.

5   Describe the challenges to ecommerce for small businesses and how they can be overcome.

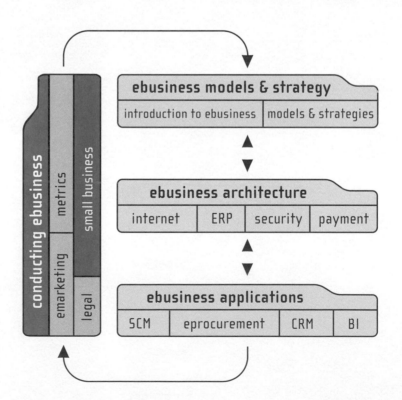

INTRODUCTION

Ecommerce has brought a great deal of growth and opportunity to the small business sector. The potential to reach new markets, reduce costs of operations, and compete against larger competitors brought the potential of ecommerce to the forefront of news during the late 1990s and early 2000s. At that time, high profile dot-com startups such as Amazon.com and eBay, no longer small businesses, generated fortunes for their founders and raised expectations to unrealistic levels. However, that time was followed by several equally high-profile dot-com failures, such as eToys.com and Pets.com, which significantly lowered expectations and even produced many sceptics about the opportunities for the small business sector to become involved in ecommerce. Nevertheless, there have been thousands of successful dot-com startups in recent years, as well as thousands of cases where established businesses have expanded their operations by developing an ecommerce initiative. In this chapter we will consider the importance of ecommerce to small businesses and consider different ways in which these companies can use the internet and other ebusiness technologies to their advantage.

The importance of the small business sector to the economy of Canada and, in fact, to the economies of many countries throughout the world cannot be overstated. In Canada, 98 percent of all businesses have fewer than 100 employees, and much of the job growth in the country can be attributed to these small enterprises.[1] The number of small businesses, combined with their importance to the economy, has led to much interest in developing the use of ecommerce in the small business sector. Evidence of this interest can be found, for example, in the government of Canada's information website developed by Industry Canada, which includes specific information for small companies. Many regional and provincial government agencies have developed seminars and other incentives for helping small business get started in ecommerce. In addition, many technology service providers and online services have developed products and services that are designed specifically for the small business sector.

Soon after the ecommerce era began, large organizations and many high-growth firms shifted their focus from the business-to-consumer (B2C) market to the business-to-business (B2B) market and left a massive opportunity for the right individuals wishing to launch ebusinesses in the B2C arena. Since then, innumerable businesses have started new B2C business with considerable success, and many of the larger players have returned to the B2C arena, seeing the tremendous potential in it. (See the Ebusiness in Global Perspective box for an example of a successful B2C strategy.) While initially B2C was held up by the limited availability of the internet to many people, as well as security concerns, these issues have largely been overcome. The internet is now ubiquitous, with high speed reaching most customers and mobile internet access the norm. Many businesses are targeting mobile users with innovative approaches. Security remains an issue, especially as it relates to viruses and phishing, but more safeguards are in place, and the general population is much more sophisticated in detecting such threats than they once were. Online purchasing is a significant portion of the overall retail trade. Canadians ordered $15.1 billion in goods and services on the internet in 2008, up from $12.8 billion in 2007.[2]

Ebusiness in Global Perspective

Building a Business from a Blog

When Eric Nakagawa, a software developer in Hawaii, posted a picture of a cat on a website he created, he had no idea that he was starting a new business. In fact, it started as just a joke for a few friends. The picture showed a fat, smiling cat, with the caption, "I can has cheezburger?" The lingo is curious—a mixture of net-talk and baby talk. Eric noticed the hits increasing, and first he was amazed but then decided to try it again as a blog, with some new photos and funny captions. In his blog, readers could comment on the photos. The hits increased, starting out at 375,000 hits per month and quickly increasing to 1.5 million. The blog, I Can Has Cheezburger, settled out at around 500,000 page views per day.

With this kind of traffic, Nakagawa decided to sell ads on the site, and businesses began to buy them at prices ranging from $500 for a week to nearly $4,000. Nakagawa took on running Cheezburger as his full-time job.

As the site evolved, it went beyond readers commenting on the photos to submitting their own photos and writing funny captions on them. Readers vote on the submissions, and the ones gaining the highest votes get posted on the main page. Readers also rate each post based on a scale of one to five cheeseburgers. Traffic kept going up.

Nakagawa and his associates also monitor traffic to see when people log in and time their posts for when users are most likely to be available, such as early morning, lunch time, and in the evenings.

Blogs and other sites often focus on the idea of building a community around user-supplied content. Fewer businesses are built this way.

Blogging, when fully implemented as an interactive medium, creates a connection between authors and readers, a community, and many businesses seek to do this same thing with their customers. Nakagawa's attitude is that he knows he is on to something, but doesn't know how big it can get. Part of the challenge of his new business is to find that out.

I Can Has Cheezburger
http://icanhascheezburger.com

Questions

1. Are there ways that Cheezburger could improve its business model?

2. What can more conventional businesses learn from the Cheezburger experience?

Source: J. Tozzi, "Bloggers Bring in the Big Bucks," *BusinessWeek*, July 13, 2007, www.businessweek.com/print/smallbiz/content/jul2007/sb20070713_202390.htm.

OPPORTUNITIES FOR SMALL BUSINESS

ALTHOUGH THE INTERNET AND OTHER EBUSINESS TECHNOLOGIES OFFER SIGNIFICANT opportunities to small business, 75 percent of small businesses underutilize these technologies.[3] To stimulate small business ecommerce in Canada, it is important to make small business owners aware of the many opportunities and benefits it can offer. The small business owners must also look to how other small businesses have overcome some of the challenges of matching technology and ecommerce use to the small business setting. For example, about 25 percent of small business owners use an integrated mix of desktops, laptops, and mobile devices connected to the internet and running software that enables employees to share information, produce client deliverables, and manage customer relationships.[4] Over the past few years, the use of mobile devices has become a much more important part of this mix.

The opportunities for ecommerce use in small business are many, and have been realized across numerous industries and geographic regions of the world. The benefits can include access to new markets, improved customer responsiveness, increased flexibility, enhanced profits (through cost reductions and revenue increases), increased innovation, and better-managed resources.[5] The number and amount of benefits received in any of these categories will depend of course on factors such as the industry, products or services sold, and estrategy chosen.

The use of the internet can be of benefit to small businesses across many functional areas. To illustrate the types of benefits that can be obtained, we will look at ecommerce and internet usage across a number of areas and provide examples where appropriate. The use of the internet can be valuable in the key areas of marketing, customer support, market intelligence, procurement, operations, sales transactions, public relations, and employee retention and morale.[6]

Marketing

The capability to market products and services to a wide audience at a reasonable cost was one of the first drivers of businesses to the internet. While some may question the value of online marketing, many examples exist of the successful use of online marketing and advertising tools. In addition to attracting new customers, small businesses have found that online advertising has provided valuable, targeted marketing campaigns that have resulted in increased business. One small business operator in the tourism industry is Outside Expeditions of Charlottetown, Prince Edward Island. The owner, Bryon Howard, stated, "Yes, we have landed lots of new business as a result of our website. People have booked tours as a result . . . Others have phoned for information, and rather than wait up to 10 days for a brochure to get to the U.S.—I can give them my website address . . . and voilà, a reservation is the result, the very same day."[7] Many businesses have had similar findings—the value of an online presence for marketing can at times outweigh other marketing efforts. From finding new customers to building a customer database, the internet offers businesses a cost-effective means of marketing in a new way. See table 14.1 for some of the uses of the internet for small business marketing efforts.

Table 14.1 Marketing Aspects of the Internet

- Provide product or service information
- Find new customers
- Develop new export markets
- Educate customers
- Reduce marketing costs
- Enhance your image
- Build a customer/potential customer database
- Encourage requests for information
- Support traditional media campaigns
- Distribute frequently changing information
- Build brand image

Customer Support

One of the key reasons the internet is valuable to small businesses for customer support is the availability of websites 24/7. While many small businesses pride themselves on personal support, quite a few enquiries can often be handled without any human contact, and the customer is just as happy to be served in a timely fashion. If, for example, a customer from Montreal is looking for product details at 9 a.m. their time, it is unlikely that a business in California would be open. Rather than having to wait until the afternoon, the customer can find the information immediately if the supplier has a website. This form of self-service often leads to satisfaction, since it is timely and can reduce the cost of calling long-distance to another business. The customer is now informed of all important product features (assuming a well-designed, useful website exists) and may call or place an order online.

One of the main tools that will reduce routine questions over the phone is a frequently asked questions (FAQ) page on the web. The FAQ page should pose questions in a manner consistent with how customers would typically ask them by phone or in person. Responses can be in basic text format or can integrate text and multimedia to give visual aids to users. The use of an FAQ page to reduce phone queries can benefit both the customer and the business by reducing the time and cost of dealing with these concerns individually.

Market Intelligence

PR Newswire
www.ewatch.com

The internet offers numerous tools whereby small businesses can more easily gather market intelligence. Monitoring industry information and competitors can be a time-consuming and costly task, but many internet sites allow this task to be carried out quickly and at a low cost. For example, online services such as eWatch offered by PR Newswire allow users to search for news by company name and even subscribe to receive email notification when press releases or news items occur for selected companies. These types of services range in cost but can be invaluable to businesses in industries where timeliness and competitor monitoring are of crucial importance.

Industry Canada
www.ic.gc.ca

The internet also holds great potential for small businesses trying to gather data relevant to their online and offline marketing efforts. For example, the Industry Canada site is host to a massive volume of data from Statistics Canada and other reliable sources. It contains industry statistics, demographics, business listings, and a great deal of other information. Many others, such as the sites for the *Globe and Mail* and the *National Post*, offer the ability to search some archives for free and more distant archives for a fee. The wealth of information online (discussed in more detail later in this chapter) provides useful access to data that may assist business owners in decision making for everyday issues and in establishing growth strategies during times of change.

Procurement

The use of the internet and ecommerce can help small businesses save money on procurement of virtually everything they purchase, turning those savings into lower prices and increased market share. Through the internet, a small business can locate a broader range of suppliers, giving it more opportunity to find lower prices or greater value. With emarket-places, a small business may be able to join with other small businesses to aggregate its purchasing to receive volume discounts that are otherwise available only to large companies. Eprocurement also helps to streamline the process by managing purchases electronically.

Operations

The internet and ecommerce offer small businesses the opportunity to achieve efficiencies for operations in numerous ways. Some of the easiest cost savings to achieve are reduced long-distance telephone charges (due to email and VoIP-based services such as Skype), reduced postage (due to email, websites, and downloads), and the time savings related to these everyday business tasks. Online payment processing through credit card companies and services such as PayPal can be more efficient, less expensive, and more reliable.

The use of the internet for sharing business information with business partners can lead to better inventory management, better service delivery, greater efficiencies, and improved lines of communication. For example, Trail Blazer, a family-owned business in Nova Scotia that manufactures camping, hunting, and gardening supplies, communicates almost entirely through the Canadian Tire extranet, thus saving time, phone costs, and frustrating automated message machines in the process. Canadian Tire prefers this means of communication, and in many cases demands that suppliers (large and small) utilize the technology. All communication through this channel is timely, and in many cases more accurate, than other communication media.

Many small businesses also rely on the internet to find ideas on how to operate their business better.

Sales Transactions

The internet offers small businesses many tools they can use to generate potential sales leads and/or conduct online sales transactions. The growth of the B2C market has been somewhat slower than anticipated, but some small businesses have been very successful in building a profitable online sales store. For example, Rogers' Chocolates Ltd. of Victoria, British Columbia, decided in 1996 to make its "brochureware" site transactional to reduce the administrative time required to complete sales and create a stronger online presence. In addition to strong growth in its B2C market, the company found that the B2B (wholesale) market increased substantially with its new web presence (see the Estrategy box).

Many large enterprises and government agencies require their suppliers to connect with them via the internet. They see this as a way to streamline their own procurement processes. (See also the discussions on eprocurement in chapter 8.) Most small businesses have found that they need to be online-savvy or risk being cut out of this type of lucrative supply chain.

The potential for online sales transactions will depend upon the industry in which the small business operates, as well as the reputation that the company is able to build. Companies that have operated previously in catalogue-sales operations, such as Rogers' Chocolates, have an easier transition to online sales than those who have no history in the area. Customers will be familiar with the business, and the company will have established logistics and distribution mechanisms in place.

From Bricks to Clicks at Rogers' Chocolates

Rogers' Chocolates Ltd. opened originally as a grocery store in Victoria, British Columbia, in 1885. After a short time in operation, the entrepreneur decided that the most popular product, chocolates, should become the focus of the entire business, but the existing supplier was unable to consistently provide the product at a reasonable cost. Then Rogers' soon developed its own brand of chocolates and quickly shifted the focus of the business to selling only chocolates to a local market as well as a growing number of tourists visiting the area.

Rogers' realized around the turn of the last century that the tourists who had visited the store and been very impressed by the quality products represented an important market. In attempting to continue the company's growth, a mail-order marketing effort began to get the tourists who visited the shop to consider buying more products after they returned home. This represented an early form of "permission marketing," since visitors to the store were asked if they would be willing to receive catalogues and advertisements at home. Growing steadily, the mail-order business came to represent an important market to Rogers' and continues to be a strong component of today's company.

In 1995, 110 years after the business was established, www.rogerschocolates.com was developed as a marketing site with basic company information and advertising. The company decided to make its website transactional in 1996, and today the website is a full ecommerce site with secure ordering capabilities, Flash-based promotional materials, visual tours, and more. Rogers' Chocolates was an early small business to progress through the major stages of website development.

The website has resulted in ecommerce sales growing rapidly and continuing to grow since then. Along with the growth in sales, Rogers' has developed a high rate of repeat customers in the B2C marketplace—a significant factor in becoming profitable.

The internet's growth and the success of the B2C strategy at Rogers' led the company to begin development of a B2B strategy as well. The same website is now used to allow potential retailers to contact the company. The wholesale side of Rogers's business grew from just 5 percent of sales in 1989 to over 40 percent of sales by 2004. In addition to utilizing the internet, Rogers' uses EDI links with major suppliers and has embraced the capabilities of technology to enhance and improve its business.

The success at Rogers has led to excellent growth in both B2B and B2C markets, increased profile, a global expansion, and development of an important volume of repeat customers. From a mom-and-pop grocery store in 1885 to a successful ecommerce business today, Rogers' Chocolates has shown how a reasonably staged approach can lead even small businesses to capitalize on the internet. In the future the company aims to establish a secure extranet and to expand the functionality and services available through the existing website.

Rogers' Chocolates
www.rogerschocolates.com

Questions

1. Why was the transition to ecommerce a smooth one for Rogers' Chocolates?

2. What uses will an extranet have for www.rogerschocolates.com?

3. What additional services or features could be added to the website?

Sources: J. Andrews, "The More Things Change . . . ," *CA Magazine* (March 2000); www.rogerschocolates.com.

Businesses that provide services rather than products may or may not be able to provide those services with only online communication. For many products and services, the value of ecommerce is the generation of sales leads online. For example, Oven Head Salmon Smokers of St. George, New Brunswick, found that its web presence actually led to enquiries from potential customers, who were seeking orders beyond their existing capacity.[8] This type of lead generation is invaluable to any business seeking growth and future profitability.

Conducting online sales transactions and generating sales leads, combined with the value of online marketing, makes ecommerce a very significant tool for most small businesses. Whether the sale actually takes place over the internet is less significant than whether sales occur that would not have otherwise taken place—and much evidence exists to suggest that this does happen.

Public Relations

Most small businesses rely on word of mouth as the main way of promoting their companies and products or services. However, the internet offers small businesses the opportunity to more easily broadcast their message to the media and other users in an effort to create positive PR. Many newspapers and online media channels offer email addresses where businesses can send press releases and other information that may be published. By preparing press releases and notifying the media, small businesses may gain exposure in local or even national newspapers that can lead to increased business or traffic to a website. The website can also include PR items that are considered of importance to the local community, such as testimonials from well-known community members as well as information on fundraising initiatives the company is involved in, corporate donations, and community events. Social networking sites, such as Facebook, LinkedIn, and Twitter, offer tremendous opportunities for small business to get their message out. Many businesses are using social media for PR purposes. The cost is minimal and the reach can be quite large. The potential for the internet to generate positive PR is limitless if the business is innovative in its use, and may potentially lead to improved brand image and/or increased sales.

Employee Retention and Morale

Retaining talented employees is challenging for most small businesses. How can ebusiness help? Small companies can use web-based services to offer the same kinds of benefits as larger firms. Online training programs provide a cost-effective way to boost the knowledge of staff, giving them the skills they need to be more productive. Also, the use of ebusiness technologies for marketing, supply-chain management, and other business functions can help employees feel challenged in a small company.

GETTING STARTED WITH A SMALL EBUSINESS
Developing an Estrategy

Small businesses can go into ebusiness in two basic ways—by starting up as a "pure play" dot-com business or by launching an ebusiness initiative within an established business. Either way, it is important for a small business to develop a strategy for ecommerce, implement that strategy effectively, and constantly evaluate and revise the strategy. It is also important to plan the action steps that are required to successfully implement a small ebusiness.

Trail Blazer, the company mentioned briefly earlier, decided to use its website to market its products and help customers find retailers rather than to actually sell its products online. Within each business, considerations such as these need to be thought through so as to avoid unintended consequences. One of the difficulties often found when dealing with small business owners, however, is that they tend not to use traditional planning and strategy-setting techniques. Therefore, it is important that consultants, government agencies, and other advisers encourage owners to think about the important issues with regard to going online. The Canadian Snapshots box provides another example of an internet startup and some of the issues that arise.

Canadian Snapshots

Hal 2000: Automating the Home

Drew Fraser and his wife, Wendy, started up HAL 2000 Canada out of their home in Springhill, Nova Scotia. Hal 2000 is an operating system they invented that is designed to automate all the functions in a home, such as heating, lighting, cooking, and refrigeration. Moreover, it is designed to accept voice commands. Yes, you can talk to your house and have it do your bidding. You can also talk to it over Skype or the telephone from anyplace in the world. It's a dream many of us have had from time to time, but Drew and Wendy made it a reality for their customers.

Of course, when you have a new product to sell, you need to get the word out that you have it and that it does what you say it does and that they need it. These are tall orders, especially in the case of automating a house, which is something not many people have even seen.

To get the marketing ball rolling, the Frasers started by implementing their system in their own home, which they could then use to demonstrate their product. "Imagine being able to say 'run my bath' and setting off a chain of events that would fill the tub to the desired height and temperature," Drew said, "or calling out for the television or lights to come on simply by asking."

Drew and Wendy invited the public, the press, schools, and organizations to HAL's Heritage House—their house— where the visitors could experience the full impact of a technologically enhanced house. They followed this up with presentations, newspaper articles, and televised interviews. Their marketing campaign was very self-driven.

In the next phase of their marketing strategy, Drew and Wendy targeted people with disabilities. This appeared to them to be a logical niche market for them. Individuals with disabilities could benefit greatly from having a house in which they could operate controls through voice, without reaching for switches and buttons on the walls.

Targeting individuals with disabilities appealed to Drew for altruistic reasons as well. "I am sure that people I show HAL to would like to see someone they know have a bit better quality of life. With a product like HAL hundreds and thousands of people will benefit. The inner strength gained by helping others is a great motivator."

Drew had a goal of selling the product to 1 percent of the population within his reach. He recognized that contact needs to be made with this diverse group on an anytime, anyplace basis. Therefore, a good website and email are important ingredients of his marketing strategy. The marketing strategy also recognizes that people contact matters in the end, so targeted marketing is also part of his approach: finding out who are the best people to contact, who knows who, and going after potential customers.

Starting a business is not easy and famously involves long hours of work without pay, at least during the start-up phase and likely for a good length of time afterwards. But Drew's advice was to "find something that's unique, look for a niche market, grab the bull by the horns, and anticipate a wild ride. Know what you are willing to do to make your dreams possible. You could be in for the wildest ride of your life, if you stay on!"

HAL 2000
www.automatedliving.com

Questions

1. What applications for HAL 2000 might be feasible in the future?

2. Should this product be directed to a niche market or to a general market?

Sources: S. Ward, "Canadian Small Business of the Month, Drew Fraser: HAL 2000 Canada," About.com: http://sbinfocanada.about.com/library/weekly/aa022801a.htm; HAL 2000 Website, www.automatedliving.com

Getting Connected

The first step in becoming involved in ecommerce for small businesses that are not already connected is to establish an internet connection. It is not absolutely necessary for a business to have a connection if all aspects of ecommerce are outsourced, but it would be unlikely that a business could understand ecommerce and take advantage of all of its potential without email and web use within the firm. Numerous alternatives exist for businesses as well as consumers to connect to the internet through an internet service provider (ISP) such as dial-up, cable, asymmetrical digital subscriber line (ADSL), satellite, and other advanced connection forms. In choosing one of the alternatives from an ISP, a small business needs to consider its needs and then balance a number of trade-offs.

Most businesses would want high-speed internet. Most of the ISPs, including telephone companies such as Bell or cable companies such as Rogers, offer high-speed internet connections in urban areas. There are still some rural areas of the country that do not have high-speed connections, but can obtain satellite connections through operators such as Bell ExpressVu. Such satellite connections generally are high speed only for downloads, not uploads, which still work at telephone modem speeds. However, satellite connections are sometimes the best option for a business operator located in a rural area.

Many ISPs exist, and the range of services can vary widely. The ISP used to gain access to the internet does not have to be the one used to host the business website. Most ISPs offer a variety of services, including website hosting, but it is wise to research the various hosting sites available, especially their cost and reliability, before making a decision. It may be preferable and less costly to bundle services with one service provider, but this is not always the case. Many Canadian telecommunications companies bundle their internet and phone packages, which can provide a discount for services. An overall review of the needs of the business as the strategy is implemented will be worthwhile. The selection of a service provider is not necessarily a long-term decision, and ISPs can often be switched with one month's notice. However, while it is fairly easy to switch the ISP providing internet access, it is not so easy to switch the hosting provider, as it will then be necessary to transfer the website to the new host's server, which may lead to difficulties in the functionality of the site. Most companies must be careful to avoid possible service interruptions, and a switch in web hosting can lead to costly outages and downtime.

Domains and Domain Name Registration

Before actually having the website hosted, a business must select and register a domain name. The process of domain name registration and some of the related marketing considerations are set out in chapter 11.

The selection of a domain name is extremely important, as this is the name that the company will be known by on the internet and the name customers and potential customers must use to access the business's website. Ideally it should be one that evokes the name of the business and is easy to remember and to enter into a web browser. Most hosting sites will help with domain name selection and registration.

Getting Hosted

Moving a small business online involves establishing both a website location and a website design. These activities can either be performed internally or may be outsourced, depending on the capabilities and goals of the firm. The hosting of an internet site internally requires technologies that many small businesses do not have or wish to invest in; however, many small technology firms do host their own sites due to their expertise in the area. To host a website, the company would require a fast, stable, and permanent internet connection so that users can visit the site at all times. The company would also require high-performance hardware, specific software applications (e.g., web server software), and other technologies, such as routers and firewalls. This requirement brings with it a number of concerns such as security risks, system performance, and internal expertise, all of which can be costly issues. Professional web hosting packages for businesses are now available for less than $20 per month, and most small businesses find outsourcing to be the best approach.

The development of an internet presence requires close communication between the small business and the provider. As with other services, service levels can vary significantly from one provider to another. Some providers develop and host a website, whereas others offer discounted hosting-only solutions.

When looking for a service provider, it is critical that business owners ask for detailed information on how the project will progress as well as evaluating the types of services provided. The dissatisfaction that occurs in many outsourcing arrangements is due to a misunderstanding between the firms involved—spending more time up front can reduce the likelihood of a poor outcome.

Building an Ecommerce Presence

The implementation of an estrategy requires a small business to consider numerous issues. Since small businesses are less likely than larger corporations to have their own information technology departments, chances are that a great deal of the work involved in building an ecommerce presence will be outsourced. In addition, small businesses must often continue to service and capitalize on existing markets while attempting to utilize ecommerce opportunities without additional staffing. The result of the unique aspects of small businesses entering into ecommerce is that a staged approach (see figure 14.1) is often adopted, where firms develop a basic website and then later enhance the site with additional features and capabilities. This growth mimics the stages of website evolution discussed in chapter 11.

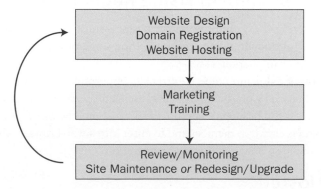

Figure 14.1 Building an ecommerce presence

The process of developing an ecommerce presence can be broken down into a continuous process of design and improvements.

ONLINE SERVICES FOR SMALL BUSINESS

THE INTERNET OFFERS A WEALTH OF INFORMATION THAT CAN BE USEFUL TO SMALL business owners. Much of the information available online is free or low in cost. Information available online can be used to evaluate the competition, gain a better understanding of the industry, research tax and other issues, and monitor governmental programs and services.

As with the use of any external sources, it is important that online information be evaluated in terms of the validity of the source, its timeliness, and its accuracy. The wealth of information can be overwhelming, and the process of sifting through it can be very time-consuming. It is therefore important that web users become familiar with search techniques and develop an understanding of which sources are most relevant to the business. The sources of available information vary widely and can include government, professional firms, media, industry organizations, and many others. An estimated half-million people make a full- or part-time living by auctioning products on the internet using sites such as uBid.com, Bidville.com, ePier, and, of course, the largest of them all, eBay.

New Business Models
A New Kind of Family Farm

Family farms have been in trouble for a few decades. Many of them are burdened with debt, having to use heavy doses of chemicals to maintain high levels of production, and are highly dependent on marketing boards and intermediary buyers from the big food companies, who pay prices that depend on faraway futures markets. No wonder the farms have been closing down.

In other industries, we have seen the internet lead to new business models, in which customers can be reached directly, intermediaries eliminated, and supply chains streamlined with more direct interaction between customers and the business.

Now, similar business models are beginning to emerge for family farms. There is even hope that these new models may reverse the trend to factory farms. The consuming public would be a big beneficiary of such a shift in terms of the quality of the food they consume.

A good example, and a leader in this field, is Polyface Farm, a 550-acre spread in the Shenandoah Valley of Virginia, which produces beef, chickens, and pork. It is a family farm with 10 employees, and it is thriving.

Polyface has a website that provides a full description of the farm, its techniques, and its products. However, the website is not interactive because Polyface does not sell its products via the site. The company does sell some products, but they are non-food products, such as t-shirts. Polyface does not ship food anywhere. Instead, the farm encourages people to seek out local producers in their own area. Nevertheless, people come from miles around to buy food from Polyface because it is so good.

The company employs technology such as moveable electronic pens to enable their livestock to graze together on fresh grass each day. Each day they are moved to a new location, where the grass is fresh and unsoiled. The manure provides a natural fertilizer, and the moving technique allows Polyface to graze four times as many cattle on a given space as a conventional farm.

The company established a buying club with its own website. People can join the club and place their orders for food items, but they need to go pick them up at the farm because there is no delivery. Polyface also delivers meat eight times a year to specific drop points in the region, where members can pick it up.

To avoid the need to obtain bank loans, Polyface personnel maintain constant flows of cash by giving seminars on their style of farming and selling books

>

and guides on how to do it. This is consistent with their philosophy of encouraging local farms to grow and be prosperous in other areas, which of course will not be competitors to them. The seminars teach farmers and prospective farmers the techniques used at Polyface, including dressing chickens, grazing management, handling egg layers, composting, and soil management. The sessions are offered at $550 per person, excluding transportation and lodging.

Much of Polyface's marketing occurs through the website and by way of email. The farm deals with the end consumers of the food and not the big-food-chain companies. In this way, it has eliminated the intermediaries that have traditionally plagued the farming industry. The high quality of the products Polyface offers has enabled the farm to build a loyal following of consumer and restaurant customers. In the span of two years, the buying clubs grew from 200 families to 900 families within a 100-mile radius.

Polyface, Inc.
www.polyfacefarms.com

Buying Club Website
www.polyfaceyum.com

Questions

1. What are the parallels of this new business model with others of the information age, such as the travel industry?

2. How could the web and web technology be used to improve this model?

Source: D.E Gumpert, "A New Push to Make Farming Profitable," *Bloomberg Business*, August 10, 2007, www.businessweek.com/smallbiz/content/aug2007/sb2007088_984272.htm.

Imagine This Sold
www.imaginethissold.com

In addition, for individuals and stores using sites such as eBay, intermediary services have been developed to help them use the sites effectively. For a fee, intermediaries such as Imagine This Sold Ltd. take in products for auctioning, assess them, photograph them, write up descriptions, and then work through the eBay process, remitting payment to the customer and taking a cut of the selling price; for example, 35 percent of the first $200 and 20 percent of the balance of the selling price, plus the applicable eBay fees and payment-processing fees.[9]

The Government of Canada provides a useful website for small business called Canada Business (www.canadabusiness.ca). The site includes a wealth of information on numerous topics targeted to ebusiness B2B users. The site provides users with case studies, statistics, and the ability to ask an expert about issues related to ebusiness. Several other sections of the site provide information relevant to ecommerce and small business, and include useful guides, information, and data related to such topics as retailing on the internet, ecommerce in service industries, and emarketing.

Grant Thornton LLP
www.grantthornton.ca

A common theme on the internet is the provision of free information, and many professional service firms have excellent websites for small business owners. For example, accounting firm Grant Thornton LLP has a website that includes a complete section dedicated to owner-managers, with news and advice on a broad range of issues. Some of the "management issues papers" address important issues that are relevant to small business owners. Many of the major accounting and law firms also provide a large amount of information at no cost that can be of significant value to small businesses.

The media are another major source of information on the internet—including the websites of television and print media, as well as online-only media outlets. A number of newspaper sites (e.g., globeandmail.com) provide free access to current and recent Canadian news content, and television media (e.g., CNN Money) provide access to up-to-date financial news at no cost. Other online media (e.g., *CNET* and Wired News) are also great resources for technology and ebusiness news.

OPERATING A SMALL EBUSINESS

Application Service Providers (Software as a Service)

The explosive growth of internet-based products and services has included the development of application service providers (ASPs) with solutions aimed particularly at small businesses. These ASPs—increasingly referred to as providers of software as a service (SaaS)—offer services such as accounting systems, website tools, payroll applications, and many others. The benefits of utilizing an ASP include reduced need for internal expertise, software upgrades, and administration.

One notable SaaS provider that has targeted the small business sector is NetSuite, which provides an integrated suite of products that handle accounting/finance, customer relationship management, employee management, and the company's web presence (see figure 14.2). The NetSuite SaaS provides a system that is extremely powerful, fully web-integrated, and relatively hassle-free. The integration with the web allows small organizations to provide customers with the option to review their account online, pay bills, and submit orders—services that can be very valuable. In addition, the integration allows a custom web store to be designed using information from the accounting system that can control inventory, pricing, and other issues. Multiple sites can be created (for example, one for retail and one for wholesale customers) and each one is capable of multi-lingual product descriptions and multi-currency payments (e.g., for Canadian customers a site can describe products in English and price them in Canadian dollars, and for French customers the site can describe them in French and price them in euros). All sites can draw from the same inventory. In addition, NetSuite provides important support services, such as tracking shopping-cart abandonments, automated up-sell/cross-sell recommendations, and referral tracking (organic search engine referrals vs. pay-per-click ads).[10]

NetSuite
www.netsuite.com

Marketing and Selling

The marketing efforts required by small businesses can capitalize on many of the tools available on the internet. Chapter 11 identified and described many of the marketing and online advertising approaches that can be valuable to small and large businesses. The difficulties small businesses may encounter will include search engine optimization, developing a community, and reaching new markets. The promise of global markets through ecommerce is not untrue, but is commonly misunderstood—since the "build it and they will come" approach doesn't work on the internet, where billions of websites exist. Whereas large organizations may have employees and automated tools monitoring such issues as search engine placement, many small businesses will need to outsource their website redesign or may have fewer resources available. Developing an understanding of how major search engines work will help the company draw traffic to its site.

Experience has shown that the approaches to marketing in small businesses must include the use of traditional media and advertising efforts and direct marketing. Personal referrals remain a major source of business for businesses of all sizes. Social networking sites are a growing medium for marketing by businesses of all sizes. It is relatively easy for a small business to establish a presence on Facebook and LinkedIn, for example, and then

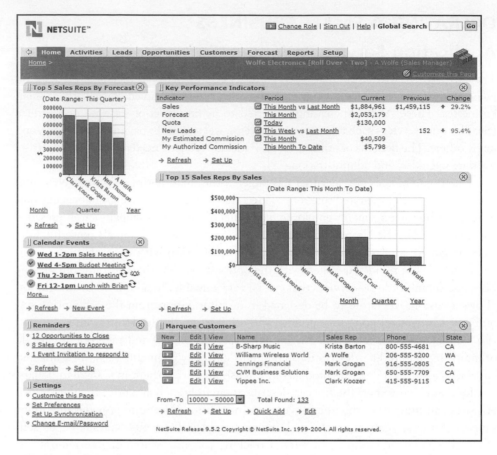

Figure 14.2 Illustration of a SaaS for a small business

NetSuite business software allows small and mid-sized businesses to maintain a powerful set of financial records, manage sales and service, and develop sophisticated ecommerce capabilities with reasonable costs and relative ease.

Source: Courtesy of NetSuite, Inc.

seek to expand its numbers of "friends" and also integrate it with Twitter to reach even more people.

Most small businesses include their website address on business cards, packaging, and on brochures that customers may see. The internet allows small businesses to be innovative in their approach to developing existing customer relationships as well as in attracting new customers.

Trading Exchanges and Online Marketplaces

As discussed in chapter 8, internet-based trading exchanges and marketplaces are an important area where small businesses can market and sell their products or services. Trading exchanges allow B2B commerce to take place efficiently and effectively online.

Canadian trading exchange MERX, for example, specializes in public sector contracts from across Canada. The site, which requires a paid membership, lists daily opportunities from the provincial and federal governments as well as MASH (municipal, academic, school, and hospital) sectors from across Canada. According to MERX, over 80 percent of its customers are small and medium enterprises with less than 50 employees. Another interesting feature of the site is the "document request list" where subscribers can find out what other companies have ordered documents about a particular business opportunity. The potential is obvious: competitors and partnership opportunities can be easily identified.

Small businesses that offer numerous products may look to trading exchanges as a means of selling excess products, or may use them as a day-to-day sales channel. The key to success is to choose a strategy that the business can support and implement well—with a focus on customer service and profitability.

Upon devising a strategy for the use of a trading exchange, a company must first determine which exchanges (and how many) they should utilize, and then register and become familiar with how they work. The exchanges need to be monitored on an ongoing basis, similar to any other sales channel, to determine what is working and what is not.

Receiving Payment—Credit Card Processing

Accepting credit cards online has come a long way since the early days of the internet. Initially, only the largest online stores were able to process credit card transactions. Today, even very small ebusinesses can quickly set up credit card processing for their websites through a variety of banks and merchant account providers. Canadian banks were quite hesitant in the beginning to provide small businesses doing business over the internet with **merchant accounts**, that is, accounts that were able to accept credit card transactions (e.g., Visa and MasterCard). Due to the new nature of ecommerce, many of the banks required small businesses to establish holding accounts of $5000 to $25,000 to ensure that fraudulent transactions would not be defaulted to the bank itself. In addition, some merchant account providers established **holdbacks** of specified amounts, such as 10 percent, that would be retained in the holding account for up to six months on a rolling basis to reduce the risk of bad debts and fraudulent credit card use. Another major issue at the early stages of ecommerce, which to some degree exists even today, was the high discount rate charged by some merchant account providers. The **discount rate** is the amount that the merchant account provider takes as a percentage of sales conducted through credit cards. Normally, it would be less than 4 percent. Early online entrepreneurs, however, were sometimes faced with fees of up to 15 percent due to the high perceived risk. As a result, small businesses faced a major reduction in cash flow and were deterred from becoming involved in ecommerce.

Customized services have developed that cater to small business payment processing over the past several years. One example of such a service is InternetSecure Inc., a leading Canadian payment service provider, which established itself as an important alternative for small businesses during the period when it was very difficult to obtain an online merchant account. InternetSecure allows its customers to join the service by paying an enrolment fee, starting at approximately $300, and guarantees them merchant account

merchant account:
An account held by a business to collect payment through credit cards.

holdback:
An amount that credit card companies keep in escrow to reduce the risk of bad debts and fraudulent credit card use.

discount rate:
The amount that the merchant account provider takes as a percentage of sales conducted through credit cards.

InternetSecure
www.internetsecure.com

status without dealing with banks or other service providers. The company looks after all payment processing and offers various methods of approving transactions, such as integrated, online approval. Users of the InternetSecure service can choose from a number of packages that offer Canadian and/or U.S. currency support. The discount fee charged by InternetSecure is comparable to those of other merchant account providers. Numerous other payment service providers, who simplify the process of accepting payments compared with traditional bank/merchant account providers, have developed services similar to those offered by InternetSecure.

The banks' response to the pressure from small businesses and other lobby groups has since led to major improvements in merchant accounts. Most of the major banks now offer merchant accounts that allow internet transactions with little or no required holding amounts, as well as additional ebusiness-related services. For example, CIBC has partnered with Global Payments Inc. to provide small businesses, web businesses, and large businesses with the ability to accept credit cards online. In this partnership, CIBC is the merchant account provider and banking solution, while Global Payments offers the technology that allows businesses to integrate their ecommerce solution with a secure payment-processing technology. This is a common method by which businesses establish their ecommerce systems and allow a company that specializes in transaction processing to handle that end of payment processing.

The growth of ecommerce and demand for payment-processing mechanisms has given way to a wide variety of services being developed. The important features for small businesses to consider in selecting a payment-processing system are ease of integration, currency, and security. If the site is being outsourced or developed in-house, it is important that the payment mechanism be easy to integrate with the shopping cart or purchasing mechanism the website uses. Some services, such as the Canada Post Sell Online solution for small businesses, provide an easily integrated shopping cart technology. The Canada Post service is provided in partnership with Clic.net and allows web designers to simply cut and paste customized HTML codes into their website to integrate the shopping cart and payment process. Services such as this allow even novice web designers to create powerful, integrated ecommerce sites.

The ability to deal in multiple currencies can be of importance to online retailers operating in global markets. It is not necessary to deal in foreign currencies, but some Canadian businesses have found that allowing their U.S. customers to make purchases with the American dollar resulted in increased sales. For this reason it is important when establishing a merchant account to give consideration to the currencies that will be accepted and how they will be handled. Although credit card processing is only one small component of an ecommerce presence, it is one that is of critical importance, and should be fully considered as an estrategy is being developed. The time involved in establishing a merchant account can also be several weeks for many businesses, and therefore this process should begin early.

Procurement

The purchase of goods and services online by small businesses represents another important aspect for an estrategy. The number of firms, both large and small, that are targeting goods and services to small businesses through their own websites, as well as through trading exchanges, affiliate sites, and other means, has grown substantially as the internet has evolved. This growth has resulted in fierce competition in many areas, thus leading to cost reductions and opportunities for the small business owner.

Small businesses can acquire a wide range of products and services online, from office supplies and computers to internet services such as web design and hosting. The key to the use of eprocurement in small business is to evaluate the market and then negotiate prices (with local suppliers if they are preferred). For example, Staples (and many other firms) offers many office supply products online, where the small businesses can review the prices easily and then demand lower prices from an existing local supplier. Other savings, especially time savings, can also be achieved by using eprocurement to acquire goods through the internet, by creating electronic processes, and by using technological tools to speed up the entire process.

Training

The implementation of an ecommerce initiative may also require training for employees. The amount and type of training that will be required will vary by organization according to its size, the type of strategy being pursued, the level of internal expertise required, and the owner–manager's commitment. The implementation of any ecommerce activities should at least be accompanied by basic training sessions that provide employees with an understanding of how the company's own website works, what it offers, and the impact on internal processes, so they can effectively deal with customers. In many circumstances it is also beneficial to offer employees general internet training as well, so they may evaluate competitors, understand the industry, and possibly make useful suggestions. The necessity for internet training is declining as internet use becomes more widespread, but it is still of benefit to many organizations.

Training efforts may also be necessitated by the adoption of ecommerce, depending upon the technologies being utilized and the level of outsourcing being used. For example, a business may decide to outsource initial website development but train employees to maintain the site and make minor modifications. In this instance an employee or a few employees may be trained in basic website design principles using an HTML editor. The key to training efforts is to ensure that employees are comfortable with and understand the technologies being employed and know the business processes related to the ecommerce initiative.

CHALLENGES TO ECOMMERCE FOR SMALL BUSINESS

The small business sector in Canada has been relatively slow to adopt ecommerce and the use of the internet despite the growth of online commerce. Small businesses are often characterized by the ability to adapt to change quickly and to be innovative, which has created some confusion over their limited adoption of ecommerce. Many studies have concluded that the development of ecommerce in Canadian small businesses has been slower than that in other countries, particularly the United States, and is therefore a concern for the entire economy. The slow development of ecommerce in the small business sector can be attributed to several barriers, notably technological, financial, organizational, and operational barriers.

Technological Challenges

The technological barriers to ecommerce for small business continue to evolve as technology and the internet evolve. Initially, poor internet access combined with other factors was one of the major barriers to ecommerce. However, internet access and technology in general have declined in cost, and Canada is now one of the most connected countries in the world.

The common barrier to technology often found within small businesses is an internal lack of knowledge of computers, the internet, and technology generally. Small business owners are often very pressed for time just to deal with the core aspects of the business, and therefore cannot dedicate time to learning about technologies not considered of crucial importance to the business. The growth of ecommerce has, however, brought attention to the importance of the internet and sparked the interest of many small businesses.

The complexity of becoming involved in ecommerce is often overstated and misunderstood. Many small business owners interviewed in research studies have indicated that the task of becoming involved in ecommerce seemed too technical, and they lacked internal expertise.[11] However, as described in this chapter and throughout this book, it is possible to become involved in ecommerce with only limited technology skills, and many skills can be learned quickly through practice. As businesses increase in size, it becomes more likely that an internal individual may have the capability to implement and manage an ecommerce strategy. Therefore, businesses with more than 75 employees are more likely than smaller enterprises to be involved in ecommerce.

Financial Challenges

Small businesses and many large businesses must balance their financial investments across numerous activities, and ecommerce investments to date have often been considered a non-essential investment. As owners are learning the importance of developing an ecommerce strategy and an internet presence, the costs associated with the investment need to be considered. The costs of implementing an ecommerce strategy can vary widely and may include costs for hardware, software, web design, training, outsourcing, or internet access.

Organizational Challenges

The introduction of change into a small organization is likely to cause as much anxiety, confusion, and resistance as in large organizations. The major difference for small organizations is that if the owner is promoting the change it is much more likely to be accepted than if a manager is promoting change in a large business. If the owner is not the leader of change, however, small businesses may run into many of the difficulties experienced by large ones in implementing new technologies and making business process changes.

The keys to overcoming the organizational barrier of ecommerce implementation are leadership and communication. The owner–manager is in a strong position to positively affect change if he or she is able to clearly communicate the plan to employees. Employees must understand what implications ecommerce will have on the organization as well as their own job responsibilities. The industry, organization size, and many other factors will also influence the changes necessary to become a small "e" business.

Operational Challenges

The small business sector can often experience difficulty in dealing with the operational aspects of becoming an ebusiness. The impact that establishing an ecommerce strategy has on everyday operations may include global issues, fulfillment and logistics needs, hours of operation issues, and several other necessary changes. These issues should all be thought through before the decision to pursue ecommerce is being made.

The impact on everyday business operations can be tied into the organizational issues if employees are not prepared for the changes that are likely to occur. For example, the introduction of a B2C ecommerce website by a manufacturing company may require a complete change in the fulfillment and shipping area of the firm. This could lead to employee dissatisfaction and result in poor performance in the traditional market, the new market, or both. In establishing the estrategy, small businesses must attempt to plan for all impacts of the implementation on operations.

Other potential issues could include language and cultural barriers if operations are expanding globally, as well as currency exchange issues. The types of problems will largely depend upon the operations of the firm prior to its ecommerce activities. For example, businesses with an established catalogue or 1-800 sales channel will often find the move to ecommerce simpler, since the delivery channel is already well established, customer service representatives are trained and knowledgeable, and comfort exists with selling to customers who are not present at the retail outlet. The type of industry and product or service will substantially impact the operational issues that the organization will face.

CHAPTER SUMMARY

Ecommerce represents a significant opportunity for small businesses. Not only does the internet allow small businesses to increase market reach, but it can also provide them with an opportunity to gather a wealth of valuable information. In addition, the use of the internet to conduct operational processes such as procurement and billing represents a great opportunity for small businesses to reduce their costs.

Developing a strategy for small business ecommerce requires planning and analysis similar to any other business decision. The small business must determine what opportunities exist, what costs need to be incurred, and what level of management's involvement will be required. The major issues that small businesses may have to address include overcoming technical weaknesses and ensuring that the costs involved are justified by expected outcomes.

Small businesses may use the internet to gather competitive intelligence and other useful data, or for other purposes. For example, the number of services available to small businesses is expanding rapidly, and they can "rent" applications from application service providers or take advantage of other online tools. The internet has assisted in reducing the in-house technical requirements for many small businesses by converting much software into simple point-and-click solutions.

The use of social media for marketing and for establishing a relationship with customers is rapidly increasing.

The ecommerce strategy and presence for a small business can take numerous forms. The website can be a simple "brochureware" page or, with reasonable costs, can become a fully transactional online presence. The small business must determine which strategy is most appropriate for its industry and customer base.

Key Terms

discount rate (p. 343)

holdback (p. 343)

merchant account (p. 343)

MyEbusinessLab	Tools for Online Learning

To help you master the material in this chapter and stay up to date with new developments in ebusiness, visit the MyEBusinessLab at www.pearsoned.ca/myebusinesslab. Resources include the following:

- **Pre- and Post-Test Questions**
- **Additional Chapter Questions**
- **Author Blog**
- **Recommended Readings**
- **Commentaries on Current Trends**
- **Additional Topics in Ebusiness**
- **Internet Exercises**
- **Glossary Flashcards**

Endnotes

1. InnovaQuest, "The State of Electronic Commerce in Atlantic Canada," Atlantic Canada Opportunities Agency, March 2000.

2. www.cbc.ca/consumer/story/2010/09/27/con-internet-shopping.html#ixzz17SRWBsbk.

3. D. McLean, "Small Business Loves IT, but Could Be Doing More," *Globe and Mail*, October 21, 2006, B14.

4. D. McLean, "Small Business Loves IT, but Could Be Doing More," *Globe and Mail*, October 21, 2006, B14.

5. J. Davis, "Mom and Pop Go Online," *InfoWorld* (May 28, 2001).

6. J. Carroll and R. Broadhead, *Small Business Online* (Toronto: Prentice Hall, 1998).

7. S. McCue, "Small Firms and the Internet: Force or Farce?" *International Trade Forum* 1 (1999), 27.

8. J. Carroll and R. Broadhead, *Small Business Online* (Toronto: Prentice Hall, 1998), 180.

9. M. Strauss, "Taking the 'E' Out of E-Commerce: Meet the eBay Middleman," *Globe and Mail*, October 6, 2004, p. B1.

10. R. Morochove, "NetSuite Can Help Take the Next Step," *Bottom Line* (March 2007), 20.

11. G. Hunter, M. Diochon, D. Pugsley, and B. Wright, "Small Business Adoption of Information Technology: Unique Challenges," Proceedings of the Information Resources Management Association 2001 Conference.

Developed by Research In Motion Ltd. (RIM), of Waterloo, Ontario, Canada, the BlackBerry started life in 1998 as an email-only handheld PDA device. Now, after several iterations, it is a full-fledged portable email terminal, wireless communications solution, and a cellphone. It's the archetypical device for busy executives and others to keep in touch with their business or organization. It's also very popular in government circles. It's become so important on Capitol Hill in Washington that a senator said a failure in the BlackBerry network could be a national security crisis. A member of Parliament in Ottawa, during a rare blackout of BlackBerry email, was quoted in late 2006 as saying "Without my BlackBerry, I'm nothing!" It's not nicknamed "The CrackBerry" for nothing.

Clearly, the BlackBerry fills a fundamental need—the need to stay connected with other people in this fast-moving, modern, technology-fuelled world. With the BlackBerry, you can get email, browse the internet, access corporate data applications, maintain your calendar, and pick up the latest news and weather. It has a full, albeit very small, QWERTY keyboard, a colour screen, and a very appealing design. A significant feature of the BlackBerry is that it has a very long battery life. The email employs push technology, which means that it automatically pushes your emails to the device so that when you look at it, the emails are already there—you don't need to do anything to get them. That's a major advantage that not all similar devices have.

EVOLUTION OF THE BLACKBERRY

The first BlackBerry came with its well-known full keyboard along with a black-and-white LCD screen. It was an email/PDA product that even then made use of push technology. Current versions of the BlackBerry, such as the popular Model 8700, include a state-of-the-art cellphone, enhanced PDA functions, and growing numbers of applications, such as news services and a colour screen. It also enables SMS messaging, a full-featured organizer with a calendar, an address book, and an alarm clock. A thumb-operated track wheel is used to select icons and functions. The rechargeable lithium battery provides four hours of talk time and 10 days of standby time. Memory is 16-Mbyte flash and 2-Mbyte SRAM. The BlackBerry supports Java 2 Micro Edition (J2ME) for handling applications. It can utilize various communications networks, including EDGE, GSM, GPRS, and CDMA2000 technology, and consequently is available through such suppliers as Rogers, Bell, TELUS, AT&T, Cingular, Nextel, T-Mobile, Verizon, and many others outside North America.

A key advantage of the BlackBerry is that it offers full international roaming anywhere that GSM/GPRS networks exist, which means most populated areas of the world. International calling is automated by the system, so that travellers don't need to remember international country codes and don't need to know about local telephone systems in order to make calls. This means travellers can land in a foreign country and start making calls while they wait for their luggage.

BlackBerrys connect with PCs through a USB cable connection for purposes of backup and data synchronization. Through this means, users can synchronize their email with that on their PC and also with their business servers. BlackBerry users with a BlackBerry Enterprise Server have automated and synch with corporate email systems and calendering/PIM systems.

USERS

There are currently more than 10 million BlackBerry users, and the number is growing quickly. The user community consists largely of corporate executives, managers, government and military officers, and the financial and legal communities. The BlackBerry offers them connectivity without having to carry laptops, an advantage that appeals particularly to senior executives, who often don't like carrying a laptop and don't want to be tagged as techie geeks. With a high-end cellphone and email terminal combined in one package, the BlackBerry is a natural.

Another big BlackBerry user is the financial and securities industry. It's a way to keep in touch with key developments on an ongoing basis. The U.S. Department of Defense and other U.S. agencies regularly use the BlackBerry because it's safe and encrypted. Its security features are generally underutilized by regular users.

Lawyers are important users of the BlackBerry, and many big law firms have adopted it for full communications among partners as well as to maintain continuous contact with clients during crisis periods. One advantage of it is that they can send SMS messages in the court room, where communications are likely to be limited.

HOW IT WORKS

There is more to the BlackBerry than the little handheld unit you see people carrying. That is the tip of the iceberg, which actually is an information system, consisting of, besides the handheld, enterprise server software, desktop software, and a wireless web client.

The BlackBerry Enterprise Server software plays an important role in the usefulness of the BlackBerry. The software runs on the corporate email server and is designed to work primarily with Microsoft Exchange, IBM Lotus Domino, or Novell Groupwise. It is this software that manages message synchronization, enables wireless access to corporate data, provides encryption, and lets corporate administrators manage BlackBerry deployment as a part of the overall corporate networking system.

The BlackBerry Internet Service software permits access to as many as 10 email accounts from the handheld. It pulls emails from those accounts and places them on the handheld. The system is set up in advance and does not erase the emails from the main server. However, when the user returns to the office, he or she does not have a big pile of unanswered emails to wade through.

When the BlackBerry Enterprise Server is used, the software goes into the Microsoft Exchange or IBM Lotus Domino server inbox, retrieves a copy of the message, and then compresses and encrypts it. The encrypted message is sent over the internet and through a wireless network provider to the handheld. The user chooses the means of being notified of an email's arrival, which can be by a ring tone, a vibration, or an LED light. When called up, the BlackBerry decrypts and decompresses the message and displays it. Replies also work like this, only in reverse.

STRATEGY FOR THE BLACKBERRY

RIM has a host of engineers continually working on improvements for the BlackBerry. It needs to revise and update the product to meet changing wireless carriers' needs. It also needs to constantly focus on the needs of its customers in the corporate and public sectors. The BlackBerry has also moved to high-speed systems like EDGE and CDMA to make sure it transmits data fast enough. The demand for fast data transmission seems insatiable. Eventually, there will be a model that works with the thousands of 802.11 Wi-Fi wireless LAN hot spots that now exist around the world. The latest models also have GPS tracking capabilities.

There is competition out there, but so far there has been none that has been so effectively directed to the corporate/government market. Palm and Dell have their handhelds and have been seriously considering a run at RIM. Microsoft introduced its smart phone. Even the ubiquitous Apple iPhone, has not had a large impact on the corporate market The iPhone has strong communications capabilities and new interface characteristics that appeal to the non-techies in the market, such as touch-screen commands and camera and video capabilities, but it doesn't have the enterprise server type of capabilities that would appeal to big organizations.

The shortcoming of the BlackBerry at present seems to be in the area of consumer applications that can be downloaded and run on it. There are several, but nothing like what's available for Palm OS PDAs, Pocket PCs and those running Google\s Android system. They have been increasing in number though.

One source of BlackBerry applications is Handango, an online store where applications can be downloaded for a number of devices, including those designed for specific models of the BlackBerry. Handango has more than 900 applications that people can put on BlackBerrys. By comparison, however, Handango also sells more than 25,000 Palm applications and more than 20,000 Windows Mobile applications.

For the corporate or government user, playful applications are simply not important. However, useful ones can add to the appeal, and so BlackBerry needs to be able to keep up with demand in this area. More recent models have, and so there are more third-party applications available for them. These applications include utilities such as the Verichat universal instant messaging client, the WorldMate travel assistant, card games such as Texas Hold'em, and Google Maps specifically designed for mobile systems. These are known as "prosumer" applications to differentiate them from the custom enterprise and corporate-oriented programs that the corporate and government types want and need. On the other hand, recent BlackBerry surveys indicate that the range of users is broadening. Customers include the corporate and government mainstays, but now there are also more sole practitioners, small businessmen, and moms buying BlackBerrys. This could mean a higher demand for applications. In any event, any company needs to at least look at broadening its market base as a strategy.

Finding and installing applications for the BlackBerry has been a problem in the past. There are few applications, for example, on the Rogers website, one of the major carriers of BlackBerrys in Canada. And many of the applications that are available don't download directly into the handheld, but rather need to be downloaded into a PC and then transferred through a USB port and then installed. This is improving, though; the 8700 model, for example, can download a number of applications, such as Google Maps, and have them running in minutes.

To deal with this issue, Handango developed a free BlackBerry application of its own that can be used to browse, buy, and install other BlackBerry applications. Handango InHand can be easily acquired by pointing a BlackBerry browser to mobile.handango.com and following the prompts. It can deliver such applications as Expense Manager, a $6 business expense tracker, and a $5 puzzle game called Oasis.

BlackBerry has a well-established and growing market for its product. The market in which it operates is changing fast, with cellphones coming out with new capabilities like camera, music, and video and, more importantly for the business market, new ecommerce capabilities and applications such as payment systems. There is every indication that the use of cellphones and PDA-type handhelds has changed forever, and that they will play a much larger role in the future, both for personal and for business use. BlackBerry must continue to keep up with the times.

Questions for Discussion

1. Why has connectivity become such an important need for the contemporary business and government community?

2. What should be RIM's strategic thrust with the BlackBerry over the next five years?

Sources

www.blackberry.com
www.rim.com
Y Arar, "BlackBerry Software Story," *PC World* (May 12, 2005).
M. Frenzel, "The BlackBerry Success Story: Mike Lazaridis, President & Co-CEO," *ED Online* (March 29, 2004).

CASE STUDY 1 YouTube

HISTORY

YouTube was launched early in 2005 in the same way that many other great tech companies started—in a garage, by a couple of "under thirties" with no real money. Google, Microsoft, Apple, and eBay all started this way, too. The founders of YouTube were Chad Hurley, Steve Chen, and Jawed Karim, who met when they worked for PayPal.

It is said that Hurley, Chen, and Karim became frustrated with trying to email video clips, so they decided to set up a video-sharing site on the web. The story is that they fleshed out the basic infrastructure for their video-sharing platform in a couple of hours. They were computer science graduates, and they were able to quickly pull together the technology necessary to build a rudimentary video-sharing site.

The **www.youtube.com** domain name was registered February 14, 2005, and the site was opened to the public by May. It was an instant hit and simply took off from there. Hurley, Chen, and Karim did little advertising, and much of the site's growth came from word of mouth. They began to get requests for new, faster and better functionality and quickly realized that while there was an obvious opportunity here for them, they would need to respond to these requests if they were to capitalize on that opportunity.

The growth and interest in the site was so spectacular that the founders managed to attract funding from Sequoia Capital—a global venture capital company that had provided financing for Apple, Google, Oracle, Yahoo!, and others. Sequoia provided the impressive sum of $3.5 million initially. A few months later, it invested another $8 million. Bringing in outside investors like that is a big move for a startup, and growth that is too fast can lead to serious management and organizational problems. However, YouTube's popularity was such that if the company hadn't brought in enough cash to grow its infrastructure, it is likely that the servers would have bogged down, new features couldn't have been added, and users would have migrated quickly to emerging competitors.

Like many other internet startups, YouTube had no clear business plan. And in fact, at first there was little or no revenue—the classic mistake of the dot-com bubble startups. All the newfound capital from Sequoia went into infrastructure and responding to user requests for additional features.

YouTube made some important decisions during this period—strategies consistent with the idea of sharing rather than trying to develop a closed system. Also, the company went way beyond the simple idea of video sharing, although that remained the core of the system. It added such functions as short links to videos, which would be easy to email, "tell-a-friend" functions, and embedding of videos in profiles of other social networking services. YouTube also added a voting system, showing the numbers of times a video was viewed and the ratings given it by viewers. This provided some interactivity and participation to the site, helping to create a sense of community among the users.

Because the videos are provided by the public, and they include not only original content but also copies of previously published videos, copyright has been an issue from the beginning. The original content has been tremendously popular. For example, the Evolution of Dance video was posted in 2006 and by mid-2007 had been viewed more than 52 million times. The easy availability of the copyright content may have been an important factor in the popularity of YouTube as well. People of all ages can view videos of their favourite performers from decades ago. Numerous clips of Elvis Presley, for example, exist on YouTube, from his early days in the late 1950s to the closing days of his career. Most performers up to the present day are represented. Some, such as Justin Bieber, have actually had their start on YouTube.

The strategic response of YouTube managers to the inevitable copyright legal challenges has been brilliant. They extended olive branches to some of the copyright owners in the form of revenue-sharing partnerships. This means that some of the content has effectively become licensed. To users, this makes no difference, and to the copyright owners, it means an opportunity to make some profits. In addition, YouTube locked into the Safe Harbor Provisions of the Digital Millennium Copyright Act (DCMA).

In 1998, the U.S. Congress had passed the On-Line Copyright Infringement Liability Limitation Act in an effort to protect service providers on the Internet from liability for the activities of its users. Codified as Section 512 of the DMCA, this new law exempted online service providers that meet the criteria set forth in the safe harbour provisions from claims of copyright infringement made against them that resulted from the conduct of their customers. If a service provider qualifies for the safe harbour exemption, only the individual infringing customer is liable for monetary damages.

To safeguard the copyright of video owners as best it could, YouTube installed software that could identify the soundtracks in the videos posted by users and then shared with the copyright owner the advertising revenue that runs along with the video. Advertising revenue is the central part of YouTube's business model. Nevertheless, lawsuits continued to roll in.

On October 9, 2006, Google acquired YouTube for $1.65 billion in exchange for stock in Google Inc., which provided enough clout to quell many of the lawsuits. The founders had taken their new venture from $0 in the garage to $1.65 billion in just under two years—an amazing story.

For Google, the YouTube deal was an immediate success, and investors loved it. The deal was paid for with Google shares, which meant Google did not have to actually expend cash. Shares of Google gained $8.50 on news of the deal. As a result, Google made more than $400 million on the deal the very day it was done.

There are issues to deal with going forward. Google needs to reconcile this venture with those it already has under way, particularly its partnership with News Corp. Google had agreed to pay News Corp. $900 million to put its advertising systems to work on MySpace and other social networking sites. There is a potential for conflict in that YouTube and MySpace are both after the same users and the same objectives—bringing together communities of users and getting them to post content. Even though the content is different, they may conflict unless their strategies are aligned with each other.

The other major issue is the likelihood of continuing copyright lawsuits. While Google has deeper pockets than YouTube to deal with them, this issue will probably keep Google's lawyers busy for quite some time.

The biggest issue, however, is the potential for future competition. No business can enjoy the tremendous success that YouTube has experienced without attracting the interest of other entrepreneurs. Companies such as Microsoft, Time Warner, Walt Disney Co., and NBC are looking at their video strategies. And numerous smaller upstarts could become targets of acquisitions by bigger players, thus forming serious competition.

A natural extension of video hosting and sharing sites is a useful video search engine that can search the whole web to find particular movies. Such a search engine does not yet exist, even though rudimentary searches can be made with popular search engines such as Google. It would be too expensive to host them all, although YouTube boasts that it plans in future to host all the music videos ever produced. Movies are a different challenge from the so-called snack-sized videos, however, because of their size (and arguably more difficult copyright issues). There are several illicit and illegal movie-sharing sites on the internet, but they are not viable businesses and will eventually be forced to shut down. Finally, showing advertisements on video sites is problematic because of the difficulty of showing advertisements in conjunction with videos.

Eventually these issues will be addressed by the many video startups now on the scene. The following are just a few of these companies:

■ **VideoEgg**—This is a user-friendly video upload site initially financed by Starbucks Chairman Howard Schultz. It entered into partnerships with popular social networking sites such as Bebo and Hi5 and created an advertising model that allows users to choose whether they want to watch an ad. This approach, together with the attractive layout, may give the company a viable business model. The company makes an ideal acquisition target for a larger company with content but no good way to distribute it.

■ **Metacafe**—This new video site is growing rapidly, with traffic nearly doubling over a six-month period. NielsenNetRatings places it in ninth place in popularity among video sites. The Israeli founders have put $20 million into it, with the intention of building a bigger and better YouTube. Their advertising strategy is to run "pre-roll" video ads that show up at the start of each movie, an approach rejected by several other video sites, as many viewers consider forced video ads to be a nuisance.

■ **Break.com**—This site targets a particular audience—20-year-old guys. So far, it has attracted an audience of about 3 million monthly viewers. Contributors to the upload site try to outdo each other with videos of wild antics and pranks. Although its market is limited, the company may be attractive to another wanting to bring in the ready-made audience.

■ **Revver**—This site has an unusual approach: Pay the contributors. It offers content creators a 50–50 split on revenues from their creations. The advertising model involves running ads alongside the videos.

■ **Blinkx**—This company may have an edge in terms of video search capability. Its founder, Suranga Chandratillake, has another company that specializes in video search technologies. It uses audio recognition and image analysis technologies for search queries. It has partnerships with AOL and Microsoft, which show that those big operators believe that video searching rather than hosting may be the way to go in the long term. Some industry pundits insist that the company that breaks into the market in the video search end will make it big.

■ **Veoh**—This company is moving beyond snack-sized videoclips to longer, higher-resolution video—eventually to be viewed on a television set rather than a monitor. Veoh allows users to download content rather than stream it. Time Warner and Disney are both funding Veoh, which shows that big companies have an interest in video downloading.

Any of these startups and innumerable others could be targets for takeovers by larger, established companies, creating powerful competitors for YouTube. It seems clear that the Google/YouTube alliance has some work to do.

Questions for Discussion

1. What were some good and bad aspects of the strategies YouTube followed in getting its business started?
2. What strategies should YouTube follow in future, given the competition it is likely to face?

Sources: www.youtube.com; M. Bloch, "YouTube—An Online Success Story,"Taming the Beast; www.wikipedia.org/YouTube.

CASE STUDY 2 cars4u

HISTORY

In 1999, Carriage Automotive Group Inc. had been in the automotive industry for over 30 years. It had seen the industry change many times in the past but knew that there would be many more changes ahead. As internet technologies developed, consumers were demanding more from industry retailers, and some were demanding online purchasing, due to its convenience. Carriage understood that, with so much emphasis being placed on technology prior to the new millennium, there would be potential for new forms of competition associated with the emergence of ecommerce. The reasoning was that, since businesses were investing in more sophisticated technologies, these new technologies would allow car dealerships easier access to ecommerce capabilities, which would enable them to compete in new ways. Carriage believed that manufacturers were going to help drive ecommerce in the automotive industry by being able to deal directly with the consumer through the internet and, in turn, by being able to reduce costs and increase savings for the consumer.

As a result of these changes, Carriage decided that it would need to be able to offer its products and services online. It felt that it wasn't enough for a dealership to simply have a website. Instead, it concluded that consumers who were able to reach it via the internet would want the opportunity to use this medium for the whole purchasing process. Following Carriage's strategic decision to enter the ebusiness market, the business changed its name to cars4U Ltd.

When cars4U launched its website (**www.cars4U.com**) on September 6, 2000, it became the first online car dealership in Canada that allowed consumers the opportunity to purchase or lease a vehicle online at a competitive price. All necessary actions could be handled online, from research (prices, features, etc.) to payment and delivery arrangements. The site, although accessible worldwide, offered online purchases only within the Ontario region.

It wasn't long before cars4U had over 1 million hits, and it received over 200 orders within the first nine months of operation, putting it on track to exceed the annual volume of the average Canadian dealership.

THE PROCESS

One of the issues businesses face in ecommerce is developing an attractive website, one that is easily navigated by consumers. Even more importantly, if customers are serious about a purchase, they usually want to complete their transactions quickly and without any inconvenience.

cars4U's website is simple and appealing. When searching for a car, consumers have three options: They can search for a specific make and model; they can look for a car that meets specific characteristics; or they can begin their search through a workbook. The purpose of a workbook is to allow consumers a secure area to save personal vehicle profiles, which makes it easier to compare prices and features each time they visit the site.

Once the consumer indicates the make, model, and price he or she is looking for, the site lists and displays the vehicles currently available. To compensate for models that are currently unavailable, it has a section called "coming soon," which describes the new models that will be available at cars4U in the near future.

Once a vehicle is chosen, the customer can customize it by simply browsing a list of options and checking those they wish to include on their vehicle. The vehicle is then priced automatically, where every component of the final price, including Canadian taxes, appears on the left side of the screen. The right side, which holds both lease and finance calculators, gives consumers the opportunity to compare the two payment options, as well as try out different terms, rates, and down payments.

cars4U offers financing through several financial institutions. The calculators automatically offer the most attractive terms available from this collection of lenders. This entails less hassle for consumers, because they can see exactly how much money the car will cost them. This also avoids the negotiations that some consumers face when they buy at the usual dealer locations. After clicking the cash, the finance, or the lease button on the bottom of the pricing page, the consumer puts down a refundable $350 deposit using a credit card, which completes the loan application. There is also a real-time chat room available at this point where customers can get quick answers to any questions or concerns. cars4U then locates the vehicle and contacts the buyer for purchase verification and approval. Once the buyer gives the go-ahead, the deposit becomes non-refundable. Consumers can choose delivery at the dealership, at their home, or at their office.

SUPPLY-CHAIN MANAGEMENT

For cars4U to be able to offer consumers the opportunity to purchase online without any problems, it needs full participation from its suppliers. To achieve a close-knit relationship with its suppliers, cars4U has purchased several physical dealerships. These dealerships allow it to maintain good relations with the manufacturers, which is necessary for it to be able to offer consumers the best possible price.

cars4U owns Toyota, Acura, and Honda dealerships in Ontario. It also has various other affiliate dealerships that provide it with particular makes and models not available at these dealerships. cars4U has established a close relationship with its affiliate dealers.

Currently, it allows these dealers to become a part of cars4U free of charge. At the same time, cars4U gets a percentage of the profit from each sale. This way, each dealer gets more exposure on the web, which increases revenues for both affiliate dealers and cars4U.

THE BUSINESS MODEL

cars4U online follows a model that allows the customer to be in control, by providing comfort, convenience, and choice. cars4U found that clients feel they are *not* in control in a traditional dealer environment, but are rather at the mercy of the seller. "For the first time in automotive dealing in Canada, consumers have control over a process they never had control over before," said Barry Shafran, cars4U's CEO. Lilly Buchwitz, the very first customer of cars4U, certainly agreed. She knew she wanted a new Volkswagen. But she had neither the time nor the inclination to visit a dealer and haggle over price. "I don't believe anyone enjoys haggling over a car," she said. "It just really fills you with dread."

cars4U is also able to increase sales opportunities by giving consumers the chance to shop 24 hours a day, 7 days a week, all year long. Over holiday seasons, Canadians take advantage of the fact that the cars4U's edealer never closes. In its first season, as many orders were placed with cars4U in December and January as there had been in the previous three months. This growth was even more striking given that December and January are typically the slowest months of the year for automotive retailing. Additionally, spending on advertising in these two months was substantially reduced from previous levels.

In addition to providing customers with the opportunity to shop around the clock, cars4U has also improved the efficiency of its internal business processes. The whole process of ordering a vehicle now takes just a few minutes, and delivery takes only a little longer than a week if the specific vehicle is available in the manufacturer's inventory.

In the long term, as it continues to develop its business model, cars4U may develop greater cost-effectiveness by reducing concessions. For instance, by reducing costs, cars4U may eventually be able to afford more extensive delivery service for consumers. Large numbers of orders would make neighbourhood delivery by truck possible, straight from the factory to private homes. However, its current model is to start a new distribution centre, which aims not to replace traditional car dealerships but rather to develop new sales channels online. This can be accomplished by targeting those customers who are looking for more comfort, convenience, and choice and are willing to shop online.

STRATEGY

cars4U has moved from a 30-year-old brick-and-mortar company to a complete clicks-and-mortar organization. To finance growth, the company went public on the Toronto Stock Exchange in May 2000.

The corporate strategy chosen by cars4U online was "launch and learn." To be the first online car dealership in Canada, cars4U's management chose to launch an incomplete site on September 6, 2000, one that was not totally integrated. However, this launch-and-learn strategy allowed cars4U to become the first online car dealer based in

Canada. This decision was influenced by such competitors as Carpoint (now Sympatico/MSN Autos), the little brother of Carpoint owned by Microsoft (now MSN Autos), and Megawheel.com, which was also in the starting blocks for this type of ecommerce. cars4U felt that being the original automotive ebusiness in Canada would be a significant benefit to it. It hoped this would influence customers to perceive it as the most experienced leader in the industry.

cars4U's divisions, brick-and-mortar and online, seek to satisfy consumers in their automotive investments through quality products and service. cars4U realized that, although both of its divisions share the same goals, they follow very different strategies to achieve these goals. Their brick-and-mortar strategy involves expanding the physical dealership network to further satisfy consumers who are not comfortable with the ebusiness concept. On the other hand, cars4U's online strategy is to offer customers more comfort and efficiency by enabling them to make their choices conveniently in the comfort of their own home or office.

cars4U decided it had to maintain and continue to expand its brick-and-mortar business in order to maintain the loyalty of those customers who enjoy the experience of visiting and buying from new car dealerships. For instance, it acquired its Acura dealership in November 1999, only a few months before launching its ebusiness division.

The pricing structure online follows a strategy different from pricing in its traditional dealerships. cars4U stresses that the customer is in control because there is no haggling or pricing when shopping online. The price customers see is the price they get. As indicated by Lilly Buchwitz, cars4U's price was $700 cheaper than the lowest price quoted by any traditional dealer she visited. How does cars4U make money, offering such discounts? It's a matter of perception. This firm gives customers a fixed price, unlike traditional car dealers, where staff members "structure" sales according to how much they think they can get.

ADVERTISING AND PROMOTION

Another major issue cars4U faced was advertising and promotion. Since it has two separate business models for its divisions, it needed to develop a strategy that would promote its new online store while not giving its physical dealerships a negative return. Advertising and promotion strategy was designed to focus on being Canada's first-ever edealer. During the first quarter of 2001, cars4U invested $450,000 in advertising. Because of this investment, it experienced a $212,000 loss compared with its $68,353 net earnings during the first quarter of 2000. cars4U plans to continue advertising, but feels it must develop a marketing strategy that will result in an overall profit for cars4U's online and brick-and-mortar divisions.

PRIVACY AND SECURITY

When trying to tackle the issues that are relevant to consumers, cars4U had to spend a significant amount of effort on security and privacy concerns. Due to the issues of fraud and hacking, it is in the best interest of consumers to be sure that they shop only on secure sites. cars4U has outlined several areas where it has taken precautionary steps to help make its site more secure and trustworthy in a privacy statement posted on its website.

All financial information is kept completely confidential. Only information that is necessary in processing the customer's order will be made available to additional parties. These parties may include the alliance dealership that supplies the customer's vehicle, the credit card company, or the institution that finances or leases their new vehicle purchase.

When placing an order with cars4U, a customer must give his or her name, email address, mailing address, and phone number so that the company can contact the customer regarding the order and its delivery. This information ensures that the customer is located in an area that cars4U can service. Unfortunately, cars4U still does not service areas outside of Ontario. After the customer has placed an order, cars4U will require the customer's driver's license number, insurance company, and policy number.

While cars4U does indicate that it may provide aggregate statistics about its customers, sales, traffic patterns, and related site information to reputable third-party vendors, it ensures that no personally identifying or financially sensitive information will be passed on.

When customers place an order or access their account information, cars4U uses a secure server to transfer the data back to them. The secure server software is designed to provide encrypted communications on the internet.

All information customers send through the internet is encrypted before it is sent to cars4U to reduce the likelihood of unauthorized access. cars4U maintains secure data networks protected by industry-standard backups, such as firewalls and password-protection systems. These software investments protect against the loss, misuse, and alteration of the information.

Barry Shafram, CEO of cars4U, was quite pleased with the progress of the company's new online division. He knew, however, that there were many challenges ahead to gain a strong position in the market. For example, the company has been criticized for expanding its "bricks" operations as it expanded online. In addition, increasing competition from U.S. sites like Carpoint, which were well financed and growing quickly, has caused some concerns over growth and market share. Shafram needed some innovative ideas on how to strengthen cars4U's ebusiness.

On February 16, 2006, cars4U was wrapped into Chesswood Income Fund, a financial services trust. Operating activities of the fund started on May 10, 2006. That move marked the completion of conversion of cars4U to an income trust, and the $57 781 930 initial public offering by the fund, the proceeds of which were used for the acquisition of Pawnee Leasing Corporation of Colorado, enabling an expansion into the United States.

The fund is an unincorporated, open-ended, limited-purpose trust established under the laws of the Province of Ontario pursuant to a declaration of trust. The fund was created to indirectly acquire all of the shares in Pawnee, a Colorado company, and all of the shares of cars4U, pursuant to a plan of arrangement under the Business Corporations Act (Ontario).

This brought a substantial amount of capital into the enterprise, and enabled substantial income tax savings. In late 2006, however, the Canadian government announced that it would be taxing income trusts, launching the Chesswood Income Fund into a crisis to determine its ultimate structure.

The cars4U website, however, continues as before.

Questions for Discussion

1. Does the continued growth of cars4U's "bricks" presence make sense for an online company?

2. What alternatives could cars4U pursue instead of increasing its dealership network?

3. What can cars4U do to fight off competition from U.S. competitors?

4. How can the company develop an advertising strategy that builds on both the online and offline divisions?

5. cars4U would like to expand its operations. Should the company expand nationally or provincially, and why? What about global or U.S. opportunities?

Source: This case was originally prepared by Myra Cholmondeley, April Wells, and Yves Leblond under the supervision of Professor David Pugsley for the sole purpose of providing material for classroom discussion. The authors do not intend to illustrate either effective or ineffective handling of a managerial situation.

CASE STUDY 3 Monster

It was almost midnight on the eve of Monster.com's July 2007 quarterly board meeting, and CEO Sal Iannuzzi continued to wrestle with what position he would present to the board in less than 12 hours. Monster, the flagship brand of Monster Worldwide Inc., sat at a critical point in its existence. Despite user levels that had reached record highs, due in large part to the company's massive advertising efforts as well as numerous strategic partnerships with major online portals and expansion into new parts of the globe, the company had lost its leadership position to CareerBuilder.com.

Sal Iannuzzi had come to Monster only three months before and had spent the past two weeks preparing two different proposals for the upcoming meeting, one of which he would present to the board. Iannuzzi saw Monster as being at a crossroads. For most of its early life, like most internet companies, Monster had operated at a loss, focusing on its long-term growth. It seemed that no sooner had it become profitable than it ran into headwinds. Sal Iannuzzi was looking at the quarter's results and they weren't pretty.

Second-quarter profit fell. Net income slid 28 percent to $28.6 million, or 21 cents a share, from $39.6 million, or 30 cents, a year earlier. Although sales rose 20 percent to $331.1 million, they missed the $337 million average estimate of 15 analysts.[1] The company's shareholders were looking for increased profitability and evidence of sustainable competitive strength, and these results would not help. This led Iannuzzi to wonder whether perhaps this would be the year to cut back on the company's expansion plans and focus on increasing profitability. On the other hand, he saw the need for investing in untapped markets such as China and India, as well as for funding new advertising initiatives in North America and Europe to maintain the customer base. The company also needed to spend up to $80 million to upgrade technology, such as software to let employers place more ads without help, to rekindle growth in North American job listings, its largest business, and to improve the company's gross margin. Competitors were devoting much effort to self-service features to maintain their gross margins. Maybe now was not the time to put the brakes to the company's past marketing strategy and spending on technology. Iannuzzi decided that he would examine all relevant evidence one more time and then arrive at a decision.

THE ARRIVAL OF ONLINE RECRUITING

Monster is the flagship brand of Monster Worldwide Inc., with more than 8500 employees in 33 countries and 26 local language and content sites in 24 countries.[2] Monster was retooled in January of 1999 as a result of a merger of The Monster Board (**www.monster.com**) and Online Career Center, founded in 1994 and 1993, respectively. Monster.com was acquired in 1995 by TMP Worldwide (TMPW) in a move to penetrate the new online career services market. TMPW was one of the most aggressive companies on the acquisition trail during 2001 and 2002, scooping up beleaguered competitors such as FlipDog.com and Europe-based Jobline.net. It also paid $800 000 for the domain name of defunct site Jobs.com as part of a bid to create a network of regional sites focused on non-professional jobs. However, Monster failed to obtain HotJobs.com itself due to regulatory concerns. Instead, HotJobs.com was sold to Yahoo!.

The association between TMPW and Monster.com was so successful that TMPW entirely revamped its strategy, making Monster.com its primary focus. To reflect this change in strategy, TMPW renamed itself Monster Worldwide in 2003. Headquartered in New York, it is not only the world's largest recruitment advertising agency network, and one of the world's largest search and selection agencies, but also the world's largest Yellow Pages advertising agency and a provider of direct marketing services. The company's clients include more than 90 of the *Fortune* 100 and approximately 465 of the *Fortune* 500 companies.

Based in Maynard, Massachusetts, Monster.com has 12 million unique visitors per month, a database with more than 50 million résumés, and over 150 000 member companies.[3] Monster.com offers value to recruiters and employers by helping them attract, source, connect with, hire, and retain best-fit employees through the use of their strong, global brand. This results in lower recruiting and retention costs, shorter job fulfillment cycles, lower turnovers, and increased employee satisfaction. At the same time, Monster.com provides value to job seekers by allowing them to proactively search for better career options. It is free to list a résumé on Monster.com and to peruse its job listings; however, Monster.com also offers job seekers additional value-added for-fee services, such as My Monster Premium.[4]

MONSTER'S COMPETITION
Yahoo! HotJobs

Yahoo! HotJobs is a leading career-search site on the web. It earns revenues through monthly subscription fees from its 8000-plus business users, and the company would like to boost the software-based services it offers to enable businesses to manage the recruitment process from their desktops. HotJobs possesses global career portals in the United States, Canada, and Australia. The home page has links to 26 career channels, including entry-level jobs, positions with startups, and a channel for job seekers fresh out of college. Although it attracts only a fraction of the visitors that Monster does, HotJobs is quick to call attention to the fact that its clientele is not merely internet companies but also major international corporate players, including 80 of the *Fortune* 100.

Like many other dot-com companies, HotJobs relies on offline advertising, such as the Super Bowl ads that constituted a major portion of its ad budget in earlier years. Managers at HotJobs believed that they could strengthen their company's credibility and acknowledgement through strong offline advertising and growing word-of-mouth support. They also had a high regard for the power of television. The company's outdoor and print campaign reflected an optimistic tag line: "Onward, upward." However, Marc Karasu, director of advertising at HotJobs, believed that television slots were key for developing an overall brand. "Outdoor ads work in conjunction with the television campaign," he said.

HotJobs was trying to target university and college students. Under a partnership with Student Advantage, the company established a presence at big campus events, such as homecoming day.

A continuous objective of HotJobs was to improve its site by adding new and innovative services that would provide more convenience to its customers. Shopping carts and company blocking are examples of additional services that were included to enhance customer expediency.

A driving force behind the success of online recruiting companies, like Monster and HotJobs, is their ability to offer more than the traditional offline recruiting services, such as newspapers, as well as to operate with much lower expenses.

Workopolis

Although it is not a global competitor to Monster, Workopolis is one of the many formidable "local" job sites that Monster competes with in Canada. Workopolis is co-owned by Toronto Star Newspapers Ltd. and Gesca Ltd., the newspaper-publishing subsidiary of Power Corp. Workopolis provides many of the same features as Monster, within a more focused geographic arena. In 2004, Workopolis teamed up with CareerBuilder. com, a Chicago-based jobs site owned by the Tribune, Gannett, and Knight-Ridder newspaper chains, and featuring jobs from the classified sections of more than 130 U.S. newspapers. CareerBuilder.com features more than 9 million résumés and more than 400 000 jobs from over 25 000 of the top employers in the United States. According to Patrick Sullivan, president of Workopolis, the arrangement makes it easier for customers to post jobs in both Canada and the United States, making Workopolis a one-stop shop. Since Workopolis and CareerBuilder.com are the dominant online players in Canada and the United States, respectively, they represent a significant challenge to Monster.[5]

Hiring managers, Monster's most important customers, were becoming weary of sifting through thousands of online résumés in search of the perfect applicant. Competitors such as Jobster, Craigslist, and Kforce were eager to turn that dissatisfaction into dollars through a combination of technology, personalized services, and better local focus.[6]

MAKING A NAME FOR ITSELF: ADVERTISING STRATEGY

Monster strives to be the advertising leader among online recruiting firms. Over the past several years, the method of internet advertising has been changing. Banner ads have been decreasing in popularity due to the success of search engine marketing, promoted by Google and other more targeted and performance-based advertising models. Online companies also realized the importance of offline advertising, relying on television advertising and other methods. As the most widely viewed annual event, the National Football League's Super Bowl is considered a powerful advertising opportunity. But because airtime costs millions of dollars per 30-second spot, advertisers must make sure that their marketing campaign generates a return on their investment. The most important goal for Super Bowl advertisers is to make sure that it's really their company that is talked about, and not just a catchy ad. It's easy to be caught up in the entertainment and lose sight of brand recognition. Often, there are many great ads during the Super Bowl, but people do not remember the next day what they were or what they were advertising. The number of dot-com advertisers has dropped drastically from the heyday of the dot-com boom (e.g., from 17 to just 3 from Super Bowl XXXIV to Super Bowl XXXV). But Monster continued to spend millions on 30-second ads during the broadcast in the hopes of attracting new clients to their electronic résumés. For Monster, advertising during the Super Bowl appears to have paid off. Traffic peaked in the 24 hours following Super Bowl XXXV, as 2.2 million job searches were conducted, up from half a million the week before. And about 40 000 job seekers posted their résumés on Monster the week after.

Monster's advertising division has proposed an advertising budget of US$200 million for their advertising campaign for the current year, centred on five TV spots. The ads would focus on the positive impact that work can have on the viewer's life. All of the commercials would be skits that highlight work life and how it corresponds with life overall. The underlying message would be that when work is good, life is good.

These advertising spots would also feature "Trump," the company's colourful signature monster. Trump would be a signature signoff, intended to strengthen brand name. Trump was developed by United Virtualities in New York, and was based on "Shoshkeles," which is a new technology featuring animation or photography that works across all platforms and requires no plug-ins. Unlike static banner ads, at the top or bottom of a page, Shoshkeles remains in the viewer's sight even when he or she scrolls around the page. Yet it only stays on the page for a few seconds, an important selling point for people who may leave the site if they feel annoyed by advertising.

Other advertising plans this year included visits by the Monster "ground crew" to college football games and tailgating parties in five key markets starting in the third quarter. Monster also wanted to continue its relationship with AOL and the Monster Show, a 30-second direct-response TV effort. An email push to 11 million MyMonster.com members and a direct mail to 150 000 companies in its job bank would round out Monster's advertising efforts this year.

Monster has an effective marketing strategy through combining both online and offline advertising in order to attract clientele. It has built strong brand awareness, encouraging customer loyalty by delivering quality services. As online recruiting firms continue to arise, Monster has become the standard and leader in this industry.

EXPANDING AUDIENCES: MONSTER'S ALLIANCES

The advent of mergers, strategic partnerships, and high-profile deals between web companies is a phenomenon that has taken hold in the ecommerce arena while, at the same time, leaving much of the corporate community confused. The intangible, virtual nature of the deals inked by online enterprise executives often leaves many to wonder what it is exactly that these giants are actually exchanging, and what impact the agreements will really have on their bottom lines and the competitive internet landscape altogether. These alliances materialize in a variety of forms: fixed-sum arrangements, revenue-sharing agreements, "pay as you go" deals through methods such as per-click or per-sale compensation, barter arrangements where one company will trade advertising space with another, and the out-and-out acquisition of one company by another.

While many may believe that the benefits of these deals are not measurable, and thus are often quantified inaccurately and overly optimistically, others such as Bryan Rutberg, director of the internet investment group at an investment bank that regularly advises web companies in these matters, believe that, "The contracts for these deals often have built-in performance guarantees. And the companies have tracking mechanisms to make sure they're met."[7] These online collaborations have proved indispensable, as they open companies to new markets that otherwise would likely not have been reached.

For example, Monster's four-year US$100 million deal with America Online (which took a painstaking five years of negotiations) provided Monster with a contextual integration into AOL sites made available to over 19 million members. Prior to this, Monster's aggressive offline marketing campaign had been the primary method of generating awareness. This arrangement enabled it to reach a new key demographic: online users who are merely a click away from accessing Monster.

Advice and services from Monster were featured daily on the AOL properties, including the heavily trafficked main screen of the WorkPlace Channel (AOL Keyword: WorkPlace). Content from Monster also was featured in the Channel's industry areas, where professionals in a variety of fields meet, trade, and conduct research online.

While AOL was Monster's most significant partner in terms of user span, Monster had aligned itself with several other key portals that enabled it to target a wider variety of audiences. Links through major portals such as iWon.com, ESPN, AT&T Worldnet, and World Pages provide the company with increased avenues for traffic and collectively constitute a major portion of its visitors.

DECISION TIME

Sal Iannuzzi knew that he had to make some decisions. Could Monster thrive in the eyes of the market without a positive bottom line? Did it have enough of an edge on the competition to stay dominant if advertising were cut back? Could he afford to cut back on offline advertising? If advertising wasn't cut, what could be? Could he delay investing in technology? Were there more potential partners that Monster could benefit from?

Questions for Discussion

1. What impact do you think the history of Monster Worldwide may have had on the development of Monster as an online competitor?

2. What benefits are there to being a "global online recruiting network"?
3. Given the nature of Monster's competitors, does it seem worthwhile to spend large amounts of money on television advertising campaigns? Why or why not?
4. What are the pros and cons of advertising during the Super Bowl?
5. What should Sal Iannuzzi do about the serious decline in profitability?

Source: This case was adapted by Efrim Boritz from a case originally prepared by James Blackburn, Maher Markabi, and Arlene Pino under the supervision of Professor David Pugsley for the sole purpose of providing material for classroom discussion. The author does not intend to illustrate either effective or ineffective handling of a managerial situation.

Endnotes

1. http://money.cnn.com/2007/07/30/news/companies/bc.monster.results.reut/, accessed August 5, 2007 [link no longer active].
2. http://about.monster.ca/6268_en-CA_p1.asp, accessed August 4, 2007.
3. www.caslon.com.au/jobsearchprofile1.htm, accessed August 6, 2007.
4. www.careertrainer.com/Request.jsp?lView=ViewArticle&Article=OID:31340&Page=OID:31341, accessed August 6, 2007.
5. "Workopolis Teams Up with U.S. Jobs Site," *Globe and Mail*, February 19, 2004.
6. http://money.cnn.com/magazines/fsb/fsb_archive/2007/05/01/100003829/index.htm, accessed August 6, 2007.
7. B. Zerega, "Web Deals Are Different," *Red Herring*, March 31, 2000, www.redherring.com/Home/8776.

CASE STUDY 4 Mountain Equipment Co-operative

In January, 2001, Geoff Campbell, president and chairman of the board at Vancouver, BC-based Mountain Equipment Co-operative (MEC), sat at his office desk and contemplated the feasibility of establishing an online website. Over the past two years Campbell had been pleased with the performance of the organization, which had reached annual sales of $500 000 by specializing in outdoor recreation and the sale of sporting equipment,[1] but he felt that there were markets that were not being reached. Campbell was beginning to think a website might be what his organization needed to get wider exposure.

Although his main job kept him from committing 100 percent of his time to researching this potential opportunity, he did have an entrusted and supportive group that he could work with. They all respected Campbell and together they all wanted to see MEC grow globally as well as nationally.

COMPANY BACKGROUND

Mountain Equipment Co-operative was spawned by a lack of mountaineering stores in Vancouver in the late 1960s. At that time, most mountaineers in need of gear would make pilgrimages to REI, which was based in Seattle. Although this worked for a time, problems arising with Canadian Customs produced a need for a similar facility north of the border. Therefore, in the spring of 1970 a group of six Canadians began to organize what would later be known as Mountain Equipment Co-operative.

In the beginning the decision was made to restrict business to the sale of high-quality equipment for mountaineering, rock climbing, ski mountaineering, touring, and hiking. The organization later expanded to include paddling and bicycling equipment due to strong demand in these areas. The first store was built in Vancouver, and afterwards the organization expanded eastward to 10 different locations. The Vancouver store also hosted the head office.

Four years later, another store was opened in Calgary to serve the Prairie provinces. The Calgary store established an initial presence out of a U-Haul trailer loaded with gear driven out from Vancouver. Then a storeroom was established in a cramped office space above a record store and finally the Calgary store moved into an independent building downtown. The new store was the second one to employ environmentally friendly building features, such as high-efficiency heating, ventilation, and air-conditioning systems, as well as low-consumption water fixtures.

The next step in MEC's expansion was into central Canada with the creation of a Toronto store in 1985. In this huge market the new store was extremely successful, and on March 31, 1998, a new location was needed to accommodate the high traffic volumes and the increasingly diverse product offerings. The new facility was 42 000 square feet and, like the others, was committed to environmental sustainability, the principles of which guided design and construction.

Because of high demand, a second store was needed to serve the Ontario market. Thus in 1992 the first Ottawa store was built in the shell of an old movie theatre. This store quickly became known because of its location, and in a short time sales were phenomenal. As with Toronto, volume grew very quickly, leading to the need for a larger capacity. In June of 2000, the Ottawa store moved to a reconditioned building, which solved the problem with ease, and operations once again continued to grow unabated.

In May 1998, a team of market analysts determined that Edmonton, Alberta, would be a profitable location for MEC's fifth store, as it would help to expose the company to northern Alberta and perhaps even the Territories. By converting a vacant Safeway store, MEC became a part of a changing shopping district in the neighbourhood of Old Glenora. The building was a good example of MEC's core value of respecting and protecting the natural environment. An attractive and functional facility provided the aesthetics to draw in customers. Business grew, and once again the design was consistent with its objective of controlling the impact on the surrounding neighbourhood.

Throughout its first 30 years, MEC has changed both in the size of its stores (from closet to aircraft hangar) and hours (Wednesday through Friday evenings to seven days a week). This has been directly correlated to the growth of the membership. To continue growing, MEC opened its sixth store, in Halifax, Nova Scotia, in the summer of 2001. Other stores later opened in North Vancouver, Winnipeg, Montreal, and Quebec City.

MARKET ANALYSIS

The market for outdoor sporting equipment consists of several overlapping groups, primarily young adults and sporting enthusiasts. Changing demographics were causing MEC to think in terms of a broader market, particularly families, surrounding businesses, and, to a lesser extent, senior citizens.

Campbell identified five major market segments:

1. *Young adults*—This group consists of individuals aged 18 to 35. The majority of this group are single male and female sport enthusiasts who enjoy weekend excursions and other adventurous activities to get away from city or college life and their stresses.

2. *Retired*—These are people in their 60s and 70s who enjoy active outdoor activities and weekend outings as well as vacations in a nature setting. Many of them are financially secure and stable and enjoy spending money for premium products.

3. *Families*—They search for opportunities to escape from the city life and spend time together in natural surroundings. They purchase camping equipment such as sleeping bags, tents, and outerwear in multiple quantities to accommodate family members.

4. *Businesses*—These are individuals in the workplace who share the same interests but are competitive with one another and desire top-of-the-line products. For example, if someone buys MEC equipment, they convince their co-workers that it is a premium product and that, in turn, stimulates referral purchases.

5. *Gift buyers*—This group consists of people purchasing equipment for their sons, daughters, other relatives, and special friends at Christmas, birthdays, graduations, etc. For that reason, this market is aggressively pursued in and around holidays.

There are also groups interested in this equipment for more specialized purposes, such as outdoor adventure groups who provide and coordinate nature expeditions. The growth of MEC coincided with general trends across Canada towards more active lifestyles.

Despite the obvious interest shown by many people in the company and its products, however, all was not positive. The head office in Vancouver was receiving high volumes of letters from people who were interested in finding out more about MEC's products but, because of their location, couldn't visit one of the stores. Potential customers were being lost because they were either unaware of MEC or didn't want to go to the trouble of giving their credit card and personal information on the phone and then having to wait six to eight weeks to receive their products. Therefore, MEC was losing sales because customers were going to the competition.

Campbell and the rest of the board realized that there was potential to reach many more Canadians. However, with their current structure and style they could not reach a majority of this market, so a change was necessary. That was when they began thinking seriously about a website.

COMPETITIVE ANALYSIS

MEC's equipment essentially served two customer functions. It could be used as gifts for family or friends, or for those who showed great interest in rafting, canoeing, rock climbing, camping, or any other outdoor events that required top-quality gear.

Competition came from all other sporting equipment stores, but mostly was based on cheaper prices for lower-quality gear. The main direct competition was traditional retail chain stores that can provide similar gear that still satisfies consumer needs, but at an exceptionally low price. However, many of these customers were becoming unhappy with the quality and were looking for alternatives. They found that they were constantly replacing and returning their equipment because it was simply not durable enough for the terrain in which they were using it. Interestingly enough, most purchasers of these cheaper products were aware of MEC's product line and did buy some of their equipment from MEC through mail-order catalogues. However, most found this to be a huge inconvenience, because they did not want to wait for the product to come in the mail. Market analysis indicated that the indirect competitors consisted of equipment recyclers like Play-It-Again-Sports who go one step further than the traditional outlet by offering second-hand, mediocre equipment at extremely discounted prices.

In a survey conducted of its members, MEC asked if, by improving the accessibility of its products, members would increase their purchases at MEC. The response was that close to 85 percent preferred MEC gear to the competition and would increase their purchases of the gear if it was made more easily accessible to them.

FINANCES

Before determining how to solve their exposure problems, Campbell and the rest of the board decided to review MEC's earnings for 1999 and evaluate the feasibility of expanding its operations, either online or through traditional brick-and-mortar establishments. In examining the costs associated with opening more store locations as opposed to setting up a website, the board determined that, although opening more stores would be a good way to increase sales, the cost and time associated with opening more locations was extremely high. With a website the startup costs were not even close to those of opening a new location, and Campbell was positive that it would be a success. He also felt that by having a website, MEC customers could share their experiences with one another. The only problem with a website is that some people would not feel comfortable giving their credit card number online, so Campbell felt the company would have to address this issue carefully to ensure the security and privacy of all their customers' information.

DISTRIBUTION

After a good deal of discussion, the board decided to go with a website. Campbell and the rest of the board then had the task of implementing several activities that would promote the success of the new website. The first of these was to determine how to expand MEC's supply-chain logistics to facilitate the extra business. The company's mail-order catalogue as well as its telephone service required an extensive delivery system that transferred the product to each individual purchaser upon receipt of payment. With the new website, it would be inevitable that customer orders would increase and necessitate a more comprehensive delivery system. Therefore, nurturing their already existing relationship with FedEx was mandatory, as success would ultimately depend on their combined efforts. Campbell and his associates felt strongly that the organization needed to focus on reducing the delivery time of orders. And the expectations of the online customers would, they knew, be higher than those of other customers with regard to fast turnaround.

CONCLUSION

MEC has made a significant commitment to its Canadian customers, and developing a website increased the quality of its service and allowed continued growth in its market. Although the company felt that it was capable of expanding the number of store locations, it also felt that it was unnecessary and costly.

As Campbell sat back in his chair, he felt confident and satisfied with the decision to implement a website, because of the low investment needed to receive a potentially high payback. Even if the performance of the website were to fall below expectations, the initial investment would be minimal, certainly less than that required to open new stores.

Questions for Discussion

1. How should the different market segments impact the website and ecommerce strategy?
2. Would startup costs for an ecommerce strategy necessarily be lower than opening an additional brick-and-mortar store?
3. What factors should be considered in deciding between an investment in a brick-and-mortar store vs. a website?
4. What supply-chain management concerns must MEC overcome?
5. What types of integration between bricks and clicks should be made in terms of supply-chain management?

Endnote

1. Based on Mountain Equipment Cooperative's 1999 Income Statement.

Source: This case was originally prepared by Steve Benvie and Michael Halliday under the supervision of Professor Gerald Trites for the sole purpose of providing material for classroom discussion. The authors do not intend to illustrate either effective or ineffective handling of a managerial situation.

CASE STUDY 5 TD Canada Trust

The banking industry has been transformed by technology, particularly by the internet. At one time, when people wanted to withdraw or deposit money in the bank, they had to go to a local branch, fill out a paper slip and sign it, wait in line for a teller, and then conduct their business. Banks had large numbers of branches everywhere, and most banks had a number of tellers to be able to handle the volume and not keep people waiting too long.

The first major change to all this was the advent of automated teller machines (ATMs). Very familiar to everyone today, in the 1970s and to some extent the '80s they were a unique and powerful convenience. Now people could go to the machine and do their banking without having to wait for normal banking hours. So if they didn't have enough money to last the weekend, they could go to the ATM any time of the day or night and withdraw some more (provided they had it in the bank!). While it was true they still had to wait in line sometimes, nevertheless, the convenience of 24/7 banking was undeniable. Gradually, the bank cards they used for access to the ATMs morphed into debit cards, and merchants began to accept them for payment. Now people didn't even need cash; they could pay with their debit cards.

With these changes, banks found they didn't need as many tellers in their branches. Indeed, they found they didn't even need as many branches, as people didn't go to them as much. Instead, they closed many of their small branches and installed ATMs or kiosk banking locations. In this way the structure of banks began to change dramatically.

During the early 1990s, the internet gained prominence and began to attract the interest of banks. They introduced internet banking, where people could log in and do much of their banking online, such as payment of bills and transfers between accounts. Of course they still needed to go to an ATM or branch to deposit or withdraw cash, but now there were a lot of things they could do on their own.

Internet banking has been tremendously popular with the general public. Although there were initial concerns about security, banks addressed this issue head on and were early adopters of 128-bit high encryption techniques. Also, people tended to trust banks, so the security issue did not impede the development of internet banking significantly.

While all of the Canadian banks have gone into online banking, and they are all good, TD Canada Trust stands out as a leader in online banking in Canada. It has consistently won major awards for the quality of its online banking offering. For example, *Global Magazine* has been conducting a contest for several years, and in 2007 rated TD Canada Trust as the "Best Consumer Internet Bank in Canada." In 2008, 2009, and 2010, however, this award was won by the Canadian Imperial Bank of Commerce. The contest was based on the following criteria: "strength of strategy for attracting and servicing online customers, success in getting clients to use web offerings, growth of online customers, breadth of product offerings, evidence of tangible benefits gained from Internet initiatives, and web site design and functionality."

Online banking provided by the TD is referred to as EasyWeb. Presentations on EasyWeb for both personal and small business banking are included at **www.tdcanadatrust.com**.

SECURITY

There is a strong emphasis on security in EasyWeb. TD claims to be the first Canadian bank to offer its customers a security guarantee. The EasyWeb Security Guarantee provides that customers will receive 100 percent reimbursement of any losses that occur as a result of unauthorized activity. They have also established an Online Security Centre that summarizes the steps that TD takes to protect online customers and then provides guidance on steps that customers can take to protect themselves.

Among these steps, TD mentions their Privacy Code and the fact that it sets out the commitment of the bank to protect its customers' information. They also mention their Technology Risk Management and Information Security Group, which has responsibility for security standards applicable to the systems and information contained therein. They ensure that appropriate security controls are built into the bank's procedures, systems, and software, and they monitor the systems. Of course, the bank also operates firewalls to control outside access.

The bank also makes use of cookies for customer login purposes. These include "session cookies" and "persistent cookies." The session cookies exist only as long as the user is logged into the site. They record an ID for the browser, and thus authenticate any requests as legitimate during the session.

Persistent cookies are placed on a user's hard drive and last until they expire. It includes the information that the user has agreed to have saved, such as the login ID. When the user logs in next time, the system will use the cookie to call up the information and facilitate the login process.

The bank system also offers the customers "EasyWeb IdentificationPlus," which is a multi-level authentication system under which the customer provides five security questions that are asked for future logins, particularly for sensitive transactions or when the customer is using a computer that is not the normal one used by that customer. The bank has also formed an alliance with Norton under which tools that enhance the security of internet usage are offered at a discount or for a free trial period.

The site offers customers some guidance on conducting their own activities when using the internet. Many of these are standard fare for experienced internet users. They include watching for online fraud such as phishing, using passwords and safeguarding them, using a firewall on their own computer, installing and using anti-virus and anti-spyware software, encrypting their own home wireless network, and using only encrypted networks offsite for accessing online banking.

FUNCTIONALITY

The EasyWeb system offers a broad range of functions to customers. It includes all the usual items, such as the ability to access their accounts and view all the transactions, the ability to transfer money between accounts, and the ability to pay bills. In addition, the system provides "single sign-on" access to online investing through WebBroker. Single sign-on means, of course, that the customer only needs to sign on once for these various services.

Customers can review up to 18 months of transaction activity on their chequing, savings, and line of credit accounts and up to 6 months of activity on their Visa accounts. Moreover, they can sort the transaction activity by such factors as date, description, and type.

The site has a bill presentment service as well, meaning customers can register their bills with the service and have their statements come to them electronically, through a service called View Bills. They can also process payments through their accounts, as well as recurring and post-dated payments, and then cancel them later if they wish. Finally, they can transfer money between their Visa and other bank accounts.

As with many other banks, TD offers Interac Email Money Transfer service for customers to make money transfers from their personal bank account to someone else's account. This is carried out through email. Within the secure area, an email is sent to another person, along with a security question that only the customer and the other person know. When the other person receives the email, the money can then be deposited by using their own online banking service, regardless of which bank it is carried with. This is a popular service and is useful for a variety of purposes, from sending money to family members (okay, from parents to students!) to payment of independent contractors.

The TD Canada Trust online banking service also offers a number of features that facilitate paperless record keeping. This includes, in addition to the ability to capture transactions on record, the ability to download account activity to Quicken or Microsoft Money for record-keeping purposes. In addition, there is an ability to view cheques for those who sign up for paperless document management and bill presentment.

Of course, people can purchase a variety of products from TD online, including ordering cheques online for personal chequing and savings accounts, and applying for Visa cards and new accounts.

One of the long-term visions for online banking is to be able to do all the things that one does with banks offline. At present, some such functions are excluded. The most obvious one is that customers cannot withdraw cash from their accounts, simply because there is no way to deliver cash online.

This is likely to change, however, when non-cash means of payment become more common. For some time, banks and others have been experimenting with the use of "smart cards" such as Mondex, which would be about the size of normal debit or credit cards but a bit thicker and would contain memory that could contain units of currency in electronic form. These cards could be refilled by inserting them in an appropriately configured and equipped ATM. It would also be possible to refill them over an internet connection to an online banking system if the user were equipped with the appropriate piece of hardware. However, banks have not managed to achieve consumer acceptance of such smart cards, largely because they would require a considerable investment in infrastructure in order to work, and also because consumers have not seen a real need for them.

More recently, there have been initiatives to make use of cell phones for payment purposes. Such cell phones could communicate with cash registers using a wireless means such as Bluetooth and actually pay a bill wirelessly. In the same way it would be possible to use cell phones with, say, Bluetooth capability to transmit currency back to the phone and then store it there for use in the stores. This would not require any additional hardware because the connections would be wireless. It is not difficult to envisage online banking systems that would incorporate the ability to refill cell phones or other wireless devices like the Blackberry using Bluetooth.

Other services that the current online banking systems do not offer are loans. While it is possible to apply for credit cards through online banking, it is seldom possible to apply for loans through those means. Apparently, the banks wish to meet the people who borrow money from them.

While online banking sites have taken some business away from the bank branches, at the same time, the branches have expanded their businesses. For example, many of them now offer individualized investment advice, insurance, personal financial planning, estate planning, and estate management, including executorships. The banks had wished for some years to expand their business to encompass the three pillars of financial activity—banking, insurance, and investments. They have accomplished that.

The issue then becomes whether online banking systems can be expanded to accommodate these new services—whether they can eventually accommodate all of the services that are offered by banks. As the world of commerce becomes more and more electronic, it is easy to envisage that this might be possible. The only exceptions might be where services are offered that require a lot of personal interaction, or can only be offered on a face-to-face basis; this might be the case with investment planning and with such activities as estate planning and acting as estate executors. For everything else, online banking should be possible.

Questions for Discussion

1. How feasible is it for online banking services to provide cash deposit and withdrawal services?
2. What additional services could feasibly be added to the online banking offerings of TD Canada Trust over the next year?
3. Compare the TD Canada Trust online banking site to that of another major Canadian bank. Comment on the differences.

Sources: www.tdcanadatrust.com; TD Press Release—"TD Canada Trust EasyWeb Named 'Best Consumer Internet Bank in Canada,'" September 27, 2007.

CASE STUDY 6 ValueClick

Google startled the online marketing industry when it announced that it was buying DoubleClick in April 2007. Shortly afterwards, 24/7 Real Media agreed to be taken over by WPP Group, and Microsoft acquired Aquantive. After a brief flurry of stock market activity, disappointing second-quarter 2007 results, and slightly lower guidance, ValueClick's shares plummeted. It was the last of the publicly traded online marketing companies that hadn't been taken over. What did the future hold for ValueClick?

COMPANY OVERVIEW

ValueClick LLC was established in May 1998 as a subsidiary of Web-Ignite Corporation, an internet-based advertising firm based in Delaware. The company has offices in the United States, the United Kingdom, Germany, France, and Japan. ValueClick has grown its business by investing in research and development and searching out other complementary technologies and media solutions to acquire. The following is a list of companies that ValueClick has acquired over the past several years: 2000: onResponse (Nov.); ClickAgents (Dec.); 2001: ZMedia (Jan.); Mediaplex/AdWare (Oct.); 2002: Be Free (May); 2003: Search123 (May); Commission Junction (Dec.); Hi-Speed Media (Dec.); 2004: Pricerunner (Aug.); 2005: E-Babylon (June); Web Marketing (June); Fastclick (Sept); 2006: Shopping.net (Dec).

These acquisitions represented competencies such as email-based advertising, ad serving, online promotions and purchase rewards, broadband convergence, web analytics and other technologies used to provide enhanced online marketing services to advertisers and advertising agency customers. As a result of these acquisitions, the company is a single-source provider of media, technology and related services that enable more than 5000 advertisers and more than 50 000 internet publishers and ad agencies to reach consumers in all major online marketing channels—display/web advertising, search marketing, email marketing, and affiliate marketing. Additionally, the company provides software that assists advertising agencies with information management regarding their financial, workflow, and offline media buying and planning processes. The company possesses a database of more than 97 million opt-in email profiles and can address 140 million internet users in the United States and 80 million in the United Kingdom each month.

ValueClick derives its revenue from four business segments as summarized in Table 1 below. ValueClick Inc. plans to grow its business by continuing its investment in research and development and searching out other complementary technologies and media solutions to acquire. ValueClick also plans to expand its client base and improve partnerships with advertising agencies and respected companies.

Table 1 ValueClick's Business Segments

Segment	Activity	How the Company Makes Money
Valueclick Media	Display Advertising: Provides advertisers with access to network of publishers and internet users and 18 content channels for display advertising (Fastclick).	Advertisers and agencies pay for targeted display ad campaigns that generate impressions, clicks and leads.
	Lead Generation Marketing: Generate qualified customer enquiries for an advertiser's product or service (HiSpeed Media; Web Marketing).	Advertisers pay per customer enquiry for an offer or opt-in to being contacted by the advertiser.
	Email Marketing: Enables advertisers to target prospective customers with email campaigns (HiSpeed Media; Web Marketing).	Advertisers pay per email delivered; commissions on sales of products directly to customers.
	Ecommerce: Sells consumer products to end-user customers (HiSpeed Media; E-Babylon).	End-user customers pay for products.
Affiliate Marketing	CJ Marketplace enables advertisers to load offers to affiliates and advertisers and affiliates to assess each other's effectiveness (Bee Free; Search 123; Commission Junction).	Advertisers pay percentage commissions paid to affiliates plus consulting fees and program management fees.
	Search Marketing enables advertisers to find customers and manage keyword search campaigns (Search 123).	Advertisers pay commission for revenue generated; per click for search terms.
Comparison Shopping	Enables consumers to compare products from thousands of online and offline merchants (Pricerunner).	Merchants pay per click for traffic delivered to their sites.
Technology	ASP model enables advertisers to implement and manage display advertising and email campaigns and online publishers to manage their website inventory (Mediaplex).	Advertisers, ad agencies and website publishers pay for ad serving, email and reporting tools on a CPM basis plus consulting and implementation fees.
	ASP model delivers web-based enterprise systems to advertising, communications and public relations companies (Mediaplex Systems).	Ad agencies and advertisers pay monthly service fees.

THE ONLINE MARKETING INDUSTRY

Over the past decades, competition has increased dramatically throughout the major industries in the world. Small, medium, and large businesses have been seeking new methods to attract and retain their customers over the last century. Print media, radio and television have been the classic forms of advertisement; however, recently the internet has been drastically gaining pace as an advertising medium. According to Forrester Research, online advertising and marketing spending would reach $26 billion by the year 2010, more than double the 2005 level. This phenomenal anticipated increase is due to the shift by marketers towards use of the internet in place of traditional media such as television, radio, magazines, and newspapers.

Today, online consumers spend more of their free time online than they spend watching TV, but only 4 percent of advertising budgets are allocated to online ads vs. the 25 percent spent on TV ads. Marketers and advertisers are recognizing the shift in consumer behaviour and are beginning to address it through their ad spending. According to Forrester, the reluctance of marketers to choose online advertisement has mainly been due to the lack of personalized or the hands-on experience with the various forms of online advertising such as search engine marketing, online display ads, and email marketing. According to TheEconomist, the combined advertising revenues of Google and Yahoo! will soon rival the combined prime-time ad revenues of America's three big television networks, ABC, CBS, and NBC. The online advertising giants Google, Yahoo!, MSN, and AOL have started introducing new methods of marketing, which include; auction-based service for display advertising and more effective payment methods. The following are some other key statistics from Forrester:

- Search engine marketing would reach US$11.6 billion by 2010.

- Display advertising, which includes traditional banners and sponsorships, would grow to US$8 billion by 2010.

- New advertising channels will draw interest and spending from marketers. Sixty-four percent of respondents are interested in advertising on blogs, 57 percent through RSS and 52 percent on mobile devices, including phones and PDAs.

- Marketers are losing confidence in the effectiveness of traditional advertising channels and feel that online channels will become more effective over the next three years. Seventy-eight percent of survey respondents said they think search engine marketing will be more effective, compared with 53 percent of respondents who said TV advertising would become less effective.

- The only non-digital advertising channel to reach the same level of confidence as online channels with marketers is product placement.

SUPPLIER POWER

There are large numbers of suppliers in the online marketing industry and the rate at which new entrants are entering in the supplier industry further reduces the suppliers' power. These suppliers often compete with each other to attract online marketing companies. This reduces the cost for the companies in the online marketing industry to switch to new suppliers. Another factor which further strengthens the online marketing industry's position is the fact that their business is not restricted by geographical barriers. This gives additional leverage to the industry to explore new areas for better deals.

BUYER POWER

The buyers of online marketing services are from diversified industries, such as computer software and hardware providers, insurance companies, and the automobile industry. It is easy for buyers to switch from one online marketing company to another, which gives buyers a high degree of bargaining power. Also, since there is tough competition in most of the industries, buyers are very price sensitive, especially with regard to their expenditures on marketing.

THREATS OF SUBSTITUTES

The substitutes for online marketing are direct marketing such as direct mail, telemarketing and door-to-door selling, and other traditional marketing methods such as advertising on television, radio, newspaper, and magazines. There are many advantages that online marketing has over the other marketing methods that make the threats from substitutes weak. Online marketing is less expensive than the other methods mentioned above. It not only can reach more people in different countries but can also provide detailed analysis of advertising campaign effectiveness instantly to the marketers.

Web technologies enable marketers and online publishers to create rich, creative, and interactive advertisements that grab online surfers' attention in a way that traditional media cannot. Also, web-based services provide more and more detailed tracking and performance information with reduced delay, so that marketers can rapidly analyze the effectiveness of each advertisement by capturing the amount of time spent viewing an ad, the number of times the ad is viewed/clicked, when, and in which locations.

As more people use the internet and as the technologies of the internet become more mature, online marketing will grow, since the threats from traditional marketing are weak.

BARRIERS TO ENTRY

Startup costs for an online marketing company are not high. A startup company only has to register for a domain name and build its website to operate. However, in spite of the low startup cost, there are significant barriers to entry. Online marketing companies need to have contracts with websites that are well known and have lots of traffic in order to attract advertisers. Because of the brand factor, it will be hard for start-up online marketing companies to gain reputation since the well-known online marketing companies have a majority of the market share. They may have contracts with popular websites such as msn.com, yahoo.com, and ebay.com that millions of users visit every day.

Moreover, existing online marketing companies have the advantages of enormous databases and expertise, which can help them implement better customized advertising strategies to suit marketers' needs. The management and leveraging of large amounts of data require advanced, large-scale, real-time technology infrastructures. In addition, a company needs significant advertiser and publisher relationships to generate the data used to target and optimize online ad campaigns.

Also, the well-known companies can lower their prices while providing the same services to eliminate any new entrants, as they have more resources to do so. Hence it is easy for companies to enter the online marketing industry but hard to be successful in the industry.

COMPETITIVE RIVALRY

Rivalry is the intensity of competition among existing firms in an industry. Highly competitive industries generally earn low returns because the cost of competition is high. In the online marketing industry there are many firms and the competition is strong.

Questions for Discussion

1. Is online marketing an attractive industry? Why or why not?
2. What changes, if any, should ValueClick anticipate in light of Microsoft's and Google's acquisitions of two of its key rivals?
3. How should ValueClick compete against Google and Microsoft, given the comprehensiveness of their offerings?

Sources: Forester Research Inc., www.forrester.com/ER/Press/Release/0,1769,1003,00.html; www.doubleclick.com; www.investopedia.com/features/industryhandbook/porter.asp; www.247realmedia.com/about/financial.html; http://finance.yahoo.com (ticker symbols: TFSM and VCLK); www.valueclick.com/Investor_Relations.shtml; "The Online Ad Attack," Economist.com, April 27, 2005.

APPENDIX GLOSSARY OF ONLINE MARKETING AND ADVERTISING REVENUE TERMS

"PFP—Pay for Performance"—Types of advertising target:

- *Broad*—banner ads (CPM—cost per thousand, lowest cost)
- *Focused*—banner ads on topical sites (CPM)
- *Interested*—clicks (CPC—cost per click), leads (CPL—cost per lead) (e.g., $0.30 per click or lead for delivering a visitor to customer's website)
- *Actionable*—action (CPA—cost per action, most expensive) (e.g., $20 per action for delivering a customer who fills out a mortgage application at a financial institution's website)

SEM—Search Engine Marketing

- *Pay for Placement*—bid for positioning among the top spots in the "sponsored links" section of search results pages
- *Paid Inclusion*—pay fee to be indexed and ranked by search engines on a priority basis
- *SEO (Search Engine Optimization)*—improve architecture and content of website to enable the search engines to index the website more effectively and achieve a higher ranking in the "natural results" section of the search page

Glossary

ad hoc query: The ability for users to generate any type of query or report they wish within the system.

adviews: A measure of the number of times a page with a banner ad or another advertisement is viewed during a period of time.

affiliate program: An agreement between website operators whereby delivery of customers or prospective customers to another company's site results in compensation becoming due.

animated graphic interchange format (GIF): A file format that consists of a series of frames that are shown in a particular sequence.

Anticybersquatting Consumer Protection Act (ACPA): U.S. legislation that requires a trademark holder to simply demonstrate that a domain name has been registered in bad faith and that it has been used in an attempt to make a profit.

asynchronous transfer mode (ATM): A switching technology that organizes digital data into 53-byte cell units and transmits them using digital signalling technology. A cell is processed asynchronously relative to other related cells; in other words, not necessarily in a pre-specified sequence.

asynchronous: A term for activities that are not conducted in real time but that involve delays.

authentication: The property that confirms a particular person or server is, in fact, the person or server that is identified in a transaction.

automated teller machines (ATMs): User-friendly, kiosk-based computers that enable bank customers to carry out their own banking transactions.

balanced scorecard: A scorecard that includes performance indicators related to accounting and finance, human resources, internal processes, and customers.

banner ad: An icon containing an advertising messages that, when clicked, takes the user to the site of the advertiser.

biometrics: Access controls that rely on physical characteristics such as signatures, fingerprints, palmprints, voice recognition, and retina scans to authenticate the identity of a user before permitting access.

blog: A website containing personal posts available to be read by web surfers.

blog: A website maintained by individuals or a group to provide an ongoing stream of information about personal experiences, opinions, or some specific topic of interest.

brand: A name, term, sign, symbol, design, or combination of these attributes that is used to differentiate a product or service from its competitors.

brochureware phase: An early stage of the internet's development, in which commercial enterprises primarily put existing marketing brochures in digital format.

brokerage site: A site that brings together buyers and sellers to facilitate business transactions on the web.

business continuity plan: A plan which ensures that a business can continue to operate after a disaster or other event occurs that could otherwise disable the computer systems for a lengthy period of time.

business intelligence (BI): A powerful application, or set of applications, that allows businesses to capture, analyze, interpret, and report on data across an enterprise, thus creating valuable information for the enterprise.

business model: The manner in which a business organizes itself to achieve its objectives, which normally involve the generation of profits.

business process reengineering (BPR): A fundamental rethinking and radical redesign of existing business processes to add value or prepare for new technologies.

buy-side: The purchasing end of the supply chain, which consists of suppliers and the processes that connect with them.

Canadian Internet Registration Authority (CIRA): A not-for-profit Canadian corporation that is responsible for operating the .ca internet country code top-level domain.

CAPTCHA: Completely automated public Turing test to tell computers and humans apart.

cash-to-cash cycle: The length of time from purchasing materials until a product is manufactured.

certificate authority (CA): An organization that issues digital certificates and signs them with digital signatures to establish the authenticity of the certificates.

channel conflict: A situation in which various sales channels for a single organization operate in competition with each other.

check digit control: A control that performs a calculation on a set of digits, such as an employee ID number, and then adds the result of that calculation to the number.

click-stream analysis: A method by which a user's path through a website can be tracked and analyzed.

clickthroughcount: The number of users who have been shown a banner ad and who have clicked on it to take them to the website to which it refers.

click-wrap agreement: The online equivalent of a standard agreement included in shrink-wrapped software bought in physical locations.

client: A computer that is used by a network user to gain access to and operate applications on the network.

client-server system: A network configuration that evolved from networks built around central computers (servers) to provide computing power to the users on their own desktop computers (clients).

collaborative commerce (c-commerce): The application of technologies that allow trading partners to synchronize and optimize their partnerships and that are performed in collaboration.

collaborative systems: Information systems that interact between enterprises to enable them to work together on common business initiatives and ventures.

Common Gateway Interface (CGI): A method used by a web server to pass a user's request that has come over the internet to an application. It also receives data from the application that can be sent back to the user.

computer telephony integration (CTI): A technology that allows telephone systems to integrate with computer systems to aid in customer service and data capture.

control total: A total based on a count of records, monetary values, or hashes that is used to reconcile inputs and outputs and thereby control completeness and accuracy of processing.

control: A preventive, detective, or corrective measure that is designed to reduce the risk of error, fraud, malicious acts, or disaster to an acceptable level.

conversion rate: Proportion of click-throughs that actually result in the purchase of goods or services.

cookie: A small text file stored by a website on an individual computer that allows the site to track the movements of a visitor.

copyright: A category of intellectual property that includes literary and artistic works such as books, poems, films, and musical works.

core technologies: Those technologies that provide the basic infrastructure for business intelligence.

cost per thousand (CPM): A standard measure of impressions in online advertising. Charges are set for each thousand users who visit a site or see an advertisement.

cross-selling: The process of encouraging customers to purchase complementary or additional products or services from the firm.

customer intelligence: The use of CRM applications to explore data to identify relevant customer information.

customer relationship management (CRM): The set of strategies, technologies, and processes that enable a business to continuously improve offerings to customers.

cybersquatting: Registering a domain name with the intention to use the name for financial gain without legal rights to its use.

data cube: A multi-dimensional database structure that allows quick drill-down and reformatting of data.

data mining: The analysis of data for relationships that may not have previously been known.

data warehouse: A central data repository utilized to organize, store, analyze, and report upon data for decision-making purposes.

daughter window: Another name for inter-stitial or pop-up window.

deep linking: The creation of a link on one website to a specific part or page (not the homepage) of another website.

digital certificate: An electronic document that contains the identity of a person or server and the related public key.

digital signature: An encrypted message digest that can only be decrypted by a key that authenticates the sender's identity.

digitized word of mouth: Mechanisms for recording feedback about ecommerce sites, products, and market participants and sharing such feedback with others.

disaster recovery plan: A detailed plan of action that enables an information system to be recovered after a disaster has made it inoperable.

disaster: An act of nature such as a flood, storm, tornado, earthquake, fire, power failure, or other event that can lead to destruction of assets and disruption of business activities.

discount rate: The amount that the merchant account provider takes as a percentage of sales conducted through credit cards.

disintermediation: A change in the supply chain where the manufacturer or service provider and consumer interact directly with each other, thereby eliminating the need for an intermediary.

domain name service (DNS): An internet site that provides a table for translating domain names into IP addresses.

domain name system: A method of translating names into IP addresses.

Dutch auction: An auction that uses a descending price format, whereby the auctioneer begins with a high price, and buyers can bid on specific quantities of inventory as the price falls.

dynamic pricing: The use of market-based, negotiated prices for transactions.

electronic data interchange (EDI): A structured way of creating electronic "forms" that can be transmitted between trading partners to execute business transactions without the need to generate any paper.

electronic wallet: A file that securely stores a user's information, such as name, address, credit card number, and ship-to address, for frequent use in executing ecommerce transactions.

emarketing: The utilization of internet and electronic technologies to assist in the creation, implementation, and evaluation of marketing strategy.

enabling technologies: Technologies that enable BI applications to interact and perform tasks within the core technologies, such as the data warehouse.

encryption: The use of a mathematical formula (an algorithm) that is applied to electronic data to render it illegible to anyone without the decoding key.

English auction: An auction in which the bidding occurs through an ascending price process when buyers gather in a common location (physical or digital) during specified periods of time.

enterprise application integration (EAI): The process of planning, implementing, and managing the ability of applications in an enterprise to share information efficiently, often including legacy systems and ERP systems.

enterprise-wide system: An information system used throughout an enterprise with the intention of enabling a consistent type of functionality as well as enterprise-wide access to data.

eprocurement: The complete business process of acquiring goods and services through electronic means, from requisition through to fulfillment and payment.

error: An unintentional act or omission that leads to undesirable consequences.

Extensible Markup Language (XML): A markup language similar to HTML in that they both contain symbols to describe the contents of a page or file; but while HTML describes the content only in terms of how it is to be displayed and interacted with, XML describes the content in terms of what data is being included.

Extensible Markup Language (XML): A tool that is similar to HTML and is compatible with it but does not rely on single pre-set tags to identify information.

extraction, transformation, and loading (ETL): The process of gathering data from a system, such as an ERP system, which can be simplified and stored within the data warehouse.

extranet: A computer network that makes use of internet technology and includes users from outside the organization as well as inside.

fibre optics: The transmission of information as light impulses along a glass or plastic wire or fibre.

firewall: A separate, highly secure computer, along with related software, policies and procedures, through which access to a network from the internet is exclusively directed.

fraud: An intentional act that relies on deception to misappropriate assets or obtain other benefits.

general control: A control that is not unique to a particular application or applications.

hash: A total based on a field that is not expected to change (e.g., total of all employee number fields in a file) and that is useful for ensuring that no unauthorized additions, changes, or deletions have occurred in a file of records containing that field.

hit: A single download of any information from a website.

holdback: An amount that credit card companies keep in escrow to reduce the risk of bad debts and fraudulent credit card use.

horizontal trading exchange: A trading exchange that has a product or service focus, such as computers or office equipment, and that does not target any specific industry.

HyperText Markup Language (HTML): A specialized coding language that is used to encode content so it can be displayed in a web browser.

HyperText Markup Language (HTML): The programming language used to create webpages.

HyperText Transfer Protocol (HTTP): A set of rules used in exchanging files (such as text, graphics, sound, and video) for display on the World Wide Web.

industrial property: A category of intellectual property that includes patents, trademarks, and other industrial designs.

influencer: individual or website that is at the hub of conversations

input mask: A means to establish formats for input areas in a screen that allow certain numbers of characters and/or digits to be entered.

integrated systems: Information systems that are joined together in such a way that they can easily share data with each other.

intellectual property: A creation of the mind such as an invention, artistic work, symbol, name, image, or design used in commerce.

intelligent agent: An automated tool that can help users find products or information throughout a site and can contribute to up-selling and cross-selling of products.

interactive phase: A stage of the internet's development in which websites began to allow two-way communication through email and web forms.

internet backbone: An organized and managed communications system, often based on fibre-optic cables, that forms the central connection for a section of the internet.

internet business model: The way in which a business uses the internet to support, amplify, or develop an overall business model.

Internet Corporation for Assigned Names and Numbers (ICANN): A domain name registrar that holds control over the primary -top-level domains.

Internet Protocol (IP): A protocol that uses a set of rules to send and receive messages at the internet address level.

internet service provider (ISP): A company that offers internet access and related services to individuals and businesses for a fee. Connections are offered through telephone lines, cable, satellite, or wireless technology.

interstitial: A Web-based window that pops up as a user enters an internet site, aiming to catch the user's attention.

intranet: A computer network within an enterprise that makes use of internet technology.

intrusion detection system (IDS): A system that monitors devices and processes for security threats and can alert security personnel of the occurrence of unusual activity as it occurs.

IP address: An address used in a scheme that provides an address for every physical device on the internet to enable any device to communicate with any other device.

Java: A programming language that was originally invented for the purpose of enhancing webpages and is used to create animations and moveable, interactive icons.

key performance indicators (KPIs): Important standards against which a company measures its performance in relation to goals, competitors, and the industry.

legacy system: An old, usually outdated, application that has not yet been replaced or upgraded.

log file analysis: The process of analyzing information regarding the movements of users throughout a site based upon data captured in server log files.

log file: A file stored on a web server containing details of every action that has occurred.

logical access control: A control that is included in software to permit access by authorized personnel in accordance with the privileges granted to them and to prevent access by unauthorized personnel.

logistics: The process of planning, implementing, and controlling the efficient and effective flow and storage of goods, services, and related information from point of origin to point of consumption.

malicious act: An intentional act that leads to the destruction of facilities, hardware, software, or data or unauthorized disclosure of confidential or private information.

market segment: A group of customers who share common needs and/or characteristics that the selling firm may be able to satisfy.

mashup: A website or application that combines content from simple existing web services to create a new service.

maverick buying: The unauthorized purchase of goods by employees through non-routine and poorly controlled means, such as acquiring office supplies with petty cash.

megabits per second (Mbps): A measure of speed for data transmission. Megabits means a million bits per second and states the number of data bits that are transmitted per second on a particular medium.

merchant account: An account held by a business to collect payment through credit cards.

message digest: A unique number calculated from the content of a message that can then be added to the message and checked by recalculating the number to ensure that the message has not been tampered with.

metadata: A structured definition of data; it is data about data.

middleware: Any software or programming that links together or communicates between two separate and different programs.

near-field communication (NFC): Technology that uses magnetic field induction to transfer data between a mobile phone and a reader device.

non-repudiation: The property that confirms a particular person did indeed send a message and cannot deny that fact.

online analytical processing (OLAP): A process that provides the ability for users to perform detailed, summary, or trend analysis on data and allows for drill-down into that data.

online transaction-processing (OLTP) system: A program that facilitates and manages transaction-oriented applications, typically for data entry and retrieval transactions across a network.

order fulfillment: A set of processes involved in delivering a product to the customer. It consists of procedures grouped into the main areas of order processing, warehousing, and shipping and transportation planning.

order processing: A set of activities that take place during the fulfillment of an order. These include credit checks, inventory availability determination, accounting, billing, and replenishment requests.

passive versus active test: A standard that attempts to place the website of an online business along a continuum, based on the interactivity of the website, to determine if operations within a jurisdiction were planned.

patent: A document issued by the government that grants an inventor or a patent owner the right to make and use an invention for 20 years after the patent is filed.

PayPal: A payment system, owned by eBay, that allows money transfers over the internet in a variety of currencies.

pay-per-action: Measures and rewards actions that result from click-throughs rather than the number of click-throughs themselves.

pay-per-call: Measures and rewards the number of calls placed by visitors during a specific time frame.

permanent establishment: A term in Canadian law and in international tax treaties that is used to determine where a business is located for tax purposes.

Personal Information Protection and Electronic Documents Act (PIPEDA): Canadian legislation that has provided privacy protection for personal information since coming into full effect on January 1, 2004.

personal information: Information that could identify an individual and could potentially be used to discriminate against that person or invade his or her privacy.

personalization phase: A stage in the internet's development in which websites began to develop one-to-one marketing techniques through the use of cookies and other tracking tools.

physical access control: A measure to secure the physical safety of a resource by restricting access to it.

physical presence: A term for a test under U.S. law and internationally that is used to determine whether a business has a permanent establishment in a jurisdiction and hence considered to be subject to taxation in that jurisdiction.

point of presence (POP): An access point to the internet that has a unique IP address.

primary data: Information that is gathered in an effort to better make a specific decision.

principle of least privilege: A principle which suggests granting to each individual the minimum privileges he or she requires to complete the tasks he or she is responsible for and no more.

private exchange: A trading exchange that limits participation to specific buyers and sellers—normally related to the exchange provider's supply chain.

private key: A set of data used to encrypt and decrypt data transmissions that is known to one person only.

public exchange: A trading exchange in which buyers and sellers register to join, and there are few limitations to joining.

public key infrastructure (PKI): A system that stores and delivers keys and certificates as needed and also provides privacy, security, integrity, authentication, and non-repudiation support for various ebusiness applications and transactions.

public key: A set of data used to encrypt and decrypt data transmissions that can be shared with anyone.

pull system: A supply chain in which the production of suppliers is determined by the needs of customers who request or order goods, necessitating production.

push system: A supply-chain model in which suppliers produce goods based upon their efficiencies and push them to customers, rather than relying on demand to determine production.

radio frequency identification (RFID): Technology that uses radio waves to transfer data between a reader device and an item such as a smart card.

reintermediation: The process of using the internet to reassemble buyers, sellers, and other partners in a traditional supply chain in new ways.

relational database system: A logical database model that relates data in different tables within the database by sharing a common data element (or field) between them. The common data element can serve as a reference point in the tables to other data elements in a data record.

relational database: A database that uses numerous tables and can relate fields or tables within the database to one another, and can easily be reorganized or extended.

remarketing (or retargeting): The process of tracking customers who don't complete a purchase by placing cookies on their computer to make it possible to make repeat offers for the abandoned item on other websites that the customers visit.

remarketing (or retargeting): The process of tracking customers who don't complete a purchase by placing cookies on their computer to make it possible to make repeat offers for the abandoned item on other websites that the customers visit.

request for proposals (RFP): The first stage in a procurement process, whereby the buyer communicates its needs to potential suppliers, who will then submit tenders based on the requirements.

reverse auction: An auction that uses a descending price format, but the buyer creates the auction to receive bids from potential suppliers.

reverse logistics: The internal processes for handling customer returns, either for a refund or for repair or replacement under warranty.

RFID tag: A radio frequency identification tag placed on a shipping crates or pallet containing embedded electronic product codes that can be used for tracking and identifying items at the individual crate and pallet level.

risk: The probability of an event occurring and leading to undesirable consequences.

sales force automation (SFA): The process of simplifying sales in the field and the integration of sales activity into the corporate information structure.

scalability: The ability of a system to maintain a set rate of performance as the number of users or volume of usage increases.

scorecard: A multi-dimensional measurement tool aimed at capturing a variety of key performance indicators.

sealed-bid auction: An auction that is often used for products/ services where price is only one consideration in the decision. The buyer will consider capabilities, product quality, timelines, and past experience with the seller before awarding the contract.

search engine optimization (SEO): A field that specializes in driving traffic from search engines to websites.

search engine ranking: A measure of closeness to the top of the list of links returned by a search engine.

secondary data: Data that have not been developed specifically for the task at hand, but that may be useful for decision making.

Secure Electronic Transaction (SET) protocol: A method of securing credit card transactions using encryption and authentication technology.

Secure HyperText Transfer Protocol (S-HTTP): A security protocol for use with HTTP that provides security for transmission of messages over the World Wide Web.

Secure Sockets Layer (SSL) protocol: A security protocol associated with TCP/IP that establishes a secure communications channel between web clients and servers.

sell-side: The selling end of the supply chain, which consists of customers and the processes that connect with them.

semantic web: A version of today's web that will include technology to understand and process human language.

server: A large central computer that forms the nucleus of a network and contains the network operating system, as well as case-specific network-based applications.

shipping and transportation planning (STP): The process of transporting finished goods to the consumer quickly and efficiently.

shrink-wrap agreement: An agreement printed on the outside of shrink-wrapped software packaging which says that the use of the software product is subject to license terms.

site stickiness: A term describing the likelihood that users will stay on a particular website, and the amount of time they will spend there.

smart card: A card, not much bigger than a credit card, which contains a computer chip that is used to store or process information.

sniffing: The use of electronic devices attached to transmission lines that can detect and capture data transmissions on those lines. Newer models of sniffing devices can work on wireless transmissions as well.

Social CRM: The use of social media in deploying Customer Relationship Management.

social media: blogs, opinion sites, chat rooms, photo, music, video and game sharing sites and other sites promoting social interaction.

social network: A loosely linked community of individuals with some common interest.

social networking website: A website that enables subscribers to link with other subscribers to share personal, professional or commercial interests.

software as a service (SaaS): Software made available over the internet by independent providers to users who pay on a subscription or pay-as-you-go basis.

software as a service (SaaS): Software that is provided for rent to businesses over the internet.

spam: Unsolicited email sent in an attempt to gain commercial advantage.

SSL/HTTPS protocols: Protocols for sending encrypted data from a web browser to a server.

strategy: The sum of all the choices that a business makes to offer unique value to its customers that differentiates its business model from those of its competitors.

stress testing: A process of high-volume entry, processing, and output of test data designed to determine whether the system has the capacity to handle the volumes that will be required of it.

superstitial: An internet advertisement spot that loads into a user's browser while the internet connection is idle and then launches as a daughter window, showing a short, TV-like advertisement.

supply chain: The set of processes that encompasses purchases of raw materials or resources through to final delivery of a product or service to the end consumer.

supply-chain management (SCM): The process of coordinating and optimizing the flow of all products or services, information, and finances among all players of the supply chain.

systems integration: The bringing together of various business systems that have different technologies, functions, and platforms so they can conduct business processes in such a way that the user does not see that different systems are being used.

systems sizing: The process of ascertaining the volume and processing requirements that will be placed on a new information system, and thereby determining the size of system required, including hardware and software.

TCP/IP: A set of protocols based on Transmission Control Protocol (TCP) and Internet Protocol (IP).

threat: A condition or force that increases the risk of error, fraud, malicious acts, or disaster.

time stamping: The process of adding a tag containing the time that a record is created, modified, or moved.

time: A measure of a visitor's engagement with a website.

trademark: A distinguishable feature such as a word, symbol, picture, logo, or design that can be used to identify the products or services of a specific individual or organization.

Transmission Control Protocol (TCP): A protocol that uses a set of rules to exchange messages with other internet points at the data packet level.

trustmark, service mark, or seal: A graphic representation similar to a logo that is placed on websites to indicate that the entity complies with certain recommended ecommerce practices and is therefore a trustworthy business partner.

tunnelling: A process in which data packets are transmitted over the internet by including an additional header that establishes its route through the internet.

uniform resource locator (URL): The address of a resource on the World Wide Web.

up-selling: The process of encouraging customers to purchase higher-priced products or services.

user: A visitor who registers on a website by providing at least their email address.

user: A visitor who registers on a website by providing at least their email address.

value-added network (VAN): A privately owned network that is rented to users, along with a package of related services, to operate their EDI systems by providing an environment within which they can work, and by connecting them to their customers and suppliers.

vendor-managed inventory (VMI): A process by which suppliers take over monitoring inventory levels through the use of technology and are responsible for replenishment of stock.

vertical trading exchange: A trading exchange that has an industry or specific market focus, such as health care or energy products and services.

Vickrey auction: An auction that uses an ascending price format in which the highest bidder wins the auction but must pay the price submitted by the second-place bidder.

virtual private network (VPN): A secure and encrypted connection between two points across the internet.

virus: A computer program that is inserted into computer systems on an unauthorized basis, unknown to the system owner or user, and with the intent to take some action on that computer that can be mischievous or malicious.

visit: A collection of webpages a visitor views in a time period while on a website.

Voice over Internet Protocol (VoIP): A set of protocols for carrying voice signals/telephone calls over the internet.

Voice over Internet Protocol (VoIP): A set of protocols for carrying voice signals/telephone calls over the internet.

warehousing: Tasks involved with handling inventory. These processes include receiving orders of inventory from suppliers, as well as picking, organizing, and packaging goods for delivery.

web browser: Software with a user-friendly, graphics-capable interface that enables users to connect to and navigate websites on the internet.

web bug (clear GIF): An image file embedded in a webpage that can track user movements without the user's knowledge.

web server: A server attached to a network; it is dedicated to specific applications that must be run on the World

Wide Web, used by web users, or interfaced very closely with the web.

web services: A mechanism for applications to communicate with each other from different systems across the internet.

website framing: The use of HTML and browser technology to split a page into segments, which is useful for facilitating ease of use and building impressive websites.

WEP (Wired Equivalency Privacy): A security protocol designed to provide a wireless local area network with security and privacy comparable to that of a wired local area network.

World Wide Web (WWW): The user-friendly, graphics-capable component of the internet.

Y2K: An abbreviation referring to the year 2000 to categorize the computer glitches that were widely predicted to take place when the calendar turned to the year 2000.

Yankee auction: An auction format similar to an English auction, except that multiple items are sold by price, quantity, and earliest bid time. This form of auction can be used by businesses that are buying products where price is not the only factor to consider and quantity available is a key consideration.

Index

Note: Key terms and pages on which they are defined are referenced in **bold**.

Privacy Commissioner of Canada, Office of, 19
private exchanges, 178, 185
private key, 99
privilege management, 107
PR Newswire, 332
Proactis, 181
processing controls, 97–98
process redesign in customer relationship management (CRM), 209–210
Pro-C Ltd., 309
Procter & Gamble (P&G), 5, 153, 161
Global eXchange Services (GXS) and, 179
procurement, 332–333, 344–345
costs of, 17
paper-based, 177
procure-to-pay cycle, 181
production items, eprocurement and, 174–175
product value, redefinition of, and ebusiness models, 8
profitability, trading exchanges and, 184
project management, 234–235
promotions, 263–264
in auctions, 191
protocols, 52, 62–63
psychographics in market segmentation, 246
public exchange, 179
public exchanges, 185
public key, 100
public key cryptography, 116
public key infrastructure (PKI), 101
public relations, 265–269, 335
defined, 265
Public Works, decision against reverse auction, 175–176
pull system, 150
purchase agreement, 176
purchase order (PO), electronic drafting of, 176
pure play ebusinesses, 27–28
pure plays, 26–27
Purolator, outsourcing and, 164
push system, 147
Pyra Labs, 46

R
radio buttons in surveys, 247
radio frequency identification (RFID) tag, 164

radio-frequency identification (RFID) technology, 128
as supply-chain management efficiency measure, 148
random-access memory (RAM), 148
Rappa, Michael, 29
Raytheon, 171
realignment, 161
Real Media, 374
real-time business intelligence (BI), 237
real-time chat, 204–205
Recording Industry Association of America (RIAA), 313
reengineering, 158
Reengineering the Corporation (Hammer and Champy), 157
referrer analysis, 286
Regional Advanced Networks (RANs), 53
reintermediation, 152
relational databases, 75, 76, 228–229
relational OLAP (ROLAP), 224
Reliable Tools Inc., 140
remarketing, 249
reporting state of customer relationship management (CRM) implementation, 211
request for proposal (RFP), 188
request for quotation (RFQ), 176
Research in Motion Ltd. (RIM), 2, 11, 99, 349
resource management, 37–38
Retail Link, 153
retargeting, 249
return on investment (ROI), 235, 288
maximizing, 278
revenues, 287
reverse auctions, 26, 36–37, **188**
deciding against, 175–176
reverse logistics, 166–167
Revver, 355
Rhapsody, 31
rich media, 256
risk, 89
Robertson v. Thomson Corp S.C.J. No. 43, 314
RoboShopper, 37
Rogers' Chocolate Ltd., 27, 57, 333, 334
Rose, Kevin, 25
Roxio, 35
Royal Bank of Canada, 28
RSA, 259
RSS, 67

S
Safaricom Kenya, 117
Safe Harbor Provisions of the Digital Millennium Copyright Act (DCMA), 354
SafeWeb, 306, 307
Sage Software, 80
sales
analysis of, 287
ebusiness in increasing, 15–16
goals of, 201
transactions in, 333–335
sales force automation (SFA), 201
Salesforce.com, 26, 67
Samsung Electro-Mechanics Company, 165
Sanger, Larry, 8
Sanmina-SCI Corporation, Gmail at, 64
SAP, 11, 12, 74, 76, 78, 184, 216
introduction of Business Warehouse (BW), 155, 218
Strategic Enterprise Management suite of, 226
SAP R/3, 77
SAS.com, 216
SAS Institute, 155, 216
scalability, 231–232
scheduling in auctions, 191
Schultz, Howard, 355
Schwab.com, 14
scorecard, 225
balanced, 225
sealed-bid auction, 188
seals, 266
Search123, 374
search ads, click fraud and, 278
search agents, 37
search engine optimization (SEO), 254
search engine ranking, 281
search engines
in marketing, 260–261
registration with, 254
Sears, 5, 28, 30, 140, 147
secondary data, 246–247, 249
Second Life, 47
Secure Electronic Transaction (SET) protocol, 121–122
Secure HyperText Transfer Protocol (S-HTTP), 100
Secure Sockets Layer (SSL) protocols, 100
security, 18–20, 162, 232–233
administration of, 106
management of, 93
monitoring of, 109–110
payment systems and, 18–20

supply-chain synchronization, 146
supply-side streamlining, 145
supply web, 144
support, 283
surveys, 247
    online, 247
SWOT analysis, 246
Sybase, 81
Symantec, 306
Sympatico, 57, 265
Sympatico/MSN Autos, 359
Sysomos, 284–285
system acquisition or development
    controls, 96–97
system architecture, 234
system maintenance and change
    controls, 96
systems integration, 10–12
    tools for, 12–13
systems sizing, 77

T

tactical plans, 41
Tandem, 79
Tapscott, Don, 9
target markets, 250
taxation, 322–324
TCP/IP, 50, **52,** 54, 63, 144, 228
TD Canada Trust, 370–374
TD Waterhouse WebBroker, 35
technological challenges for small
    businesses, 346
technological concerns for customer
    relationship management (CRM)
    implementation project, 208
technologies
    integration of, 152–157
    privacy and, 306–307
Teleglobe Canada, 52, 53
TellApart.com, 249
Telpay Inc., 129
terabits, 53
terrorism, fighting, with business
    intelligence software, 225
Texas Instrument, eprocurement
    and, 172
Thiel, Peter, 124
Thomson Consumer Electronics
    Inc., 153
threat, 92
3D software, 47
three-tier client-server system, 75
Ticketmaster v. *Tickets.com*, 322
Timberland, 240
time, 281

time stamping, 98
time to market, supply-chain
    management and, 149
Time Warner, 354, 355
TMP Worldwide (TMPW), 362
Tor Hidden Services, 306
Toronto, 123
Toronto Star Newspapers Ltd., 363
Torvalds, Linus, 317
Toyota Motor Sales U.S.A. Inc., 140,
    357
Toys "R" Us, 164, 265
Trademark Dilution Act, 310
trademarks, 308–309
Trade-marks Act, 309
Trade Ranger, 182
trade secrets, 162
trading exchanges, 35, 178–181,
    183–185, 342–343
    evolution to software as a service
        (SaaS), 179–181, 183
    horizontal, 178
    issues for providers, 183–185
    vertical, 178
traffic, website, 282
traffic metrics, 279–282
Trail Blazer, 333, 335–336
training, 345
transaction brokers, 37
transaction costs, minimizing,
    277–278
transaction databases, 294
**Transmission Control Protocol
    (TCP), 50**
Travelocity.com, 152
travel services, eprocurement
    and, 173
Treo™, 11
Tribune, 363
TripAdvisor.com, 269
Trojan program, 91
Trump, 364
TRUSTe, 266, 267
trustmark, 266
Tucows Inc., 309
Tungsten™, 11
tunnel, 65
tunnelling, 65
TweetMeme, 25
Twitter, 2, 25, 27, 32, 67, 202, 269,
    335, 342
    innovation and, 283
    as social networking website, 294
    social network metrics and, 283
two-tier client-server systems, 75

U

uBid.com, 339
Uniform Domain Name Dispute
    Resolution Policy (UDRP), 311
unique visitors, 280
Unisys, 105
United Nations Commission on
    International Trade Law
    (UNCITRAL), 321
United Parcel Service (UPS), 164–165
    outsourcing and, 164–165, 167
    tracking of packages on Internet
        and, 167
U.S. Bank, extension of business
    intelligence to customers, 222
U.S. PATRIOT Act, 237
U.S. Super Bowl, 246
United Virtualities, 364
Universal Ad Package, 256
Universal Description, Discovery, and
    Integration (UDDI), 184
universality of Internet, 50
universal resource locator (URL), 57
up-selling, 198
UPS Logistics Group, 165
upstream partners, 29
USA Today, 44
user, 280–281
    measurement of, with Mint.com,
        281–282
user behaviour analysis, 248–249
user profile analysis, 287
user profile databases, 294
utility model, 29, 31

V

ValuClick, 374–378
value-added networks (VANs), 12,
    115, 165–166, 171
valuechain.dell.com, 145
value-chain management, 146
ValueClick, 260
Vancouver Hospital and Health Services
    Centre, 235–236
vendor-managed inventory (VMI), 63,
    161
Veoh, 355
Veronica, 58
vertical trading exchanges, 178
VHL, 67
Viacom, 67
Vickrey auction, 188
VideoEgg, 355
virtual corporations, creation of, 9